THE ENGLISH CHURCH AND THE CONTINENT
IN THE TENTH AND ELEVENTH CENTURIES

The English Church and the Continent in the Tenth and Eleventh Centuries

Cultural, Spiritual, and Artistic Exchanges

VERONICA ORTENBERG

CLARENDON PRESS

1992

Oxford University Press, Walton Street, Oxford OX2 6DP

Oxford New York Toronto
Delhi Bombay Calcutta Madras Karachi
Petaling Jaya Singapore Hong Kong Tokyo
Nairobi Dar es Salaam Cape Town
Melbourne Auckland
and associated companies in
Berlin Ibadan

Oxford is a trade mark of Oxford University Press

Published in the United States
by Oxford University Press, New York

British Library Cataloguing in Publication Data
Data available

Library of Congress Cataloging in Publication Data
Ortenberg, Veronica.
The English Church and the Continent in the tenth and eleventh
centuries : cultural, spiritual, and artistic exchange / Veronica
Ortenberg.
p.   cm
Includes bibliographical references and index.
1. England—Church history—Anglo Saxon period, 449–1066.
2. England—Church history—Medieval period, 1066–1485.   3. Church
history—Middle Ages, 600–1500.   4. England—Civilization—To 1066.
5. England—Civilization—Medieval period, 1066–1485.
6. Civilization, Medieval.   7. England—Civilization—European
Influences.   I. Title.
BR749.O78   1992
274.2'03—dc20   91–39369
ISBN 0–19–820159–1

Typeset by Pentacor PLC, High Wycombe, Bucks

Printed and bound in
Great Britain by Biddles Ltd,
Guildford and King's Lynn

TO MY PARENTS

ACKNOWLEDGEMENTS

This book owes its existence primarily to two scholars and two institutions. Without the encouragement, constant support, and tireless help of Professor Christopher Brooke, it would have been neither begun nor pursued; his having read it in its entirety and commented on it as thoroughly and constructively as he used to do when he was my supervisor has been more than I would have ever dared to hope for. The invaluable inspiration which I gained from my discussions and friendship with Dr Henry Mayr-Harting have enabled me to enjoy writing it and to avoid potential mistakes in handling the material. I was exceptionally lucky in being able to carry out this project, not only at Oxford but, more specifically, at St Hugh's College, first as the Joanna Randall McIver Junior Research Fellow, then as a British Academy Post-Doctoral Fellow, between 1987 and 1990. I am grateful to the British Academy for awarding me this Fellowship, which has enabled me to finish this book; above all, I remain deeply indebted to my college for providing me not only with the material comforts and practical help throughout these years, but also with the outstandingly congenial atmosphere and friendliness which have made this time so enjoyable.

It would be impossible to name every person who has given me help and advice. Let them all know how grateful I am to them, even if only a few are cited here, who have read parts of the book or discussed it with me: J. Campbell, J. Cowdrey, R. Deshman, J. Dunbabin, B. Hamilton, J. Howard-Johnston, S. Keynes, R. Krautheimer, K. Leyser, P. Llewellyn, and B. Ward-Perkins. I owe a special debt of gratitude to Patrick Wormald, who most kindly agreed to read the entire final draft of the book; his customary learning has helped me avoid numerous pitfalls, and his perceptive insights have often led me to a deeper understanding of particular issues. The two successive history editors of Oxford University Press, R. Faber and A. Morris, should also be thanked for their support and trust. Last but not least, I should like to express my thanks to the staff of the numerous libraries where I have worked during my research, in England, France, and Italy; and, especially, to that of the Bodleian Library in Oxford, whose help, patience and courtesy have never failed me since I first came to Oxford as a student in 1981.

V.O.

Oxford, 1990

CONTENTS

LIST OF PLATES

Grateful acknowledgement is made to the following institutions, which have supplied the photographs and given me permission to reproduce them: Boulogne-sur-Mer, Bibliothèque Municipale for Pl. 14*c*; Florence, Biblioteca Medicea Laurenziana for Pl. 8*a*; Hildesheim Cathedral Library for Pl. 2*b*; London, British Library for Pls. 1*a*, 3*a*, 5*a*, 6*a*, 9*a*, 10*a*, 11*a*, 12*a*, 13*a*, 14*a* and 14*b*; the Victoria and Albert Museum for Pl. 12*b*; Madrid, Patrimonio Nacional for Pl. 3*b*; Montecassino, Biblioteca for Pl. 6*b*; Paris, Bibliothèque Nationale for Pls. 9*b* and 10*b*; Rouen, Bibliothèque Municipale for Pls. 2*a*, 4*b* and 7*a*; Trier, Stadtbibliothek for Pls. 1*b* and 5*c*; Vatican, Biblioteca Apostolica for Pl. 5*b* and Fabbrica di S. Pietro for Pl. 8*b*. Pls. 5*a*, 7*b*, 11*b*, 11*c*, and 13*b* are my own photographs.

ABBREVIATIONS

AASS	Acta Sanctorum.
AB	*Analecta Bollandiana.*
Aelfric's Lives of the Saints	W. W. Skeat (ed.), *Aelfric's Lives of the Saints: Being a Set of Sermons on Saints' Days* (2 vols.; London, 1881–1900).
Aethelweard	A. Campbell (ed.), *Chronicon Aethelwardi: The Chronicle of Aethelweard* (London, 1962).
Annales Monasterii de Wintonia	H. R. Luard (ed.), *Annales Monasterii de Wintonia* (AD *519–1277*) in *Annales Monastici*, ii. 3–125 (London, 1865).
ASC	D. Whitelock *et al.* (eds.) *The Anglo-Saxon Chronicle: A Revised Translation* (London, 1961).
ASE	*Anglo-Saxon England.*
Asser	W. H. Stevenson (ed.), *Asser: Life of King Alfred . . .* (Oxford, 1904, rev. edn. 1959).
BAR	H. A. Wilson (ed.), *The Benedictional of Archbishop Robert* (HBS 24; London, 1903).
B. A. R.	British Archaeological Reports.
Beckwith, *Ivory Carvings*	J. Beckwith, *Ivory Carvings in Early Medieval England* (London, 1972).
Benedictional of St Aethelwold	G. F. Warner and H. A. Wilson (eds.), *The Benedictional of St Aethelwold* (Oxford, 1910).
BHE	B. Colgrave and R. A. B. Mynors (eds. and trs.), *Bede's Ecclesiastical History of the English People* (Oxford, 1969).
CCCC	Corpus Christi College, Cambridge.
CED	A. W. Haddan and W. Stubbs (eds.), *Councils and Ecclesiastical Documents Relating to Great Britain and Ireland* (3 vols.; Oxford, 1869–71).
Chronicon Abingdon	J. Stevenson (ed.), *Chronicon Monasterii de Abingdon* (2 vols.; London, 1858).
Chronicon Evesham	W. D. Macray (ed.), *Chronicon Abbatiae de Evesham ad annum 1418* (London, 1863).
Chronicon Rameseiensis	W. D. Macray (ed.), *Chronicon Abbatiae Rameseiensis* (London, 1886).
Claudius Pontificals	D. H. Turner (ed.), *The Claudius Pontificals* (HBS 97; London, 1971).
Codex Egberti	H. Schiel (ed.), *Codex Egberti der Stadtbibliothek Trier* (Basel, 1960).
Collected Writings	F. Wormald, *Collected Writings* i: Studies in Medieval Art from the Sixth to the Twelfth Centuries, ed. J. J. G. Alexander, T. J. Brown, and J. Gibbs (Oxford, 1984).

CSD	D. Whitelock, M. Brett, and C. N. L. Brooke (eds.), *Councils and Synods: With Other Documents Relating to the English Church*, Vol. 1, pt. i: AD 871–1066; pt. ii: 1066–1204 (Oxford, 1981).
Drogo-Sakramentar	W. R. W. Koehler (ed.), *Drogo-Sakramentar: manuscrit latin 9428, Bibliothèque Nationale, Paris: Vollständige Faksimile-Ausgabe im Originalformat* (2 vols.; Graz, 1974).
EEMF	Early English Manuscripts in Facsimile.
EETS	Early English Texts Series.
EHD	D. Whitelock (ed.), *English Historical Documents*, i: *c.*500–1042 (2nd edn.; London, 1979).
EHR	*English Historical Review.*
Encomium	A. Campbell (ed.), *Encomium Emmae Reginae* (London, 1949).
Florence	B. Thorpe (ed.), *Florence of Worcester: Chronicon ex Chronicis* (2 vols.; London, 1848–9).
Foreville, *William of Poitiers*	R. Foreville (ed. and tr.), *Guillaume de Poitiers: Histoire de Guillaume le Conquérant* (Paris, 1952).
Gervase	W. Stubbs (ed.), *Chronica*, in *The Historical Works of Gervase of Canterbury* (2 vols.; London, 1879–80), i. 3–594.
Hampson, *Kalendarium*	R. T. Hampson, *Medii Aevi Kalendarium: Or Dates, Charters and Customs of the Middle Ages* (2 vols.; London, 1841).
HBS	Henry Bradshaw Society.
HCY	J. Raine (ed.), *The Historians of the Church of York and its Archbishops* (3 vols.; London, 1879–94).
HTA	Goscelin, *Historia Translationis S. Augustini episcopi Anglorum Apostoli*, P L 155, 13–46.
Hugh Candidus	W. T. Mellows (ed.), *The Chronicle of Hugh Candidus, a Monk of Peterborough* (Oxford, 1949).
Ideal and Reality	*Ideal and Reality in Frankish and Anglo-Saxon Society: Studies Presented to J. M. Wallace-Hadrill*, ed. P. Wormald, D. Bullough, and R. Collins (Oxford, 1983).
JEH	*Journal of Ecclesiastical History.*
JWCI	*Journal of the Warburg and Courtauld Institutes.*
LE	E. O. Blake (ed.), *Liber Eliensis* (London, 1962).
Learning and Literature	*Learning and Literature in Anglo-Saxon England; Studies Presented to P. Clemoes on the Occasion of his Sixty-Fifth Birthday*, ed. M. Lapidge and H. Gneuss (Cambridge, 1985).
Leofric Collectar	E. S. Dewick and W. H. Frere (eds.), *The Leofric Collectar* (2 vols.; HBS 45, 56; London, 1914, 1921).
Leofric Missal	F. E. Warren (ed.), *The Leofric Missal as Used in the Cathedral of Exeter* AD 1050–1072 (Oxford, 1883, repr. Farnborough, 1968).
LP	L. Duchesne (ed.), *Le Liber Pontificalis* (2 vols.;

	Paris, 1886–92, and vol. iii, rev. C. Vogel (Paris, 1957)).
McGurk, 'Metrical Calendar'	P. McGurk (ed.), 'The Metrical Calendar of Hampson: A New Edition', *AB* 104 (1986), 79–125.
MC	M. D. Knowles (ed.), *Decreta Lanfranci monachis Cantuariensibus transmissa* (Siegburg, 1967), Vol. iii of *Corpus Consuetudinum Monasticarum*, gen. ed. K. Hallinger.
Menologio	*Il Menologio de Basilio II: Codex Vaticano Greco 1613* (2 vols.; Turin, 1907).
MGH	Monumenta Germaniae Historica.
AA	Auctores Antiquissimi.
SRG	Scriptores Rerum Germanicarum.
SS	Scriptores.
SSRM	Scriptores Rerum Merovingicarum.
MNM	D. H. Turner (ed.), *The Missal of the New Minster, Winchester* (HBS 93; London, 1962).
MRJ	H. A. Wilson (ed.), *The Missal of Robert de Jumièges* (HBS 11; London, 1896).
Ohlgren, *Iconographic Catalogue*	T. H. Ohlgren (ed.), *Insular and Anglo-Saxon Illuminated Manuscripts: An Iconographic Catalogue c.AD 625–1100* (New York, 1986).
Orderic	M. Chibnall (ed. and tr.), *The Ecclesiastical History of Orderic Vitalis* (6 vols.; Oxford, 1968–80).
P L	Patrologia Latina.
Portiforium	A. Hughes (ed.), *The Portiforium of St Wulfstan* (2 vols.; HBS 89–90; London, 1958–60).
RB	*Revue Bénédictine.*
RC	K. Hallinger (ed.), 'Regularis Concordia Anglicae Nationis', in 'Consuetudinum saeculi X/XI/XII', *Monumenta Non-Cluniacensia, Corpus Consuetudinum Monasticarum*, VII/3 (Siegburg, 1984), 61–147.
RED	Rerum Ecclesiasticarum Documenta.
Religious Houses	D. Knowles and R. N. Hadcock (eds.), *Medieval Religious Houses: England and Wales* (London and New York, 1971).
Rella, 'Continental'	F. A. Rella, 'Continental Manuscripts Acquired for English Centres in the Tenth and Early Eleventh Centuries: A Preliminary Checklist', *Anglia*, 8 (1980), 107–16.
Rituale	U. L. Lindelöf (ed.), *Rituale Ecclesiae Dunelmensis: The Durham Collectar* (Surtees Society, 140; London, 1927).
RS	Rolls Series
Settimane	*Settimane di studio del Centro di Studi sull'Altomedioevo, Spoleto.*
Stubbs, *Memorials*	W. Stubbs (ed.), *Memorials of St Dunstan Archbishop of Canterbury* (London, 1874).
Symeon	T. Arnold (ed.), *Historia Dunelmensis Ecclesiae*, in

	Symeonis Monachi Opera Omnia (2 vols.; London, 1882–5), i. 3–135.
Temple, *ASM*	E. Temple (ed.), *Anglo-Saxon Manuscripts 900–1066*, Vol. ii of *A Survey of Manuscripts Illuminated in the British Isles* (London, 1976).
Vita Aedwardi	F. Barlow (ed. and tr.), *The Life of King Edward* (London, 1962).
Winchester Troper	W. H. Frere (ed.), *The Winchester Troper* (HBS 8; London, 1894).
Winterbottom, *Three Lives*	M. Winterbottom (ed.), *Three Lives of English Saints* (Toronto, 1972).
WMGP	N. E. S. A. Hamilton (ed.), *William of Malmesbury: De Gestis Pontificum Anglorum libri quinque* (London, 1870).
WMGR	W. Stubbs (ed.), *William of Malmesbury: De Gestis Regum Anglorum libri quinque* (2 vols.; London, 1887–9).
WMHG	J. Scott (ed. and tr.), *The Early History of Glastonbury: An Edition, Translation and Study of William of Malmesbury's 'De Antiquitate Glastonie Ecclesie'* (Woodbridge, 1981).
WMVW	R. R. Darlington (ed.), *The Vita Wulfstani of William of Malmesbury* (London, 1928).
Wormald, 'Eleventh-Century'	F. Wormald, 'An English Eleventh-Century Psalter with Figures, British Museum Cotton MS Tiberius C.VI', *The Thirty-Eighth Volume of the Walpole Society*, 1960–2 (Glasgow, 1962), repr. in *Collected Writings*, 123–37.
Wormald, *Kalendars*	F. Wormald (ed.), *English Kalendars Before AD 1100* (HBS 72; London, 1934).

᛭ Monastic House

• Urban centre with several churches

0   200   400 KM

INTRODUCTION

England and the Continent in the tenth and eleventh centuries: a continuation of Wilhelm Levison's work? The question has been asked of me several times, and a most flattering one it is. Like the medieval chronicler, I too wish to acknowledge my debt to my predecessor, the scholar whose name has become identified with this particular topic for the early Anglo-Saxon period.[1] But the comparison is, needless to say, extremely misleading. Levison's book was the intellectual Last Will and Testament of a master craftsman, his skills honed by decades of careful work on the intransigent sources for Frankish history. It set a standard of scholarly knowledge and judgement across a vast range of issues, which has never been matched and will probably never be surpassed. This, on the other hand, is a first book by a journeyman apprentice, in which anything gained by way of youthful enthusiasm is likely to be more than cancelled out by the corresponding inexperience. Nevertheless, there are two reasons why I have thought it possible and useful to write at this stage.

The first is that I am naturally attempting much less. When Levison wrote his Ford Lectures, his knowledge of the subject was so comprehensive that he could incorporate both a study of the exchanges between England and the Continent, and an analysis of parallels between those areas. My aim here is to provide a study of the first of these type of connection by looking at exchanges and links; at a later stage, I would hope to be able to speak more knowledgeably about parallel developments too. Furthermore this is a book very largely about *ecclesiastical* relationships and the type of cultural contact that arose mainly in an ecclesiastical *milieu*. However, within these self-imposed limitations it has seemed desirable, first of all, to bring together the evidence scattered throughout the sources and, secondly, to carry out a study on a larger scale, destined to cover all those parts of the Continent with which English or Continental sources show some such exchanges to have been in existence. The only area of exchanges which I have deliberately omitted is Scandinavia, since the problems posed by Anglo-Scandinavian history would require too much space and special expertise to fit within the confines of this book. Equally necessary seemed to me the attempt to pursue the study of these connections in depth, going

---

[1] W. Levison, *England and the Continent in the Eighth Century* (Oxford, 1946).

beyond the cataloguing of facts, in such manner as to reassess the direct evidence found in the narrative, diplomatic, liturgical, and didactic sources, and also to identify the indirect evidence for these contacts. Such indirect evidence consists of all the themes and motifs which can be traced to foreign texts, devotions, and art, and for which little, if any, direct evidence can be found. My task will be to trace back to their original sources such features and to uncover and analyse probable exchanges of which no extant written evidence makes any mention. The coverage I have given to the Continental background may seem occasionally too extensive: I have felt it to be essential to define quite precisely the political, religious, cultural, artistic, and, in some cases, economic situation in those European centres with which English centres were in contact, directly or indirectly. This appeared to be the only possible way to show, if not actually prove, why I believe an English theme, cult, or artefact to have been imported from or inspired by a particular European centre at that precise moment. Moreover, English cultural features which reached the Continent are also best highlighted by determining the importance of the European centres to which they were exported. And because this work does not purport to be an examination of the *English Church*, but of the *English Church and the Continent*, the European material is of equal importance to the English, provided it relates to English matters. The ultimate aim of this study is to examine the repercussions of the contacts between late Anglo-Saxon and early Anglo-Norman England and the Continent on both English and European culture, spirituality, and art, taking into account every possible textual and visual testimony to their existence.

My second reason for attempting anything so ambitious is that writing after a lifetime's experience need not be the only way to open up a challenging and important subject. I would be the last to deny the inspiration I have drawn from the pages written by other scholars on various aspects of the exchanges between England and the Continent in general histories of Anglo-Saxon England, the Anglo-Saxon Church, and Anglo-Saxon monasticism. Sir Frank Stenton mentions numerous examples of such exchanges from the narrative and diplomatic sources,[2] while Margaret Deanesly insists on the debt of early Anglo-Saxon churchmen to Rome.[3] The most illuminating account for both the traditionally well-known and the subtler and less obvious influences from the Mediterranean world, Western and Eastern, on early Anglo-Saxon England is to be found in Henry Mayr-Harting's study on the Conversion of England,[4]

[2] F. M. Stenton, *Anglo-Saxon England* (3rd edn.; Oxford, 1971).
[3] M. Deanesly, *The Pre-Conquest Church in England* (London, 1961).
[4] H. Mayr-Harting, *The Coming of Christianity to Anglo-Saxon England* (London, 1972).

further complemented in art-historical terms by Fritz Saxl and Rudolf Wittkower's comprehensive book on English art and the Mediterranean.[5] For the tenth and eleventh centuries, David Knowles's study of late Anglo-Saxon and early Anglo-Norman monasticism includes notable references to the Brogne, Gorze, Cluniac, and Norman contribution in England,[6] while Frank Barlow's books on the English Church in the eleventh century and a recent seminal article by Patrick Wormald[7] are particularly rich in discussions about the Continental background of some English ecclesiastics and their continuous links with European centres. Also in the field of the tenth-century monastic reform, several authors such as Donald Bullough, Thomas Symons, Christopher Hohler, Henry Taylor, and Jonathan Alexander, writing in a collection of essays commemorating the millennium of the *Regularis Concordia*, emphasized the Continental background of tenth-century English culture.[8] It was my great fortune to be able to read Barbara Raw's definitive study on the Anglo-Saxon Crucifixion iconography, published shortly before I finished writing my own book: her work covers a wide scope and many of her conclusions parallel mine, and she has provided a very rich supply of material and focus for discussion.[9]

More specific studies have been made of the exchanges between England and some particular areas of the Continent during the period 600 to 800: such are, for example, Levison's for Gaul and Germany, and Wilfred Moore's remarkable essay on the 'Schola Saxonum' in Rome.[10] On the other hand, two areas alone have been investigated in this respect for the late Anglo-Saxon period: Flanders, in the classic article by Philip Grierson, who catalogued almost every single piece of evidence mentioning contacts with England,[11] and Germany, in another classic article by Karl Leyser, whose breadth of scope covers numerous aspects of Ottonian and West Saxon connections during the tenth century in particular.[12] Finally, some

---

[5] F. Saxl and R. Wittkower, *British Art and the Mediterranean* (London, 1942).

[6] D. Knowles, *The Monastic Order in England* (2nd edn.; Cambridge, 1963).

[7] F. Barlow, *The English Church 1000–1066* (2nd edn.; London, 1979) and *The English Church 1066–1154: A History of the Anglo-Norman Church* (London, 1979); P. Wormald, 'Aethelwold and his Continental Counterparts: Contacts, Comparison, Contrast', in B. Yorke (ed.), *Bishop Aethelwold: His Career and Influence* (Woodbridge, 1988), 13–42.

[8] These essays are edited by D. Parsons in *Tenth-Century Studies* (London and Chichester, 1975).

[9] B. Raw, *Anglo-Saxon Crucifixion Iconography and the Art of the Monastic Revival* (Cambridge, 1990).

[10] W. J. Moore, *The Saxon Pilgrims to Rome and the Schola Saxonum* (Fribourg, 1937).

[11] P. Grierson, 'Relations between England and Flanders before the Norman Conquest', *TRHS*, 4th ser. 23 (1941), 71–112 (repr. in R. W. Southern, *Essays in Medieval History* (London, 1968), 61–92.

[12] K. J. Leyser, 'Die Ottonen und Wessex', *Frühmittelalterliche Studien*, 17 (1983), 73–97.

aspects of the interplay of influences between England and Normandy have been mentioned in Donald Matthew's book on the Norman monasteries and also in Jonathan Alexander's study on the illumination of Mont Saint Michel.[13] The only work which discusses other exchanges in this period comes from an art historian, Charles Reginald Dodwell, whose interests are wide-ranging and spread as far as Aquitaine, southern Italy, and Byzantium.[14]

Many of these distinguished scholars could no doubt have written this book, and done it better than I could ever hope to. But it is a fact that none has. Donald Bullough's 'unwritten work of early medieval historiography' has remained unwritten. There must be a hope that someone brash enough to take this plunge may inspire stronger swimmers to follow. Though I have naturally tried to read around as well as through the vast mass of primary and secondary material, it is inevitable that not all the evidence I have used in this book is equally secure. Much (I hope not *too* much) of what I now think may need modification, even correction. On the other hand, much can and will, I assume, be added. My hope that this book will inspire further reasearch is therefore not the equivalent of the medieval 'humility *topos*' that it so often seems in modern works of scholarship. At the same time, I would claim that the cumulative effect of the evidence I have assembled is significant. The sheer quantity of often incidental information, understated as it surely is by the almost invariably inadequate evidence, is such as to place the English Church of the tenth and eleventh centuries where it certainly saw itself but is too rarely seen by its later historians: in the mainstream culture of Western Christendom.

[13] D. J. A. Matthew, *The Norman Monasteries and their English Possessions* (London, 1962), and J. J. G. Alexander, *Norman Illumination at Mont Saint Michel 966–1100* (Oxford, 1970).
[14] C. R. Dodwell, *Anglo-Saxon Art: a New Perspective* (Manchester, 1982).

THE EVIDENCE

I. THE SOURCES

1. English and Continental sources available

Specific occasions during the course of which exchanges of people, books, relics, and other artefacts took place are mentioned essentially in the narrative sources. Under this heading, I encompass chronicles, annals, saints' lives and other biographies written in England, and some accounts of English events in a few sources from the Continent.

Among English sources, the *Anglo-Saxon Chronicle*, together with its various continuations until the middle of the twelfth century, remains the main narrative document.[1] Apart from this anonymous compilation, begun in the ninth century but going back to the Creation and, more usefully, to the Conversion of England, there are other monastic annals from the tenth century onwards, some contemporary and some incorporated in later texts. Such are the annals of Evesham, Abingdon, and Ramsey, and one set of secular annals, the chronicle written by the Ealdorman Aethelweard, who died about 998.[2] Of a slightly different kind, between the annalistic record and the more detailed chronicle written by one or several known authors, are the histories of Glastonbury, Canterbury, Wells, Durham, Peterborough, Bury, and Westminster, put together by William of Malmesbury (*c*.1095–*c*.1143), Gervase of Canterbury († *c*.1210), Giso of Wells (1060–88), Symeon of Durham († after 1129), Hugh Candidus (*fl.* late twelfth century), Herman of Bury, and Sulcard of Westminster (*c*.1076–85).[3] The twelfth-century accounts among these often incorporate earlier material. Other chronicles are the anonymous *Liber Eliensis* and the chronicle of Battle Abbey, the latter begun with the foundation of the abbey by William the Conqueror in 1067; the chronicle known under the name of 'John' of Worcester, of the early twelfth

---

[1] *ASC*. See also the new edition and study: *The Anglo-Saxon Chronicle: A Collaborative Edition*, gen. eds. D. Dumville and S. Keynes, esp. vol. iii, ed. J. Bately (Cambridge, 1986) and vol. iv, ed. S. Taylor (Cambridge, 1983).

[2] *Chronicon Evesham; Chronicon Abingdon; Chronicon Rameseiensis; Aethelweard.*

[3] *WMHG; Gervase;* J. Hunter (ed.), Giso of Wells, 'Historiola de primordiis episcopatus Somersetensis', in *Ecclesiastical Documents* (London, 1840), 9–20; *Symeon; Hugh Candidus;* Herman in T. Arnold (ed.), *Memorials of St Edmund's Abbey* (3 vols.; London, 1830–6) i; B. W. Scholtz (ed.), Sulcard of Westminster, 'Prologus de construccione Westmonasterii', *Traditio*, 20 (1964), 59–91.

century; and the histories of the kings of England by William of Malmesbury, and of the bishops—those of England by William of Malmesbury and those of the see of Canterbury by Gervase—all three going back to the Conversion in their scope.[4] Also interested in Canterbury and the history, saints, and relics of Christ Church, was the monk Eadmer († c.1130) who, in the first part of the twelfth century, wrote several short histories and tracts on these topics.[5]

Of a more biographical turn, the first work of interest in this context, though slightly earlier than the period covered in this book, is Asser's life of King Alfred.[6] It provides some interesting information on the first renewed contacts with the Continent after the difficult times of the ninth century in England. King Edgar's 'Establishment of Monasteries' is a contemporary account.[7] Apart from William of Malmesbury's history of the kings of England, any other information about later Anglo-Saxon kings comes from hagiographical texts, such as the two lives of Edward the Confessor, one by a monk of St Bertin, probably Goscelin, who lived in England from 1058 to his death in the early twelfth century, and the other by Osbert of Clare, written in the first half of the twelfth century.[8] Ecclesiastical biographies of Archbishops Lanfranc and Anselm were written, the first one in the twelfth century by Milo Crispin of Le Bec and the second before 1100 by Eadmer, an eyewitness.[9] Eadmer, Osbern, who was a monk of Christ Church, and William of Malmesbury wrote Lives of St Dunstan, but the first Life of the founder of the monastic reform had been composed not long after his death in 988 by a foreign, probably Flemish or Lotharingian, cleric, once in the service of the bishop of Liège.[10] Other foreign ecclesiastics throughout the period were commissioned to compose or revise Lives of English saints. Examples of these are Lantfrid, a monk at Winchester possibly coming from Lotharingia, as his name seems to indicate, who wrote a Life of St Swithun before the middle

---

[4] *LE*; E. Searle (ed.), *The Chronicle of Battle Abbey* (Oxford, 1980); *Florence*; *WMGR* and *WMGP*; Gervase's *Actus Pontificum Cantuariensis Ecclesiae*, in Stubbs, *Gervase*, ii. 325–414.

[5] A. Wilmart (ed.), 'Eadmeri Cantuariensis Cantoris Nova Opuscula de Sanctorum Veneratione et Obsecratione', *Revue des sciences religieuses*, 15 (1935), 207–19, 362–70, 371–9.

[6] *Asser*.

[7] *CSD* I. i. 143–54.

[8] *Vita Aedwardi*; M. Bloch (ed.), 'Vita beati ac gloriosi regis Anglorum Eadwardi', *AB* 41 (1923), 5–63.

[9] J. A. Giles (ed.), 'Vita Lanfranci autore Milone Crispino', in *Lanfranci Archiepiscopi Cantuariensis Opera Omnia* (2 vols.; Oxford, 1844) i. 281–313; this Life is based on that of Gilbert Crispin, tr. in *EHD* ii. 626–31; for Anselm, see M. Rule (ed.), *Eadmeri Historia Novorum in Anglia* (London, 1884) and especially R. W. Southern (ed.), *Eadmer: The Life of St Anselm, Archbishop of Canterbury* (Oxford, 1972).

[10] All four Lives of St Dunstan are edited in Stubbs, *Memorials*; on this foreign cleric, who signs only as 'B', see pp. x–xxvi.

of the eleventh century;[11] Abbo of Fleury, who was asked by the monks of Bury to write a Life of St Edmund around 985;[12] and Goscelin, commissioned to write Lives of St Edith of Wilton, St Ivo of Ramsey, St Wulfsige of Sherborne, St Wulfhild, and St Mildrith, as well as a *Liber Confortatorius* and a history of the abbey of St Augustine's at Canterbury.[13] His contemporary and compatriot Folcard of St Bertin also spent some time in England and was commissioned to compose a Life of St John of Beverley.[14] Other hagiographical material was produced locally, some by anonymous authors who rewrote the Lives of early Anglo-Saxon saints whose bodies were rediscovered or translated in the eleventh century, and whose original foundations were then rebuilt, as in the cases of Modwenna of Burton or Werburgh of Chester. Other English authors contributed the Lives of the other two monastic reformers, St Oswald and St Aethelwold: the monk Byrhtferth of Ramsey and Eadmer for Oswald, and Wulfstan as well as Aelfric abbot of Eynsham and author of numerous homilies, for Aethelwold, who had been his master.[15] The Life of the most prominent eleventh-century bishop, Wulfstan of Worcester, was compiled by William of Malmesbury on the basis of an earlier Life by a contemporary of Wulfstan, Coleman.[16]

The wealth of eleventh-century hagiographical material is not to be doubted. Equally interesting is the large Continental contribution to English hagiography, which implies not only the existence of regular contacts with Continental centres and traditions, but also a prolonged and

[11] E. P. Sauvage (ed.), 'Sancti Swithuni Wintoniensis episcopi translatio et miracula', *AB* 4 (1885), 367–410; M. Lapidge, 'Three Latin Poems from Æthelwold's School at Winchester', *ASE* 1 (1972), 105–6, and *The cult of St Swithun* (Oxford, forthcoming) expresses doubts about Lantfrid's Lotharingian origin and suggests that he may have been Frankish.

[12] Edited in Winterbottom, *Three Lives*, 67–87; Aelfric used this Life when he wrote his Old English Life of this saint, edited in *Aelfric's Lives of the Saints*, ii. 314–35.

[13] A. Wilmart (ed.), 'La Légende de Ste Édith en prose et en vers par le moine Goscelin', AB 56 (1938), 5–101 and 265–307; W. D. Macray ed., *Miracula S. Ivonis* in *Chronicon Rameseiensis*, pp. lix–lxxxiv; C. H. Talbot (ed.), 'The Life of St Wulfsi of Sherborne by Goscelin', RB 69 (1959), 68–85; M. Esposito (ed.), 'La Vie de Ste Wulfhilde par Goscelin de Cantorbéry', *AB* 32 (1913), 10–26; D. Rollason (ed.), 'Goscelin of Canterbury's account of the Translation and Miracles of St Mildrith (BHL 5961/4): An Edition with Notes', *Mediaeval Studies*, 48 (1986), 139–210; C. H. Talbot (ed.), 'The *Liber Confortatorius* of Goscelin of St Bertin', *Studia Anselmiana*, 37 (1955), 1–117; *HTA*. A Life of St Swithun, traditionally ascribed to Goscelin (E. P. Sauvage (ed.), 'Vita Sancti Swithuni Wintoniensis episcopi auctore Goscelino, monacho Sithiensi', *AB* 7 (1888), 373–80), has now been attributed to a different author, see Barlow in *Vita Aedwardi*, 111.

[14] J. Raine (ed.), 'Vita sancti Johannis episcopi Eboracensis auctore Folcardo' in *HCY* i. 239–60. On both Folcard and Goscelin, see also A. Gransden, *Historical Writing in England c. 500 to c. 1307* (London, 1974), 63–6, and *Vita Aedwardi*, xlv–li and li–lix.

[15] Both Lives of St Oswald are edited in *HCY* i. 399–475 and ii. 1–40. The 'anonymous' Life has now been proved to have been written by Byrhtferth. The Life of Aethelwold is in Winterbottom, *Three Lives*, 17–29.

[16] *WMVW*.

thorough knowledge of the respective political and cultural situation of
both English and European affairs on both sides. A look at contemporary
narrative sources from the Continent confirms this familiarity of specific
European centres with England, whose affairs were followed and regis-
tered in quite a few of the extant sources. The most important of these are
the Annals of St Bertin from Flanders, the Chronicle of the Counts of
Anjou, Richer's History of France, the Annals and the History of the
Church of Reims by Flodoard, the Histories by Rodulfus Glaber,
Adalbero of Laon's poem to King Robert and the Life of Gauzlin by André
of Fleury.[17] From northern Germany the Chronicle of Thietmar of
Meerseburg and the Life of Bishop Bernward of Hildesheim by Thangmar
and Adam of Bremen's History of the Church of Bremen are of interest;[18]
and from Italy the *Liber Pontificalis* naturally, but also the Chronicle of
Monte Cassino and Liutprand of Cremona's *Antapodosis*.[19] From the
Eastern Empire Anna Comnena's *Alexiad* and the Book of Ceremonies of
Constantine VII Porphyrogenitus are of relevance.[20] Equally interesting
are other Continental documents which also report exchanges with the
English: the accounts of the council and dossier relating to the cult of St
Martial at Limoges,[21] letters of English kings and ecclesiastics to and from
popes,[22] the archbishop of Reims Fulk, the Count of Flanders, the duke

---

[17] F. Grat, J. Vielliard, and S. Clémencet (eds.), *Les Annales de St Bertin* (Paris, 1964);
L. Halphen and R. Poupardin (eds.), *Chronique des comtes d'Anjou et des seigneurs d'Amboise*,
(Paris, 1969); R. Latouche (ed.), *Richer: Histoire de France 888–995* (2 vols.; Paris, 1964–7);
P. Lauer (ed.), *Les Annales de Flodoard* (Paris, 1906); M. Lejeune (ed.), *Flodoard: Histoire de
l'Église de Reims* (2 vols.; Reims, 1854); N. Bulst (ed.), with J. France and P. Reynolds trs, *Rodulfi
Glabri Historiarum Libri Quinque: Rodulfus Glaber, 'The Five Books of the Histories'* (Oxford, 1989);
C. Carozzi (ed.), *Adalbéron de Laon: Poème au roi Robert* (Paris, 1979); R. H. Bautier and
G. Labory (eds.), *André de Fleury: Vie de Gauzlin, abbé de Fleury* (Paris, 1969).

[18] I. M. Lappenberg, rev. F. Kurze (eds.), *Thietmar Merseburgensis Episcopi Chronicon*, MGH
SRG (Hanover, 1889); O. Holder-Egger (ed.), *Vita Bernwardi Hildesheimensis Episcopi auctore
Thangmari*, MGH SS iv. 754–82; B. Schmeidler (ed.), *Adam von Bremen: Hamburgische
Kirchengeschichte*, MGH SRG (Hanover and Leipzig, 1917).

[19] *LP*; H. Hoffmann (ed.), *Chronica monasterii casinensis*, MGH SS xxxiv (Hanover, 1980);
J. Becker (ed.), *Liudprandus: Opera*, MHG SRG (Hanover and Leipzig, 1915)

[20] E. A. S. Dawes (tr.), *The Alexiad of the Princess Anna Comnena* (London, 1967); Constantin
VII Porphyrogénète, *Le Livre des Cérémonies* (2 vols.; Paris, 1967).

[21] On St Martial and England, see Adémar of Chabannes, *Historiarum Libri Tres*, P L 141, 56
and 66; *Commemoratio abbatum Lemovicensium*, ibid. 84; *Epistola de apostolatu S. Martialis*, ibid.
99; *Sermo III*, ibid. 122; and *Acta Concilii Lemovicensis* ii, P L 142, 1368–69.

[22] Omitting the texts usually regarded as spurious, there are four letters sent by popes to a king
and to several ecclesiastics in England in the late 9th c.: three from Pope John VIII to Burgred,
king of the Mercians (873–4), to the English clergy (873–5), and to Archbishop Aethelred
(877–8), and one from Pope Formosus to the bishops of England (891–6), see *CSD* 1. i. 1–2,
2–3, 3–6, 35–8. After this, there are no more letters until 960, the date of a privilege of Pope John
XII to Archbishop Dunstan accompanying the grant of the *pallium*, ibid. 88–92. Between 960
and the end of the 11th c. we have nine letters from popes to English kings and ecclesiastics, and
five in the other direction. These are: a letter from Pope John XII allowing Bishop Aethelwold
to eject the secular canons from Winchester cathedral (963), one from a Pope John to Ealdorman

of Aquitaine, and a variety of monastic houses asking for alms, such as St Samson's at Dol, St Peter's at Ghent, St Ouen at Rouen, Ste Geneviève in Paris, and St Bertin.[23] A variety of other sources mention casually grants of land or benefactions, such as St Denis', to whom King William I gave some money for the building of a tower, and the presence of Anglo-Saxon artists or architects, such as one Gautier 'Coorland' at Poitiers.[24]

By the same token, English non-narrative sources can sometimes offer an insight into some of the exchanges which took place during this period. Such sources are the extant laws of the kings Edward, Edmund, Aethelstan, Edgar, Aethelred, Cnut, and William I, which occasionally make provision for foreigners visiting England or, more subtly yet, display at least a knowledge, if not occasionally an imitation, of certain Continental formulae and legal features, Lombard or Carolingian.[25] The same could be said of royal writs and sometimes of private charters.[26] The latter are interesting also from the point of view of their contents, particularly after the Conquest, when an increasing number of donations of land to Norman abbeys becomes notable. Even more important for my purpose are the

---

Aelfric (982–98), one from Pope John XV concerning the peace between King Aethelred and Duke Richard I of Normandy (991), one from Pope Leo IX to King Edward about the transfer of the see from Crediton to Exeter (1050), two from Pope Victor II to that same king, giving privileges to the abbeys of Chertsey and Ely (1055–7), two from Pope Nicholas II confirming Giso of Wells and Wulfwig of Dorchester in the rights of their sees (1061), and one from Pope Alexander II to King William I in 1071 after the legatine council of Windsor in 1070, ibid. 109–13, 173–4, 177–9, 524–5, 543–4, 544–5, 548–50, 550–2, and *CSD* I. ii. 579–80. In the other direction, only one letter survives from the Pre-Conquest period, that of the English bishops to the pope in 1020, protesting against the obligation to go to Rome to fetch the *pallium*, see *CSD* I. i. 441–7. For the Post-Conquest period, four letters are extant, three from Lanfranc to Popes Alexander II and Gregory VII (1071, 1072, and 1080) and one from King William I to the latter pope (1080), see *CSD* I. ii. 572–73, 597–601, 628–9.

[23] Fulk of Reims's letters to King Alfred and Archbishop Plegmund (885–6 and 890–1) are in *CSD* I. i. 6–12, 12–13, and 13; that from the Count of Flanders Arnulf to Dunstan (961 or 966), ibid. 93–5. For those from St Samson's to King Aethelstan (*c*.927), from Abbot Wido of St Peter at Ghent to Dunstan (981–6), from St Ouen's and Ste Geneviève's to Kind Edgar and from Abbot Odbert of St Bertin to Archbishop Sigeric (990), ibid. 38–40, and that of Odbert, ibid. 175–7; and Stubbs, *Memorials*, 380–1, 363–4, 366–8 for the others.

[24] S. McK. Crosby, *The Abbey of St Denis 475–1122* (New Haven, 1942) i. 79, 186; Gautier is mentioned in the *Chronicon Sancti Maxentii Pictaviensis*, cited in V. Mortet and P. Deschamps (eds.), *Recueil de textes relatifs à l'histoire de l'architecture . . . en France au moyen-âge* (Paris, 1911–29), 141.

[25] A. J. Robertson (ed.), *The Laws of the Kings of England from Edmund to Henry I* (Cambridge, 1925). Most of the laws addressing ecclesiastical issues are edited in *CSD* I. i and ii. On the Carolingian parallels see, for example, J. Campbell, 'Observations on the English Government from the Tenth to the Twelfth Centuries' in his *Essays in Anglo-Saxon History* (London, 1986), 43–54.

[26] F. E. Harmer (ed.), *Anglo-Saxon Writs* (Manchester, 1952); A. J. Robertson (ed.), *Anglo-Saxon Charters* (Cambridge, 1939); and P. H. Sawyer (ed.), *Anglo-Saxon Charters: An Annotated List and Bibliography* (London, 1968).

extant wills, which give accounts of people going abroad to Rome and to the Holy Land, and occasionally record bequests from people who had been abroad and left to family, friends, or acquaintances objects acquired during their travels. So did, for example, the bishop of London Theodred (*c.*942–51), himself a foreigner to England, who went to Rome and brought back from Pavia some ecclesiastical vestments, which he left to kinsmen and friends in England.[27]

Equally rich are the numerous letters preserved from and to foreign correspondents. Some examples of the first category have been already mentioned above. Other examples of letters from English kings and ecclesiastics to popes, princes, and ecclesiastics abroad have been preserved, in most cases concerned with alms or with problems of ecclesiastical discipline such as those relating to the primacy of the see of Canterbury under Lanfranc.[28] More personal or pastoral letters are sometimes also of interest, either because they were written by foreign bishops governing English sees, as were those of Herbert Losinga bishop of the newly established see of Norwich but a Lotharingian by birth,[29] or those written by one English cleric to another, such as those of Aelfric to Wulfsige, bishop of Sherborne, and Wulfstan, archbishop of York.[30]

Both Wulfstan and Aelfric wrote numerous homilies. Wulfstan's deal mostly with theological and moral themes and were written for special occasions.[31] Aelfric's collections, by contrast, include numerous feasts of the saints and it is particularly interesting to analyse his choice of non-English saints.[32] Two tenth-century sets of homilies, the Blickling and the Vercelli

[27] D. Whitelock (ed.), *Anglo-Saxon Wills* (Cambridge, 1930), 2–5. Theodred's will is also edited in *CSD* I. i. 76–81.

[28] Other examples of letters sent abroad from England are: a letter from English ecclesiastics to the Count of Flanders Arnulf, asking him to let them have back a book stolen from Winchester and taken to Flanders, where the Count bought it; a letter to Dunstan from Fleury, possibly written by an English monk living there, who asked for a book to be returned to him (974–88); and one from Abbo to Dunstan about his completing the Life of St Edmund (985–88); a letter from Abbot Fulrad of St Vaast of Arras to Archbishop Aethelgar (988–90) and another, also to Aethelgar, from Odbert of St Bertin, asking for alms (988–90); a letter from a prelate in Rome to Dunstan, thanking him for a present, possibly a relic (959–88) and one from a foreign visitor putting himself under Dunstan's protection; and a letter attached by Abbot Wulfric of St Augustine's to a MS of the Life of St Dunstan which he sent to Abbo at Fleury, asking him to put it into verse (1000–4), see Stubbs, *Memorials*, 361–2, 376–7, 378–80, 383–4, 384–5, 370–1, 374–6, 409. For Lanfranc's letters and the dispute relating to the primacy of Canterbury, see V. H. Clover and M. Gibson (eds.), *The Letters of Lanfranc, Archbishop of Canterbury* (London, 1979), nos. 1–5, pp. 30–59.

[29] The East Anglian see was transferred from Thetford to Norwich in the 1090s. On Herbert Losinga, see E. M. Goulbourn and H. Symonds (eds.), *The Life, Letters and Sermons of Bishop Herbert de Losinga* (2 vols.; London, 1878).

[30] CSD I. i. 191–226, 242–302.

[31] D. Bethurum (ed.), *The Homilies of Wulfstan* (Oxford, 1957).

[32] B. Thorpe (ed.), *The Homilies of the Anglo-Saxon Church; The Homilies of Aelfric* (2 vols.; London, 1844–6); J. C. Pope (ed.), *Homilies of Aelfric; A Supplementary Collection* (2 vols.; London, 1967–8); and most important for this study, *Aelfric's Lives of the Saints*.

collections, are less interesting from this point of view, since they also include exclusively texts for the major feasts;[33] however, the second set is revealing from another point of view, as its very name indicates. The homilies were written in a book of Anglo-Saxon prose and poetry, which reached the north Italian city of Vercelli by the eleventh century, undoubtedly brought there by a traveller who would have to go through this town on his way to Rome, for example:[34] the city was by no means negligible at the time, being not only a centre for Irish pilgrims and monks, but also important enough to have been chosen by the pope for the meeting of a council in 1050, which the Norman bishop of Dorchester, Ulf, attended.[35]

After the narrative, diplomatic, epistolary, and didactic sources, two other kinds remain to be considered: the liturgical and the artistic. They are the least 'direct' and 'immediate' of all sources, and the evidence they present requires skills of interpretation and sometimes almost detective reasoning. But the wealth of indications they offer for the knowledge of foreign contacts and influences is immense, both in the forms and texts they borrow and in the feasts they adopt, for the liturgy, and in the iconography and stylistic motifs for art. The liturgical texts first. Some of the books used in England were imported from abroad and adapted for English usage, such as the first part of the 'Leofric Missal', written at St Vaast of Arras in the ninth century and brought to England, where it reached Glastonbury by the later tenth century, a path also followed at about the same date by the 'Utrecht Psalter', this time from Reims to Canterbury.[36] Other books were replicas of Continental ones, as were most Anglo-Saxon collectars, such as those of Leofric and Wulfstan, of the second half of the eleventh century, modelled on the famous book of collects of the tenth-century canon Stephen of Liège.[37] The main interest

---

[33] R. Morris (ed.), *The Blickling Homilies of the Tenth Century* (London, 1874–80); M. Förster (ed.), 'Die Vercelli Homilien', in C. W. M. Grein (ed.), *Bibliothek der angelsächsischen Prosa* (1st edn. R. P. Wülker, 13 vols.; Cassel and Göttingen, 1872–1933, xii; repr. Darmstadt, 1964) or the facsimile edition by C. Sisam, *The Vercelli Book*, EEMF XIX (Copenhagen, 1976).

[34] M. Halsall, 'Vercelli and the *Vercelli Book*', *Proceedings of the Medieval Languages Association*, 84 (1969), 1545–7; A. M. Tommasini, *Irish saints in Italy* (tr. London, 1937), 246.

[35] *ASC*, E1047 (= 1050), 116.

[36] The 'Leofric Missal' is Oxford, Bodleian Library, Bodley MS 579, edited by Warren, *Leofric Missal*. The traditional attribution of the first part to St Vaast is confirmed by E. M. Drage in a detailed study of the MS in her thesis 'Bishop Leofric and Exeter Cathedral Chapter (1050–1072): A Reassessment of the Manuscript Evidence', D.Phil. thesis (Oxford, 1978), 83–4 and not challenged by R. Deshman, 'The Leofric Missal and Tenth-Century English Art', *ASE* 6 (1977), 145–73. On the route followed by the Utrecht Psalter, see S. Dufrenne, 'Les Copies anglaises du Psautier d'Utrecht', *Scriptorium*, 18 (1964), 185–97; and also Wormald, 'The Utrecht Psalter', in *Collected Writings*, 36–46, and D. Tselos, 'English MS Illustration and the Utrecht Psalter', *The Art Bulletin*, 41 (1959), 137–49.

[37] Leofric's Collectar is British Library, Harleian MS 2961, edited by Dewick and Frere, *Leofric Collectar*; Wulfstan's Collectar is CCCC MS 391, edited by Hughes, *Portiforium*. On Stephen of Liège, see A. Auda, *L'École musicale liégeoise au Xe siècle: Étienne de Liège* (Brussels, 1923), 27–38, 42–66 and my ch. 3.

of the liturgical material, however, remains that of the texts and order of the celebrations, in particular for the feasts of non-English saints. Through them, it is possible to trace the import of particular saints or of particular liturgical formulae from specific European centres, where these saints were venerated or these formulae used. To the impact of the tenth-century Continental Benedictine reform on England and, later, to the arrival of several Lotharingian bishops on English sees in the eleventh century, correspond two successive waves of European saints from the regions concerned in the English liturgy.[38] Equally, we find strong elements reminiscent of Continental coronation orders, pontifical rituals and monastic customaries in English coronation orders, pontificals, and in the two main customaries of the period, the *Regularis Concordia* and Lanfranc's *Monastic Constitutions*. The first of these incorporates elements from Fleury and Ghent, and the second elements from Cluny and also from Bec.[39] It must be noted, however, that most of these texts were adapted for use in England, with the addition of English stresses, themselves revealing for the spirituality of the English Church. Moreover, in not a few cases, the borrowings were also working the other way round, especially after the Conquest, when Norman abbeys came into contact with English cults and texts, but also before then, on account of the liturgical texts sent from England to the Continent, such as the 'Winchcombe Sacramentary', a late tenth-century book written at either Winchcombe or Ramsey and sent from there to the abbey of Fleury.[40]

Exchanges in both directions, with an emphasis on influences from England on Flemish and Norman illumination, are also most common and significant in English tenth- and eleventh-century art. Through the illuminated manuscripts, ivories, and sculpture of the period, it is possible to trace iconographical themes from Early Christian, Eastern and Byzantine, Carolingian and Ottonian art. It is often difficult to isolate these elements, since it is not uncommon for Early Christian themes to have reached England through the medium of Carolingian art, and for Byzantine illustrations to be found in English art in the form they have taken in Ottonian art, rather than having been introduced in this country directly from Rome or southern Italy and Byzantium. First, we find an obvious indication of significant influences from Carolingian and Ottonian art in England. We deduce it from the presence of a manuscript such as the Utrecht Psalter in England, and it is confirmed when studying together

---

[38] See below, chs. 2 and 3.

[39] The coronation orders have been studied by J. L. Nelson, *Politics and Ritual in Early Medieval Europe* (London, 1986). The two customaries are *RC* and *MC*.

[40] The 'Winchcombe Sacramentary' is Orléans, Bibliothèque Municipale MS 127.

the illuminations of manuscripts and ivories from the School of Metz, such as those of the 'Drogo Sacramentary' and those of a 'Winchester School' manuscript like the 'Benedictional of St Aethelwold', or Ottonian manuscripts from the Trier School, such as the 'Gregory Register' and the eleventh-century 'Claudius Pontifical'.[41] It is possible, however, to prove that there were also some direct influences from more remote centres in Italy and Constantinople, for example, if we compare the Benedictional of St Aethelwold with Greek menologioi from the point of view of its iconography as well as of its presentation, and again some of the compositions of the Crucifixion scenes on English Crosses to those found in Eastern manuscripts.[42] Equally, we find once again examples of motifs first expressed in Anglo-Saxon art, such as the iconography of the Nativity with the midwife Salome and of the Ascension with the disappearing Christ, then introduced in Continental art.[43] And the iconography of St Benedict could have reached this country from Monte Cassino, the only centre where it is illustrated in a particular way, but it is not impossible that it was actually first established in England and was passed on to Monte Cassino itself from here, since we know that both manuscripts and craftsmen from Britain were highly regarded at St Benedict's own foundation in the eleventh century.[44] The Anglo-Saxon art of embroidery, possibly first introduced into England by craftsmen familiar with Byzantine techniques, had reached great heights here in the eleventh century and was greatly prized as far as Italy and also, nearer home, in Normandy.[45] Equally famous was Anglo-Saxon metalwork, especially when inset with precious stones, and, in this particular field, exchanges of techniques and designs were common with Scandinavia.[46]

2. Method of study

The sketch of the sources has adumbrated the double nature of the evidence available. On the one hand, we find direct accounts of events such as embassies, trade relations, missions, official and sometimes private travels and pilgrimages, briefly mentioned or described at length in the narrative sources, and occasionally referred to in the hagiography,

---

[41] *Drogo-Sakramentar*; *Benedictional of St Aethelwold*; for the 'Gregory Register' and the 'Claudius Pontifical', which is a part of British Library, Cotton MS Claudius A.III, see *Claudius Pontificals*; and see below, ch. 3.

[42] See below, ch. 4.

[43] M. Schapiro, 'The Image of the Disappearing Christ: The Ascension in English Art around the Year 1000' (1943), repr. in his *Late Antique, Early Christian and Medieval Art: Selected Papers* (London, 1980), iii. 280–5.

[44] See below, ch. 4.

[45] See below, chs. 4 and 7.

[46] Dodwell, *Anglo-Saxon Art*, chs. 2 and 7.

biographies, letters, law codes, and private documents such as the wills. From such documents, we hear about the identity and the social and professional standing of the people involved in these travels, about their business, and sometimes about the objects (books, relics), artefacts, gifts or goods which, one way or the other, changed hands on the occasion of these exchanges. In some cases, this information is given in as complete a way as possible: in the account of the embassy sent by Hugh of Paris to King Aethelstan to ask for the hand of one of the latter's sisters for Hugh, both William of Malmesbury and French sources such as Flodoard's *Annals* mention in detail the gifts of relics brought by Hugh's envoys to England.[47] In others, we can infer the existence of possible exchanges from the simple recording of an event in a fairly laconic way: when the *Anglo-Saxon Chronicle* records the presence of three English ecclesiastics at the papal council of Reims in 1049, we are entitled to suppose that, having spent their time meeting European bishops and abbots, talking to them, attending the papal Translation of the relics of St Rémi, and viewing the building in progress of the church of the abbey, they would have become familiar with some of these people's preoccupations, devotions, intellectual and artistic tastes.[48] Hence, for both examples cited above, it becomes necessary to draw an outline, albeit brief, of the European background which would have been accessible to such visitors, for example, the importance of the abbey of St Rémi within Reims, itself a highly prosperous centre during the tenth and eleventh centuries in economic success, religious observance, and intellectual energy, especially when Gerbert's school was in its full bloom in the 990s.[49]

These sources convey the basic information, from which a wider panorama can be constructed, with the help of additional information about the places visited by Englishmen abroad or about the royal court, monastic and episcopal centres in England, to which visitors from abroad are known to have come, for example, Abbo of Fleury to Ramsey (986–8) and a Venetian nobleman to Ramsey.[50] The second category of sources offers exclusively what I would call *indirect* information, because never given for its own sake, but always in passing, and, in some cases, the artistic evidence for example, only when it can be traced back to its source by the historian. Here, my task is not simply to identify and point out these

---

[47] *WMGR* i. 149–51; Lauer, *Flodoard*, 36.

[48] *ASC*, E1046, D1050, 111–12, 115.

[49] See below, ch. 7.

[50] HCY i, Byrhtferth's Life of Oswald, 431–2, and ii, Eadmer's Life of Oswald, 22–3. Abbo describes his visit in the prologue to his *Quaestiones Grammaticales*, ed. A. Guerreau-Jalabert (Paris, 1982); on the Venetian at Ramsey, see the 'Miracula S. Ivonis' in *Chronicon Rameseiensis*, p. lxvii.

passing comments, and place them within the context of our knowledge, or lack of it, from other sources. It is also to retrace the remaining evidence back to its foreign origins, if it appears indeed to have originated abroad, from our knowledge of the parallel evidence from foreign sources, and to trace its way into England or from England on to the Continent as best I can. Effectively, it means deducing from elements or images encountered in England, for example, not only where the origin of these elements or images is to be found, but also how they came to be adopted and adapted in English books and art. The representation of the Magi as kings in the Benedictional of St Aethelwold appears within exactly the same five or ten years (late 970s–late 980s) in an Ottonian manuscript, the *Codex Egberti*, and in a Byzantine menologion, that of Basil II.[51] Did it circulate from one manuscript to another, and if so, in which direction, when, and how? In other words, what does this contemporary representation in these three books say about the links between England, the Ottonian and the Byzantine Empires?

The two kinds of evidence are obviously complementary and help piece together the different strands of knowledge about the contacts between England and the European scene. Hence, they are not to be treated separately, but together; the determining factor for this study will be the geography of these exchanges as revealed by the sources.

The presentation of the evidence in chapters 2 to 7 follows the geographical pattern imposed by what the sources indicate regarding the contacts between the English Church and the Continent: Flanders, the German Empire including in particular the kingdom of Burgundy, the Rhineland, and Lotharingia, Italy (northern, central, and southern, but excluding Rome itself), Rome, the Byzantine Empire and the East and, finally, France, which includes Brittany, Normandy, Aquitaine, the Île de France, and the duchy of Burgundy. Each chapter gives first a survey of the geographical area encompassed by the overall title of the chapter itself, delineating the history and cultural status of those episcopal sees, major monastic and urban centres within this area, for which some evidence of links with England is available. For evident reasons, other centres on the Continent, however important in their own right, will be omitted as a rule. The second part of each chapter presents a survey of the available factual evidence for contacts: reports of political events, matrimonial alliances, visits, and cultural exchanges. The third, fourth, and fifth parts analyse respectively the cultural, devotional, and artistic exchanges, from both

---

[51] *Benedictional of St Aethelwold*, fo. 24v; *Codex Egberti*, fo. 29; *Menologio*, fo. 272; on this matter see below, chs. 5 and 6.

narrative and allusive sources, between the geographical areas covered in the chapters and England.

3. Problems relating to the sources

Like almost every medieval historian, the historian who tries to describe the outlook and components of Anglo-Saxon culture finds it difficult not to complain about the problems posed by the sources, the first being their sparsity. This is particularly true for the indirect evidence such as that of the liturgical books and of works of art. C. R. Dodwell has analysed in detail the reasons for the disappearance of works of art, destroyed by fire throughout the Middle Ages, carried away by the Normans to their French possessions as war loot, or deliberately taken to pieces for the bullion value of the metal and precious stones.[52] Ely manuscripts and ecclesiastical objects were removed to Normandy after the Conquest;[53] the single sizeable example of possibly the most famous Anglo-Saxon craft, that of embroidery, has survived only in the Bayeux tapestry. Reliquaries and sacred vases were melted even in Anglo-Saxon times when a series of bad crops brought the threat of famine close, and Bishop Aethelwold did not hesitate to sacrifice such objects for cash;[54] what contemporaries and later medieval conflicts, robberies, and fires had left intact, the Reformation further destroyed or scattered. This was particularly true of books as well. The Norman ecclesiastical staff of the twelfth century often looked down on Anglo-Saxon liturgical and theological manuscripts and, on account of the liturgical changes introduced then, numerous Anglo-Saxon Church books were either lost or, more often, erased and written over to save the parchment. The majority of surviving books are the illuminated manuscripts, preserved on account of their artistic value or of their reputed connection with specific saints, such as the 'St Dunstan Pontifical' or the 'Portiforium of St Wulfstan'. In the case of the diplomatic evidence, charters and wills only survive in the archives of monasteries and churches well enough organized to have preserved them in their cartularies or single sheets: hence the slightly distorted vision we may have of the success and popularity of East Anglian monasteries during the eleventh century, because so many of these documents include bequests to Ely and Bury in particular. It is, in fact, more probable that bequests were made to all monastic centres and churches, but that only the best organized of these preserved such documents in their archives.

---

[52] Dodwell, *Anglo-Saxon Art*, 4–12.

[53] *LE*, 194–5; evidence for such removals is also found in Norman sources, see Foreville, *William of Poitiers*, 222–7.

[54] Wulfstan's Life of St Aethelwold in Winterbottom, *Three Lives*, 50.

Hence, the second problem posed by the survival of the evidence is its haphazard nature. It is sometimes difficult to tell whether one centre was more active than another in furthering exchanges with European centres. A centre may then appear to reflect wide contacts, whereas, in fact, this impression is due to some accident instrumental in the destruction of the evidence from other centres, perhaps equal or more active in that respect. No liturgical books, and hardly any manuscripts at all, survive from either Ely or Glastonbury, two of the most important Anglo-Saxon cultural and spiritual centres: since we know about the looting of Ely manuscripts after the Conquest and the destruction of Glastonbury's immensely rich library at the Reformation, it is obvious that their manuscript production must have been considerable, and probably reflected a wealth of cultural exchanges.[55] We only hear about Abbot Manni of Evesham, one of the greatest and most famous goldsmiths of his age, known at least as far as France, through a random entry in the Chronicle of Evesham, since his works have not survived;[56] we also have little knowledge of how impressive Anglo-Saxon cathedrals and monastic churches may have been, except through textual descriptions, since so many were pulled down by the Normans, as were Winchester, Bury, and Durham, to make room for churches built by them. We are left under the impression that Anglo-Saxon architects and builders could only build the small churches left from that period, in villages where Norman taste did not impose, or lack of money prevented, the new building style and size.[57] Thus, it is wise always to remember such examples of losses and destructions before making specific statements about Anglo-Saxon tastes and openness of culture.[58]

II. THE SPREAD OF CONTINENTAL INFLUENCE IN ENGLAND

1. *The Continent and English centres*

Reference has already been made to some of the ways in which cultural exchanges were promoted. Examples of these are the embassies, such as that of Hugh to Aethelstan, that of Otto to Edgar, that of Cnut to the Duke of Aquitaine, and that of Bishop Ealdred to the imperial court at Cologne in 1054.[59] The pilgrimages, such as those of Archbishop Sigeric to Rome

[55] J. P. Carley, 'John Leland and the Contents of English Pre-Dissolution Libraries: Glastonbury Abbey', *Scriptorium*, 40 (1987), 107–20.
[56] *Chronicon Evesham*, 86–7.
[57] On these two issues, see Dodwell, *Anglo-Saxon Art*, 55, 58, 65–7, 231–4.
[58] A. Ayton and V. Davies, 'Ecclesiastical Wealth in England in 1086', in W. J. Shiels and D. Wood (eds.), *The Church and Wealth*, (Studies in Church History, 24; Oxford, 1988), 47–60.
[59] For Hugh and Aethelstan see above note 47; for Otto's gifts, see *Florence*, i. 139; for Eadred, see *ASC*, CD1054, 129, and *Florence* i. 212.

in 990 and of Ealdred to the Holy Land, and trade, which we know Flemish and Norman merchants to have carried out in London, provide two other examples.[60] On these occasions, books, relics, and valuable objects were exchanged: Hugh sent to Aethelstan the Holy Lance, Otto sent to Edgar several manuscripts, and Cnut sent a book containing saints' lives to William of Aquitaine.[61] Inspiration was found abroad for new devotions and for artistic styles: the pilgrimage to Rome reinforced the cults of some Roman and other saints, venerated in churches on the way to Rome, such as St Rémi of Reims, St Vaast of Arras, and St Maurice of Agaune, and was sometimes instrumental in introducing a saint little known in England but venerated in centres on the pilgrimage route, such as St Christina of Bolsena or St Caprasius of Aullà; Ealdred deliberately introduced the style of Rhineland metalworkers, which he admired from having seen it in Cologne, in the church he restored at Beverley.[62] Other kinds of exchanges are more rarely mentioned, but some examples exist to confirm their activity. During his three years in France with Queen Emma on her exile, Abbot Aelfsige of Peterborough toured various monasteries and on his visit to Bonneval, on the Loire valley, he acquired the relics of their patron saint, Florentinus, which he later brought to Peterborough.[63] Cnut, Edward, and William I all appointed Lotharingian and Norman bishops throughout the century to English sees; some, such as Leofric at Exeter and Giso at Wells, introduced in the liturgy of their cathedrals various German and Burgundian saints, and Abbot Thurstan attempted but failed to introduce the Norman style of liturgical chanting at Glastonbury in 1083.[64] Other kinds of exchanges can only be deduced from passing comments in various texts: merchants from abroad, a Greek 'bishop' at Malmesbury in the late-tenth century, soldiers spending some time in Constantinople in the Varangian guard, exiles to Flanders and Normandy, such as Earl Godwine's son Swein and even the future King Edward himself, returned exiles from even further afar, such as the Aetheling Edward and his family reared in Hungary, matrimonial alliances, such as those of Aethelred, then Cnut, with Emma of Normandy, Earl Tostig and William I, both of whom took wives from the family of the count of Flanders, and Godwine's wife the Danish Gytha, not to mention the numerous alliances of Aethelstan's sisters in the early tenth century. All these bear witness to the diversity and wealth of contacts between England

---

[60] Sigeric's pilgrimage diary is still extant, see Stubbs, *Memorials*, 391–5; on Ealdred's pilgrimage, see *Florence*, i. 218; on trade, see Robertson, *Laws*, IV Aethelred 5 and 6, 73.

[61] *Acta Concilii Lemovicensis*, ii. 1369.

[62] *Chronica pontificum ecclesiae Eboracensis Pars I auctore anonimo* in *HCY* ii. 353–4.

[63] *Hugh Candidus*, 48–9.

[64] See below, chs. 3 and 7; on Thurstan's attempt, see *ASC*, E1083, 160, and *WMHG*, 156–8.

and its neighbours during this period, and the opportunities for exchanges of influences in the cultural, devotional, and artistic fields.

Such links as these are specifically mentioned in various texts, and are placed in the context of the history of a religious or political centre: embassies were received most of the time at Winchester, a main royal residence, exiles went to other courts, relics and devotions were brought to the churches under the control of the abbots or bishops who venerated these saints and acquired these relics. Can we then assume that these contacts were also operative in the less famous, poorer, more retired centres, or are we to conclude that only the mainstream towns and abbeys were thus exposed to Continental influences?

2. *Foreign influences within England*

The evidence available makes it quite clear that contacts between English religious houses and the court at Winchester, and among religious houses themselves, were frequent and intensive. In the late tenth century, monks from the reformed monasteries, such as Abingdon, Winchester, and especially Glastonbury, became bishops at Sherborne, archbishops of Canterbury, abbots at Evesham, Thorney, and Ramsey, to cite only the most famous examples. Bishops and abbots spent quite a lot of time at court, and King Edward appointed his chaplains such as Giso and Hermann and his doctor the monk Baldwin of St Denis as bishops of Wells, Ramsbury, and abbot of Bury. Monks were educated in one abbey and became abbots of another, such as Wulfsige of Sherborne, educated possibly at Westminster, or Wulfstan of Worcester, later archbishop of York, educated at Evesham and Peterborough. An episode in the Life of Wulfstan exemplifies the circulation of manuscripts: when a pupil at Peterborough, he used to learn on a specific psalter, which Cnut subsequently removed from this abbey to offer as a present to the Emperor. While an ambassador in Germany, Ealdred of York recovered this book and brought it back, offering it to Wulfstan:[65] this manuscript, now CCCC 9, a Worcester homiliary, has an Evesham calendar bound into it though it remained at Worcester.[66] The careers of both Wulfstan and Ealdred, not

[65] *WMVW* 5, 15–16.

[66] I have accepted and followed F. Wormald's dating and attributions in his edition of the calendars, with one reservation, included by himself, in his attribution of calendar 18 to St Mary's, Worcester: this reservation arises from the absence of Oswald's feast on 15 April, not entered in this calendar, as one would have expected it to have been by then. This may have been the reason for Wormald's question mark. He nevertheless chose Worcester on account of the origin of the MS itself, CCCC 9, an Homiliary from Worcester. The only significant English saint in the calendar—entered in capitals—is Ecgwin, who was venerated at both Worcester and Evesham. Wormald's calendar 16 has been ascribed by Sir I. Atkins to Worcester where, according to him, it was copied by Wulfstan from a Peterborough calendar, see 'An Investigation of two Anglo-

to mention that of Oswald himself, were intermingled with the history of at least two episcopal sees, Worcester and York, and, in the case of Ealdred, briefly of Hereford as well. These random examples are sufficient to explain how we come to find manuscripts written in the main *scriptoria* of Winchester and Canterbury adapted for the use of other less prestigious houses, how saints popular at Winchester came to be venerated at Sherborne and throughout other Wessex houses under the influence of Winchester, or the liturgical parallels between East Anglian and West Mercian houses, and how relics were given by kings to abbeys of their choice. In fact, it becomes clear that a centre does not have to have had documented contacts with Continental ideas and influences for it to display a knowledge of them: the knowledge comes to it sometimes second-hand, through the intermediary of another major religious centre or town. This is particularly obvious in the case of rather remote influences, Greek or southern Italian for example, of which some more obscure churches in Wessex or the Fenland may not have known directly, but which are displayed in occasional litanies or calendars. Since the problem we are concerned with here is that of the general influx of European culture into England and vice versa, the channels of circulation of these exchanges are not the principal object of this study. It is sufficient to note that they exist and are active, thus demonstrating the force and popularity of these exchanges.

Saxon Kalendars (Missal of Robert of Jumièges and St Wulfstan's Homiliary), *Archaeologia*, 78 (1928), 219–54. His long and rather complex argument, based on superficial similarities of this calendar with that in the missal of Robert, which he also unconvincingly ascribes to Peterborough, does not take into account the six highly ranked feasts of Evesham saints: Wystan, Credan, Ecgwin, and Odulph, as opposed to only two entries of St Oswald, who was also highly venerated at Evesham. The Evesham provenance seems hard to challenge, and links between the two centres would account for it being inserted in a Worcester MS.

FLANDERS

I. GEOGRAPHICAL OUTLINE

For the purpose of this study, Flanders is the area encompassing the largely Flemish-speaking dioceses in the area controlled partly by the counts of Flanders and, nominally if not always in reality, by the king of France.[1] It may seem superfluous to devote a separate short chapter to it, rather than encompass it within the kingdom of France; my reason for doing so is the particular frequency and wealth of exchanges between late Anglo-Saxon England and the main Flemish centres, the first and closest points of contact of English people arriving on the Continent, or leaving it, after and before crossing the Channel. These dioceses are, from North to South, the sees of Noyon–Tournai, Thérouanne, and Arras–Cambrai. There was a great concentration of religious houses of major importance in this area.[2] The abbeys founded by the 'apostle' of Flanders, St Amand, had prospered: St Peter's and St Bavo's at Ghent and St Amand's itself. Other foundations were the monasteries St Bertin's at St Omer, Bergues St Winnoc, Corbie, St Josse of Montreuil, St Vaast's at Arras, and Centula-St Riquier; and the canonical house of St Donatian at Bruges and the nunnery of St Aldegund of Maubeuge are also known in English sources. The patron saints of these monastic houses, reformed by Gérard of Brogne in the tenth century, were all venerated in England. Furthermore, some of these abbeys had contributed to the establishment of monastic boroughs with flourishing markets or ports in the towns concerned, in some cases as early as the Merovingian period. Ghent, Arras, and Montreuil had developed along these lines, especially the last, through which passed the luxury goods imported into England from the Continent, such as silks and spices, and those exported from England, timber, linen, wool, hemp, tin, cheeses, and horses.[3]

Although the Count of Flanders' court was mostly based at Bruges, the spiritual capital was Ghent. Its two abbeys of St Peter's and St Bavo's had

[1] On the history and contemporary significance of these centres, see E. de Moreau, *Histoire de l'Église en Belgique* (6 vols.; 2nd edn.; Brussels, 1945–52), i and ii.

[2] On the abbeys of Flanders, see J. Lestocquoy, 'Des Origines historiques à la fin du règne de Charlemagne', 28–31, in C. Debray *et al.* (eds.), *Histoire des territoires ayant formé le département du Pas-de-Calais* (Arras, 1946).

[3] J. Lestocquoy, 'The Tenth Century', in *Études d'histoire urbaine: Villes et abbayes: Arras au Moyen Âge* (Arras, 1966), 43–4.

both been founded by St Amand himself, and St Bavo's possessed the relics of St Bavo, who had been a monk at St Peter's. Both abbeys were reformed in the tenth century by Gérard of Brogne. St Amand's, whose first name had been Elnone, had been founded during the reign of King Dagobert, before his death in 639. It possessed the relics of St Amand, and its three churches were dedicated to St Peter, St Martin, and St Andrew. St Bertin's had been founded about 648–9 under the name of Sithiu by Bertin and two of his companions. The abbey was reformed in 1021 and rebuilt after a fire in 1035; by the ninth century, the city around the abbey was rapidly expanding and trading with England in cloth and wool.[4]

The renowned abbey of Corbie had been founded by the English-born Merovingian Queen Balthild about 660, with monks from St Columbanus' monastery at Luxeuil.[5] It became one of the great centres of the cultural revival during the Carolingian period: its abbots Maurdramnus, Adalard, and Wala and two of its members, the theologians Ratramnus and Paschasius Radbertus, exerted great influence on the movements of ideas.[6] Balthild had placed some of her compatriots at Corbie, and in the eighth and the ninth centuries, there was a strong Anglo-Saxon presence in the *scriptorium* of the abbey, possibly directed by an Englishman about 750. The abbey church was dedicated to SS Peter and Paul, and two other churches were added, one in 662, dedicated to St Stephen, and another at the end of the eighth or beginning of the ninth century, dedicated to St John the Baptist.[7] The new standard Carolingian script, perfected at Corbie, was introduced into England in the tenth century.[8]

The abbey of St Vaast's at Arras[9] contained three churches, dedicated to St Vaast, St Peter, and the Virgin. The first had fourteen, the second thirteen, and the third three altars, with dedications to various major, as well as local, saints. After the first monastic reform of Gérard of Brogne and his disciple Hildebrand, a second attempt at reform was made under Count Baldwin IV (988–1035) by Richard of St Vannes and the abbey was rebuilt in 1030 after a fire.[10] Other churches at Arras were those of St

---

[4] G. Espinas, *Les Origines du capitalisme*, iii: *Deux fondations de villes dans l'Artois et la Flandre française (X^e–XVe siècles): St Omer et Lannoy du Nord* (Lille and Paris, 1946), 3–145.

[5] P. Cousin, 'Les Origines et le premier développement de Corbie', in *Corbie, Abbaye Royale: Volume du XIIIe centenaire* (Lille, 1963), 20–2.

[6] Ibid. 24–30, and the papers by H. Peltier, G. Mathon, and R. Béraudy in *Corbie*, 61–104 and 135–80.

[7] Cousin, 'Origines', in *Corbie*, 22.

[8] G. Ooghe, 'L'Écriture de Corbie', in *Corbie*, 278.

[9] On Arras, see Lestocquoy, *Études*, 85–6, 92, and 127–35, and on St Vaast's itself, 'Les Saints et les églises de l'abbaye de St Vaast d'Arras au VIIIe siècle', ibid. 85–92.

[10] J. Dhondt, 'Les Seigneuries du IXe au XIIIe siècle,' in Debray, *Histoire*, 46–7 and 57–9.

Stephen, St Maurice, and St Médard, of the eighth century. In 965, the relics of St Maellon were brought from Paris and a church was built to house them at the end of the century. The cathedral had a hospice, though it only appears in the texts in the eleventh century.

St Riquier[11] had been re-founded by Abbot Angilbert, Charlemagne's 'son-in-law', some time between 790 and 799. Its three churches were dedicated to the Saviour and St Riquier, St Benedict, and the Virgin with all the Apostles. The abbey church contained numerous altars with dedications to twenty-three different saints, and a set of painted stucco representations from the life of Christ.

Ghent, Arras, and Montreuil, as well as St Omer and Noyon, saw an impressive growth in their population during the tenth century. The town of Arras expanded from the seventh century onwards and Italian merchants were already trading there by 1027; the port of Ghent, destroyed by the Vikings was rebuilt in the mid-tenth century and there is a first mention of a fair there in 996, while at Noyon, there was one by the ninth century; merchants from St Omer mixed with English pilgrims going to Rome in the tenth century, and Corbie merchants were actively trading with their English counterparts from Bristol, Southampton, and London by the end of the period.[12] Montreuil replaced the once flourishing port of Quentovic, destroyed by the Viking invasions, and the abbey of St Josse, given by Charlemagne to Alcuin,[13] was a popular stopping point for English pilgrims, possibly on account of this English association.[14]

II. THE FACTUAL EVIDENCE FOR CONTACT

The first example of renewed contacts with Flanders pre-dates slightly the period covered by this study, since it comes from the time of King Alfred, whose daughter Aelfthryth married the count of Flanders Baldwin II some time between 893 and 899,[15] but it is important as a first stage in what becomes a steady link throughout the tenth and eleventh centuries with the abbey of St Bertin. Having asked the archbishop of Reims Fulk, who was

[11] C. Heitz, *L'Architecture religieuse carolingienne* (Paris, 1980), 51–62.

[12] Lestocquoy, 'Tenth century', in *Études*, 45, 48, 50; M. Chibnall, 'Corbie et l'Angleterre', in *Corbie*, 223–7.

[13] L. Levillain (ed.), *Correspondance de Loup de Ferrières* (2 vols.; Paris, 1907) i. 104.

[14] A text from the second half of the tenth century suggests that there might have been there a guild of merchants organized on the model of English guilds, see Lestocquoy, 'Les Saints', in *Études*, 97–9.

[15] *Aethelweard*, 2; *WMGR* i. 129 and n. 1, and 133. It may be worth noting that Baldwin was the son of Baldwin I and his wife Judith, daughter of Charles the Bald, who had been first married to two successive kings of England, Aethelwulf († 858) and Aethelbald († 860), and therefore not only knew England well, but was in fact related to King Alfred.

also the abbot of St Bertin, for a suitable and scholarly monk, who could restore learning and the monastic discipline in England, Alfred received in reply a letter from Fulk, which set out guidelines for the English Church and recommended the monk Grimbald of St Bertin as a suitable candidate to lead the English revival of learning in the last years of the ninth century.[16] Grimbald became the head of the community at Winchester, where he remained until his death in 901 or 903.[17] This was the first example of frequent and very successful imports of monks from St Bertin's to England, for educational and literary purposes. Grimbald himself was honoured as a saint at the New Minster at Winchester, where his relics were preserved.[18]

The first tenth-century example of Flemish presence in England is the arrival, also at Winchester, of a group of monks from St Josse in 901, who had been forced to flee the exposed abbey of Montreuil on account of Viking raids. They brought with them St Judoc's head, a relic greatly venerated at Winchester until the twelfth century, when St Josse's claim to have regained possession of it succeeded in superseding the claim of the New Minster.[19] The next example comes from almost forty years later, when we hear about an Englishman who, prompted by a vision, went to Ghent and helped rebuild St Bavo's in about 940 after the return there of this saint's relics from St Omer the previous year.[20] About that time, in a less edifying incident, a visiting monk to Flanders, possibly knowing King Aethelstan's interest in relics, attempted to steal those of St Bertulph from Boulogne in order to sell them in England.[21] Aethelstan himself is said to have been grateful to the monks of St Bertin, who had buried his brother

---

[16] *CSD* 1. i, 7–12.

[17] On Grimbald, see P. Grierson, 'Grimbald of St Bertin's', *EHR* 55 (1940), 529–61, and J. M. Bately, 'Grimbald of St Bertin's', *Medium Aevum*, 35 (1966), 1–10.

[18] His name is entered in five Winchester calendars between 1023 and 1060, see Wormald, *Kalendars*, nos. 9 to 12, and in the sacramentary of Robert of Jumièges, of the 1st half of the 11th c., now Rouen, Bibliothèque Municipale MS Y.6, edited by Wilson, *MRJ*; he is celebrated with a mass at New Minster in Winchester, entered in the missal of this abbey, written in the 2nd half of the 11th c., now Le Havre, Bibliothèque Municipale MS 330, edited by Turner, *MNM*, and with a benediction in the 'Benedictional of Archbishop Robert', also from New Minster but of the late 10th c., now Rouen, Bibliothèque Municipale MS Y.7, edited by Wilson, *BAR*. A mass is also recorded in the sacramentary of Bishop Giso of Wells, British Library, Cotton MS Vitellius A.XVIII, and parts of the office for the feast in Wulfstan's collectar, see *Portiforium*.

[19] *ASC*, F903, 60, and see Grierson, 'Relations', 78. The New Minster continued to venerate the relics of St Judoc throughout the 11th c., entering him in five calendars with feasts both of his *Natale* and of his translation to Winchester, celebrating both feasts in the missal and the benedictional of the abbey, which Giso's sacramentary also does, and Wulfstan's portiforium for parts of the office. St Josse claimed to have recovered the relics, whereas the New Minster cult seems to have died out by the 12th c., while it flourished increasingly at St Josse, see *Orderic*, ii. 156–69.

[20] Grierson, 'Relations', 94 and id., 'The Early Abbey of St Bavo's, Ghent', *RB* 49 (1937), 57.

[21] Grierson, 'Relations', 94.

Edwin, drowned when crossing over.[22] A relative of the count of Flanders certainly found refuge at his court.[23] But the new count, Arnulf, after supporting the claims of Aethelstan's nephew Louis IV, subsequently turned against him, and relations with the English court deteriorated as a result. Only a few years later, in 944, some monks from St Bertin's who refused to live there after the monastery had been reformed by Gérard of Brogne, acting under the authority of the count of Flanders, came to the abbey of St Peter at Bath and joined the community there.[24] In 956–7, Dunstan had to leave England and he spent the exile into which he had been forced by King Eadwig at St Peter's at Ghent, a gesture which illustrates the hostility between the two courts.[25] During the time he spent there, he met the count of Flanders, as a letter from the latter to the future archbishop makes clear.[26]

Dunstan's encounter with the reformed monasticism prevailing at Ghent and his respect for it probably prompted him to invite some monks from St Peter's when the problem of drawing up a monastic customary for English houses arose at the council of Winchester in 970–2: the Proem of the *Regularis Concordia* agreed upon at the council mentions the presence of these monks from Ghent and the text of the *Concordia* bears witness to the introduction of some of the customs prevailing at St Peter's, such as the manner of offering at mass, the Maundy Thursday ceremonies carried out by children, the practice of confession on Christmas Eve and on Maundy Thursday, the singing of psalms during manual labour and the recording of the names of dead monks.[27] King Edgar showed his gratitude to St Peter's in a more practical way too, by granting land at Lewisham in Kent to Ghent.[28] His liking for the Flemish, however, was not popular with everyone; the *Anglo-Saxon Chronicle* criticizes him for being too favourable to 'foreigners' at his court, possibly meaning, among others, the Flemish.[29] Relations between the two courts themselves may not have been at their best, but we continue to have further evidence of links with Ghent from the last twenty years of the century and the early years of the next century. In 982–5, we hear of the presence of an English nun living at Ghent whilst, in the other direction, the name of the abbot Womar of

[22] O. Holder-Egger, *Folcuini Diaconi Gesta Abbatum Sithiensium*, MGH SS xiii, 629.
[23] *WMGR* i. 150.
[24] Holder-Egger, *Folcuini Gesta*, 629.
[25] Adelard's Life of St Dunstan in Stubbs, *Memorials*, 59–60; Grierson, 'Relations', 89.
[26] *CSD* i. i, 93–5, and above, ch. 1 n. 23.
[27] *RC* 78, 20, 62, 31, 39, 25, 68, and p. i.
[28] Sawyer, *Anglo-Saxon Charters*, no. 728.
[29] *ASC*, DEF 959, 75.

Ghent was entered in the *Liber Vitae* of New Minster, as a result of the visit he made to Winchester before his death in 980.[30]

Both archbishops of Canterbury Aethelgar and Sigeric maintained relations with two other Flemish abbeys, St Bertin's and St Vaast's. Aethelgar actually visited St Bertin's and left there a reputation for liberality, which prompted Abbot Odbert to invite Sigeric for a visit which he, however, does not seem to have paid.[31] Odbert's letter of invitation is still extant, as is the correspondence between Aethelgar and Abbot Fulrad of St Vaast.[32] Sigeric, on the other hand, most certainly visited and stayed at St Vaast's on his return journey from Rome in 990, since Arras is specifically named on the list of his stays in the travel diary compiled on the occasion of his pilgrimage to Rome, together with Bruay-en-Artois, Thérouanne, Guisnes south of Calais, and the then still active port of Wissant.[33] James Campbell has stressed the importance of English involvement with Flemish abbeys, particularly at the end of the tenth century, when these seem almost to expect continuous support from English ecclesiastics through gifts: they appear to have been 'in [English] patronage'.[34]

The first example of attested contacts with Flemish centres in the eleventh century originates once again at St Bertin's. In 1027, King Cnut, on his way to Rome, stopped at St Omer, a stay recorded in the history of the abbey.[35] Meanwhile, Flemish merchants probably continued to trade in England, as they had probably been doing under Cnut's predecessor, King Aethelred, since a set of laws ascribed to this king mentions the presence of such merchants paying tolls at the bridge of Billingsgate in London.[36] Edward's sister married a vassal of Count Baldwin V of Flanders, Eustace of Boulogne, who was to play a not unimportant part in the rebellion which caused Earl Godwine's family to be exiled.[37] Unsurprisingly, on their exile, various members of this family went themselves to the court of Flanders. Earl Swein had already spent some time there in 1048 and 1049;[38] in 1052, Earl Godwine with his wife Gytha

---

[30] Grierson, 'Relations', 94; W. de Gray Birch (ed.), *Liber Vitae: Register and Martyrology of New Minster and Hyde Abbey, Winchester* (London, 1892), 24; J. Gerchow, *Die Gedenküberlieferung der Angelsachsen* (Berlin and New York, 1988), 323, 177; and H. Vollrath, *Die Synoden Englands bis 1066* (Paderborn, 1985), 232 n. 136. His *obit* was entered in the C recension of the Anglo-Saxon Chronicle; see J. Earle and C. Plummer (eds.), *Two of the Saxon Chronicles Parallel* (2 vols.; Oxford, 1892–9 repr. 1952) i. 124, under the year 981.

[31] See above, ch. 1 n. 23.

[32] See ch. 1 n. 23.

[33] Stubbs, *Memorials*, 395.

[34] Campbell, 'England', in *Essays*, 203–4.

[35] *Encomium*, 36–7.

[36] Stevenson, *Laws*, IV Aethelred 6, 73.

[37] *ASC*, E1048 and D1052 = 1051, 116–21; *Florence* i. 204–6.

[38] *ASC*, E1045 = 1048, 110 and C1049, E1046 = 1049, 114.

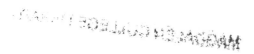

and three of their sons Harold, Gyrth, and Tostig went to Baldwin on their exile,[39] Tostig being already married to a close relative of the count's, Judith, sister or cousin of Matilda of Flanders, William the Conqueror's wife.[40] There were, also for political reasons, other refugees from England, beginning with Edward himself as an exile. He was at Ghent in 1016 and in Bruges in 1037–8, as was Queen Emma herself, who took refuge there when she was sent away by King Harold in 1037; she was joined by her son Harthacnut in 1039.[41] Others were Cnut's kinswoman Gunnhild, who went to Bruges first, before moving on to Denmark,[42] and the nobleman Osgod Clapa, involved in the incidents of 1049 on the side of Godwine, with his wife.[43] Gytha, Godwine's wife and Harold's mother, left England in 1067, after Harold's defeat at Hastings, with Judith, and another daughter of the family, who is recorded to have bequeathed in 1087 a psalter to St Donatian's at Bruges, where she presumably stayed.[44]

These examples appear to confirm the hypothesis of rather strained relations between the English and Flemish courts during the eleventh century too, since we usually hear of the count of Flanders as a protector of political exiles who fled from England. The phenomenon seems to have become well established since, for example, Edward went to the Flemish court several times during his exile on the Continent before becoming king but, once he did become king of England, he was an ally of the Emperor Henry III against Duke Godfrey of Lorraine and Baldwin V of Flanders in 1049.[45] As a result, Baldwin supported Godwine's family and went as far as to open his ports to the enemies of England; once Harold became king in 1066, the count of Flanders found himself on the side of William the Conqueror, his brother-in-law, against Harold. As a result no doubt of these almost consistently strained relations between the two courts of England and Flanders before the Conquest, the *Anglo-Saxon Chronicle* shows considerable interest in all matters connected with Flanders in the first half of the eleventh century, far above any concern with Normandy, for example, a perfectly understandable interest if Flanders was to be seen as potentially dangerous.[46] Of no less interest is the fact that, political problems notwithstanding, the links of English ecclesiastics and religious centres with Flemish ones remained considerable during the eleventh

[39] *ASC*, C1051, D1052, E1048 = 1051, 116 and 120–1; *Florence*, ii. 2.
[40] *ASC*, D1052 = 1051, 119.
[41] *Encomium*, 48–9; *ASC*, 1037, 104; C1039 and 1040, 105; *Florence*, i. 192–3.
[42] *ASC*, D1045 = 1044, 108.
[43] *ASC*, D1050, C1051 = 1051, 113.
[44] *ASC*, D1067, 148; *Florence*, i. 223–4 and ii. 2; Grierson, 'Relations', 109.
[45] *Vita Aedwardi*, 10.
[46] F. Barlow, 'Edward the Confessor and the Norman Conquest', in *The Norman Conquest and Beyond* (London, 1983), 101.

century. In 1038, a certain Balger offered some relics of St Oswald and St Eadburgh of Winchester to the abbey of St Winnoc at Bergues, and also at Bergues, we hear of the presence of Bishop William of London in 1060, when the relics of St Ursmer were exhibited there, a ceremony at which were also present the count and the countess of Flanders and the bishop of Thérouanne.[47] We hear of St Bertin's again when Bishop Herman of Ramsbury left England in 1053: he went to this abbey, where he spent several years and where he took the monastic habit, before coming back to England to resume his episcopal functions, bringing Goscelin with him.[48] After the Conquest too, political links were not the only ones to remain, although these were strengthened by William I's close kinship with the counts of Flanders. Another ecclesiastic took up the tradition of seeking refuge in Flanders, this time fleeing to put himself and his valuable library under the protection of the abbot of St Vaast after the Conquest. Thus the library of Abbot Seiwold of Bath finally ended up at Arras at the end of the eleventh century.[49] The abbot of St Riquier Gervinus, who had been in contact with King Edward and Edith and was given lavish presents by them, including some lands in England, came to England in 1068 and was granted various lands by the Conqueror in a diploma cited by Hariulf.[50]

The county of Flanders was perhaps the most important partner for Anglo-Saxon England, as a political ally or enemy, as well as for economic purposes. The wealth of contacts is not necessarily paralleled in cultural terms, perhaps because of the fragmented nature of individual contacts, due to a certain hostility at high level and, perforce, the presence in Flanders of people having left England as refugees.

III. CULTURAL EXCHANGES BETWEEN ENGLAND AND FLANDERS

The two areas illustrating the influence of Flemish culture in England are that of hagiographical writing and that of the circulation of manuscripts. Hagiographical production in England was more than once boosted by the influx of *Vitae* written by Flemish authors in Flanders or in England itself. To the first category belongs the Life of St Dunstan by a monk of Ghent,

---

[47] Grierson, 'Relations', 101; O. Holder-Egger (ed.), *Miracula S. Ursmari*, MGH SS xv (2), 839–40.

[48] *Florence* i. 214.

[49] On this library, see P. Grierson, 'Les Livres de l'abbé Seiwold de Bath', *RB* 52 (1940), 96–116 and, more recently, M. Lapidge, 'Surviving Booklists from Anglo-Saxon England', in *Learning and Literature*, 58–62.

[50] F. Lot (ed.), *Hariulf: Chronique de l'abbaye de St Riquier* (Paris, 1894), 237–8, 240–5.

Adelard, composed *c*.1006–11. Of all the extant Lives of the great reformer, this one may well be the most accurate, since it was written by a contemporary, who must have known the saint when the latter spent a year in Ghent. The remaining Lives were composed, one by a contemporary cleric from Lotharingia, but who may have simply been given the commission to rewrite in a superior style an Anglo-Saxon text, in the way Abbo of Fleury was asked by the monks of Bury to add some cosmetic touches when revising a Life of St Dunstan in verse. The other Lives of the saint were put together from the twelfth century onwards. Adelard's Life is particularly interesting for the details it gives about Dunstan's year in Ghent, his activities at St Peter's, and his contacts with the Flemish court.

Somewhat similar in its history is another text, not properly speaking a hagiographical one, but rather hovering between biography, panegyric, and hagiography, a composition from St Bertin's of 1040–2, known as the *Encomium Emmae*. The St Bertin's monk who wrote it in praise of Queen Emma, a Norman princess married first to King Aethelred then to the Danish king of England Cnut, can be taken to provide a good indication of what Emma would have wished to hear about herself. Hence, its stress is on Cnut's reign rather than on Aethelred and on his son Edward, whom Emma seems to have disliked somewhat, since more than once she fought against him, first in favour of her son by Cnut, Harthacnut, then plotting with Bishop Stigand to invite King Magnus of Norway to invade England.[51] On the whole, despite the respectful English attitude towards the style of foreign writers, which led Anglo-Saxon monasteries to commission works from them, it cannot be said that there was a particular significance in this style, which led to adaptation or imitation in England. The main value of some of these texts, such as Adelard's Life of Dunstan and the *Encomium Emmae*, consists in the information they supply on the Flemish sojourn of their protagonists.

The same comment applies to the Flemish writers of the latter half of the eleventh century. Another handful of hagiographical texts relating the Lives of a variety of English saints were written by two Flemish monks while they were staying in England. Folcard of St Bertin spent a few years here and is the author of a Life of St John of Beverley and of some responses for the office of this saint, commissioned by Archbishop Ealdred. The other St Bertin's monk, Goscelin, spent the years from 1058 when he came to England to possibly the 1120s, when he died at St Augustine's at Canterbury, in this country. He had various commissions to provide Lives

---

[51] On Emma's attitude to Edward see below, ch. 7; *ASC*, E1042, CD1043, 107; Rollason, 'Translation of St Mildrith', 176.

of English saints: Edith, Wulfsige of Sherborne, Mildrith, and Wulfhild, as well as one of St Ivo and a summary of those of the patron saints of St Augustine's at Canterbury.

Apart from these examples of Flemish authorship of texts used in England, there are other cases of texts produced in Flanders and used in England, which they reached some time during these two centuries. The most famous of these is the manuscript known as the Leofric Missal, a sacramentary probably written at St Vaast's of Arras in the late ninth century and brought to England sometime during the tenth century, since it was at Glastonbury by the later tenth century. Some masses were added to it there and the manuscript finally reached Exeter, where it was by the time of Bishop Leofric who, in turn, added masses and other liturgical material to it. We know of two other manuscripts, one a Prudentius from St Bertin's and the other a collection of letters, including one from Charlemagne to the Emperor Michael Paleologus, from Corbie, which were both in England at the turn of the tenth and eleventh centuries.[52]

It has already been noted that a major contribution of Ghent to the late tenth-century English scene was the presence of monks from the abbey of St Peter at the Winchester council at which the *Regularis Concordia* was drawn up. Elements from the monastic life and customs introduced by Gérard of Brogne in the monasteries he reformed, especially St Peter's at Ghent, found their way into the *Concordia*, undoubtedly suggested or supported by these monks. But Gérard's reform was by no means of equal importance in its original features and innovations as were the reforms promoted by Gorze and Cluny, even when it shared some of their characteristics; while some Brogne customs were undoubtedly introduced in the *Concordia*, the impact of these relatively minor elements was less than that of the other movements of monastic reform in Europe.

Other Flemish monastic centres also contributed to the cultural developments in England, most notably Corbie.[53] Part of the contribution of this abbey was not direct. Corbie had taken the lead during the Carolingian 'renaissance' in devising the standard Carolingian script, the caroline minuscule, which had become the standard one in tenth- and eleventh-century Europe.[54] The other contribution of Corbie was that of its adaptation of the Gregorian sacramentary reformed and added to by Benedict of Aniane and known as the *Hadrianum*, and two copies of the Corbie version of the sacramentary, commonly called the Missal of

[52] Rella, 'Continental', nos. 3 and 16.

[53] Chibnall, 'Corbie', in *Corbie*, 226, emphasized the similarities between some of the customs in *RC* and those in a 9th c. *ordinarium* from Corbie.

[54] Ibid. 224–9, and Ooghe, 'L'Écriture', in *Corbie*, 278; see also C. W. Jones, 'The Scriptorium of Corbie', *Speculum*, 22 (1947), 191–204, 375–94.

St Eligius and the Sacramentary of Ratold, are still extant.[55] Copies of these were probably known in England, since there are examples of masses

[55] Of the earlier MSS used as sources for the English books, the essential ones were the two great Roman Sacramentaries, the Gregorian and the Gelasian. The eighth-century Gelasian had been compiled in Gaul from a mixture of pre-seventh-century Roman masses and eighth-century Gallican material. The most recent edition of the eighth-century Gelasian Sacramentary is that of K. Mohlberg, *Das Fränkische Sacramentarium Gelasianum* (Münster, 1971). Numerous studies have been made of this text, from the first recognition of its importance by E. Bishop in 'The earliest Roman Mass-Book (the Gelasianum)' in *Liturgica Historica* (Oxford, 1918), 39–62, to the most recent study by B. Moreton, *The Eighth Century Gelasian Sacramentary: A Study in Tradition* (Oxford, 1976). Other studies are included in general works on the early liturgy, such as E. Bourque, *Étude sur les sacramentaires romains* (ii, 2 vols.; *Le Gélasien du VIIIᵉ siècle*, Quebec, 1952; Vatican City, 1958); K. Gamber, A. Dold, and B. Bischoff, *Sakramentartypen: Versuch einer Gruppierung der Handschriften und Fragmente bis zur Jahrtausendwende* (Beuron, 1958); and K. Gamber, *Codices liturgici latini antiquiores* (2 vols.; 2nd edn.; Fribourg, 1968). The Gregorian Sacramentary, then regarded as the work of Gregory the Great, contained in reality later additions, and represented the state of the liturgy used by the pope in Rome about 784, when Pope Hadrian sent a copy of it to Charlemagne. The most recent edition of the *Hadrianum* and its Supplement is by J. Deshusses, *Le Sacramentaire grégorien* (3 vols., Fribourg, 1971, 1979, 1982). For a detailed discussion on the up-to-date debate on the Carolingian reforms of the Roman Sacramentary, see R. McKitterick, *The Frankish Church and the Carolingian Reforms 789–895* (London, 1977), 123–35 and J. M. Wallace-Hadrill, *The Frankish Church* (Oxford, 1983). At Charlemagne's command, a collection of supplementary texts was produced, to adapt it to the needs of the Frankish Church, either by Alcuin or, more probably according to modern scholars, by Benedict of Aniane. This revised version of the Gregorian Sacramentary, the *Hadrianum*, together with the Supplement which included essentially texts from the eighth-century Gelasian Sacramentary, was later used throughout the western Church, and it returned in this form to Rome, where it was adopted in the ninth and tenth centuries; on this evolution see also the general histories of the liturgy, for example, J. Lechner and L. Eisenhofer, *The Liturgy of the Roman Rite* (tr. London, 1961), 7–13, esp. 12–13. It had become the standard collection of masses and benedictions by the tenth century in the western Church, although it was by no means compulsory, but rather adaptable to local needs. The liturgical usage still allowed great freedom of choice, so that, in addition to the *Hadrianum* and its Supplement, and some English compositions, the compiler of a liturgical book could borrow elements from the collection of masses now known as the Leonine or Veronese Sacramentary, the local revisions of the eighth-century Gelasian, the purely Gallican collections now known as the *Missale Francorum*, the *Missale Gallicanum Vetus*, and the *Missale Gothicum*, and other local variations of the Gallican masses and benedictions, and even occasionally from the Ambrosian (Milanese) liturgy. The Leonine Sacramentary is edited by L. C. Mohlberg *et al.*, *Sacramentarium Veronense (Codex Bibl. Capit. Veron. LXXXV [80])* (Rome, 1956). For the Gallican Sacramentaries, see L. C. Mohlberg *et al.* (eds.), *Missale Francorum* (Rome, 1957), and *Missale Gallicanum Vetus* (Rome, 1958); and L. C. Mohlberg (ed.), *Missale Gothicum* (Rome, 1961). On the Benedictions, see J. Deshusses, 'Le Bénédictionnaire Gallican du VIIIᵉ siècle', *Ephemerides Liturgicae*, 77 (1963), 169–82, and the catalogue of benedictions in B. Moeller (ed.), *Corpus Benedictionum Pontificalium* (2 vols. in 4.; Turnhout, 1971–9). The majority of English masses and benedictions, though mostly copied from the Gregorian Sacramentary (*Hadrianum*) and the eighth-century Gelasian Sacramentary, occasionally borrow forms from Gallican Sacramentaries and also from the various versions of the tenth-century Romano-German liturgy, as represented, for example, by the Romano-German Pontifical. On the Romano-German Pontifical, see C. Vogel and R. Elze (eds.), avec utilisation des collations laissées par M. Andrieu, *Le Pontifical romano-germanique du dixième siècle* (3 vols.; Rome, 1969 and 1972). Both the Missal of St Eligius (Paris, Bibliothèque Nationale MS lat. 12051, of the second half of the ninth century) and the sacramentary written at Corbie for Ratold (Paris, Bibliothèque Nationale MS lat. 12052, of *c*.972–86) were mixed Gregorian and Gelasian books; see Gamber, *Codices latini*, ii. 409–10 and iii. 213, and Bourque, *Étude*, ii. 2, nos 197 and 201, 258 and 261. On the vagaries of the Ratold Sacramentary through northern France, Brittany, and Flanders, and its close links with England,

from them in English manuscripts, such as the mass for St Benedict's feast of the Deposition in the missal of Robert of Jumièges.[56] Another contribution of Corbie to the English liturgy was the chant as practised in the abbey, which had such a reputation for having preserved the Roman style of the early centuries that, when St Aethelwold wished to teach the newly reformed English monasteries the proper way of chanting according to the Roman tradition, which they had forgotten, he sent one of his monks to re-learn it from Corbie.[57] By the eleventh century, the musical part of the collectar of Wulfstan was modelled on the Corbie antiphoner. The contribution of Corbie to the liturgy of Anglo-Saxon England was by no means the only one to come from Flanders; numerous other examples of additions to the liturgy of the *Sanctorale* also originated in Flemish abbeys.

IV. LITURGICAL AND DEVOTIONAL EXCHANGES BETWEEN ENGLAND AND FLANDERS

The first example of devotional influences between the two countries goes back to the earlier Anglo-Saxon period and operates in the direction from England to Flanders, at a time when the latter was a part of the Carolingian Empire. As such, it is probably through the presence of Anglo-Saxon ecclesiastics and intellectuals carrying out Church reforms within the Empire that the cult of the most popular saint in England, St Peter, was not introduced but rather reinforced, throughout the Empire. By the tenth century, St Peter was the most venerated saint in the West and, when we find manuscripts such as the collection of Saints' Lives from St Bertin's which enters celebrations of St Peter in gold capitals throughout the manuscript,[58] we can only look upon it as a manifestation of a devotion by then paramount everywhere and confirmed by dedications to the saint of major abbeys such as that of Ghent. It is of interest, however, to note that, if numerous monastic houses and churches among the most prestigious in the West are dedicated to the saint, that dedication is often to 'SS Peter and Paul', as we find, for example, at Cluny or Reichenau. On the other hand, dedications to St Peter alone are less common, and remind us more of a particularly English feature, the great veneration to Peter alone, rather

---

where it may have been for a short time before returning to Corbie, see C. Hohler, 'Some Service-Books of the Later Saxon church', in Parsons, *Tenth Century Studies*, 64–9. The Missal of St Eligius is printed in P L 78, 25–582.

[56] *MRJ*, 167–8.

[57] *Chronicon Abingdon*, i. 129; see Chibnall, 'Corbie', in *Corbie*, 225–7.

[58] Boulogne, Bibliothèque Municipale MS 107, of the 11th c.

than to the more traditionally Roman standard combination of Peter and Paul. Interestingly, it is often abbeys in areas of contact with England, such as Ghent, or those founded by Englishmen, such as Fulda, which have a dedication to St Peter alone, on the English model.[59] Other English devotional elements were doubtless transmitted to Flanders throughout the period; it will be sufficient to cite one from the end of the eleventh century, when some English prayers to the Virgin dating from the middle of that century found their way into a Cambrai manuscript of the late eleventh century.[60]

More notable and closer to the period discussed are the cults of local saints from Flanders found in English devotional and liturgical texts. Most important of these are the founders of major Flemish abbeys, SS Amand, Bertin, Bavo, Omer, and Vaast, venerated at St Amand's, St Peter's at Ghent, St Bertin's, and St Bavo's at Ghent. Others are St Austroberta of Abbeville, St Aldegund of Maubeuge, the bishops Salvius of Valenciennes, Médard and Eligius of Noyon, Silvinus of Thérouanne and Piato of Tournai, and St Riquier. All these names are found in English liturgical books, calendars, and litanies. In some cases, they are entered by tradition and have little devotional significance, as in the case of Bavo and Aldegund, for example. Aldegund is still entered in tenth-century calendars at Glastonbury and in the West Country, as well as in two calendars from the second half of the eleventh century at Exeter and Wells, in the latter together with Balthild, who gradually dislodges her in the other fourteen calendars of that period.[61] Bavo's name appears in the Wells, Evesham,

---

[59] There were sixteen churches dedicated to St Peter, either on his own or with other saints, before 1100: Abbotsbury, Bath, Cerne, Chertsey, Coventry, Ely, Eye, Gloucester, Hackness, Leominster, Monkwearmouth, Peterborough, Westminster, Whitby, the New Minster at Winchester, and Worcester. Another eleven were dedicated to St Peter and St Paul: Aethelney, Bardney, St Augustine's at Canterbury, Hereford, Malmesbury before its re-dedication to the Virgin Mary and Aldhelm in 1078, Minster-in-Thanet, Muchelney, Pershore, Shrewsbury, the Old Minster at Winchester, and the Cluniac Priory of Montacute, founded *c.* 1078. In the early Anglo-Saxon period, dedications to St Peter were the most common ones: Levison, *England and the Continent*, App. V, 260–1, counted twenty-two, and we know from literary sources that, for example, St Modwenna dedicated one of her two churches at Burton-upon-Trent to SS Peter and Paul, that Malmesbury, Chester, and, possibly, Sherborne, were dedicated to St Peter before changing dedications in the late eleventh century, and that Shrewsbury was founded on the site of a previous chapel dedicated to St Peter; on these dedications, see D. Knowles, V. C. M. London, and C. N. L. Brooke, *Heads of Religious Houses: England and Wales 940–1216* (Cambridge, 1972), 58–81, and A. M. Binns, *Monastic Dedications of Houses in England and Wales c.1066–c.1216* (Woodbridge, 1989), 61–91; also R. Morris, *The Church in British Archaeology* (Oxford, 1983), 35–8. Evidence for the existence of churches, chapels, and altars dedicated to St Peter appears occasionally: there was a Pre-Conquest church in Sudbury, see Binns, *Monastic Dedications*, 86; a chapel at Ramsey, see the *Miracula S. Ivonis* by Goscelin in *Chronicon Rameseiensis*, p. lxiv; and an altar at Christ Church, see *Gervase*, i. 15.

[60] M. Clayton, *The Cult of the Virgin Mary in Anglo-Saxon England* (Cambridge, 1990), 79–81.

[61] Wormald, *Kalendars*, nos. 2, 4, 7, 8; her cult appears to have been localized in the South-

Bury, and Crowland calendars, and is included in the mass for the *Natale* of SS Rémi, Germanus, and Vaast in the missal of Robert of Jumièges and in the office for that feast in Wulfstan's collectar. In the cases of SS Amand, Omer, Bertin, and especially Vaast, the entries increase in frequency at the end of the tenth century, probably because of the stronger links between England and the abbeys founded by these saints, St Amand's, St Bertin's, St Vaast's of Arras, and St Riquier.

St Amand,[62] the 'Apostle of Belgium' (first years of the seventh century –674–5), became bishop of Tongres in 639, and moved his see to Maastricht. He was a great missionary and traveller, who went several times to Rome. He founded several monasteries among which are St Peter's of Mont Blandin and St Bavo's at Ghent, and died at Elnone, which later became St Amand's. His body was translated at Elnone fifteen years after his death and again when his relics returned from St Germain des Prés, where they had been moved to protect them from Vikings *c*.872–84. In 1066 a fire destroyed St Amand's except for the relics in the crypt, and a journey with the relics was undertaken by the monks in order to raise funds for the rebuilding of the basilica, consecrated in 1088. Ely possessed some relics of the saint, incorporated in a crucifix made *c*.980.[63] St Bertin,[64] first a monk at Luxeuil, then a missionary for the bishop of St Omer, founded the monastery of Sithiu, later St Bertin's. He died in 698 and a document of 745 already mentions him as a saint. St Vaast[65] (second half of the fifth century–*c*.540), bishop of Arras *c*.500 and a missionary, consecrated by St Rémi, founded the abbey later dedicated to him, restored by Alcuin *c*.790–808. His cult started very early, since he appears in the earliest litanies, and he was celebrated on 6 February with St Amand and on 5 October. Bruges had relics, and so had Ely by the late tenth century. St Omer,[66] after being a monk at Luxeuil and a missionary with St Bertin and St Mummolinus, later bishop of Noyon or Tournai, became bishop of Thérouanne and died *c*.670. His cult was already well developed by the eighth century.

West, since she is only entered in calendars from that region, where she is still remembered in the eleventh century, long after the general English custom had assigned this day to Balthild, treated as an English saint.

[62] On St Amand, see L. van der Essen, *Étude critique sur les Vitae des saints mérovingiens de l'ancienne Belgique* (Louvain and Paris, 1907), 341–51, and *Le Siècle des saints (625–739)* (Brussels, 1948), 47–59; de Moreau, *Église en Belgique*, i. 79–90, 134–5 and, especially, his *Saint Amand, apôtre de la Belgique et du Nord de la France* (Brussels, 1927).

[63] *LE* 124. The crucifix also contained relics of St Vaast.

[64] On St Bertin's, see de Moreau, *Église en Belgique*, i. 155–6.

[65] On St Vaast's, see de Moreau, *Église en Belgique*, i. 54–8; van der Essen, *Étude critique*, 211–19 and *Siècle des saints*, 28–33; and J. Lestocquoy, *Le Diocèse d'Arras* (Arras, 1949), 6–9.

[66] On St Omer's, see van der Essen, *Étude critique*, 400–9 and de Moreau, *Église en Belgique*, i. 63–4.

St Amand's feasts were entered in English calendars throughout the period, the main feast which was on the same day as that of St Vaast's appearing in almost all of them with the exception of those from Winchester, and the second feast in six calendars from various centres spread out throughout the period.[67] There are no liturgical celebrations but most litanies enter the name. The diminishing number of entries of the secondary feast, after the initial enthusiasm at the end of the tenth century, is significant of a trend which we will encounter on several occasions. While the extremely widespread links with numerous Flemish abbeys in the aftermath of the reform prompted an increasing interest in their saints, the attempt to provide a more standardized list of celebrations, in keeping with a general trend towards order and more clearly defined hierarchies after 1030, contributed to limiting random entries and feasts perceived as being of minor importance, by comparison with the major ones. As a result, Amand's second feast gradually disappeared, to be superseded in importance by his fellow-saint on that day, Vaast, whose prestige in England was greater, even though this was only Vaast's secondary feast.

St Vaast's main feast fell on the same day as those of SS Rémi, Germanus of Auxerre, Bavo, and Piato. It was entered in all calendars except the late tenth-century ones; which tends to confirm the generalization of the cult by the middle of the eleventh century. Whereas, as we shall see later, his companion saints Rémi and Germanus were highly venerated in their own right in England, and remained equal to Vaast in the celebrations of that day, the other two minor saints Piato and Bavo, after the initial impetus from Flanders in the late tenth century, suffered the fate of Amand and gradually disappeared from the celebrations. This pattern is further confirmed by the celebrations themselves: masses at Winchester in the missal of Robert and that of New Minster, and at Wells in Giso's sacramentary, and a collect for the office in Wulfstan's collectar, all books of the eleventh century, as well as benedictions in four late-tenth-century benedictionals (that of St Aethelwold and two others from Winchester and Christ Church, as well as the 'Lanalet Pontifical' from Cornwall), and in three eleventh-century ones from Canterbury, Exeter, and Worcester.[68] The mass used at Wells is taken from the Corbie version of the *Hadrianum*,

---

[67] Wormald, *Kalendars*, nos. 1, 2, 4, 6, 8, 13, 17, 18, 19, 20, and Hampson, *Kalendarium*, A and B; the second feast only in 1, 2, 4, 16, 18, 19, and *MRJ*.

[68] *Benedictional of St Aethelwold*; the other two 10th-century benedictionals are in Paris, Bibliothèque Nationale MS lat. 943, of the 2nd half of the 10th c., possibly written at Christ Church, and MS lat. 987, of the last quarter of the 10th c. from Winchester; and the 'Lanalet Pontifical' is Rouen, Bibliothèque Municipale MS A.27, of the very early 11th c. possibly from St Germans or Crediton; the 11th c. benedictionals are British Library, Harleian MS 2892, of the 1st half of the 11th c., edited by R. M. Woolley, *The Canterbury Benedictional* (London, 1917); Additional MS 28188, of the 2nd half of the 11th c.; and *Claudius Pontificals*, Claudius I.

the sacramentary of Ratold, as is also the case for the only mass for the feast of St Omer in the missal of Robert.

For this saint too, there are two feast-days entered in the calendars, one in practically all tenth-century calendars and in those of Bury and Crowland, and the second date in the tenth-century calendars from, possibly, the North, Wessex, St Augustine's, and Winchester. Once again, we have a case of a cult which reaches its peak in the late tenth and early eleventh century, probably as a response to particularly close links with St Bertin's, notably at the time of Abbot Odbert, and which gradually recedes during the eleventh century. Most cults of secondary saints of Continental abbeys, as opposed to the principal patron, suffer this fate.

The main St Bertin's saint, however, was Bertin himself. Since his name only appears in the Old English Martyrology and in Aethelstan's Psalter, his entry in all tenth- and eleventh-century calendars is clearly due not so much to tradition as to a reinforced veneration at this period, confirmed by the entry of his Translation at St Bertin's in the tenth-century calendars from Wessex, Glastonbury, and St Augustine's. This increase in the cult is probably related to the links between England and St Bertin's in the late tenth century. However, the evidence from the calendars is not confirmed by that from the other liturgical sources, since St Bertin is entered in seven litanies alone, of which only one dates from the tenth century, all the others belonging to the mid- or second half of the eleventh century, and four of which come from Exeter. If the uniformity in the calendars is due to the establishment of the cult in the late tenth century and to the historical links between Winchester, Canterbury, and St Bertin's at that time, the devotion to the main saint of the abbey must have grown in the eleventh century, possibly under the influence of the two monks from St Bertin's then at work in England, Goscelin and Folcard. The liturgical texts also show an increase of the cult in the second half of the eleventh century, since the earliest liturgical forms for St Bertin are two collects in Wulfstan's collectar and a mass at New Minster. Wulfstan and his collectar have been previously shown to have had close Continental connections and to have been open to Continental saints; and New Minster possessed relics of the saint, which may explain the existence of a mass.[69]

There was another reason for the cults of some Flemish saints such as SS Austroberta and Salvius. Here the cult is particularly visible in texts from Christ Church, Canterbury, which claimed to possess the heads of these saints as relics. Entries in the calendar of the abbey, as well as

[69] A third saint venerated at St Bertin's, the abbot and bishop of Noyon–Tournai Mummolinus, was entered in the so-called Northern early 10th-c. calendar but not afterwards.

benedictions in the Canterbury benedictional, bear witness to these cults.[70] The possession of relics by the New Minster at Winchester justifies the cults of SS Grimbald and Judoc there.[71] Other Flemish saints have more random entries, due either to a tradition of veneration in the Carolingian world or to personal contacts with some of the centres which they patronized. Médard, Eligius, and Silvinus are entered respectively in all calendars except the Winchester ones for Médard, in the tenth-century West Country and those of Wells and Evesham for Eligius, and in the verse martyrology, the West Country, Wells, and Christ Church calendars for Silvinus, as well as at Wells and Evesham for Piato. Eligius has a benediction in the Claudius Pontifical, while Médard, in addition to one such benediction, also has a mass in Giso's sacramentary and a collect for the office in Wulfstan's collectar.

Finally, two saints provide examples of cults adopted on account of an English link. Two saints conflated into one, Wulgan, both reputedly English, crossed the Channel in the other direction and became established in the area where they were supposed to have lived as hermits, one near St Vaast, the other near St Riquier at Monstrelet, after having supposedly been an archbishop of Canterbury. The first's relics were kept at Lens, then allegedly translated to St Ouen's in Rouen about 1060, and a saint of that name is entered in the Christ Church calendar.[72] Another seventh-century hermit and founder of the abbey of Samer, St Wulfmar, whose relics were at Ghent, appears in calendars from Wessex, Wells, Winchester, Christ Church, Evesham, Worcester, and Bury, and has a collect in Wulfstan's collectar. It is difficult to know whether the cult was popular on account of its Ghent connection or rather because King Ceadwalla of Wessex was reputed to have visited this saint on his way to Rome on pilgrimage in 688,[73] but the confusion itself is of interest, showing how eager Anglo-Saxon ecclesiastics were to seize on any historical, real or supposed, connections with the Continent and Flanders especially.

---

[70] Austroberta was also entered in the martyrology from Aethelstan's Psalter, see Hampson, *Kalendarium*, 397–420, and McGurk, 'Metrical Calendar', 93, and in two calendars, the mid-10th-c. West Country one and that of Giso, see Wormald, *Kalendars*, nos. 2 and 8; and Salvius appears in the former as well as at St Augustine's, Evesham, Bury, and in 11th-c. Wessex, ibid., nos. 2, 5, 16, 19, and 3.

[71] Birch, *Liber Vitae*, 149 and 161; 92.

[72] On Wulgan, see J. Corblet, *Hagiographie du diocèse d'Amiens* (5 vols.; Amiens, 1869–75), iii. 226–42.

[73] C. Plummer (ed.), *Venerabilis Baedae Opera Historica* (2 vols.; Oxford, 1896), ii. 279.

V. ARTISTIC EXCHANGES BETWEEN ENGLAND AND FLANDERS

In art also the links between England and Flanders go back to the Carolingian period, when the 'Hiberno-Saxon' style of illumination from Northumbria reached the abbeys of Corbie and St Vaast's in particular, but also Tours where Alcuin was abbot, through the means of English manuscripts taken to the Continent by Anglo-Saxon scholars. Such manuscripts as the Corbie Psalter, of the beginning of the ninth century, the Evangeliary from Prüm and that of St Vaast, of the mid-ninth century, and the second Bible of Charles the Bald, of the third quarter of the ninth century, coming from the *scriptoria* of Prüm, St Vaast, Corbie, and the court of Charles the Bald, clearly show the influence of the Insular style of illumination, especially in the decoration of the capitals, as late as 900.[74]

Meanwhile, one of the common Carolingian features adopted in England was the innovation of the Westwork or double-ended church with a raised end and apse on the west as well as on the east side, on the model of the abbey church of Corvey, for example.[75] The best representative of this style of basilica in the western part of the Carolingian Empire remained the abbey church of Centula–St Riquier,[76] which has been shown to have had a direct influence on the building of the church at Sherborne and probably also at Deerhurst.[77] The most evident example of a genuine Westwork in England, together with that at Deerhurst, is the Old Minster at Winchester, while the church of St Oswald at Gloucester was also following Carolingian architectural models.[78]

By the end of the tenth century, the leading role in artistic terms has returned to England. It gives us the only example of genuine direct artistic influences between England and Flanders. At St Bertin's, the style of late tenth-century Anglo-Saxon illumination appears to have been particularly popular.[79] Under Abbot Odbert, one or more Anglo-Saxon monks worked

---

[74] A. Boinet, *La Miniature carolingienne* (Paris, 1913), pls. CXLVIII–CXLIX; XXXVII; XCIII–XCVI; and C–CIII. On Insular influences on Carolingian art, see also A. Goldschmidt, *German Illumination* (Florence and Paris, 1928; Eng. tran.), i. 15; and G. L. Micheli, *L'Enluminure du Haut Moyen Age et les influences irlandaises* (Brussels, 1939), 127–43.

[75] Out of the vast literature on this subject see, for example, C. Heitz, *L'Architecture religieuse carolingienne* (Paris, 1980), 148–56.

[76] C. Heitz, *Recherches sur les rapports entre architecture et liturgie à l'époque carolingienne* (Paris, 1963), passim.

[77] A. W. Klukas, 'Liturgy and Architecture: Deerhurst Priory as an Expression of the *Regularis Concordia*', *Viator*, 15 (1984), 85–91.

[78] E. Fernie, *The Architecture of the Anglo-Saxons* (London, 1983), 99–106 and 74–89. A further development of this Carolingian style as seen at St Gall, Xanten, and Nivelles is exemplified in Ottonian architecture in the churches of Hildesheim, Werden, Essen, and Gernrode; their direct influence on English architecture was more limited, ibid. 46–89.

[79] On 10th- and 11th-c. exchanges with Flanders, see A. Boutémy, 'L'Enluminure anglaise de l'époque saxonne (x^e et xie siècles) et la Flandre française', *Bulletin de la Société Nationale des*

in the *scriptorium* of the abbey and contributed to the illumination of at least two books written by Odbert and owned by him, known as the 'Boulogne Gospels' and the 'Boulogne Psalter'.[80] Other such travelling artists were also influenced, more or less directly, by the illumination of Corbie and St Vaast such as we see it in the mid-eleventh-century St Vaast Bible, a source of inspiration for the artists of the three Gospel-books belonging to the Countess Judith, particularly the Anhalt–Morgan Gospels.[81] In this manuscript, written at St Vaast's or Corbie, the Evangelists' portraits were added by some of these travelling Anglo-Saxon artists in one of these three abbeys. As a result, we find at St Bertin's, in the 'Channel School', a mixture of the abstract patterns inherited from the Carolingian Franco-Saxon style in the decoration of initial capitals with the iconographic elements and stylistic features of the Winchester School of the late tenth century.[82] This style found its way into the Rhineland, where echoes of it appear in the Trier–Echternach School, then in northern Italy and at Monte Cassino.[83]

Political and economic contacts with Flanders were numerous during the tenth and eleventh centuries. By contrast, the cultural and artistic exchanges were of rather limited importance and, apart from a few monastic customs, some relatively indifferent hagiographical writings, and the traditional cults of local patron saints, they brought little to England, which herself exported there the artistic style admired throughout Europe. The reason for the modest impact of Flemish culture in England may well

---

Antiquaires de France, (1956), 42–50. For Corbie, see A. Hauttecoeur, 'Les Enluminures', in *Corbie*, 249–62 and H. Swarzenski, 'The Anhalt–Morgan Gospels', *The Art Bulletin*, 31(2) (1949), 79–80.

[80] The 'Boulogne Gospels', now Boulogne, Bibliothèque Municipale MS 11, of the late 10th c. were illuminated by an English monk of Ramsey (with the exception of two illuminations attributed to Odbert himself), who visited both Fleury and St Bertin's, see A. Boutémy, 'Un monument capital de l'enluminure anglo-saxonne: le manuscrit 11 de Boulogne-sur-Mer', *Cahiers de civilisation médiévale*, 1 (2) (1958), 181–2; J. Backhouse identified him with the illuminator of the 'Ramsey Psalter', a contemporary manuscript from either Ramsey or Winchester for the use of Ramsey, now British Library, Harleian MS 2904, see J. Backhouse, D. H. Turner, and L. Webster (eds.), *The Golden Age of Anglo-Saxon Art 966–1066* (London, 1984), 60, 65. The illuminations of the 'Boulogne Psalter', in the same library, MS 20, of the same period, used to be attributed to an Anglo-Saxon artist, see J. O. Westwood, *Facsimiles of the Miniatures and Ornaments of Anglo-Saxon and Irish Manuscripts* (London, 1868), 104–7, and E. G. Millar, *English Illuminated Manuscripts from the Tenth to the Twelfth Century* (Paris and Brussels, 1926), 17. Doubts were later expressed on this attribution, but it has now come back in favour, see Temple, *ASM*, 23 and 100 and A. Wilmart, 'Les Livres de l'abbé Otbert', *Bulletin historique de la Société des Antiquaires de la Morinie*, 14 (1922–4), 169–88, and I agree with it. On the Channel School, see Temple, *ASM*, 12, 24; and Micheli, *Enluminure*, 152–64, esp. 162–4.

[81] Temple, *ASM*, 24 and Swarzenski, 'The Anhalt–Morgan Gospels', 78–80; on the St Vaast Bible, see Micheli, *Enluminure*, 163, pls. 254–5.

[82] Ibid. 162–4.

[83] Ibid. 155–7, 164–8.

reside in the lack of a significant cultural output in Flanders itself or, at any rate, one which could compare with that of other West European areas and of England itself. Meanwhile, the not infrequent hostility between the English and Flemish courts contributed to the strengthening of the alliance between England and, beyond Flanders, Germany, one of the most brilliant cultural centres of tenth- and eleventh-century Europe.

3

THE EMPIRE

I. GEOGRAPHICAL OUTLINE

The area covered by the name of Empire in this chapter encompasses the regions of Lotharingia, the Rhineland, the duchies of Saxony, Franconia, Swabia, and Bavaria, the kingdom of Burgundy, and reaches as far as the kingdom of Hungary in the East. It excludes Italy, to which a separate chapter is devoted. This geographical survey follows the general rule adopted in this book, which consists of including only those parts of a unit which have been found to be relevant to the topic under scrutiny, namely their connections with England; other areas, towns, or monasteries, however important in their own right in the history of the Empire, are ignored. Politically speaking, we are discussing the Ottonian–Salian Empire, established in 962 with the coronation of the duke of Saxony and German king, Otto, son of Henry the Fowler, as Emperor. Lotharingia, the old Carolingian Middle Kingdom, was a duchy by the early tenth century, wavering in its allegiance between the French and German kings until 924, when it was permanently taken over by the latter. However, it continued to have its own dukes under imperial authority, first Rénier, his son Gislebert, and their family in the tenth century, then, from the middle of the eleventh onwards, those of the house of Alsace, Gérard and Dietrich.[1] The core of the Empire remained Saxony, with its principal cities of Quedlinburg, Magdeburg, and Goslar and its ports of Hamburg and Bremen. In the early eleventh century, the Emperor Henry II attempted to establish a 'capital' at Bamberg in Franconia, where we find a major ecclesiastical centre in the wealthy city of Mainz. Aachen, Cologne, and Liège were in Lower Lotharingia, and Trier, Metz, Verdun, Toul, and Gorze in Upper Lotharingia; and Besançon in the kingdom of Burgundy, which covered part of present-day south-east France and Switzerland. Franconia, Swabia, Bavaria, and Burgundy were part of the Empire and under imperial authority, the latter only in the eleventh century, but they also had their own local dukes or kings, such as Bavaria,

---

[1] E. H. Huhn, *Geschichte Lothringens* (2 vols.; 2nd edn.; Berlin, 1877), i. 77–83; R. Parisot, *Les Origines de la Haute Lorraine et sa première maison ducale 953–1033* (Paris, 1909); and E. Hlawitschka, *Lotharingien und das Reich an der Schwelle der deutschen Geschichte* (Stuttgart, 1968), 185–220 and *Die Anfänge des Hauses Habsburg-Lothringen* (Saarbrücken, 1969).

governed by the Luitpolding then the Babenberg dukes. Hungary, founded as a kingdom by King Stephen in 1000 after more than a century of fighting by its population of pagan Magyars against the German rulers, had close political as well as family links with the Empire.

Quedlinburg, Magdeburg, Bamberg, and Goslar were not the only centres of Ottonian power. This relied on three main components, well studied by Karl Leyser: the itinerary, the royal chapel, and the imperial crown-wearings.[2] The first two are the most relevant to our purpose. The itinerant nature of the court meant a continual move from one palace to another, where the Emperor spent part of the year and appeared crowned in glory on major feast-days. Otto I stayed mostly at Cologne, Mainz, and his own foundation at Magdeburg; Otto II in Saxony and Franconia; and Otto III travelled a great deal, but his favourite palaces were those of Ingelheim near Frankfurt and later Aachen, on account of its associations with Charlemagne; while Henry II concentrated on Bamberg, which he tried to establish as an imperial 'capital', and Henry III on Goslar.[3]

The constant movement of the court implied also the movement of the royal chapel, which accompanied the Emperors. The chapel was the intellectual and spiritual centre, from the ranks of which were appointed the bishops of major sees; some of the greatest personalities came to these appointments after having been chaplains and chancellors, such as Egbert of Trier and Willigis of Mainz, and the main policies on cults supported by the Emperors and on monastic reforms in imperial abbeys, to cite but two examples, had their roots there.[4]

The episcopal sees and religious centres with close connections with the court and chapel are numerous; of relevance on account of their documented links with England are, from West to East and from North to South, those of Liège, Cologne, Bremen, Hildesheim, Magdeburg, Verdun, Metz, Trier, Mainz, Bamberg, Toul, and Besançon. Some were of exceptional importance: Liège, Cologne, and Trier for their great economic and cultural pre-eminence,[5] Metz and Aachen for their Carolin-

---

[2] K. J. Leyser, 'Ottonian Government', in *Medieval Germany and its Neighbours 900–1250* (London, 1982), 69–101 and *Rule and Conflict in an Early Medieval Society: Ottonian Saxony* (London, 1979), 102–7. The main study of the itinerant court of the Ottonians is that by K. Brühl, *Fodrum, Gistum, Servitium Regis* (2 vols.; Cologne and Vienna, 1968), i; and of the chapel in J. Fleckenstein, *Die Hofkapelle der deutschen Könige* (2 vols.; Stuttgart, 1966), ii.

[3] Fleckenstein, *Hofkapelle*, 134–43; G. Zimmermann, 'Bamberg als königlicher Pfalzort', *Jahrbuch für fränkische Landesforschung*, 19 (1959), 203–22, esp. 212–13, has shown how the attempt by Henry II to collect relics of saints from all regions of the Reich in the altars at Bamberg is a manifestation of this programme.

[4] Fleckenstein, *Hofkapelle*, 127–31, 220, 260–75.

[5] On the role of these cities in the Rhine and Mosel valleys as European economic centres see, for example, M. Lombard, 'La Route de la Meuse et les relations lointaines des pays mosans entre le VIIIe et le XIe siècle', in P. Francastel (ed.), *L'Art mosan: Journées d'études, Paris 1952* (Paris, 1953), 9–28.

gian past and associations, Bremen as a missionary centre for northern Europe, Bamberg as well as Cologne and Magdeburg as imperial residences, and Hildesheim, Toul, and Besançon for individual prestigious bishops in the persons of Bernward, Gérard, and Hugh of Salins. The role of these often aristocratic bishops, wielding considerable worldly power and closely associated with the ideals of Ottonian kings in their role as protectors and rulers of the Church since they were both laymen and clerics, has been often discussed and on occasions diminished, but never denied.[6] Before looking at some of these personalities, a brief survey of the main centres which had links with England is needed, in order to highlight particular features of their architecture and devotions subsequently imported into England by visitors.

At first a small village in the diocese of Tongres-Maastricht, Liège saw its fortunes ascend considerably after the translation there of the relics of Bishop Lambert in the first quarter of the eighth century. From 924 onwards, it passed under the authority of the German king, and gradually, as first the dukes of Lower Lotharingia, then the counts of Maastricht, Tongres, and Huy were evicted, its bishops became the sole ruling authority in matters both secular and ecclesiastical, dependent on the Emperor alone. Governed by capable bishops, Bruno of Cologne (955–65), brother of Otto I, for a while, then Hugh abbot of St Maximin at Trier, Farabert abbot of Prüm, Rather, and Heraclius, it became a strong imperial stronghold by the time Bishop Notker received it in 972. He began to build the episcopal power into a political state, which it was to remain until the end of the Middle Ages. From the second half of the tenth century onwards, Liège, together with other Meuse valley cities such as Huy, reached an exceptional degree of economic prosperity, with a group of servants in the service of episcopal and imperial administration, and of merchants, who blended together to form the nucleus of an expanding urban patriciate. Under Bishops Bruno, Heraclius, and especially under Notker, the six Liège schools, one of the cathedral and five associated with collegiate churches, flourished, particularly after Wazo took over the cathedral school from c.1003 onwards. Students from several parts of Europe attended these schools, where mathematics, history, and theology were the main subjects of study. Among these students were Heriger,

---

[6] L. Santifaller, 'Zur Geschichte des ottonisch-salischen Reichskirchensystcm', *Abhandlungen der phil.-hist. Klasse der österreichischen Akademie der Wissenschaften*, Sitzungsberichte 229 (1954), and T. Reuter, 'The "Imperial Church System" of the Ottonian and Salian Rulers: A Reconsideration', *JEH* 33 (1982), 347–74, exemplify the two positions respectively emphasizing the deliberate attempt by the Emperors to set up an 'imperial Church' with which they could govern and the denial of the existence of such a plan; see also H. Hoffmann, *Buchkunst und Königtum im ottonischen und frühsalischen Reich* (Stuttgart, 1986), 24–37, and F. Lotter (ed.), *Die Vita Brunonis des Ruotger* (Bonn, 1958), 78–90.

Rupert, future abbot of Deutz, and eight other future bishops and abbots, as well as one future pope and Hubald, who was to become the first master of the school of Ste Geneviève in Paris. Whilst under the influence first of Anglo-Saxon and Irish art, then of Carolingian art of the Aachen Palace School and the Metz School, whose most famous patron was Bishop Drogo, also abbot of St Trond, Liège became an important artistic centre by the late tenth century, closely associated with the art of the Rhineland. The first churches in Liège were the cathedral of St Lambert and the church of St Peter, built by Bishop Hubert at the beginning of the eighth century. Destroyed by the Vikings, St Peter's was rebuilt during the first half of the tenth century, while the cathedral was later also rebuilt by Notker. Other churches were built in the tenth centuries, both monastic and parochial, particularly by Notker, who had a parish church dedicated to his recently canonized friend Adalbert of Prague. Notker also founded the canonical church of St John, to which he gave relics of SS Vincent, Fabian, and Sebastian, which he had acquired in Rome; and he restored the cathedral, which enshrined the tombs of St Laurence and other early bishops of the see in its crypt. Some of these churches were decorated with paintings, none of which have survived, by an Italian artist, John, who had worked in Aachen before coming to Liège. Several churches were founded during the eleventh century, the collegiate church of St Bartholomew in 1016, the abbey of St James in 1017, and that of St Laurence under Bishop Reginold (1025–38). In 1056, some relics of St James were brought to Liège from Spain, and some of St Laurence from Rome. Around 1070, as the city was expanding, other churches were founded in the suburbs, some dedicated to saints whose cults were then growing, such as St Christopher, St Giles, and St Leonard.[7]

Liège was closely associated with the see of Trier, one of the most significant German cities in Ottonian and Salian times.[8] Imperial residence in the Late Roman period and main Roman outpost in Germany, the city remained relatively prosperous under the Merovingians and, after a relative decline during the Carolingian period, lived through its greatest era between the tenth and the twelfth centuries. It was a successful trade

[7] On the history of Liège, see G. Kurth, *La Cité de Liège au Moyen Âge* (3 vols.; Paris, 1905), i, 17–50; id., *Notger de Liège et la civilisation au* x[e] *siècle* (2 vols.; Paris, Brussels and Liège, 1905), i. 6–30, 137–321; and Auda, *École*, 12–21, 76–7.

[8] On the history of Trier, see G. Kentenich, *Geschichte der Stadt Trier von ihrer Gründung bis zur Gegenwart* (Trier, 1915); S. J. Beissel, *Geschichte der Trierer Kirchen* (Trier, 1887–9); E. Herzog, *Die ottonische Stadt* (Berlin, 1964), 125–46, 243–4; H. Planitz, *Die deutsche Stadt im Mittelalter* (Graz and Cologne, 1954), 39, 63; also, more specifically, E. Boshof, *Das Erzstift Trier und seine Stellung zu Königtum und Papstum in ausgehenden 10. Jahrhundert: Der Pontifikat des Theuderichs* (Cologne and Vienna, 1972), and J. Jacobi, 'Erzbischof Poppo von Trier', *Archiv für mittelrheinische Kirchengeschichte*, 13 (1961), 9–26.

city on the Mosel valley and on the road leading from Metz to Aachen, Bruges, and England. It remained mostly a clerical and episcopal centre, around its numerous churches and abbeys.

The ecclesiastical centre was that of the double complex of the church of the Virgin and the cathedral of St Peter, built in the sixth century by Italian workmen and rebuilt by Archbishop Poppo (1016–47). The main churches in the city, however, were the three fourth-century foundations, later abbeys, of St Eucharius, St Maximin, and St Paulinus, while the founding of another church, the Holy Cross, was also traditionally attributed to that period and more specifically, to the Empress Helena. St Maximin, allegedly founded under Constantine, contained the tomb of Bishop Maximinus (336–46), and an abbey was already attached to its church by 500, the oldest abbey in Germany. It was also the largest and most influential, and the main intermediary for the spreading of the Gorze reform into the rest of Germany in the tenth century, when it was rebuilt in 934. The church of St Mary, founded in the late fourth century, changed its name when Bishop Felix brought there the relics of St Paulinus; it was rebuilt in the fifth century, became the burial place of the bishops of Trier, and was again rebuilt in the eleventh century and dedicated by Pope Leo IX on his visit to Germany in 1049. At St Eucharius', the church of St John the Baptist contained the relics of the first bishops of the city, Eucharius, Valerius, and Maternus, since *c.*455; the abbey church was entirely rebuilt by Archbishop Egbert (977–93) on a Greek cross plan with a chapel of St Maternus on the top floor, and was reformed by monks from St Bavo's at Ghent. Other churches in the city were the abbey of St Irmina, founded in the seventh century, and that of St Maria ad Martyres, dating from the turn of the seventh and eighth centuries, built on a Greek cross plan and subsequently restored by Archbishops Dietrich (965–77) and Egbert. Archbishop Egbert added a chapel dedicated to St Andrew in the cathedral, containing the highly venerated relic of the sandal of the Apostle. In the eleventh century, a few new churches were built and Archbishop Poppo founded a basilica on the spot where the hermitage of his friend the Greek monk St Simeon had been, after the hermit's death in 1035. This basilica, dedicated in 1042, was on the second floor of the Porta Nigra.

With the exception of a few years when Archbishop Bruno was reigning in Cologne, the archbishops of Trier were primates of Lotharingia and often also archchaplains at court. Trier prided itself on its apostolic descent and the emphasis on it was strengthened by its claim to possess the relics of the staff of St Peter, which it shared with Cologne, as well as those of the Holy Nail from the Cross and the sandal of St Andrew, in the

cathedral. The climax of the archiepiscopal power occurred under Archbishops Dietrich and Egbert, when Trier was also a major artistic centre
on account of the exceptional quality of manuscript production and
metalwork from the episcopal workshop. Examples of these are manuscripts such as the *Registrum Gregorii* and the *Codex Egberti*, and the
reliquaries made for the above-mentioned relics.[9] The next great archbishop of Trier was Poppo, a royal chaplain educated in the milieu of the
Gorze reform and provost of Bamberg before becoming archbishop of
Trier. He went on a pilgrimage to the Holy Land, accompanied by a monk
of Mount Sinai, Simeon, whom he subsequently persuaded to take up
residence at Trier in a hermitage inside the Porta Nigra, later transformed
into a basilica. These archbishops had very close links with the Ottonian
and Salian courts and played a considerable part in the political and
cultural life of the Empire.

An even more important role within the Empire, however, was that of
the archbishop of one of the three main imperial cities with Magdeburg
and Mainz, Cologne.[10] This Roman city contained an imperial palace and
was also one of the most important market towns under the Ottonians. It
was at the heart of the trade route on the Rhine between England and
Scandinavia and the south of Europe, as well as being itself engaged in
manufacturing glassware. Its merchant organization, based on guilds with
a provost and comprising their own laws, regulations, and feasts, was very
similar to that of English guilds, and Cologne proved to be at the forefront
of the communal movement from the middle of the eleventh century
onwards.

Tradition ascribed the founding of the Church of Cologne to St Peter
himself. Its first ecclesiastical foundations were the church of St Gereon,
companion of St Maurice and the other martyrs of the Theban Legion,
and that of the Eleven Virgins, among whom were the two British
princesses Ursula and Pinnosa. Both these churches were cemeterial
basilicas built on the tombs of these martyrs in the fourth century. They
subsequently became abbeys and St Ursula's was rebuilt in the eleventh
and twelfth centuries, when the saint's relics were found and translated
anew; by then the legend of the British origin of the saints, whose number
had augmented to eleven thousand by the ninth century, was well
established, and would be developed in the twelfth century in England by

---

[9] *Codex Egberti*; for the relic of St Andrew and its reliquary, see J. Beckwith, *Early Medieval Art: Carolingian, Ottonian, Romanesque* (London, 1964), 137–8 and ill. p. 21.
[10] On the history of Cologne, see W. Neuss and F. W. Ödiger, *Geschichte des Erzbistums Köln* (3 vols.; Cologne, 1964), i. 36–257, 282–85, 374–85, 464–5; Herzog, *Die ottonische Stadt*, 235, 246; Planitz, *Deutsche Stadt*, 39, 75–8, 98–111.

Geoffrey of Monmouth.[11] A third Early Christian foundation of the fourth century was the basilica of St Severinus of Bordeaux, associated with Cologne and greatly venerated there. The next foundations belonged to the seventh and eighth centuries: St Clement's, later St Cunibert, built by the latter, who was closely involved with the Merovingian kings, contained the relics of the two English missionary brothers Ewald; Pépin of Herstal and his wife Plectrud founded the nunnery of St Mary, rebuilt in the eleventh century and known from that time onwards as Scta Maria im Kapitol. The cathedral, originally the church of St Martin, was dedicated to St Peter by St Boniface, who had intended Cologne to be his see before he moved to the metropolitan see of Mainz. Cologne itself became an archbishopric under Charlemagne. One of its greatest archbishops was Bruno I (953–65), youngest brother of Otto I and his closest counsellor, as well as for a time Duke of Lotharingia.[12] Educated in Lotharingia and by the Irish bishop Isaac and Bishop Rather of Verona, he was a widely learned man and a supporter of the Gorze reform movement. Under his reign, not only the suffragan dioceses of Cologne itself, Minden, Bremen, Osnabrück, and Utrecht, were under his authority, but also those of Trier, Liège, Verdun, Metz, and Toul, the bishops of the latter two, Dietrich and Gérard, both being his appointees, ex-Cologne clerics and trained in the royal chapel. Bruno brought to Cologne the relics of the staff of St Peter from Metz and the bodies of SS Eliphius and Patroclus, Gregory of Spoleto, and Pantaleon from Italy. The latter he deposited in the church of that name, to which he attached a monastery in 957, whose first abbot came from St Maximin at Trier. Other foundations include the church of Great St Martin, converted into a monastery for Irish monks in 988. The next important archbishops during our period were Heribert (999–1021), chancellor of Italy under Otto III, educated at Gorze and founder of the abbey of Deutz, dedicated in 1020; and Herman II (1036–56), founder of the cathedral of SS Simon and Jude at Goslar, who had great influence at court and received Leo IX on his visit to Cologne in 1049. Herman's father had been the founder of the abbey of Brauweiler, dedicated c.1028 and given to monks of Stavelot first and of St Maximin afterwards. Archbishop Anno II (1056–75) founded the abbey of Siegburg in 1071–2, inspired by the rule of Fruttuaria and with monks from the Italian abbey.

Metz and Toul belonged to the province of Trier, except under the reign of Bruno. Metz had been one of the main Carolingian cities in the ninth century, especially under Bishop Drogo, who promoted learning and art in his cathedral. Witnesses of this School of Metz art are manuscripts such

[11] See below, n. 141.
[12] On his career, see Lotter, *Vita Brunonis, passim.*

as the Sacramentary of Drogo and various ivory plaques, all displaying the characteristic features of this art workshop, which mixed late antique inspiration with the fluid drawing of the Reims School and colours derived from another major Carolingian centre, Tours.[13] Apart from the cathedral St Stephen's, Metz had several important abbeys such as St Arnulf's and St Symphorien.[14] Its great eighth-century bishop Chrodegang had been responsible for drawing up a rule for the use of canons in cathedral communities, based on a mixture of the Augustinian and Benedictine Rules, ensuring the enforcement of a communal life among canons serving the cathedrals.[15] This rule was widely adopted in tenth-century Europe, including in England. Meanwhile, most monastic communities at Metz and in the diocese had been reformed along the lines of the Gorze customs.[16] At Toul, the monastic reform had been carried out by William of Volpiano, and the greatest of the city's bishops were Gérard, and Bruno, who became Pope Leo IX, the first of the leading eleventh-century reforming popes. Toul, whose main abbeys were St Aper's and St Mansuetus', was also a trade and market city, as was Verdun, whose monastic life was reformed both from Gorze and by Richard of St Vannes, who had close links with Liège and its schools.[17] Its main abbeys were St Vanne and St Paul's, dedicated in 974.

Aachen, the capital city of Charlemagne and Louis the Pious, still preserved the imperial palace, with the round Palatine chapel, built on the model of S. Vitale of Ravenna and of the Late Antique imperial *aula* at Trier, and the tomb of Charlemagne himself.[18] Otto III had a nunnery attached to the church of St Saviour in 997, founded the church of St

---

[13] *Drogo-Sakramentar*; on the ivories, see A. Goldschmidt (ed.), *Die Elfenbeinskulpturen aus der Zeit der karolingischen und sächsischen Kaiser VIII–XI Jahrhundert* (4 vols., Berlin, 1914–26), i. 38–59 and pls. XXIX–LII; for a discussion of the Metz School see, for example, W. R. W. Koehler, cont. F. Mütherich, *Die karolingische Miniaturen im Auftrage des deutschen Vereins für Kunstwissenschaft* (6 vols.; Berlin, 1930–77), and J. Hubert, J. Porcher, and W. Volbach, *Carolingian Art* (tr. London, 1970), 71–260, esp. 158–61, 233–8.

[14] M. Parisse, *La Lorraine monastique au Moyen Âge* (Nancy, 1981), 18–135.

[15] Wallace-Hadrill, *The Frankish Church*, 171, 174–9, 264; R. McKitterick, *The Frankish Kingdoms under the Carolingians 751–987* (London, 1983), 44, 56, 58–9, 112; and various articles in *Saint Chrodegang: Communications présentées au colloque tenu à Metz à l'occasion du douzième centenaire de sa mort* (Metz, 1967), esp. G. Hocquard, 'La Règle de St Chrodegang', 55–89.

[16] On the reform in Lotharingia, the best recent studies are in J. Choux, *La Lorraine chrétienne au Moyen Âge* (Metz, 1981) and D. Iogna-Prat and J.-C. Picard (eds.), *Religion et culture autour de l'An Mil: Royaume capétien et Lotharingie* (Paris, 1990).

[17] On the history of Toul and Verdun, see Parisse, *Lorraine*, 24–6, 57.

[18] On the chapel, see Hubert, Porcher, and Volbach, *Carolingian Art*, 45–6 and pls. 35–9, and the articles by G. Bandmann, F. Kreusch, and L. Hugot in W. Braunfels and H. Schnitzler, *Karl der Grosse: Lebenswerk und Nachleben* (3 vols.), iii: *Karolingische Kunst* (Düsseldorf, 1965), 424–62, 463–533, 534–72.

Adalbert, completed by Henry II, and built the abbey of Burtscheid *c.*1000 for his Greek teacher and friend Gregory of Cassano.[19]

The first Ottonian resided mostly in Saxony. Magdeburg, already a market town under the Carolingians, expanded when Otto I made it his favourite imperial residence.[20] He gave it as a dowry to his English Queen, Edith, and they both lived there often. In 937 he dedicated the church he had founded with Edith to St Maurice and his companions, both as a family monastery and as a centre for the Slav mission. In 968, it became the cathedral and Otto had a palace built with materials brought from Ravenna, with a round chapel dedicated to the Virgin Mary then to St Gangolf, in an attempt to emulate Aachen.[21] Magdeburg was also an important centre for trade, with merchants' guilds. Edith herself was sufficiently interested in the market to prevail upon her husband to move its site to a more convenient location in the city, and the Elbe, flowing into the North Sea, could provide a trade link with England.

On the trade route from Cologne to Magdeburg was the episcopal city of Hildesheim.[22] Apart from the cathedral, it had several churches built under its greatest bishop, Bernward (993–1022), the abbey of St Michael, and the churches of St Maurice and St Bartholomew, both of these eminently Ottonian saints, particularly venerated by the imperial family. Bernward was not only a builder, but also interested in the decoration of his churches, and he commissioned artefacts of metalwork, the best known of which are the doors of the cathedral and the column at St Michael's, depicting New Testament scenes in a deliberate imitation of the column of Trajan in Rome.

Bamberg was made into an imperial city by Henry II, and became also an episcopal see in 1007.[23] But the main religious centre of Franconia and southern Germany remained the city of Mainz. Mainz's first church was the basilica built on the tomb of the martyr Alban. After its main eighth-century bishop, the Anglo-Saxon missionary Boniface, the greatest occupant of the see was Archbishop Willigis (975–1011).[24] Archchancellor,

[19] Herzog, *Die ottonische Stadt*, 248.

[20] D. Claude, *Geschichte des Erzbistums Magdeburg bis in der 12. Jahrhundert* (2 vols.; Cologne and Vienna, 1972), i. 17–379.

[21] E. Nickel, 'Magdeburg in karolingisch–ottonischer Zeit', in H. Jankuhn, W. Schlesinger, and H. Steuer (eds.), *Vor- und Frühformen der europäischen Stadt im Mittelalter* (Abhandlungen der Akademie der Wissenschaften in Göttingen, phil.-hist. Klasse, 3rd ser. 83, 2 vols.; Göttingen, 1973), i. 316–31, esp. 321–2 on the Byzantine features of the palace.

[22] On Hildesheim, see Herzog, *Die ottonische Stadt*, 237–41.

[23] Ibid. 171–81.

[24] A. P. Brück (ed.), *Willigis und sein Dom: Festschrift zur Jahrtausendfeier des Mainzer Domes 975–1975* (Mainz, 1975), and H. Büttner, 'Erzbischof Willigis von Mainz (975–1011)', in *Zur Frühmittelalterlichen Reichsgeschichte am Rhein, Main und Neckar*, ed. A. Gehrlich (Darmstadt, 1975), 301–13.

primate of Germany, he had the cathedral rebuilt and dedicated in 1009, and founded other churches. Willigis was a respected counsellor of Otto II and Otto III, who went to Italy with the Emperor in 983, 996, and 999; he crowned Otto III in Aachen and later, Henry II and Cunigunde in 1002 at Mainz. Apart from maintaining his position at court, he was also a theologian and administrator of the see, and most concerned with the eastern mission, as shown by his attempts to force Adalbert of Prague back to his diocese after the latter's repeated withdrawals to Rome. The other churches of Mainz were the two main abbeys of St Alban and SS Sergius and Bacchus. At Besançon, the cathedral, founded possibly in the fourth century, was dedicated to St Stephen in the fifth, when an arm of the saint was translated there, and rebuilt in the ninth century with a dedication to St John the Evangelist.[25] The patron saints of the town, SS Ferriolis and Ferritiolis, saw their cult develop from the fifth century onwards, a cult already mentioned by Gregory of Tours. In the tenth century, the links between Besançon and Cluny were strong.

Within these dioceses were some of the most prestigious monastic centres. Stavelot–Malmédy was founded by St Remaclus in the seventh century, and the cult of this saint developed there between the ninth and the eleventh centuries, as well as the cults of SS Nicasius, Quirinus, and Cubiculus translated from Rouen in 876 and that of St Justus translated some time between 909 and 933–4, leading to a peak of popularity of the pilgrimage to these shrines during the tenth and eleventh centuries.[26] The abbeys had close links with the papacy as well as with the bishops of Cologne and Liège, especially under Notker, and the basilica was rebuilt at the end of the tenth century.[27]

St Hubert, originally Andage, was founded by Beregisus and named after the seventh-century hermit Hubert, who had lived there and whose cult developed at the abbey. St Trond, founded c.660 by the saint of that name, had close links with Metz. Abbot Adelard II (1055–82) rebuilt the abbey church with workmen from Cologne. In 1082, following the contested election of the new abbot, some monks left the abbey to find refuge in Flanders, Germany, and England.[28]

Bilsen was founded in the seventh century by St Landrada, consecrated by St Lambert, and Nivelles at the same period, by two women, St Gertrud and her mother St Jutta; Gertrud invited Irish monks there, and the abbey

---

[25] On Besançon, see B. de Vregille, 'Les Origines chrétiennes et le Haut Moyen Âge', in C. Fohlen (ed.), *Histoire de Besançon* (2 vols.; Besançon, 1964), i. 155–237.

[26] F. Baix, *L'Abbaye et la principauté de Stavelot-Malmédy* (Brussels, 1981), 45, 212–15, 98–9, 119, 127.

[27] Ibid. 141–3, 147.

[28] E. G. Millar, *The St Trond Lectionary* (Oxford, 1949), 4–14.

remained closely connected with Ireland and a centre of the cult of St Patrick on the Continent. Further east, Essen was founded in the middle of the ninth century, but saw its hour of glory during the tenth and eleventh centuries, when it was most closely associated with Cologne.

Gorze, an abbey founded by Chrodegang of Metz, had been reformed in 933 by Bishop Adalbero of Metz with clerics from Toul and Irish monks. It was taken over in the tenth century by John of Vandières, abbot after 967, who pursued a specifically monastic reform. John spent some time in Italy, where he knew and admired basilian monasticism, and among the main tenets of the reform were a strong emphasis on eremitism, poverty, manual labour, and private devotion, within the ideal of a return to the purity of the apostolic life.[29] The Gorze reform spread to Germany and Lotharingia: it influenced to a certain extent the reforms at St Maximin and St Eucharius' at Trier in 934 and 977, Echternach in 974, and Reichenau in 1006, as well as Stavelot in 938, St Hubert's *c.*942 and the Toul, Metz, and Verdun abbeys between 934 and 1000.[30]

In Saxony, Gandersheim, the family abbey of the Liudolfings, was a great cultural centre at the time of Abbess Gerberga, niece of Otto I, then of Abbess Sophia, the Empress Theophano's daughter. It had strong links with the imperial family and its most famous member was the nun Hroswith, author of a panegyric of Otto the Great, a history of her abbey, and several plays modelled on classical authors such as Terence.[31]

Fulda, in Franconia, one of the main cultural centres under the Carolingians, as well as a trade centre, recovered all its prestige under the Ottonians, when it was once again a major artistic centre, producing numerous manuscripts such as the Fulda Sacramentary and the Codex Wittekindeus.[32]

Founded in 724 by St Pirmin, the abbey of Reichenau was another major centre of learning and monastic life under the Carolingians and the home of the writer Walafrid Strabo (838–49).[33] It was reformed in the last quarter of the tenth century from the neighbouring monastery of Einsiedeln, under Henry II, and Abbot Immo (1006–8) was from Gorze. Before him, Abbot Witigowo (985–97) had been a great builder, who rebuilt the main abbey

---

[29] Life of John of Gorze in MGH SS iv. 337–77; see K. Hallinger, *Gorze-Kluny* (2 vols.; Rome, 1950–1), i. 51–9, and J. Leclercq, 'Jean de Gorze et la vie religieuse au xᵉ siècle', in *Saint Chrodegang*, 133–52, as well as the classic F. Chaussier, *Histoire de l'abbaye de Gorze* (Metz, 1894) and a very good insight in Wormald, 'Aethelwold', 26–9.

[30] Hallinger, *Gorze–Kluny*, i. 49, 59–92 and J. Choux, 'Décadence et réforme monastique dans la province de Trèves 855–959)', in his *La Lorraine chrétienne au Moyen Âge*, 53–72.

[31] P. de Winterfeld (ed.), *Hrosvithae Opera*, MGH SRG (Berlin, 1902).

[32] On the Fulda production, see Hoffmann, *Buchkunst*, 132–80.

[33] For Reichenau, see K. Beyerle (ed.), *Die Kultur der Abtei Reichenau* (2 vols.; Munich, 1925) and H. Maurer (ed.), *Die Abtei Reichenau* (Sigmaringen, 1974).

church. A Roman-plan basilica, this church, situated on the middle island, was dedicated to the Virgin Mary whilst the church of Oberzell, of the ninth century, was dedicated to St George and that of Niederzell, of the eighth century, to SS Peter and Paul. Witigowo was especially close to Otto III, went to Italy in 989–90 and 996 at the Emperor's coronation, and was honoured by the pope with the gift of a relic of the Holy Blood, a visit at Reichenau in 998, and the privilege of wearing the sandals and the dalmatic. The artistic summit of the Reichenau School corresponded partly with Witigowo's abbacy: it extended from *c*.950 to *c*.1020, when the production of nearly 500 manuscripts and ivories comprised the manuscripts of the Eburnant and Ruodprecht groups, represented by the Gero Codex and the Egbert Psalter, and both the manuscripts and ivories of the Liuthard group, examples of which are the two Gospel books of Otto III, the Pericopes book of Henry II, the Bamberg Apocalypse and the Lorsch Sacramentary.[34] Reichenau was at the forefront of the Ottonian artistic movement, promoting a strong renaissance of Late Antique and Early Christian iconographic themes and style, as well as displaying a staunch predilection for the treatment of christological narrative cycles, as seen in the most important contribution of the abbey to Ottonian monumental painting, the wall-paintings of the nave of St George, Oberzell, of which some depictions of miracles of Christ are still visible today.[35]

St Gall, founded in 613 by the Irish monk Gallus, was one of the most famous Carolingian abbeys, whose reputation rested on its library, on scholars such as the Notkers, and on its perfecting a liturgical and musical invention, the tropes, which were to dominate European monastic culture for the next five centuries. It remained a major cultural centre until the 920s, when fires and attacks from Hungarians and Saracens brought about a decline, to be stopped only under a series of brilliant late tenth- and eleventh-century abbots, who brought it into the mainstream of Ottonian Renaissance culture, such as Notker Labeo (*c*.950–1022). This revival was evident in scholarship, in painting, with the decoration of the abbey church after the 937 fire, and in manuscript illumination, which produced manuscripts such as the Antiphonary of Hartker and the Sacramentary of Gottescalc.[36] Another main Burgundian centre was the renowned abbey of St Maurice of Agaune, founded in 515 and associated with the legend

[34] Hoffmann, *Buchkunst*, 303–35.

[35] K. Martin, *Die ottonische Wandbilder der St Georgskirche Reichenau–Oberzell* (2nd edn.; Sigmaringen, 1975), 23–8 and pls. 6–13.

[36] J. M. Clark, *The Abbey of St Gall as a Centre of Literature and Art* (Cambridge, 1926), 1–16, 148–99; Hoffmann, *Buchkunst*, 366–402, credits St Gall with more manuscripts than were hitherto attributed to it.

of the martyrdom of St Maurice and his companions of the Theban Legion.[37]

Whilst some of the older Carolingian foundations were less active by the beginning of the tenth century, other monasteries were at the head of the tenth-century monastic reform, which spread from Gorze and Trier within the Empire. Some of the Lotharingian and Rhineland houses were at the peak of their activity during these two centuries, especially Stavelot, St Hubert, Nivelles, and the abbeys in Trier and Cologne, whereas Fulda and Reichenau produced their most impressive output during the early eleventh century.

The Ottonians and Salians were well served by an exceptionally qualified set of bishops throughout the period. Although they may not have been primarily used by the emperors as administrators and bureaucrats, since they were frequently related to the local aristocracy, these bishops were often serving the emperors, particularly in one respect: they were the creators of the imperial ideology, which was based to a great extent on a parallel with episcopal sacrality.[38] The bishops, who ruled as 'holy men', played a considerable role in the development of ceremonial displays of power in their own cities, through their patronage of relics, liturgical feasts, buildings, and art. Through these, they exerted a strong influence on the development of ceremonial at court, where a parallel emphasis was put on relics and cults encouraged by the emperors, artistic displays, and rites such as the crown-wearings and the attendance of the court on great religious festivals. Bruno of Cologne, Otto I's own brother, Egbert of Trier, Willigis of Mainz, Bruno of Toul, later Pope Leo IX, Ulrich of Augsburg, Reginold of Eichstätt, Bernward of Hildesheim, and Notker of Liège are only the best known among these bishops. The careers of some of these, who were close counsellors of the Emperors and of great significance in the development of their own cities, can be illustrated by the examples of Notker and Gerbert. Born in Swabia about 930, first a member of the imperial chancery of Otto I with Willigis and Gerbert of Aurillac, later Pope Silvester II, Notker was consecrated at Bonn in 972 by the Archbishop of Cologne. He was involved in the succession to the throne of Otto III, whose claim had been contested by Duke Henry of Bavaria, and spent much time at imperial councils both in Germany and Italy. Whether simply with the court or on imperial missions, he went to Italy four, possibly even five times, once with Theophano in 988–90. Very close to Otto III, who visited him at Liège in 993, Notker followed him

---

[37] E. Aubert (ed.), *Trésor de l'abbaye de St Maurice d'Agaune* (Paris, 1872), 6–41.
[38] Leyser, *Rule and Conflict*, 77–91.

for his coronation in Rome in 996, which Willigis also attended. Other friends of Notker were Adalbert of Prague, whom he met in Rome at S. Alessio, the abbot of the two Ghent monasteries Womar, for whom he wrote the Life of a local saint Landoald in 980, Gerbert of Reims, and Odilo of Cluny. Notker remained a counsellor for Henry II, who also came to Liège, and he was sent on diplomatic missions to the king of France and the count of Flanders in 1005. By the time he died in 1008, he had created a strong episcopal power at Liège, as well as endowed the city with impressive buildings and good schools.[39] Another bishop of great significance in German politics, though officially reigning over a diocese which belonged to the Western Frankish area of influence, was Gerbert of Aurillac. His later career, after leaving Reims, was closely connected with the Empire. A friend of the Emperor Otto II and the Empresses Adelheid and Theophano, he became one of Otto III's tutors, remained in contact with most German bishops such as Egbert, Willigis, Notker, Everger of Cologne, and Adalbero of Verdun, and spent several years in Aachen, Magdeburg, and Reichenau, before being appointed archbishop of Ravenna then pope by Otto III.[40]

II. THE FACTUAL EVIDENCE FOR CONTACT

The first hint of contacts with Germany comes with the arrival in England at Alfred's court of a Saxon monk John, in the later years of the ninth century.[41] Serious evidence begins when Aethelstan renewed political connections with the German court by marrying one of his half-sisters, Edith, to the future Otto I, and another to someone who is not very clearly identifiable but seems to have been Conrad, son of Rudolf, the king of Burgundy.[42] The connection between English kings and the Liudolfings was to have considerable consequences for the future political situation in Western Europe during the following three centuries, when this alliance between the kings of England and the German emperors was to be renewed several times with the marriage of Mathilda, Henry I's daughter, to the Emperor Henry V in 1114, and with that of Mathilda, daughter of Henry II, to Henry the Lion in 1168, whose ultimate legacy was to be the disastrous defeat of Henry the Lion's son Otto IV at Bouvines in 1214. But it was to have more immediate consequences on the cultural exchanges

---

[39] Kurth, *Notger*, i, 32–114.

[40] H. P. Lattin (ed.), *The Letters of Gerbert* (New York, 1961), 281–99, 294–9.

[41] *Asser*, chs. 78 and 94, pp. 63 and 81.

[42] *ASC*, D (Mercian Register) 924, 68; *Aethelweard*, 2 and p. xx; *Florence*, i. 132; WMGR i. 149 and 137. On the identification of the King of Burgundy, see R. L. Poole, 'Burgundian Notes: The Alpine Son-in-Law of Edward the Elder', *EHR* 26 (1911), 313–17.

between the two countries, which both appear to have benefited from them and welcomed external innovations, especially in view of the evidently strong feelings Otto I seems to have had towards his first wife. Although both Widukind of Corvey and Thietmar make mistakes when recounting Edith's exact parentage, they both stress Otto's love for her and their son Liudolf and his distress on her death, as does also Hroswith of Gandersheim; and Thietmar terms her St Edith.[43]

The first manifestation of these exchanges is the circulation of people between the two countries. One must assume that there were at least several Englishmen among Edith's suite escorting her to Germany.[44] We have only one example recorded of a group of Englishmen in Germany in 929, that of Abbot Coenwald who, with his suite of accompanying monks, visited several abbeys throughout Germany. His visit is recorded in the books of confraternity of Reichenau and St Gall, and in these he is said to have asked for the monks' prayers for himself, his suite and King Aethelstan.[45] Not only did these monks visit what was probably quite a wide number of monastic houses, but they doubtless brought presents with them. In a way, it could be said that one book we know well was also intended to be sent as a present to Germany, this time by the English earl who wrote it, Aethelweard, to his kinswoman the abbess of Essen Mathilda, niece of another Mathilda, abbess of Quedlinburg, to whom Widukind of Corvey dedicated his work.[46] We do not know whether Mathilda was more English than German but living in Germany, or a German relation, though the second alternative is more probable. Within this context, it does not matter; the most important fact is precisely the obliteration of the nationality in favour of the stronger ties of kinship, 'communis prosapia', since it was of no relevance to Aethelweard whether she was directly related to Otto or to Edith and hence to Aethelstan. Another kinsman of the English royal family seems to have been one

---

[43] Thietmar, *Chronicon*, 18–20; *Widukindi monachi Corbeiensis rerum gestarum saxonicarum libri tres*, ed. H. E. Lohmann rev. P. Hirsch, MGH SRG (Hanover, 1935), 54, 99–100; Hroswith, *Gesta Ottonis*, 206–28.

[44] Among them may have been the cleric Thorketil, see Pseudo-Ingulf in *Ingulfi Croylandensis Historia*, in W. Fulman and T. Gale, *Rerum Anglicarum Scriptorum Veterum*, i (Oxford, 1684), 38.

[45] This text, first edited by J. Armitage Robinson, 'The Saxon abbots of Glastonbury', in *The Saxon Bishops of Wells* (London, 1921), 40–1, 60–2, is now discussed in *CSD* I. i. 40–3 and especially by S. D. Keynes, 'King Aethelstan's books', in *Learning and Literature*, App., 198–201. It is also edited in the confraternity books themselves, P. Piper (ed.), *Libri confraternitatum Sancti Galli, Augiensis, Fabariensis*, MGH (Berlin, 1884), 136–7, 238. One of the monks in his suite has a German name, Conrad: he would have been either a guide from Germany or, possibly, a German living in England. On this visit and Aethelstan's links with Germany, see M. Wood, 'The Making of King Aethelstan's Empire: An English Charlemagne?', *Ideal and Reality*, 250–64.

[46] *Aethelweard*, pp. xii–xiii; on this and the links between the two works, both on account of the closeness between Essen and Corvey and between the two abbesses, see Campbell, 'England', in *Essays*, 194–5.

Gregory, who became abbot of Einsiedeln in the kingdom of Burgundy, and who was said to be of English royal descent.[47]

Some evidence for the continuous links with imperial lands around the middle of the tenth century is given to us in the biography of Archbishop Egbert of Trier, whose mother is said to have been an Englishwoman.[48] He was archbishop of Trier from 977 to 993 and he may have inherited from his mother, who must have lived in Germany at about the time of Aethelstan and Edith, his sympathy for things English, expressed in his artistic tastes and in his activities. Egbert's role was pre-eminent in the development of one of the most famous cultural and artistic Ottonian centres in the 980s and 990s, both stimulated and promoted by the archbishop's privileged relations with the court of Otto II as well as with the Empress Theophano. He may have known of, and possibly been instrumental in, furthering the diplomatic relations between King Edgar and Otto I or II, sealed by an exchange of gifts, related by John of Worcester.[49] John's account tantalizingly stops at this point without elaborating on the nature of these gifts. Several manuscripts from Germany were in England by the end of the tenth century and the exchanges continued during the eleventh century.[50] Other ambassadors to Germany are also likely to have brought gifts from there and taken some back. Both Richer and Flodoard mention the presence of English ambassadors at the Aachen court in 949, where they met Greek and Italian ambassadors.[51] Queen Gerberga, sister of Otto I and wife of King Louis IV, Aethelstan's nephew and protégé, sent messengers to both her brother and King Edmund after her husband's imprisonment to ask for their help in fighting against Duke Hugh of Francia.[52] Under Edmund, we hear again of German ambassadors in England, and Edgar sent two envoys, Abbot Aetherius and the thegn Wulfmaer, to the Emperor's court, to whom they gave presents and received some in return.[53] The last piece of evidence for the tenth century records the presence of a monk of Trier, Benna, who

[47] Armitage Robinson, *Saxon Bishops*, 67 and 154 and Wood, 'Making', *Ideal and Reality*, 261 n. 53.

[48] E. Freeman, *A History of the Norman Conquest* (6 vols.; 3rd edn. of vol. i; Oxford, 1877), i. 644.

[49] *Florence*, i. 139. John does not specify which Otto it was or when the exchange took place and, since Edgar died in 975 and Otto I in 973, it could have been either of the two emperors. Wood, 'Making', *Ideal and Reality*, 260 suggests that the Brunswick Casket as well as a Metz ivory cover of the early ninth century, depicting the Crucifixion, may have been part of such imperial gifts to English kings.

[50] See below, ch. 3.

[51] Richer, *Histoire*, 275; Flodoard, *Annales*, 949.

[52] Richer, *Histoire*, 207–8.

[53] *Vita Dunstani auctore B*, 23; *Vita Oswaldi auctore anonimo*, i. 435. We do not know whether this embassy is different from the one mentioned by John of Worcester.

came to England probably some time between 961 and 975 and was entrusted with supervising the education of the princess, later saint, Edith of Wilton. A painter and goldsmith, Benna painted the wall-paintings in Edith's new church at Wilton and, when returning from a short visit to Trier, he brought with him a relic of the Holy Nail from that city to England.[54]

Throughout these two centuries, a variety of people from Germany and Lotharingia are recorded in England. Some were merchants, such as those from Huy, Liège, Nivelles, and the 'subjects of the Emperor', trading in wool, cloth, animals, gloves, pepper, and vinegar in London on a permanent basis in the early eleventh century and were protected by the laws ascribed to Aethelred.[55] Other merchants on their way to England are recorded in Bremen by Thangmar.[56] Others were ecclesiastics of various kinds. Before 933, there were three German clerics belonging to the *familia* of New Minster and another one at Christ Church; Bishop Theodred of London, probably a German, surrounded himself with clerics bearing German names, Gundwine, Odgar, another Theodred, and Gosebriht; a priest Godescalc was put in charge of the royal chapel at Abingdon by Aethelstan; and a Cologne nobleman was sent on an embassy to Canterbury, and heard there about the cult of Ursula, which he is credited with having introduced at Cologne.[57] The author of the first Life of St Swithun was a certain Lantfrid, whose name could be German.[58] In the early eleventh century, an abbot of Ramsey, Wythman (1016–20), was German; and we hear of a nun with an English name, Aelfgifu, becoming the abbess of a nunnery likely to have been Nunnaminster, after having spent several years at Cologne.[59] Two other clerics from imperial lands, Ingelric and Albert of Lorraine, became canons of St Paul's in London in the middle and late eleventh century.[60] Other categories of people, some obviously

---

[54] Wilmart, 'Légende de Ste Édith', 50. On Benna's connection with England, see T. Kempf, 'Benna Treverensis Canonicum de Sancti Paulini Patrocinio', in *Mainz und der Mittelrhein in der europäischen Kunstgeschichte: Studien für W. F. Volbach zu seinem 70. Geburtstag* (Mainz, 1966), 180–93.

[55] Stevenson, *Laws*, IV Aethelred 8–10, 73.

[56] *Vita Bernwardi; Miracula Sancti Bernwardi*, 784.

[57] M. Lapidge, 'Some Latin Poems as Evidence for the Reign of Aethelstan', *ASE* 9 (1981), 93 n. 143 and 93–7; F. M. Stenton, *The Early History of the Abbey of Abingdon* (Reading, 1913), 38; Hroswith, 408–10.

[58] *CSD* 1. i. 93 n. 8.

[59] *Chronicon Rameseiensis*, 121; for the Life of St Edburgh by Osbert of Clare, see M. Lapidge, 'The Origin of CCCC 163', *Transactions of the Cambridge Bibliographical Society*, 8 (1981), 27 n.16. She was a contemporary of Aelfwine of Winchester (1032–47); S. J. Ridyard, *The Royal Saints of Anglo-Saxon England* (Cambridge, 1988), 34, gives an edition of this saint's Life in her App. I, 259–308, esp. 265–6, 296.

[60] J. H. Round, *The Commune of London and Other Studies* (London, 1899), 28–38, and C. Brooke and G. Keir, *London 800–1216: The Shaping of a City* (London, 1975), 310–11.

pilgrims or visitors, are also recorded, apart from the ambassadors of the
Emperor Henry III to Edward the Confessor on his accession.[61] William
of Malmesbury mentions a German cured at Glastonbury, Osbern talks
about another called Clemens, Eadmer knows of a Saxon penitent at
Worcester, and pilgrims from Saxony and Cologne are recorded in
Goscelin's Life of St Ivo.[62] Also among the ecclesiastics who came to
England from Germany or Lotharingia were several bishops appointed to
English sees. The first of these, Bishop Theodred of London, was in office
from *c*.942 to *c*.951.[63] Cnut appointed Duduc as bishop of Wells in 1033,
where he stayed until 1060.[64] Following him in this see was another
Lotharingian, Giso (1060–88), who gave his collection of relics and books
to his cathedral and wrote a history of the see.[65] Other bishops from the
same area were also appointed by King Edward: Herman to the see of
Sherborne in 1045, Walter to that of Hereford in 1060, and Leofric, a
Cornishman educated at Liège, to that of Exeter in 1046. Giso had been
educated at St Trond, then at Liège under Wazo, Bishop Notker's
schoolmaster, who became himself bishop of that city after Notker's death,
and then taught Leofric among his pupils.[66] We know little about Herman,
except that he left his see for three years to become a monk of St Bertin,
and returned to England in 1056.[67] Leofric, a learned man, took great
pains with his see at Exeter, which he reformed, introducing the offices of
Stephen of Liège and the canonical Rule of Chrodegang of Metz instead
of the Benedictine Rule in the abbey of St Peter, which became a secular
cathedral in his time. He was a collector of books and these, together with
others he commissioned, some probably from his own chaplain from
Liège, Lambert, he bequeathed to Exeter.[68] After the Conquest, clerics
from Lorraine continued to be appointed as bishops in England: Robert
(1070–95), who became a close friend of Wulfstan, at Hereford, which had
been Walter's see, Walcher at Durham (1071–80) and Herbert Losinga

---

[61] *Vita Aedwardi*, 10.

[62] *WMHG* 134–5; Stubbs, *Memorials*, 135; *HCY* ii. 44; *Chronicon Rameseiensis*, p. lxviii.

[63] His will is in *CSD* 1. i. 76–81.

[64] *ASC*, E1061 = D1060, 135.

[65] Ibid.; *Florence*, i. 218; *WMGP* 194; Hunter, 'Historiola', 9–20.

[66] *Vita Aedwardi*, 35; see also Barlow, *English Church 1000–1066*, 82–3, and C. W. Jones, *St Nicholas of Myra, Bari and Manhattan: Biography of a Legend* (London and New York, 1978).

[67] *ASC*, C1045, D1046, 108; *Florence*, i. 199, 214; *WMGP* 182–4; *Vita Aedwardi*, 47.

[68] *ASC*, C1045, 109 and D1047, E1044, 109; *Florence*, i. 199; *WMGP* 201; and Barlow, *English Church 1000–1066*, 83–4. On Leofric, see also F. Barlow, 'Leofric and his Times', 1–16 and L. G. Lloyd, 'Leofric as Bibliophile', 34–42, in F. Barlow, K. Dexter, A. M. Erskine, and L. J. Lloyd (eds.), *Leofric of Exeter: Essays in Commemoration of the Foundation of Exeter Cathedral Library in AD 1072* (Exeter, 1972); M. Förster, 'The Donations of Leofric to Exeter', in R. W. Chambers et al. (eds.), *The Exeter Book of Old English Poetry* (London, 1933), 10–32; Drage, 'Bishop Leofric', 2–7; and Lapidge, 'Booklists', 64–9.

(1087–1119) at the by then newly moved East Anglian see of Norwich.[69]

However, examples of people of one country visiting, or living, in another country do not limit themselves to Germans in England. English people travelled to Germany extensively. Above all, pilgrims to Rome had to go via Besançon and St Maurice of Agaune, even if they took the most direct route, via Champagne, the Rhineland, Burgundy and the Alps, as we know that Archbishop Sigeric in 990 and possibly Aelfstan of St Augustine's (1022–47) did.[70] Many did not take such a short trip, and had time to travel via the Rhineland, as did Earl Tostig and his wife Judith, who spent some time there and went even as far as Saxony.[71] Bishop Brihtheah of Worcester was sent to Germany by Cnut to accompany the king's daughter Gunnhild/Cunigunde, when she went there to marry Conrad II's son, the future Emperor Henry III, in 1036.[72] This marriage had probably been arranged in 1027, when Cnut had gone on a pilgrimage to Rome and had met there Conrad II at his coronation and exchanged valuable presents of gold and silver vessels and costly vestments with him.[73] On his way to Rome, Cnut had met the king of Burgundy Rudolf and negotiated an understanding with him, to the effect that English as well as Danish merchants and pilgrims should not be harassed, but exempt of taxes and offered security when travelling through Rudolf's lands on their way to Italy.[74] King Edward also had family links with Henry III: the latter presented him with gifts on his accession and, in 1049, a German army fought alongside the English fleet against Baldwin of Flanders.[75] In 1054, the bishop of Worcester, later archbishop of York, Ealdred, was sent on an official mission to the court at Cologne, possibly to negotiate the return of the aetheling Edward to England, since King Edward was clearly without an heir. He spent a year there, where he was received with honour and entertained by the Emperor Henry III and Herman II, archbishop of Cologne.[76] The aetheling had fled England after the death of his father

[69] *WMGP* 300, 271, 151; on Walcher and his two compatriots Gilbert and Lebuin and his assassination, see *Florence*, ii. 10, 13–16; *ASC*, E1080, 160; *WMGR* ii. 330; and *WMGP* 271–2. On Herbert, cf. ch. 1. n. 29.

[70] *HTA* 31.

[71] *ASC*, D1061, 135; *Florence*, i. 218; *Vita Aedwardi*, 34.

[72] T. Hearne (ed.), *Hemingi Chartularium Ecclesiae Wigornensis* (2 vols.; Oxford, 1723), i. 267; H. Bresslau (ed.), *Die Werke Wipos*, MGH SRG (Hanover and Leipzig, 1915): *Gesta Chuonradi II Imperatoris*, 54, 93 (Annals of St Gall).

[73] *ASC*, DEF1031 = 1027, 101; *Florence*, i. 186; *WMGR* i. 229–30., For the date of the journey, see F. Barlow, 'Two notes: Cnut's Second Pilgrimage and Queen Emma's Disgrace in 1043', *EHR* 73 (1958), 649–51, repr. in his *Norman Conquest*, 49–51 and for the presents cf. *CSD* 1. i. 509.

[74] Ibid. 509–10.

[75] *ASC*, D1050 = C1049, 111–12; *Florence*, i. 201.

[76] *ASC*, CD1054, 129; *Florence*, i. 212; *WMVW* 15–16.

Edmund Ironside and taken refuge at the Hungarian court, where he married a princess of the imperial family, Agatha.[77] By the 1050s, he already had three children brought up there, two girls and a boy. After their return to England in 1057, one daughter, Christina, became a nun at Wilton or Romsey, the other, Margaret, married the king of Scotland Malcolm in 1067, and her son Edgar became the new aetheling and rival claimant to the throne at the time of the Norman Conquest, his father being by then dead.[78]

Ealdred did not limit himself to spending some time in Cologne on his embassy; he continued his travels as far as the Holy Land, crossing Bavaria and also Hungary, possibly in order to meet the aetheling.[79] Being a great collector of works of art, rather in the mould of some of his episcopal colleagues in Germany and Italy, he not only made and received presents to and from his hosts, but was inspired by some of the crafts he encountered on his journeys, especially by that of Rhenish metalworkers, and introduced it into England when he had a pulpit made in the 'German style' for Beverley Minster.[80] One of his most notable predecessors and colleagues, whose tastes for the visual arts is well known, was Bishop Bernward of Hildesheim, who is described by Thangmar as being an admirer of Anglo-Saxon artefacts, greatly reputed throughout western Europe, which he could see at the Imperial court,[81] another proof of the importance of such gifts passing between the English and the German rulers. The abbot of St Augustine's, Canterbury, Aelfstan, who travelled to Rome in 1022, is said to have met there the Emperor Henry II, who made him a gift of relics, according to Goscelin.[82] After the Conquest, the Countess Judith, of the family of the counts of Flanders and wife of Earl Tostig of Northumbia, married as her second husband the Duke of Bavaria and before her death in 1094, took the veil at the abbey of Weingarten, to which she bequeathed three Gospel-books probably at least illuminated, if not written, by Anglo-Saxon scribes,[83] and possibly also a portable altar

---

[77] *ASC*, D1057, 133 and ED1067, 146–8; *WMGR* i. 218. The links between Germany and Hungary were close ones, on account of the marriage of the first Hungarian king Stephen with a sister of the Emperor Henry II, see Wipo, *Gesta Chuonradi*, 43.

[78] *WMGR* i. 278; *Florence*, ii. 19; *ASC*, DE1067, 146–8. On the Aetheling Edgar's life, see N. Hooper, 'Edgar the Aetheling: Anglo-Saxon Prince, Rebel and Crusader', *ASE* 14 (1985), 197–214.

[79] *Florence*, i. 217.

[80] *HCY* ii. 354: 'Supra ostium etiam chori pulpitum opere incomparabili, aere, auro argentoque fabricari fecit, . . . et in medio supra pulpitum arcum eminentiorem crucem in summitate gestatem, similiter ex aere, auro, et argento, opere Theutonico fabrefactos erexit'.

[81] *Vita Bernwardi*, 760.

[82] *HTA* 31.

[83] M. Harssen, 'The Countess Judith of Flanders and the library of Weingarten Abbey', *Papers of the Bibliographical Society of America*, 24 (1930), 1–13.

now in the Musée de Cluny in Paris.[84] In the last years of the century, an Irish monk from Worcester, Marianus, left England for the abbey of Great St Martin 'of the Scots' at Cologne.[85]

III. CULTURAL EXCHANGES BETWEEN ENGLAND AND THE EMPIRE

Throughout the period, manuscripts travelled frequently between the two countries. During the age of Aethelstan, two Ottonian manuscripts seem to have found their way into England. One, a manuscript of the Gospels written at Lobbes in the late ninth century, now British Library, Cotton MS Tiberius A.II, was a present of Otto I to Aethelstan, who gave it to Christ Church, Canterbury. Another Gospel-book, written at Metz *c.*860, may also have been a gift to Germany from the English king, as a return present for Tiberius A.II; this manuscript, now Coburg, Landesbibliothek 1, later returned to Germany to the abbey of Gandersheim, but we know of its probable sojourn in England on account of the Old English additions made to it in the tenth century. In view of the links of Aethelstan's family with the Empire, we can imagine a variety of ways in which such a manuscript may have been sent to England. Significantly, as Hoffmann has argued very convincingly, it was England which was the leading light in manuscript production: Otto I sent old books, not having any contemporary sumptuous ones available which could match the Anglo-Saxon production, and Aethelstan had to have at least one of these touched up with gold additions before he thought it worthy of being offered as a present to Christ Church.[86] Another possibility has been put forward by Simon Keynes, who suggests that it was unlikely for Abbot Coenwald to have returned empty-handed from his tour of German abbeys, since it is more than likely that he himself went there with presents, and that it is quite possible to imagine both the Gandersheim Gospels and another manuscript, such as the Aachen book comprising the Acts of the Sixth Council of Constantinople of 680, also a present from Otto I to Aethelstan, who offered it to Bath, to have been brought back to England in Coenwald's baggage.[87] We do not know when the Gandersheim Gospels

---

[84] E. Okasha and J. O'Reilly, 'An Anglo-Saxon Portable Altar: Inscription and Iconography', *JWCI* 47 (1984), 32–51, esp. 51.

[85] *Florence*, i. 143, 197–8, 215.

[86] Hoffmann, *Buchkunst*, 9–10.

[87] Keynes, 'King Aethelstan's Books', 147–53, 189–93, and Rella, 'Continental', nos. 7 and 11. On the importance of Coenwald's trip with regard to both books and possibly people he recruited in Germany, see Wood, 'Making', *Ideal and Reality*, 256–61.

was taken back to Germany, but we know the date and circumstances underlying the arrival in Germany of other English manuscripts in the eleventh century. Some time during the second quarter of that century, Cnut sent two books, a psalter and a sacramentary, which he had obtained from Peterborough, to the Emperor as a present. These manuscripts happen to have been those used by St Wulfstan when, as a young man, he had studied at Peterborough. This is how the Life of the saint comes to mention the existence of these manuscripts, the circumstances of their departure from England, and of their return here, brought back from Cologne by Archbishop Ealdred on his return in 1056 and sent to Wulfstan by him.[88] Ealdred also brought back two pontificals from Cologne, modelled on the Romano-German Pontifical of Mainz, and another pontifical was copied around the middle of the century at Winchester from the prototype of the Mainz book.[89] Deshman has argued that another English manuscript, known as the Arenberg Gospels, was also sent to Cologne by Cnut,[90] and earlier on, a manuscript which had reached England from Germany, and acquired its decoration here, was sent back there, where additions were made to it about 1000.[91] Another set of manuscripts consists of three Gospel-books, possibly written on the Continent but illuminated in England on the commission of the Countess Judith, which she took with her when leaving England in 1067 and which she bequeathed to the abbey of Weingarten. Slightly different is the case of a Gospel-book, now in Besançon, a Continental manuscript to which one or several English visitors at Besançon added some rubrics in Old English, thus incidentally confirming the considerable role of this city as a stopping point for English visitors to Germany or Italy.[92] It has been shown that occasionally English works, such as Aldhelm's *De Virginitate*, were imported into England from Germany, in this instance from a Würzburg copy of the work and, furthermore, that the Genesis poem in Bodley MS Junius 11 is, in fact, an Old English translation of an Old German text.[93] This has been confirmed by the study of the illustrations in Junius 11, which were designed to illustrate the Old German text.[94] A

---

[88] *WMVW* 5, 15–16.

[89] M. Lapidge, 'Ealdred of York and the MS Cotton Vitellius E.XII', *Yorkshire Archaeological Journal*, 55 (1983), 11–25, and 'Origin of CCCC 163', 18–28. On the Romano-German Pontifical, see Vogel and Elze, *Pontifical*, 467–548.

[90] R. Deshman, '"*Christus rex and magi reges*": Kingship and Christology in Ottonian and Anglo-Saxon England', *Frühmittelalterliche Studien*, 10 (1986), 392.

[91] Anhalt–Morgan Gospels, see Swarzenski, 'Anhalt–Morgan', 81–2.

[92] Temple, *ASM*, 93–4.

[93] Wood, 'Making', *Ideal and Reality*, 261–3.

[94] B. Raw, 'The Probable Derivation of Most Illustrations in Junius 11 from an Illustrated Old Saxon *Genesis*', *ASE* 5 (1976), 133–48.

final significant fact is the provenance of the oldest manuscript of the Old German poem *Heliand* from England in the late tenth century, where it was written either by an English scribe or, more probably, by a German scribe working in England for some time, as his familiarity with Old English spelling shows; moreover, the *Heliand* may have been originally composed at Werden, an Anglo-Saxon foundation, which had close links with a neighbouring monastery with English connections in the tenth century, Essen.[95]

Cultural links were not limited to exchanges of manuscripts. The influence of the widely spread reforms of John of Gorze in Germany and of Gérard of Brogne in Lotharingia on the customs put together in the *Regularis Concordia* is made clear from such borrowings as the use of secular services for Holy Week and Easter Week based on the *ordo Romanus primus* and not of the monastic office, and some specific rites for Holy Week, Easter week, and Nocturns on Whit Sunday borrowed from the customs used at Verdun and Toul.[96] A Worcester manuscript of the late tenth or early eleventh century includes a few verses from a poem by one Israel, whom Neil Ker identified with a teacher of the court of Archbishop Bruno of Cologne, and who is known to have written a grammatical poem now extant in three manuscripts only, one of which is the Worcester copy.[97] Some knowledge of English affairs in the eleventh century is shown by Thietmar, who recounts the Danish raids in England under King Aethelred and Cnut's invasion of 1016, by the author of the Annals of Lobbes and by Lampert of Hersfeld, who was exceptionally aware of events in England in 1066.[98] Most of the other cultural links between England and the imperial lands seem to have been associated with what was admittedly one of the most brilliant cultural and scholarly European centres, Liège. The 'B' author of the Life of St Dunstan had been a cleric at the court of the bishop of Liège.[99] Not long after his time, both bishops Leofric of Exeter and Giso of Wells studied in Liège with

---

[95] Wood, 'Making', *Ideal and Reality*, 263, and Campbell, 'England', in *Essays*, 195–6.

[96] T. Symons (ed.), *Regularis Concordia Anglicae Nationis Monachorum et Sanctimonialiumque* (London, 1953), pp. xlix–l. This is the first example of the use of the *ordo Romanus primus*, known via Lotharingia, in England.

[97] Worcester Cathedral Library MS Q.5, fo. 71ᵛ. The other two MSS are in the Bibliothèque Ste Geneviève in Paris and in the Vatican Library. The identification appears in a letter by N. Ker inserted in J. K. Floyer, rev. S. H. Hamilton, *Catalogue of Manuscripts Preserved in the Chapter Library of Worcester Cathedral* (Oxford, 1906). On Israel, see Lotter, *Vita Brunonis*, ch. 7 and 75–7, and C. Selmer, 'Israel, ein unbekannter Schotte des 10. Jahrhunderts', *Studien und Mitteilungen zur Geschichte des Benediktinerordens*, 62 (1950), 69–86.

[98] Thietmar, *Chronicon*, 214–18; *Annales Laubienses*, ed. G. H. Pertz, MGH SS iv, 20; and O. Holder-Egger (ed.), *Lamperti Monachi Hersfeldensis Opera: Annales*, MGH SRG (Hanover and Leizig, 1894), 103.

[99] Stubbs, *Memorials*, pp. x–xxvi.

Notker and Wazo: Giso produced a history of the Church of Wells, while Leofric removed his see from Crediton to Exeter minster. Both converted their churches into cathedrals where they enforced the canonical rule of Chrodegang of Metz: Giso specifically mentions that he built communal buildings, cloister, refectory, and dormitory at Wells.[100] Leofric occupied himself with restoring the property of his see and also with endowing it spiritually, commissioning liturgical manuscripts and bequeathing his considerable library to it, which comprised, apart from about thirty-five service-books, works by Boethius, Porphyry, Prosper, Prudentius, Isidore, Bede, Persius, Sedulius, Arator, Smaragdus, Amalarius, and Chrodegang of Metz.[101] The attention he paid to local cults at Exeter, relying on the rich relic-collection bequeathed by King Aethelstan[102] whilst, together with his priest Lambert of Liège, he introduced new cults and liturgical texts as well as the Rule of Chrodegang, illustrates the effect of this harmonious collaboration between Lotharingia and England at its best.

IV. LITURGICAL AND DEVOTIONAL EXCHANGES BETWEEN ENGLAND AND THE EMPIRE

The first instance of these exchanges may seem, to the modern mind, to belong to the history of political ideas rather than to that of the liturgy. Janet Nelson's work has made it obvious that the connection between these two areas is so close as to be indistinguishable, in her work on English coronation orders. She argues most convincingly that, both in the field of ideas and in that of the texts themselves, Ottonian concepts of imperial power were of considerable importance in the development of such *ordines* in England. It was this idea which underlay the evident increase of the use of the words *imperium* and *basileus* by tenth-century English kings; it was the coronation of Theophano in Rome in 972, when Bishop Oswald was there for his *pallium*, which prompted the ceremonies making Edgar's Queen Aelfthryth a crowned sovereign together with her husband; and it was the use of the orb by the Ottonians which served as a model for the

[100] Hunter, 'Historiola', 19. Doubtless Leofric followed the same policy, see Barlow, *Leofric of Exeter*, 9–11, and D. Blake, 'The Chapter of Exeter', *Journal of Medieval History*, 8 (1982), 1–11.

[101] Chambers in *Exeter Book*, 18–32; *CED* I. i. 693–4; and the most recent study in Lapidge, 'Booklists', 65–6.

[102] This list is entered in an 11th-c. Gospel-book from Exeter, now Oxford, Bodleian Library MS Auctarium D.12.16, fos. 8–14, and was edited by M. Förster, *Zur Geschichte des Reliquienkultus in Altengland* (Munich, 1943), 63–80.

iconography of King Harold on Anglo-Saxon coinage.[103] Most important of all, the coronation *ordo* used by William the Conqueror was probably written by Archbishop Ealdred, using liturgical elements which he had borrowed from the Romano-German Pontifical.[104] This situation is, in a way, the reverse of that which had led the first Saxon kings to seek a matrimonial alliance with the English kings in the person of Aethelstan, an alliance which broke the tradition of marriages with daughters of the German aristocracy in a deliberate attempt to enforce a new legitimacy and an increased prestige of the recently established dynasty.[105]

The main set of offices used in northern Europe by the middle of the eleventh century was the collectar or office-book of the tenth-century canon of Liège, Stephen (902–20), the *Liber Capitularis*. This collectar was known in England quite soon after its composition, since we find extracts from it in an early tenth-century English collectar.[106] Its consistent use as a model for English books becomes evident in two collectars written about the middle of the eleventh century, Leofric's from Exeter and Wulfstan's from Worcester. While Leofric's book is made for secular use, Wulfstan's is for monastic use; they share the two sets of chapters and collects common to both uses, but not the antiphons, responses, and versicles, which differ. The chapters and collects are close to those of a whole group of Low Countries breviaries based on the model of Stephen's *Liber Capitularis*; Leofric's collectar is particularly close to it, while Wulfstan's is less so in relation to both Leofric's and Stephen's. The source of Leofric's collectar was obviously taken directly from Liège whilst Wulfstan's is more indirectly dependent on Stephen's, suggesting that its sources were drawn from an archetype from the Low Countries.[107] Wulfstan had often been in contact with the Lotharingian bishops at Edward's court and he is known to have been a close friend of Robert of Lorraine, bishop of

---

[103] H. Kleinschmidt, *Untersuchungen über das englische Königtum im 10. Jahrhundert* (Göttingen, 1979); Nelson, 'Inauguration Rituals', 301–3; 'The Second English *Ordo*', 373; and 'The Rites of the Conqueror', 395, in *Politics and Ritual*.

[104] Ibid. 382–93. This view has been recently challenged by G. S. Garnett, '*Franci et Angli*: The Legal Distinction between Peoples after the Conquest', *Anglo-Norman Studies*, 8 (1985), 110 n. 8, and in his doctoral thesis 'Royal Succession in England: 1066–1154' (Cambridge, 1987) App. A, 482–524, on grounds of dfferences between the 3rd recension of the *ordo* and the manuscripts of the Romano-German Pontifical said to have been brought by Ealdred to England. The general argument is not, however, invalidated by these differences, in my opinion, since the likelihood of Ealdred having had access to other copies of the Romano-German Pontifical, as well as that of his having adapted the text for English needs, as English ecclesiastics always did, is very great.

[105] Leyser, 'Die Ottonen', 73–92.

[106] Durham, Cathedral Library MS A.IV.19, written in the South of England in the early 10th c. then removed first to Chester-le-Street, then to Durham, where it was by 1000. It is edited by U. L. Lindelöf, *Rituale*.

[107] *Leofric Collectar*, ii, pp. xxi–lvii on the precise divergences between the two collectars.

Hereford; a knowledge of the liturgy and of cults of Lotharingian origins will appear clearly on several occasions in Worcester sources, knowledge probably acquired through the personal ties of the bishop of Worcester with his south-western colleagues.

Other influences on the English liturgy come from further east in Germany. The earliest one is that of the system of tropes and other additions to the texts of the gradual and the offices, modelled on the development of these texts during the ninth century at the abbey of St Gall, under the aegis of Notker the Stammerer, and adopted in the two surviving tropers from Winchester and Canterbury.[108] Other tropes have been traced to the Rhineland, where English prelates of the early eleventh century were looking for models which they saw as authoritative.[109] During the eleventh century, not only are there two copies of the Romano-German Pontifical available in England, but also English pontificals are modelled on it. In the case of offices not found in Stephen's Collectar, for example for recently introduced saints in the Latin liturgy, collects are copied from those written towards the middle of the century by the German bishop Reginold of Eichstätt. This is the case for the offices of St Nicholas and St Blaise, both cults being particularly popular in Germany itself.[110] A mid-eleventh-century passional from Worcester contains the whole office of Reginold for the feast of St Nicholas.[111]

In the cults of major saints we also see the result of reciprocal influences between the two countries. The examples of SS Andrew, John the Baptist, Stephen, and Laurence illustrate the possible reinforcement of major devotions of the Church in Anglo-Saxon England on account of their popularity in the German Empire. The Apostle Andrew was a popular saint in England on account first of his link with his brother, Peter, the most highly venerated saint throughout the Anglo-Saxon period, and his cult was further enhanced by the great devotion which Pope Gregory the Great was known to have for him and which led him to dedicate his monastery in Rome on Mount Coelius to this Apostle. The cult was strong generally in Rome and English pilgrims such as Wilfrid in the late-seventh

---

[108] The two manuscripts from the Old Minster at Winchester, now CCCC 473, of the first half of the 11th c., and Oxford, Bodleian Library MS Bodley 775, of the late 10th c., were edited together by Frere, *Winchester Troper*, and have been further discussed by J. Handschin, 'The Two Winchester Tropers', *Journal of Theological Studies*, 37 (1936), 34–49, 156–72. On the history of the tropes on the Continent, see *Winchester Troper*, pp. vi–xxxvii, esp. xii–xiii, xxi–xxii. The Canterbury MS from the mid-11th c. from Christ Church, now British Library Cotton MS Caligula A.xiv, has not been published but parts of it are compared with the Winchester material by Frere, 101–24.

[109] A. E. Planchart, *The Repertory of Tropes at Winchester* (2 vols.; Princeton, 1977), i. 167–240.

[110] C. W. Jones, *The Saint Nicholas Liturgy and its Literary Relationships (Ninth to Twelfth Centuries)* (Berkeley, 1963), 6–8, 69–73; and Jones, *Nicholas of Myra*, 112–13.

[111] British Library Cotton MS Nero E. I.

century, could pray at altars dedicated to him there.[112] Much more popular even was Laurence, one of the three patron saints of Rome with Peter and Agnes, and numerous churches were dedicated to him there, the most important of which pilgrims such as Archbishop Sigeric visited.[113] Clearly the cults of these saints were already among the most popular in England and had a long history behind them, partly on account of this Roman connection. However, it is not at all impossible that the cult of Andrew may have been further strengthened by, on the one hand, the considerable development of the devotion to this saint in ninth- and tenth-century Constantinople under the Macedonians, who were then attempting to make him the Apostle of the city as a rival to St Peter, patron saint of Rome,[114] and, on the other hand, by the devotion to the saint at Trier as a result of the acquisition by the cathedral of a relic of his sandal.[115] In the same way, the cult of Laurence may well have been enhanced by his newly acquired status as a patron of the Ottonians following his alleged intervention in helping Otto I's army to gain its major victory at the Lechfeld in 955.[116]

The Byzantine devotion to Andrew and the Trier cult could well have been connected, since we only hear of the relic in the tenth century in the reign of Archbishop Egbert, and this was the time when links between the two imperial courts were at their closest, following on Princess Theophano's marriage to Otto II. It is quite possible to imagine that influences from Constantinople were also at work in the Western Empire in the case of the cult of John the Baptist, the most venerated saint in the Greek world.[117] The Precursor was evidently highly regarded in the Latin world, but this regard appears to be somewhat formal rather than devotional until he becomes one of the popular saints at Trier, once again, and at Liège. The links of both cities and of their bishops Egbert and Notker with the

---

[112] B. Colgrave (ed.), *The Life of Wilfrid by Eddius Stephanus* (Cambridge, 1927), 12–13. There were at least three churches in England dedicated to St Andrew, two by Wilfrid himself, Hexham and Oundle, and Rochester, see *Life of Wilfrid*, 44–7, 140–1, and *BHE* 530–1, 142–3. The popularity of this saint in early Anglo-Saxon England is confirmed by at least two texts relating his passion, based on apocryphal sources, the poem *Andreas* and a Life in the vernacular, see *Andreas*, ed. K. R. Brooks, *Andreas and the Fates of the Apostles* (Oxford, 1961), 1–55. See also the Introduction of this book for other Old English versions of the legend of St Andrew, especially the text in CCCC 19, ed. C. W. Goodwin, *The Anglo-Saxon Legends of St Andrew and St Veronica* (Cambridge, 1851), 2–25.

[113] See below, ch. 5.

[114] F. Dvornik, *The Idea of Apostolicity in Byzantium and the Legend of the Apostle Andrew* (Cambridge, Mass., 1958), 138–299.

[115] On the relic and the reliquary made to enshrine it by one of Archbishop Egbert's goldsmith, see Beckwith, *Early Medieval Art*, 137–8 and ill. p. 21.

[116] Thietmar, *Chronicon*, 23–4; see also Leyser, 'The Battle at the Lech', in *Medieval Germany*, 66, and H. Beumann, 'Das Kaisertum Otto der Große: Ein Rückblick nach Tausend Jahren', *Historische Zeitschrift*, 195 (1962), 529–73, esp. 552–66.

[117] See below, ch. 6.

Graecophile German court have been already underlined, and it comes as no surprise to find the Byzantine saint *par excellence* gain in popularity in this area. Equally popular in Lotharingia and particularly at Liège were the cults of two other major saints of the Church, Stephen and Martin. The hypothesis is obviously not that these saints were made known in England through the German channel, but only that their special popularity in the area of Liège and the Rhineland cities, with their close links with the imperial court, may have contributed to enhancing a more personal devotion to these already considerable liturgical cults. One such case in point is that of St Stephen.

St Stephen's original feast in the West on 26 December was supplemented by a second feast, of the Invention of his relics, on 2–3 August. This feast only entered the calendars and liturgical texts in the tenth century and, significantly, is found in all English calendars, like the main feast of his Passion. It was entered in capitals at Crowland and with XII lessons at Christ Church. Meanwhile, the main feast appears as a high-rank entry in almost all calendars with liturgical distinctions, and some add the octave of the Passion. St Stephen heads the group of the martyrs in almost all litanies, his name is written in capitals in four in the eleventh century, and he is also the first of the martyrs in prayers which address them all. In such cases where the local saint of a monastery was also a martyr, as St Kenelm was at Winchcombe, then the saint's name could be capitalized but still took second place after that of St Stephen, in the litany of this abbey. The liturgical celebrations for the Passion are amongst the most important for any saint, with long masses, particularly in Leofric's missal, possibly as a result of Leofric's special devotion to a saint greatly venerated in the Liège area, where a popular office for St Stephen's feast had been composed by his namesake, the canon Stephen.[118] The feast was troped, hymns and the whole office are entered in all books.

For the feast of the Invention, Leofric again added more masses to the existing ones in his missal. Most of the office is included at the end of Harley 3271 at fos. 114–114v, a manuscript containing grammatical treatises, from the first half of the eleventh century, unfortunately of unknown origin; this is composed essentially of parts of the office of Stephen of Liège for that feast. The addition of a separate office in a non-liturgical book suggests a personal as well as an official cult, and purely devotional prayers are included in most eleventh-century psalters.

The same deduction of imperial influence could be applied to saints whose cults only became popular in England in the late tenth or the early

[118] Auda, *École*, 27–35, 42–66 on Stephen of Liège and his office, which had a great impact on Leofric, 37–9.

eleventh century. One such example of a saint already celebrated in the West in a low key, mostly around the prestigious abbey founded in the fourth century and containing his relics at Agaune and in some parts of the Empire, is St Maurice. Under Otto I, however, his cult increases as he becomes one of the patrons of the Ottonians. Trier remained one of the centres of the German cult, with several altars dedicated to St Maurice and relics at St Maximin, whereas Cologne also claimed relics in the church of St Gereon from the late sixth century onwards.[119] The cult was just as strong in the diocese of Constance, especially at Reichenau and St Gall, while Constance itself had a basilica of St Maurice built in 976. At Magdeburg the English Queen of Otto I was a co-founder, with her husband, of an abbey dedicated to the saint in 937. It is worth remembering that Queen Edith was Aethelstan's half-sister, and that a relic of St Maurice was given to Exeter by Aethelstan. It is difficult to know whether it was the German cult, supported by Otto partly in order to tighten the links of the Liudolfings with Burgundy, which prompted Aethelstan's interest, or whether the English relic sustained Queen Edith's interest in the saint in Germany. The cult was further strengthened after the translation in 960 of the saint's relics to Magdeburg.[120]

We can follow the steady progression of this devotion in Ottonian Germany through the tenth and eleventh centuries, by which time St Maurice, like St Laurence, but to a far greater extent, had become a 'Reichspatron'. In A. J. Herzberg's words, 'the patronage of St Maurice for this dynasty [the Ottonians] was made manifest' and 'under Henry II [Maurice] became the patron saint of the Empire'.[121] During the twelfth century, the Emperors were crowned by tradition at the altar of St Maurice in St Peter's in Rome and the chapel in the palace at Pavia was also dedicated to him. This cult, which may have originally appealed to the Ottonians in the same way that it and other similar cults of military saints such as St Sebastian and St George appealed to the nobility in the rest of Europe, had become an imperial cult by the eleventh century. Its importance was later reinforced by the Emperors' claim to possess St Maurice's lance, given to them by Rudolf of Burgundy, according to Liutprand of Cremona, and increasingly identified with St Longinus' Holy Lance from

---

[119] Beissel, *Geschichte der Trieren Kirchen*, 16–33, and on the relics at St Gereon's at Cologne, ibid. 145.

[120] Thietmar, *Chronicon*, 28–9.

[121] A. J. Herzberg, *Der heilige Mauritius: Ein Beitrag zur Geschichte der deutschen Mauritius-Verehrung* (Düsseldorf, 1936), 37, and 65 (my translation); also Leyser, 'The Battle at the Lech', 66. The role of St Maurice as 'Reichspatron' is well expressed in an ivory plaque of *c*.980, now in the Castello Sforzesco in Milan, depicting Otto II and Theophano between the Virgin Mary and St Maurice, see P. Lasko, *Ars Sacra 800–1200* (Harmondsworth, 1972), pl. 85.

the thirteenth century onwards.[122] One may wonder why Otto I should have chosen Maurice as a protector and dedicated his foundation at Magdeburg, the newly founded imperial cathedral, to this saint, even admitting that Maurice was one of the military saints well suited to provide such protection. It is, therefore, necessary to search a little further, and one is then led to observe that the cult developed after Otto's marriage to Edith. It would be assuming too much to argue that it was Edith who prompted the development of this German cult, but it is not unlikely that, knowing about it on account of the saint's popularity in England because of the position of Agaune on the pilgrimage route to Rome, she may have supported her husband's attempts to take over this cult. Thus, in the late tenth and the eleventh centuries, the combined prestige of the saint of Agaune, also venerated at Fleury,[123] with which English monasteries were in close touch, and of the imperial patronage of Maurice, may have combined to enhance the English cult. By the tenth century it was general, with the saint's name entered in all calendars and in twenty litanies; even the calendar in an English manuscript of the tenth century, of indeterminate date and origin, which has few non-gregorian saints, includes it, and at Christ Church, the feast was celebrated with XII lessons, a very high ranking.[124] All sacramentaries include masses for the saint, Wulfstan's collectar one collect, and the Exeter benedictional one benediction. Lives of the saint have survived, one in Latin, added in an eleventh-century Malmesbury copy of Gregory's *Pastoral Care*, and one in the vernacular by Aelfric, as well as a private prayer added in a Christ Church psalter of the first quarter of the eleventh century.[125]

In the same way, two other cults popular in the Empire seem to have acquired additional weight in England, although in both cases the English devotion pre-dated the German cults. The veneration for St Mary Magda-

---

[122] Herzberg, *Der heilige Mauritius*, 56, 108. On the question of the Holy Lance see, for example, W. Holtzmann, *König Heinrich I und die heilige Lanze* (Berlin, 1947) and Leyser, *Rule and Conflict*, 84, 88. The difficulties about the Holy Lance are numerous, since it was also supposed to have belonged to Charlemagne and to have been given as a gift to Aethelstan by Count Hugh of Paris, and this, St Longinus' Lance, was later claimed as a possession of the English kings. The confusion between St Longinus' and St Maurice's lances, both identified as the Holy Lance, complicated the matter even further. On the English side, see Leyser, 'The Tenth-Century', 116–17; L. Hibbard Loomis, 'The Holy Relics of Charlemagne and King Aethelstan: The Lances of Longinus and St Mauricius', *Speculum*, 25 (1950), 440–56 and 'The Aethelstan Gift-Story: Its Influence on English Chronicles and Carolingian Romances', *Modern Languages Association Pub.*, 67 (1952), 521.

[123] At Fleury, the cults of Agaune saints, Maurice and his companions and King Sigismund of Burgundy, were held in high regard, which suggests that the insistence on these names in the litany of the Winchcombe Sacramentary was due to Oswald's privileged links with Fleury, see below, ch. 7.

[124] Paris, Bibliothèque Nationale MS lat. 7299, fo. 7; Wormald, *Kalendars*, no. 13.

[125] CCCC MS 361, fo. 104^v; *Aelfric's Lives of the Saints*, ii. 158–69; British Library Arundel MS 155.

lene in England had long preceded her eleventh-century cult in the West, based mostly on the discovery of her relics at Vézelay about 1050, because the cult had been introduced into this country in the early eighth century from its eastern centre at Ephesus, possibly by Willibald, who may have brought back a relic of the saint later donated to Exeter by Aethelstan.[126] There is no doubt, however, that her cult was greatly reinforced from the middle of the eleventh century onwards, thanks to the Burgundian devotion. But before the latter was actually launched, others had timidly begun to dedicate churches to her during the first half of the eleventh century, the two most significant ecclesiastics in this respect being Bishop Ermenfrid of Halberstadt and Bishop Hugh of Salins of Besançon.[127]

The cult of St Nicholas provides an even clearer example of a devotion introduced into the West from the Greek world, where it was based on a major pilgrimage centre at Myra in Asia Minor, and which was actively promoted by the Empress Theophano and her son. They dedicated the abbey of Burtscheid to him, and introduced Greek monks from southern Italy into it, under Gregory of Cassano. They spread the cult at court, in the cities whose bishops were closest to the court, such as Notker of Liège and Willigis of Mainz, and from there further on as far as England, long before the existence of the Bari cult after 1087. St Nicholas was often said to compete with St Martin for the title of the most popular saint in the West. His cult met with increasing success in western Europe from the tenth century onwards, due essentially to the popularity of his legends.[128]

The cult had been of importance in Constantinople as early as the beginning of the sixth century, when the Emperor Justinian built the church of St Nicholas, Blacherne, followed in the seventh century by an oratory dedicated to the saint in the imperial palace itself. Constantinople had twenty-five churches dedicated to St Nicholas, who appears to have been the third most popular saint after the Virgin Mary and St John the Baptist. Meanwhile, the reputation of the pilgrimage to Myra, where the saint's relics exuded the famous manna or oil, was steadily increasing.

---

[126] C. H. Talbot (tr.), *The Anglo-Saxon Missionaries in Germany* (London, 1954), 160, and cf. I. G. Thomas, 'The Cult of the Saints' Relics in Medieval England', Ph.D. thesis (London, 1975), 430.

[127] V. Saxer, *Le Culte de Marie Madeleine en Occident des origines à la fin du Moyen Âge* (2nd edn.; Auxerre, 1959), 54–5, 60–5.

[128] The first of these, the *Vita per Michaelem*, was written in Greek, at the beginning of the ninth century. It was followed by two other Greek Lives, the compilation by Methodius, *Methodius ad Theodorum*, of c.842–6, and the Life written in the second half of the 10th century by Simon Metaphrastes. A Latin version adapted from the Greek was produced during the third quarter of the 9th century by the deacon John of Naples and remained the basis of he cult until Jacob of Voragine's Golden Legend. The Lives of St Nicholas are edited in N. C. Falconius, *Scti Confessoris Pontificis . . . Nicolai Acta Primagenia* (Naples, 1751).

C. W. Jones described, in great detail, how the cult was originally brought
to Germany by Theophano and how her entourage spread it by dedicating
churches to the saint, as did, for example, the bishops Willigis of Mainz
and Notker of Liège in the late tenth century.[129] The imperial foundation
of Burtscheid was governed by a Greek abbot and filled with Greek
treasures and icons, and Brauweiler had the same patron saint. The most
ardent supporter of the cult was Notker, a man who often accompanied
Theophano, and whose artistic inclinations were 'clearly Rhenish' and who
probably built the first chapel of St Nicholas at Liège. It is, therefore, not
surprising that 'the weight of evidence points directly to Lorraine, not
Normandy as the source of [the] Nicholas cult [in England]'[130] since five
of the south-western bishops in England in the eleventh century were from
Lotharingia, and another of the promoters of the cult, Wulfstan, was prior
and bishop of Worcester, a centre in close touch with the sees governed
by the Lotharingian bishops.[131]

Most of the English evidence for St Nicholas' cult in the eleventh
century comes in the first place from the south-western centres. The links
with Lotharingia are further confirmed by the adoption, at Worcester in
the 1060s, of the office written in Bavaria by Reginold of Eichstätt, which
circulated in Lotharingia.[132] This adoption demonstrates Wulfstan's
devotion to the saint, visible in his collectar and evident in the re-naming
of his favourite pupil Aethelred as Nicholas, according to William of
Malmesbury. William used several features from the Life of St Nicholas
in his Life of Wulfstan, comparing Wulfstan to the bishop of Myra in his
pastoral zeal and miracle of saving the sailors from shipwreck.[133]

In England, St Nicholas' name was added to the Glastonbury calendar
and to the early Worcester one in the eleventh century, the other entries
being all contemporary ones in the Exeter, Wells, Sherborne, Wessex,
Winchester, Evesham, and Crowland calendars. In the latter three, it was
entered in capitals, and also in blue at Winchester. The additions date from
the twelfth century in the Christ Church and later Worcester calendars,
and are in red in the latter. The devotion was clearly connected with the
Continent, and more specifically with Germany, as can be seen from the
Exeter, Wells, and their associated Evesham and Worcester entries, and

---

[129] On Theophano's support of her cult and its favour with German bishops, see Jones, *The Liturgy*, 86–8, and Jones, *Nicholas of Myra*, 108–11.

[130] Jones, *Nicholas of Myra*, 140–4 and *The Liturgy*, 88 n. 35: 'I believe that Liège . . . was a centre for the dissemination of the cult of St Nicholas to France and Britain.'

[131] Ibid. 11.

[132] Ibid. 6–8, 69–73; and Jones, *Nicholas of Myra*, 112–3.

[133] Jones, *The Liturgy*, 6–8. Aethelred became prior of Worcester. For the comparison of Wulfstan with Nicholas in the *Vita Wulfstani*, see *WMVW* 90, 156.

from those at Winchester. These calendars reveal the progression of the cult in the eleventh century, before it was inserted, as a rule, with distinctions, in all twelfth-century calendars in which both feasts were entered. From a liturgical point of view, this cult appears to have been, virtually from the outset, as much a great individual cult for the English as an official, formal one. We find a mass in the Leofric Missal, that of Wells, and that of St Augustine's, as well as in CCCC 422, an unusual manuscript from the mid-eleventh century, of uncertain, but possibly Winchester, origin. No gradual has survived, but the pericope was Matt. XIII, known from an addition to the list of liturgical Gospels in Auct. D.2.16. Two hymns to the saint are given in Rouen A.44, thus confirming the importance of St Nicholas at St Augustine's and, incidentally, of the cult itself in Norman Canterbury.

The more individual or devotional aspects of the cult are of special interest. Although there is no office for the saint in Wulfstan's collectar, we find him invoked in the list of martyrs and protectors of the English Church in the *orationes privatae*. From Worcester under Wulfstan comes the earliest surviving manuscript of the office. The absence of the office from the Portiforium is puzzling and even more so is its omission in Leofric's collectar. Part of it was entered in the late eleventh century at Durham in a late tenth-century pontifical.[134] However, the most interesting aspect of the devotional cult is represented by the existence of three prayers addressed to St Nicholas, which are amongst the longest in the whole Anglo-Saxon liturgical corpus. One is in Laud. lat. 81, a second lengthy one in Arundel 60 and an exceedingly long one is found on fos. 76 to 79 of Titus D.XXVI.[135]

A variety of cults of minor saints, mostly local ones in individual dioceses, cities, and abbeys of the Empire, also appear in English liturgical texts of the eleventh century. The majority of them were obviously brought over in the baggage, as it were, of the Lotharingian bishops and clergy established in England at the time. From Liège and its diocese come the cults of St Lambert, patron of the city. Lambert, bishop of Tongres–Maastricht from c.670, then of Liège, where he moved his see in 682 and was martyred c.705, was already a major saint a few years after his death

---

[134] Sidney Sussex College, Cambridge, MS 100, fo. 14ᵛ.

[135] The three religious houses dedicated to him before 1100 were Exeter (1087), Yarmouth (before 1100), founded by Herbert Losinga as a dependency of the Cathedral Priory at Norwich, and Spalding (1052) granted to St Nicholas' of Angers in 1074, see Binns, *Monastic Dedications*, 71–2, 91, 105. Another of Lanfranc's foundations at Canterbury, a leper hospital, was dedicated to St Nicholas, ibid. 24. A church in London was also dedicated to him around the middle of the century, St Nicholas Acon, see Brooke and Keir, *London*, 129. On the cult of St Mary Magdalene, see ch. 7.

since he was entered in the martyrologies of Willibrord and Bede and in a probably northern calendar and appears in all late Anglo-Saxon calendars with the exception of two from St Augustine's and Bury, and in all litanies; both Leofric and Wulfstan have his office in full in their collectars and a mass is recorded in Giso's sacramentary.[136] Also from Liège we see Beregisus, founder of the abbey of St Hubert, and Hubert himself, its patron saint, Remaclus of Stavelot, Gertrud and her mother Jugata of Nivelles, Landrada of Bilsen, and the early bishops of the see Servatius, Munulf, Gundulf, Sulpicius, and Domitian. Beregisus and Hubert are entered by Leofric, and Hubert, together with Remaclus and Gertrud, by Giso, in their calendars. Gertrud also appears in an Evesham calendar and in the Canon of the mass in the sacramentary of Robert; but there is no mass for her in this book, whereas Giso includes one, as does another mid-eleventh-century sacramentary from Winchester, and litanies of that period at Exeter, Winchester and in Wessex feature her name.[137] Leofric included an office for Gertrud's mother, Jugata or Jutta, in his collectar, even though there is no entry for her in the official calendar of his church. He also added the names of the early bishops of the see of Tongres–Maastricht Servatius, Munulf, and Gundulf, in the Glastonbury calendar attached to the Leofric Missal, by then at Exeter, and those of the latter two saints in his own calendar. In it, he also promoted the cult of Domitian, and in an Exeter litany, that of Landrada. Giso also included Servatius in his calendar, while another early bishop of that see, Sulpicius, is entered in an eleventh-century Winchester litany. Sulpicius appears already in Willibrord's martyrology; and Servatius, founder and first bishop of the see of Tonges, a dedicated anti-Arian fighter, whose relics were translated

---

[136] On the cult, see van der Essen, *Étude critique*, 20–34, 38–43; id., *Siècle des saints*, 65–76; de Moreau, *Eglise on Belgique*, i. 94–8, 104–5; and for the cult outside Liège in Lotharingia and the Rhineland, M. Zender, *Räume und Schichten Mittelalterlicher Heiligenverehrung in ihrer Bedeutung für die Volkskunde* (Düsseldorf, 1959), 27–60. The martyrology of St Willibrord is edited by H. A. Wilson, *The Calendar of St Willibrord* (London, 1918), and Lambert's name was added only a few years after his death, p. xi; the martyrology of Bede is edited in H. Quentin, *Les Martyrologes historiques du moyen-âge* (2nd edn., Paris, 1908), 47–56, and in J. Dubois and G. Renaud (eds.), *Édition pratique des martyrologes de Bède, de l'Anonyme lyonnais, et de Florus* (Paris, 1976); the northern calendar in Wormald, *Kalendars*, no. 1. There may have been an office in the Durham Collectar also but that part of the MS is missing; Lindelöf, *Rituale*, pp. xiv–xix, deduced its existence from the similarities of this MS with the *Liber Capitularis*. There seems to be a strong case for Cnut having chosen Lambert as his baptismal name, see Adam of Bremen, *Hamburgische Kirschengeschichte*, 112; L. M. Larson, *Canute the Great 935–1035 and the Rise of Danish Imperialism during the Viking Age* (New York and London, 1912), 164–5, and Gerchow, *Gedenküberlieferung*, 256.

[137] This (possibly) Winchester sacramentary, known as the 'Red Book of Darley', now CCCC MS 422, is edited by R. J. S. Grant, 'Cambridge, Corpus Christi College 41: The Loricas and the Missal', *Costerus*, n.s. 17 (Amsterdam, 1973). Gertrud's entry in the Canon of the mass remains, to my mind, still unsatisfactorily explained.

to Maastricht by Munulf, saw his cult extend by the eighth century outside the diocese of Liège to Cologne and southern Germany and become an imperial cult under Otto I, who translated his relics anew to the imperial city of Quedlinburg.[138]

From the diocese and city of Trier, we find the first bishops and martyrs of the city, Valerius, Maximinus, Paulinus, Eucharius, and Géry, included by Leofric in the Exeter litany. In his calendar, he also entered the name of Goar, an Aquitanian who spent his life in a hermitage near Trier, where Charlemagne had a church built.[139] From Cologne, similarly, we have one of the first bishops, Severus, and also SS Cunibert, archdeacon of Trier and archbishop of Cologne, Gereon, one of St Maurice's companions, Pantaleon, and Ursula and the 11,000 virgins. Of the Trier saints, Giso had only included Severinus, whose name appears also in calendars from Glastonbury, the West Country, Evesham, and Worcester and in litanies from Winchester and Exeter. While Leofric only included Cunibert of Cologne, Giso also had Gereon and Ursula with the virgins, but both featured Pantaleon, whose name is generally not included in the late tenth-century calendars but appears in most eleventh-century ones.[140] Pantaleon has masses in both the New Minster missal and the Wells sacramentary and a collect in Wulfstan's collectar, and his name appears in the litanies of Winchester, with that of Gereon, and of Exeter, together with both Gereon and Cunipert. Only the latest missal in our period, that of St Augustine's of the very end of the eleventh century, includes a mass for Ursula and the Eleven Virgins.[141] The latter two cults illustrate the

---

[138] On Servatius, see de Moreau, *Église en Belgique*, i. 31–9, and Zender, *Räume*, 61–70.

[139] Géry had been a bishop of Cambrai who finished his life as a deacon at Trier; on Goar, see Beissel, *Geschichte der Trieren Kirchen*, 166; he was also entered in the Evesham calendar.

[140] On this cult at Cologne, see E. P. Baker, 'The Cult of St Alban of Cologne', *The Archaeological Journal*, 94 (1937), 208–9.

[141] This missal, now CCCC MS 270, was edited by M. Rule, *The Missal of St Augustine's Abbey, Canterbury* (Cambridge, 1896). This cult had only just begun its astonishing rise in the 11th c., to become a major devotion of Cologne by the end of the Middle Ages. The compiler of the MS may have taken his information from a text which entered the cult as it had been correctly known at first: 'de sanctis virginibus XI'. At a later stage, somebody mistakenly read a martyrological entry for XI MV, 'XI m[artyres] virgines' as 'XI m[ilia] virgines', and the cult became that of the Eleven Thousand Virgins. However, this had already happened by the eleventh century, since the entry in the Wells calendar reads 'In Colonia XI milium virginum' and the Invention of the Relics of the Virgins at Cologne in 1106—which gave much impetus to the cult—was also that of Eleven Thousand Virgins. In this light, the St Augustine's entry is unusual. One of the additions to the legend of St Ursula and her companions was her British origin. Although it may not have made her cult in England a very popular one, this story may have helped establish it in the early stages of its development in Cologne, since it was reputed to have been brought there by a German ambassador to England, see above, 57. On this cult, see W. Levison, *Das Werden der Ursula-Legende* (Cologne, 1928); M. I. Tout, 'The Legend of St Ursula and the Eleven Thousand Virgins' in T. F. Tout and J. Tait (eds.), *Historical Essays* (Manchester, 1907), 17–56; and Zender, *Räume*, 196–9.

closeness of the links between England and Cologne during the second half of the century, the period when Archbishop Ealdred spent a year there, since Pantaleon's cult had developed there not long before, and Ursula's was only just becoming a major one. Gereon is also entered in the Worcester calendar and in the litany from the Winchcombe Sacramentary. The cult of Agaune saints was particularly strong at Fleury, which could explain the special honouring of Maurice, Gereon, and also of Sigismund, King of Burgundy, in the litany and in the latter case, in the entry of a mass for this feast. The privileged Fleury links with Winchcombe or Ramsey, both foundations of Oswald and possible *scriptoria* of that manuscript, have already been mentioned. Other Burgundian saints are Gengulf, Mamertus of Vienne, and two saints who, however, were already entered in Bede's and Willibrord's martyrologies, Ferriolis and Ferritiolis of Besançon. Gengulf was adopted by Giso in his calendar, and he is entered in a Winchester litany; Mamertus and the two Besançon saints in one late tenth-century calendar and in the Exeter litany. From Lotharingia come the cults of Mansuetus of Toul and of the patron saint of Metz, St Arnulf. Both are entered in Giso's calendar and Arnulf also has a mass at Wells and a collect in Wulfstan's collectar. Finally, we find two saints from southern Germany, SS Afra of Augsburg and Florian, venerated in Austria and south Germany,[142] Afra in the Glastonbury calendar and in the Exeter and Wessex litanies. Florian is recorded in the two West Country calendars of the late tenth and early eleventh century, but this entry is clearly a left-over from the Hieronymian Martyrology, under the heading 'Floriani in Africa'. Much more interesting is the mass included by Giso in his sacramentary. Since this book belonged to Giso and since only the bishop himself could have allowed the celebration of a mass in the liturgy of his cathedral, we may safely assume that Giso himself held Florian in particular regard, thus showing him to have been exceptionally far-reaching and knowledgeable in his widespread devotional interests.

It is possible to wonder to what extent some isolated entries of such saints in a few English sources, especially if they come from Exeter and Wells, can be said to reflect a wide knowledge of and veneration for them in England. Although it is not possible to estimate the degree of popularity of these saints in terms of popular devotion, it could be said that, whilst the most unfamiliar remained as isolated entries alone, others saw their cults develop for a variety of reasons, as in the case of Nicholas, Mary Magdalene, Lambert, Ursula, or Pantaleon. Those who did so achieved

---

[142] Florian had a cult at Reichenau since his name is entered in the calendar of Egbert's Psalter, H. V. Sauerland and A. Haseloff (eds.), *Der Psalter Erzbishof Egberts von Trier* (2 vols.; Trier, 1901), 39.

fame either on account of the development of a European cult, as in the first two cases, or sometimes on account of a strong link between an area of the Empire, such as Liège or Cologne, with England, in the case of the other three; sometimes relics were donated by foreign patrons, to Wells by Giso after his death, to Durham by the Emperor Henry II, who allegedly gave some relics of St Gereon.[143] In the case of cults adopted by Wulfstan, a thorough Englishman, we can identify those Continental saints whose success in England was more than superficial; their adoption by an English bishop shows them to have been more than solely a passing whim of foreign ecclesiastics. Ultimately, the important factor for the purpose of this investigation is the evidence of imports of saints from or through the Empire and, thus, the evidence for the devotional influence of the imperial lands on cultural developments in England.

It would, however, be erroneous to think that devotional influences operated only from Germany to England. Enough evidence exists to show that English devotions were also taken up in the Empire. Already in the eighth century, Anglo-Saxon missionaries to Frisia, then to Saxony under the first Carolingians, established there one of the two most popular cults in England, that of Gregory the Great and, from the eleventh century onwards, of the British martyr Alban at Cologne, where he became identified with St Alban of Cologne after the translation of his relics from Rome to St Pantaleon's in 984.[144] Moreover, they also introduced the two most popular English saints into Germany, St Cuthbert and the saintly king Oswald of Northumbria. Both these cults prospered and remain in evidence in tenth- and eleventh-century German sources, for example, in the calendars of Trier and Cologne and in that of Essen, whose links with England through Abbess Mathilda are well known.[145] That of Oswald saw a revival of its popularity in Bavaria in the second half of the eleventh century, as a result of the Countess Judith's stay there, implying that she had fully adopted one of the most popular saints of her first husband's homeland.[146] He was also venerated at Hildesheim, where his head was claimed to have been brought from England.[147] The missionaries themselves became the objects of a cult, mostly but by no means solely in the cities or abbeys with which they had been associated, Willibrord at Utrecht

[143] Thomas, 'Cult of Saints' Relics', 107–8.

[144] Baker, 'Cult', 211–18.

[145] P. Miesges (ed.), *Der Trierer Festkalender* (Trier, 1915), and G. Zilliken (ed.), *Der Kölner Festkalender* (Bonn, 1910); see also the entries for Cuthbert and Bede in the Egbert Psalter litany, Sauerland and Haseloff, *Der Psalter*, 192.

[146] P. Clemoes, *The Cult of St Oswald on the Continent* (Jarrow Lecture, 1983), 7–10; and Leyser, 'Die Ottonen', 78.

[147] F. J. Tschan, *St Bernward of Hildesheim* (3 vols.; Notre Dame, 1943, 1951–2), ii. 107.

and Echternach in Lorraine, which he had founded, Boniface at Mainz and Fulda, his monastic foundation, as well as Lebuin and the two brothers Ewald, and Willehard.

Apart from favouring specific saints, whose cults reached England, Ottonian Germany contributed to the development of English spirituality in a different way. Under the influence of the Gorze reform, whose promoter John was particularly noted for his devotion to Christ,[148] then of Reichenau, German spiritual trends show strong interests in the Cross, the earthly life of Jesus, and the Virgin Mary. Bernward was particularly devoted to the Cross, as was Ulrich of Augsburg, whose veneration for the Virgin is also noted in his Life; Bishop Heribert of Cologne was devoted to Mary, and Hroswith of Gandersheim wrote up with relish the stories of the Virgin, the Nativity and Ascension of Christ; Bernward was equally reputed for his insistence on the notions of repentance and penance and on the Crucifixion and Salvation.[149] Above all, Otto III himself, and other members of the imperial family, the Empresses Agnes and Cunigunde, and Henry III, were strongly influenced by the Italian monastic piety, first of Greek origin, then by that of the Italian reformers St Romuald and St Peter Damian, who insisted on a personal, ascetic piety, focusing on individual salvation through devotion to Jesus.[150] The atmosphere at the imperial court, particularly from the time of Otto III onwards, was one of intense spiritual awareness, with a strong accent on penance, tears, sin and forgiveness, all elements displayed in court art and in the success of relatively new cults, such as that of St Mary Magdalene. This christological, New Testament-focused, interest was certainly not new in Anglo-Saxon England; indeed, it had been a constant feature of Anglo-Saxon spirituality from the very beginning, as we can see from early Anglo-Saxon texts both directly associated with monasticism, such as the prayers in the eighth-century Book of Cerne, and in vernacular ones, such as the poem *The Dream of the Rood*. The Anglo-Saxon emphasis on the devotion to the Cross, the crucified Christ and His life on earth, and the veneration for His mother, mostly originating in the close links of the English Church with the eastern Mediterranean and Byzantine world, notably through

---

[148] *Life of John of Gorze*, 344, 354–5, 358.

[149] Tschan, *St Bernward*, ii. 762; *Gerhardi Vita Sancti Oudalrici*, MGH SS iv. 389; *Vita Heriberti archiepiscopi Colonienses*, ibid., 746; Hroswith, 5–34; *Vita Bernwardi*, 430–4, and Tschan, *St Bernward*, ii. 439–40.

[150] An example of the importance of this theme and others derived from it is the parallel made between sin and penance, expressed as the dual concept of *humilitas* and *humiliatio–exaltatio*, which becomes an *imitatio Christi* for the Emperor following Christ; see the *Vita Mahthildis posterior* and Wipo's *Gesta Chuonradi*, as well as the artistic illustration of the theme in the Lothar Cross, all studied by L. Bornscheuer, *Miseriae Regum: Untersuchungen zum Krisen- und Todesgedanken in der Herrschaftstheologischen Vorstellung der ottonisch–salischen Zeit* (Berlin, 1968).

Ireland, remains a major feature of late Anglo-Saxon spirituality. In this sense, it is not possible to attribute such developments primarily to the contacts with the Ottonian world; however, there is no denying that the trend set by the new spiritual movements issuing from Gorze, Reichenau, then the north Italian monastic reforms such as those of Fruttuaria, implemented in Germany notably at Siegburg, probably contributed to reinforcing this sensibility in England. In this respect also, England and Germany, both under the influence of Byzantium to a greater or lesser degree, moved along parallel lines. More evidently, this European trend of the eleventh century, created by parallel movements in England, Germany, and Italy, contributed to drawing England into the European devotional mainstream. Clearly these spiritual inclinations were corresponding with the English tradition, in the way that another western European contemporary trend, the eremitic revival, which had little success in England, did not: the lack of interest in the eremitic features of the Vézelay cult of St Mary Magdalene demonstrates this.[151] This way of proceeding was typical of English relations with the Continent: the English Church was ready to adopt specific Continental features, but the most successful of these imports were often those which had already some basis in England and corresponded to native traditions of devotion, partly, it is to be surmised, because of their being already familiar. The most obvious links between English and Ottonian spirituality are in the field of art.

V. ARTISTIC EXCHANGES BETWEEN ENGLAND AND THE EMPIRE

Examples illustrating the circulation of artists and works of art between the two countries have reached us in written evidence. A German cleric, Benna, came to Wilton sometime between 961 and 975, where St Edith had the abbey church rebuilt and consecrated in 984.[152] Benna was a canon of St Paulinus at Trier, a painter and goldsmith, who worked both for St Paulinus, itself and possibly for Archbishop Egbert's cathedral workshop. Though almost certainly not the 'Gregory Master' himself,[153] he may have been one of the artists, or at least a member of the workshop, which produced the most famous art pieces to come from Trier under Egbert, the *Registrum Gregorii*, the shrine for the relic of St Andrew and possibly

---

[151] Cf. ch. 7.

[152] Wilmart, 'Légende de Ste Édith', 50–1, 87; H. Westermann-Angerhausen, in a paper which she gave in Oxford in 1989, thinks that Benna must have been in England before King Edgar's death.

[153] Hoffmann, *Buchkunst*, 103–26.

even the top of the Basle portable altar, since he himself was both a painter and a metal worker; these three artefacts display similarities with one another and exhibit some Anglo-Saxon stylistic influences.[154] He went back to Trier at least once during his stay in England, and on his return he brought with him not only the relic of the Holy Nail, but also German artistic models to England from the flourishing Trier School.[155] Benna painted a cycle of the life of Christ for Edith at Wilton, the only such cycle that we know of in England, which appears to have resembled quite closely the Ottonian narrative illustrations found in Gospel books and Gospel lectionaries.[156] Equally, he may also have found some inspiration in the English artistic themes and style of the flourishing Winchester School to take back to Trier. One of the most famous manuscripts produced at Trier under the reign of Egbert was the *Registrum Gregorii*. In it, there is a miniature representing a portrait of Gregory. The figure of the saint is very clearly a product of the Ottonian style of illumination, with its possibly Byzantine frontality and magnificence; but watching him from a hole in a side-curtain is a deacon Peter whose figure is drawn in a much more fluid and sinewy manner, while the curtain is knotted in a way characteristic of the Anglo-Saxon style (Pl. 1*a*, *b*). If Benna worked at Trier during the production of this manuscript there by the 'Gregory Master', it is not impossible that he should have been able to talk about some of the models which he had seen in England. Westermann-Angerhausen has proved that the lions inserted in the medallions on Egbert's shrine were of English manufacture.[157] She thinks they were sent to Trier at Egbert's request, since Egbert was himself related to the West-Saxon royal house through his mother, though Benna may also have had some role to play in this connection. We know that there were in the Empire 'collectors' of English works of art, such as Bernward of Hildesheim himself, and there is material proof that such works of art reached Germany at that time: for example, an ivory T-cross carved in England in the late tenth or the early eleventh century was taken either to Cologne or to the neighbouring abbey of Deutz,

---

[154] Kempf, 'Benna', 179, 181–96. Goscelin said that the paintings and metalwork of Benna could still be seen at Wilton in his time, about 1080, which implies that for the whole period they would have been available as models for English artists. After Egbert's death in 993, Benna left Trier for Mainz, where he may have worked for Bishop Willigis, see Hoffmann, *Buchkunst*, 73; thus, Anglo-Saxon features could also have been conveyed further than Trier into Germany in this way.

[155] On the Trier School, see Hoffmann, *Buchkunst*, 444–509.

[156] Wilmart, 'Légende de Ste Édith', 51.

[157] H. Westermann-Angerhausen, 'Spolie und Umfeld in Egberts Trier', *Zeitschrift für Kunstgeschichte*, 50 (1987), 526–32.

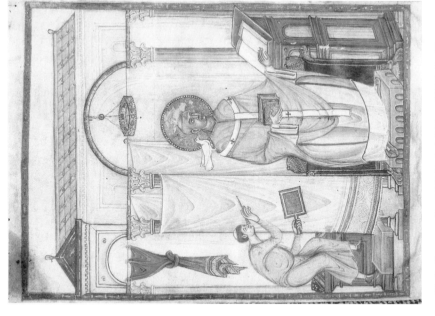

PLATE 1 (a) St Gregory, British Library, Cotton MS Claudius A.III, fo. 8.

(b) St Gregory, Stadtbibliothek Trier, MS 171a (Gregory Register), fo. 2.

and is still part of the Cologne cathedral treasury.[158] Its iconography features two of the most popular themes in England, the Three Maries and the Harrowing of Hell, of which numerous representations in manuscript, ivories and sculpture are still extant.[159] Another Ottonian reliquary cross has an ivory Christ from tenth-century England attached to it,[160] although some art historians have described the whole piece as English[161] and others as German:[162] the possible confusion is in itself a proof of the closeness of the two areas, particularly in the art of metalwork. Barbara Raw thinks it may have reached England, where its type was subsequently adapted in the Crucifixions from the Arenberg Gospels and the Sherborne missal.[163] The best documented example of a direct link between England and Cologne is the visit of Archbishop Ealdred there in 1054; in his Life of John of Beverley, Folcard stated that Ealdred was so impressed with the art of the Rhenish metalworkers that he commissioned a pulpit for the restored church at Beverley to be made 'in the German manner'. Such inspiration could be at the root of the similarities between an eleventh-century chalice from the area of Hexham with the chalice held by Ecclesia in a tenth-century Fulda illumination,[164] and a gold plate excavated at Winchester displays filigree work said to be of Rhenish origin.[165] The example of the Ottonian bishops, powerful worldly figures and patrons of the arts, could well have had some impact on English bishops such as Aethelwold, Ealdred, and Stigand, who were adopting precisely that pattern of art patronage.[166] The role of the bishops in England was not entirely similar to that of their Ottonian colleagues, in so far as they were

---

[158] Beckwith, *Ivory Carvings*, no. 30, p. 124, pl. 80, and Goldschmidt, *Elfenbeinskulpturen*, iv, nos. 10a–b. The iconography of the cross is as follows: on one side a Crucifixion with the Virgin, St John, Sol, and Luna, on the other Christ in Majesty with four angels; the silver mount is engraved with the two scenes of the Three Maries at the Sepulchre and the Harrowing of Hell, and with an inscription describing the contents of the cross as relics of the Virgin and St Christopher.

[159] Boulogne Ps, fo. 109; *Benedictional of St Aethelwold*, fo. 51ᵛ; *BAR*, fo. 21ᵛ, reproduced in Temple, *ASM*, pl. 89; Harleian 603, fos. 8, 24, 71; Missal of Robert, fo. 72ᵛ, reproduced in *MRJ*, pl. VIII; Tiberius C.VI, fos. 13ᵛ and 14, reproduced in Wormald, 'Eleventh-Century', pls. 15, 16, and pls. 138 in *Collected Writings*. In Harleian 603, as in the Utrecht Psalter, some of the scenes have only two Maries, a fairly common occurrence in Continental MSS.

[160] H. P. Mitchell, 'English or German?—A Pre-Conquest Gold Cross', *Burlington Magazine*, 47 (1925), 324–30.

[161] M. C. Ross, 'An Eleventh-Century English Bookcover', *The Art Bulletin*, 22 (1940), 84.

[162] Raw, *Crucifixion*, 113–15; she shows that its closest parallels are to be found in the Lothar Cross, the Crucifix of Bernward, and the Gero Cross.

[163] Ibid. 112–115.

[164] R. N. Bailey, 'The Anglo-Saxon Metalwork from Hexham', in D. P. Kirby (ed.), *St Wilfrid at Hexham* (Newcastle, 1974), 155.

[165] D. M. Wilson, 'The Gold Plate', in M. Biddle and R. N. Quirk, 'Excavations near Winchester Cathedral', *The Archaeological Journal*, 119 (1962), 187.

[166] Wormald, 'Aethelwold', 36–8, and Barlow, *English Church 1000–1066*, 79–80, 87–90.

probably even more closely involved with royal power, which they served in the first instance, being its representatives and tools. However, the parallel with Ottonian bishops is relevant on two counts. English bishops also played a part in the development of the sacral aspects of royal power and royal ceremonial, clearly seen in the composition of the coronation *ordines* for King Edgar by Aethelwold and possibly of King William I by Ealdred, as well as in the royal–christological parallels in some of the images in the Benedictional of St Aethelwold. Secondly, the link between art patronage and support of royal cults, particularly at Winchester, by English bishops from Dunstan to Ealdred, was also reminiscent of the Ottonian court. There is no denying that these developments are the result, less of mutual influences than of a similar response in a similar situation, and represent essentially a parallel evolution. Nevertheless, it is worth noting that both Aethelwold and Ealdred had been, at some time or other in their life, aware of the German situation through direct or indirect contacts with the Imperial court.

The Washing of the Feet scene in the psalter Tiberius C.VI, where Christ is depicted washing St Peter's feet whilst the other Apostles sit as spectators in the background, is another example of possible iconographical exchanges between English and Ottonian art.[167] The Washing of the Feet was depicted from the Early Christian period onwards, and appears in Syrian, Byzantine, Carolingian, and Ottonian art, either as an action scene depicting Christ in the act of performing this rite, in the Early Christian tradition, or as a dialogue between Christ and St Peter in the Ottonian tradition. In the eleventh century, a new iconographical representation, which occurs simultaneously in the Trier School, in a manuscript such as the Gospel-book of Henry III, made for Speyer at Echternach, a *scriptorium* closely linked with Trier, about 1043–6,[168] and in England in Tiberius C.VI, shows Christ bending or kneeling in front of St Peter, in the process of washing his apostle's feet (Pl. 2*a*, *b*). This representation was modelled on the Maundy ceremony, during which the abbot washed the monks' feet on Maundy Thursday. Apart from illustrating the monastic character of the iconography, this innovation in both Germany and England exemplifies the close links existing between these two areas. It is difficult to know which artistic school first introduced this iconography, since both were intent on illustrating Gospel scenes. But the interest in practical, emotional details, together with the strong monastic

---

[167] Tiberius C.VI, fo. 11ᵛ, reproduced in Wormald, 'Eleventh-Century', pl. 11, and pl. 134 in *Collected Writings*.

[168] A. Boeckler (ed.), *Das goldene Evangelienbuch Heinrichs III* (Berlin, 1933), 11 and pl. 149; on the Echternach *scriptorium*, see Hoffmann, *Buchkunst*, 509–16.

PLATE 2
(a) The Washing of the Feet, British Library, Cotton MS Tiberius C.VI, fo. 11ᵛ.

MISIT IHC AQVAIN PELVIM · ET COEPIT LAVARE PEDES DISCIPVLORVM SVORVM ·

(b) The Washing of the Feet, Madrid, Biblioteca del Escorial, MS Vitrinas 17 (*Codex Aureus* of Henry III), fo. 152ᵛ.

background in England, led Meyer Schapiro to view this variation as English.[169]

Yet another iconographical innovation in the tenth century is the draped lectern found in practically all Evangelist portraits in England alone. But we find this theme in a golden pulpit given by Henry II to Aachen: Nordenfalk attributes it either to the presence of an Englishman in Germany or Benna's visit to England, or to the availability of an English manuscript such as the Arenberg Gospels, which was given as a present to Archbishop Heribert, in the Empire.[170] If one of the models for the Arenberg Crucifixion had been originally German, the wheel had turned full circle.

A theme common to English and Ottonian iconography is also that of the representations of the ruler and of royal power, in the context of a 'Christ-centred theory of kingship'.[171] Robert Deshman has drawn a parallel between the theories of imperial power and the innovations made in England in the Benedictional of St Aethelwold, which depicts, for the first time, the crowned Christ, Magi, and Virgin.[172] These changes were subsequently adopted in Ottonian circles under the influence of Egbert at Trier and Bernward at Hildesheim, possibly through the intermediary of Benna of Trier, who had been closely involved with the circle of Edgar and Aethelwold at Winchester.[173] Interestingly, however, Anglo-Saxon art rarely represented the ruler himself; Hoffmann has counted five portraits, two of Aethelstan, one of Edgar, one of Cnut and one of Emma, as against the many more such representations of the Emperor crowned in German art, particularly of Otto III.[174] The reason for this may be worth pursuing. The representation of the ruler crowned in glory was originally a Byzantine one, whereas the Western tradition, modelled on Late Antique images, depicted the king or emperor being presented to Christ. The English representations follow the Western,

---

[169] Schapiro, 'The Image', 281–8. This opinion could be further supported by a parallel example of a Gospel scene whose illustration was strongly influenced by a monastic ceremony in England, the Three Maries at the Sepulchre, in which it is the Easter Drama which is usually depicted. On the early representations of the Washing of the Feet in Early Christian and Roman (4th-c. Sarcophagus, St Augustine's Gospels), eastern (Codex Rossanensis), Carolingian (Müstair), and Ottonian (Codex Egberti, Book of Pericopes of Henry II) art, see G. Schiller, *Iconography of Christian Art* (2 vols.; tr. London, 1971–2), ii. 43–5, and on the new iconography of the 11th c., 46–7.

[170] C. Nordenfalk, 'The Draped Lectern', in *Intuition und Kunstwissenschaft: Festschrift für Hanns Swarzenski zum 70. Geburtstag am 30. August 1973*, P. Bloch et al. (eds.) (Berlin, 1973), 81–97.

[171] Deshman, ' "Christus rex" ', 389.

[172] Ibid. 367–90.

[173] Ibid. 390–405.

[174] Hoffmann, *Buchkunst*, 7–41, esp. 23–4.

Carolingian model, with the exception of the Benedictional of St Aethelwold, with its christological parallels between the king and Christ; one more element confirming the importance of the Byzantine and Ottonian elements in this manuscript and in Aethelwold and Edgar's circle at Winchester. The English court used the Ottonian model by depicting the ruler, but the iconography of these images remained that inherited from the Western tradition. It is worth noting, however, that the first portraits in England are those of Aethelstan, whose important part in the development of royal sacral power based on powerful relics such as the Holy Lance and the production of sumptuous books has been well studied by Karl Leyser.[175] It is therefore not impossible that the influences here could have been those of Aethelstan on the German emperors in the first place. The second king depicted in England is Edgar, whose links with the Ottonians have been shown, particularly through Aethelwold's artistic production and ceremonial language in the titles, coronation *ordo*, and coinage; and the third is Cnut, who was not only attempting to imitate the Anglo-Saxon tradition of kingship, but was also particularly involved with the German emperors, after having attended Conrad II's coronation. On the other hand, Aethelred and Edward, for example, did not try to fit into this framework, theirs being a more characteristically western Frankish attitude towards kingship, particularly in the case of Edward. His power was not a parallel kind of episcopal power: his chosen patron saint for the English king was none other than St Denis, the capetian saint, his building of Westminster as a royal abbey was not unlike the establishing of the abbey of St Denis by the French kings as their royal necropolis, as was the burgeoning theory of the power of the king to cure the King's Evil, paralleled in Robert the Pious's Life in France.[176] Whatever the influences at work, it remains to explain why the actual Byzantine–Ottonian form of representation of the crowned ruler in majesty, on the model of Christ, was never shown in England; could it be that the influence of Bede, and beyond him, of Gregory the Great, who insisted on the importance of humility for kings as well as bishops and made it difficult to accept the ideological exaltation of the ruler to the level of Christ himself, remained paramount in England and did not allow such developments as the Ottonian court encouraged?[177]

[175] Leyser, *Rule and Conflict*, 88.

[176] See ch. 7, p. 231

[177] I am indebted to Patrick Wormald for this suggestion and for a stimulating discussion on this subject. The importance of this concept in Anglo-Saxon art has been discussed by Raw, *Crucifixion*, 129–46, who stresses the link between royal power and glory and humility, expressed in the representations of the crowned Christ in Anglo-Saxon art. The association between the royal function and humility, however, was also present in Ottonian art, see Bornscheuer, *Miseriae Regum*.

One particular feature of Ottonian iconography, to be related to the christological and New Testament-oriented piety already mentioned, is the frequency of cycles representing either the public life of Jesus, such as those on the Column of Bernward of Hildesheim, in the *Codex Egberti*, the Golden Evangeliary of Echternach, the Speyer Gospel-book of Henry III, and the Reichenau cycle of wall-paintings at Oberzell; or His Passion, as in the Gospel-book of Otto III. These narrative cycles, which belong to the Late Antique tradition of, for example, the Rossano and St Augustine's Gospel-books, had become relatively rare under the Carolingians, when they appear only a few times, for example in the Bible of San Paolo fuori le Mura and the Vivian Bible, and then only for the Old Testament. Carolingian art was more interested in illustrating the psalter (Stuttgart and Utrecht Psalters) or specific scenes from the life of Christ rather than cycles, such as those in the Sacramentary of Drogo; meanwhile, Byzantine art had taken a different direction and preferred to illustrate *liturgically*, in other words, to follow the liturgical year by depicting the events in the Gospels which related to specific feasts and explained them, Nativity, Epiphany, Crucifixion, Ascension, and so on.[178] The importance of this distinction cannot be too strongly emphasized, and it has been repeatedly stressed by Barbara Raw, who interprets the contrast between *illustrative* and *iconic* images as a reflection of the different theological and devotional emphases between the Late Antique narrative tradition followed by Ottonian art and the highly charged symbolic and emotional contents of Anglo-Saxon images such as those in the Tiberius Psalter and the Benedictional of St Aethelwold.[179]

English art as a whole provides a mixture of the two types. While the Benedictional of St Aethelwold is essentially a liturgical manuscript of the Byzantine type, the missal of Robert of Jumièges comprises narrative cycles, such as that of the journey, adoration, dream, and warning by the angel of the Magi. However, there is a difference with Ottonian cycles in that we do not in England find cycles of the public life of Jesus, on the model of those mentioned above, and at most occasional illustrations of some particular scenes or parables, such as that of the Gadarene swine in the leaves previously belonging to the Museum at Damme in Belgium.[180] Some images, apart from the Washing of the Feet, are however clearly common: the Adoration of the Magi, the Nativity with the midwife Salome, the Ascension with the 'disappearing' Christ (Pl. 3*a*, *b*), in

---

[178] On this problem of narrative and liturgical choices in the different traditions, see K. Weitzmann, 'The Narrative and Liturgical Gospel Illustrations', in H. L. Kessler (ed.), *Studies in Classical and Byzantine Manuscript Illumination* (Chicago and London, 1951), 247–70.

[179] Raw, *Crucifixion*, 7–39, 68–85.

[180] Temple, *ASM*, pl. 174.

PLATE 3
(*a*) The Ascension, Rouen,
Bibliothèque Municipale, MS Y.6
(Benedictional of Archbishop
Robert), fo. 81ᵛ.

(*b*) The Ascension, Hildesheim Cathedral Library, MS 18 (Bernward Gospels),
fo. 175ᵛ.

Schapiro's view an English innovation,[181] Pentecost with the rays of the Holy Spirit being directed towards each apostle individually, 'portraits' of St Peter, and the Nativity of John the Baptist. The Adoration in the Benedictional of Aethelwold and the Victoria and Albert Museum ivory can be paralleled in Bernward's Evangeliary, on his doors and in the Echternach Gospel-book, which includes also the Dream of the Magi, as does the missal of Robert.[182] The Nativity with Salome, which we see in the Benedictional, the missal of Robert and the Liverpool ivory, for example, is also carved on Bernward's doors.[183] The Entry into Jerusalem in the Benedictional and in Tiberius C.VI is also shown in a similar way, Christ followed by the Apostles riding and the people of Jerusalem spreading their cloaks before Him, in Bernward's Evangeliary, the Echternach and Henry III's Gospel-books, the *Codex Egberti*, and on Bernward's Column.[184] Bernward's Evangeliary and the *Codex Egberti* have the Ascension scene with the 'disappearing' Christ, as in the Benedictional and missal of Robert.[185] The Three Maries at the Sepulchre, a particularly common scene in England, in the benedictionals of Aethelwold and of Archbishop Robert and the missal of Robert is similarly shown in the Echternach Codex, the *Codex Egberti*, and Bernward's doors.[186] The Pentecost scene, depicted in England in the benedictionals of Aethelwold and Robert and in the missal of Robert, is close to that in the two Ottonian manuscripts just mentioned, which also contain 'portraits' of St Peter, as does the missal of Robert.[187] The Nativity of John the Baptist, a not very common representation, occurs in England in the Hereford Troper, and in Germany in the Gospel-book of Henry III and the Evangeliary of Bernward.[188] It will come as no surprise to realize that, of all Ottonian

---

[181] Schapiro, 'The Image', 277–9.

[182] *Benedictional of St Aethelwold*, fo. 24ᵛ; Beckwith, *Ivory Carvings*, pls. 12, 122; S. Beissel (ed.), *Der heilige Bernward Evangelienbuch im Dome zu Hildesheim* (Hildesheim, 1891), pl. VI, and Tschan, *Bernward*, iii, pl. 126; P. Metz (ed.), *The Golden Gospels of Echternach* (London, 1957), pl. 30; *MRJ*, fo. 37, pl. 4. On the Echternach Codex, see also R. Kahsnitz, V. Mende, and E. Rücker (eds.), *Das goldene Evangelienbuch von Echternach* (Frankfurt, 1989).

[183] *Benedictional of St Aethelwold*, fo. 15ᵛ; *MRJ*, fo. 32ᵛ, pl. I; Beckwith, *Ivory Carvings*, pl. 56; Tschan, *Bernward*, iii, pl. 125.

[184] *Benedictional of St Aethelwold*, fo. 45ᵛ; Wormald, 'Eleventh-Century', pl. 10, and pl. 133 in *Collected Writings*; Beissel, *Evangelienbuch*, pl. XXIII; Metz, *Echternach*, fo. 83; Boeckler, *Evangelienbuch*, pl. 55; *Codex Egberti*, fo. 66; Tschan, *Bernward*, iii, pl. 190.

[185] Beissel, *Evangelienbuch*, pl. XXIV; *Codex Egberti*, fo. 101; *Benedictional of St Aethelwold*, fo. 64ᵛ.

[186] *Benedictional of St Aethelwold*, fo. 51ᵛ; *BAR*, fo. 21ᵛ; *MRJ*, fo. 72 Pl. VIII; Metz, *Echternach*, fo. 85; *Codex Egberti*, fo. 86ᵛ; Tschan, *Bernward*, iii, pl. 130.

[187] *BAR*, fo. 29ᵛ reproduced in Temple, *ASM*, frontispiece; Metz, *Echternach*, pl. 86; *Codex Egberti*, fos. 103, 19; *MRJ*, fo. 132ᵛ, pl. XI.

[188] Caligula A. XIV, fo. 20ᵛ; Boeckler, *Evangelienbuch*, pls. 110, 111; Beissel, *Evangelienbuch*, pl. XVI.

manuscripts, the Evangeliary of Bernward is the one closest to the spirit of most Anglo-Saxon liturgical manuscripts in its unique mixture of almost literal illustration of the Gospel with the doctrinal and symbolic significance.[189] A final and convincing proof of the combination of an Ottonian-style narrative cycle of the life of Christ and the devotional meditative attitude to it in England is provided by the Wilton cycle, painted by the German Benna for Edith, 'as she had pictured [it] in her heart'.[190]

A common characteristic of these artefacts is the constantly increasing number of characters from the Gospels and the Apocrypha which they depict: Anne, Elizabeth, Joachim, Joseph, Peter, Andrew, John and James in the Calling of the Apostles, Thomas and his Doubting, Mary Magdalene and Lazarus and numerous others. This common feature further confirms the parallels between English and German devotional trends, responsible for the increase in veneration for evangelical figures; a trend, however, about which the English Church was particularly enthusiastic, witness the very early development of such cults as those of Joseph in England and the representation of such scenes as the Deposition from the Cross in the Boulogne Gospels and the missal of Robert. It is no mere coincidence that the artefacts which seem to be the closest to English ones are the products of either the Trier–Echternach School or Hildesheim, the two centres whose links with England were particularly strong at the time; there are less features in common between English manuscripts and the other Ottonian schools, such as those of Regensburg or even Cologne.[191]

Possibly the most significant influence of an imperial school in artistic terms remains that of the Carolingian Metz School of illumination and ivory-carving of the ninth century, illustrated by manuscripts such as the Sacramentary of Drogo and ivories such as the Brunswick Casket.[192] The sacramentary, with its use of Early Christian iconographic themes adapted by Carolingian artists and its nervous, fluid style of drawing as well as the delicate pattern of colours and gold filigree, was certainly a source of inspiration to the illuminators of the Benedictional of St Aethelwold. They borrowed iconographic themes from it, such as the Martyrdoms of St Laurence, St Peter, and St Paul, and from the

---

[189] Raw, *Crucifixion*, 73–5.

[190] Wilmart, 'Légende de Ste Édith', 87, and see Raw, *Crucifixion*, 60.

[191] Goldschmidt, *German Illumination*, ii, and P. Bloch and H. Schnitzler, *Die ottonische Kölner Malerschule* (2 vols.; Düsseldorf, 1970).

[192] *Drogo-Sakramentar*; the Brunswick casket is reproduced and discussed in Goldschmidt, *Elfenbeinskulpturen*, i, no. 96, pp. 52–3, pl. XIV*a*. On the influence of the Metz School in England, see O. Homburger, *Die Anfänge der Malschule von Winchester im X. Jahrhundert* (Leipzig, 1912), 8–33, and his 'L'Art carolingien de Metz et l'école de Winchester', *Gazette des Beaux-Arts*, 62 (1963), 35–46.

Brunswick Casket the Baptism of Christ, including the river-god and the angels presenting the folded linen, and possibly details in the Nativity of Christ, seem to have been borrowed. The illuminations of the cycle of the Magi in the missal of Robert, unusual in England in the form of a cycle of images, may also have been inspired by a Metz ivory depicting their journey to Herod, their gifts, and their sleep, from which an angel awakes them.[193]

An image in the Benedictional presents us with a problem. The Adoration of the Magi depicts the three Magi as kings, wearing crowns, which is one of the earliest examples of this iconographical change from their Early Christian representation wearing Phrygian bonnets, as they had been depicted from the earliest times in frescos in Rome in the catacombs of Priscilla, of Peter and Marcellinus, and in a mosaic at Sta Maria Maggiore, as well as at Sant'Apollinare Nuovo at Ravenna, then throughout Carolingian art, in the late eighth-century Munich Gospels, on the ivory cover of the Lorsch Gospels and in the sacramentary of Drogo.[194] This representation is preserved in England in the missal of Robert and in the 'Bury Psalter' (Pl. 4*a*, *b*).[195] However, at the same moment in time, the 970s, two other manuscripts also depict them in this way. One is a Greek menologion, of Basil II, the other the Ottonian *Codex Egberti*.[196] Either the miniature in the Menologion is the first example of the scene, an iconography possibly known in Byzantium, but which we do not find before then on account of the destroying of manuscripts during the iconoclastic period, and the motif was borrowed by both the Ottonian and the Anglo-Saxon manuscripts from a book such as the Menologion; or the Benedictional borrowed it from the *Codex Egberti*; or the Benedictional borrowed it directly from a book such as the Menologion, since so many other features of its iconography show the influence of a Greek liturgical manuscript; or possibly the Benedictional was the first manuscript to use

---

[193] Goldschmidt, *Elfenbeinskulpturen*, i, no. 95, pls. XLI–XLIII.

[194] On the iconography of the Magi, see H. Kehrer, *Die 'Heiligen drei Könige' in der Legende und in der deutschen bildenden Kunst bis Albrecht Dürer* (Strasburg, 1904), and G. Vézin, *L'Adoration et le cycle des Mages dans l'art chrétien primitif* (Paris, 1950), 33–5, 59–62, 64–5. For the Catacombs of Priscilla and Peter and Marcellinus, see J. Wilpert, *Roma sotterranea: Le pitture delle catacombe romane illustrate* (2 vols.; Rome, 1903), i. 176–8 and ii. pl. 60 for the Peter and Marcellinus fresco, and G. Wilpert, *Fractio panis: la plus ancienne représentation du sacrifice eucharistique à la 'Cappella Greca'* (Paris, 1896), 62, pl. VII for the Priscilla fresco. On the mosaic at Sta Maria Maggiore see below, ch. 5 p. 142, and on that at Sant'Apollinare Nuovo, see M. van Berchem and E. Clouzot, *Mosaïques chrétiennes du ivᵉ au xᵉ siècle* (Geneva, 1924), pl. 178; Boinet, *La Miniature carolingienne*, no. I; for the ivory cover, see Beckwith, *Early Medieval Art*, Ills. 28, 36; *Drogo-Sakramentar*, fo. 34ᵛ.

[195] *MRJ*, fo. 37, pl. IV; the 'Bury Psalter', produced *c.* 1050 either at Bury or at Christ Church for Bury, is now Vatican Library MS Reginensis 12, see R. M. Harris, 'The Marginal Drawings of the Bury St Edmunds Psalter', Ph.D thesis (Princeton, 1960).

[196] *Menologio*, fo. 272; *Codex Egberti*, fo. 17.

PLATE 4 (*a*) The Adoration of the Magi, Doors of Sta Sabina, Rome.

(*b*) The Story of the Magi, Rouen, Bibliothèque Municipale, MS Y. 7 (Missal of Robert of Jumièges), fos. 36ᵛ and 37.

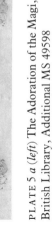

PLATE 5 *a* (*left*) The Adoration of the Magi,
British Library, Additional MS 49598
(Benedictional of St Aethelwold), fo. 24ᵛ.

b (*above right*) The Adoration of the Magi,
Biblioteca Apostolica Vaticana, MS Greco 1613
(Menologion of Basil II), fo. 272.

c (*below right*) The Adoration of the Magi,
Stadtbibliothek Trier, MS 24 (*Codex Egberti*),
fo. 17.

the motif, on account of its royal connections, and then it reached Trier from England (Pl. 5 *a*, *b*, *c*).[197] According to Deshman, the innovation is English, since he chooses to interpret the crowns of the Magi as 'oriental tiaras' rather than actual crowns in the Greek manuscript, and he further dates the *Codex Egberti* to the second half of Egbert's reign, that is after *c*.985.[198] Whatever the answer is, the problem illustrates by itself the close links between England and Germany, or England and the Byzantine world through the intermediary of the German Empire, a cultural route which we encounter again when examining both north and south Italian connections.

[197] R. Deshman, 'The Iconography of the full-page Miniatures of the Benedictional of St Æthelwold', Ph.D. thesis (Princeton, 1969), 128–33, and '*Christus rex*', 396–404.

[198] Ibid. 377–96.

4

ITALY
(EXCEPT ROME)

I. GEOGRAPHICAL OUTLINE

The areas covered here under this general name represent in effect the whole of present-day Italy, with the exception of Rome, discussed in the next chapter. During the period we are concerned with, however, the political geography of the peninsula was far from unified. Areas of Lombard rule remained: the duchies of Spoleto, Apulia, and Benevent and the principality of Capua. Northern and central Italy, that is to say the area extending from the Alps to the papal lands as far as Latium and Rome, was under three different rulers, the Emperor as far south as a line stretching from southern Tuscany and Liguria to Ancona in the Marches through northern Umbria, where the Patrimonium of St Peter, the papal lands, began. A third authority dominated, at least in theory, the lands centred on Ravenna and Venice, the Emperor of Byzantium. His authority had extended nominally over some of the lands south of the Patrimonium since the conquest of Italy by the Carolingians in the late eighth century. But this authority had been heavily challenged, both in the south of Italy itself and in Sicily, first by the establishment of Saracen pirates during the ninth and tenth centuries, then by the gradual conquests of the Norman noblemen of Robert Guiscard in Apulia and Richard in the principality of Capua. The former was officially accepted as king of the territories he had mastered by the popes and, under duress, by the German Emperors themselves, during the eleventh century.[1]

Among the cities visited by pilgrims once they had crossed the Alps, those known to us are Aosta; Ivrea and Vercelli in Piedmont; Pavia and Piacenza in Lombardy; Pisa, Siena, and Lucca in Tuscany; Luni in

---

[1] The political facts of Italian history are presented in great detail in general works on European history such as C. Brooke, *Europe in the Central Middle Ages 962–1154* (2nd edn.; London, 1987), and J. H. Mundy, *Europe in the High Middle Ages 1150–1309* (London, 1973); more specifically, in those on Italian history, such as *Storia d'Italia*, ii: *Della caduta dell'impero romano al secolo XVIII* (Turin, 1974), 5–142, 447–516, 1085–1142, and G. Galasso (ed.), *Storia d'Italia* (Turin, 1980), i. ii. On the history of the Church, see also G. Penco, *Storia della Chiesa in Italia* (2 vols.; 2nd edn.; Milan, 1978), i. 144–319. The best account in English on the development of the Patrimonium of St Peter is P. Partner, *The Lands of St Peter: The Papal State in the Middle Ages and the Early Renaissance* (London, 1972), 1–137; for Sicily, see D. Mack Smith, *A History of Sicily: Medieval Sicily 800–1713* (London, 1968), 3–23.

Liguria; and Bolsena, Sutri, and Viterbo in the Patrimonium. All these
are cited in the travel diary of Archbishop Sigeric of Canterbury, who went
to Rome for the *pallium* in 990. Earlier evidence corroborates the importance of Pavia and Lucca as two essential stops on the route to Rome.
Although not always mentioned by name, pilgrims and travellers could
well have come in contact with some of the famous abbeys situated on their
way, such as the Sagra di San Michele, Fruttuaria, Bobbio and Nonantola
and Farfa.

Bobbio, founded in 612 by St Columbanus, Nonantola, established
under the aegis of the Lombard king Astolf and Farfa, founded in 705 by
the dukes of Spoleto, together with the Sagra in Lombardy, were the main
economic, political, and cultural monastic centres in Lombard, Carolingian and, after recovering from the troubles of the ninth century, Imperial
Italy.[2] They had impressive buildings and libraries, and played an
important role in the Investitures Controversies at the end of the eleventh
century. Fruttuaria, on the other hand, was a new foundation, set up by
William of Volpiano on the lands of the Marquess of Ivrea, and it belonged
to the eleventh-century reform movement associated with the names of St
Romuald, Peter Damian, and John Gualbert.

Sigeric's Itinerary shows that, for example, pilgrims stopped at the
abbey of St Benedict at Montelungo in Tuscany, and the abbey itself as
well as the area around Pontremoli were dependent on Bobbio, which
owned most of the land there, as it also owned churches in Pavia and its
diocese. Further south, Nonantola was known to pilgrims, since a ninth-
century fly leaf containing a mass for St Ambrose written there was inserted
in a tenth- or eleventh-century Christ Church manuscript of Arator's
Historia Apostolica, and a prayer is found in a Nonantola psalter as well as
in a Winchester one, British Library, Cotton MS Tiberius D. XXVII, but
nowhere else, unfortunately without it being possible to tell in which
direction the exchange was made.[3] Farfa, whose area of influence extended
to include Viterbo, which was a main stopping-place before Rome, was
also possibly visited or known by Englishmen. Italian culture, both
monastic and secular, was in the process of being once again strongly
revitalized during the eleventh century, when Peter Damian, William of
Volpiano, and numerous other historians and lawyers were active, at the
same time as a strong spiritual revival was developing in monastic circles.[4]

South of Rome, an area less frequented by Englishmen, unless they were

---

[2] Penco, *Chiesa*, 200–90.
[3] Cambridge, Trinity College MS B.14.3; the Nonantola psalter is Rome, Vatican Library MS
Vat. lat. 84.
[4] Penco, *Chiesa*, 218–94.

on their way to Jerusalem or on special business, two places are specifically mentioned: Apulia, in particular Bari once it became the main European centre for the cult of St Nicholas at the end of the eleventh century, and Monte Cassino, St Benedict's foundation north of Naples.[5]

Monte Cassino was destroyed by the Lombards in 581 and refounded *c*.718, then fell again under the blow of the Arab invasion in 883; the monks, exiled at the time, only returned at the end of the ninth century, when Byzantine power was re-established in the area.[6] From that period onward and until the end of the eleventh century, Byzantine influence was to be considerable at the abbey, particularly under the reign of its most prestigious abbot, Desiderius (1058–87), who then became Pope Victor III.[7] Desiderius had the basilica rebuilt after 1066 and consecrated in 1071, on the model of Early Christian and Byzantine basilicas, and he imported decorators, painters, and other skilled craftsmen from Constantinople to decorate it with wall-paintings and mosaics, and teach his monks new skills in 'mosaic, marble, gold, silver, bronze, iron, glass, ivory, wood, alabaster and stone'.[8] An idea of the wall-paintings in the abbey, two Old Testament and fifteen New Testament scenes, of which ten relate to the infancy of Christ, can be obtained from the only surviving south Italian fresco cycle, inspired by that of Desiderius, in the church of Sant'Angelo in Formis.[9] The two most famous artefacts obtained by Desiderius came from Byzantium, the altar antependium made of gold, gems and enamels, depicting New Testament scenes and episodes from the life of St Benedict, and especially, the bronze doors of the abbey, also lost now; their iconography would have probably been similar to that of the two other contemporary sets of Byzantine bronze doors from Constantinople brought to Italy, those of S. Paolo fuori le Mura in Rome, and Monte Gargano, incorporating scenes from the life of Christ and the Apostles.[10] Monte Cassino was a major cultural centre during most of the eleventh century. It had considerable prestige as a house of learning, especially in the fields of history and law, with the chroniclers Leo and Peter the Deacon, and people such as Alphanus of Salerno and Constantine the African spending time there. It also possessed an impressive school of illumination,

---

[5] Out of the considerable literature on both Bari and Monte Cassino, the best accounts are: F. Schettini, *La basilica di San Nicola di Bari* (Bari, 1967) and H. E. J. Cowdrey, *The Age of Abbot Desiderius: Monte Cassino, the Papacy and the Normans in the Eleventh and Early Twelfth Centuries* (Oxford, 1983).

[6] Cowdrey, *Age*, pp. xiv–xxxiii, and H. Bloch, *Monte Cassino in the Middle Ages* (3 vols.; Rome, 1987) i. 5–14.

[7] Ibid. i. 3, 12–14, and Cowdrey, *Age*, 1–45 on Desiderius' reign.

[8] H. Hoffman (ed.), *Chronica monasterii casinensis*, 718; Bloch, *Monte Cassino*, i. 41–53.

[9] Ibid. 58–62, 89.

[10] Ibid. 65–8, 141–51, 187–90 and iii, figs. 64–5, 85–90, 126–8, 150–7.

illustrated by the two manuscripts of the Life of St Benedict of *c*.1071–2, now Vaticano latino 1202 and Monte Cassino H. H. 99; it remained at the heart of religious, political, and artistic links between Italy and Byzantium, and became one of the supporters of ecclesiastical reform within the Church and papacy in the second half of the eleventh century.[11]

Other centres, however, were of great significance as sources of cultural, particularly Greek, influences on northern Europe: the abbey of S. Vincenzo al Vulturno, the main Western sanctuary of St Michael at Monte Gargano, and Naples. S. Vincenzo, founded at the beginning of the eighth century by monks from Farfa, was closely linked with the Lombard dukes of Benevento, then with the Carolingians; destroyed by the Saracens in 881, it was rebuilt around the middle of the tenth century, and its closer links from then on were with Monte Cassino and with the Norman rulers of Apulia.[12] The crypt of the original basilica of the ninth century survives, and is renowned for its wall-paintings, depicting, among other scenes, the Annunciation, Nativity, Assumption of the Virgin, Crucifixion, the Three Maries at the Sepulchre, the martyrdoms of Stephen and Laurence, and Christ between these two saints.[13]

The sanctuary of St Michael on Monte Gargano, founded in the late fifth century following an alleged apparition of the Archangel, suffered under Lombard and Saracen attacks, but retained some of its early artefacts, in particular the oldest representation of St Michael, in an icon of *c*.600; in it, and in a relief of about 858, the Archangel is shown standing, holding a spear and, in the relief, piercing with it the head of the dragon.[14] The basilica itself, built over the grotto of the apparition and enlarged under the Carolingians, was given a set of bronze doors cast in Constantinople in 1076, similar to those of S. Paolo fuori le Mura in Rome and Monte Cassino; they included several scenes from the story of St Michael.[15]

By the seventh century, Naples under Byzantine rule had preserved a cultural tradition inherited from the past. The quality of its school was exemplified by the training of one ecclesiastic whose career we know reasonably well thanks to Bede, Abbot Hadrian.[16] This episcopal school

---

[11] Bloch, *Monte Cassino*, i. 93–110, 73–82; Cowdrey, *Age*, 47–106, 73–99.

[12] N. Cilento, 'S. Vincenzo al Vulturno e l'Italia meridionale longobarda e normanna', in F. Avagliano (ed.), *Una grande abbazia altomedioevale nel Molise: San Vincenzo al Volturno* (Montecassino, 1985), 43–53.

[13] F. de' Maffei, 'Le arti a S. Vincenzo al Volturno: Il ciclo della cripta di Epiphanio', in Avagliano, *Una Grande abbazia*, 269–352, figs. 1–21, 26–9.

[14] A. Graf von Keyserlingk, *Vergessene Kulturen in Monte Gargano* (Nurenberg, 1968), 19–23, 38, 36; and frontispiece and pl. 56. Also now G. Otranto and C. Carletti, *Il Santuario di S. Michele arcangelo sul Gargano dalle origini al X secolo* (Bari, 1990), 13–55 and 79–89.

[15] Ibid. 32 and pl. 35; Bloch, *Monte Cassino*, iii, pls. 85–90.

[16] *BHE* 328–9. On Hadrian and the Neapolitan school in the 7th c., see M. Fuiano, *La cultura*

experienced a considerable revival at the end of the ninth and in the tenth centuries, focusing in particular on history and hagiography; its main representative at the time was John the Deacon. On account of its bilingual Greek and Latin tradition, Naples became a crossroads between East and West, both in its cultural and devotional outlook, as a centre for the translation into Latin of Greek hagiographical texts and for the growing cult of the Virgin Mary.

The cultural and particularly the devotional influence of these major south Italian houses and cities had already been felt in England during the early Anglo-Saxon period to a considerable extent.

II. THE FACTUAL EVIDENCE FOR CONTACT

The earliest contacts of the Anglo-Saxon Church with the Continent, apart from those with Rome itself, were with southern Italy in the seventh century. The arrival of Archbishop Theodore and Abbot Hadrian, one Greek and the other from North Africa, had momentous consequences for the development of Anglo-Saxon culture, spirituality, and art. The school founded by the two prelates at Canterbury taught Greek and was more celebrated than those of the Irish for the quality and breadth of its learning, according to Bede and Aldhelm.[17] From a devotional point of view, it is probable that at least one cult popular in Naples found its way into English devotions, that of St Mary the Egyptian. Its presence in liturgical books, combined with the knowledge of the seventh-century Greek Life by Sophronius well before the tenth century, when it became popular in the Latin West, points to Theodore and Hadrian as the instigators of the cult, as well as the channels through which hagiographical, as well as classical, patristic, and disciplinary texts reached England.[18] One such text may have been the bilingual copy of the Acts of the Apostles, used by Bede, which came to England from Italy around the beginning of the eighth century.[19] Hadrian's influence on English devotions is made obvious by the introduction of Neapolitan feasts in two lists, one preceding the Gospel

a Napoli nell'alto medioevo (Naples, 1961), 23–4, 30, 35–52, 137–51; N. Cilento, *Civiltà napoletana del Medioevo nel secoli VI-XIII* (Naples, 1969); J. M. Sansterre, *Les Moines grecs et orientaux à Rome aux époques byzantine et carolingienne (milieu du* VI*ᵉ siècle–fin du* IX*ᵉ siècle)* (Brussels, 1983); and M. Lapidge, 'The School of Theodore and Hadrian', *ASE* 15 (1986), 45–72.

[17] *BHE* 332–5; and Aldhelm, 'Letter to Ecfrith', in M. Lapidge and M. Herren (trs.), *Aldhelm. The Prose Works* (Cambridge, 1979), 160–3, esp. 163. On the south Italian background of this school, see A. Guillou, 'L'École dans l'Italie byzantine', *Culture et société en Italie byzantine* (VI–XI*ᵉ siècle*) (London, 1978), 299–301.

[18] Fuiano, *Cultura*, 131–51.

[19] Oxford, Bodleian Library Laud. gr. 35, dating from the late 6th or early 7th century; on this and on Theodore, see C. Mango, 'La Culture grecque et l'Occident au VIII*ᵉ* siècle', *Settimane*, 20 (1973), 685–90.

of Mark in the Lindisfarne Gospels, and one in an eighth-century Gospel-book from Southumbria; other manuscripts of English origin, the Echternach Gospels, the calendar of Willibrord, and the Gospels of Burchardt in Würzburg, also show links with the Neapolitan liturgy, as does the division in *capitula* of the Lindisfarne Gospels, according to the use of Naples.[20] Also from the south of Italy comes the inspiration for some of the illumination found in Insular Northumbrian manuscripts: one such link is known to us through one of the illuminations of the Bible pandect now known as the Codex Amiatinus, written at Jarrow under the abbacy of Ceolfrid, who took it, with other manuscripts, to offer to the pope on his last Roman pilgrimage.[21] This illumination of the prophet Ezra composing his work has been shown by art historians to have been inspired by a similar illustration in a manuscript of Cassiodorus, produced at his monastic foundation of Vivarium.[22] Similarly, the sources for the Evangelist portraits in both the Lindisfarne Gospels and the Copenhagen Gospels, in particular that of Matthew, are to be found in south Italian manuscripts of the Cassiodoran type, just as the text of the Lindisfarne Gospels was copied from a Neapolitan archetype.[23]

Of equal importance during the late seventh and eighth century were the north Italian centres on the route to Rome, where pilgrims stopped and spent some time. By far the most famous of these was Pavia, at the time at the peak of its glory as the capital of the Lombard kingdom, especially during the eighth century under King Liutprand (712–44). Among the pilgrims having stayed there, we know of Bishop Wilfrid, collector of books and relics in Rome but probably also elsewhere, who was in Pavia.[24] We hear incidentally of two princesses who died there, Eadburgh wife of King Beorhtric of Wessex, driven away from England for her crime of murdering him; and Aethelswith, sister of King Alfred, on her way to Rome in 888.[25] Boniface also spent some time in Pavia, enough to be able to realize that a number of local prostitutes were of Anglo-Saxon origin.[26] It is no coincidence that the first to mention the

[20] Fuiano, *La cultura*, 28–9, and G. Morin, 'La Liturgie de Naples au temps de St Grégoire d'après deux évangéliaires du VIIe siècle', *RB* 8 (1891), 481–93, 529–37.

[21] *Bedae Vita Abbatum*, 402.

[22] On this MS, see J. J. G. Alexander (ed.), *Insular Manuscripts: Sixth to the Ninth Century* (London, 1978), 32–5, and G. B. de Rossi, *La Bibbia offerta da Ceolfrido Abbate al sepolcro di San Pietro* (Rome, 1887).

[23] R. L. S. Bruce-Mitford, 'The Sources of the Evangelist Portraits' and T. J. Brown, 'The Origin of the Latin Text', in T. D. Kendrick et al. (eds.), *Evangeliorum Quattuor Codex Lindisfarnensis* (2 vols.; Olten, 1960), ii. 142–57, 47–58.

[24] *Life of Wilfrid*, 54–5.

[25] *Asser*, 14; *ASC*, C889 = 888, 53.

[26] E. Emerton (ed.), *The Letters of St Boniface* (New York, 1940), letter 62, addressed to Archbishop Cuthbert of Canterbury, 140.

translation of the relics of St Augustine of Hippo from Sardinia to Pavia by Liutprand, was Bede.[27] These relics, given to Pavia's most famous abbey, possibly founded and at any rate enriched by Liutprand, San Pietro in Ciel d'Oro, together with the tomb of Boethius in the crypt of the church, were to become one of the main attractions of the city throughout the Middle Ages.[28] Other churches in the ex-capital of the Lombards were dedicated to St Mary (nine, of which four were nunneries), the Saviour, and, in order of foundation, SS Gervase and Protasius, SS Nazarius and Celsus, St Eusebius, St John (two), St Ambrose, St Peter (three, one of which was attached to a hospital), St Agatha, St Romanus, St Hadrian, St Gregory, St Sabinus, St Felix, St Stephen, St Michael (three), St Germanus, St Pontianus, St Marinus, St Tecla, St Thomas, St Columbanus, St Pancras, St Laurence, St Maurice, St Romulus, St Victor (two), St Christina (two), St Euplius, St Quiricus, St Mostiola, St James, St George, St Theodore, St Vitus, St Maiolus, and St Martin.[29] Of these four were abbeys for monks and nine were nunneries. Anglo-Saxon pilgrims may have stayed at the *xenodochium* of Sta Maria *Brittonorum*, founded in 868. Not far was the famous abbey of Nonantola, which possessed several churches in Pavia itself. Other important monasteries also had churches belonging to them in Pavia: Bobbio, St Martin's of Tours, Sant'Ambrogio in Milan, and Cluny, as did some of the neighbouring episcopal sees. In 924, Pavia was devastated by one of the worst Hungarian attacks on the Western world, narrated by Liutprand and by other Continental writers such as Flodoard, who described the city as 'populosissima [. . .] atque opulentissima⟨m⟩' and spoke of 'opes periere innumerabiles, aecclesiae XLIIII succensae'.[30] By the end of the century, it had fully recovered and was once again not only economically prosperous, but also still a great political capital under the Ottonians; in 990 both Empresses Adelheid and Theophano were briefly in residence at Pavia, probably in the old palace

---

[27] D. Hurst (gen. ed.) (based on C. W. Jones), 'De Temporum Ratione Liber LXVI: Chronica Maiore seu de Sex Aetatibus Mundi', *Bedae Venerabilis Opera* (Turnhout, 1977), 532.

[28] On the abbey and its relics, see A. Addeo, *Pavia e Sant'Agostino* (Pavia, 1950). The probably 12th-c. church of St Augustine Papey was named after the Pavian abbey, see Brooke and Keir, *London*, 141. Interestingly, the only representation of Boethius as a saint is found in a MS from Fleury, of the last quarter of the 10th c., illuminated by an Anglo-Saxon artist, now Paris, Bibliothèque Nationale MS lat. 6401, fo. 158ᵛ, reproduced in *Golden Age*, 64.

[29] B. Ward-Perkins, *From Classical Antiquity to the Middle Ages; Urban Public Buildings in Northern and Central Italy* (Oxford, 1984), App. II, 244–5; D. Bullough, 'Urban Change in Early Medieval Italy: The Example of Pavia', *Papers of the British School at Rome*, 34 (1966), 82–130; P. Hudson, 'Pavia: L'evoluzione urbanistica di una capitale altomedioevale', in *Storia di Pavia*, a cura della Banca del Monte di Lombardia (Milan, 1987), ii: *L'alto medioevo*, 237–315; id., *Archeologia urbana e programmazione della ricerca: L'esempio di Pavia* (Florence, 1981), 23–32, 63–6.

[30] *Liutprand*, 74–7; *Flodoard*, 924.

of Theodoric, later restored by Otto III.[31] In the eleventh century, the schools of Pavia, where Lanfranc probably studied, were particularly renowned for the study of the trivium, as Liège and Reims were for the quadrivium from the third quarter of the tenth century onwards.[32]

Pilgrims also stopped at Lucca, the two most notable among them having been the two brothers Willibald and Winnibald with their father, on their way to Rome about 720.[33] The father died in Lucca and was buried there in S. Frediano, whilst the sons continued their pilgrimage as far as the Holy Land. But the tomb of this pilgrim, together with the Volto Santo, remained the two highlights of the stay in Lucca for English pilgrims of subsequent centuries. Lucca [34] was a major crossroads, where most pilgrimage routes met, and was already then fighting against Pisa to preserve this advantage, since Pisa was attempting to attract more traffic to herself; it had already begun to develop its trade in precious stuffs since the 980s.[35] Lucca had a great many churches and monasteries, the most important of which were the church of SS Vincenzo e Frediano, which possessed the relics of the patron saint of the city, St Fredianus, and the cathedral San Martino. In the cathedral were kept the relics of St Regulus and the Volto Santo, and the apse mosaic depicted Christ enthroned and the Four Rivers. Other churches within the city were dedicated to various saints, apart from those under the patronage of the Saviour and the Virgin. Among these, the most popular were St Peter's, St Michael's, and St George's, given to Monte Cassino to become a monastery in 1056, whilst SS Pantaleon, Julia, Romanus, and Alexandrus represent less common dedications, as do those to SS Columbanus, Donatus and Gervasius and Protasius for the suburban churches outside the walls of the city. Out of these churches, many were monastic, some belonging to St Peter's in Rome and one to Monte Cassino, four at least had *xenodochia* and hospices attached to them, of which San Silvestro was the most popular since 720. The most prestigious attraction of the city was the image known as the *Volto Santo*, a Byzantine crucifix which may have reached the city in the eighth century, and was greatly venerated as a miraculous image and

---

[31] On Pavia's economic and political role, see A. A. Settia, 'Pavia carolingia e postcarolingia', in *Storia di Pavia*, 69–158, esp. 95–8.

[32] On the schools of Pavia, see M. Gibson, *Lanfranc of Bec* (Oxford, 1978), 11–15.

[33] Talbot, *Missionaries*, 157–8; on this trip, see also H. Schwarzmaier, *Lucca und das Reich bis zum Ende des 11. Jahrhunderts* (Tübingen, 1972), 33.

[34] On Lucca, see I. Belli Barsali, 'La topografia di Lucca nei secoli VIII–X', *Atti del 5. Congresso Internazionale di Studi sull'Alto Medioevo (Lucca)* (Spoleto, 1973), 461–554; Ward-Perkins, *From Classical Antiquity*, App. II, 245–9; and Schwarzmaier, *Lucca*, 19–70, 335–411.

[35] F. P. Magoun Jr., 'An English Pilgrim Diary of the Year 990', *Mediaeval Studies*, 2 (1940), 239; see also D. J. Osheim, *An Italian Lordship: The Bishopric of Lucca in the Late Middle Ages* (Berkeley, 1977), 1–12; Lestocquoy, 'The Tenth Century', in *Études*, 43.

admired by pilgrims, particularly from the eleventh century onwards.[36] A sign of early Anglo-Saxon presence in Lucca was the church of San Dalmazio, first mentioned in 771 and sold in 782 to *Adaltruda*, the daughter of King Aethelwald Moll of Northumbria.[37]

Strong links with Pavia are attested for our two centuries. The tenth-century bishop of London Theodred travelled to Rome through Pavia, where he bought several church vestments and possibly also books, which he bequeathed to a countryman and a fellow priest in his will of *c*.951.[38] In the early eleventh century, the Archbishop of Canterbury Aethelnoth also made a purchase at Pavia, this time of relics from the body of St Augustine, an arm which he offered to Coventry on his return.[39] Other items than purely religious ones could be bought in Pavia, since a law-text mentions the presence of English merchants trading in wool and horses in the city on a regular basis.[40]

Before arriving at Pavia, Anglo-Saxon travellers went through Aosta, whose main church and hospice were dedicated to St Ursus and where several *sceattas* and pennies of the eighth and ninth centuries have been found.[41] Vercelli, a city important enough for the pope to hold a council there in 1050, attended by the bishop of Dorchester Ulf, also had Irish connections and a church dedicated to St Eusebius, while the *hospitale scottorum*, attached to a church of St Brigid and documented in the eleventh century, may have already existed in the tenth.[42] The presence of Anglo-Saxon pilgrims at Vercelli is further confirmed by the existence of the Old English collection of poetical and homiletical texts left there some time in the eleventh century, known as the Vercelli Book.[43] Pilgrims travelled through Ivrea too, whose links were also with St Ursus, to whom the

---

[36] On the problems relating to the dating of the relic, see Schwarzmaier, *Lucca*, 337–68, and D. M. Webb, 'The Holy Face of Lucca', *Anglo-Norman Studies*, 9 (1986), 227–37.

[37] Belli Barsali, 'Topografia', 528, and Schwarzmaier, *Lucca*, 32. The 'Aethelbald of Mercia' mentioned in the Italian charter was probably Aethelwald Moll usurping King of Mercia (759–65/6 then again 774–81). Alcuin had close links with this family and, since we know the date of his meeting with Charlemagne in Pavia to have been precisely 782, it is quite possible that he was there as an escort for Adeltruda/Aethelthryth, this king's daughter.

[38] See above, ch. 1.

[39] *WMGR* i. 224.

[40] A. Hofmeister (ed.), *Instituta Regalia . . . Camerae Regum Longobardorum*, MGH SS xxx(2), 1452.

[41] Tommasini, *Irish Saints*, 271–2; *La Moneta dall'antichità ad oggi*, pub. by Regione Val d'Aosta and the Circolo Numismatico Valdostano (Aosta, 1984), and M. Orlandi, *Antiche monete in Val d'Aosta* (Aosta, 1983), 110–12. I am grateful to Mr. J. Rivolin, Keeper of the Archives in Aosta, for these references.

[42] L. Gougaud, 'Sur les routes de Rome et du Rhin avec les 'peregrini' insulaires', *Revue d'histoire ecclésiastique*, 29(1) (1933), 257.

[43] See above, ch. 1 n. 33.

church and hospice were dedicated.[44] Further south, Lucca also remained a major stop and an eleventh-century pilgrim, the abbot of Bury Leofstan (1044–65), spent enough time there to be so impressed by the Volto Santo as to have it used as a model for the great rood he had made for the church of Bury on his return. The next abbot of that abbey, Baldwin, also stopped at Lucca in 1071, bringing with him relics of St Edmund, which he left to the cathedral; an altar was dedicated to this saint there and later, a confraternity established with Bury.[45] Various other towns, abbeys, and hospices are mentioned by the most informative of all itineraries to Rome, that of Sigeric, such as Luni in Liguria, Siena, Bolsena, and Viterbo, and possible effects of the pilgrims' stays there can be observed in an indirect manner from specific devotional or artistic innovations in late Anglo-Saxon England, as will be shown below.

Contacts with Italy were carried out in other ways too. Linking the north of Italy and the Greek south, we find evidence in Goscelin's Life of St Ivo for the presence of a pilgrim from Venice at Ramsey i, the eleventh century.[46] Another Italian, the bishop of Benevento, came to England about 1020–35, as part of a fund-raising campaign through Europe, to collect alms for his city stricken by famine, and he sold to Queen Emma a relic of the arm of St Bartholomew, which she then donated to Christ Church; in return, he was offered as a present a cope embroidered in the style of the *opus anglicanum*.[47] Other Englishmen went to southern Italy. The chronicle of Monte Cassino mentions an English goldsmith working at the abbey at the time of Abbot Desiderius, and English embroiderers were highly regarded there, as they were on the Continent in general.[48] In 1085, when he lost all hope of regaining the English throne, the aetheling Edgar took refuge in Apulia.[49] In 1095, a monk of Christ Church,

[44] Tommasini, *Irish Saints*, 275. A sacramentary, written and illuminated *c.*1000 at Ivrea, now Ivrea, Biblioteca Capitolare cod. LXXXVI, ed. L. Magnani, *Le miniature dell'Sacramentario d'Ivrea e di altri codici warmondiani* (Rome, 1934), has several iconographical motifs in common with some early 11th-c. English MSS, which is especially interesting since the bishop who commissioned it, Warmund, was a near contemporary of Sigeric.

[45] *Registrum Album Monasterii S. Edmundi* in British Library, Additional MS 14.847, fo. 21; Arnold, *Memorials of St Edmund*, 68. See Schwarzmaier, *Lucca*, p. 397–9.

[46] *Chronicon Rameseiensis*, p. lxvii.

[47] Rule, *Eadmer*, 107–10. At an earlier time, one of the churches of Benevento, St Sophia's, is alleged to have provided some inspiration for the church of the Holy Wisdom at York in the 8th c., see R. Morris, 'Alcuin, York and the *alma Sophia*', in L. A. S. Butler and R. K. Morris (eds.), *The Anglo-Saxon Church* (Cambridge, 1986), 83–4. If the church was known in England, Rome would provide the link, but the model for the York church is surely more likely to have been the church of Justinian in Constantinople.

[48] *Chronica monasterii casinensis*, 712; on the taste for English ornaments, see Foreville, *William of Poitiers*, 224–5, who mentions such ornaments 'quae Byzantium percara haberet' being sent to Pope Alexander II.

[49] *Florence*, ii. 19.

Aethelwine, when going on a pilgrimage to the Holy Land, travelled through Apulia and presumably crossed by sea from Bari to Jerusalem, as could have done numerous other pilgrims who had chosen the sea-route, possibly Ulf and Madselin in 1066–8.[50] Also at the end of the century, the monk Eadmer from Christ Church went to Bari with Archbishop Anselm, to attend the council of 1098. At Bari, he was pleasantly surprised to see one of the other prelates wear an English cope, which he assumed from its design and workmanship to be that offered to the bishop of Benevento.[51] By the twelfth century, frequent political and personal links developed between England and southern Italy and Sicily, both ruled by a Norman aristocracy and kings.

III. CULTURAL EXCHANGES BETWEEN ENGLAND AND ITALY

These exchanges were carried out through the circulation of manuscripts and through that of people. By tradition, Italian manuscripts such as the model for the Codex Amiatinus, and English manuscripts such as the Codex Amiatinus itself, were brought over or sent from one country to the other. In the same way, two English liturgical manuscripts, a Christ Church Gospel-book of the first half of the eleventh century and a Gospel lectionary of *c*.1050, seem to have reached respectively Monte Cassino and Florence by the end of the eleventh century, not long after their composition.[52] Another manuscript found its way to Vercelli, probably in some pilgrim's bag, for reasons still unknown. Vercelli was a city of quite considerable significance during the eleventh century, since a papal council took place there, and it catered for pilgrims, in particular Irish and English pilgrims, on a large scale, since the founder of its main hospice in the seventh century, St Eusebius, was deemed to have been an Irishman. A few other manuscripts are known to have reached England during the course of this century, a fly leaf or a perhaps complete mass-book from Nonantola, the Farfa Codex, and an eighth-century copy of Juvencus. A late ninth-century collection comprising works by Augustine, Ambrose, Cassiodorus, Ebbo of Metz, and Halitgar of Cambrai, written in the north of Italy, reached Brittany or Wales first and was in England at the beginning of the eleventh century.[53]

[50] Stubbs, *Memorials*, 245–6; Whitelock, *Anglo-Saxon Wills*, 95.

[51] Rule, *Eadmer*, 107–10.

[52] These are now Monte Cassino Library MS 437–9 and Florence, Biblioteca Medicea Laurenziana MS Pluteo XIV.20, cf. Temple, *ASM*, nos. 95, 69.

[53] Rella, 'Continental', nos. 4, 27.

Not far from Vercelli is Aosta, which was not only a stop on the pilgrimage route, but also the birth place of one of the greatest prelates and theologians of the time, Anselm, abbot of Bec in Normandy, then archbishop of Canterbury.[54] His predecessor in the see of Canterbury had also been an Italian from Pavia, Lanfranc, educated in the newly developing law schools of northern Italy.[55]

It is very likely that some of the new eleventh-century movements of monastic reform and eremitism pervasive in the north and central Italy, associated with the names of St Romuald at Camaldoli, St Peter Damian at Fonteavellana and St John Gualbert at Vallombrosa, were at least known in England, although there is no direct evidence available to confirm this supposition. Some evidence exists to show that there were hermits in Anglo-Saxon England. Several seem to have been associated with Evesham: Wulfsige, a layman from Crowland in the eleventh century, was given permission by the prior to become a hermit near Evesham, and it was from this abbey that the movement of refounding of Northumbrian monasteries at Jarrow, Wearmouth, and Whitby in 1073–4 was instigated by the monks Aldwin, Reinfrid, and Aelfwig.[56] The other two hermits of the eleventh century were attached to the abbeys closest to Evesham, Worcester and Ramsey: Mantat, who lived near Worcester, and Whythman, once abbot of Ramsey, who left it to retire to a hermitage.[57] Whythman may have been a German, and both Evesham and Worcester had strong links with the Lotharingian world through Wulfstan and the circle of foreign bishops in the west of England. Lotharingia was one of the areas where the new eremitic trends were extremely active, around foundations at Liège, Affligem in Cambrai under the aegis of the archbishop of Cologne, and at least one hermit was living near Trier, of whom St Norbert himself had been a disciple.[58] The link with the Italian movements could have been a direct one, or a roundabout one, via Lotharingia or via the Ottonian court, where Otto III had close links with the reformers, whose disciples were his spiritual advisers; and Queen Margaret of Scotland, together with her brother and sisters, had been brought up in the circle of the Empress Agnes, particularly close to John of Fécamp and Peter Damian.[59] Margaret was very keen for Lanfranc to

[54] Anselm's biography was written by Eadmer, see Southern, *Vita Anselmi*, 3.

[55] *Orderic*, ii. 248–9; the most recent biography is by Gibson, *Lanfranc*.

[56] *Chronicon Evesham*, 322; *Symeon*, 108–13; on this, see H. Leyser, *Hermits and the New Monasticism* (London, 1984), 13, 36.

[57] Whitelock, *Anglo-Saxon Wills*, 66–7; *Chronicon Rameseiensis*, 125.

[58] Leyser, *Hermits*, 35–6.

[59] On the links of Agnes of Poitou with Peter Damian, see Cowdrey, *Age*, 17–19, 34–6, and J. Leclecq, *St Pierre Damien ermite et homme d'Église* (Rome, 1960), 127–30; and of Agnes with John of Fécamp, see J. Leclercq and J-P. Bonnes, *Un maître de la vie spirituelle au XIe siècle: Jean de Fécamp* (Paris, 1946), 18, 211–17.

be her spiritual father in her later life.[60] At any rate, it seems highly likely that not only specific customs but also some of the monastic ideals of Fruttuaria may have reached England, since the reform of William of Volpiano was implemented in several places where Englishmen were frequent visitors: at the abbey of Siegburg in Cologne, at Dijon, in Normandy at Fécamp, and, through Abbot Suppo of Fruttuaria, at Mont St Michel, in the second half of the eleventh century. Lanfranc had spent some time at Mont St Michel when Suppo was abbot there, and the customs of Bec were based on those of Fruttuaria, even though the *Monastic Constitutions* themselves were much closer to the customary of Cluny.[61] One of the main leaders of the reform in France was the nephew of William of Volpiano, who had come with his uncle from Fruttuaria: John of Ravenna later known as John of Fécamp, reformer, theologian and spiritual master, abbot of St Bénigne at Dijon between 1052 and 1054 and of Fécamp from 1028 to his death in 1078.[62] John visited England in 1054, where Fécamp owned some land, and met then King Edward, who gave him presents.[63] Some of the themes put forward by the spiritual reform in Italy: the ideal of the *vita apostolica* of the primitive Church, poverty, charity, private devotion, and penitential asceticism, together with the contemplative, mystical and eremitical spirituality of love and grace and personal communion with God, which appear in England in the eleventh century, may have been reinforced by the Italian trends. Anselm's spirituality was certainly close in its contemplative and christological style to that exemplified by John of Fécamp.[64] However, these traditions had already been present in English spirituality previously, often without links with eremitic movements. These were not of major consequence in England before the end of the eleventh century; for example, the concept of charity in the Life of Edward the Confessor is a royal attribute, and one of the most characteristically eremitical cults of that century, that of St Mary Magdalene, was not successful on that account in English texts, but on account of being a Gospel cult.[65] We can be at least certain that some of these ideals of personal conversion were highly regarded at the Norman court at the end of the century from the veneration and respect shown by

[60] Gibson, *Lanfranc*, 127; cf. Lanfranc's letter to her, ed. in Clover and Gibson, *Letters*, no. 50, pp. 160–3.

[61] Gibson, *Lanfranc*, 20–1, 27.

[62] Leclercq and Bonnes, *Un maître*, 14–19.

[63] Ibid. 14.

[64] G. R. Evans, 'Mens Devota: The Literary Community of the Devotional Works of John of Fécamp and St Anselm', *Medium Aevum*, 43 (1974), 105–15.

[65] The earliest version of the story of Edward's charity to the beggar is in an addition to the *Vita* by Osbert de Clare, see M. Bloch, 'Vie de S. Edouard', 124–8, but the story appears to have been based on an earlier tradition, see F. Barlow, *Edward the Confessor* (London, 1970), 273–4; on Mary Magdalene, see ch. 7.

William and Mathilda in particular towards one of the most representative among the leaders of the new eremitic trend, the nobleman Simon of Crépy.[66] Mathilda sent valuable presents to Simon's tomb in Rome and his monastic conversion had made a great impression on the whole aristocratic milieu of northern France.[67] The spirituality of Anselm was clearly linked with these devotional developments, but cannot be said to have initiated them; Thomas Bestul has shown, in a remarkable article, that Anselm's prayers are to be seen within a long-standing Anglo-Saxon tradition of a subjective, emotional emphasis on the sufferings of Christ, the notions of personal sin, tears, compunction, and love, and devotion to the Virgin Mary, already found in the eighth-century prayer-books of Cerne and Nunnaminster, which exerted considerable influence in Europe as late as the eleventh century.[68] While doubtless corresponding to the mood of the period, as we see it in the meditations of John of Fécamp and Maurilius of Rouen, for example, Anselm's prayers clearly show, in their composition, vocabulary and preoccupations, a close link with the Anglo-Saxon tradition of piety, influential in both northern Italy and Normandy.

IV. LITURGICAL AND DEVOTIONAL EXCHANGES BETWEEN ENGLAND AND ITALY

One notes with surprise that in terms of liturgical borrowings as such, there is little Italian influence in English books, if we leave aside the Roman one. The cults of some major saints of the Church may well have been reinforced in England on account of their general popularity in the West and in Italy, as in the case of Martin, Michael, Benedict, Mary the Egyptian, John the Baptist, and the Greek Fathers (especially Basil), venerated respectively in Lucca, the Sagra and Monte Gargano, Monte Cassino, Naples and the south of Italy. Some of these cults had probably been introduced into England in the seventh and eighth centuries, Michael's from Gargano and Rome directly or via Ireland, and Mary the Egyptian's from Naples by Theodore and Hadrian.

St Michael was probably the most popular of the great saints in England, after St Peter; not only the liturgy, but also other texts confirm this

---

[66] H. E. J. Cowdrey, 'Count Simon of Crépy's Monastic Conversion' (forthcoming). I am grateful to Mr Cowdrey for having drawn my attention to this matter and for allowing me to read the proofs of this article.

[67] Ibid.

[68] T. H. Bestul, 'St Anselm and the Continuity of Anglo-Saxon Devotional Traditions', *Annuale medievale*, 18 (1977), 20–41; such Anglo-Irish influence is found, for example, in the prayer-book of Bishop Arnulph of Milan (988–1018).

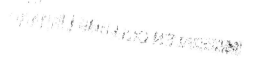

popularity: some of the late Anglo-Saxon homilies, one by Aelfric, and one in the Blickling set, celebrating only the greatest feasts of the year.[69] This tradition of veneration can be traced back to the beginning of the English Church and to its Irish background.[70] The Archangel was highly venerated in Ireland from the sixth or seventh century onwards, when the first, and later renowned, monastery of Sceilig Mhichil was dedicated to him. Hymns and prayers were also composed for him in the eighth century, and the cult was reinforced in the eleventh century as the dedications of churches, the *Second Vision of Adomnan* and various homilies demonstrate. It is probable that St Wilfrid's vision of the Archangel at Meaux, when he was about to die, was linked with his Irish training at Lindisfarne, however much the romanizing bishop was attempting to discard it, rather than with an Italian source. Ultimately, however, in England as well as in the rest of Europe, it is to Italy that we must turn to find the origin of the cult, and beyond Italy to the Egyptian and Greek East, since the devotion reached Ireland itself through this channel.[71] The two distinct facets of St Michael's personality were the 'general of the heavenly armies' and the 'chief of the legions of angels', as Dionysius described him, and the guide of the souls of the dead, to be weighed by him at the Last Judgement. While various elements of the cult, such as the Fight with the Dragon and the Weighing of the Souls, may, as has been suggested, have had Egyptian and Persian origins, the Christian St Michael, whose cult developed first in the Byzantine world, was associated above all with the Book of Revelation, a text which had an immense impact on the Early Christian and medieval world. From Byzantium, where the Emperor Constantine built the first known church dedicated to the Archangel, the cult spread to Greek Italy, and secured permanent recognition through the apparition of the Arch-

---

[69] Aelfric's in Thorpe, *Homilies*, i. 502–19; Morris, *Blickling*, 196–211. In another homily by Aelfric, he is associated with the departed souls and intercession in the Other World, see the homily on the Vision of the Departing Souls in Pope, *Homilies*, ii. 775–80. He is again associated with intercession on Judgement Day, together with the Virgin and St Peter, in the *Vercelli Homily XV*, see Förster, *Vercelli Homilien*, 100–21.

[70] On the Irish cult, see H. M. Roe, 'Ireland and the Archangel Michael', in M. Baudot (ed.), *Millénaire monastique du Mont Saint-Michel*, iii (Paris, 1971), 481–7.

[71] On the eastern sources of the cult, see A. Baumstark, *Comparative Liturgy* (tr. London, 1958), 137, and P. du Bourgnet, 'Origines lointaines d'images de Saint Michel', in Baudot, *Millénaire*, 37–8. O. Chadwick, 'The Evidence of Dedications in the Early History of the Welsh Church', in N. K. Chadwick (ed.), *Studies in Early British History* (Cambridge, 1954), 182–4, offered another interpretation, saying that the cult did not reach England from the Celtic world but was brought by the Roman missionaries from Italy and that it is wrong to trace it from Gaul to Ireland and then to England. But he did not seem to envisage the possibility of an early direct link between Ireland and the south of Italy, from where the cult seems to have travelled. I am grateful to Dr H. Mayr-Harting for having drawn my attention to this paper.

angel in a grotto on the summit of Monte Gargano, where a church was subsequently built and consecrated on 8 May 492.[72]

Two churches followed at Rome, one being the sixth-century basilica on the Via Salaria, dedicated on 29 September, and the other in the Mausoleum of Hadrian, as a result of an apparition of St Michael foretelling the end of the plague, famine, and Lombard attacks on the city. From this time onwards, under the impact of the two apparitions of Monte Gargano and Rome, the echoes of which reached as far as Ireland, the cult developed in a spectacular manner throughout Italy in the sixth and seventh centuries. From Italy and, possibly, various other locations such as Lérins, it reached Ireland, whence it was then brought to England. Apart from Eddius, Bede also mentions the cult at Hexham, Wilfrid's church, where a cemetery chapel dedicated to the Archangel existed at the time of St John of Beverley, while another such chapel seems to have been in existence in the eleventh century at Lichfield.[73] Both the Book of Cerne and the Book of Nunnaminster, written under Irish influence, have prayers addressed to St Michael, and the cult became relatively important in the eighth century on the Anglo-Welsh border. The mixture of the Irish and Italian influences in England promoted the devotion in the early Anglo-Saxon period but, according to Olga Rojdestvensky, it was mostly the Anglo-Irish influence which was responsible for the development of the cult in Carolingian Europe, culminating in the foundation of various monasteries by Irish monks, the most prestigious of which was to become Mont St Michel.[74] The Carolingians developed the cult, not only as a result of the Irishman John Scot Eriugena's translation of Dionysius, but also under the influence of Bede's martyrology and later, of Alcuin, who was asked to compose a variety of liturgical forms, establishing the cult as a major component of the Carolingian imperial idea. The Archangel was a patron saint of Carolingian kings and the numerous dedications to him show his popularity.[75] First in the wake of the Anglo-Saxon missionaries, then as a Carolingian heritage, the cult moved to Germany, where the Ottonian Emperors also used it by placing themselves under the Archangel's patronage, as witnessed, for example, by the legend of Henry II's

---

[72] On the beginnings of the cult in the West, see M. Baudot, 'St Michel dans la liturgie chrétienne' and 'Origine du culte de St Michel', in Baudot, *Millénaire*, 23–7, 15–22; also O. Rojdestvenski, *Le culte de St Michel et le Moyen Âge latin* (Paris, 1922), 6–28.

[73] On the early history of the English cult, see R. Finberg, 'The Archangel Michael in Britain', in Baudot, *Millénaire*, 459–69, and Rojdestvenski, *Le Culte*, 18–28.

[74] Rojdestvenski, *Le Culte*, 26–33.

[75] Ibid. 29, and M. Baudot, 'Saint-Michel dans la légende médiévale', in Baudot, *Millénaire*, 34; also M. Baudot, 'Diffusion et évolution du culte de St Michel en France', in Baudot, *Millénaire*, 109–12.

vision on Monte Gargano.[76] Meanwhile, the cult found another centre in the west of France, at Mont St Michel, refounded by Bishop Avitus of Avranches in 966 and dedicated on 16 October.[77] The devotion to the Archangel became important for the Normans and increased when they conquered the south of Italy and took possession of Monte Gargano, thus uniting under the same authority the by then two most famous centres of the cult in Europe.

The main festival of St Michael was 29 September, already entered in the Leonine Sacramentary as the date of the dedication of the Roman basilica on the Via Salaria. Gradually, the dedications of Monte Gargano and the chapel in Hadrian's Mausoleum also came to be celebrated on that date.[78] The English early tenth-century verse martyrology also enters 8 May, the correct date of the Monte Gargano dedication, since the legend was well known and very popular in Ireland, as is demonstrated by the account of it in several Irish homilies. But the liturgical offices in England are different from those of both Mont St Michel and the second great centre of St Michael's cult, in northern Italy, San Michele della Chiusa or Sagra di San Michele, the Piedmontese abbey.[79]

The 29 September feast appears in all calendars, with liturgical distinctions whenever the calendars use them. Liturgical celebrations exist for this feast alone, the most important being the masses in all sacramentaries, to which are added part of the gradual in the missal of St Augustine's and numerous tropes in both tropers. Three or four hymns are given in the hymnals and one or two benedictions in the benedictionals. The office is given in its entirety in all three collectars and is particularly detailed in Leofric's.[80] St Michael is not only the most important figure in Heaven after Christ on the Day of Judgement, which accounts for his presence in the litanies immediately after Christ and the Virgin Mary, but also the most popular saint after St Peter in devotional prayers. He is invoked after the Virgin Mary, and before St Peter and St Andrew, in the prayers at the end of the psalter in the Bury Psalter, and is the only saint to be mentioned

[76] Rojdestvenki, *Le Culte*, 35–43.

[77] J. Laporte, 'L'abbaye du Mont Saint-Michel aux xᵉ et xiᵉ siècles', in Laporte, *Millénaire*, 53–80. Mont St Michel claimed to possess as relics the sword and shield of the Archangel, see J. Dubois, 'Le Trésor des reliques de l'abbaye du Mont Saint-Michel', in Laporte, *Millénaire*, 578.

[78] Baudot, 'Diffusion', 111.

[79] J. Lemarié, 'Textes relatifs au culte de l'Archange et des Anges dans les bréviaires manuscrits du Mont-Saint-Michel' and 'Textes liturgiques concernant St Michel', *Sacris Erudiri*, 13 and 14 (1962 and 1963), 113–52 and 277–85.

[80] It is worth noting that the benedictionals which have two benedictions are the two from St Germans and Exeter; coupled with the emphasis on the cult in Leofric's collectar, this appears to strengthen the hypothesis of a very strong cult in the Celtic areas of Britain, which is not surprising in view of the Irish connections of the cult.

in the long prayers in another mid-eleventh-century English psalter.[81] In a third psalter, Arundel 60, he is again invoked with the Virgin Mary and St Nicholas, and he heads the group of the archangels in a prayer in British Library Cotton MS Vespasian D.XII, a mid-eleventh-century Christ Church hymnal. Various prayers are addressed to him alone in five psalters, the theme of which is invariably the intercession of the saint on Domesday. Aelfric's 'Visions of the Souls' homily and the Vercelli Homily XV also recall this function of St Michael on the Day of Judgement, when he intercedes together with the Virgin Mary and St Peter.

The two themes of St Michael fighting the dragon and the Weighing of the Souls are the two representations of the Archangel in art.[82] Both have been traced back to original Egyptian motifs which reached Greece and culminated in the prototype of the Fight with the Dragon represented in a seventh-century fresco at Monte Gargano.[83] The Fight with the Dragon, based on the Book of Revelation, appeared at first as a static illustration in Byzantine art, in a seventh-century Monte Gargano icon and on the eleventh-century Byzantine bronze doors, as well as in the Menologion of Basil II.[84] It became an action scene in the north of Europe, possibly under the influence of Viking art, though the Carolingian early ninth-century Corbie Psalter already depicts it in this way.[85] Various English representations of the combat scene, in which St Michael is shown with a spear and shield, are found, for example, in the psalters Tiberius C.VI, Harleian 603, and Douce 296, and in the Wadham Gospels.[86]

[81]   Paris, Bibliothèque Nationale MS lat. 8824.

[82]   C. Lamy-Lasalle, 'Les Représentations du combat de l'Archange en France au début du Moyen-Âge', and J. Fournée, 'L'Ange de la Mort et du Jugement', in Baudot, *Millénaire*, 53–61, 66–9.

[83]   Rojdestvenski, *Le culte*, 9. The first representation of the Weighing of the Souls in the West may have been that found on a 10th-c. cross at Monasterboice in Ireland, within a series of carvings of the Last Judgement.

[84]   Rojdestvenski, *Le Culte*, 9; on the bronze doors, E. Bertaux, *L'Art dans L'Italie méridionale de la fin de l'Empire romain à la conquête de Charles d'Anjou* (2 vols.; Paris and Rome, 1903, repr. 1968), i. 408; and A. Grabar, 'La porte de bronze byzantine du Mont Gargan et le 'cycle de l'Ange''', in *L'Art du moyen-âge en Occident*, 355–61 and pls. xxxiii-xxxv; *Menologio*, i. 7–8 and ii. pl. 17. On these representations, see Lamy-Lasalle, 'Les représentations', 53–64, and Rojdestvenski, *Le Culte*, 43–5.

[85]   Boinet, *La Miniature carolingienne*, no. CXLVIII.

[86]   Tiberius C. VI, fo. 16, reproduced in Temple, *ASM*, pl. 310; see also, for example, Harleian 603, fos. 71ᵛ, 72ᵛ, 73; Bodleian Library MS Douce 296, of the mid–11th c. from Crowland, fo. 40ᵛ, and Oxford, Wadham College MS 2, of *c*.1020–31, fo. 67, which has the Byzantine static representation. The illumination in the Benedictional of St Aethelwold is now lost, see Deshman, 'Iconography', 5. This is all the more unfortunate since it would have enabled us to see whether, in this respect as in others, this MS followed the Byzantine rather than the western iconography when depicting this scene. The Byzantine iconography modelled on the representations at Monte Gargano was common in Ottonian art, for example, on the Golden Altar of Basle and in the Echternach Gospels, see Alexander, *Norman Illumination*, 87–8. On the early representations of St Michael and the dragon in English sculpture, see C. E. Keyser, 'Note on a Sculptured Tympanum at Kingswinford Church, Staffordshire, and Other Early Representations in England

The Irish and subsequent Anglo-Saxon devotion to the angels and to their leader St Michael found its way to the Continent during the early Middle Ages but remained meanwhile a deeply rooted English feature. St Michael was the first among the archangels, but all angels were venerated in England, an ancient and particularly strong cult, which can be paralleled to that of the angels in the Greek world and, beyond it, the Eastern and Old Testament traditions. The cult of St Michael belongs to these traditions, whose other main representation and prototype in the West are illustrated by the cult and pictorial expression in the south Italian Exultet Rolls.[87]

Strongly based at Monte Cassino, the cult of its founder, St Benedict, was determinedly and exclusively western. A feast of the saint on 21 March, the date of his Deposition, was already in evidence by the early eighth century. It had been probably established first in Italy, but the earliest evidence for its existence is to be found in an early eighth-century English source, the martyrology of St Willibrord, where, according to Dom J. Chapman, it was added as soon as St Augustine brought the feast to England on his conversion mission.[88] It is probable that St Augustine of Canterbury himself was devoted to St Benedict, since the archbishop had been abbot of St Andrew's on Mount Coelius, St Gregory's foundation in Rome.[89] After the Translation of St Benedict's relics to Fleury in the seventh century, the feast of the Translation was celebrated there on its original date of 4 December and then, on account of a copying mistake which spread from one monastery to another and finally infiltrated even Fleury, on 11 July. Consequently, the 4 December decreased in importance and became a rather confused celebration of either the *Tumulatio* of the saint by Abbot Mummolinus of Fleury, the instigator of the Translation, or the *Illatio*, the return of the relics after the Viking incursions. The feast of 21 March may have been the last of the three to establish itself in Gaul, while it remained the only one in Italy and in England for a considerable length of time, and was still the most important of the three even after the introduction of the other two dates.[90]

of St Michael the Archangel', *The Archaeological Journal*, 62 (1905), 137–46. There was also a representation of St Michael among the sculptures in the New Minster tower, see Birch, *Liber Vitae*, 10.

[87] M. Avery (ed.), *The Exultet Rolls of Southern Italy* (Princeton, 1936).

[88] *Calendar of St Willibrord*, 5. J. Chapman, 'À propos des martyrologes: B. Les Fêtes de St Benoît aux VII–IXᵉ siècles', *RB* 20 (1903), 295–313.

[89] The issue of the knowledge of the Rule of St Benedict in Rome in the early Middle Ages is a much-discussed one, see Ch. 5 n. 100. However, we are not talking here of the *knowledge* of the Rule itself, but of the *devotion* to St Benedict, based on Gregory's *Dialogues*.

[90] On the problems related to the feasts of St Benedict, see Chapman, 'À propos', see n. 88 above; and H. Leclercq, *St. Benoît sur Loire, les reliques, le monastère, l'église* (Paris, 1925), 21–

St Benedict's cult was among the oldest English devotions, since we find the feast of 21 March in both Willibrord's and Bede's martyrologies. The original success of the cult in England was due, to a great extent, to the popularity of Gregory's *Dialogues* and to Gregory's veneration for the saint. In view of the English devotion for Gregory the Great, any saints whom he had venerated, such as St Benedict and St Andrew, were in turn revered in England. The founder of Wearmouth took the name Benedict, and the early English devotion to the Monte Cassino saint may well have contributed to encouraging the Carolingian interest in the application of the Rule in the Empire, as the romanizing tendencies of such English ecclesiastics as Boniface and Alcuin had contributed to shaping Carolingian Church policies. The oldest copy of the Rule in existence is found in an eighth-century English manuscript, Hatton 48, in the Bodleian Library, Oxford.[91] The 21 March Deposition is in all calendars, usually strongly emphasized by means of capitals and colours, first at Winchester and Canterbury, and then everywhere else by the second half of the eleventh century. The feast of the Deposition has no Vigil in any calendar, that in the missal of Robert included, which makes it all the more surprising to note the mass for the Vigil in that book, which is the mass used in the Corbie Sacramentary of Ratold for the July Translation.

The missal uses this Ratold Mass for the Vigil and, in part, for the Deposition itself, the rest of the mass for the Deposition being borrowed from the Ratold mass for the March feast. This is the mass used by all other sacramentaries, being a particularly long one in that from Winchcombe. The gradual is given in the New Minster missal, and the feast is troped in the Winchester and Canterbury books. The office is represented solely by the four collects in Wulfstan's collectar. The considerable importance of this cult, associated in England with Monte Cassino until well into the eleventh century, when most of Western Europe came to associate it with Fleury, is underlined by the interest in another, Greek, Father of the Church, whose disciple Benedict had considered himself to be, St Basil. His name was entered in the calendars, even in capitals in that from Crowland. There are masses for him in the missal of Robert and in Giso's sacramentary, and a collect in Wulfstan's collectar. His cult had begun in the West with his entry in the martyrologies, but it was promoted

39, 60–1, 115. Among the first known Italian texts including a feast on 21 March is a Monte Cassino calendar of the end of the 8th c., see E. A. Loew, *Die ältesten Kalendarien aus Monte Cassino* (Munich, 1908), 16, and the 9th-c. Calendarium Marmoreum of Naples, ed. D. Mallardo in *Ephemerides Liturgicae*, 58–60 (1944–6), 115–77, 233–94, 217–92.

[91] D. H. Farmer (ed.), *The Rule of St Benedict: Oxford, Bodleian Library MS Hatton 48* (Copenhagen, 1968), 22–6.

more specially through the influence of Basilian monasticism in Italy, for example, at the abbey of Grottaferrata and in Rome, to which was added his prestige as a monastic founder, venerated and cited by St Benedict in his Rule.[92] It is probable that contacts with Basilian monasticism in the south of Italy and Rome contributed to maintaining this cult at a time when other Greek Fathers saw theirs fade away gradually by the end of the eleventh century, particularly after 1054.

Naples was a centre from which a variety of devotions particularly popular in the Greek world found their way into England, either directly or via Rome. In the case of Mary the Egyptian, a saint whose cult may have arrived in England with Theodore, a direct link can be seen, a link which may well have continued at a later stage, since the Greek Life of the saint by Sophronius, translated by John the Deacon in Naples, reached England by the end of the ninth century, but no other northern European countries.[93] Its success in England is well attested by the existence of at least two Lives of the saint in the vernacular, one of the ninth century, and one of the late tenth-century, ascribed to Aelfric.[94] The connection with Naples seems to be confirmed by the date of her entry in English calendars, since the usual date, after Usuard, was 2 April, whereas the ninth-century Calendarium Marmoreum of Naples has 9 April, the date found in twelve Anglo-Saxon calendars as contrasted with 2 April which is given in two. Her name appears in most calendars, except for some from Winchester, St Augustine's, Christ Church and Crowland, and thus seems to have progressed during the eleventh century. She was placed second to St Mary Magdalene in the litanies in which her name was entered. Her cult, however, was not well established in the official liturgy, since no celebrations were provided for her feast. The cult of St Mary was destined to flourish in the twelfth century, as we see from the emphasis on her name in the litanies or from the existence of two Anglo-Norman Lives, a not

---

[92] It is not impossible that St Basil's cult in England may have been increased by such contacts with basilian monasticism in Rome. However, the most probable explanation for the popularity of the saint remains St Benedict's Rule. The translation by Aelfric into Old English of some of St Basil's works confirms this supposition. Aelfric compiled a work from extracts from Basil's and Bede's works, with additions of his own, as well as translating Basil's *Admonitio*. Both are edited by H. W. Norman, *The Anglo-Saxon Version of the Hexameron of St Basil and the Saxon Remains of St Basil's 'Admonitio ad Filium Spiritualem'* (London, 1848), the Hexameron, 2–29, and the *Admonitio*, 32–55. In the latter, the author explicitly links St Basil with St Benedict (who had been devoted to the Greek bishop, as his Rule shows), 32–3.

[93] On her cult in Naples, see Fuiano, *Cultura*, 131–52.

[94] J. Earle, *Legends of St Swithun and Sancta Maria Aegyptiaca* (London, 1861), 102–13 and, possibly by Aelfric, *Lives of the saints*, ii. 2–53. On these, see K. Kunze, 'Studien zur Legende Mariae Aegyptiacae', *Philologische Studien und Quellen*, 49 (1969), 38–9; and C. Chase, 'Source Study as a Trick with Mirrors: Annihilation of Meaning in the Old English Mary of Egypt', in P. Z. Szarmach and V. Darrow Oggins (eds.), *Sources of Anglo-Saxon Culture* (Kalamazoo, 1986), 23–33, esp. 27–31.

altogether surprising evolution since she was a symbol of an eremitical life
of penance, a theme particularly cherished by twelfth-century monasticism.[95] At that date, she was not seen as a rival of St Mary Magdalene, and
was only later confused with this saint and finally absorbed into her cult.

In the same way, the tradition of inspiration from Naples is again visible
in England in our period, when cults popular in Neapolitan circles reach
this country, in particular those of various figures such as Anne, Joseph,
and Longinus, that is to say the close family of, and other people associated
with, Jesus. It could be said, therefore, that a Greek current of devotion
to the human Christ and the characters who played a part in His earthly
life, was first introduced in Anglo-Saxon piety by the Irish, who had strong
connections with the Eastern Mediterranean and Byzantium through
southern Italy and Spain, and then by Theodore and Hadrian in the
seventh and eighth century, and gave a specific and unusual tone to Anglo-
Saxon devotions, centred on the veneration for Gospel characters, both of
the recognized synoptic texts and of the most popular apocrypha, such as
the Protoevangelium of James and the Gospel of Nicodemus.[96] St Joseph's
cult started in Palestine in the fourth century, and was entered in various
Greek calendars, for example, in that of St Sabas in Palestine and in the
Menologion of Basil II, without a particular feast or date.[97] In the West,
it was first entered on 19 March in a few tenth-century calendars from
Fulda, Stavelot and Reichenau. The cult started effectively at the end of
the eleventh century, when a relic was brought back by the Crusaders from
Palestine to Chiusi, and an oratory was dedicated to the saint in the
cathedral at Parma. His entry in the five eleventh-century English
calendars, two from Winchester and three from Sherborne, Evesham, and
Worcester, as early as the 1020s at Winchester, is among the earliest in the
West, and bears witness to the enthusiasm of English monks for the

---

[95] A. T. Baker, 'Vie de Sainte Marie l'Egyptienne', *Revue des langues romanes*, 59 (1916–7),
152.

[96] On the role of eastern Mediterranean devotions known in England via Italy or Spain and
Ireland see below, ch. 6. These were possibly the most popular apocryphal texts of the Middle
Ages. They are both translated in M. R. James, *The Apocryphal New Testament* (2nd edn.; Oxford,
1953), 38–48, 94–146. An Old English copy of the Gospel of Nicodemus survives in one of
Leofric's Exeter MSS, see Förster, 'The Donations of Leofric to Exeter'. This MS is a Gospel-
book of the third quarter of the 11th c. (Cambridge, University Library MS Ii.2.11). See also
W. H. Hulme, 'The Old English Gospel of Nicodemus', *Modern Philology*, 1 (1904), 579–614.

[97] On 25 December in the Menologion, see Migne, Patrologia Graeca 117, 227–8. On the cult
of St Joseph, see J. Seitz, *Das Josephfest in der lateinischen Kirche in seiner Entwicklung bis zum
Konzil von Trient dargestellt* (Freiburg, 1908), 3–14; P. Lucot, *St Joseph, étude historique sur son
culte* (Paris, 1875) (to be used with caution); D.C.A., 'Le Développement historique du culte de
St Joseph', *RB* 14 (1897), 104–14; R. des Fourmeils, *St Joseph, son culte en France, en Palestine
et à Rome* (Paris, 1912); J. Duserre, *Les Origines de la dévotion à St Joseph* (Montreal, 1954); and
P. Grosjean, 'La Prétendue origine irlandaise du culte de St Joseph en Occident', *AB* 72 (1954),
357–62.

increasing cult of the Holy Family. Longinus, identified with the lance-bearer of the Crucifixion and subsequently with the Church, as the sponge-bearer Stephaton was identified with the Synagogue, had a cult in the West from the earliest times, which identified him with three Gospel characters rolled into one: the lance-bearer, the centurion who confessed Christ, and the first of the Sepulchre guards.[98] Theologically, he was regarded as the first converted Gentile and the piercing of Christ's flank was interpreted as the beginning of Salvation since Christ forgave St Longinus, who became a symbol of the Gentiles just as Stephaton was the symbol of the Jews. Later, another legend, first told by Gregory of Nyssa, took root, making St Longinus the missionary and martyr of Cappadocia.[99] Latin Passions followed in the West, such as those by Hrabanus Maurus and Notker. The Hieronymian Martyrology enters him on three different dates, 15 March, 23 October, and 22 November, and, although the first gradually became the most important, the three were still entered in English calendars. The cult flourished in the eleventh century, when the relic of the chalice containing the Blood of Christ, supposedly brought by St Longinus to Mantua, became known, thus making him the patron saint of this city. In England, 'Longinus qui latus Domini aperuit' is entered on the latter two dates from the Hieronymian Martyrology at Glastonbury, and the feast on 15 March for 'Sanctus Longinus martyr' is entered at Wells, Winchester, Sherborne, and Bury.

St Anne's name was entered in first position in the choir of the Virgins in the litany in Wulfstan's collectar and again among the first, inserted between those of St Cecilia and St Lucy, in an Exeter litany. Like all female saints, except the Virgin Mary herself, St Anne also belongs to the choir of the Virgins. She has a mass with the pericope added in the missal of St Augustine's. St Anne's cult started in the East, relying on the Protoevan-gelium of James since no part of the story belongs to the Gospels, with the dedication of a church to her at Constantinople around 550.[100] Relics of St Anne were supposed to have been kept in Rome from the eighth century onwards, but the cult only started in the West in Naples in the tenth century. Once again, England seems to have been in advance of the

---

[98] L. Réau, *Iconographie de l'art chrétien* (6 vols.; Paris, 1955–8), ii (2). 495–7, and esp. iii (2). 812–4.

[99] His main role in the Greek Church was this one, see *Menologio*, i. 32, ii, fo. 117. His feast was on 16 October.

[100] H. Aurenhammer, *Lexikon der christlichen Ikonographie A-Chr* (Vienna, 1959–67), 141. On the development of the cult of St Anne in the East, see also P. V. Charland, *Madame Ste Anne et son culte au Moyen Âge* (2 vols.; Paris, 1911–13), i. 77–348; in the West, see A. Wilmart, 'Chants en l'honneur' and 'Les Compositions', in *Auteurs spirituels et textes dévots du Moyen Âge latin* (Paris, 1932), 46–55, 261–3.

Continent since, through a knowledge of the south Italian cult, the devotion to St Anne flourished here earlier than in the rest of Europe. We may wonder whether the remarkably early development in England in the late tenth century of the feast of the Conception of the Virgin may have been responsible, in part, for the cult of the Virgin's mother, the relation between the two being thus further assimilated to that of the Virgin and her Son. The theological doctrine of the Conception developed in England first, in the early twelfth century; although the treatise which argued the case circulated under the name of Anselm, it was in fact the work of an English monk from that circle, Eadmer; and Sir Richard Southern has explained how the piety preceded the theology in Anglo-Saxon England, which is not surprising in view of the English tradition of devotion to the Virgin.[101]

This peculiar nature of English devotions in the early period continued into the late Anglo-Saxon centuries, when the cults of these Gospel figures, as well as their representations in art, show them to be extremely popular representatives of a form of piety centred on the earthly life of Jesus, which was to develop in the rest of Europe from the eleventh century onwards, partly under the influence of the Ottonian emperors, to whom it may well have been given a boost by the Greek ecclesiastics of Theophano.[102] This emphasis is further confirmed by other cults, such as those of Mary Magdalene and Lazarus, of whom more will be said below, and also by the introduction in England, from the eleventh century onwards, of two new feasts of south Italian origin, that of the Conception and the Oblation in the Temple of the Virgin Mary.[103] A liturgical entry for the first is found in several calendars from Glastonbury, St Augustine's, New Minster (1020–35), Old Minster (c.1030), and in the Canterbury benedictional. It may be of some significance that the entry in the Winchester calendars, a city with particularly close royal associations, appears to coincide with the dates suggested for the visit of the bishop of Benevento to England, who had been warmly welcomed by Cnut and Emma. The devotion to the Virgin had been strong in England from the seventh century onwards, and eighth- and ninth-century prayer-books such as the

---

[101] Southern, *Anselm*, 290–6.

[102] H. Beurath, *Die Kaiserin Theophano* (Stuttgart and Berlin, 1940).

[103] Gasquet and Bishop, *Bosworth Psalter*, 43–52, and M. Clayton, 'Feasts of the Virgin in the Liturgy of the Anglo-Saxon Church', *ASE* 13 (1984), 229–33, or her Ch. 2 in *Cult of the Virgin*, 25–51; E. Bishop, 'On the Origins of the Feast of the Conception of the Blessed Virgin Mary', in *Liturgica Historica*, 238–59; Wilmart, *Auteurs spirituels*, 263–5, 49; A. W. Burridge, 'L'Immaculée Conception dans la théologie de l'Angleterre médiévale', *Revue d'histoire ecclésiastique*, 32 (1936), 570–97; S. J. P. van Dijk, 'The Origin of the Latin Feast of the Conception of the Blessed Virgin Mary', *Dublin Review*, 118 (1954), 251–67, 428–42; and H. F. Davis, 'The Origins of the Devotion to Our Lady's Immaculate Conception', ibid. 375–92.

Book of Cerne and the Book of Nunnaminster display this personal attachment to her in their prayers, many written in England and subsequently taken to the Continent. The circulation of some such prayers to the Virgin seems to have been permanent between England and both Italy and France. A very interesting example is the presence of the same prayer in two books alone, one the New Minster Psalter of *c.*1060 Arundel 60, and the other a psalter from Nonantola, of the eleventh century.[104] Since other prayers from the Nonantola psalter are found in this book, it seems likely that the English text copied the Italian one.[105] Barré suggested that English travellers may have come across them at another Italian abbey, which was a pilgrimage centre on the route to Rome and strongly influenced by Nonantola, S. Michele at Poggibonsi; this is not impossible, but it is worth remembering that we have evidence that another manuscript, now in Trinity College Cambridge, reached England from Nonantola, and prayers or even whole psalters may have also done so.[106] In other instances, however, the circulation of prayers and texts went from England to Italy: a Winchester prayer of the second half of the tenth century was incorporated into a Monte Cassino book of the end of the eleventh century and another in a manuscript from Fonteavellana in the twelfth century.[107]

The veneration for St Joseph has already been mentioned in connection with Naples. His cult, however, was also developing in central Italy, especially after the arrival of the Chiusi relics. The other cults from this area and from northern Italy were known in England for having been encountered on the pilgrimage route to Rome, and they are all cults of saints popular in the West from the eleventh century onwards. It is all the more interesting to see them appear so early in Anglo-Saxon documents: whilst the cult of St Christopher had already been known in Europe from the fifth century onwards, though only with limited local success, as at Lucca where a hospice was dedicated to him, those of St Christina and St Margaret developed mostly during the course of the eleventh century, in relation to their relics kept at Bolsena, north of Rome. This is almost certainly the place where English pilgrims encountered them, well before the sudden growth of St Margaret's cult in the wake of the Crusaders' establishment at Antioch. Depicted in the catacombs of S. Gennaro at Naples together with St Catherine and other saints, St Margaret was

---

[104] This MS is Rome, Vatican Library, Vat. lat. 84. On these prayers, see H. Barré, *Prières anciennes de l'Occident à la Mère du Saveur des origines à St Anselme* (Paris 1963) , 135–42, 210–11; and Clayton, *Cult of the Virgin*, 112.

[105] Barré, *Prières*, 142.

[106] Ibid. 236–44, and see above, p. 96

[107] Ibid. 117, 222.

venerated in the East under the name of Marina, on 17 or 18 July. St Margaret (as she became known in the Latin version of her Passion) is first found in the West in Hrabanus Maurus' martyrology on 20 July. Her popularity in the West was based on the subsequent legend of the dragon which swallowed her. By the twelfth century, she had already been identified with the princess saved by St George, as we can see from a tympanum at Ault Hacknall, on which she is shown above St George fighting the dragon.[108] This cult, although boosted by the Crusades, had nevertheless begun as early as 908, when the saint's relics were translated from the East to S. Pietro della Valle on Lake Bolsena. Pilgrims to Bolsena would have become acquainted not only with the cult of St Margaret, but also with that of St Christina, the martyr of Bolsena, celebrated on 24 July.[109] She was venerated at Bolsena from the fourth century onwards, was depicted among the Italian virgins in the sixth-century mosaics at Sant'Apollinare Nuovo in Ravenna, and a Latin Life was written in the ninth century.[110] In the liturgy, St Margaret appears on the Greek date of 18 July in the Glastonbury, Wessex, and West Country calendars, and is entered once as St Marina in the tenth-century West Country calendar. The West Country calendar also entered her on 20 July, the date in Hrabanus Maurus' martyrology, thus perhaps demonstrating that in the early tenth century, the cult was still no more than martyrological and that, in all probability, it was not quite clear to the compiler who the saint was. From the late tenth century onwards, possibly as a result of the intensification of the Roman pilgrimage, St Margaret was entered in all calendars, except two from Winchester and Worcester, on 20 July, with XII lessons at Christ Church and Worcester and in blue capitals at Crowland. We find here a clear example of the way in which an initially rather vague cult became increasingly more definite by the eleventh century with the establishment of the 20 July feast in the eleventh century, whereas two close late tenth-century calendars, such as the Glastonbury and St Augustine's ones, could still choose to adopt two different dates, one, the Greek and the other, the Western. St Christina's cult was equally widespread. She was entered at the usual date at Wells, Crowland, and Winchester, on 24 July, with capitals in the Crowland calendar. The Wessex, Evesham, Worcester and Bury calendars, along with one from

---

[108] C. E. Keyser, *Norman Tympana and Lintels* (4 vols.; 2nd edn.; London, 1927), pp. lxxviii. Some doubt has been expressed more recently, however, as to whether the two components of the tympanum were actually conceived to go together from the start.

[109] P. Paschini, 'Richerche agiografice: S. Cristina di Bolsena', *Rivista d'archeologia cristiana*, 2 (1925), 167–94.

[110] For the mosaic of the Virgins at Sant'Apollinare Nuovo, see van Berchem and Clouzot, *Mosaïques chrétiennes*, 138–41, pl. 173.

Winchester, have her name on 19 July, whereas the old early-tenth-century verse martyrology with additions records her on 17 July. The only form of liturgical celebration for St Christina are the three collects in Wulfstan's collectar. St Margaret, on the other hand, has simple masses at Exeter and Wells, and a group of collects in a Winchester manuscript. Both saints appear in late tenth-century litanies, mostly from the south-west, Wessex, and Exeter. By the second half of the century, St Margaret appears in almost half the litanies, and St Christina in a significant number. These two cults, reinforced in the first place by the pilgrimage, were later promoted by the Crusades, especially that of St Margaret.

St Christopher was celebrated in the Greek liturgy, in the *Codex Rossanensis*, in two eighth-century and tenth-century menologioi, and in the ninth-century Calendarium Marmoreum; a church was dedicated to him in Ravenna in 743. Of great influence on English devotions was the powerful north Italian cult.[111] St Christopher became one of the patron saints of pilgrims in Italy, because of the number of hospices dedicated to him on the pilgrimage route: Fano, Altopascio, Pavia, and Siena had such hospices built in the course of the eleventh century. The two strongest centres of the cult were Milan and Lucca. At Milan, St Christopher's name appears in the Ambrosian liturgy from the fifth century onwards, on 28 April, as it later does in Bede's martyrology, in both cases as a result of Syrian influence. At Lucca, there was a church dedicated to the saint by 812 and in this town famous for its hospices, one of the greatest was St Christopher's. From Lucca, the cult spread through Tuscany. Many of the places cited above, and especially Lucca, were stopping-places on the pilgrimage route and would presumably have brought Anglo-Saxon pilgrims in contact with the cult. Only one eleventh-century English calendar from Wessex preserves the Syrian/Ambrosian/Mozarabic date found in Bede's martyrology, 28 April. All other calendars use the date from Jerome's martyrology, 25 July, on which St Christopher is entered in most except the Glastonbury, Evesham, and two Winchester calendars. The saint's name was not entered in calendars before the end of the tenth century, since it is missing from the verse martyrology. It is also missing from the calendar in Robert's missal, possibly because of the reluctance of the compilers of this manuscript to accept relatively little-established saints. At Christ Church, St Christopher was celebrated in copes, at Worcester with XII lessons and is in capitals in a Winchester calendar.

[111] H. F. Rosenfeld, *Der heilige Christophorus, seine Verehrung und seine Legende* (Leipzig, 1937), 30–49. On the English cult and a text of the Passion of St Christopher from *c.*1000, found in the Beowulf manuscript, see K. Sisam., *Studies in the History of Old English Literature* (Oxford, 1953), 68–72.

There are masses at Winchester, St Augustine's, and Wells, and three collects in Wulfstan's collectar. St Christopher entered the liturgy at a remarkably late date, since none of these texts is earlier than the second half of the eleventh century, a feature to be expected in Anglo-Saxon books, generally reluctant to provide a liturgical celebration for the as yet less official and accepted saints. Although known in the tenth century, since the saint's name appears in some early calendars and in some litanies, St Christopher's cult was not yet widespread but it developed in the early eleventh century, possibly in response to the pilgrimage or to the stronger links with the Continent, and became general by the end of the century, when the saint's name appears in most litanies, and as the second name in the general prayer to the martyrs in Wulfstan's collectar.

In the late eleventh century, there were, once again, strong links with the south of Italy. Of these, we have not only the direct evidence, but also such indications as the increasing cult of St Nicholas, already strong in England on account of the Byzantine–German–Lotharingian channel, but nevertheless reinforced by the Translation of his relics to Bari in 1087.[112] Another example is the entry of Bede, considered to be the English national saint, in some Italian books.[113]

IV. ARTISTIC EXCHANGES BETWEEN ENGLAND AND ITALY

The only direct evidence we have regarding artistic exchanges relates to the south of Italy, in the account of the presence of the English goldsmith at Monte Cassino and of the English cope Eadmer saw at Bari; and also to Lucca, where Leofstan of Bury saw the Volto Santo and had the rood at Bury modelled on it, a stylistic innovation which may have been at the root of the popular iconography of the 'draped' Christ of Langford.[114] Of the art of embroidery, more will be said later; but metalwork was one of the skills for which Anglo-Saxon craftsmen were best known, though few of the ornate, gem-studded vessels, reliquaries, and crucifixes described in the sources are still extant.[115] Some of these artefacts reached the Continent and possibly contributed to patterns of decoration there. But the most

---

[112] Jones, *Nicholas of Myra*, 175–209.

[113] In the litany from a breviary from S. Vincenzo al Volturno, for example, in the late-11th c., Rome, Vatican Library MS Chigi D.V.77.

[114] T. D. Kendrick, *Late-Saxon and Viking Art* (London, 1949), 52, and E. Coatsworth, 'The Iconography of the Crucifixion in Pre-Conquest Sculptures in England', Ph.D. thesis (Durham, 1979), 165–69, as well as her more recent article in Yorke, *Aethelwold*, 'Late Pre-Conquest Sculptures with the Crucifixion South of the Humber', 190.

[115] *LE* 196–7, 223–4; *WMHG* 96–7, 130–1; *Chronicon Abingdon*, i. 443, 474; *Chronicon Evesham*, 86–8; see also Dodwell, *Anglo-Saxon Art*, 188–215.

influential English art form in Europe was that of book-illumination. It exerted strong influence in Flanders and France, but may also have contributed some ideas in Monte Cassino. Indeed, we know that an English Gospel-book reached Monte Cassino before the middle of the eleventh century, not long after having been produced in England. This book has illustrations of the Evangelists at the beginning of each Gospel, as was by then common. Since this manuscript reached Monte Cassino, though we do not know how, it is not impossible to imagine others doing the same. We could then explain a puzzling fact: how can an English psalter of the first quarter of the eleventh century contain an illumination of a monk presenting a copy of the Rule to St Benedict in an open book with the words 'Ausculta filii precepta' inscribed on it, an image similar in some of its iconographical elements to that of the frontispieces of a manuscript of the Rule now in Monte Cassino and one of the Life of St Benedict now in the Vatican Library, written at the time of Abbot Desiderius around 1071–2 (Pl. 6*a*, *b*)?[116] In the Monte Cassino manuscript, we see Abbot Desiderius introducing a monk John, who presents the codex to St Benedict, at whose feet John's nephew Leo kneels. In one of the two images in Arundel 155, Benedict is presented with a copy of the Rule by several monks. Both illuminations have in common the enthroned saint, who blesses the holder of the book; the saint is holding a staff and a small figure kneels at his feet. There are differences in the orientation of the image, the cowled saint being on the left in the Monte Cassino manuscript and holding his staff in the left hand, while the reverse is true in Arundel 155; and in the presence of one monk offering a closed codex, presumably that of the Vita itself, whereas several monks offer an open book containing the Rule in England. These differences may be partly the result of adaptations of the same theme and, in the case of the Arundel manuscript, significant of the English interest in the revival of the Rule, not a major issue at Monte Cassino itself. However, this particular iconography in association with St Benedict does not appear before the age of Desiderius at Monte Cassino. Either there was such an image there before the time of Desiderius, which is now lost, and which inspired a hypothetical traveller to the abbey, who brought it back to England in a very short space of time; or the image was first created in an English *scriptorium*, at a time when English monks were particularly keen to establish what they viewed as the pure Benedictine Rule, in the wake of the monastic reform of the tenth

---

[116] Monte Cassino Library, Codex H.H.99, fo. 3, see P. d'Ancona, *La Miniature italienne du* X*e au* XVI*e siècle* (Paris and Brussels, 1925), 5; Vatican Library MS Vaticano lat. 1202, fo. 2ᵛ, reproduced in M. Avery and M. Inguanez, *Miniature cassinensi del secolo* XI *illustranti la 'Vita di San Benedetto'* (Monte Cassino, 1934).

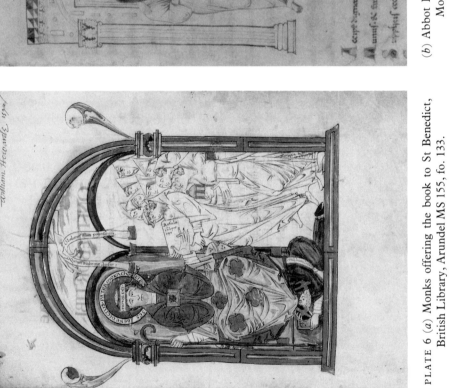

(b) Abbot Desiderius offering the book to St Benedict, Montecassino Abbey, MS H.H.99, fo. 3.

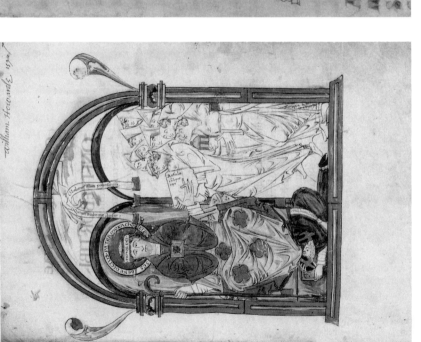

PLATE 6 (a) Monks offering the book to St Benedict, British Library, Arundel MS 155, fo. 133.

century. In the Benedictional of St Aethelwold, St Benedict is one of the three confessors in the choir to be identified by an inscription on his *pallium*, with St Gregory and St Cuthbert.[117] He is depicted, on one side of Christ in majesty, while St Gregory stands on the other, in a manuscript in the Bibliothèque Municipale in Orléans, no. 175, a copy of St Gregory's *Homilies on Ezekiel*, written at Fleury in the tenth century but illuminated by an Anglo-Saxon monk.[118] These representations of St Benedict dressed as a monk, enthroned, holding a book and a pastoral staff, were originally modelled on the portrait-type images of saints in Byzantine art, which became quite common in Europe during the Carolingian, then Ottonian periods, for example, on the portable altar from Adelhausen, of the late eighth century, and the golden altar of Henry II, dating from the beginning of the eleventh century.[119] Two miniatures in Arundel 155 and one in Tiberius C.III depict St Benedict enthroned, either giving or expounding the Rule to several monks, some of whom are kneeling and kissing his feet— a form of representation of Benedict not apparently common on the Continent.[120] The saint wears either a diadem or a mitre, which in one case is inscribed with the words 'Sctus Benedictus pater monachorum et dux' and 'Timor Dei' (Arundel 155); and in the other 'Pater', 'Benedictus'. In Arundel 155, he carries a staff and wears a breastplate inscribed with the word 'iust'. He also holds the book of the Rule in this manuscript, while in Tiberius C.III, it is placed next to him on a tripod table. The second illustration contained in Arundel 155 and its subsequent Monte Cassino success has already been discussed.

Another Italian source of inspiration from the point of view of the iconography is an Ottonian manuscript, written around 1000 in Ivrea, for, and possibly by, the then bishop of the city, Warmund. This sacramentary, which illustrates the main feasts with events of the Gospels, contains in particular ink drawings of St Gregory and Peter the Deacon, the Nativity and the Bathing of the Child, the Annunciation to the Shepherds, the Stoning of Stephen, the Massacre of the Innocents, the Adoration of the Magi, the Baptism of Christ, the Presentation in the Temple, the Entry into Jerusalem, the Washing of the Feet, the Last Supper, the Crucifixion, the Anastasis, the Three Maries at the Sepulchre, the Incredulity of Thomas, the Ascension, Pentecost, the Nativity of St John the Baptist, the Martyrdom of SS Peter, Paul, and Laurence, the Death of the Virgin,

---

[117] *Benedictional of St Aethelwold*, fo. 99ᵛ.
[118] fo. 149, reproduced in Temple, *ASM*, pl. 144.
[119] Both altars are reproduced in Lasko, *Ars Sacra*, pls. 9 and 130, the second also in H. Jantzen, *Ottonische Kunst* (Hamburg, 1959), no. 38.
[120] Arundel 155, fo. 10 and fo. 133, reproduced in Temple, *ASM*, pl. 213; Tib.C. III, fo. 117ᵛ.

St Michael and the Dragon, and portraits of the Evangelists, altogether twenty-four out of the thirty-three illuminations of the Proper and the Sanctoral, whose iconography is remarkably close to that of several Anglo-Saxon manuscripts.[121] Gregory and Peter are depicted in the Claudius Pontifical; the Nativity of Christ though without the Bathing of the Child, the Stoning of Stephen, the Adoration of the Magi, the Baptism, the Entry into Jerusalem, the Anastasis, the Three Maries, the Incredulity of Thomas, the Ascension, Pentecost, Death of the Virgin, and Martyrdom of the three saints in the Benedictional of St Aethelwold; the Stoning of Stephen and the Nativity of John in the Hereford Troper; the Massacre of the Innocents in the Bury Psalter; the Washing of the Feet, Michael and the Dragon, and the Entry into Jerusalem in Tiberius C.VI; the Last Supper in the Boulogne Gospels; and the Harrowing of Hell on the 'Bristol slab'. The Nativity, Three Maries, Ascension, and Pentecost are common representations in English art, which have some specific features such as the presence of the midwife Salome arranging a cushion behind the Virgin's head, the upward 'disappearing' Christ in the Ascension scene, and the central position of St Peter in the Pentecost image; and other scenes such as the Death of the Virgin with her soul shown as a child swathed in cloths being taken upward are proper to Continental iconography; whilst some features are common to English and Ottonian art such as the kneeling Christ washing Peter's feet in the Washing of the Feet, already discussed, and the individual tongues of fire over the apostles' heads in the Pentecost representation, seen in the Benedictional of Robert.[121] The Warmund Sacramentary was perhaps in the process of being completed precisely at a time when ecclesiastical pilgrims to Rome were common, Sigeric of Canterbury in 990 and, after him, the archbishops Aelfric, Aelfheah, Lyfing, Aethelnoth, Eadsige, and Robert. It is not at all impossible that they should have come to see a manuscript of that kind on their way, just as it seems likely that they should have seen Greek liturgical manuscripts, such as the menologioi of the type of that of Basil II, with which the Benedictional of St Aethelwold has numerous affinities in its presentation as well as in its iconography. And the likeliest place for English pilgrims to have observed such manuscripts was most certainly Rome itself.

[121] Magnani, *Le miniature*, fos. 8ᵛ, 17ᵛ, 20, 21, 22ᵛ, 26ᵛ, 27, 32, 48ᵛ, 50, 57ᵛ, 65, 67, 71, 78, 82, 88, 90ᵛ, 98, 100, 107ᵛ, 221ᵛ, 222ᵛ. On the iconography of Salome, the 'disappearing Christ' and the Washing of the Feet, see Schapiro, 'The Image', 280–5, and Schiller, *Iconography of Christian Art*, i. 63–6 and 67, and ii. 46–7.

—◆◆◆—

5

ROME

I. ROME IN THE TENTH AND ELEVENTH CENTURIES

Before undertaking to examine what foreign pilgrims brought back with them from Rome to their native countries by way of spiritual and artistic inspiration, a short survey of what they could and would have seen in Rome at the time of their visit there seems necessary. Most sources from the period between the eighth and the twelfth century give few indications about the monuments of republican and imperial Rome left standing after the successive invasions, pillages, and other sources of destruction of such monuments, such as the re-use of building materials for the purposes of either domestic or military defence architecture and the conversion of Roman buildings into churches, fortresses and, on occasion, private dwellings, between the fifth and the twelfth century.[1] Apart from the archaeological evidence, our knowledge of the history of these buildings during the early medieval period relies principally on a text of the early eighth century, known as the Itinerary of Einsiedeln, of which the earliest version now extant is in Einsiedeln, Abbey Library MS 326, and dates from the ninth century; it was probably written in Germany. From it, from entries in the *Liber Pontificalis*, and from fleeting references in Gregory the Great's letters, we know that such monuments as the theatre of Pompey, the Roman Forum and Trajan's Forum, the statue of Constantine, the baths of Commodus, Constantine, Trajan, and Diocletian, the markets of Livia, and some of the triumphal arches were still standing undisturbed.[2] Some of the buildings of imperial Rome had been converted and put to a different use. The most common of these conversions were into churches, beginning with the early changes from pagan civic buildings such as the library of Augustus in the Forum into the church of Sta Maria Antiqua and of the Curia into the church of St Adrian. Subsequently temples and imperial mausolea such as that to all the gods, the Pantheon, the Temple

---

[1] R. Lanciani, *The Destruction of Ancient Rome* (New York and London, 1899) and H. Grisar, *History of Rome and the Popes in the Middle Ages* (3 vols.; London, 1911–12); generally on the topography and history of the city, see R. Krautheimer, *Rome: Profile of a City 312–1308* (Princeton, 1980), and P. Llewellyn, *Rome in the Dark Ages* (London, 1971).

[2] Lanciani, *Destruction*, 142–53. Examples of such references in the letters are those to Hadrian's Mausoleum and to remaining libraries in Rome, see D. Norberg (ed.), *S. Gregorii Magni Registrum Epistularum* (2 vols.; Turnhout, 1982), i. no. I.23, p. 21, and ii. no. VIII.28, p. 549.

of the Urbs, and Hadrian's Mausoleum were converted into the churches of St Mary and All the Martyrs, that of SS Cosmas and Damian, and the papal castle with a church dedicated to St Michael.[3] But the conversion into churches was not the only possible use for imperial buildings and, if Hadrian's Mausoleum contained a church, it was also a fortified castle, which stood the popes in good stead during both the outsider attacks of the Lombards and Saracens, for example, during the latter's main effort in 846,[4] and the enemies within Rome itself. Other buildings retained their original administrative function: those of the Annona were taken over for similar purposes of grain distribution to the people, from the *diaconiae*; and the palaces on the Palatine, after being abandoned by the Byzantine dukes of Rome and other officials representing the exarch of Ravenna when they stopped functioning during the eighth century, were used again briefly by Otto III during his stay in Rome.[5] Others again were taken over for the simple purpose of habitation, such as the theatre of Marcellus, on top of which was built the palace of the Pierleoni family, or for trade and workshops: the Basilica Julia was used by the rope-makers and the Circus Flaminius by the lime-burners.[6]

Far more information is available for the history of the churches of Rome throughout the early Middle Ages. Both the documents concerning these churches, such as acts of councils, martyrs' passions, letters, itineraries and descriptions, and the main narrative source for the history of Rome during that period, the *Liber Pontificalis*, allow us to reconstruct the history of ecclesiastical foundations during the first seven centuries of their existence. These churches, their relics and artistic treasures were the main objects of interest for English pilgrims, though they no doubt also noticed remaining pagan monuments.

From the fifth century onwards, the influx of originally non-Roman features in Rome was due partly to military events, as in the case of the Ostrogothic and Lombard elements, and partly to the peaceful foreign presence of the 'protectors' of the city, as in the case of the Greek, Carolingian, and Ottonian characteristics.[7] These became gradually part

[3] *LP* i. 317 and 268 n. 36.

[4] Ibid. ii. 99–101.

[5] C. Brühl, 'Die Kaiserpfalz bei St Peter und die Pfalz Ottos III auf dem Palatin', *Quellen und Forschungen aus Italienischen Archiven und Bibliotheken*, 34 (1954), 1–30.

[6] Lanciani, *Destruction*, 82–5, 157.

[7] On the history of Rome, its buildings and churches, see M. Armellini, *Le chiese di Roma dal secolo IV al secolo XIX* (2 vols.; Rome, 1887, 2nd edn. rev. C. Cecchelli, 1942); C. Huelsen, *Le chiese di Roma nel Medio Evo* (Florence, 1927); R. Krautheimer *et al.*, *Corpus Basilicarum Christianarum Romae: The Early Christian Basilicas of Rome IV–IXth Centuries* (5 vols.; Vatican City, 1937–70); Krautheimer, *Rome*; id., *Early Christian and Byzantine Architecture* (3rd edn.; Harmondsworth, 1979); O. Marucchi, *Églises et basiliques de Rome*, vol. iii of *Éléments d'archéol-*

of the cultural outlook of the city to the point of *being* Roman culture between the fifth and the eleventh centuries. Despite the removal of his court and capital from Rome to Constantinople, Constantine and his family continued to contribute to the monumental development of Rome by initiating the construction of several basilicas on the tombs of the most venerated martyrs, Peter, Paul, Laurence, and Agnes. Neither the Sack of Rome in 410 nor the subsequent barbarian attacks actually destroyed the buildings, especially the churches, built during the fourth and fifth centuries. These included Sta Maria Maggiore, then known as the Liberian basilica, or the old *tituli* officially transformed into churches, for example, that of Eudoxia, which became under her husband, the Emperor Valentinian III, the church of S. Pietro in Vincoli, and that of Sabina, which became *c*.422–32 the church of Sta Sabina, or even churches outside the walls, such as S. Sebastiano near the catacombs of Callixtus on the Appian Way. Between 476 and 553, under Theodoric and the Ostrogothic kings, other monuments were erected, churches such as S. Stefano Rotondo, Sta Bibiana, S. Martino ai Monti, and Sta Agata dei Goti. Some of the Roman architectural creations, when they fell into disrepair, began to be re-used for new buildings, and the process continued on an increasing scale during the period of Byzantine occupation of Rome after the consolidation of Justinian's reconquest in 553, particularly after the last visit of an Emperor to Rome, that of Constans II in 663, when he ordered all bronze ties to be removed from ancient buildings as well as the bronze tiles of the Pantheon, to be melted for military use. Imperial buildings, now stripped of their marble and crumbling because they lacked support, were however still used sometimes for their initial purpose, since Greek officials and civil servants governing Rome in the Emperor's name, appointed by the exarch at Ravenna, still resided on the Palatine. Several churches founded at the time in the vicinity of the Palatine, between the republican Forum and the Tiber, where the centre of most of the economic and social life of imperial Rome had been, such as Sta Maria Antiqua and S. Teodoro, followed the pattern of occupation of the soil and replaced the services of the Annona with *diaconiae* whose role became that of supplying food to the population. Despite troubled relations with Constantinople on account

ogie chrétienne (Paris and Rome, 1902); E. Mâle, *The Early Churches of Rome* (tr., London, 1960); G. Matthiae, *Le chiese di Roma dal iv al x secolo* (Rome, 1962); also useful is G. Ferrari, *Early Roman Monasteries* (Rome, 1957); F. Hermanin, *L'arte in Roma dal secolo viii al xiv* (Bologna, 1945); G. Matthiae, *La pittura romana del medioevo* (2 vols.; Rome, 1965–6); id., *Musaici medievali di Roma* (Rome, 1962); J. Wilpert, rev. W. N. Schumacher, *Die römischen Mosaiken der christlichen Bauten vom IV zum XIII Jahrhundert* (Freiburg, Basle and Vienna, 1976); W. Oakeshott, *The Mosaics of Rome from the Third to the Fourteenth Century* (London, 1967); and S. Waetzoldt, *Die Kopien des 17. Jahrhundert nach Mosaiken und Wandmalereien in Rom* (Vienna and Munich, 1964).

of the monothelite position defended by the emperors until 692, and afterwards of the iconoclastic debate, the popes not only succeeded in upholding the principle of the primacy of the Roman see, but also saw their position improve considerably in the West, due to the considerable development of the cult of St Peter among the Lombards, Visigoths, irish, Anglo-Saxons, and Franks, and also in Rome itself, where dislike for the Byzantine occupation led both the people and the army to rely on the bishop of the city as a replacement both in religious and in secular political, administrative, and military leadership. Papal dominance was further made possible by the abandonment of imperial institutions such as the senate, the prefecture of the city, and the Annona after Gregory the Great, as well as the incapacity of the Byzantine government to ensure the defence of the city against Lombard attacks. The popes became responsible for keeping bridges, aqueducts, walls, and other civic buildings in a state of repair. They also erected new churches at S. Lorenzo, S. Gregorio, S. Adriano and the oratory of the Forty Martyrs of Sebasta in the Forum; rebuilt older ones such as S. Agnese; built some to house the relics of martyrs which had reached Rome at the time from the East, Anastasius' at SS Vincenzo e Anastasio, George's at S. Giorgio in Velabro and the Dalmatian martyrs in the oratory of S. Venanzio in the Lateran Baptistery, and others for relics brought inside the walls from the catacombs, of Simplicius, Faustinus and Beatrix in a small church near Sta Bibiana in 682–3 and of Primus and Felician in S. Stefano in 642–9. They also built churches for the Greek monastic population, which had reached Rome from the Eastern provinces, led there by both the Arab and Persian attacks and the imperial monothelite decrees, for example, S. Saba for monks of the Great Laura in Palestine. Frescos and mosaics from this period, at S. Cesario on the Palatine, Sta Maria Antiqua, S. Saba, S. Crisogono, S. Valentino, the cemeteries of Callixtus and of Felicity, and at S. Lorenzo, Sant'Agnese, S. Venanzio, S. Stefano, S. Teodoro, and the chapel of John VII in the Vatican basilica, display a strong Byzantine influence, with decoration in the Alexandrian style. Liturgical changes were made in Rome during this period, such as the enforcement of processions from St Apollinare to St Peter's on Saturdays under Pope Honorius (625–38), the singing of the Agnus Dei at Mass, and the celebration of the feasts of the Virgin, Annunciation, Assumption, Nativity and Presentation in the Temple, with processions, under Sergius I (687–701). Various new saints were introduced among the new dedications, most of them of Greek origin, such as Theodore, Sergius and Bacchus, Athanasius, George, and Eufemia. Icons painted in the East were brought to Rome for Sta Maria Maggiore, Sta Maria in Cosmedin, S. Boniface, and the Pantheon, and eastern painters settled in the city.

By the middle of the eighth century, under the pressure of renewed Lombard attacks and with no help from the Emperor, papal policies changed from being moderately favourable to the Emperor to being more radically western-oriented, and the Franks were appealed to. The link gradually forged between these newly found supporters of the papacy, who defeated the Lombards, and the papacy led to the coronation of Charlemagne as western Emperor and the presence of Carolingian officials in Rome. They also contributed to the monumental landscape of the city, first by ensuring the completion of the Leonine wall in 852, then by adding to churches already in existence or by building new ones. Additions were made to Sta Sabina, S. Silvestro, and Sta Maria in Cosmedin; St Petronilla's mausoleum in St Peter's was transformed into the chapel of the Franks, who adopted her as a patron saint, S. Martino was rebuilt, and SS Nereo e Achilleo, Sta Prassede, Sta Maria Nova, and SS Quattro Coronati were founded or re-founded. To all these, sculpture, frescos, and mosaics were given.

During the first Carolingian period, Rome was comparatively peaceful, despite repeated Saracen attacks. By the late ninth century, however, the Carolingian kings of Italy failed to preserve the peace in the city, and the Ottonian emperors after 962 until the death of Otto III in 1002 repeatedly repressed several attempts by the Roman nobility, particularly the Crescentii family, to take hold of the government of the city as self-styled senators. Popes whose allegiance was given alternately to the Roman aristocracy and to the German Emperors succeeded each other during one and a half centuries, until Leo IX and Nicholas II proceeded to reform the electoral procedure, which was to detach the office from the vagaries of both aristocratic and imperial parties, making way for, on the one hand, an attempt at a general reform of the Church during the second half of the eleventh century, and on the other, a change of alliances which was to make Rome and the by then well-established *Patrimonium* of St Peter the fighting ground for emperors and Norman rulers of Apulia from the middle of the eleventh century onwards. Recent research has emphasized, however, that the apparent weakness of tenth-century popes was not to be taken too literally, and that, although the Roman nobility held major posts in the Lateran, they were presided over by officers appointed by the pope, such as the *vestararius* and the *bibliothecarius*, who prepared the way for the recovery of the principle of papal sovereignty by developing ideological and religious positions, in particular in relation to western rulers.[8] Relatively little was built in Rome during the tenth and eleventh centuries.

---

[8] P. Llewellyn in a letter to me. The most recent discussions of the papal reform are those in C. Morris, *The Papal Monarchy: The Western Church from 1050 to 1250* (Oxford, 1989), 79–108, and I. Robinson, *The Papacy 1073–1198* (Cambridge, 1990).

Some additions were made to the churches of SS Alessio and Bonifazio and Sta Pudenziana. The tomb of Otto II in the Vatican basilica, with its mosaic, the icon of Sta Maria in Aracoeli and the bronze doors of S. Paolo, brought from Constantinople, come from this period, and two new churches were built, S. Bartolomeo in Isola, to receive the relics of the apostle after their translation from Benevento in the south of Italy, and S. Cosimato.

How would Rome have looked to an Anglo-Saxon pilgrim of the tenth and the eleventh century? For the pilgrims who came to Rome via the Alps, the road to the city was the Via Cassia, one of the few of the Roman ways still in good state of repair. Afterwards, they walked or rode along the other main arteries leading to the churches of the martyrs outside the walls, the Flaminia for S. Valentino, the Nomentana for S. Agnese, the Tiburtina for S. Lorenzo, the Appia Antica for S. Sebastiano, the Ostiense for S. Paolo, and the Aurelia for S. Pancrazio, all of which were obviously practicable. Before beginning this tour, they would have had to reach their lodgings, noticing on the way the Aurelian Wall and, from the middle of the ninth century onwards, the walls which encircled St Peter's and its dependent churches and houses, forming the *borgo* and known as the Leonine City. Unlike his pre-eighth-century predecessors, but like his contemporaries from other parts of Europe, the Anglo-Saxon pilgrim would not have had to stay in a hospice attached to a monastery, a *xenodochia*, but could stay in that of his own Schola in the *borgo*, just as the Greeks, Lombards, and Franks stayed respectively in the Scholae Graeca, Longobardorum, and Francorum. The founding, development, and prosperity of the Schola Saxonum under the aegis of successive popes provides the clearest evidence for the interest of the papacy in promoting and supporting friendly relations with the English Church. Moore's masterly study of the Schola will suffice to show the nature, history, and role of this institution.[9]

Like its other three counterparts, the Scholae of the Lombards, the Franks and the Greeks, the Schola of the Saxons was the quarter, the village, in Roman terms the *burg* or *borgo*, of the Anglo-Saxons in Rome. Its foundation was approximately contemporary with King Ine's stay in Rome in 726, and its function consisted in catering for English pilgrims visiting or living in Rome. It was situated at the gates of St Peter's itself, where one finds nowadays the Ospedale di San Spirito in Sassia.[10]

There are several references to the Schola in the *Liber Pontificalis* from

[9] Moore, *Saxon Pilgrims*, ch. 4.

[10] The name 'Sassia', ultimately deriving from the Schola Saxonum, illustrates the impact of this institution in Rome.

the end of the eighth century onwards, two of them related to fires which destroyed the *borgo*. After the first fire, *c*.817–24, the pope had given food to the pilgrims and money to rebuild the Schola.[11] After the second fire in 847,[12] Pope Leo IV built the church which was to become the church of the Schola, 'S. Maria qua vocatur Schola Saxonum' or 'Sca Maria in Saxia'.

In the *Liber Pontificalis*, the term 'Schola Saxonum' was used to signify the body of Anglo-Saxon pilgrims living in or visiting Rome, and the name of the district where they lived. This, consequently, brings up the question of the nature of the institution itself. A Bull of Pope Leo IV in 854, which can be completed from a later Bull of Pope Leo IX in 1053, more or less repeating the first one, enables us to distinguish the main features of the Schola. In Moore's words:

The Schola clearly consists of a pilgrim community with considerable property, unified by a centralized organization of a quasi-monastic character. The centre of the Saxon colony is the church of S. Maria, which, as a pontifical foundation, is declared to be dependent on the Chapter of St Peter's . . . The appointment of the Archpriest of S. Maria is considered important enough to be reserved to the Pope himself. The church possessed its own cemetery and all Saxons, 'divites et pauperes, nobiles et ignobiles', who die within the limits of the Schola, have the right to be buried there . . . we find unmistakable evidence in this Bull of a definite Saxon hospice or hospices for pilgrims, attached to the church of S. Maria.[13]

From the time of King Alfred, and perhaps even from that of King Offa, a tax was levied more or less regularly in England, known as Peter's Pence or Romscot, the profits of which were to be sent to Rome, to be shared between the pope and the service of St Peter (meaning mainly the provision of lights for St Peter's) and the upkeep of the Schola and of its residents and pilgrims. 'The regular visits of Saxon almoners to Rome bearing the Romscot', Moore explained, 'must have tended to maintain a close rapport between the Saxons in Britain and their compatriots in Rome. Similarly, the not infrequent visits of Archbishops-Elect of Canterbury and York throughout the tenth and eleventh centuries must have produced the same effect.'[14] Both the Schola Saxonum and the others were used by the popes for the defence of the city and, in particular, that of the *borgo*,

---

[11] *LP* ii. 53–4.
[12] Ibid. 110–11.
[13] Moore, *Saxon Pilgrims*, 109–10.
[14] Ibid. 115. On the origins and the history of Peter's Pence, see F. Cancellieri, 'La visita de'sacri limini ed il danaro di San Pietro', *Giornale Arcadico*, 10 (1821), 264–82; P. Fabre, 'Recherches sur le denier de St Pierre au Moyen Âge', *Mélanges G.-B. de Rossi* (Paris and Rome, 1892), 159–82; O. Jensen, 'The "Denarius Sancti Petri" in England', *TRHS*, n.s. 15, (1901), 171–98; and H. R. Loyn, 'Peter's Pence', *Friends of Lambeth Palace Library Annual Report 1984*, 10–29.

centred on the Castel Sant'Angelo, which had become a fortress, while other main churches outside the walls were also fortified, such as S. Lorenzo and S. Paolo.

The pilgrims' main interest was, evidently, in the churches and their relics. In the *borgo* itself, they saw St Peter's and the church of the Schola Saxonum, Sta Maria in Saxia. St Peter's had been originally a Constantinian basilica, built to shield the tomb of the Apostle, and it was relatively little altered between the fourth century and its demolition during the fifteenth and sixteenth centuries. A fair amount of its decoration is known to us, mainly through drawings made before it was destroyed, especially those of Grimaldi.[15] The mosaic on the façade, made under Leo I (440–61) and restored under Sergius I (687–701), and known to us through the Farfa codex,[16] showed on its upper level the Agnus Dei with the symbols of the Evangelists and the Apostles, and on its lower level the Twenty-Four Elders standing between the cities of Bethlehem and Jerusalem.

Inside the basilica, there were more mosaics and frescos. On the walls of the nave, painted at various times between the fourth and the ninth century under Pope Formosus, were depicted on the right at the upper level, Old Testament scenes from the lives of Noah, Abraham, Isaac and Moses, among which were Abraham and the three Angels, the Sacrifice of Isaac and the Plagues of Egypt; and at the lower level, various prophets.[17] On the left wall, the upper level had scenes from the life of Christ, of which the Baptism, the Resurrection of Lazarus, the Descent into Hell, and the Apparition to the Disciples are known, and the lower level had portraits of various popes. In the middle of the wall, stretching across two levels, was a gigantic Crucifixion. On the triumphal arch was a mosaic depicting Christ between St Peter and Constantine, the latter possibly shown presenting to Christ a model of the church; this mosaic dated from either the fourth or the ninth centuries. The apse mosaic represented the *Traditio Legis*.

The most famous chapel in the basilica was that built and decorated by Pope John VII (705–7), renowned both for its decoration and its treasures, and well known in England because it was mentioned in Bede's *De Temporum Ratione*.[18] The wall of the apse contained a large mosaic representation of the Virgin as an *orans*, with John VII presenting the

[15] G. Grimaldi, *Descrizione della basilica antica di San Pietro in Vaticano, Cod. Barberini lat. 2733*, ed. R. Niggl (Vatican City, 1972).
[16] For the 11th-c. Farfa codex, now in the Library of Eton College, see the relevant folio reproduced in Krautheimer, *Corpus*, v, fig. 199.
[17] J. Garber, *Wirkungen der frühchristlichen Gemäldezyklen der alten Peters und Pauls-Basiliken in Rom* (Berlin and Vienna, 1918), 22–8 and figs. III–IV.
[18] Hurst-Jones, 'De Temporum', 530.

model of the oratory to her, and she was surrounded by scenes from the life of Christ. These fourteen scenes, divided into seven panels, depicted the Annunciation and the Visitation, the Nativity of Christ and the Adoration of the Shepherds, the Adoration of the Magi, the Presentation in the Temple and the Baptism of Christ, two healing miracles, the Raising of Lazarus, the Entry into Jerusalem and the Last Supper and, finally, the Crucifixion, the Three Maries at the Sepulchre, and the Descent into Hell. Under an arch were shown the Virgin and Christ with Peter and Paul. On the left wall of the chapel were represented scenes from the life of St Peter: his preaching in Antioch and Rome, Peter and Paul before Nero with Simon Magus, the Flight of Simon and his Fall, the Martyrdom of Peter crucified head-downwards and that of Paul beheaded.[19] The right wall may have depicted further scenes from the lives of Peter and Paul. This chapel contained one of the greatest treasures of the basilica, the *Veronica*, a piece of cloth bearing the image of the face of Christ.

Other treasures in the basilica were the Chair of St Peter, with a huge cross with two large iron keys suspended from it, where lights would have been lit on festive days, and the relics of SS Simon and Jude, Gregory the Great, Processus and Martinian, Petronilla, John Chrysostom, and Gregory of Naziansus. These relics were kept in various altars around the basilica. Of specific interest to Anglo-Saxon pilgrims, apart from the tomb of Gregory the Great, were the tombs of the two English kings Ceadwalla and Offa, who had died in Rome and had been buried at St Peter's, and that of St Pega, St Guthlac's sister, also said to have died in Rome.[20] For all pilgrims, the ultimate goal of the pilgrimage remained the *confessio* under the main altar, which enshrined the tomb of St Peter. It was reached through an arcaded portico, with ninth-century mosaics and statues of Christ, the Apostles, and angels. It was preserved under a *ciborium*, surrounded by ornaments and lights, and a ninth-century mosaic over the tomb depicted Christ holding the Gospel-book. One of the functions of Peter's Pence was precisely to share in the cost of providing some of these lights for the tomb of the Apostle.[21]

The church of the Schola Saxonum, Sta Maria in Saxia, founded either

[19] W. Tronzo, 'Two Roman Wall Decorations', *Dumbarton Oaks Papers*, 41 (1987), 489–92, suggests that this cycle may have been added in the Later Middle Ages; his argument, based on his view that the figures drawn by Grimaldi have a 'Gothic sway', does not seem to me very convincing.

[20] On Pega's tomb, see Armellini–Cecchelli, *Le chiese*, ii. 921; however, their statement is based on a spurious Crowland text of the later Middle Ages, the Pseudo-Ingulf, see B. Colgrave (ed.), *Felix's Life of St Guthlac* (Cambridge, 1956, repr. 1985), 192–3.

[21] *Asser*, ch. 16, p. 15. Armellini–Cecchelli, *Le chiese*, ii. 858–951; Huelsen, *Le chiese*, 417–18; Krautheimer, *Corpus*, v. 165–279; and C. Galassi Paluzzi, *La Basilica di San Pietro* (Bologna, 1975), 67–99.

at the same time as the Schola itself, or by Pope Leo IV *c.*850, was clearly
mentioned for the first time in the *Liber Pontificalis* in connection with the
rebuilding of the Schola after the fire of 847. The church contained a
reputedly miraculous image of the Virgin, thought to have been offered to
it by King Ine.[22] Its priest was appointed in theory by the monastery of
San Martino in the Vatican, to which it had been assigned by Pope Leo's
Bull of 854.[23] King Burghred, who went to Rome in 855 and died there,
was buried in the church.[24]

After them, the pilgrim visited the churches outside the walls, mostly
Constantinian foundations. The first of them was Sant'Agnese. The
original basilica had been built in the fourth century by Constantina, the
Emperor's daughter, who was particularly devoted to St Agnes. The old
basilica was rebuilt entirely nearby *c.*625–38 by Pope Honorius I, who had
the apse mosaic laid, which shows St Agnes as a Byzantine princess, richly
vested and crowned, with a pope on her right (Symmachus) and another
on her left (Honorius), one of whom offers her a model of the restored
church. Under the altar is St Agnes' tomb. In the ninth century, the relics
of St Agnes' foster-sister, St Emerentiana, were removed from the
cemetery on the Via Nomentana, and placed next to those of St Agnes in
the church, but the cemetery was still visited in the tenth century.[25]
Another image of St Agnes in the basilica is a fourth-century low relief
showing her as an *orans*.

Next door to the basilica is the Mausoleum of Constantina (Costanza),
which the pilgrims must also have visited. This fourth-century building
was erected around the princess's tomb and it contained contemporary
mosaics in the cupola, showing scenes from the Old Testament. To the
New Testament belong one of Christ's healing miracles and two mosaics
in the niches on the right and the left, the *Traditio Legis* and the *Traditio
Clavis*. St Agnes was the most popular female saint in Rome and hers was
also the third most popular cult after St Peter and St Laurence. She was
celebrated with two feasts in the Roman calendar and had three basilicas
dedicated to her in Rome by the tenth century.[26]

At S. Lorenzo, the original Constantinian basilica was built on the tomb
of St Laurence, to whose relics were later added those of St Stephen. It
later developed into a monastery, encircled by a whole ecclesiastical

---

[22] F. A. Gasquet, *A History of the Venerable English College, Rome* (London, 1920), 9–10.
[23] This was one of the four monasteries within the Vatican itself.
[24] *Aethelweard*, 41. Armellini–Cecchelli, *Le chiese*, ii. 951–3; Huelsen, *Le chiese*, 363–4.
[25] G. B. de Rossi, *Roma sotterranea cristiana descritta ed illustrata* (2 vols.; Rome, 1864–97), i. 221–2.
[26] Apart from the basilica on the Via Nomentana, the other two were Sant'Agnese *ad due furna*
and Sant'Agnese in Agone, on the alleged place of her martyrdom. Armellini–Cecchelli, *Le chiese*,
ii. 1063–71; Huelsen, *Le chiese*, 170, 238–9; Krautheimer, *Corpus*, i. 14–39.

complex of churches and houses, a *borgo*, later walled. The Catalogue 'Salisburgense', a seventh-century Itinerary found in a manuscript now in Salzburg,[27] described San Lorenzo as two churches next to each other: the old *basilica maior*, originally the Constantinian church restored by Sixtus III, and the *basilica nova*, built by Pope Pelagius II (579–90) and incorporating the tomb and shrine of the saint. The mosaic on the triumphal arch represented Christ in glory with St Peter, St Laurence, and Pope Pelagius on his right, and St Paul, St Stephen, and St Hyppolitus on his left. The *basilica nova* was dedicated in the eighth century to the Virgin and later the two churches were joined by Hadrian I (772–95). This was the centre and the major focus of the cult of St Laurence in Rome, and the cemetery attached to the basilica was still known in the tenth century. The monastery of St Laurence itself was reformed by Odo of Cluny *c*.950.[28]

At S. Paolo the original Constantinian basilica had been built to replace a small memorial on the tomb of the Apostle Paul. It was rebuilt by the three emperors Theodosius, Gratian and Valentinian II and Theodosius' daughter Galla Placidia in 385–6, then completed by the emperors Theodosius, Arcadius, and Honorius. Here, too, there was a monastery with a *borgo*, walled since 880 against Saracen attacks, containing houses and oratories. In 937, the monastery was reformed by Odo of Cluny. In the basilica, on the triumphal arch, was a mosaic given by Galla Placidia, one of the few items to have escaped the fire which destroyed San Paolo almost completely in 1823. It represents Christ, the symbols of the Evangelists, the Twenty-Four Elders, and St Peter and St Paul. The apse mosaic was divided into two levels: the upper level showed Christ with St Peter and St Andrew on his left and St Paul and St Luke on his right, and the lower level depicted the Agnus Dei enthroned with the Four Rivers of Paradise. On the left of the throne were represented SS James, Bartholomew, Thomas, Simon, Matthew, and Mark, and on the right, SS John, Philip, Mathias, James, Jude, and Barnabas, altogether a rather unusual iconographical pattern.[29] The façade also carried a mosaic, of which some remains were later placed in the wall at the back of the triumphal arch, indicating that St Peter, St Paul and the symbols of the Evangelists around a bust of Christ in a medallion were represented. Along the walls of the nave were depicted cycles of scenes from the Old and New

---

[27] Huelsen, *Le chiese*, 3–4, and R. Valentini and G. Zuchetti (eds.), *Codice topografico della città di Roma* (4 vols.; Rome, 1940–53), ii. 106–31.

[28] Armellini–Cecchelli, *Le chiese*, ii. 1075–86; Huelsen, *Le chiese*, 285–6; Krautheimer, *Corpus*, ii. 1–144; Ferrari, *Roman Monasteries*, 182–9.

[29] The importance of St Andrew and St Luke needs underlining; the popularity of St Peter's brother in England, a saint venerated second only to his brother, was originally based on the devotion to him in Rome, especially from the age of Gregory the Great onwards.

Testaments, in fresco.[30] The two registers on the right wall had forty-two episodes from the Old Testament, of which those extending from the Separation of Light from Darkness to the Death of the first-born of the Egyptians are known. The left wall depicted scenes from the Acts of the Apostles, with special reference to the life of St Paul, from the Meeting of the Seven Deacons to the Meeting of St Peter and St Paul in Rome. Over the arches of the transept were fifth-century medallions with the portraits of the popes from St Peter onwards.[31]

Some of the churches outside the walls were of a later date. One was S. Sebastiano. Until the ninth century, this church was commonly known as 'Sanctus Sebastianus ad Catacumbas'. The *Liber Pontificalis* recalls the fact that the basilica was built on the spot where the bodies of St Peter and St Paul had provisionally rested in the third century at the time of Valerian's persecution. Its first name was *titulus Petri et Pauli*.[32] In the fifth century, it became the monastery *in Catatymbas*, the oldest monastic foundation in Rome, dedicated to St Sebastian, whose relics were venerated in the cemetery. After the ninth century, the catacombs of St Sebastian were amongst the few to remain a centre of pilgrimage, chiefly because of their associations with St Peter and St Paul.[33]

The monastery of Tre Fontane, SS Vincenzo e Anastasio, also called *ad Aquas Salvias*, at the spot where St Paul is supposed to have been martyred, was built by Pope Honorius in 625, to honour its two titular martyrs, and was a Greek monastic church of great repute in Rome, especially in the ninth century, and although somewhat in decline in the tenth century, still visited by St Nilus himself in 998.[34] Theodore may well have been a monk there, since the monastery was mainly staffed by refugees from Tarsus, and we know that Bede was particularly attached to St Anastasius, whose Life he had at his disposal in England and spent some time editing.[35] St Anastasius had been a Persian monk and martyr of the seventh century, whose relics were brought to Rome by eastern refugees fleeing from the

[30] Garber, *Wirkungen*, 7–22, figs. I–II and pls. 2–27, based on the drawings in Vatican MS Barberini lat. 4406.

[31] Armellini–Cecchelli, *Le chiese*, ii. 1151–62; Huelsen, *Le chiese*, 415–16; Krautheimer, *Corpus*, v. 93–164.

[32] This tradition is recorded in various early sources such as Philocalus, the Acts of St Sebastian, of the 5th c., and Gregory the Great's letters.

[33] Rossi, *Roma sotterranea*, i. 225–9. This cemetery was by then already known as 'St Callixtus''. The church itself was further associated with Gregory the Great, who reputedly preached his famous 37th Homily on the Gospel there. Armellini–Cecchelli, *Le chiese*, ii. 1112–28; Huelsen, *Le chiese*, 460; Krautheimer, *Corpus*, iv. 99–147; Ferrari, *Roman Monasteries*, 163–5.

[34] B. Hamilton, 'The City of Rome and the Eastern Churches in the Tenth Century', in *Monastic Reform, Catharism and the Crusades (900–1300)* (London, 1979), 7, and Ferrari, *Roman Monasteries*, 33–48.

[35] Ibid. 39–41, and Bede, *Chronica minora* ed. T. Mommsen, MGH AA xiii (3), 310–11.

Muslims. In the church, pilgrims would have seen a greatly venerated image of this saint.[36]

The basilica of S. Valentino, built in the fourth century by Pope Julius I at the first milestone on the Via Flaminia, on the tomb of the martyr Valentine, was decorated with frescos by either Pope Theodore (642–9) or Pope Benedict II (683–5), or in the early eighth century. The cemetery was one of the few to be still visited by pilgrims in the tenth century.[37] On the tomb of the martyr, there were frescos depicting the Visitation, the Nativity of Christ with the Bathing of the Child and the midwife Salome, and the Crucifixion.[38] In the tenth century, S. Valentino became a cell of the monastery of S. Silvestro in Capite, which was possibly, but by no means certainly, still Greek, one of the richest and most influential monastic houses in Rome.[39] The abbot of S. Silvestro Theobald restored S. Valentino *c*.1060. This basilica was a major station during the *Laetania Maior* procession in Rome.[40]

The last of these churches was S. Pancrazio. An original building had been erected on the tomb of St Pancras, a fourth-century martyr, by Pope Symmachus.[41] It was rebuilt entirely by Pope Honorius I, who had the apse mosaic made. The catacombs were among those still visited in the tenth century.[42]

The other churches visited were all inside the walls, some dating back to the age of Constantine, such as S. Giovanni in Laterano and Sta Croce, others built between the mid-fourth and the seventh century. S. Giovanni was the first church and the cathedral of Rome, 'mater caput ecclesiae', as well as the church of the Lateran Palace, the official residence of the pope. It had been originally dedicated to the Saviour, but, after the fourth century, the names of St John the Evangelist and St John the Baptist were added, from the name of a neighbouring monastery. Little by little, this latter name was substituted to the original dedication, and the evolution was completed in the tenth century. The first great restoration was credited

[36] Armellini–Cecchelli, *Le chiese*, ii. 1168–70; Huelsen, *Le chiese*, 173.

[37] Rossi, *Roma sotterranea*, i. 222.

[38] J. Osborne, 'Early Medieval Wall-Paintings in the Catacomb of San Valentino, Rome', *Papers of the British School at Rome*, 49 (1981), 82–90.

[39] Hamilton, 'The City of Rome', 8–9 and 'The Monastic Revival in Tenth-Century Rome', 39–40, in *Monastic Reform*; Ferrari, *Roman Monasteries*, 336–40, 302–12.

[40] Deshusses, *Sacramentaire Grégorien*, 211. Armellini–Cecchelli, *Le chiese*, ii. 1044–9; Huelsen, *Le chiese*, 496–7; Krautheimer, *Corpus*, iv. 289–312.

[41] St Pancras was popular in England because some of his relics had been sent to King Oswiu of Northumbria by Pope Vitalian in the seventh century, see *BHE* 320–1. Furthermore, a church dedicated to him formed the east end of the alignment of St Augustine's, Canterbury since the seventh century, see Fernie, *Architecture*, 37.

[42] Armellini–Cecchelli, *Le Chiese*, ii. 1181–7; Huelsen, *Le chiese*, 409; Krautheimer, *Corpus*, iii. 153–74; Ferrari, *Roman Monasteries*, 341–4.

to Pope Sergius III in 904–11, who gave it its nave mosaics, figuring scenes from the Old and the New Testaments, in the usual allegorical arrangement. Some of the scenes represented were: Adam driven out of the Garden of Eden and Christ in Heaven, the River of Sin and the Baptism of Christ, the Sacrifice of Isaac and Christ bearing his Cross, Joseph and his brothers and Christ and Judas, Israel crossing the Red Sea and the Descent into Hell, and Jonah in the belly of the whale and the Ascension of Christ. The columns in the nave carried mosaics depicting the Prophets, the Apostles, and the Evangelists' symbols, whilst the apse mosaic, subsequently restored in the thirteenth century, represented a bust of Christ surrounded by the Dove of the Holy Spirit and angels. This upper part of the mosaic has survived, having been incorporated within the restored apse. The façade mosaic depicted Christ between St Michael and St Gabriel. Near the basilica was the Baptistery, built and decorated under Pope Hilarius (461–8), comprising the oratories of St John the Evangelist, St John the Baptist, and the Holy Cross.

Archbishops and other pilgrims who actually met the pope spent some time in the Lateran Palace itself. The palace had two *triclinia*, both extensively decorated with mosaics and frescos since the time of Leo III. In the first there was a mosaic of Christ with the Four Rivers of Paradise at his feet and five Apostles on either side. Two of the side apses had frescos, whilst a spandrel displayed a mosaic depicting St Peter enthroned giving Charlemagne a standard and Leo III the *pallium*, both pope and emperor kneeling at his feet. The second *triclinium* had one main apse and ten smaller ones off the 'nave', all probably decorated with mosaics and frescos. The main apse showed Christ, the Virgin Mary, Peter, Paul, and other saints; on its walls were depicted the Twenty-Four Elders and the 144,000 Elect of the Revelation, as well as a bust of Christ and the symbols of the Evangelists. Two other pictures represented St Peter saved from the waves and St Paul saved from shipwreck.

Within the palace, two chapels held objects of veneration: the chapel of St Silvester, which had an icon of Christ, decorated with pictures of saints, and the oratory of the Holy Cross, of the fifth century, with a relic of the Cross in a golden Crucifix. The greatest treasures of the palace were kept in the chapel of St Laurence, of the fourth century, known as the Sancta Sanctorum on account of the great number of relics it possessed, some enclosed in a casket made under Leo III and some walled in.[43] This chapel, whose mosaic decoration was entirely refurbished in the thirteenth century,

[43] On the Sancta Sanctorum, see P. Lauer, 'Le Trésor du Sancta Sanctorum', *Monuments et mémoires publiés par l'Académie des Inscriptions et Belles-Lettres*, 15 (1906), 7–140, and H. Grisar, *Die römische Kapelle Sancta Sanctorum und ihr Schatz* (Freiburg, 1908).

also contained a sacred image of Christ, dating from the fifth century, known as Acheropoita. The main relics, first listed by John the Deacon, were the heads of SS Peter, Paul, Laurence, and Agnes, the patron saints of Rome, and parts of the bodies of SS John the Evangelist, John the Baptist, Eufemia, Eulalia, Praxedis, Aldegund, and Zachariah. The crosses and reliquaries in the chapel were also prized treasures. Most noticeable was the processional cross used for the Good Friday procession to Santa Croce and for the feast of the Exaltation of the Cross.[44] It depicted scenes from the life of Christ: the Annunciation, Visitation, Nativity, Presentation in the Temple, and Baptism on the long arm, and the Flight into Egypt and the Adoration of the Magi on the short arm. From the eighth century onwards, it was venerated in its own right. Other crosses depicted the Crucifixion, and on the silver mount of a ninth-century one were represented the Wedding at Cana, the Incredulity of Thomas, and Christ appearing to the Holy Women. The most ornate reliquaries were of the seventh century, showing Christ between Peter and Paul, and another, of the ninth century, made of silver, possibly an Anglo-Saxon work,[45] had representations of the Virgin Mary, St Peter, and the Resurrection with the Holy Women at the Sepulchre.[46]

Sta Croce was founded under Constantine by his mother the Empress Helena, in her Sessorian Palace. It was first called 'Sancta Hierusalem', then became Santa Croce after Helena brought back from Jerusalem the greatly venerated relic of the Cross. The possession of the relic of the Cross made this basilica one of the major Roman churches for devotional purposes. It was equally important from a liturgical point of view, since a major papal procession went from the Lateran to Santa Croce on Good Friday, and it was also a major stational church for various feast-days throughout the year. A chapel of the fourth century, dedicated to St Helena, had a mosaic, and on the upper level of the nave walls were depicted the ancestors of Christ in mosaic.[47]

At Sta Maria Maggiore, a basilica was founded by Pope Liberius (352–6), known as the Basilica Liberiana. Pope Sixtus III built a basilica dedicated to the Virgin, which an erroneous entry in the *Liber Pontificalis* identified with Liberius' basilica. The name of 'Sancta Maria *ad Praesepe*', the one recorded in the Itinerary of Einsiedeln, began to be used in the sixth or the seventh centuries. This name derived from its possession of

[44] The Good Friday procession is described in the Appendix to the Itinerary of Einsiedeln.

[45] Grat, *Annales de St Bertin*, anno 864, p. 106.

[46] Armellini–Cecchelli, *Le chiese*, i. 121–49; Huelsen, *Le chiese*, 272; Krautheimer, *Corpus*, v. 1–92.

[47] Armellini–Cecchelli, *Le chiese*, ii. 981–9; Huelsen, *Le chiese*, 243; Krautheimer, *Corpus*, i. 165–94; Ferrari, *Roman Monasteries*, 107.

one of the most popular relics in Rome: the cradle of Christ. It appears for the first time as 'Sancta Maria Maior' in the *Liber Pontificalis* in the ninth century. Sixtus III gave it its series of mosaics covering the walls of the nave and representing scenes from the Old and the New Testaments, many emphasizing St Mary's status as the Mother of God.

On the upper level of the nave walls, the mosaics represent scenes from the Old Testament, running in chronological order from the left wall with its remaining twenty-eight scenes from the lives of Abraham, Isaac, and Jacob to the right wall with its remaining twenty-four scenes from the lives of Moses and Joshua, and ending with the triumphal arch scenes depicting scenes from the Infancy of Christ, based on the New Testament and the Apocrypha. These are the Annunciation and the Dispelling of Joseph's doubts, the Presentation in the Temple, the Flight into Egypt, the House of Joseph, the Magi before Herod, the Adoration of the Magi, Aphrodisius and his household receiving Jesus and his parents, and the Massacre of the Innocents. In the centre was depicted the bejewelled throne with the royal insignia and the Seven Seals, placed between SS Peter and Paul, the Four Beasts, and the cities of Bethlehem and Jerusalem as symbols either of the Churches of the Gentiles and the Jews or of the Church Militant and the Church Triumphant.[48]

At S. Pietro in Vincoli, there had been an earlier Christian building on this spot, a rich *domus*. The church was built under Pope Sixtus III with the help of the Empress Eudoxia, wife of Valentinian III. Three objects were greatly venerated there: the Chains of St Peter, a mosaic of *c.*680 showing St Sebastian as a protector against the plague and, by tradition, the relics of the Seven Macchabee Brothers.[49] S. Lorenzo in Panisperna goes back to Constantinian times, and tradition described it as being built on the spot where St Laurence had been martyred.[50]

Sta Sabina was founded in the fifth century, under Pope Celestine I (422–32). It had mosaics on the inside wall above the entrance door, representing allegories of the Church of the Gentiles and the Church of the Jews, as well as symbols of the Evangelists. On the apse arch, there were mosaics showing the busts of Christ and the Apostles, and the walls probably also carried mosaics or frescos. The other notable feature of the church was its main cypress-wood door, with fifth-century carvings of Old

---

[48] Armellini–Cecchelli, *Le chiese*, i. 281–94; Huelsen, *Le chiese*, 342; Krautheimer, *Corpus*, iii. 1–60. On the mosaics, see B. Brenk, *Die frühchristlichen Mosaiken in Sta Maria Maggiore zu Rom* (Wiesbaden, 1975).

[49] Armellini–Cecchelli, *Le chiese*, i. 260–3; Huelsen, *Le chiese*, 418–19; Krautheimer, *Corpus*, iii. 178–231.

[50] Armellini–Cecchelli, *Le chiese*, i. 249–51; Huelsen, *Le chiese*, 292–3; Krautheimer, *Corpus*, ii. 185.

and New Testament scenes. Recognizable among these are the Crucifixion, the Holy Women at the Sepulchre, the Adoration of the Magi, the Disciples at Emmaus, the Healing of the Blind Man, the Multiplication of the Bread, the Wedding at Cana, Christ's miracles in the Desert, Pentecost (?), the Ascension, the Denial of Peter, Jesus before Caiaphas, before Pilate, and carrying His Cross, and scenes from the lives of Moses, Zachariah, Habakuk and Elijah.[51]

At Sta Cecilia, the *Hieronymian Martyrology* mentioned the *titulus Ceciliae*, which, therefore, must have already existed in the fourth century. Pope Paschal I (817–24) translated the relics of St Cecilia from the cemetery on the Via Appia, and built the church, whilst also founding the monastery of St Cecilia and St Agatha. The relics of SS Valerian and Tiburtius were also venerated in the church, and the two saints were represented in a mosaic in the porch. The apse mosaic in the basilica depicted Christ, on his right, St Paul, a crowned St Cecilia, and Pope Paschal with the square halo of the living, and on his left, St Peter, St Valerian and St Agatha.[52]

Already mentioned in the list of the Roman council of 499,[53] the *titulus*, then basilica, of S. Crisogono was restored in 731 by Pope Gregory III, who added frescos on the walls of the aisles and in the apse, representing the titular saint, SS Felicissimus and Agapitus, and others. During the course of the tenth century, a new set of frescos was added in the right aisle, relating the story of St Benedict. Still visible in the old (now the lower) church, are three scenes: Benedict saving Placidus, healing a leper, and a monk being assaulted by a wild beast. A monastery was attached to it, Greek before it was reformed by Odo of Cluny.[54]

Tradition ascribes the foundation of a Christian basilica at Sta Maria in Trastevere to Pope Calixtus (217–22). The first reference to the subsequent basilica is in the *Liber Pontificalis*, which ascribed its building to Pope Julius I in 340. In the eighth century, Pope John VII restored it and gave it its frescos and there was from the early eighth century onwards an icon of the Virgin of Mercy, with the Child and angels, of the *Maria Regina* style.[55]

---

[51] Armellini–Cecchelli, *Le chiese*, ii. 709–15; Huelsen, *Le chiese*, 430–1; Krautheimer, *Corpus*, iv. 72–98.

[52] Armellini–Cecchelli, *Le chiese*, ii. 825–8; Huelsen, *Le chiese*, 229; Krautheimer, *Corpus*, i. 95–112; Ferrari, *Roman Monasteries*, 23–5.

[53] Ed. Huelsen, *Le chiese*, 124–5.

[54] Armellini–Cecchelli, *Le chiese*, ii. 847–9; Huelsen, *Le chiese*, 238; Krautheimer, *Corpus*, i. 144–64; Ferrari, *Roman Monasteries*, 92–5.

[55] Armellini–Cecchelli, *Le chiese*, ii. 783–96; Huelsen, *Le chiese*, 371; Krautheimer, *Corpus*, iii. 65–71; Ferrari, *Roman Monasteries*, 228–9. On the icon and its western, as opposed to Byzantine, iconography, see C. Bertelli, *La Madonna di Santa Maria in Trastevere* (Roma, 1961) and R. Deshman, 'Servants of the Mother of God in Byzantine and Medieval Art', *Word and Image*, 5 (1989), 33–70.

The origin of S. Lorenzo in Lucina is unknown, but it probably goes back to the third or fourth centuries. It was a presbyteral *titulus* by 365 and the church dates from the time of Sixtus III (432–40). Its main interest for pilgrims was the relic of the *craticula*, the gridiron upon which St Laurence had been martyred. The apse decoration, remade in the twelfth century but possibly preserving the previous iconography, represented Christ in the middle between St Peter, St Laurence, and Lucina on the right and St Paul and two saints on the left.[56] The devotion to St Laurence was pervasive in Rome, where the saint was venerated second only to St Peter and St Paul, and where four great basilicas and numerous chapels and smaller churches were dedicated to him.[57]

Sta Maria ad Martyres or Sta Maria Rotonda was Agrippa's Pantheon, transformed by Pope Boniface IV into a church in 608–15, and normally called 'Sancta Maria ad Martyres' until the end of the tenth century, when the name 'Sancta Maria Rotonda' became the more usual one. Here, too, there was an icon of the Virgin and Child of the eastern type.[58]

The old *titulus* of SS Apostoli was founded by Pope Pelagius I (555–60) to enshrine the relics of the Apostles Philip and James, brought to Rome. Its name became increasingly understood as a dedication to all the Apostles, until this became its common name by the end of the Middle Ages. The most precious relics in the church were those of the Apostles Philip and James in the *confessio* and, from the ninth century onwards, those of the martyrs Chrysantius, Daria and their companions.[59]

Finally, the pilgrim could also visit some of the Greek churches and communities, other than SS Vincenzo e Anastasio. There was the church called S. Bonifazio, first cited in the *Liber Pontificalis* in the sixth century, together with the monastery, and originally dedicated to the martyr Boniface alone. The name of Alexis was added in the tenth century, when the cult of this saint developed and from the tenth century onwards, especially from the time of the second Greek abbot of the community, Leo, the two names were always used. The first abbot, Sergius, probably brought the relics of St Alexis to Rome in 977, and Abbot Leo promoted the cult of this saint, which subsequently became very popular there. In 977, Pope Benedict VII gave the church and the monastery to the Greek

---

[56] It was reconstructed by C. R. Morey, *Lost Mosaics and Frescoes of Rome in the Medieval Period* (Princeton, 1915), 6–15.

[57] Armellini-Cecchelli, *Le chiese*, i. 355–8; Huelsen, *Le chiese*, 288; Krautheimer, *Corpus*, ii. 159–84.

[58] Armellini–Cecchelli, *Le chiese*, i. 589–92; Huelsen, *Le chiese*, 363 and C. Bertelli, *La Madonna del Pantheon* (Rome, 1961).

[59] Armellini–Cecchelli, *Le chiese*, i. 309–12; Huelsen, *Le chiese*, 201–2; Krautheimer, *Corpus*, i. 78–83.

Metropolitan Sergius and the monastery became half Benedictine and half Basilian, under the name of *Blacherne*. This was derived from an area of Constantinople, where a miraculous image of the Virgin was to be seen. An icon of the Virgin of Blacherne is still venerated in this church, but there is no evidence to show whether this eighth-century icon was at Sant'Alessio at that date. The reputation of Greek monasticism and learning was once again very high in Rome in the late tenth century, and the mixed monastery of Sant'Alessio in particular was 'the most distinguished in Rome in the last quarter of the tenth century', and held privileges from Emperors and Popes.[60] The year 990 was a significant one in the history of this house: advised by St Nilus, whom he had met at Valleluce, St Adalbert of Prague entered the community and spent several years there before undertaking his mission of conversion of the Slav peoples. The monastery became even more famous on account of St Adalbert's stay there, though already renowned on account of the learning and asceticism of the community under its Greek abbots.[61] Then came Sta Maria in Cosmedin, founded in the sixth century on the ruins of part of the *Statio Annonae*, which became in the seventh century the church of the Greek colony, the 'Schola Graeca', stretching over this whole area called 'Ripa Graeca'. It was rebuilt and enlarged by Pope Hadrian I, when it took the name *in Cosmedin*, a common one for Greek churches in Italy. In the church, there was a greatly venerated icon of the Virgin and Child.[62]

All these churches are mentioned in Sigeric's Itinerary of 990. They are evidently far fewer than even the most important of the Roman churches known to us through the lists of the councils of 499 and the catalogues, prominent amongst which are the seventh-century Catalogue 'Salisburgense', the late eighth-century Itinerary of Einsiedeln,[63] and the Catalogue of Leo III (795–816) in the *Liber Pontificalis*.[64] A list of Roman churches, now presumed to date back to the seventh century, was included by

---

[60] Hamilton, 'City of Rome', 15–20 and 'Orientale lumen and magistra latinitas: Greek Influences on Western Monasticism (900–1100)', 188–9 and 209–11 in *Monastic Reform*; Ferrari, *Roman Monasteries*, 78–87.

[61] Ferrari, *Roman Monasteries*, 213–15; 'City of Rome', 15–24 and 'Monastery of S. Alessio', 265–310, esp. 282–91. Armellini–Cecchelli, *Le chiese*, ii. 715–19; Huelsen, *Le chiese*, 171–2; Krautheimer, *Corpus*, i. 41–2. On Adalbert's journeys in Italy and his interests in Greek monasticism, see *Vita Sancti Adalberti auctore Iohanne Canapario*, ed. G. H. Pertz, MHG SS iv, chs. 14–17, pp. 587–9. The *Ex Miraculis Sancti Alexii*, ibid. 619–20, written before 1012, show the beginnings of the community in Rome.

[62] Armellini–Cecchelli, *Le chiese*, ii. 735–43; Huelsen, *Le chiese*, 327–8; Krautheimer, *Corpus*, ii. 277–307.

[63] Huelsen, *Le chiese*, 4–5; Valentini–Zuchetti, *Codice*, 176–201; see also C. Huelsen, *La Pianta di Roma dell'Anonimo Einsiedlense* (Rome, 1907).

[64] *LP* ii. 1–34.

William of Malmesbury in his *Gesta Regum Anglorum*: it may have been compiled under Pope Honorius I (625–38), and was in any case produced probably before 682.[65] Sigeric's Itinerary is not just a catalogue or a guide book, but a personal diary: his choice expressed the preferences of an Anglo-Saxon ecclesiastic and pilgrim. Since it is known how considerable was the number of such pilgrims to Rome, the importance of this list of preferences can be easily perceived. Leo III's Catalogue is part of the *Liber Pontificalis*, whose existence was certainly known in England since Bede uses it in his *Ecclesiastical History*, and whose subsequent additions after Bede's time may well have reached England after 806, the probable date of the compilation of the Catalogue. The Catalogue 'Salisburgense' lists twenty-six churches, the Itinerary of Einsiedeln sixty-six, William of Malmesbury's list approximately forty, and Leo III's Catalogue 117, including monasteries, *diaconiae* and oratories. Sigeric's list of twenty-three churches includes sixteen of those mentioned in 'Salisburgense', eighteen from the Itinerary of Einsiedeln, ten from Malmesbury, and no less than twenty-one, possibly twenty-two, from Leo's Catalogue. His choices acknowledge, not necessarily these lists themselves, but the implicit importance of some of these churches in Rome, such as the major basilicas. It can be argued, however, that he may also have made some personal selections, probably dictated by what returning pilgrims or compatriots living in Rome may have told him. Clearly, the choice of these twenty-three churches out of an existing number of at least 117 means that, apart from major pilgrimage goals such as the Vatican and the Lateran basilicas, he made deliberate decisions as to what he wished to see.

Among the other churches, however, a pilgrim could have also visited, for example, Sta Pudenziana, S. Stefano Rotondo, SS Cosma e Damiano, SS Giovanni e Paolo, S. Clemente, Sta Maria in Domnica, S. Teodoro, and Sta Suzanna, all mentioned in the list of popes which Sigeric brought back to Rome, S. Gregorio, Gregory the Great's monastic foundation on the Coelius, and some recently built or rebuilt churches, such as Sta Prassede and SS Quattro Coronati. Gregory's monastery on the Coelius, dedicated to SS Andrew and Gregory, and reformed from being a Greek community by Odo of Cluny, was extremely wealthy and influential in Rome.[66] Sta Pudenziana, older than 398, when it was restored by Pope Siricius, had an apse mosaic representing Christ, the Twelve Apostles, and the saintly virgins Pudenziana and Prassede, and another, of the ninth century, in a chapel, showing St Peter between the two virgins, preaching

[65] Valentini–Zuchetti, *Codice*, ii. 138–53.
[66] Ferrari, *Roman Monasteries*, 138–51.

from his chair to his flock. S. Stefano was the only early Roman church built in the round; founded in the fifth century, it was partly rebuilt in the seventh, when the bodies of the martyrs Primus and Felician were brought there, and it acquired a mosaic over their tomb, representing them with a bust of Christ and a bejewelled cross; it also had some association with Gregory the Great, reputed to have preached there. One of the oldest churches, since it had been built by Pope Felix IV (526–30) in parts of the Forum of the Peace of Vespasian, of the Temple of the Urbs where the archives were kept, and of the Temple of Romulus, SS Cosma e Damiano possessed an apse mosaic showing Christ between St Peter, St Cosmas, and Theodore, and St Paul, St Damian and Felix, with the Agnus Dei enthroned, symbols of the Evangelists, and the Twenty-Four Elders, and the relics of the two patron saints. SS John and Paul had been martyred in their house on the Coelius and were for a long time the only martyrs to be buried in a Roman church, built over their house, first a *titulus* then a church since at least 398; the 'house' contained frescos and the church had, attached to it, one of the earliest pilgrims' hospices in Rome. S. Clemente was a *titulus c.*200 and Pope Siricius (384–99) dedicated it as a church; there were numerous frescos of different periods there, a Virgin and Child of the sixth century, a Last Judgement with Michael, Gabriel, Andrew, Clement, Cyril, and Methodius (Cyril's tomb was in the church), an Ascension or Assumption of the Virgin, the Holy Women at the Sepulchre, the Wedding at Cana, and the Descent into Hell, all of the ninth century, and several scenes from the life of St Alexius and St Clement, a Christ between Michael and Clement, and Gabriel and Nicholas, and a Crucifixion of St Peter, all of the second half of the eleventh century. Sta Maria in Domnica, of Constantinian origin and residence of the archdeacon of Rome, was rebuilt by Pope Paschal I, who gave it its apse mosaic. S. Teodoro, first mentioned under Gregory the Great and dedicated to a martyr of Pontus, had an apse mosaic dating from the sixth or seventh century, of Christ between Peter and Theodore, and Paul and Cleonicus. A *titulus* since the fourth century and rebuilt by Leo III, Sta Suzanna also had a tribune mosaic of that period, showing Leo III with a model of the church and Charlemagne, both with the square halo of the living. Sta Maria Antiqua, possibly the first church to which a *diaconia* was attached in the seventh century, was built in the library of Augustus in the Forum, decorated by Pope John VII but burnt down in the late ninth century and rebuilt nearby as Sta Maria Nova. Sta Prassede was a fifth-century *titulus*, completely rebuilt by Paschal I, who gave it its arch mosaics and two chapels dedicated to St John the Baptist and St Zeno; the main mosaic shows Christ with angels and elect in the heavenly Jerusalem, together with fifteen saints among whom are SS Peter, Paul, John the Baptist, Prassede, and the other Apostles. SS Quattro Coronati, founded in the fifth century, was also rebuilt in the ninth by Leo IV (847–55) and again after being burnt down by Robert Guiscard and the Normans in 1080. Other influential monasteries were SS Cosma e Damiano in Mica Aurea, founded in the mid-tenth century, S. Agata in Suburra, whose church had been founded by the Arian Goth Flavius Ricimer *c*.462–70 and reconsecrated as a catholic church by Gregory the Great, and S. Andrea Catabarbara, founded in the fifth century and given to the German abbey of Fulda after 1044; the latter two had apse mosaics depicting Christ and the Apostles.[67] This is quite enough to sustain a view of Rome during the Anglo-Saxon period as, in the first place, a repository of books and relics, further a font of spiritual benefits, and not least a major attraction for her artistic treasures and liturgical splendour.

II. THE FACTUAL EVIDENCE FOR CONTACT

The evidence of the early Anglo-Saxon period includes numerous references to close intercourse between England and Rome. Augustine, the prior of St Gregory's monastery on the Coelius, was sent by the pope and reached England with several helpers in 597, not only to ensure the conversion of the Angles and the Saxons, but also to implement Gregory's ideas in terms of ecclesiastical organization, liturgy, and pastoral techniques. These were subsequently enforced by Augustine's successors Laurentius, Mellitus, Justus, and Honorius at Canterbury, Paulinus at York, and even, in a way, Birinus in Wessex, all sent by Rome to England.

The first pilgrims to Rome belong to the next generation after the Conversion, and came from Northumbria, Benedict Biscop founder of the monastery of Monkwearmouth, and Wilfrid, bishop of the whole of Northumbria first, then of Hexham. Until the late seventh century, it was still considered regular practice for the archbishop of Canterbury to be appointed directly from Rome and when the first English archbishop-elect Wigheard died there before returning to England with the *pallium*, Pope Vitalian appointed a monk from Tarsus present in Rome, Theodore, as the new archbishop in 668, and sent him to England with the African abbot Hadrian; the regard in which Theodore was held in Rome appears clearly from the letter of the Roman council to the Emperor, assuring the latter that Theodore had to be consulted on the issue of monothelitism since, despite Rome being at that point a Greek cultural centre of considerable

[67] Ferrari, *Roman Monasteries*, 103–6, 19–22, 51–7.

importance on account of the presence of a large community of refugees from the East, he alone was deemed able to understand it.[68] Matters of ecclesiastical discipline were still settled in Rome, as numerous letters from and to the pope to and from English kings and ecclesiastics show. When Wilfrid, whose influence had been instrumental in settling the controversy between the 'Roman' and the 'Irish' parties with regard to the date of celebration of Easter and the shape of the tonsure in favour of the 'Roman' style, at the council of Whitby in 664, opposed Theodore who wished to divide the Northumbrian diocese into two smaller ones, he appealed to the pope for the solution of the conflict, a procedure as yet rather uncommon in the West.

Pilgrims to Rome followed in the wake of the first two. Kings set the example: Caedwalla of Wessex who, after being baptized in Rome, died there and was buried in the Vatican basilica, where his tomb became one of the highlights of the visit to Rome for later pilgrims; Ine of Wessex, who, together with his wife Ethelburgh was reputed to have founded the Schola Saxonum, and who died there in 726; Coenred of Mercia and Offa of Essex in 709; and Burghred of Mercia, who also died there and was buried in the Schola Saxonum. Archbishops of Canterbury, such as Cuthbert *c.*740 and Bregwin in 751, followed, as did other ecclesiastics: bishops Daniel of Winchester in 721, Egbert of York in 733 and 735 and Cuthwin of East Anglia *c.*750; Hwaetberht and some of his fellow monks from Wearmouth *c.*700, Aldhelm *c.*701, Ceolfrid and some monks from Jarrow in 716, Willibald and Winnibald, together in 721 and 730 and the first on his own in 739, a priest from London Nothelm *c.*725, Abbot Forthred in 757, Alcuin twice in 767 and 780, another priest, Odberht, in 795, and an abbot Wada in 797. Laymen also went, such as the two thegns Cildas and Ceolbert in 798, and even women: some Northumbrian nuns *c.*713, Wethburgh *c.*716, who 'retired' to lead a quiet life near the shrine of St Peter, two friends of Eangyth and Bugge *c.*722 and the latter herself in 738, when she met Boniface there and toured the shrines of the martyrs in his company.[69] In Bede's words, 'nobles and common, layfolk and clergy, men and women' went to Rome.[70] The Anglo-Saxon Church was a staunch preserver of the Roman liturgy and chant in England and no saints were as highly regarded as those associated with Rome, St Peter, St Gregory, and St Laurence. When Boniface and Willibrord undertook their

---

[68] J. M. Mansi (ed.), *Sacrorum Conciliorum Nova et Amplissima Collectio* (31 vols.; Florence and Venice, 1759–98), xi. 235c, see Mango, 'Culture', 702 and generally, 694–721. The importance of Rome as a centre of transmission for Greek culture has also been emphasized by J. Howard-Johnston (ed.), *Byzantium and the West c.850–c.1200* (Amsterdam, 1988), 2–15.

[69] Moore, *Saxon Pilgrims*, 126–7; *Boniface*, 35, 56, 58, 177.

[70] *BHE* 473.

missions, they did so after visiting Rome and receiving the pope's blessing. It may be no coincidence that two of the three reformers and thinkers who moulded the Frankish Carolingian Church into a Romanizing spirit were English, Boniface and Alcuin, even in such details as the introduction of papal exemption privileges of the type English monasteries possessed, for example at Boniface's foundation of Fulda.[71] The orthodoxy of the English Church was in no doubt, as Pope Agatho found from its emissaries at the synod of Rome in 680.[72]

During the tenth and eleventh centuries, these close links with the city of St Peter were maintained and reinforced. Englishmen of all ranks and status from the kings down continued to go to Rome. In 855, King Aethelwulf of Wessex went on pilgrimage with his son Alfred, whom he had previously sent to Rome alone in 853.[73] In 1027, it was King Cnut, baptized when already of mature age, who followed the English tradition and went on pilgrimage.[74] When in Rome, he used the opportunity to do some business as well, meeting the pope, asking him to allow the archbishops coming for the *pallium* to obtain it without having to pay extortionate sums for it in gifts, and also meeting Abbot Odilo of Cluny and attending the coronation of the Emperor Conrad II, with whom he arranged a marriage between his daughter Gunnhild and Conrad's son, the future Henry III.[75] The archbishops Plegmund in 909, Aelfsige in 955–6 (who died on his way in the Alps), Dunstan in 960, Sigeric in 990, Aelfric in 997, Aethelnoth in 1020, Robert of Jumièges in 1051 and the archbishops of York Cynesige and Ealdred in 1033 and 1061 went to take the *pallium* or on business to Rome.[76] The only archbishop of Canterbury who did not take his *pallium* in Rome and is expressly said not to have done so was Stigand, appointed by King Edward in 1052, whom the 'correctly' elected Pope Leo IX had refused to consecrate, and who was sent the *pallium* in 1058 by the anti-pope Benedict X.[77] In this refusal of a pope to

---

[71] Wormald, 'Aethelwold', 25; Fulda was the only German monastery to preserve this privilege throughout the Carolingian period. There is one example, however, of an exemption privilege of this kind even earlier, that of Bobbio, see P. Wormald, 'Bede and Benedict Biscop', in Bonner, *Famulus Christi*, 146–8; it confirms the attachment of the Irish, as well as the Anglo-Saxons, to Rome, see below n. 159.

[72] *BHE* 384–91.

[73] *ASC*, AB853 and C854, 43; *Asser*, chs. 8, p.7 and 11–12, pp. 8–10.

[74] *ASC*, DEF1031 = 1027, 101 and *Florence*, i. 185; on the problems relating to the date of this journey, see Barlow, 'Two notes', repr. *Norman Conquest*, 50–1.

[75] *CSD* I. i. 509.

[76] *Aethelweard*, 52; Lives of St Dunstan by 'B' and Osbern in Stubbs, *Memorials*, 38–40, 108; *ASC*, EF989 = 990, 82; F997, 84; CDE1022, 98; C1051, E1048, 116; D1055, 130; D1061, 135; D1051, E1047 = 1050, 116.

[77] *ASC*, E1052, 127; E1048, C1051, 116–17; DE1058, 134.

approve the choice of a royal candidate are made apparent the first attempts of the papacy to obtain control over episcopal elections. The papacy's arguments in this case were that Stigand had been appointed by the king despite the fact that the incumbent of the see, Robert, was still alive at the time, even though exiled. Stigand's irregular position was further weakened by William I's refusal to be crowned by him. The knot was untied only in 1070, on the initiative and to the satisfaction of the papal reforming party, by the two papal legates sent to England to depose Stigand.[78]

Other ecclesiastics of lower rank went on pilgrimage too, such as Bishop Herman of Ramsbury and Abbot Aelfwine of Ramsey, who attended the council of 1050, together with Ealdred; and Abbot Aelfstan of St Augustine's, who spent some time in Rome in 1022 and met the Emperor Henry II.[79] Among the laity, both the higher ranks, such as the earls Harold and Tostig with his wife, and the lower, such as the simple *thegn* mentioned in the Life of St Swithun by Lantfred, and Aelfric Modercope, were represented.[80] A nobleman who had entered an illicit marriage condemned by Dunstan went to Rome to ask the pope for a letter addressed to Dunstan, which would support his claim.[81] The statutes of an Exeter guild of the first half of the tenth century mention the pilgrimage to Rome of its members as a fairly common occurrence.[82] Despite Boniface's warning as to the fate of women and nuns going to Rome on pilgrimage and ending up in Italian cities as prostitutes,[83] women continued to go to Rome; we know of one Sifflaed, who made a will before leaving, and another one is mentioned by Symeon of Durham among the visitors to the shrine of St Cuthbert at Durham.[84]

Visits from ecclesiastics from Rome to England are also attested, both from papal legates, in 1061 and 1070. In the first instance, they came back with Ealdred from Rome to solve the problem of his own irregular position as a holder of the two dioceses of York and Worcester, and only consecrated him archbishop of York when he resigned the see of Worcester

---

[78] See the important discussion in Barlow, *English Church 1000–1066*, 302–8.

[79] *ASC*, D1051, 116 and *Florence*, i. 204; *HTA* 29–31. Aelmer, the abbot who preceded Aelfstan between 1006 and 1022, may also have visited Rome, ibid.

[80] *Vita Aedwardi*, 33–4 and n. 5; *ASC*, D1061, 135, and *Florence*, i. 204, 218; Sauvage, 'Swithuni . . . translatio', ch. 16, p. 397; Whitelock, *Anglo-Saxon Wills*, 74–5.

[81] Adelard's Life of Dunstan in Stubbs, *Memorials*, 67. But the English clergy were not blindly following Roman directives: Dunstan refused to obey the pope's envoy in this case.

[82] *CSD* 1. i. 59–60. Examples of penance which involved going to Rome contributed probably to the frequency of pilgrimages, see, for example, *LE* 60 and *Hugh Candidus*, 29–30. Collections of penitential letters are extant, see *CSD* i. 230–7.

[83] ch. 4, n. 26.

[84] Whitelock, *Anglo-Saxon Wills*, 94–5; *Symeon*, 82.

to Wulfstan.[85] Then, as later in 1070 with the visit of the cardinals John and Peter and Bishop Ermenfrid of Sion, to resolve the question of Stigand's position, the action of the Roman reforming party can be seen at work, attempting to enforce the principles laid down by the popes of the second half of the eleventh century from Leo IX to Gregory VII, in the matter of appointments to episcopal sees and stricter ecclesiastical discipline.[86] During the early years of Lanfranc's archiepiscopate, links between England and Rome were exceptionally close, and few legates in England had as much power and influence as Ermenfrid of Sion, who contributed to ecclesiastical legislation at William's councils of 1072, 1074–5, and 1076, reflecting the preoccupations of Roman reformers.[87] One of these, the issue of clerical marriage, was specifically dealt with in 1076.[88] On the whole, however, it must be noted that the papal directions were no longer ultimate law in England, once the Norman kings became powerful enough, though their conquest of England had been legitimized by the popes in the first place, since William of Poitiers claimed that the pope had given Duke William the standard. Thus, although William accepted to pay all the arrears of Peter's Pence when Pope Alexander II asked him to do so, he remained firmly opposed to the placing of his kingdom under the feudal authority of the popes, and continued to refuse to bow to Gregory VII's demands in the matter of episcopal elections, to the point of attempting to forbid his clergy to go to Rome on any pretext after 1080.[89] Both Lanfranc and William remained closely involved in papal politics, however, and their support was sought by both contenders to the papacy Clement III and Urban II, after Gregory VII's death, on political as well as financial grounds.[90] Sometimes, the popes tried to intervene in English affairs, for example, in a matrimonial case in the diocese of Chichester or in a claim to land made by St Mary's at Wilton; in the first case, it was Lanfranc who eventually solved the case.[91] Interestingly, the appeal in the second case emanated from among the Anglo-Saxon aristocracy: this seems

---

[85] *WMVW* 17–18.

[86] On the visit of 1070, the deposition of Stigand and the rest of the business discussed at the two councils of Winchester and Windsor, see *CSD* 1. ii. 563–80.

[87] Gibson, *Lanfranc*, 113, 131–3, 142. On the 'Investitures Contest' in England, the most recent survey is in U. R. Blumenthal, *The Investiture Contest: Church and Monarchy from the Ninth to the Twelfth Century* (Philadelphia, 1988), 142–59.

[88] C. N. L. Brooke, 'Gregorian Reform in Action: Clerical Marriage in England 1050–1200', *Cambridge History Journal*, 12 (1956), 1–21, esp. 6.

[89] Letters of Alexander II and Gregory VII in ch. 1, n. 22; Gibson, *Lanfranc*, 131–7.

[90] H. E. J. Cowdrey, 'Pope Gregory VII and the Anglo-Norman Church and Kingdom', in *Popes, Monks and Crusaders* (London, 1984), 105–14. One of the main reasons for this diplomatic move was the need for the pope to benefit from the collection of Peter's Pence, which represented an important part of the papal revenues.

[91] Gibson, *Lanfranc*, 150, 137–8.

to confirm the impression that it was the Anglo-Saxon tradition, with its sentimental link with St Peter and Rome, which was much more strongly attached to the Roman tradition than the Norman one, despite the efforts of a reformed papacy.

Also part of the 'Gregorian' movement was the tendency to increase the process of standardization in liturgy and iconography, part and parcel of the wider movement towards hierarchy within the Church. This trend is evident in the papacy's attempt to separate and identify the clerical order from the rest of the world and in the removal of the haphazard and idiosyncratic features of particular churches and local traditions.

Letters also continued to be exchanged between English ecclesiastics and popes. Some came from the pope for the purpose of granting privileges or confirming episcopal elections; one from John XII accompanied the grant of the *pallium* to Dunstan in 960 and two from Victor II to Giso and Wulfwig of Dorchester confirmed the privileges of their sees.[92] Others allowed various administrative changes: the ejection of secular canons from the Old Minster at Winchester and their replacement with monks by Bishop Aethelwold in 963, and the removal of sees to new centres, as in the case of Leofric's from Crediton to Exeter in 1050.[93] Others circulated on the occasion of the quarrel regarding the supremacy of the see of Canterbury over that of York, instigated and won by Lanfranc.[94] In this instance, as in others before, letters were also sent and received by the kings themselves. From the late ninth century onwards, with the letter of John VIII to Burghred of Mercia of 873–4 on marriage practices, and those to and from that pope to King Alfred, to those from Victor II to Edward the Confessor, granting privileges to the abbeys of Chertsey and Ely, sometime between 1055 and 1057, and that sent to William I by Alexander II on matters ranging from the supremacy of Canterbury over York to the right of the king to appoint bishops, such letters were numerous and wide-ranging in their subject matter, covering both political and disciplinary problems relating to the life of the Church in general.[95]

III. CULTURAL EXCHANGES BETWEEN ENGLAND AND ROME

The paramount importance of cultural exchanges with Rome during the seventh and eighth centuries has been noted and studied on numerous

---

[92] *CSD* 1. i. 90–2, 548–52.
[93] *CSD* 1. i. 109–13; and 524–5, though for the transfer to Exeter the letter was actually sent to King Edward.
[94] *CSD* 1. ii. 586–601; Clover and Gibson, *Letters*, nos. 1–5, pp. 30–59.
[95] *CSD* 1. i. 1–2, 3–4, 543–5, and 1. ii. 579–80.

occasions previously. Only a brief summary of its main outlines is necessary. In the first stage after the Conversion, guidance for ecclesiastical organization and pastoral theology was sought in Rome; together with the devotion to St Peter, the main practical reason leading the first pilgrims Benedict Biscop and Wilfrid to go to Rome several times was the desire to learn the Roman liturgical practices and chant, and the need to obtain books, relics, and images to bring home to England.[96] Books were brought by the missionaries themselves to begin with and one of these, the Gospels perhaps owned by St Augustine, a manuscript probably written and decorated in the south of Italy, still survives.[97] Biscop and Wilfrid also brought home books. Among those collected by Biscop must have been at least one manuscript from Cassiodorus' south Italian monastery at Vivarium, on which a subsequent copy of the Bible made in Abbot Ceolfrid's time was modelled, and a copy of the Rule of St Benedict, familiar also to Wilfrid, who may have visited Gregory the Great's foundation on the Coelius, since the earliest surviving manuscript of the Rule comes from eighth-century England.[98]

Although Benedictine monasticism as such did not become the predominant form of monastic life in the West before the reforms of Benedict of Aniane at the beginning of the ninth century,[99] and before the tenth-century reform in England, great veneration for St Benedict himself was already common by the eighth century in England, rooted in the veneration shown towards the saint by Gregory the Great in his *Dialogues*. This undoubtedly expresses the devotion of the English for Gregory himself, which was considerable and out of proportion with the feelings of the Roman clergy itself towards this pope and St Benedict's model of life he sought to promote in his foundation on Mount Coelius.[100] It was, to a certain extent, the English devotion which contributed to making both the Roman Church and the western world aware of Gregory as worthy of veneration, both on account of the production of the first Life of the

---

[96] *BHE* 72–115, 388–91, 468–73; *Vita Abbatum Bedae*, 364–87, and *Vita Abbatum Anonimo*, 388–404.

[97] Ed. F. Wormald, *The Miniatures in the Gospels of St Augustine, Corpus Christi College, Cambridge, MS 286* (Cambridge, 1954), repr. *Collected Writings*, 13–35.

[98] The Jarrow Bible Pandect is now Florence, Biblioteca Medicea Laurenziana MS Amiatino 1; the Rule is in Oxford, Bodleian Library MS Hatton 48, possibly written at Canterbury, see ch. 4, n. 91.

[99] P. Schmitz, 'L'Influence de St Benoît d'Aniane dans l'histoire de l'ordre de St Benoît', *Settimane*, 4 (1957), 401–16, and McKitterick, *The Frankish Kingdoms*, 108–24.

[100] On the cool reception of Gregory's attempt by the Roman clergy and their hostility to popes with a monastic background, see P. Llewellyn, 'The Roman Church in the Seventh Century: The Legacy of Gregory the Great', *JEH* 25 (1974), 363–8, 378–80, and K. Hallinger, 'Papst Gregor der Grosse und der heilige Benedikt', *Studia Anselmiana*, 42 (1957), 231–319.

Apostle of the English at the abbey of Whitby about 700,[101] and of the favour in England of the Rule of St Benedict, and its promotion in the Carolingian Empire by the Anglo-Saxon missionaries. For English pilgrims, Rome was not only the city of St Peter, but also that of Gregory, and devotion did not stop at the writing of the pope's Life but remained constant through the study of Gregory's writings, theological, pastoral, and homiletical, as well as through the influence of Gregorian spirituality, hagiographical techniques and pastoral outlook derived from the homilies, commentaries on the Gospels, *Dialogues*, *Pastoral Care*, and correspondence with St Augustine of Canterbury.[102] These influences are perceived in the works of Bede, Aldhelm, Alcuin, and later Anglo-Saxons, which rely on the libraries begun at Wearmouth–Jarrow, Canterbury, and York by Biscop and Ceolfrid, Hadrian and Theodore, and Wilfrid, Egbert, and Egbert's successor Bishop Aelberht, comprising a body of theological, patristic, historical, pastoral, hagiographical, classical, and scientific texts.[103] All three libraries had copies of Jerome, Gregory the Great, Sedulius, Juvencus, Prosper, and Isidore at their disposal, while Canterbury and Jarrow also had Cassian, Eusebius in Rufinus' translation, Virgil, and Augustine; at Wearmouth–Jarrow and York were found Hilary, Ambrose, Orosius, Fulgentius, Cassiodorus, Victorinus, Pompeius, Prudentius, Paulinus, Arator, Fortunatus, Lactantius, Donatus, Servius, Paulinus of Nola, as well as Pliny and the Greek Fathers Athanasius, Basil, and John Chrysostom. Interestingly, Bede's knowledge included a variety of minor theological authors of Late Antiquity, the best known of which are Arnobius, Cyprian, Dionysius Exiguus, Macrobius, Origen, Pelagius, as well as Josephus, Gregory of Naziansus, and Gregory of Tours, while Alcuin's taste seems to have led him to favour the mentioning of classical writers in his description of York library: Aristotle, Cicero, Statius, Probus, Priscian, and Porphyry, as well as Leo the Great, Boethius, Venantius Fortunatus, Sulpicius Severus, and Prosper of Aquitaine;

---

[101] B. Colgrave (ed.), *The Earliest Life of Gregory the Great by an Anonymous Monk of Whitby* (Lawrence, 1968, repr. Cambridge, 1985); on the impact of this text, see also C. W. Jones, *Saints' Lives and Chronicles in Early England* (New York, 1947), 64–7, and H. Thurston, 'The Oldest Life of Gregory', *The Month*, 104 (1904), 337–53; and on this devotion, S. Mosford, 'A Critical Edition of the *Vita Gregorii Magni* by an Anonymous Member of the Community of Whitby', D.Phil., thesis (Oxford, 1988), pp. xxv–xxx.

[102] *BHE* 78–107.

[103] M. L. W. Laistner, 'The Library of the Venerable Bede', 237–66 and W. Levison, 'Bede as a Historian', 111–51, in A. Hamilton Thompson, *Bede: His Life, Time and Writings* (Oxford, 1935); M. L. W. Laistner, *Thought and Letters in Western Europe AD 500 to 900* (2nd edn.; London, 1957), 155, 161–3, 165; N. Brooks, *The Early History of the Church of Canterbury: Christ Church from 597 to 1066* (Leicester, 1984), 94–5; Alcuin, *The Bishops, Kings and Saints of York*, ed. P. Godman (Oxford, 1982), 108–27 and pp. lxx–lxxi; J. D. A. Ogilvy, *Books Known to the English 597–1066* (Cambridge, Mass., 1967), 1–5; and Gransden, *Historical Writing*, 15–23.

Canterbury added to this classical collection copies of Juvenal and Lucan. Bede's work shows other influences of Roman preoccupations and style, since the *Ecclesiastical History* was based on the model of both the standard work of this kind in Europe, Eusebius' *Ecclesiastical History*, which he would have known in its Latin translation by Rufinus, and the type of national histories which remained fashionable through Cassiodorus, Jordanes, Isidore, and Gregory of Tours.[104] Moreover, a knowledge of Roman contemporary history was made even more direct to him since he used direct sources such as the *Liber Pontificalis* and archives, of which he asked a pilgrim to Rome, the priest Nothelm, to bring him copies.[105] Also available in England were copies of the acts of the Lateran council of 649, which the precentor John, whom Biscop had brought back from Rome, took to England and had copied at Wearmouth, as he did with the instructions given to him by the pope; Bede cites Theodore of Pharan from these acts. Admittedly, Wearmouth–Jarrow may have had closer links than other English monasteries with Rome on account of Biscop's travels and those of his successors Eosterwine and Ceolfrid. But Canterbury was equally well placed for maintaining a strong link. The manuscripts brought back by Wilfrid, probably at least copies of the Bible, theological works and service-books, also show his Roman inclinations,[106] as do a little later the choice of works, classical, theological, and patristical, described by Alcuin in the York library.[107] The fidelity to the *Vetus Latina* in England for a long time, when most of western Europe was using the Vulgate, and to the Roman rather than the Gallican Psalter until well into the eleventh century, confirms an attachment to Roman customs dating back to the Conversion, which the study of the liturgy will confirm.[108] The cultural attachment was doubtless strengthened by the success of the school opened by Theodore and Hadrian at Canterbury in the later years of the seventh century, where the teaching of grammar, rhetoric, metrics, Roman law, classical literature, astronomy, mathematics, and music as well as that of the scripture and patristic texts was that obtainable in Rome and possibly,

---

[104] R. A. Markus, *Bede and the Tradition of Ecclesiastical Historiography* (Jarrow Lecture, 1975).

[105] *BHE* 4–5. A copy was given to Theodore and parts of the text were inserted among the acts of the council of Hatfield in 680, which were then taken to Rome and reassured the pope as to the orthodoxy of the English Church before the last anti-monothelite Roman synod of 692, see *CED* iii. 140–51.

[106] M. Roper, 'Wilfrid's Landholdings in Northumbria', in Kirby, *Wilfrid*, 69.

[107] *Alcuin*, ed. Godman, 121–7.

[108] B. Smalley, *The Study of the Bible in the Middle Ages* (3rd edn.; Oxford, 1983); of Ceolfrid's three Pandects, two were of the *Vetus Latina* and only one of the Vulgate, see *Historia Abbatum Bedae*, 379–80; on the attachement to the Roman Psalter, see K. Wildhagen, 'Studien zum Psalterium Romanum in England und zu seinen Glossierungen', *Festschrift für L. Morsbach*, ed. F. Holthausen and H. Spies (Halle, 1913), 418–72.

even better, since tuition in Greek was also given.[109] Abbot Hwaeberht of Wearmouth himself had studied in Rome during the reign of Pope Sergius and may have known a little Greek, as did Bede. This, and a knowledge of Roman events in England, is shown by Bede's correction of an already existing translation in England of the Greek Passion of St Anastasius, a saint whose relics were brought to Rome by Greek refugees in 643 and became the object of a major cult at SS Vincenzo e Anastasio and generally in the city.[110] Although a knowledge of Greek was not exclusively of Roman origin in England, since Aldhelm was taught it by Irish teachers, and was not so widespead as to enable so romanizing a churchman as Wilfrid to learn it and to understand it when it was spoken at the 692 synod he attended in Rome,[111] people such as Aldhelm were prompt enough to switch allegiance from the Irish schools to that of Canterbury, whose prestige relied on the quality of its teachers as well as on its Roman origins. Aldhelm was strongly committed to Roman spiritual models, as his choice of saints in the *De Virginitate* shows, with its emphasis on Roman virgin saints and martyrs. Nevertheless, these Roman models in pastoral and disciplinary terms were themselves occasionally mixed with the Germanic and Celtic ones under the influence of Irish penitentials and perhaps Anglo-Saxon law-codes, and Theodore himself did not hesitate to use these law-codes by moulding the penitential texts he was responsible for on their pattern,[112] at the same time doing no more than Gregory the Great had recommended to Augustine about adapting his methods to the people he was attempting to convert. When Boniface wrote to Bishop Daniel of Winchester, to seek his advice on missionary techniques to use in Germany, Daniel's recommendations were to use exactly the kind of Roman methods of conversion through discussion and argument that Gregory had recommended to Augustine; and one of the books which Boniface insistently asked his friends in England to send him was precisely the *Liber Responsionum* of Gregory.[113]

[109] *BHE* 332–5; Aldhelm, 'Letter to Ecfrith'; for example, the two bishops Albinus and Tobias were proficient in Greek; on the school and its teaching, see Brooks, *Early History*, 94–7 and Lapidge, 'School of Theodore'.

[110] *BHE* 24; on this text, see P. Meyvaert and C. Vircillo-Franklin, 'Has Bede's Version of the 'Passio S. Anastasii' Come Down to us in "BHL" 408?', *AB* 100 (1982), 373–400, whose conclusion is that it probably has. Bede also used a Roman 'computus annalis', the calendar of Polemius Silvius, an inscription from a Christmas candle from Rome in 701, and a cosmography from Rome, see Levison, 'Bede', in Hamilton Thomson, *Bede*, and *Historia Abbatum Bedae*, 380.

[111] *Life of Wilfrid*, 112–13.

[112] Theodore's Penitential is edited in *CED* iii. 173–204; for a recent discussion, see A. J. Frantzen, *The Literature of Penance in Anglo-Saxon England* (New Brunswick, 1983), 62–78. Equally, Bede considered that the English had been the first Germanic peoples to have written down their laws under King Ethelberht of Kent, 'iuxta exempla Romanorum', cf. *BHE* 150.

[113] *Boniface*, 48–50, 114–21, 62–3. Boniface also asked one of his Roman friends to copy for him Gregory's letters, and send them to Germany, 90–1.

At a time when the influence of the papacy was rather weak in the Roman Empire it was still attached to, and when the monothelite conflict and other problems made it appear as though even its moral authority was challenged,[114] it was the growing prestige of the pope in the West on account of his direct link with St Peter, among the Lombards, Franks, Visigoths, and especially Anglo-Saxons, which maintained his position of primacy. This link with England was a privileged one, and both parties saw it as such. Thus, to a certain extent, the maintaining of the authority of Rome in Europe was due to the English devotion to the Roman Church and pope, through the veneration for St Peter, Gregory the Great, and St Benedict, which caught on in Rome and was particularly emphasized in the Carolingian Empire, and the respect for Bede's writings and for Anglo-Saxon scholarship in the eighth century, spread onto the Continent by the Anglo-Saxon missionaries and reformers of the Carolingian Church Willibrord, Boniface, and Alcuin, who upheld the theory of their authority as derived from Rome and, more generally, Roman traditions and primacy. Boniface in particular emphasizes very strongly his role as representative of St Peter and the pope and 'disciple of the Roman Church' in Germany, in several of his letters, so many of which are direct communications with several popes.[115] He was the main upholder of the principle of the *Roman* character of St Peter in a territorial sense, thus deflecting the attempts to break the link between city and saint, which the Franks had been trying to do on the ground that the saint had followed them in their success.[116] In view of his role both in the conversion of Germany and the reform of the Frankish Church, Boniface's influence in disseminating these feelings in the West cannot be underestimated.

Both in terms of learning and of respect for Rome, the period which followed on the ninth-century slowing-down follows the same pattern as the earlier Anglo-Saxon one. The first works to be put into circulation by King Alfred were Gregory's *Pastoral Care*, Augustine's *Soliloquies*, Orosius' *History of the Pagans*, and Boethius' *Consolation of Philosophy*.[117] The next generations of scholars under Aethelstan and Edgar continued to write within the Roman theological framework adapted by the Carolingians, and to use the same texts previously mentioned, which we know from surviving book catalogues. These are, for example, Isidore, Persius,

[114] O. Bertolini, *Roma di fronte a Bisanzio e ai Longobardi* (Bologna, 1941), 287–416, and G. Arnaldi, *Le origini dello stato della Chiesa* (Turin, 1987), 55–72.
[115] Bertolini, *Roma*, 41, 53, 131–2, 136, 181. On Boniface and the Roman Church, see Wallace-Hadrill, *The Frankish Church*, 143–90, esp. 150–61.
[116] P. Llewellyn, 'The Popes and the Constitution in the Eighth Century', *EHR* 101 (1986), 60–1.
[117] Keynes and Lapidge, *Alfred the Great*, 124–52.

Donatus, and Sedulius in the library of a grammarian Aethelstan, who lived in the second half of the tenth century, and Jerome, Augustine, Julian of Toledo, Paulinus of Nola, Isidore, Alcimus Avitus, and Cyprian in the catalogue of books given by Bishop Aethelwold to Peterborough.[118] The tenth-century monastic reform and the *Regularis Concordia* enforced the Rule of St Benedict and, in addition to it, as close a set of monastic customs as possible to those of the Rule of St Benedict, with the addition of some features from the Cluniac and Lotharingian reforms. Moreover, according to Janet Nelson, the choice of Bath by Edgar for his coronation in 973 was a deliberate attempt to revive the imperial past in one of the English cities where it was most present and still visible.[119] Although by then Carolingian theologians were increasingly copied and studied, Gregory the Great's writings remained the most popular and frequently copied texts. In theological terms, the English must have been aware of some of the contemporary debates in the eleventh century, for example of Berengar of Tours' eucharistic heresy, which was discussed both at the Roman council of 1050, which Ealdred, Herman and Aelfwine of Ramsey attended, and at that of Vercelli.[120] At this council, as well as at that of 1049 at Reims, the English envoys were bound to become aware of the reforming drive in the Church under Leo IX and probably met some of the reformers at these councils, such as Humbert of Moyenmoûtier.

English hagiography also remained faithful to Roman models and saints. Most significant in Aelfric's collections of Lives are those of St Peter, St Andrew, St Gregory, St Benedict, and the Roman martyrs. Some of these were used as references and models for English saints. Wulfstan in his Life of St Aethelwold compares this saint's charity not with the standard example of ecclesiastical charity in the West, St Stephen, but with St Laurence, the Roman deacon and martyr, when the bishop of Winchester had some of the valuable vessels of his church melted down to feed the poor during a famine; and in the Life of St Edmund, a parallel is drawn between him and St Laurence, whose persecutors were immediately destroyed as a result of laying hands on him.[121] All Lives of St Dunstan

---

[118] Lapidge, 'Booklists', 50–2, 52–5.

[119] Nelson, 'Inauguration Rituals', in *Politics*, 301. If she is right about King Alfred's leading Asser mistakenly to incorporate an anointing ceremony by the pope on the child Alfred when he was a pilgrim there, the reason for such a falsification could have been a desire to confer the aura of papal approval on the authority of the king, Nelson, 'Problem', in *Politics*, 315–27. Personally, I would view this with caution and, if her version of the anointing account is correct, I would see it rather as an imitation by Asser of Einhard's account of Charlemagne's coronation.

[120] H. Leclercq and C. J. Hefele, *Histoire des conciles d'après les documents originaux* (11 vols.; Paris, 1911), iv. 1040–61, and J. de Montclos, *Lanfranc et Bérenger: la controverse eucharistique du XIᵉ siècle* (Louvain, 1971), 53–83.

[121] Winterbottom, *Three Lives*, 50, 85–6.

insist on his personal devotion to SS Peter, Paul, and Andrew.[122] Unsurprisingly, the English liturgy favours in an equal manner the Roman saints above all others.

IV. LITURGICAL AND DEVOTIONAL EXCHANGES BETWEEN ENGLAND AND ROME

From the very first, the Anglo-Saxon Church had adopted Roman liturgical customs, introduced by St Augustine and reinforced by the addition of the 'correct', that is, Roman practices by men such as Wilfrid and Benedict Biscop, who brought from Rome liturgical books, a teacher of the papal style of chanting, John the archcantor, liturgical objects for the veneration of the people, and relics.[123] In the name of St Peter, the 'Roman' party triumphed over the 'Celtic' at the synod of Whitby, and enforced the Roman style for the calculation of Easter. Bede and Willibrord in their respective martyrologies used the Hieronymian Martyrology, compiled in Rome in the fourth century,[124] as a model for the Anglo-Saxon liturgical calendar.[125] The books used, sacramentaries and pontificals, then as in our period, were closely modelled on the Roman, that is, 'Gregorian' Sacramentary then attributed to Gregory the Great, and on the *ordines* used by the popes themselves, going as far as to preserve the entries of the station churches in Rome, and the names of purely Roman feasts such as those of Sta Maria ad Martyres (dedication of the Pantheon) and S. Iohannes ante portam latinam.[126] Another liturgical feature, which Rome alone kept and England in its wake, was the practice of having the first two Ember days move with Easter and Whitsun. The basis for the office in Aelfric's Eynsham customary was the *ordo romanus* XIIIA, written in the first half of the eighth century in the Lateran.[127]

In an article which attempts to set the Ruthwell Cross in the liturgical

---

[122] Stubbs, *Memorials*, 30–1, 57, 96–7, 185–6.

[123] *Vita Abbatum Anonima*, 391. On the importance of the archcantor of St Peter and the distinction between basilical and papal liturgy in Rome, see S. J. P. Van Dijk, 'The Urban and Papal Rites in Seventh and Eighth-Century Rome', *Sacris Erudiri*, 12 (1961), 448–86.

[124] However, the earliest copy we possess comes from Auxerre in the 8th c.

[125] Apart from Bede's and Willibrord's martyrologies, another such text from 9th-c. Mercia, known as the Old English Martyrology, was also based on the Hieronymian Martyrology; it was edited by G. Kotzor, *Das altenglische Martyrologium* (2 vols.; Munich, 1981).

[126] On the complex problems of the evolution of the Roman liturgy through the Carolingian period, see ch. 2 n. 55.

[127] J. R. Hall, 'Some Liturgical Notes on Aelfric's Letter to the Monks of Eynsham', *Downside Review*, 93 (1975), 297–303, and M. McC. Gatch, 'The Office in Late Anglo-Saxon Monasticism', in *Learning and Literature*, 341–62. The *ordo* is edited in M. Andrieu, *Les Ordines Romani du haut Moyen Âge* (5 vols.; Louvain, 1931–61), ii. 469–88.

context of Northumbrian monasticism, Éammon Ó'Carrágain demonstrates the origin of the iconographical programme of the Cross in the then recent developments of the feast of the Exaltation of the Cross and the Good Friday procession from the Lateran to Sta Croce in Rome.[128] The importance of the veneration for the Cross throughout the Anglo-Saxon period will be discussed further; but the point to emphasize here is the speed with which such Roman liturgical innovations under Pope Sergius, feast of the Cross, singing of the Agnus Dei at Mass, and celebration of the four feasts of the Virgin, reached English centres within less than twenty years of their introduction or enforcement by the papacy.

Wilfrid and Benedict Biscop had brought large collections of relics from Rome. Others were sent to English kings by the popes, such as those of SS Pancras, Laurence, Gregory, and John and Paul sent to King Oswiu of Northumbria by Pope Vitalian in the seventh century or those of the Holy Cross, sent to King Alfred by Pope Marinus.[129] Archbishop Plegmund brought back some relics of St Blaise from Rome in 909, later given to Canterbury, and Abbot Aelfstan also brought some back from his pilgrimage, which he gave to St Augustine's in 1022.[130] The importance of these relics is easily perceived from the importance of liturgical celebrations for the respective saints in the English churches where they are kept, as in the case of St Blaise, whom a pontifical from Christ Church celebrates with a special benediction.[131] The martyrs Pancras and John and Paul were celebrated with somewhat more elaborate texts than those of the numerous Roman local martyrs, for whom a simple Gregorian or Gelasian mass was usually entered in English sacramentaries. The complete text of the gradual is entered in the missal of New Minster— which occurs only for quite important saints in this book—and eleventh-century manuscripts often separate the three saints celebrated together, Nereus, Achilleus, and Pancras, by placing the first two together and Pancras separately, as do the missal of St Augustine's, Giso's sacramentary, and Wulfstan's collectar, these two masses being neither Gregorian nor Gelasian, but written in England—an unusual feature for such a minor saint. In addition, the mass for these saints in the Winchcombe Sacramentary is exceptionally long, with seven collects, instead of the usual three or

---

[128] É. Ó'Carrágain, 'Liturgical Innovations Associated with Pope Sergius and the Iconography of the Ruthwell and Bewcastle Crosses', in *Bede and Anglo-Saxon England*, R. T. Farrell (ed.), (Oxford, 1978), 131–47.

[129] *BHE* 320–1; *ASC*, 885, 52, and *Asser*, ch. 71, pp. 53–4.

[130] *Gervase*, ii. 350–1; *HTA* 29–31.

[131] *Claudius Pontificals*, fo. 139ᵛ, p. 76 ; also at Canterbury, but at St Augustine's, a mass for this saint is added in the missal, probably in the early 12th century, *Missal of St Augustine's*, fos. 79ᵛ–80.

four. SS Cosmas and Damian have only the standard short masses, but for them also the gradual is entered at New Minster, as well as a benediction at Canterbury. There were relics of these three saints at New Minster,[132] which may have been related to those sent to England in the seventh century, but none at St Augustine's, Wells or Bury; hence, it could be imagined that part of the popularity of these saints came from the visits made by pilgrims to the churches containing their relics in Rome, SS Cosma e Damiano and S. Pancrazio.[133]

The veneration for the saints known in England on account of the pilgrimage route to Rome has already been emphasized in other chapters: Christina and Margaret of Bolsena, Maurice of Agaune, Rémi of Reims, Vaast of Arras, and Bertin and Omer, to cite only the most important among them. However, apart from the Roman saints whose relics were in English churches and from those encountered by pilgrims, another category of saints was venerated on account of its origins: that of some major saints of the Church, whose cults had been brought to England by the Roman missionaries. These were by far the most popular among the saints venerated in the English Church, far and above the English saints themselves.

Among these, the first and foremost was St Peter. The devotion to St Peter rested upon his role as the Prince of the Apostles and as the 'doorkeeper of Heaven';[134] access to Heaven, therefore, depended on him, as King Oswiu of Northumbria explained when he had to decide between the Roman and the Irish parties at the Council of Whitby in 664. The two parties regarded themselves as the representatives of the traditions of St Peter on the one hand, and of St Columba on the other hand, in the controversial issue regarding the correct calculation of Easter. King Oswiu asked whose power was greater in the Kingdom of Heaven, St Peter's or St Columba's, and was answered by the synod that it was St Peter's, since Christ had told him 'Tu es Petrus . . . '. On hearing this reply, Oswiu made his decision:

Ille est hostiarius et clavicularius, contra quem conluctationem controversiae non facis nec facientibus consentio et iudiciis eius in vita mea in nullo contradicam.[135]

This attitude had not changed by the eleventh century: in his letter to the

---

[132] Birch, *Liber Vitae*, 150–1.

[133] In the 7th c. already, we hear of churches dedicated to St Pancras and the Four Crowned Martyrs (Quattro Coronati) at St Augustine's Canterbury, see *BHE* 156–9 and Fernie, *Architecture*, 37.

[134] T. Zwölfer, *Sankt Peter, Apostelfürst und Himmelspförter: Seine Verehrung bei den Angelsächsen und Franken* (Stuttgart, 1929), 52–7.

[135] *Life of Wilfrid*, 22.

English people, King Cnut justified his pilgrimage to Rome because of St Peter's power to bind and loose. Through its association with St Peter, Rome, always regarded as the Apostle's city, became the major goal of numerous Anglo-Saxon pilgrims who desired to die near the tomb of the Apostle, 'ad limina Sancti Petri', thereby securing almost certain access to Heaven. The devotion for the 'owner' of the city, St Peter, ensured the continuous success of the pilgrimage, prompting many pilgrims to visit and worship the relics of the Apostle in all the places associated with him in Rome. The pilgrims also paid their respects to the pope, who was perceived as the embodiment of St Peter on earth.[136]

Veneration for St Peter was thus originally initiated and later fuelled by England's privileged links with Rome, the original source of the conversion of England, and remained throughout the period the expression of an emotional link with the Prince of the Apostles, rather than a mere political gesture.[137] It found expression through the pilgrimage to Rome, the great number of dedications of monastic churches to St Peter and, naturally, through the liturgical cult of the Apostle, both official and devotional.

Like the rest of the Western Church, the English Church celebrated St Peter with three feasts. The first and most important of these was that of the *Natale* of both St Peter and St Paul. It is significant, however, that St Paul appears only sporadically in this double feast, which is taken over almost completely by St Peter. Some English calendars, instead of having both St Peter and St Paul on 29 June and then the separate feast of the Commemoration of St Paul on 30 June, have St Peter on 29 and St Paul on 30 June, possibly because St Peter's feast was considered too important to be shared with any other saint, even St Paul.[138]

[136] R. W. Southern, *Western Society and the Church in the Middle Ages* (Harmondsworth, 1970), 96: 'from the eighth to the eleventh centuries . . . the active force in Rome was seen as St Peter himself. It was into his presence that men came, and from him they received commands. They did not ignore the pope but they quite simply looked through him to the first occupant of his throne.'

[137] On this emotional link with the Rome of St Peter and St Gregory, see J. M. Wallace-Hadrill, 'Rome and the Early English Church: Some Questions of Transmission', *Settimane*, 7(2) (1960), 512–21, 531–2.

[138] This occurs in the Glastonbury, St Augustine's, and Bury calendars, and in that in the missal of Robert. Professor Henry Chadwick drew my attention to the fact that the feast had been already divided in this way in Rome from the time of Pope Damasus onwards, on account of the difficulties involved in walking from the Lateran to St Peter's and then to San Paolo in one day. This could be the reason for the change, but the entries of both versions of the feast in England may also mean that, since both were known, some choice was being deliberately made to break the feast into two days. Since the processional difficulty in Rome did not apply in England, the reason may have been related to St Peter's importance, especially since it occurs in two of the calendars most conscious of the hierarchical distinctions of the feasts, the missal and Bury ones, and in the Glastonbury one, highly traditional in its sympathies. I am grateful to Professor Chadwick for his comments on this problem.

The feast of the *Natale* was celebrated with a Vigil and an Octave, and was a first-rank feast in all calendars. The other two feasts of St Peter, the *Cathedra* and the Chains (Sanctus Petrus in Vinculis), were also entered in all calendars, sometimes in capitals. The existence of masses for the Vigil and the Octave emphasizes in itself the importance of the main feast of the *Natale*.

The masses for the feast are amongst the longest of *all* masses, alongside those for St John the Baptist, the Virgin Mary, and some of the most important masses of the Proper. The graduals bring out the key themes of the feast: St Peter's role as the shepherd of Christ's flock and, most notably, the 'power of the keys' based on St Peter's confession of Christ. These themes are taken up by the tropes and sequences. The importance of the mass is also visually perceptible since in some cases, as for example in the missal of Robert, the decoration of the first page of this mass is one of the richest in the whole missal, written in golden leters within a highly decorated 'Winchester' border, an honour reserved almost exclusively for the most important masses of the Proper and of the Virgin Mary.[139]

The major theme of St Peter's cult in England is thus easily identified as that of St Peter's possession of the keys, an authority interpreted as signifying the power of admission into Heaven.[140] This view is clearly expressed in the iconography of St Peter, the only Apostle to have, in his keys, a well-established attribute in art. Whatever the scene, St Peter always appears tonsured. This representation, originally seen as a copy of what was thought to be the standard Roman iconographical type portrayed in a statue which pilgrims venerated at St Peter's,[141] has been recently ascribed to England, more particularly to the Roman party here, which attempted to emphasize its point in favour of the Roman tonsure.[142] While I cannot agree with the assumption that there is no Roman representation of St Peter tonsured in Early Christian art, witness the mosaic at SS Gervasio e Protasio, this is by no means the only Roman model, and others were available; hence, it is clear that Anglo-Saxon visitors to Rome chose to reproduce this particular type in English art, possibly as a statement of the attachment of the Roman party in England to the Roman tonsure, imposed by the Council of Whitby. Furthermore, St Peter always holds

[139] *MRJ*, fo. 133.

[140] Zwölfer, *Sankt Peter*, 24–38, 56–7.

[141] F. Cabrol and H. Leclercq, *Dictionnaire d'archéologie chrétienne et de liturgie*, xiv(1) (Paris, 1939), 946–7, and J. Vielliard, 'Notes sur l'iconographie de St Pierre', *Le Moyen Âge*, 2nd ser. 39 (1929), 1–16.

[142] J. Higgitt, 'The Iconography of St Peter in Anglo-Saxon England and the St Cuthbert's Coffin', in G. Bonner, D. Rollason, and C. Stancliffe (eds.), *St Cuthbert; His Cult and his Community to AD 1200* (Woodbridge, 1989), 267–85.

the keys,[143] a detail definitely belonging originally to the Roman tradition, and obligatory in England.[144] As St Peter's most significant attribute, the keys were often greatly enlarged and depicted completely out of proportion with the rest of the image as, for example, in the frontispiece of the *Liber Vitae* of New Minster.[145] Frequently, when St Peter is depicted in plain colours, only his keys are gilded as, for example, in the Pentecost scene in the missal of Robert.[146]

St Peter's association with the 'power of the keys' is equally underlined in all the other texts for the *Natale*, hymns and benedictions. A similar concern with the main themes associated with St Peter is found in the masses for his two secondary feasts. A second kind of liturgical text is less formal than the masses and more properly devotional, whilst being also more specifically related to the monastic liturgical pattern. The collectars include the full office for the seven monastic hours for St Peter; here also it is largely the 'power of the keys' which is insisted upon. Wulfstan's contains a separate section entitled *orationes privatae*, which introduces us to the last form of liturgical texts and the most privately devotional of all: the prayers and litanies. It displays a particular devotion to St Peter, since it comprises several prayers addressed to him, as well as numerous invocations, immediately after those to the Virgin Mary, in general prayers to the Apostles or to All Saints. In practically all psalters St Peter is one of the very few saints to have special prayers addressed to him, and in some books, St Peter is invoked even in the middle of masses addressed to other saints, for example, in the mass for St Michael in Leofric's missal.[147] In every case, as is the custom for prayers to the saints—but more strongly so where St Peter is concerned because of his privileged power to bind and to loose—the prayers are mostly concerned with intercession. St Peter's function as the 'doorkeeper of Heaven' caused him to be often invoked both as an intercessor and patron. Most litanies honour his name with capitals, the only other name usually entered in this fashion being that of the direct patron saint of the monastery. In the Winchcombe Sacramentary, for example, the litany has St Peter and St Kenelm, the patron of Winchcombe, in capitals.

St Peter's intercession and patronage are best expressed in art. On a late

---

[143] Réau, *Iconographie*, ii(2), 313–15.

[144] I have found only one exception of an illumination in which St Peter has no keys in the Arenberg Gospels, fo. 12, reproduced in H. Ohlgren, *Iconographic Catalogue*, Photo 14. The English rule is significant in the light of other artistic schools since, for example, the Apostle was sometimes represented without his keys in Ottonian art, as in the late 10th-c. Solothurn Sacramentary from Reichenau, see Goldschmidt, *German Illumination*, ii. 23.

[145] British Library MS Stowe 944, fo. 6, reproduced in Temple, *ASM*, pl. 244.

[146] *MRJ*, fo. 84ᵛ, pl. x.

[147] *Leofric Missal*, fo. 8, p. 5.

tenth- or early eleventh-century ivory depicting the Last Judgement, St Peter is presented, along with the Virgin Mary, as one of the two intercessors, flanking Christ enthroned.[148] Apart from his universal power of intercession, St Peter was regarded more specifically as a patron. In King Edgar's charter to New Minster, he is shown as a protector of kings and, as usual, appears tonsured, beardless, and holding the keys. He is placed on one side of the king, whilst the other patron, the Virgin Mary, appears on the other side of Edgar.[149] Thus, the parity of their power as patrons is indicated. St Peter was also seen as a protector of monks, and appears as such in a drawing from a prayer-book dating from the latter half of the tenth century. Tonsured and beardless, he is enthroned and holds two huge keys, whilst at his feet the small figure of a cowled monk venerates him.[150] Perhaps the most significant image of St Peter as a patron is the frontispiece of the *Liber Vitae* of New Minster, which is organized into three levels. On the upper level, we can see Christ blessing, and on the lower level, King Cnut and his Queen offering a cross to Him on the altar. In between, there are the interceding figures of the Virgin Mary and St Peter, placed on either side of Christ, with St Peter holding a huge pair of keys. Brithwald's vision of King Edward being crowned by St Peter in the *Vita Aedwardi* belongs to this same tradition of patronage of the English kings by the Apostle.[151]

The Apostle appears in the Transfiguration ivory with St John and St James, as well as in the Transfiguration scene in one of the Damme leaves.[152] The popularity of this scene may have been an expression of the devotional cult of the Apostle, appearing not in his official capacity as doorkeeper of Heaven or Prince of the Apostles, but as one of the three Disciples closest to Christ, in what is essentially a mystical episode of the Gospel, eminently suited to monastic contemplative life.

The most important image for our purposes, on account of it providing the most forceful illustration of the main theme of St Peter's cult in England, remains the miniature on the verso of the frontispiece of the *Liber Vitae* of New Minster.[153] We have already seen how the Register expresses, better than any other illustration, the role of St Peter as an intercessor, on

---

[148] Last Judgement Ivory, late 10th or early 11th c., see Beckwith, *Ivory Carvings*, no. 18, 121, pl. 41.

[149] British Library Cotton MS Vespasian A.VIII, fo. 2ᵛ, reproduced in Temple, *ASM*, pl. 84.

[150] British Library Cotton MS Titus D.XXVI, fo. 19ᵛ, reproduced in Temple, *ASM*, pl. 243.

[151] *Vita Aedwardi*, 8–9.

[152] Transfiguration Ivory, late 10th c., Victoria and Albert Museum, London, see Beckwith, *Ivory Carvings*, no. 21, 122, pls. 49 and 51; Transfiguration miniature on leaf II of the Damme Lectionary leaves of c. 1000 from Canterbury, reproduced in Temple, *ASM*, pl. 173. [These leaves are now in the Paul Getty Museum in California, MS 9.]

[153] Stowe 944, fos. 6ᵛ–7, reproduced in Temple, *ASM*, pls. 247–8.

a level above all the other saints, and equal to the Virgin Mary. On the back of this official document, representing the king's view and that of his ecclesiastical counsellors, along with that of the monks of New Minster, we have two separate scenes depicting, respectively, St Peter and angels opening the gates of Heaven to admit the Elect, and then his contending with the devil for a soul, in which he is shown using his keys to strike Satan on the head.[154] We could hardly hope to find a more evocative illustration of the central theme of the Petrine liturgical cult resting upon the 'power of the keys' and its Anglo-Saxon interpretation than the 'doorkeeping of Heaven'. The *Liber Vitae* was associated with King Cnut, renowned as one of the English kings most devoted to St Peter and Rome. Cnut was an appropriate figure to express the English devotion to St Peter. Although himself a Christian, his own father, Swein, had been only a late convert and a nominal Christian,[155] and Cnut was all the more eager to learn from his English ecclesiastical entourage exactly what their main devotions consisted of, and to comply with them. It is significant that the influence of his Christian education made him a devotee of St Peter, a veneration which he expressed in many forms, including the wish for the intercession of the Apostle, special protection and favour towards some abbeys dedicated to him, such as Peterborough, and, of course, his pilgrimage to Rome.

If St Peter was venerated mostly as the gatekeeper of Heaven in the devotional texts produced within English monastic circles, he was also officially the 'Prince of the Apostles', and is shown in the liturgy even outside the Canon and the litanies. He is clearly depicted as the head of the Apostolic College in such scenes as the Death of the Virgin and the Washing of the Feet. However, the most frequent representation of St Peter as the leader of the Apostles is in the Ascension and Pentecost scenes, where he is portrayed at the head of the right-hand-side group of the Apostles, standing or sitting below Christ's mandorla or below the Holy Dove. As usual, he is tonsured, beardless, and holds the keys.[156]

The two major elements on which St Peter's cult was based, the 'power of the keys' and his rank as 'Prince of the Apostles', eventually merge into the representation of St Peter in all his glory, for example enthroned at the top of the Canon tables in Harleian 76, or in Titus D.XXVI, where he is

---

[154] The role of intercessor for the Dead, shared by St Peter with the Virgin Mary and St Michael, is clearly expressed in the Vercelli Homily XV on the Last Judgement.

[155] Stenton, *Anglo-Saxon England*, 397, 411.

[156] *Benedictional of St Aethelwold*: Ascension, fo. 64ᵛ and Pentecost, fo. 67ᵛ. *MRJ*: Ascension, fo. 81ᵛ, and Pentecost, fo. 84ᵛ, pls. IX and X; *BAR*: Pentecost, fo. 29ᵛ, reproduced in Temple, *ASM*, frontispiece; Tiberius C.VI: Ascension, fo. 15 and Pentecost, fo. 15ᵛ, reproduced in Wormald, 'Eleventh-Century', pls. 18–19, and pls. 141–2 in *Collected Writings*.

venerated by a monk; and particularly in the missal of Robert where we have a 'portrait', within a heavily decorated frame, of St Peter enthroned and giving his blessing, with his main attributes underlined in gold: the throne, the book, the halo, and the keys.[157] It is indicative of St Peter's importance that he alone, of all the Apostles, except for St Andrew in the same missal, was thus represented in his full glory. Such images may have been more common in monasteries and churches than we are now aware, since the existence of prayers for the dedication of images of St Peter, such as the ones in CCCC 163 and Vitellius E.XII, suggests that some such representations of him were certainly housed there.[158]

St Peter's cult was considerable in western Europe at the time, even outside Rome. Numerous Frankish churches were dedicated to him[159] and the German Emperors, whose imperial ideology was closely linked with their involvement with Rome, upheld it. Great imperial abbeys, such as Reichenau, were dedicated to SS Peter and Paul, as was the most prestigious abbey in the West, Cluny, favoured by both popes and emperors. The cult was flourishing in some of the centres with which English ecclesiastics were in touch, for example, at Stavelot, Ghent, and St Bertin's. In view of the contacts between England and Germany and Flanders in the early Anglo-Saxon period, the English veneration may even have been instrumental in spreading the cult by supporting extensively this Roman devotion. But, however strong the official cult may have been in western Europe outside Rome, the devotional cult appears to have been nowhere as strong as it was in England, where no local saint ever superseded it during the Anglo-Saxon period.

The English cult was underlaid by a considerable official, ecclesiastical, and royal devotion to St Peter, fostered by the Conversion, supported by the close links of the English Church with Rome, and made manifest in the liturgy, dedications, and patronage of kings such as Edgar, Cnut, and Edward. The eleventh-century reform movement of the papacy, and its insistence on the authority delegated by Christ to St Peter, may have contributed to reinforcing the English cult since at least some of the reforming ideas must have been known in England through the journeys of ecclesiastics to Rome and to the all-important council of Reims in 1049. Ultimately, however, there is little evidence of this movement having had any direct effect on the English devotion to the Apostle, so pervasive in

---

[157] Harleian 76, fo. 7ᵛ; Titus D.XXVI, fo. 19ᵛ, reproduced in Temple, *ASM*, pl. 243; and *MRJ*, fo. 132ᵛ, pl. XI.

[158] Vitellius E.XII, fos. 153–154ᵛ and CCCC 163, fos. 283–5.

[159] Zwölfer, *Sankt Peter*, 73–151. On the Irish cult, which probably contributed to both the Frankish and Anglo-Saxon ones, see J. Ryan, 'The Early Irish Church and the See of St Peter', *Settimane*, 7(2) (1960), 549–74.

England in any case, and associated with the papacy from the beginning. The association was perhaps stronger with the unreformed papacy which some Englishmen may have preferred to the late eleventh-century papacy which, after all, supported William's Conquest of England. At the same time, Ealdred's and Wulfstan's support of William may be indicative of these prelates' involvement with Continental ideas developed, for example, at Reims and in Lotharingia, and of their awareness of the papal reform, since they were the two English churchmen most familiar with the Continental movements of the late eleventh century.

The official cult of St Peter was considerable in England. But even more overwhelming was the personal devotional veneration, which in its strength is a characteristically English feature. The prayers addressed to him and his symbolic representation as a Fisher of Men in one of the Damme leaves[160] express a devotion due to his role in the process of intercession, remission of sins, and salvation, as well as to his association with Rome and his official status as Prince of the Apostles. It was St Peter, and not local or minor saints, on whom English saints focused their veneration; for example, he appears to St Dunstan in a vision, exhorting him. This very personal and emotional link, also seen in the popularity of the mystical scene of the Transfiguration, bears witness to a strong devotional cult.[161]

Second to him but also Roman in origin was the cult of Peter's brother, Andrew. Although entered only third in the list of the Apostles in the Canon and in litanies, St Andrew was the most popular of the Apostles after St Peter. His popularity was already widespread during the earlier Anglo-Saxon period, as witnessed, for example, by the dedications of Hexham and Oundle, Rochester, and Wells, and by the devotion which Wilfrid had for him.[162] It is also demonstrated by the existence of a vernacular poem, *Andreas*, based on apocryphal texts attributed to the Apostle, recording St Andrew's mission to the 'city of the cannibals' with St Matthew. In the tenth and eleventh centuries, the devotion remained

---

[160] Temple, *ASM*, pl. 176.

[161] St Peter's Denial is represented only once in England, and even this is somewhat doubtful, see the Hereford Gospels (Cambridge, Pembroke College Library MS 302), fo. 6ᵛ and Ohlgren, *Iconographic Catalogue*, 262. St Peter's weakness may not have been a favourite theme—it is never mentioned in the liturgy—although, like St Thomas' Doubting, it had a positive theological function. In any case, the range and variety of representations of St Peter in England comes close behind those from the Life of Christ and before those depicting the Virgin Mary, which also suggests a strong devotional cult.

[162] For the dedication of Rochester, see *BHE* 142–3; for Hexham, see *BHE* 530–1 and *Life of Wilfrid*, 44–7; for Oundle, *Life of Wilfrid*, 140–1. Oundle became a cell of Peterborough, since it is mentioned as such by *Hugh Candidus* in the 12th c., 110. When in Rome, Wilfrid was a most assiduous visitor at the Apostle's shrine, where he prayed for guidance, see *Life of Wilfrid*, 12–13.

strong in England. All four Lives of St Dunstan insist on this Apostle's role in the vision Dunstan had of the Three Apostles; the saint comforted Dunstan during his exile in Flanders; and Eadmer mentions Dunstan's staff, which contained a tooth-relic of St Andrew.[163] According to Eadmer, St Aelfheah's choice as bishop of Winchester was inspired by St Andrew, and in the late eleventh century, the Apostle was said to have appeared in a vision to the fisherman Godric, urging him to build a monastery—this was the legend of the foundation of Throckenholt in Cambridgeshire, dedicated to St Andrew, as well as to the Holy Trinity and the Virgin Mary.[164]

The popularity of St Andrew, based on his blood ties with St Peter, was certainly increased in England by the veneration in which Gregory the Great was known to have held the Apostle. The main feast of St Andrew is that of the *Natale* or *Passio*, celebrated in all calendars, and with masses for the Vigil and the Octave. The Vigil and the Octave have one benediction in some books and one collect for the Octave in Wulfstan's collectar. Celebrations of the day of the *Natale* itself are abundant. Most sacramentaries compile various parts from the Roman masses. There is no gradual given for any of the masses, but the tropes, sequences, and hymns are all entered. The importance of the mass is emphasized visually, once again, in the missal of Robert, by beginning it on a highly decorated title-page in golden letters.

The foundation within the Gospels of the cult is apparent from the texts of the three collectars. They recall how Jesus saw the two brothers St Andrew and St Peter fishing in Galilee and asked them to follow Him. This theme is perhaps illustrated in the Boulogne Psalter in a miniature showing Christ calling two fishermen, possibly St Andrew and St Peter. The Gospel foundation of the cult was always remembered, as well as St Andrew's relationship to St Peter. Both foundations of the cult were reiterated in the numerous personal prayers addressed to St Andrew, for example, in Wulfstan's collectar and in the psalters, and in the invocations to St

---

[163] Stubbs, *Memorials*, 30–1, 57 and 60, 96–7, 185–6. He offered the relic to Rochester, 190, 248.

[164] Stubbs, *Memorials*, 217; the 'Red Book of Thorney', cited by Binns, *Monastic Dedications*, 87. Other monastic dedications to him were those of Eynsham (possibly), Tywardreath in Cornwall, and Rochester, which only became a monastery in 1077/80. Levison, *England and the Continent*, 262, counted seven dedications to him in the 7th and 8th centuries, and Binns, *Monastic Dedications*, 23, 27, entered another nine for the period 1066–1150. On these dedications, see *Religious Houses*, 65, 79, and Binns, *Monastic Dedications*, 72, 108, 83. One secular cathedral, Wells—though a monastic community until 1033—was dedicated to St Andrew, and we hear occasionally of churches of St Andrew, for example, two in London, see Brooke and Keir, *London*, 137–8.

Andrew in general prayers. In these prayers, he always follows St Peter and St Paul, thus keeping his normal place, as in the litanies and in some lists of liturgical Gospels. In the list from Harleian 76, for example, only his name along with those of St Peter and St Paul are entered in capitals.

Two books award a special importance to St Andrew. Wulfstan's includes several private prayers to him as an intercessor, expressing an individual's personal devotion, in this case that of Wulfstan. The missal of Robert was also particularly interested in St Andrew, as the elaborate ornamentation of his mass demonstrates. Moreover, it contains one of the two attested iconographical representations of St Andrew, in a 'portrait' facing the beginning of his mass, showing him enthroned in a heavily decorated 'Winchester' frame, giving his blessing and holding a book in his left hand; the throne, halo, and book are all underlined in gold.[165] Apart from St Peter, he is the only Apostle and saint to be so venerated in this manuscript. Its calendar has an entry in capitals for the only other feast of St Andrew, his Translation. This feast is also entered in the eleventh-century Wessex calendar, the late eleventh-century West Country one, and in the Wells, Evesham, and Bury calendars. Another portrait of St Andrew enthroned is found in the Hereford Troper.[166] It seems that the celebration of St Andrew in the missal of Robert was a very special one, going beyond what was strictly required, even for a book so attentive to the proper hierarchical celebration of the most important feasts. Like St Peter's cult in England, St Andrew's was not only official and institutional, as it was throughout most of Western Europe, but also strongly devotional. It was not so much associated with a relic, as the Trier cult was, but derived from an early Anglo-Saxon devotion, probably supported by the Roman missionaries and by the Roman background of the early Anglo-Saxon Church.

In the late Anglo-Saxon period, the cult of St Andrew may have been further boosted by the devotion to this Apostle in Germany at Trier, with which close links existed. But the German and, possibly, the Greek connections, though they may have strengthened the cult in the eleventh century, only reinforced a devotion acquired in the early Anglo-Saxon period through the Roman connection, as in the case of St Peter. This underlying tradition explains the strong personal element in the cult and

---

[165] *MRJ*, fo. 164ᵛ, pl.XII.

[166] Caligula A.XIV, fo. 30ᵛ. Other representations of St Andrew occur in medallions or at the top of the Canon tables, together with the other Apostles, for example, in the Grimbald Gospels (London, British Library Additional MS 34890), fo. 114ᵛ, in the Pembroke Gospels (Cambridge, Pembroke College Library MS 301), fo. 5, and in Besançon, Bibliothèque Municipale MS 14, a Gospel-book of the late 10th c. from Old Minster, in a drawing added in the early 11th c., fos. 10ᵛ, 11ᵛ, see Ohlgren, *Iconographic Catalogue*, 197.

its popularity both in and outside the monastic world, demonstrated by the increasing importance of the feast of the Translation in calendars during the second half of the eleventh century, as well as by the story of Godric the Fisherman. The devotion to St Andrew was equally strong before and after the Norman Conquest, as this story and the dedication of Tywardreath *c*.1088 show.

Other Apostles whose relics were in Roman churches, Philip and James at SS Apostoli, Simon and Jude at St Peter's, and Bartholomew in the church of that name, also had special distinctions in the liturgy. St Paul, whose cult was much less developed and personal than Peter's, was, on the whole, mentioned very little in the texts for the shared feast of the *Natale* on 29 June. He was only occasionally recalled, usually as a parallel to St Peter, for example in the mass for the Octave of the Apostles, where St Peter's and St Paul's power over the sea is evoked; St Peter's because he could walk on the waters and St Paul's because he had been saved from shipwreck. The *Natale* was viewed, essentially, as St Peter's feast, and the celebration of St Paul was mostly expressed through the two feasts of the Commemoration on 30 June and that of the Conversion on 25 January.

Both appear in all calendars, usually in capitals. St Paul always appears second amongst the Apostles, in litanies and in those collects which name only the first three Apostles, to signify the whole Apostolic College. As in St Peter's case, there is little change or evolution in the cult of St Paul in our period, either in chronological or geographical terms. Both feasts were celebrated with the traditional Roman masses, benedictions and other formal liturgical items, such as tropes and sequences. In cases where these exist, they belong to the feast of the *Natale*.

Although the collectars show a respect for the traditional forms, the two feasts of St Paul were not viewed as compulsory: thus, the Conversion appears only in Wulfstan's. There was a certain lack of enthusiasm for St Paul's feasts, especially the Conversion, since neither in the south of England, where the Durham Collectar was written in the early tenth century, nor at Durham, to where it was brought at the end of that century, nor at Exeter under Leofric where the Leofric Collectar was written, was the monastic office for this feast entered. St Paul was described as the 'vas electionis', the 'doctor egregius', chosen by Christ to be, along with St Peter, one of the two columns of the Church. These themes also appear in the two prayers addressed to St Paul in two psalters from Winchcombe and Crowland.[167] Occasionally St Paul's intercession was invoked in general prayers, in his traditional place immediately after St Peter.

---

[167] Winchcombe Psalter, fo. 280, and Douce 296, fo. 126ᵛ.

This, second after St Peter, is the place he usually occupies in the iconography, for example, in the Choir of the Apostles in the Benedictional of St Aethelwold. He is bearded and his most common attribute is a book, rather than the late-medieval sword, which makes him difficult to recognize, since other Apostles also have books, particularly St John. His cult was still very much an institutional one: St Paul was regarded as one of the Twelve Apostles, so that it seemed natural to the illuminator of the Pentecost scene in the Benedictional of Robert to place him amongst them, forgetting that the Apostle who replaced Judas and made up the number to twelve was St Matthias, and that St Paul was not even a convert at the time of Pentecost.

The importance of St Paul in late tenth- and eleventh-century monastic circles in England was due, to a great extent, to his cult being a parallel one to that of St Peter. St Paul appears as a pendant to St Peter in Harleian 76 and in the Arenberg Gospels at the top of the Canon tables, and his martyrdom is shown, symmetrically arranged below that of St Peter in the Benedictional of St Aethelwold, and next to it in Harleian 603, on the model of the Utrecht Psalter.[168] Apart from Jarrow, no monastic house was dedicated to St Paul alone, the dedications in which he appears being joint ones to SS Peter and Paul, except the secular cathedral of London. His association with St Peter was the cause for his veneration, as the miniature depicting the two Apostles on either side of Christ in Pluteo XVII.20 in the Medicea Laurenziana Library in Florence demonstrates.[169] The association between the two 'Columns of the Church' also appears in the *Traditio Legis* scene. St Paul is symbolized by the gift of the book, and his quality as doctor and preacher explains why his cult was respected within monastic circles, in the same way as other saints 'of the book', such as St Jerome, were respected. Nevertheless, St Paul was not really a 'popular' saint, even within the monastic environment, however dutifully we find his cult to have been celebrated. He gives the impression of being associated with St Peter out of habit and tradition in Dunstan's vision of the three Apostles, and not out of any great personal feeling.

Four of the Apostles, SS Philip and James, and SS Simon and Jude, were always celebrated in the liturgy in pairs. These two feasts were entered in all English calendars in capitals, with a Vigil for SS Simon and Jude but not for SS Philip and James. SS Philip and James have the four-part Roman mass and the complete gradual. Overall, the cult appears to have been general in its official form, but still a matter of personal devotion

---

[168] Harleian 76, fo. 8; Arenberg Gospels, fo. 12; *Benedictional of St Aethelwold*, fo. 95ᵛ; Harleian 603, fo. 19.

[169] fo. 1, reproduced in Temple, *ASM*, pl. 232.

in the less formal texts: thus, there were always two hymns, but only one collect in Wulfstan's and the Durham collectars, and benedictions at Exeter and Canterbury. The psalter Arundel 155 from Christ Church has two extra hymns for Nocturns and Lauds, added to the usual ones for Vespers. It seems, therefore, that the cult was most popular at Canterbury, and in the south-west, as witnessed by the existence of a mass for SS Philip and James in CCCC 41, an Exeter book given by Leofric to his cathedral. The mass for the two Apostles is one of the very few masses added in the margins of this copy of Bede's *Ecclesiastical History*.[170] The popularity at Canterbury, if it could be confirmed, may be explained by the special links of the archbishops with Rome, where the cult of SS Philip and James was prominent and their relics venerated by Anglo-Saxon pilgrims. The Exeter cult was more likely derived from Glastonbury. In the twelfth century, the legend of the foundation of Glastonbury by disciples of SS Philip and James was known to William of Malmesbury.[171]

Both the main feast and the Vigil of SS Simon and Jude were celebrated in England, the Vigil with masses, one collect in Wulfstan's collectar, and one benediction at Canterbury and Wells. The feast has masses and was troped at Winchester. A hymn was entered in most books, one collect in the Durham and three in Wulfstan's collectar. There are two benedictions at Canterbury and Exeter and a separate one entitled 'in eodem die [as SS Simon and Jude] S. Iuda apostolo'. The cult was evenly spread in geographical terms, and it seems to have become general during the eleventh century.

Until the tenth century St Bartholomew was relatively little known in western Europe. He was not totally ignored though, since in England, for example, St Guthlac had been devoted to him, and Crowland, the abbey founded on the spot where St Guthlac's cell had once been, was from its foundation under the patronage and the dedication of St Bartholomew.[172] In the West, his cult was becoming an increasingly flourishing one by the tenth century, as a result of the translation of his relics, first from Lipari to Benevento, and then, more significantly, from Benevento to Rome in the tenth century, where they were placed by Otto III in the church now known as S. Bartolomeo in Isola, giving rise to one of the great Ottonian cults.[173] Great wonders had been reported on the occasion of these translations, concerning the miraculous journeys and preservation of the relics. The cult then developed along these lines, to which was added, as

---

[170] On the intricacies of this MS, see Grant, 'Cambridge, Corpus Christi College 41'.
[171] *WMHG* 42–7.
[172] *Life of St Guthlac*, 88–9, 106–7. Crowland was dedicated to St Bartholomew, as was Cranborne, see *Religious Houses*, 63, and Binns, *Monastic Dedications*, 31, 68–9.
[173] On this Translation and the church of S. Bartolomeo, see Mâle, *Early Churches*, 102–7.

in the case of St Andrew and St Thomas, the popularity of the apocryphal legends, relating the Apostle's mission in Armenia and India, and subsequent martyrdom.[174] Already by the late ninth century, King Alfred thought he was was sending alms to India to 'St Bartholomew and St Thomas'.[175]

To this general European background must be added a more specifically English factor, the purchase by Queen Emma of the relic of the arm of the saint from the bishop of Benevento, which initiated a Canterbury cult, supported by the presence of the relic. The cult of St Bartholomew in England should, therefore, be considered not only in its European context, based on the renowned Translations and the wonders associated with them, but also in its purely English context, supported by both the tradition of St Guthlac's devotion and the presence of the Apostle's arm in England. The feast of St Bartholomew is entered in most calendars. Another feature confirms the popularity of the cult: the introduction of the Vigil before the feast, which appears in all eleventh-century calendars but not in the tenth-century ones.

The feast was celebrated with the standard Gelasian mass and was troped at Winchester. The hymn and benediction are the standard ones in all books, except in the Canterbury Benedictional, which has three benedictions concerned with the Apostle's intercession, the sign of a more distinct Canterbury interest. Wulfstan's collectar has four collects. Although late Anglo-Saxon liturgical texts show him as essentially an official saint, other sources of evidence such as dedications,[176] and the choice of names, such as that of Bartholomew of Farne, express a personal devotion in the twelfth century.

Also associated with Rome were the other two patron saints of the city, the martyrs Laurence and Agnes, highly venerated in the liturgy. St Laurence was the most popular Roman martyr after St Peter and St Paul. This deacon was venerated soon after his death in 258, as can be seen from the entry on 10 August in the *Depositio Martyrum*. He was considered to have been the principal figure who secured the victory of Christianity over Paganism in Rome and, therefore, was venerated virtually as an equal to St Peter and St Paul, with whom he is associated in one of St Augustine's sermons, which reports how the citizens of Rome had placed themselves under their combined protection in 410. Rome put itself under his patronage, and a great number of churches were dedicated to him there.

[174] James, *Apocryphal*, 467.
[175] *ASC*, 883, 50.
[176] To the two Anglo-Saxon dedications at Crowland and Cranborne were added another two in the first half of the 12th c., see Binns, *Monastic Dedications*, 71, 86.

When the Vigil was shifted to 9 August, the main feast at S. Lorenzo fuori le Mura was celebrated with two masses, a morning mass and High Mass, in the two basilicas which together made up S. Lorenzo. The saint's name was in the Canon of the mass, a hymn was written for him by Prudentius, and in the collection of liturgical pericopes, the four weeks after St Laurence's feast were called Ebdomada I, II, III, and IV *post S. Laurentium*. They were still thus called in English lists of liturgical Gospels, such as the one in the Grimbald Gospels. The centre of the cult in Rome was S. Lorenzo fuori le Mura, but other Roman churches out of the thirty or so dedicated to the saint during the Middle Ages were also pilgrimage goals. Sigeric visited three in two days, probably following the advice of both Romans and his compatriots, the latter having been themselves once guided by the Romans in their devotional tours. We can safely assume that the cult of the saint in England, brought over by the Gregorian mission and strengthened by the continuous links with Rome during the seventh and eighth centuries, was still very much a pilgrimage devotion in the late tenth and eleventh centuries.

The feast was entered in all English calendars, usually in capitals, and was highly ranked in some, for example, that in the missal of Robert, at Bury and Crowland, and even in a New Minster calendar of *c.*1025 which apparently had not acquired the ranking habit since it contains hardly any feasts which are even distinguished, but in which St Laurence was qualified with *in albis*. Both the Vigil and the Octave were entered in all calendars, the latter in red in Wessex, and in capitals at Sherborne and Evesham. The Vigil was celebrated liturgically with the Gregorian mass in all sacramentaries, and with one benediction in most eleventh-century books.

The celebrations for the *Natale* preserved the two masses of the Gregorian tradition. The feast was troped in the two tropers and the sequence was given at Winchester and in the Durham Gradual. There is only one hymn for the saint in most books, a full office in all three collectars, and one formula in most benedictionals. The Octave was celebrated with the Gelasian mass, with one collect in the Durham collectar and two in the Wulfstan's. St Laurence's name was entered in capitals in some lists of pericopes, such as that in Royal I.D.IX, and in some litanies. His name is always found amongst those of the first ten martyrs in the litanies, and it often appears as one of the three names in the short litanies.

Relics of St Laurence existed in England at Bath, Exeter, New Minster and St Augustine's, some perhaps being part of the consignment sent by Pope Vitalian in the seventh century. The Roman background of this cult is evident in early Anglo-Saxon England, and the dedication of at least three churches to him in the eighth century is to be associated with the influence of the Roman mission and, later, of the Roman pilgrimage.[177] The cult of St Laurence belonged to the Anglo-Saxon past and tradition, being associated with Rome, like the cults of St Peter, St Andrew, and St Gregory. The popularity of the Roman pilgrimage in our period contributed to reinforcing it and Sigeric's Itinerary illustrates his interest in St Laurence's relics and churches in Rome. In the years after the Conquest the devotion was no doubt maintained but, significantly, the dedication of new churches seems to have been rare. He was a popular Roman saint as well as an institutional one, like St Peter, which may explain why he was more informally associated with the Rome of the pre-reform period; after the eleventh century, the papacy stressed the patronage of St Peter and St Paul, and thus led to a loosening of the link between St Laurence and Rome outside Rome itself. Ultimately, the Anglo-Saxon attachment to this saint may be taken to express the veneration of the English for the Church of Rome with its martyrs and relics, stronger than the subsequent link of the Anglo-Norman Church with the Roman papacy.

St Agnes, 'the most honoured female saint in the calendar', was venerated in Rome from the first half of the fourth century onwards, since her name appears in the *Depositio Martyrum*, and then in all martyrologies, calendars and sacramentaries, with both the feast and the Octave.[178] Her cult was a major Roman devotion, as the wealth of images and representations of the saint in the three churches dedicated to her in Rome demonstrates. Her relics were venerated, along with those of St Emerentiana, in the basilica on the Via Nomentana, founded by the Emperor Constantine's daughter, but her head was kept, together with the relics of other major Roman saints such as St Laurence, in the Sancta Sanctorum, the private chapel of the pope in the Lateran Palace. St Agnes has two four-part masses for her two feasts. Both masses have the gradual and the saint is celebrated with one or two collects in the Durham and Wulfstan's collectar, and in the benedictionals; and her feast was entered in golden letters in the missal of Robert, the Benedictional of St Aethelwold, and the St Dunstan Pontifical.

To them were added other Roman martyrs whose relics were kept in the Roman basilicas visited by pilgrims, such as SS Cecilia and Crysogonus, visited by Sigeric; the two Sicilian saints whose cults had been brought to Rome by Gregory the Great, Agatha and Lucy, and probably also

---

[177] Levison, *England and the Continent*, App. V, 263.
[178] V. L. Kennedy, *The Saints of the Canon of the Mass* (Rome, 1954), 175. On the cult of St Agnes, see P. Franchi de Cavalieri, 'Sant'Agnese nella tradizione e nella leggenda', *Studi e Testi*, 221 (1962), 293–354.

Prassede, Pudenziana, Emerentiana, Sebastian, Cosmas and Damian, not forgetting Clement and Silvester. The female saints first. St Cecilia, the second great Roman virgin, was mentioned in the *Depositio Martyrum* and by the Fathers.[179] Her cult was already established in Rome by the second half of the fifth century, and her feast by the early sixth century. According to a tradition, already well established by the fifth century, the basilica built in her honour in Trastevere replaced a *titulus* which she had founded in her house. There were various representations of St Cecilia in Rome, the earliest being the one in the catacombs of St Calixtus, but the most important was that in the mosaic at Sta Cecilia in Trastevere.

The other two saints, St Agatha and St Lucy, had been originally Sicilian virgins, the patron saints of Catania and Syracuse respectively, but were greatly venerated in Rome and were universally regarded as honorary Roman saints. In both cases, their cults were prompted by the popular stories of their martyrdom, and were greatly promoted by the veneration in which they were held by St Gregory, who protected the monasteries dedicated to them in their native cities and also favoured their cults in Rome. The cult of St Agatha, whose tomb was in Catania, was celebrated in both East and West, and reached Rome towards the end of the fifth or early sixth century, where it was already celebrated in the sacramentary before St Gregory's time. He dedicated the ex-Arian basilica of the Suburra to her, and two other churches in Rome were also under her patronage.[180] St Lucy's cult, centred on the monastery dedicated to her in the sixth century at Syracuse, and on her *Passio*, reached Rome in the seventh century.[181] Under St Gregory, there were already an oratory and a monastery dedicated to her in Rome, and a new abbey of St Andrew's and St Lucy's appeared *c*.600, possibly founded originally by St Gregory. Although represented rather infrequently in Rome, except for St Lucy in the eighth-century fresco at S. Sebastiano al Palatino, the two saints were venerated almost as equals with the other two genuinely Roman virgins, St Agnes and St Cecilia.

In England, these saints appear in all litanies, usually just after SS Perpetua and Felicity, and always together. In the short litanies, they frequently represent the group of the virgins. Each saint was entered in all calendars, usually with liturgical distinctions. St Lucy alone was deemed to be less important, since her name was entered second in the Winchester

---

[179] On the early cult of St Cecilia, see J. P. Kirsch, *Die heilige Cecilia in der römischen Kirche des Altertums* (Paderborn, 1910), 15–57, 60–74.

[180] On the early cult of St Agatha, see G. Consoli, *Sant'Agata vergine e martire catanese* (Catania, 1951).

[181] On the early cult of St Lucy, see O. Garana, *Sta Lucia nella tradizione, nella storia, nell'arte* (Syracuse, 1958), 18, 45, 73–4, 89, 107, 110.

and Evesham calendars, after that of the Winchester saint, St Judoc, who was himself entered in capitals at Worcester whereas St Lucy was not.

Likewise, in the liturgical celebrations, St Lucy had a mass in the sacramentaries and one collect at Worcester, but her cult may have been progressing since she has benedictions in two eleventh-century books at Canterbury and Exeter. St Agatha had a mass in most sacramentaries, as well as the gradual, but she was highly venerated at Winchester in the tenth century, since she has a seven-part mass in a tenth-century sacramentary.[182] By the eleventh century she had acquired benedictions in all benedictionals. St Cecilia has a mass in the sacramentaries, and two masses for the Vigil and the *Natale* in the Winchcombe Sacramentary; two collects in the Durham collectar, and the whole office at Worcester. She is the only one of the four to have a devotional prayer addressed to her in the psalter Arundel 155. St Agatha and St Cecilia have their feasts distinguished with golden letters in various books, all three in the Benedictional of St Aethelwold. Altogether, it is clear that even among these four saints, the two originally Roman ones were the most popular, possibly on account of the pilgrimage and their two basilicas.

A few other Roman virgins were also venerated in England, although they were not celebrated in the original Roman books, such as St Petronilla, whose legend made her the daughter of St Peter, and St Praxedis and St Pudentiana (Potentiana), whose two basilicas in Rome became increasingly well known to pilgrims after their eighth- and ninth-century restorations. St Petronilla 'filia Petri', as the Wessex calendar described her, appears in all calendars, as does St Praxedis. St Pudentiana was entered everywhere, except at Exeter, Crowland, and in one of the Winchester calendars. At Crowland and Winchester, the other feast on that day, St Dunstan's, was given in capitals. It was highly ranked at Crowland, and was perhaps considered too important to be shared with another saint.

The widespread adoption of these saints, despite the fact that they were latecomers even in Rome, can be explained by the interest in virgin saints, but also in pilgrimage saints. Most of these virgins were associated with basilicas in Rome, or with St Peter. Thus, St Emerentiana was, according to legend, St Agnes' foster-sister. Her relics had been discovered in the ninth century and placed in the same coffin as those of St Agnes, and both saints were then venerated in the basilica of Sant'Agnese on the Via Nomentana. Sta Sabina, originally not a saint but the owner of the *titulus*, was assimilated to a saint by the tenth century.

[182] F. Wormald, 'Fragments of a tenth-century Sacramentary from the binding of the Winton Domesday', in M. Biddle (ed.), *Winchester in the Early Middle Ages* (Oxford, 1976), 542.

These virgins' popularity can be clearly observed in the litanies. St Petronilla appears in all litanies except for five, in some cases immediately following the two saints who came first by tradition, SS Perpetua and Felicity. St Pudentiana's name occurs in six litanies, and St Sabina's in five, throughout the period. On the whole, these names tend perhaps to appear more often in the early litanies of the tenth century, at the time when links with Rome had regained their former strength, and to be less frequent in the litanies of the second half of the eleventh century. St Emerentiana, St Sabina, and St Praxedis had masses in the missal of Robert, St Emerentiana and St Sabina in the first part of the Leofric Missal, St Sabina and St Petronilla in the missal of New Minster, St Petronilla and St Praxedis in Giso's sacramentary, St Sabina in the Winchcombe Sacramentary and the missal of St Augustine's; and they were all given collects in Wulfstan's collectar. Their Lives were sometimes copied in England, as in the case of St Praxedis, found in a late eleventh-century manuscript from St Augustine's.[183] Only St Pudentiana had no liturgical celebration at all.

As in the cases of St Pancras and SS John and Paul, St Sebastian, SS Cosmas and Damian, and St Chrysogonus are awarded a slightly stronger celebration than the standard mass, sometimes with the full gradual at New Minster for St Sebastian, and with benedictions at Canterbury. Even more emphasized were the cults of St Clement and St Silvester. They are entered in almost all calendars and are specially distinguished in some, for example, by being entered in capitals. The liturgical celebrations for St Clement include the Gregorian mass in all sacramentaries. The Durham Collectar has one collect and Wulfstan's collectar three complete hours of the office, while all benedictionals have one benediction. The missal of Robert ranks the saint highly in its calendar. For St Silvester, we find again the Gregorian mass, with the gradual. There is one benediction for the saint at Canterbury and Exeter, and one collect at Durham and Worcester.

Last and anything but least, Gregory the Great himself was one of the most popular saints, as was St Benedict, the founder of benedictine monasticism.[184] From the first years after the Conversion, the Anglo-

---

[183] London, British Library Cotton MS Otho A.VIII.

[184] St Scholastica, St Benedict's sister, was his female counterpart as foundress, patron saint, and archetype for benedictine nuns. Her cult is recorded through masses in the sacramentaries, 11th-c. benedictions, and a collect in Wulfstan's collectar, as well as the entry of her name in all calendars and over thirty litanies. It progresses from a rather lowly ranking in early litanies, for example, that in Harleian 863 (twenty-second) either to first place in such later ones as those in the Winchcombe Psalter, CCCC 422, and Douce 296, or to third place after St Mary Magdalene and SS Perpetua and Felicity in others. In the Winchcombe Sacramentary litany, St Scholastica's

Saxon Church viewed St Gregory as the initiator of the mission to England, and he rapidly became one of the most venerated saints in the English Church. The presence of St Augustine at Canterbury, who had been prior of St Gregory's monastery on Mount Coelius, and was clearly close to him, must have increased the veneration for the pope already known as the 'Apostle of the English'. Significantly, the first Life of the saint was written in England by a monk of Whitby at the end of the seventh century, and the author used the *Dialogues*, *Moralia*, *Pastoral Care*, and the homilies on the Gospel and on Ezekiel; and Bede's chapters on St Gregory in the *Ecclesiastical History* were probably even more popular.[185] The anonymous monk may well have had access to an oral tradition in Northumbria, established by James the deacon who had accompanied Paulinus at York, since he gives details which could have only been known to someone from Rome, such as the name of Gregory's mother. Certainly, at Whitby, veneration for Gregory seems to have been promoted very early, since we hear of an altar dedicated to him in the church of St Peter.[186]

The strength of the links between England and Rome throughout the seventh and eighth centuries reinforced the veneration for the saint, and later, the first book translated by King Alfred into the vernacular was St Gregory's *Cura pastoralis*. In the early tenth century he was depicted among a few other recognizable saints on St Cuthbert's maniple, offered together with other treasures to St Cuthbert's shrine by King Aethelstan.[187] The position of eminence held by St Gregory in the Anglo-Saxon Church during the tenth century is apparent not only from the iconography of the confessors in the Benedictional of St Aethelwold, but also by the inclusion of St Gregory as one of the English additions to the originally Continental coronation order used in England in the early tenth century.[188]

name was entered in red capitals, together with those of St Praxedis and St Felicity. As with her brother, her popularity in England was based on that of Gregory's *Dialogues*, which describe St Benedict's great fondness for her.

[185] Colgrave, *Earliest Life of Gregory*. On the English veneration for Gregory see, for example, Wallace Hadrill, 'Rome and the Early English Church', 520–1, 531–2; and id., *Bede's Ecclesiastical History of the English People: A Historical Commentary* (Oxford, 1989). Bede's life of Gregory is in *BHE* 122–35.

[186] Colgrave, *Earliest Life of Gregory*, 105.

[187] On Cuthbert's stole, see G. Baldwin-Brown and A. H. Christie, 'St Cuthbert's Stole and Maniple at Durham', *Burlington Magazine*, 23 (1913), 3–17, and C. Hohler, 'The Stole and the Maniples', in C. F. Battiscombe (ed.), *The Relics of St Cuthbert* (Oxford, 1956), 396–408, reproduced pls. XXXIII and XXXIV.

[188] J. Wickham Legg (ed.), *Three Coronation Orders* (London, 1900), 60. This *ordo*, used for the coronation of an early 10th-c. Anglo-Saxon king, was based on Continental material for the coronation of a Carolingian king or emperor, but the Continental formula did not contain the name of Gregory, which is one of the English additions. The only other names invoked in the English *ordo* are those of the Virgin and of St Peter.

In 747, the Council at Clovesho decreed, in its canon XVII, that a cult was to be rendered to both St Gregory and St Augustine of Canterbury.[189] From then onwards, the feast of the saint was always celebrated on 12 March as in the rest of the Church. This feast appears in all English calendars and was entered in capitals as soon as litugical ranking became common practice, that is in the late tenth-century Glastonbury calendar and in all of the eleventh century. Some calendars awarded it special distinctions, such as those in the missal of Robert and the eleventh-century Wessex, Bury, and Crowland calendars. It should also be noted that in two calendars from Winchester, in which the name of Bishop Aelfheah of Winchester is entered on the same day, St Aelfheah is always placed second. Knowing the propensities of Winchester calendars to upgrade their local saints, sometimes by even leaving out the traditional Gregorian ones, the first place given to St Gregory indicates his importance.

St Gregory's popularity in England is further demonstrated by the existence of two supplementary feasts for this saint. A feast of the *Ordinatio* of St Gregory on 3 September was added in the eleventh century to the Glastonbury calendar, and in the early twelfth century to those of Christ Church and Worcester. At Canterbury, a feast of the Octave of the Ordination on 10 September was also added in the twelfth century: this feast may have originated from the popular story of the consecration of the pope, whose place of concealment had been revealed by God to his electors, the Roman people, by the appearance of a column of fire. This episode was recounted in all three Lives of the saint, and was also alluded to in the liturgical texts.[190] The Ordination was not a major feast before the twelfth century, and even then, it only enjoyed any real popularity in England and in those areas, such as Normandy, where English devotions were particularly influential.[191] These secondary feasts were not celebrated in the liturgical books except for the 'Leofric Missal', in which we find a mass for the 'Ordinatio S. Gregorii'.

The main feast of the saint is celebrated in all liturgical books, and all sacramentaries use the Roman mass. Both the missals of New Minster and of St Augustine's include the gradual. Most books enter one hymn, and the office is represented by one collect at Durham and Worcester, as well

---

[189] *CED* iii. 368.

[190] Colgrave, *Earliest Life of Gregory*, 12–13, and Mosford, 'Edition', 15–16; the two Lives by Paul the Deacon and John the Deacon are edited in PL 75, 41–60, 59–242.

[191] The contemporary St Evroul and St Ouen calendars in MSS A.287 and Y.21 in the Bibliothèque Municipale in Rouen both have this feast, and these abbeys clearly had links with England since saints such as St. Edmund and St Mildburgh were entered in their calendars. A third feast was included in eight calendars of various origins on 29 or 30 March.

as in CCCC 361, a Malmesbury manuscript of the eleventh century. All benedictionals have at least one benediction for the feast. The feast is not troped but has a sequence at Winchester.

The most popular themes associated specifically with St Gregory include such motifs as the column of fire and, most prominently, that of St Gregory as 'pater anglorum, doctor et apostol[us]'.[192] There is a marked absence of any reference to the Holy Spirit in the shape of a dove, providing the inspiration for his works, which became his most common iconographic motif. This theme is found, for the first time, in the Whitby Life, where it is associated with St Gregory's writing of the *Homilies on Ezekiel*. It was later reused by John the Deacon in his Life of the saint for the liturgical works attributed to St Gregory, the Sacramentary and the Antiphonal.[193]

In the Claudius Pontifical, the frontispiece image depicts St Dunstan venerating St Gregory, which shows a strong personal devotion to the Apostle of the English in monastic circles. We meet it again in prayers in various eleventh-century psalters. The popularity of the cult is confirmed by the graphic importance of the beginning of the masses and benedictions in some books, and the place of St Gregory's name in the litanies, where it is always found amongst the first of the confessors. Aelfric's homily on the saint, St Dunstan's dedication of a church to him at Winchester, altars such as that at Christ Church, and small churches dedicated to him at Sudbury and Moreville, to which should be added Lanfranc's dedication of his charitable foundation, the Priory of St Gregory at Canterbury, testify to the extent of the cult within monastic circles in England both before and after the Conquest.[194]

The cult of St Gregory was a vigorous personal devotion, due in no small measure to the highly coloured elements of St Gregory's life and to the saint's role in the Conversion of England. Its popularity was on a level with that of some major saints, such as St Peter and St Michael, and stronger than that of most other Apostles including St Paul, and of the other Fathers and Doctors of the Church including St Augustine and St Jerome. In view of the particular structure of the English Church between 900 and *c.*1040, whose personnel was composed for the greatest part of monastic bishops, St Gregory also represented a model case of the monk–bishop. Aelfric cited

---

[192] *Leofric Collectar* (fo. 233) i. 388.

[193] On the evolution of this iconographic motif, see J. Croquinson, 'Les Origines de l'iconographie grégorienne', *Cahiers archéologiques*, 12 (1962), 249–62.

[194] Aelfric in Thorpe, *Homilies*, ii. 116–33; Stubbs, *Memorials*, 15; Eadmer, 'De Reliquiis', 366; Binns, *Monastic Dedications*, 80 for Morville, a church served by canons in the Pre-Conquest period and granted to Shrewsbury abbey in 1083–6, and 86 on Sudbury, where Domesday Book records a church of St Gregory; on Lanfranc's foundation at Canterbury, see *WMGP* 72; Eadmer, *Historia Novorum*, 16, and *Gervase*, ii. 368.

him in this way, together with the other two models of the kind, St Cuthbert and St Martin.[195]

The two cults of St Gregory and St Benedict, understandable on account of the importance of these two figures, remained however rather more limited to the clerical and monastic, learned, circles, unlike the cults of St Peter and the Roman martyrs, particularly those whose churches were part of the pilgrimage routine exemplified by Sigeric's Itinerary. The churches Sigeric saw and the relics he noted have already been described, and the importance he gave to those associated with St Peter and St Laurence has been stressed. The interest of the Roman churches consisted in more than their relics alone, however; their artistic treasures were also of considerable relevance.[196]

V. ARTISTIC EXCHANGES BETWEEN ENGLAND AND ROME

Whereas we know that during the early Anglo-Saxon period, books, icons and images, vessels and liturgical vestments were brought from Rome in the baggage of pilgrims such as Biscop and Wilfrid, tenth- and eleventh-century pilgrims tended to bring back the inspiration derived from the architecture, paintings, mosaics and icons seen in Roman churches. Earlier on, architects and masons had been invited from the Continent to supervise the building of monastic churches whose features included, for example, a crypt on the model of the *confessio* in St Peter's at Christ Church[197] and twisted columns of the kind Constantine had offered to St Peter's, which supported the crypt at Repton.[198] Wilfrid's churches at Ripon and Hexham, the latter built in stone, copied 'Roman' models (although his came via Gaul), with porticos and glass in the windows,[199] as did his restorations at York on Paulinus' church, which included the insertion of glass and the leading of the roof. In the early eleventh century, Abbot

---

[195] Aelfric's first Old English letter to Wulfstan in *CSD* 1. i. 287.

[196] On the impact of Roman saints and feasts in England, a recent summary is available in D. Rollason, *Saints and Relics in Anglo-Saxon England* (Oxford, 1989), 23–69.

[197] *Eadmer*, 'De Reliquiis', 365; see Brooks, *Early History*, 41–2, and H. M. Taylor, 'The Anglo-Saxon Cathedral Church at Canterbury', *Archaeologia*, 126 (1969), 101–30.

[198] J. M. C. Toynbee and J. Ward-Perkins, *The Shrine of St Peter and the Vatican Excavations* (London, 1956), 201–4 figs. 20–1, and esp. 212–19 fig. 22; and J. B. Ward-Perkins, 'The Shrine of St Peter and its Twelve Spiral Columns', *Journal of Roman Studies*, 12 (1952), 21–33.

[199] *Life of Wilfrid*, 34–7, 45–7. These two churches, dedicated to St Peter and St Andrew, were given gifts of vessels, furniture, and books. According to Richard of Hexham, there were painted images and sculpture at Hexham, see *HCY* i. 12, but these could equally be of the 9th c. See the articles by D. H. Farmer, M. Roper, R. Cramp and E. Gilbert in Kirby, *Wilfrid*. The latter calls the Hexham crypt the 'almost unique surviving specimen of the rare Early Christian crypt', 85; E. A. Fisher, *The Greater Anglo-Saxon Churches* (London, 1962), 64–73, and Fernie, *Architecture*, 32–63.

Aelfmer of St Augustine's (1006–22) also attempted to have a rotunda built on a Roman model in his abbey.[200]

The main sources of inspiration for the English were the themes, objects, and displays seen and admired in Roman churches. Already in the seventh century, Biscop had displayed the images brought from Rome to Jarrow in a pattern copied on that of the mosaic or fresco cycles of basilicas, in a didactic manner which emphasized the role of Old Testament episodes as forerunning the history of salvation in a topological manner.[201] This kind of display is found, for example, in the cycles of mosaics and frescos at St Peter's and St Paul's. Other cycles, such as that of the Old Testament at San Paolo, seem to have had some impact on the illustration of manuscripts such as that of the illustrated Aelfric's Hexateuch from St Augustine's, dating from the second quarter of the eleventh century, particularly in the representations of Jacob's dream of his anointing the stone, Joseph describing his dream to his family and expounding Pharaoh's dream to him, and Aaron's rod transformed into a serpent swallowing the serpents of Pharaoh's magicians.[202] Individual iconographic motifs were taken, such as the Roman representation of the martyrdom of St Peter and that of St Paul, as in the chapel of John VII at St Peter's (Pl. 7*a*, *b*).[203] The two Apostles mastering the waves, as they are depicted in Leo III's *triclinium* in the Lateran Palace,[204] are found in the text of a benediction

[200] *HTA* 29–31. On the inspiration of Roman architecture, particularly on Anglo-Saxon crypts, see A. W. Clapham, *English Romanesque Architecture Before the Conquest* (Oxford, 1930), 143–58; M. Biddle, 'Archaeology, Architecture and the Cult of the Saints in Anglo-Saxon England', in Butler and Morris, *The Anglo-Saxon Church*, 16–22; and Fernie, *Architecture*, 157–9.

[201] Bede's *Vita Abbatum*, 369, 373: '[Biscop brought] picturas imaginum sanctarum quas ad ornandam aeclesiam beati Petri apostoli [i.e. Wearmouth], quam construxerat, detulit;' [here follows a detailed account of the pictures]; then again: 'imagines quoque ad ornandum monasterium aecclesiamque beati Pauli apostoli de concordia ueteris et noui Testamenti summa ratione conpositas exibuit; uerbi gratia, Isaac ligna, quibus inmolaretur portantem, et Dominum crucem in qua pateretur aeque portantem, proxima super inuicem regione, pictura coniunxit. Item serpenti in heremo a Moyse exaltato, Filium hominis in cruce exaltatum conparauit.' On these cycles, see P. Meyvaert, 'Bede and the Church Paintings at Wearmouth–Jarrow', *ASE* 8 (1979), 63–77, and R. Gem, 'Documentary References to Anglo-Saxon Painted Architecture', in S. Cather, D. Park, and P. Williamson (eds.), *Early Medieval Wall Painting and Painted Sculpture in England* (Oxford, 1990), 1–6.

[202] C. R. Dodwell and P. Clemoes (eds.), *The Old English Illustrated Hexateuch: British Library Cotton Claudius B.IV* (Copenhagen, 1974), 67 and pls. VIIc–IXd.

[203] The illumination in the Benedictional of St Aethelwold is one of the earliest representations of the martyrdom in western Art. Before it, this scene, based on the Fathers (Origen) and the Apocrypha, is found in a Greek MS of the sermons of Gregory of Naziansus reproduced in H. Omont (ed.), *Miniatures des plus anciens manuscrits grecs de la Bibliothèque Nationale du vi[e] au xive siècle* (Paris, 1929), pl. XXII, and in the 9th-c. Drogo Sacramentary, together with the Martyrdom of St Paul, reproduced in *Drogo-Sakramentar*, fo. 86; in the Utrecht Psalter, see S. Dufrenne, *Les Illustrations du Psautier d'Utrecht* (Paris, 1978), fo. 19 pl. 90 no. 28; hence, in Harleian 603, fo. 19. On this iconography, possibly inspired by a now lost mosaic in the chapel of John VII in the Vatican, see T. Sauvel, 'Le Crucifiement de Saint Pierre', *Bulletin Monumental*, 97 (1938), 337–52.

[204] See above, p. 140.

PLATE 7 (*a*) Martyrdom of St Peter and St Paul, British Library, Additional MS 49598 (Benedictional of St Aethelwold), fo. 95ᵛ.

(*b*) Martyrdom of St Peter and St Paul, Paris, Bibliothèque Nationale, MS lat. 9428 (Drogo Sacramentary), fo. 86.

for the Octave of the Apostles, common to books from Canterbury, Wells, and Worcester, first found in these English manuscripts.[205]

The Annunciation and Anastasis scenes from the chapel of John VII were the ultimate source for the Annunciation and Second Coming representations in the Benedictional of St Aethelwold (Pl. *a, b*).[206] Early Christian Nativity scenes, such as that at Sta Sabina, were probably the original models for those in the missal of Robert, the Bury and Boulogne Psalters, the Boulogne Gospels, and the ivory from Liverpool,[207] although the iconography of the Nativity was equally strongly influenced by Byzantine and Carolingian models. A similar mixture of Roman tradition and Carolingian innovation can be seen in the Presentation in the Temple in the Benedictional of St Aethelwold, where the introduction of the Prophetess Anna belongs to the latter model, whereas the rest of the iconography is that seen in the chapel of John VII. The Anglo-Saxon Harrowing of Hell, also carved on a stone slab in Bristol, may have been additionally inspired by such representations in S. Clemente and Sta Prassede (Pl. 9 *a, b*).

The Adoration of the Magi with the iconography of the type first seen in the catacombs of Priscilla and of SS Peter and Marcellinus, on the doors of Sta Sabina, and at Sta Maria Maggiore is depicted in the Benedictional of St Aethelwold, the missal of Robert, and the Victoria and Albert Museum ivory.[208] The original iconography of the Magi depicted them moving towards the Virgin and Child with the veiled hands which belong to the eastern-Persian tradition, and presenting gifts, a scene close to the classical and imperial representations of the *aurum coronarium* brought to the Emperor on the occasion of his accession to the title.[209] This iconography changed gradually from the seventh century onwards, to become a scene of Adoration, with the Magi wearing the same costume and still having veiled hands, but already arranged according to the position which was to become the standard one: the first kneeling, the second preparing

---

[205] Moeller, *Corpus*, ii, no. 1004, p. 408.

[206] On the iconography of the Anastasis, first seen in the West in the two images commissioned by John VII in his chapel and at Sta Maria Antiqua, see A. D. Kartsonis, *Anastasis: the Making of an Image* (Princeton, 1986), 69–81; subsequent Roman representations are found at S. Clemente and in the S. Zeno chapel in the church of Sta Prassede, ibid. 82–93.

[207] *Benedictional of St Aethelwold*, fo. 15ᵛ; *MRJ*, fo. 33, pl. II; Bury Psalter, fo. 93ᵛ; Boulogne Psalter, fo. 58ᵛ; Boulogne Gospel, fo. 12, reproduced in Boutémy, 'Un monument', 179; ivory no. M8060 in Liverpool County Museum, reproduced in Beckwith, *Ivory Carvings*, no. 26, 123, pl. 56.

[208] *Benedictional of St Aethelwold*, fo. 24ᵛ; *MRJ*, fo. 36ᵛ, pl. III; ivory reproduced in Beckwith, *Ivory Carvings*, no. 63, 131, pls. 12, 122.

[209] On the composition of the Adoration and the offerings, see Vézin, *L'Adoration*, 13–14, 73–4, 84–5.

PLATE 8 (*a*) The Second Coming, British Library, Additional MS 49598 (Benedictional of St Aethelwold), fo. 9ᵛ.

(*b*) Christ, Mosaic from the chapel of John VII in Old St Peter's, Rome.

PLATE 9 *a* (*left*) The Harrowing of Hell, British Library, Cotton MS Tiberius C. VI, fo. 14.

b (*above*) The Harrowing of Hell, S. Clemente, Rome.

to kneel or bowing and the third standing. Thus, on the Victoria and Albert Museum ivory, we still have the Presentation of the gifts, whereas in the Benedictional of St Aethelwold and in the missal of Robert, we see the Adoration. The other scenes in the cycle of the Magi in the missal also have Early Christian origins, for example, Herod and the Priests at Sta Maria Maggiore and several times in Carolingian art (Pl. 4*b*).

Also seen at Sta Sabina is the model of the Holy Maries at the Sepulchre, the three women led by Mary of Magdala carrying a censer and a box of ointments moving towards the sepulchre, on the stone of which sits the angel Gabriel. The scene is illustrated in such manuscripts as the benedictionals of St Aethelwold and of Robert and in Tiberius C.VI (Pl. 10*a*, *b*).[210]

The model of Christ between SS Peter and Paul, in England placed at the head of the Canon tables in Gospel-books, was first depicted in Roman art, as were two other scenes common by the tenth century, the *Traditio legis* and *Traditio clavis* of the type found in Sta Costanza, which we see, for example, in a late tenth-century ivory (Pl. 11*a*, *b*).[211] Possibly from the chapel of John VII came the illustration of a scene relatively rarely depicted in western art until then, the Calling of Peter and Andrew, in the Boulogne Psalter.[212] It was certainly in Rome that the 'portrait'-type of St Peter enthroned originated, with the tonsure and the keys, a type often found in England and ultimately based on the most famous representation of the Apostle, an Early Christian statue in the Vatican basilica, venerated by pilgrims.

Icons of Greek origins, such as those in the churches of S. Alessio, Sta Maria in Cosmedin, Sta Maria Maggiore, and the Pantheon, venerated as holy objects in their own right, contributed to increasing the devotion to the Virgin Mary, a particularly strong one throughout the Anglo-Saxon period.[213] More directly, an iconography of exclusively Roman origin, that of *Maria Regina*, which originated at Sta Maria Antiqua around the middle of the sixth century, appears for the first time outside Rome in the Assumption miniature in the Benedictional of St Aethelwold (Pl. 12*a*, *b*, *c*).[214] This particular link between Mary as queen and intercessor, and the

[210] *Benedictional of St Aethelwold*, fo. 51ᵛ; *BAR*, fo. 31ᵛ, reproduced in Temple, *ASM*, pl. 89; Tiberius C.VI, fo. 13ᵛ, reproduced in Wormald, 'Eleventh-century', pl. 15, and pl. 138 in *Collected Writings*.

[211] Paris, Bibliothèque Nationale, cod. lat. 323, reproduced in Beckwith, *Ivory Carvings*, no. 23, 122–3, pl. 53.

[212] Fo. 106.

[213] Clayton, *Cult of the Virgin*, *passim*.

[214] *Benedictional of St Aethelwold*, fo. 102ᵛ. The first appearance of this iconography in Rome at Sta Maria Antiqua, see de Grüneiseu, *Ste Marie Antique*, 276 is now unchallenged, see M. Lawrence, 'Maria Regina', *The Art Bulletin*, 7 (1924–5), 150–61; U. Nilgen, 'Maria Regina: Ein politischer Kultbildtypus?', *Römisches Jahrbuch für Kunstgeschichte*, 19 (1981), 1–33, and J. Osborne, 'Early Medieval Painting in S. Clemente, Rome: The Madonna and Child in the Niche', *Gesta*, 20 (1981), 299–310, esp. 303–6, who does mention, however, two such Byzantine images at Porec and Dyrrachum.

PLATE 10 (a) The Women at the Sepulchre, Rouen, Bibliothèque Municipale, MS Y. 6 (Missal of Robert of Jumièges), fo. 21ᵛ.
(b) The Women at the Sepulchre, Doors of Sta Sabina, Rome.

PLATE 11

a (*left*) Christ between St Peter and St Paul, Florence, Biblioteca Medicea Laurenziana, MS Plut. XVII.20, fo. 1.

b (*above*) Christ between St Peter and St Paul, Mosaic, Sta Costanza, Rome.

PLATE 12

a (left) Assumption of the Virgin, British Library, Additional MS 49598 (Benedictional of St Aethelwold), fo. 102ᵛ.

b (left below) Dormition of the Virgin (detail), Ivory no. 296-1867, Victoria and Albert Museum, London.

c (right below) Maria Regina, Icon of Sta Maria in Trastevere, Rome.

worshipper imitating her humility and becoming her servant, was first developed by Ildefonsus of Toledo, and Deshman explained how its English adoption in the 970s suggests both a link with the royal message of the book and an extremely well-developed and pervasive devotion to the Virgin in the circle of Aethelwold.[215]

The most remarkable feature concerning the Assumption iconography in the Benedictional of St Aethelwold is, in fact, the combination of two different iconographical themes, the Byzantine Koimesis, inspired by a Greek image, and the crowned Virgin, of Roman origin. The adoption of a Greek theme in this manuscript is entirely consistent with its general Byzantine inspiration; but the deliberate blending in of a Roman motif, which a pilgrim could have easily noted in the icon of Sta Maria in Trastevere, for example, underlines three points simultaneously. The first is the evident influence of Rome on artistic production in England, since the theme could not have come from elsewhere. The second shows how such artistic influences were received, never indiscriminately and slavishly, but rather thought about and incorporated by English ecclesiastics, by choice, within an existing tradition. The third supports beyond doubt every statement concerning the exceptional devotion to the Virgin in late tenth-century Winchester, where her status is enhanced even further than anywhere else in the West through this exceptional sign of her veneration as Mary the Queen of Heaven—Ottonian iconography at both Reichenau and Hildesheim, in Bernward's Gospel-book, was to adopt this theme in the early eleventh century once more after England. The traditionally accepted claim is that Rome was its source; but in view of the links already discussed between these two German centres and Winchester, we may wonder whether it could not have reached the Empire once again via England.

The same pattern applies to the devotion to the Cross: strong in Rome on account of the presence of the relic of the True Cross there at Sta Croce, it had soon become a major English devotion, as we see from the evidence of the hagiography, liturgy, and poetry. During the early Anglo-Saxon period, the importance of this devotion in the Lives of the saints and in the poem of the *Dream of the Rood* is evident.[216] Later, the celebration of the two feasts of the Cross and the elaborate ritual of Adoration of the Cross in the 'Easter play' confirm it anew.[217]

The representations of Roman martyrs in English manuscripts, such as

---

[215] Deshman, 'Servants', 33–70; on the marian devotion at Winchester, see Clayton, *Cult of the Virgin*, 65–81.

[216] M. Swanton (ed.), *The Dream of the Rood* (New York and Manchester, 1970),

[217] *RC* 115–19.

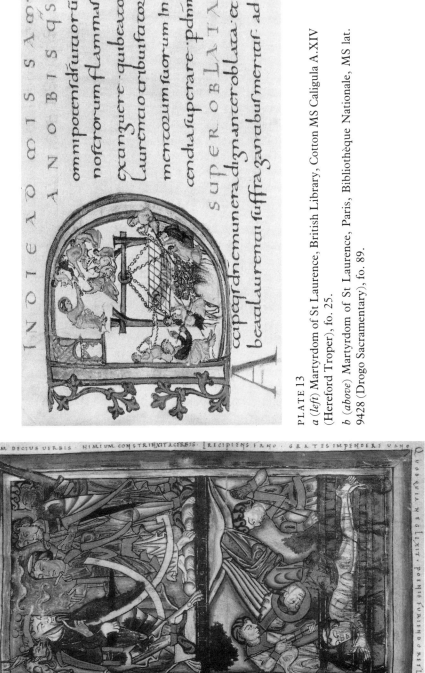

PLATE 13

a (*left*) Martyrdom of St Laurence, British Library, Cotton MS Caligula A.XIV (Hereford Troper), fo. 25.

b (*above*) Martyrdom of St Laurence, Paris, Bibliothèque Nationale, MS lat. 9428 (Drogo Sacramentary), fo. 89.

Laurence, and that of Gregory dictating his work to the deacon Peter, are yet another sign of the veneration for these saints. The oldest representation of the martyrdom of St Laurence, on the fifth-century mosaic in the Mausoleum of Galla Placidia at Ravenna, was followed by others, for example, in S. Saba in Rome, in the ninth-century frescos in the crypt of S. Vincenzo in Vulturno, and in various miniatures in Carolingian and Ottonian manuscripts dating between the ninth and eleventh centuries: the Sacramentary of Drogo, the Utrecht Psalter, the Fulda Sacramentary, and the Ivrea Sacramentary.[218] Two such images are found in England, in the Hereford Troper and in Harleian 603, the latter modelled on the Utrecht Psalter.[219] The first appears to have been modelled on a cycle, since it includes, in the upper register, St Laurence and the Emperor Decius, the latter crowned, with a devil whispering in his ear, while the saint, tonsured and dressed in clerical vestments, talks to him. Two figures, one of which bears a sword, stand behind the future martyr. The scene in the lower register shows St Laurence on the grill, with two executioners, and an angel flying down from Heaven to receive the saint's soul (Pl. 13*a*, *b*).

In some cases, themes might have reached English books through the Carolingian intermediary, for example the martyrdoms of Peter, Paul, and Laurence, represented in the Utrecht Psalter and the Sacramentary of Drogo.[220] Others, seen by pilgrims in Rome, had reached it from even further off, since these are known to have originated in the Greek and Eastern world, whose influence on Roman culture throughout the early Middle Ages was considerable. The martyrdom of St Peter, brought into Roman art by the Greek pope John VII, is an example. Some of these features arrived in England through Germany in the tenth century, some directly through the south of Italy, others through Rome; but some found their way directly from the East and from Byzantium. *Notes to Ch. V*

---

[218] For the Galla Placidia mosaic, see Wilpert-Schumacher, *Die römischen Mosaiken*, 319, reproduced pl. 74; on S. Saba's, see Krautheimer, *Corpus*, iii. 51–71, and Mâle, *Early Churches*, 127–8; on S. Vincenzo in Vulturno, see Bertaux, *L'Art dans l'Italie méridionale*, i. 94–5, fig. 31; *Drogo-Sakramentar*, fo. 89; Dufrenne, *Psautier d'Utrecht*, fo. 19, pl. 90, no. 28; Goldschmidt, *German Illumination*, ii. 109 on the Fulda Sacramentary c.997–1011 (Bamberg, Staatsbibliothek Cod. lit. 1 (A.II.52)), fo. 144; Magnani, *Le miniature*, fo. 98, pl. XXIV.

[219] Caligula A.XIV, fo. 25; Harleian 603, fo. 19.

[220] K. van der Holst and J. H. A. Engelbreght (eds.), *The Utrecht Psalter* (2 vols.; Graz, 1984), i. fo. 19, or Dufrenne, *Utrecht Psalter*, fo. 19, pl. 9, no. 28, and *Drogo-Sakramentar*, fos. 86, 89.

6

BYZANTIUM AND THE EAST

I. GEOGRAPHICAL OUTLINE

The evidence for the early Anglo-Saxon period shows widespread contacts with the eastern Mediterranean. Willibald visited not only the Holy Land but also Sicily, the Greek islands, Syria, Lebanon and Asia Minor on his way, and he was not the only one since, in the texts recounting his travels, he spoke of an old man at Emesa, who had seen many English people come to that part of the world.[1] Indirect links of Northumbria with the Greek world as well as Syria and Egypt through the intermediary of Italy or of Visigothic Spain and Ireland, were also active.[2] Greek texts, a knowledge of the language itself, and Coptic and Syriac art reached England in the first centuries after the Conversion, often through Rome. We have instanced the presence of Theodore and Hadrian at Canterbury and the school they established there, the Irish intermediary which may also have contributed to making possible the study of Greek in the British Isles, eastern motifs in the Insular artistic production, and devotional influences such as those found in the prayers of the Book of Cerne, some of which are based on texts of Ephrem the Syrian.[3] Whilst the impact of indirect Greek influence, through Italy or through Germany in the tenth and eleventh centuries, remains visible in England, direct contacts with the eastern Mediterranean seem to limit themselves to two precise areas, Constantinople and Jerusalem.

The Byzantine Empire [4] during the Macedonian period from the accession of Basil I in 867 until that of Alexius I Comnenus in 1081, had seen a recovery of its lost territories and power after the victories over the

---

[1] *Hodoeporicon of St Willibald*, in Talbot, *Missionaries*, 162, or in J. Wilkinson (ed.), *Jerusalem Pilgrims before the Crusades* (Jerusalem, 1977), 125–35, esp. 126. A great deal about the pilgrimage would have been known in England through Bede's adaptation of Adomnán's book on the Holy Places, as an independent booklet as well as in the *Ecclesiastical History*, see *BHE* 512–13, 506–13.

[2] J. Hillgarth, 'The East, Visigothic Spain and the Irish', 'Visigothic Spain and Early Christian Ireland', and 'Ireland and Spain in the Seventh Century', in *Visigothic Spain, Byzantium and the Irish* (London, 1985), 442–56, 167–94, 1–16.

[3] P. Sims-Williams, 'Thoughts on Ephrem the Syrian in Anglo-Saxon England', in *Learning and Literature*, 205–26.

[4] On the history of the Byzantine Empire, see G. Ostrogorsky, *A History of the Byzantine State* (tr, Oxford, 1968), and M. Angold, *The Byzantine Empire 1025–1206: A Political History* (London and New York, 1984); and on more general issues, C. Mango, *Byzantium: The Empire of New Rome* (London, 1980).

Arabs in Asia Minor, South Italy, Greece and the Middle East leading to the reoccupation of Antioch in 969 by Nicephorus Phocas, and the drawing into Byzantine orbit of the newly founded and christianized Russian kingdom under Vladimir in 989. Almost equally important was the final break-up of the Bulgarian state in the Balkans, overcome and absorbed into the Empire after Basil II's victory over King Samuel's army in 1014. The stronger Macedonian emperors such as Basil II attempted to impose a strong centralization of power in their hands, but were increasingly confronted with a rising aristocracy relying on its clientele and landed wealth, which was a powerful military force particularly in the eastern provinces, but was needed on account of the almost permanent state of war and was quick to profit from any weakness and instability of the central government from the death of Basil II to the accession of Alexius Comnenus. The latter put an end to the civil war, restored Byzantine power in the Balkans but had to fight the increasing Norman power in the south of Italy, thus neglecting to oppose the expanding Seljuk power in the east. The Turkish advance made pilgrimages to the Holy Land more difficult, which was a contributing factor to the western popular appeal of the First Crusade and opened the way to the establishment of new western kingdoms previously in Byzantine possession after 1099.

These two centuries saw a cultural revival in Constantinople, with the founding of higher schools of philosophy and law by Constantine IX (1041–55) and an increasing cultured class of bureaucrats keen to uphold and imitate the ideals of the hellenic past, especially of Greek philosophy discussed by Michael Psellos and John Italos in the second half of the eleventh century.[5] Classical works were copied in a more attractive and easy script, libraries were collected and anthologies of classical authors put together. Under Basil I and his son Leo VI an imposing church was built within the complex of the Great Imperial Palace in Constantinople, the Nea, which then provided the prototype for most Church architecture and decoration, a cross pattern surmounted by domes, mosaic interior decoration with the Pantocrator in the dome, the Virgin and the patron saints in the apse, Gospel and apocryphal scenes in the upper register of the walls and saints in frontal rows in the lower register, and prophets sometimes depicted within the motif of the Tree of Jesse in the narthex. Meanwhile, manuscript decoration attempted to follow classical hellenistic styles, exemplified by the presence of decorative arches, allegorical figures, the naturalistic three-dimensional representation of the human figures, and the copying of a nature background, all features exemplified in the three

---

[5] Mango, *Byzantium*, 233–81, and N. G. Wilson, *Scholars of Byzantium* (London, 1983), 136–79.

most important manuscripts surviving from that period, the Psalter and the Menologion of Basil II and a codex of Gregory of Nazianzus' sermons, now in the Bibliothèque Nationale in Paris.[6] The main churches of Constantinople by the tenth century were, according to the description of Constantine VII Porphyrogenitus in his *Book of Ceremonies*, and to other evidence, those of the Holy Apostles, St Sophia, St Polyeuctos, SS Sergius and Bacchus, the New Church or Nea, St Mary of Pharos, St Saviour in Chora, St John of the monastery of Stoudion, and St Irene.[7]

Pilgrims to Jerusalem, if they did not travel by land via Bavaria, Hungary, and Constantinople, as did Archbishop Ealdred of York, would have probably followed a route similar to that of the French monk Bernard who, in 870, left Rome for Monte Gargano, Bari, Taranto, then sailed to Alexandria, and went by land to 'Babylonia', Damietta, Gaza, Emmaus and Jerusalem.[8] Pilgrims stayed there in a hospice thought to have been founded by Charlemagne.[9] In Jerusalem, they visited first the church of the Holy Sepulchre, which possessed not only the Sepulchre itself but also relics of the Cross, the chalice, and the headcloth of Christ. This round church, prototype of all European round churches, was described in detail by many pilgrims, including Willibald and Arculf, from whom Adomnán and Bede took their descriptions.[10] Bernard mentioned the most impressive liturgical ceremony which took place there, the Holy Fire on Holy Saturday.[11] Twenty-seven other churches are noted by pilgrims in Jerusalem itself, the most important being the Holy Sion, New St Mary built by Justinian, and others where offices were held in Greek, Georgian, Syriac, Armenian, Latin, and Arabic.[12] Away from Jerusalem, another twenty-five churches were pilgrimage goals at Bethlehem, St Theodosius' where St Basil was buried, the Great Laura of St Saba's, and several near the Jordan, in Jericho, Nazareth, Cana, Tiberias, Sebasta, on Mount Tabor and Mount Sinai.

At the end of the eleventh century, the Western knowledge of the Holy Land extends to its approaches and to the places fought for, then visited, by the Crusaders, such as Antioch, taken in 1098, and the monastery of St Catherine on Mount Sinai.

[6] This MS dates from the late 9th c., Bibliothèque Nationale grec 510, see Omont, *Miniatures*, 10–31.
[7] On these churches, see Krautheimer, *Early Christian*, 201–369, esp. 331–69, and C. Mango, *Byzantine Architecture* (London, 1986), 57–140.
[8] Wilkinson, *Pilgrims*, 141–2.
[9] Ibid. 142.
[10] Ibid. 129, 95–6.
[11] Ibid. 142–4.
[12] Ibid. 137–8.

II. THE FACTUAL EVIDENCE FOR DIRECT CONTACTS

During our period, the sources mention three Greeks who visited or came to live in England. William of Malmesbury records the presence of a Greek monk, Constantine, at Malmesbury; the *Liber Eliensis* speaks of a Greek 'bishop' who came to live in England at Ely during King Edgar's reign; and the Life of Simeon the Hermit, which gives a detailed account of his travels, shows him to have also come to preach in Britain *c*.983, though no English source confirms this statement.[13]

We know a little more about Englishmen going to the East, either as pilgrims to Jerusalem or as visitors to Constantinople. Archbishop Ealdred did both, offered a gold chalice decorated with great skill to the tomb of Christ and, having met the patriarch of Jerusalem, was offered gifts by him.[14] Like Ealdred, others also travelled to Jerusalem via Germany, Hungary and Constantinople and probably visited, or at least saw, other parts of Palestine on their way, though these are not specifically mentioned. Earl Swein went to Jerusalem in 1052 from Bruges, where his family was exiled, and died on his way back in Constantinople.[15] We do not know which route the monk of Canterbury Aethelwine took in 1095, but he returned via Constantinople, Apulia, probably Bari, Rome, and Lombardy.[16] Neither are we told exactly the itinerary another monk of Canterbury, Joseph, folowed in 1089 or 1090, but he also travelled via Constantinople.[17] Other lay pilgrims of lower status, such as the couple Ulf and Madselin in *c*.1066–8, also went to Jerusalem.[18] Many probably did so, even before the Crusaders took Jerusalem in 1099, after which the pilgrimage became even easier to complete. From Orderic Vitalis and Anna Comnena's *Alexiad*, we know that one category of Englishmen went to Constantinople to settle there after the Conqueror deprived them of their English possessions in the 1080s; they were admitted into the Byzantine army from 1081 onwards, under Alexius I Comnenus, and from 1085 onwards served the Emperor in the most prestigious section of the imperial army, his personal guard known as the Varangian Guard.[19] Goscelin mentioned one such nobleman

[13] *WMGP* 415; *LE* 73; *Vita S. Simeoni monachi et eremitae*, AASS Jul. VI, 331.

[14] *ASC*, D1058, 134; *Florence*, i. 217.

[15] *ASC*, C1052, 124.

[16] Stubbs, *Memorials*, 245–6.

[17] C. H. Haskins (ed.), 'A Canterbury Monk at Constantinople, c.1090', *EHR* 25 (1910), 293–5.

[18] Whitelock, *Anglo-Saxon Wills*, 94–5.

[19] *Orderic*, ii. 202–5 and Anna Comnena, *Alexiad*, 63–4, 109, 231. On this, see A. A. Vasiliev, 'The Opening Stages of the Anglo-Saxon Immigration to Byzantium in the Eleventh Century', *Annales de l'Institut Kondakov (Seminarium Kondakovianum)*, 9 (1937), 39–69; and J. Shepard, 'The English and Byzantium: A Study of their Role in the Byzantine Army in the Later Eleventh Century', *Traditio*, 29 (1973), 53–92. K. Ciggaar, 'England and Byzantium on the Eve of the

who emigrated to Constantinople, married a local woman and built a church dedicated to St Nicholas and St Augustine, having been brought up at St Augustine's, Canterbury; this church became the rallying-point of the English community in Constantinople.[20] Many other such noblemen emigrated, according to Goscelin, who further speaks of a miracle performed by St Augustine of Canterbury in the 1070s, who saved a group of Greeks and Englishmen travelling from Byzantium to Venice by sea.[21] A Greek text, the *Admonition to an Emperor*, written by a certain Nikoulitza about 1080, displays evident hostility towards the honours and rewards showered by Alexius Comnenus on his English officers,[22] who fought the Normans at Dyrrachium in 1081 and who, later in the 1090s, were again seen helping the Emperor with an English 'fleet' stationed in the Bosphorus.[23]

III. THE INDIRECT CONTACTS WITH THE BYZANTINE GREEK WORLD

Apart from the relatively rare direct links with the Greek world, the English came to know Greek texts, devotions, and iconography through the intermediary of two areas with which they were in close touch in our period, Italy and Germany. In both cases, Greek influences were at work, in Rome and the south of Italy in the first case, in the Rhineland cities and Liège under the Ottonians and the Salians in the second case.

In Rome, pilgrims visited Greek churches, such as that of the Schola Graeca, the Greek community, Sta Maria in Cosmedin; and monastic churches served by Greek basilian monks or by a mixed community of basilian and benedictine monks, respectively Sant'Anastasio alle Tre Fontane and Sant'Alessio, possibly even S. Valentino. There, they would have come across Greek devotions, monastic customs and liturgy, especially at Sant'Alessio in the tenth century, possibly the most learned Roman

Norman Conquest (The Reign of Edward the Confessor)', *Anglo-Norman Studies*, 5 (1982), 78–96, has argued, not very convincingly, that some Englishmen went to Byzantium before the Conquest.

[20] Goscelin, *Miracula Sancti Augustini episcopi Cantuariensis*, AA Maii VI, 410.
[21] Ibid.
[22] Vasiliev, 'Opening Stages', 64–6.
[23] Anna Comnena, *Alexiad*, 63–4, and Geoffrey Malaterra, *De Rebus Gestis Rogerii Comitis*, ed. L. A. Muratori (repr. Bologna 1928), 74; on these two episodes, see Shepard, 'English and Byzantium', 73–84. The man in charge of this fleet seems to have been one Siward Barn, who had fought alongside Hereward the Wake and had to leave England afterwards, according to the evidence of a later Icelandic saga, ibid. 80–4. He was a characteristic example of a wealthy and powerful member of the Anglo-Saxon aristocracy who had to flee to Byzantium after the Conquest; we can put together a list of his landholdings in England before 1071 from Domesday Book, see J. Morris (gen. ed.), *Domesday Book*, v, *Berkshire* (ed. P. Morgan), 21.5, 11 and 18; xv, *Gloucestershire* (ed. J. S. Moore), 59.1; xxiii, *Derbyshire* (ed. P. Morgan), S. 5; xxxi, *Lincolnshire* (eds. P. Morgan and C. Thorn), T.5, 21.5, 63.7, and CW.17.

community. The intermingling of Latin and Greek traditions in Rome was still strong in the tenth century, and Rome remained one of the main centres for the transmission of Greek culture to the Latin world. Further south, not very far from Rome, other monastic communities were either of basilian tradition, such as Grottaferrata, or had particularly close links with Greek traditions and favoured the presence of Greek monks and artists within their walls, the most famous example being Monte Cassino itself under the reign of Abbot Desiderius, later Pope Victor III. Further south again, Naples had always been a city of mixed Latin and Greek culture. The south Italian Greek impact on the Anglo-Saxon Church is to be found mostly in specific devotions and liturgical features, discussed previously. While the English probably became familiar with some of these features through Rome, they may have become aware of others through the German channel.

Byzantine traditions of devotions and art were particularly favoured between the arrival in Germany of the Greek princess Theophano, to be married to Otto II in 972, and the death of Conrad II in 1039. Theophano was directly responsible for the appointment of Greek south Italian ecclesiastics, such as Gregory of Cassano, at her family's foundations of Burtscheid and Brauweiler, possibly for the markedly Byzantine features of the new imperial palace at Magdeburg, and for the Graecophile education of her son Otto III.[24] Gregory of Cassano, a Greek monk from Calabria, who had lived as an exile in Rome since 969 and had built an abbey there with the help of Theophano, was invited to Germany in 996 and given the abbacy of Burtscheid. He brought with him several disciples, a priest Andrew, a deacon Sabas, and a monk Sirius.[25] Otto III had been taught by another Greek tutor, John Philagathos, also from Calabria, abbot of Nonantola in 982, bishop of Piacenza in 988, a great favourite of Theophano and godfather of her son, on whom he exerted great influence; John was subsequently sent as an ambassador to Constantinople in 994–6 and in 997; he became the anti-pope John XVI.[26] Otto's enthusiasm for Greek and south Italian monasticism is well attested in his veneration for St Nilus and St Romuald, the disciples of these two men being among his most highly prized spiritual counsellors.

Most contacts between Greek monasticism and the Lotharingian world were carried through the Imperial court, which could not but be otherwise than in close touch with the Rhineland cities, since these were great

[24] Hamilton, 'Orientale lumen', in *Monastic Reform*, 202.

[25] N. Huyghebaert, 'Moines grecs et italiens en Lotharingie, VIIIe–XIIe siècles', in *Miscellanea Tornacensia: Annales du Congrès archéologique et historique de Tournai 1949* (Brussels, 1951), 100–1.

[26] P. E. Schramm, *Kaiser, Rom und Renovatio* (Leipzig and Berlin, 1929), 87–187.

religious, cultural, and economic centres. The bishops of these cities were often close to the court, and related to the Emperors, such as the two tenth-century archbishops Bruno of Cologne (925–65), who could speak Greek and possessed Greek artefacts,[27] and Dietrich of Trier, brother and cousin of Otto I. Notker of Liège was a counsellor of Theophano; the Emperors were often at Liège and Poppo, abbot of one of the greatest temporal and spiritual centres in Lotharingia, the abbey of Stavelot, often advised Henry III. Even simple abbots moved around Lotharingia, such as Rupert, a native of Liège, and abbot of Deutz near Cologne (*c.*1075–1127). Meanwhile, other ecclesiastics at the court also became interested and patronized Greek devotions, for example, Bishop Notker of Liège, Bishop Willigis of Mainz and Bishop Gérard of Toul. Notker and Willigis went several times to Italy with Theophano. Notker gave hospitality to a Greek bishop, Leo, at Liège in about 1000, while Gérard, who had been on pilgrimage to the Holy Land, did the same for some Greek monks at Toul; and Archbishop Poppo of Trier, after his pilgrimage to Jerusalem in 1028, invited the monk Simeon of Mount Sinai to settle at Trier in a hermitage.[28] In 1070, a group of Calabrian monks settled at Orval and another beneventan monk, Ursus, came to Sion with some relics of St James: an oratory was built and dedicated there by the bishop of Toul, which was given to the abbey of St Mansuetus.[29] Also at Liège and Aachen, we hear of an Italian painter, John, though he may have been a Roman; he decorated the chapel at Aachen then went to Liège, where he painted the crypt of the newly founded abbey of St James, where he then retired and died in 1018.[30] A little earlier in the century, John of Gorze, the reformer of Lotharingian monasticism, had travelled extensively in the south of Italy. He had been to Rome, Monte Cassino, Naples, and Gargano, had read Hilarionis, Macarius, and Pachomius, and been interested by some features of basilian monasticism, which he introduced in his reforming customs for Gorze and the abbeys reformed from it in Lotharingia and Germany.[31] Greek influence was at its strongest in Cologne under the reign of Archbishop Heribert, and there were several Calabrian monks there,

---

[27] Lotter, *Vita Brunonis, passim.*

[28] *Widrici Vita Sancti Gerardi episcopi Tullensis*, ed. G. Waitz, MGH SS iv. 488, 501; and *Ruperti Chronicon S. Laurentii Leodiensis*, ed. W. Wattenbach, MGH SS viii, 266. On Greek monks in Lotharingia, see Huyghebaert, 'Moines grecs', 95–111; and *Gesta Treverorum: Continuatio prima*, ed. G. Waitz, MGH SS viii. 175.

[29] Huyghebaert, 'Moines grecs', 102.

[30] *Vita Balderici*, 730–1; Huyghebaert, 'Moines grecs', 103.

[31] *Life of John of Gorze*, 342–4, 346, 360–1. Hamilton, 'Orientale lumen', 192. The reform from Gorze was at its strongest in the dioceses of Verdun, Liège, Trier, Metz and as far as Dijon and Arras, see Parisse, *Lorraine*, 25–6.

for example, one Elias in 1021.[32] Other German ecclesiastics, such as Adalbert of Prague, who had met St Nilus, had been to Jerusalem, Cassino, and St Saba's in Rome, were equally fascinated by south Italian spirituality, and Adalbert attempted to live by it at Sant'Alessio in Rome.[33] To these examples ought to be added the whole outlook of Otto III's reign and dreams of reconstruction of the Roman Empire since he saw himself as the heir to both the Latin and Greek thrones, as well as, for example, Conrad II's Greek sympathies. For our purpose, it is sufficient to record the wealth of Byzantine cultural elements at the court, as well as in cities such as Trier and Liège, with which the links of English centres have already been stressed.

IV. BYZANTINE AND EASTERN INFLUENCES ON ENGLISH DEVOTIONS AND LITURGY

The knowledge and absorption of some major cults of Greek origins from the south of Italy in England, such as those of St Michael, St Mary the Egyptian and the Fathers of the Desert, have already been examined. Other major saints of the Church, who were particularly venerated in the Byzantine sanctoral, such as John the Baptist, were also celebrated in a particularly solemn way in England. The position of John in the Greek Church was equal to that of St Peter in the Latin; not only was he second to none but Christ and the Virgin, he was also thought to be the only human being apart from the Virgin to have been elevated to dwell in Heaven among the angels.[34] His English cult shows an awareness of his prominent position in the hierarchy of the saints. In the liturgical texts, there was already by the fourth century a public cult of the saint, spreading from Palestine. Our first liturgical evidence in the West are the two masses for the saint's Nativity in the Leonine Sacramentary.[35] Four feasts of St John were celebrated in the western Church. The first was the Nativity, which gradually acquired a Vigil and then an Octave already celebrated by the tenth century at Cluny. This development paralleled that of Christmas, a deliberate attempt to create links between Jesus and John. This increasing devotion to St John on account of his role in the life of Christ was

---

[32] *Vita Heriberti archiepiscopi Coloniensis auctore Lantberto*, ed. G. H. Pertz, MGH SS iv. 740–53; Beckwith, *Early Medieval Art*, 118; Huyghebaert, 'Moines grecs', 101.

[33] *Vita S. Adalberti episcopi auctore Johanno Canapario*, 587–9. It is significant of Adalbert's successful commitment to this monastic outlook that his first Life was written by a monk with a Greek name.

[34] E. Kantorowicz, 'Ivories and Litanies', *JWCI* 5 (1942), 70–1.

[35] Mohlberg, *Sacramentarium Veronense*, 30–3.

superimposed upon the older eremitic side, characteristic of the earlier Middle Ages, although the eremitic remained equally strong in the new eleventh- and twelfth-century monasticism. After the seventh-century Greek influx to Rome, bringing with it the full impact of the highly developed Byzantine devotion to St John, the vigour of the cult in the West is indicated by the multiplication of the saint's feasts, on the oriental model. Three eastern feasts were gradually introduced in the West: the Decollation in the seventh century, the Conception, and then the Invention of the Head, which was one of the three Inventions of his relics celebrated in the Syrian Church.[36] By the eleventh century the Nativity, the Decollation, and the Conception were well-established feasts, whereas the Octave of the Nativity and the Invention of the Head were still only in the process of being integrated and were comparatively less celebrated.

In England, the feast of the Nativity appears in all calendars, with a Vigil, and, in the majority, is a first-class feast. The Octave is entered only in a Wessex calendar of the late eleventh century, in the Christ Church calendar, and in that in the missal of Robert. It was added at Worcester in the twelfth century, and became general in the course of that century. Both the Decollation and the Conception were entered in all calendars. Apart from the Octave, the only other feast to appear in some calendars, rather than in all of them, is the Invention of the Head, which is included in a Winchester and a Wessex calendar, and in two from the Evesham–Worcester group, all from the eleventh century.

The two feasts of the Nativity with its Vigil, and the Decollation, were celebrated in English liturgical books. The Vigil was celebrated in all sacramentaries with the Gregorian mass and the gradual is given. Other forms of celebration are the partial offices entered in the three collectars, and one of the two benedictions found in most benedictionals, either on its own or together with the main benediction for the Nativity. The main theme of the celebration is St John the Baptist's role as a prophet and Precursor preparing the way for the Messiah. It is illustrated in the Boulogne Gospels, which depicts two characters, identified as Isaiah and John by their scrolls, looking up towards Christ, while the inscription on the scroll held by John displays the words, 'Vox clamantis in deserto preparate viam domini'.[37] This is, as far as I am aware, the only scene

---

[36] On the feasts of St John the Baptist, see M. Viller *et al.* (eds.), *Dictionnaire de spiritualité ascétique et mystique*, viii (Paris, 1974), 187–9. The importance of the saint was considerable in the Syrian Church, on account of his prophetic and ascetic character, two features greatly appreciated in this milieu. He had seven feasts in his honour in that Church. The feast of the Decollation may have reached England from Naples, where it is found in the Calenderium Marmoreum, and it appears already among the feasts in the Lindisfarne Gospels.

[37] fo. 56.

representing the Precursor outside the Nativity and Baptism images in late Anglo-Saxon iconography. The illuminator may have been inspired by the Carolingian rather than the English tradition, which sometimes represented St John in this way, for example, in the St Médard Gospels.[38] Characteristically, Carolingian iconography preferred this representation of St John within his Old Testament function, whereas Anglo-Saxon iconography, like Ottonian art, was more interested in the New Testament parallels and function for St John, as the themes for the feast of the Nativity of the Baptist make explicit.

The main feast of the saint, his Nativity, was celebrated with great emphasis in all the official books of the English Church. It consists of two masses, the early-morning one and the High Mass, the texts of which are those of the two Gregorian masses. At New Minster and Exeter, where Leofric added a mass, the gradual for both masses is given and the feast was troped everywhere, displaying various liturgical embellishments such as sequences, responses, and proses. The traditional hymn is contained in all books and the collectars include the full office. The devotional trend indicated by the existence of proses and sequences is confirmed by the number of prayers either addressed to him, or in which he is invoked, in eleventh-century books from locations as varied as Worcester, Christ Church, Canterbury, Winchcombe, Crowland, and St Augustine's, Canterbury. These prayers, like the homilies for the saint in Aelfric's and the Blickling sets, repeat the themes already outlined, with additional emphasis upon the various roles of St John, as the Precursor, as a model of asceticism for monks and hermits, as the greatest among men, and also as the first martyr.[39]

The martyrdom is, naturally, the main topic of the texts for the second great feast of the Baptist, his Decollation. It was celebrated with the Gelasian mass in all sacramentaries. The office is given in a restricted form: one collect. Most eleventh-century benedictions have two benedictions for the feast, thus possibly demonstrating the increasing importance of the cult throughout that century. This is confirmed by the establishment of liturgical celebrations of the Baptist's Conception with masses at Exeter and Wells.

In the tenth century St John's cult was already substantial; in the eleventh it grew steadily in importance, as the celebration of his secondary feasts and the prayers addressed to him indicate. A devotion already strong at Winchester may have been increased in the south-west by the presence of Lotharingian bishops. The pilgrimage to Rome may have promoted the

---

[38] Boinet, *La Miniature carolingienne*, no. XIX.
[39] Aelfric in Thorpe, *Homilies*, i. 350–65 for the *Natale*; Morris, *Blickling*, 160–9.

cult, since pilgrims could see relics in various places on their way, such as Aosta, Siena, Marta on Lake Bolsena, and in Rome, in the Lateran and especially in the Scala Santa chapel. The eastern Church had always insisted that the Virgin and St John the Baptist were the only two human beings to dwell in Heaven among the angels, thus justifying the existence of the Byzantine Deesis which depicts Christ with the Virgin and the Precursor as intercessors.

Throughout its first ten centuries of existence, the Baptist's cult had various emphases put on it, which are reflected in English spirituality. Its prophetic and ascetic character, stressed in the East and in the Greek Church, was also predominant in early Anglo-Saxon England, as early saints' Lives such as the Life of St Cuthbert, the Life of Wilfrid, and the Ruthwell Cross show in their representation of St John. This emphasis was stronger than the sacerdotal and also than the role of the Precursor as a link between the Old and the New Law, which Early Christian and Carolingian art evoke. However, this second role is also present in late Anglo-Saxon liturgy. This central significance of St John within the Gospel, paralleled in Ottonian art and expressed through the popularity of the Nativity cycle and the Baptism, was the main feature of the late Anglo-Saxon cult of the saint. However, the ascetic and eremitic accent had certainly not disappeared. Aelfric's insistence on St John's chastity and Adelard and Osbern's comparison of St Dunstan with the Baptist on account of both saints' mystical visions of the Holy Spirit reveal the strong monastic character of the cult, whereas the existence of hermits in eleventh-century England, such as Mantat at Worcester or Whythman at Northeye, reminds of the uninterrupted attraction of a life associated essentially with this model for hermits *par excellence*, renewed in the eleventh century by the Italian inspiration.[40] The eremitic emphasis became even stronger in the twelfth century with the knowledge and success of the eremitic orders of northern Italy and France; an example of the renewed success of this side of the cult is given by the increase in monastic dedications to St John, four between 1066 and 1100, as against eight in the early, but only one in the late, Anglo-Saxon periods.[41] Like its counterpart, that of St Mary Magdalene, the cult retained the eremitic interest throughout the tenth and eleventh centuries, whilst it grew with every step in devotion to the Holy Family of which the saint was a member.

[40] Aelfric's first Old English letter to Wulfstan, 268 in *CSD* 1. i; Adelard and Osbern's Lives of St Dunstan in Stubbs, *Memorials*, 62, 73; Mantat's will is still extant, see Whitelock, *Anglo-Saxon Wills*, 66–7; Whythman, the abbot of Ramsey, retired to Northeye to be a hermit after resigning his abbey, see *Chronicon Rameseiensis*, 125.

[41] Binns, *Monastic Dedications*, 19–23.

Possibly of similar Greek origin, from Naples in particular, were the increasing devotions towards some saints directly related to Christ, members of his earthly family, mentioned either in the synoptic or in the apocryphal Gospels, such as Anne, the mother of the Virgin, Zachariah and Elisabeth, parents of John the Baptist, and from the eleventh century onwards, Joseph. These devotions towards the human elements associated with Christ's incarnation and life on earth, whether for persons or events, is one of the most obvious trends of eleventh-century western spirituality, but one which had already been present in the East from earlier on. It was originally as a result of the links with eastern spirituality in the early Anglo-Saxon period that the devotion towards the Virgin Mary, the Cross, and the celebration of the feasts of the Virgin and of particular episodes of the cycle of the Infancy of Christ took root in England in the seventh century, and did not disappear later, but remained a strong characteristic of Anglo-Saxon spirituality until the twelfth century. By then, the Carolingian preoccupation with the furtherance of a more collective and retributory piety had been gradually superseded by the equally personal, less formal, and more emotional preoccupation of Ottonian piety, partly under Byzantine influences. The early apparition of this kind of piety in England demonstrates the strength of this Greek inspiration, already present before the tenth century, even though the European and particularly Ottonian developments reinforced this trend. The devotion for particularly emotional episodes recounted in the Gospels is clearly illustrated in the iconography. We find it manifested towards Jesus in personal prayers, towards the Cross and its corollary, the Passion and sufferings of Christ as a subject for personal devotional meditation,[42] and towards the Virgin, exemplified by prayers, the least formal kinds of liturgical celebration, poems,[43] and by the introduction, directly from the south of Italy, of a new feast of the Conception in the eleventh century, almost two centuries before its general adoption in the West. These symptoms highlight very clearly the importance of that form of individual and emotional piety which is one of the hallmarks of Anglo-Saxon spirituality.

It is not impossible to imagine the knowledge of at least some English ecclesiastics of a Greek synaxarium or menologion, such as that of Constantinople, as illustrated, for example, in a manuscript of the type of the Menologion of Basil II. Indeed, it is likely to have existed since there are quite a few coincidences between representations of particular episodes in this menologion and the Benedictional of St Aethelwold, from an

---

[42] Raw, *Crucifixion*, 40–66, 86–102, 150–87.

[43] One such poem is edited by M. Clayton, '*Assumptio Mariae*: An Eleventh-Century Anglo-Latin Poem from Abingdon', *AB* 104 (1987), 419–26.

iconographical point of view. Greek liturgical texts sometimes reached England directly, as the presence of a litany in Greek at the end of the manuscript known as Aethelstan's Psalter shows.[44] Whether this is actually a Greek litany, one copied from an original manuscript, or a translation of a Latin litany is irrelevant—somewhere, contact with a Greek text did exist, or with someone who could translate it into Greek, which English ecclesiastics of the first half of the tenth century would probably not have felt confident enough to do. In view of the presence of several Greek ecclesiastics in England, it is not at all impossible that some Byzantine liturgical books should have been available, possibly in the baggage of those who brought to England the silks offered to St Cuthbert's shrine.[45]

Through a synaxarium, it would have been possible to learn the names of some saints highly venerated in the East though almost unknown in the West, at least outside Italy, such as St Catherine of Alexandria whose cult centre was the monastery on Mount Sinai, St Margaret of Antioch, St Blaise and, especially, St Nicholas of Myra. It is from the German and Lotharingian centres of his cult, and possibly also from Rome, that the saint's reputation reached England in the early eleventh century, becoming rapidly one of the great popular saints even by the middle of that century. Thus, the Bari cult from 1087 onwards, itself the result of a growing veneration for the saint in southern Italy, did no more than increase a cult already adopted in England from other sources, in contrast to the Norman cult, feeble to begin with and only after 1087 gathering momentum, as links between the Normans of Normandy and those who had settled in the south of Italy remained very strong.

Theophano was also responsible for the development of the cults of St Blaise and St Pantaleon, two Greek devotions which, however, appear to have been stronger in the south of Italy than in Byzantium itself by the tenth century. As for Nicholas, Reginold of Eichstätt composed an office for Blaise later adopted in England. Pantaleon's relics were brought by Archbishop Bruno to Cologne in 955, who dedicated a church to him, where Theophano was to be buried.[46] The presence of these saints in English liturgical books bears witness to the English links with the Greek world as well as with Germany and Liège. By contrast, one example alone exists of a cult known in England exclusively through Normandy and not from the eastern or Italian scene, that of St Catherine. Her relics were brought by a monk who came to Rouen from Mount Sinai, to collect the

---

[44] London, British Library Cotton MS Galba A.XVIII.
[45] On the silks see below, p. 214.
[46] Baker, 'Cult', 208–9.

alms of Duke Richard II for his abbey. The duke, who had been on a pilgrimage to Jerusalem and continued to send alms to the Holy Land on his return, placed them in the abbey of the Trinity, later renamed St Catherine's.[47] Its popularity increased greatly after the First Crusade, as did that of St Margaret and St George. Both had been celebrated before in England, George as part of the standard Gregorian sanctoral, Margaret partly on account of her cult at Bolsena, on the pilgrimage route to Rome. Clearly, however, these cults became major ones as a result of the Latin presence in the Holy Land, and late eleventh- and early twelfth-century texts as well as the iconography begin to incorporate them. The cult of St George, the martyr of Cappadocia, was already attested by the mid-fourth century.[48] After the composition of the Greek Passion in the fifth century, the cult became widespread in Palestine, where a monastery was dedicated to the saint in the sixth century, and especially in Ethiopia and Egypt. It reached Rome via the Greek Church, and the church of S. Giorgio in Velabro was dedicated in the eighth century, to which the head of the saint was translated by Pope Zacharias (741–52). The cult spread to Ravenna, Ferrara, Milan, and Naples. It is impossible, however, to trace the early channels by which the cult reached England, and, indeed, the saint was entered in the Leonine, then Gregorian and Gelasian Sacramentaries and would have arrived in this country along with the other Roman saints. However, instead of remaining simply a Roman traditional cult, the devotion to St George intensified after the First Crusade, since the saint was reputed to have helped the Crusaders, together with St Demetrios, to take Antioch in 1098.[49] The Crusaders rebuilt his basilica in Lydda, and enthusiastically brought his cult back home with them, adding to his Life the famous episode of the fight with the dragon, further embellished by naming the girl he thus saved as St Margaret and by making her a princess, as we can see on the Ault Hacknall tympanum. Thus, from the very beginning of his real cult in the West, that is to say after the First Crusade, St George's popularity among the nobility was due to his protection of the knights and his function as a military saint, like St Maurice and St Sebastian.[50]

Undoubtedly, the saint's cult was already known in England before the

---

[47] See below, ch. 7.

[48] On the cult of St George, see H. Delehaye, *Les Légendes grecques des saints militaires* (Paris, 1909), 45–76.

[49] *WMGR* ii. 420.

[50] St George had been venerated as a military saint in the Byzantine world and, together with other such saints—Demetrios and Sergius and Bacchus, for example—his cult had been particularly popular between the 7th and the 9th century, when they were regarded as members of the heavenly army which provided support to the imperial army in its fight against the enemies of Byzantium (communication by Dr Howard-Johnston).

Crusades. It was brought here from Ireland by Adomnán, who knew of it from Arculf when the latter returned from his pilgrimage to the Holy Land, and it is also found in Bede's martyrology. Aelfric wrote a homily for the feast;[51] Dunstan dedicated an altar to him at Glastonbury, and a church in Thetford was dedicated to him in King Cnut's time.[52]

Understandably, since he was a Gregorian saint, St George was entered in all calendars, with capitals at Sherborne and Crowland. He appears in sixteen litanies throughout the period and was celebrated with the Gregorian mass in the sacramentaries, except at Wells. The missal of New Minster gives the gradual, as it does for the more important among the Gregorian and Gelasian saints. The Durham and Wulfstan's collectars have collects, and the only additional celebration is found in Wulfstan's portiforium, where his name is the first in the list of martyrs in the general prayer addressed to them in the *orationes privatae*, and in Worcester F.173,[53] where his name is entered in capitals in one of the collects.

The remarkably conventional outlook of the English liturgy, hardly more noteworthy than that for the scores of Roman martyrs, is an indication of the fact that, as yet, this cult which would become of such significance from the twelfth century onwards, was simply one of many traditional Gregorian devotions, respectfully and formally celebrated, but without any of its subsequent success. His later good fortune becomes evident when we note the number of churches dedicated to the saint during the twelfth century,[54] and the popularity of the illustrations of the scene of the fight with the dragon on Norman tympana, for example, at Dameham (Wilts), Fordington (Dorset) and Hart (Durham).[55] These are probably post-First Crusade sculptures, since the episode was only then introduced in the West, even though some Greek representations at Smyrna (sixth–seventh centuries) and Mount Sinai (eighth–ninth centuries) existed before the twelfth century. When depicted in this scene, St George is shown fighting with a sword, one of the two attributes, along

---

[51] *Aelfric's Lives of the Saints* i. 306–19.

[52] Stubbs, *Memorials*, 27; on Thetford, a cell of Bury, see Binns, *Monastic Dedications*, 87. Another church dedicated to the saint before the First Crusade, in 1090, was Dunster in Somerset, a cell of Bath, ibid. 70. On the cult, see J. Hill, 'St George before the Conquest', *Report of the Society of the Friends of St George's and the Descendants of the Knights of the Garter*, 6 (1985–6), 284–95.

[53] A sacramentary of the 1st half of the 11th c., from Old Minster at Winchester, then removed to Worcester, now in the Cathedral Library in Worcester, fo. 22.

[54] The effect of the Crusade as a boost to the cult is also seen in the dedications which follow immediately after 1091, for example, in the case of a church of St George in Cambridge, probably dedicated in the 11th c., and destroyed in the early 12th c. to be replaced by that of the Holy Sepulchre, see C. N. L. Brooke, 'The Churches of Medieval Cambridge', in D. Beales and G. Best (eds.), *History, Society and the Church: Essays in Honour of Owen Chadwick* (Cambridge, 1985), 70.

[55] Keyser, *Norman Tympana*, 14, 20 23.

with the absence of wings, which enables us to distinguish him from St
Michael. Gradually, St Michael began to be represented fighting with the
sword, whereas St George later acquired a horse and a lance in the
iconography, as, for example, in Paolo Uccello's paintings.[56]

V. BYZANTINE INFLUENCES ON ENGLISH ART

Artistic features from the eastern Mediterranean, Byzantium including
Armenia, Syria, and Egypt are found in seventh- and eighth-century
'Hiberno-Saxon art', either in the form of objects from this area reaching
England or, indirectly, as sources of inspiration.[57] Coptic metalware was
found in several seventh-century graves at Taplow and in Hertfordshire,
which probably came from Egypt via Italy and the Rhine valley. Byzantine
plate was also found at Sutton Hoo, dating from the time of Emperor
Anastasius,[58] and we know that Gregory the Great sent King Ethelberht
of Kent some presents of Byzantine silver vessels.[59] It has been shown that
a specific and unusual type of leatherwork used in Egypt was also known
in Britain.[60]

Works of art from the East also provided models for Anglo-Saxon works.
The scene of Christ and Mary Magdalene on the Ruthwell Cross seems to
have been modelled on a similar scene depicted in Syriac art, for example
in a sixth-century miniature of Christ and the Woman with an issue of
blood in a Syriac manuscript; the Annunciation is not dissimilar to the
treatment of this scene in an Armenian manuscript,[61] possibly copying a
Syrian model, and an Anglo-Saxon ivory depicting the Transfiguration is
close in its iconography to that scene in the eleventh-century 'Trebizond'
Gospel.[62] Also on the Ruthwell Cross, Christ standing on the two beasts
is a theme first illustrated in Coptic art, whereas the figure of Christ himself
strongly reminds one of the figures of the prophets in Byzantine art, for
example at Sant'Apollinare Nuovo in Ravenna; the Sharing of the Bread

---

[56] J. Pope-Hennessy, *The Complete Works of Paolo Uccello* (Oxford, 1950), pls. 77–78. On the
iconography of St George, see W. Braunfels, *Lexikon der christlichen Ikonographie* (8 vols.;
Freiburg, 1968–76), vi. 375–85, and O. Grosso, *S. Giorgio nell'arte* (Milan, 1962).

[57] Saxl and Wittkower, *British Art*, 12, 14–16, 18.

[58] R. L. S. Bruce-Mitford (ed.), *The Sutton Hoo Ship Burial* (4 vols.; London, 1983), iii, ed.
A. Care Evans.

[59] Saxl and Wittkower, *British Art*, 12.

[60] R. Ettinghausen, 'Foundation-Moulded Leatherwork: A Rare Egyptian Technique also
used in Britain', in *Studies in Islamic Art and Architecture in Honour of Professor K. A. C. Creswell*
(Cairo, 1965), 63–71.

[61] Saxl and Wittkower, *British Art*, 15.5.

[62] Beckwith, *Ivory Carvings*, no. 21, p. 122, pls. 49, 51; and S. der Nersessian, *Armenian Art*
(London, 1978), 107, pl. 78.

by Paul and Anthony recounts an episode from the extremely popular Life of St Anthony by Athanasius of Alexandria, from which several early Anglo-Saxon saints' Lives were inspired, especially those of St Guthlac and St Cuthbert. The foliated vine-scroll so successful in England, as seen for example on two other crosses, at Bewcastle and Spital (*c.*700), is very close to this decorative motif in the Dome of the Rock or church of the Holy Sepulchre in Jerusalem (*c.*692) and in Coptic carving of the sixth century.[63] Lastly, the Ezra page in the Codex Amiatinus from the Jarrow *scriptorium*, copied from a Cassiodorian manuscript, has such evident links with Italo-Byzantine art, that P. J. Nordhagen was led to attribute it to the presence of an Italian painter living in this monastery, who would have been aware of seventh-century Roman artistic developments, such as we see them at Sta Maria Antiqua. Although it seems unlikely to imagine the physical presence of such an artist in England without it being clearly documented, the stylistic similarities emphasize the close relationship between Northumbrian and Italian art, probably due to the frequent exchanges of manuscripts between the two countries.[64] Another such parallel is the illumination of the Evangelist Matthew in the Lindisfarne Gospels, with its double symbol, also modelled on a south-Italian manuscript.[65]

Some motifs reached England through the intermediary of either Gaul or Ireland, so that we find, for example, the Coptic iconography for the Crucifixion on stone crosses, which depict Christ on the Cross between Longinus and Stephaton.[66] The iconography of the Crucifixion with Longinus and Stephaton has eastern origins in Cappadocia and Syria, whence it reached the south of Italy, Spain, Ireland, and Anglo-Saxon England, thus accounting for the presence of this type in the numerous early Anglo-Saxon images in manuscripts and on cross-shafts of the eighth and ninth centuries.[67] In tenth-century art, the tendency was increasingly to replace this iconography with that of the Crucifixion with the Virgin and St John, originally a Byzantine type which predominated in Italy, and

[63] A. Badawi, *Coptic Art and Archaeology* (Cambridge, Mass., 1978), pls. 3.133, 3.135; most examples of Coptic art are to be seen in Irish art of the 7th c., especially in the Book of Kells, where the Evangelist portrait of Matthew can be compared with a stone relief from Saqqara, see J. Beckwith, *Coptic Sculpture* (London, 1963), pl. 123.

[64] P. J. Nordhagen, *The Codex Amiatinus and the Byzantine Element in the Northumbrian Renaissance* (Jarrow Lecture, 1977); on this manuscript, see R. L. S. Bruce-Mitford, *The Art of the Codex Amiatinus* (Jarrow Lecture, 1967).

[65] fo. 25v.

[66] On Coptic iconography, see Badawi, *Coptic Art*, and K. Wessel, *Koptische Kunst* (Recklinghausen, 1963).

[67] C. Cecchelli, G. Furlani, and M. Salmi (eds.), *The Rabbula Gospels* (Olten, 1959), fo. 13*a*; on the Irish connection of this motif, see F. Henry, *Irish High Crosses* (Dublin, 1964), 40, and J. Reil, *Die frühchristlichen Darstellungen der Kreuzigung Christi* (Leipzig, 1904).

which became usual in Ottonian and in English art.[68] The Crucifixion with Longinus and Stephaton continued to appear in some manuscripts in the late Anglo-Saxon period, for example, in Tiberius C.VI and on two ivory crosses, with the classical motif of the personified Sol and Luna in one of them, but it remained common in the more archaic medium of the cross-shafts, five of which carry this image.[69] In the D initial to Psalm 101 in Boulogne Psalter, we find a combination of the four characters, which follows the model most commonly found on the Continent from the south of Italy (S. Vincenzo in Vulturno) to Rome (Sta Maria Antiqua), to Carolingian (Müstair, Utrecht Psalter) and Ottonian art (St Maximin at Trier, *Codex Egberti*, Ivrea Sacramentary),[70] where both the lance-bearer and the sponge-bearer are present in the Crucifixion scenes on either side of the Cross (Pl. 14a, b, c). St John was sometimes represented wearing a beard, in the wake of eastern and Irish traditions, though this became increasingly unusual in the West after the Carolingian period, but not unheard of in Anglo-Saxon iconography, since the saint is depicted with a beard in the Crucifixion drawing in Titus D.XXVII.[71]

The techniques of embroidery which were to become one of the most famous late Anglo-Saxon crafts had been originally introduced from Byzantium, and examples of Byzantine works of this kind are found as late as the early tenth century, in the stole and maniples of Frithestan, given by Aethelstan to the shrine of St Cuthbert, whose techniques and style were adapted from Byzantine textiles, and directly imported from Byzantium in the later period in some of the silks found in the coffin.[72]

Also linked with Byzantine iconography are some of the illuminations in manuscripts of the 'Winchester School' in particular those in the Benedictional of St Aethelwold. The Second Coming, originally a Cappadocian theme then known as the Byzantine Anastasis; the theme, originally Syriac,

---

[68] D. Talbot Rice, *English Art* 871–1100 (Oxford, 1952), 164, and Coatsworth, 'Iconography', 254, 278–81, 311–15, 323–6.

[69] Tiberius C.VI, fo. 13 in Wormald, 'Eleventh-century', pl. 14, and pl. 137 in *Collected Writings*; on the two ivories of the Crucifixion with Longinus and Stephaton, late 10th or early 11th c., Victoria and Albert Museum, London, see Beckwith, *Ivory Carvings*, nos. 33 and 34, 125, pls. 69 and 71. The cross-shafts are those at Almouth, Aycliffe, Hexham II, Nassington, and Penrith, the first two of the end of the 10th-c., see Coatsworth, 'Iconography', 211–12, 215, 314. For the first two, see also W. G. Collingwood, *Northumbrian Crosses of the Pre-Norman Age* (London, 1927), 62 and 79, figs. 79 and 97.

[70] Boulogne Psalter, fo. 109. Schiller, *Iconography of Christian Art*, ii. 100–2; Dufrenne, *Psautier d'Utrecht*, fo. 67, pl. 90, nos. 14, 15; *Codex Egberti*, fo. 248ᵛ, and Magnani, *Le miniature*, fo. 57ᵛ, pl. XVI.

[71] Titus. D.XXVII, fo. 65ᵛ, reproduced in Temple, *ASM*, pl. 246. This Greek tradition is still found in the Greek iconography of the south Italian Exultet Rolls, see, for example, the Exultet Roll from Bari Cathedral Arch. I, reproduced in Avery, *The Exultet Rolls*, pl. VII.

[72] Battiscombe, *Relics*, 375–525; on the other silks, see the articles by H. Granger-Taylor, C. Higgins, and A. Muthesius in Bonner, *St Cuthbert*, 303–27, 339–41, 329–37, 343–65.

PLATE 14

a (left above) The Crucifixion, British Library, Cotton MS Tiberius C.VI, fo. 13.

b (right above) The Crucifixion, British Library, MS Harley 2904, fo. 3ᵛ.

c (left below) The Crucifixion, Boulogne-sur-Mer, Bibliothèque Municipale, MS 20 (Boulogne Psalter), fo. 109.

of the Dormition of the Virgin; the Pentecost iconography with the Virgin
in the middle of the group of Apostles below Christ and Peter on the side
of Christ; the martyrdom of Peter and Paul; and details in other scenes,
such as the palms in the Entry into Jerusalem, are close to the iconography
of a manuscript such as the Menologion of Basil II, John VII's chapel, and
the Byzantine door of S. Paolo fuori le Mura in Rome, brought there in
the late eleventh century. Their iconography is either directly eastern, as
in the scenes described above, or indirectly so through the intermediary
of Roman and Carolingian art, for example, in the Ascension and Stoning
of Stephen iconography, and sometimes through Ottonian art, in the
details of the angel's stone at the sepulchre in the Three Maries, and the
Dormition. This latter scene was probably first depicted in the West in
early Anglo-Saxon art, on the eighth-century Wirksworth slab, where it
came directly from the east, before the other representation of it at Sta
Maria Egiziaca in Rome in the ninth century appeared; similarly, the
Nativity of the Virgin, based on apocryphal texts and depicted in Rome,
is based on an eastern model in England, since the animals shown are
different from those in the Greek text and must, therefore, rely on an
eastern one.[73] But the placing of the Virgin in the middle, under Christ's
mandorla and separated from the Apostles, in the Ascension scene in
Aethelstan's Psalter is a feature of Middle Byzantine art. Even closer to
Byzantine art is the representation of the choirs of the saints in the order
used in the litanies in the Benedictional of St Aethelwold, depicted
frontally as a static catalogue, as we see it at Ravenna, St Sophia, and in
the Exultet Rolls. According to Deshman, it is possible that this book may
have even included an illumination of the Byzantine Deesis with the Virgin
and St John the Baptist, now lost,[74] though this seems unlikely in view of
the much more common use in the West, especially in England, of the
alternative scene showing the Virgin and St Peter, as in the *Liber Vitae* of
New Minster. Most profoundly of all, Byzantine art influenced the
Benedictional in its attempt to provide a set of liturgical illustrations rather
than a purely narrative cycle, which was by then more in the western
tradition and can be seen in another manuscript from the same *scriptorium*,
the missal of Robert of Jumièges. The influence can be traced from the
point of view of the iconography, the stylistic features, and also the very
concept of a book illustrating the liturgical year by providing illuminations
to explain and underline the meaning of the feast and depict saints in a
static posture, rather than recounting the narrative thread of the Bible.[75]

[73] Clayton, *Cult of the Virgin*, 153–5, 172–3.
[74] Deshman, 'Iconography', 229–30.
[75] A. Guillou, 'Art et religion dans l'Italie grecque médiévale', *Chiesa*, 751; Weitzmann,

Equally significant is the Greek inspiration found by pilgrims to Constantinople, or even only the south of Italy and Rome, in the icons of the Virgin and Child, which they would have seen. These clearly provided the inspiration for the ivory panel known as the York Madonna, the iconography of the Virgin and Child being a theme not seen again in English art, after the Italian–Byzantine inspiration of the Cuthbert coffin and the Book of Kells, before the second half of the eleventh century, when this ivory was carved.

Inspiration from the East outside Constantinopolitan art is still in existence in other forms than manuscript art. From Coptic textiles, we find the motif of a figure holding a flower, as in the Alfred Jewel, whose cloisonné work reminded Fritz Saxl of south Italian metalwork. Two scenes in the 'Tiberius Psalter' bear a strong resemblance to two scenes of the seventh century representing the same subject, David and Goliath, in a fresco in Bawit in Egypt, which would seem to imply direct visual knowledge of these frescos.[76]

Altogether, most of the eastern inspiration in western Art by the tenth century came from Constantinople, which had become the arbitrator and model for the rest of the eastern Empire, while the other artistic schools, such as those of Jerusalem, Egypt, and Syria, were far less active than at the time of Carolingian Europe.[77] Thus it is that we find, both in Ottonian Germany and in England, iconographic influences from post-iconoclastic Constantinopolitan art, an art whose attraction for these two areas being not its style, often adapted to western patterns, but rather its 'iconic' qualities, which appealed to both countries and, particularly, their courts.[78] These were both stressing the royal dignity in their most lavishly decorated ceremonial manuscripts, whose aim was, to a great extent, that of emphasizing and demonstrating the magnificence and power of their respective kings.[79] It was, among other features, this awareness of the royal majesty, of paramount importance in England, which was to allow the Norman William to find legitimacy for his newly conquered English throne.

'Narrative and Liturgical Gospel Illuminations', 247–70, and 'Various Aspects of Byzantine Influence on the Latin Countries from the Sixth to the Twelfth Century', *Art in the Medieval West and its Contacts with Byzantium* (London, 1982), 15–16. On this, see ch. 3, p. 87.

[76] Saxl and Wittkower, *British Art*, and E. Chassinat (ed.), *Le Monastère et la nécropole de Baouît* (*Cairo, 1904*), pls. *XVIII, XIX*.

[77] On Byzantine illumination in general, see J. Ebersolt, *La Miniature byzantine* (Paris and Brussels, 1926), and K. Weitzmann, *Die byzantinische Buchmalerei des 9. und 10. Jahrhunderts* (Berlin, 1935).

[78] Weitzmann, 'Various Aspects', 14–19.

[79] G. Cames, *Byzance et la peinture romane de Germanie: Apports de l'art grec posticonoclaste à l'enluminure et à la fresque ottoniennes et romanes de Germanie dans les thèmes de majesté et les Évangiles* (Paris, 1966), 1–24, 118–79.

7

FRANCE

I. GEOGRAPHICAL OUTLINE

The area of France covered for my purpose is that of the northern half of the country, with a southern limit at the level of the Limousin, belonging to the duchy of Aquitaine, and the southern part of the duchy of Burgundy. There is very little evidence in English or Continental sources of any knowledge of or contacts with the lands beyond this line. Within this area, the old Carolingian west-Frankish kingdom was divided into several powerful principalities by the early tenth century and, in some cases, was even to increase its division into smaller units, the castellanies, during the course of the eleventh century.[1] The kingdom itself only covered the area known as Île-de-France, whose capital and royal centre of power was Paris. It remains throughout the period we are discussing a minor principality, where the king, despite his prestige and theoretical suzerainty at the top of the feudal pyramid, was no more than a local lord, sharing his power and rights of public authority with other powerful châtelains.[2] Several prestigious abbeys were situated in Paris: Ste Geneviève, St Germain, St Maur, and, slightly outside the city, the most prestigious of all and the necropolis of the kings, the royal abbey of St Denis.

The abbey of Ste Geneviève was dedicated to the fifth-century deaconess who had led the defence of the city against Attila in 451, and was a basilica which replaced the original oratory built over her tomb; St Germanus became bishop of Paris c.556 and founded in 558 the monastery of the Holy Cross and St Vincent, later rededicated to him, where he was translated in 754; St Maurus, a disciple of St Benedict, was sent by the latter to Gaul, according to his legend, and founded there the abbey of St Maurus of Glanfeuil on the Loire valley, but his relics were translated in the ninth century to Paris, to the abbey of St Maur-des-Fossés, which actively promoted his cult.[3] Ste Geneviève, destroyed by a fire in 856–7, had recovered some of its importance by the beginning of the eleventh century,

---

[1] On the question of the principalities and *châtellenies*, out of a vast literature, the latest work to sum up the evidence is J. Dunbabin, *France in the Making 843–1180* (Oxford, 1985).

[2] The best study on the Île-de-France and the weakening royal power remains J.-F. Lemarignier, *Le Gouvernement royal aux premiers temps capétiens (987–1108)* (Paris, 1965).

[3] On the history of Paris and of its main churches and abbeys, see J. Boussard, *Nouvelle histoire de Paris: De la fin du siège de 885–886 à la mort de Philippe Auguste* (Paris, 1976), 15–127.

but became once again a major intellectual centre only by the end of that century, which saw the foundation of one of the most prestigious schools of the next period. St Germain-des-Prés, on the other hand, although having also suffered under the Vikings, was rebuilt in 990–1014 on a lavish scale, and became active as a cultural centre from that period onward, with a school and *scriptorium* of some importance.

The first church of St Denis had been built by St Genoveva and dedicated *c*.475. In 639, King Dagobert founded a monastery on the spot where Denis and his companions the deacon Rusticus and the priest Eleutherius were said to have been martyred. By the seventh century, there was already a pilgrimage to and a fair at St Denis. By the eleventh century, the abbey had acquired some relics of the Passion of Christ, said to have been given to it by Charles the Bald, who had been a lay abbot of the abbey. In the ninth century, the monks and Abbot Hilduin were active in promoting the cult and, after centuries of Merovingian and Carolingian support, the saint gradually became the patron saint of the Capetians, who had been at first counts of Paris and were lay abbots of the abbey. The abbey was reformed *c*.996 by Odilo of Cluny, but it was less dynamic than Burgundian and Norman monasteries at that time, partly because of the weakness of the French dynasty, although Gérard of Brogne had spent some time at St Denis. The church was built in the eighth century under Abbot Fulrad and consecrated on 24 February 775, and a pilgrimage on that day became customary, as well as a fair, which was to become in the eleventh century the renowned 'Foire du Lendit'. This church presented notable Early Christian and Byzantine features. From the tenth century onwards, the abbey became the burial place of most French kings.[4]

To the north of Paris lay Amiens and Beauvais. The patron-saint of Beauvais was the martyr Lucian,[5] reputed to have been one of the twelve missionary disciples of St Denis and to have been martyred together with SS Julian and Maximian at the end of the third century. He was later said to have been bishop of Beauvais, and a basilica bearing his name was built in the seventh century. His cult flourished from the ninth century onwards. A second equally popular saint and martyr of Beauvais was St Justus, a boy-martyr beheaded near Beauvais in the third century. He was entered in an eleventh-century Auxerre Martyrology as an Auxerre saint with relics there, but Malmédy acquired a set of relics at the beginning of the tenth century, and the *Annales monasterii de Wintonia* record that Aethelstan made a gift of this martyr's head to Winchester in 924, a relic

---

[4] On the history of St Denis, see Crosby, *The Abbey of St Denis*, 41–50, 79–86, 98, 112–83.

[5] A. Renet, *St Lucien et les autres saints du Beauvaisis* (2 vols.; Beauvais, 1892–3), i. 4–179, 203–11, 331–418.

which counted as one of Winchester's most significant possessions by the late tenth century.[6] The martyr Firminus,[7] said to have been a bishop of Amiens in the fifth or sixth century, became the main saint of that city after the invention of his relics in the seventh century, and his popularity remained unchallenged in the later Middle Ages. South-west of Paris lay Orléans, whose patron saint was St Anianus, the bishop who had defended the city against Attila in 451, and who was buried in the church later dedicated to him.

Surrounding the royal domain from west to east, south of the county of Flanders, were the duchy of Brittany, the duchy of Normandy, the county of Champagne, the duchy of Burgundy, and going east again below Île-de-France, the county of Blois, the county of Anjou, and the duchy of Aquitaine, which included Poitou and the Limousin. After having drifted away from Charles the Bald's kingdom about the middle of the ninth century, Brittany had become a coherent territorial unit by the tenth century, under the government of a count.[8] The city of Dol and its abbey of St Samson and the abbey of Landévénnec are the two Breton religious centres mentioned in English sources.

The duchy of Normandy was officially founded in 911, after the peace treaty of St-Clair-sur-Epte between Charles the Simple and the Viking Rollo. The dukes remained vassals of the king of France but consolidated their power internally, on the basis of feudal allegiance, and allied themselves with the Robertian-Capetian dynasty.[9] Their power relied on their hold over the administration, justice, finances, and the Church, which they reformed in the eleventh century, and on their firm control over their own vassals, the barons, who were required to be present at the ducal court three times a year at Christmas, Easter, and Whitsun. Economic prosperity based on trade, centred on Rouen, helped maintain ducal power.[10] In relation to Normandy, we find references to the towns of Bayeux, Évreux, the duke's capital Caen, whose main abbey was St Stephen's, founded by the duke and placed under the influence of Bec; and Rouen, a rapidly expanding port, whose trade relations with England were particularly active, and whose main abbey was St Ouen.

---

[6] *Annales monasterii de Wintonia*, 10.

[7] Corblet, *Hagiographie*, ii. 31–76. There were two bishops of Amiens of that name, one of the 3rd and one of the 5th or 6th c.: the date given in English calendars corresponds to the feast of the second.

[8] A. Le Moyne de la Borderie, *Histoire de Bretagne* (6 vols.; Rennes, 1898–1914, repr. 1972), i and ii; J. Delumeau, *Histoire de la Bretagne* (Toulouse, 1969).

[9] M. de Bouard (ed.), *Histoire de la Normandie* (Toulouse, 1970); L. Musset, 'Naissance de la Normandie', 108–119.

[10] Ibid. 116–26, and Bouard, 'La Normandie ducale: économies et civilisation', in *Histoire*, 159–79.

Other monastic houses in Normandy were Jumièges, St Wandrille, Fécamp, Bec, St Évroul, and Mont Saint Michel. Jumièges[11] was founded about 654 by St Philibert; ravaged by Viking attacks in 841, it was restored about 940 by the duke of Normandy and reformed by William of Volpiano. A similar development was that of St Wandrille, founded about 649 as Fontenelle and later dedicated to its founder Wandrille, which had a main church dedicated to St Peter, and others to St Laurence, St Paul, and St Pancras. Part of Wandrille's relics were translated to St Peter's of Ghent in 944.[12] The abbey was reformed by Gérard of Brogne about 960. Fécamp, reformed by William of Volpiano under Duke Richard II, was one the main spiritual centres in Normandy, and belonged to the reforming movement of the eleventh century, developed under the influence of William and of his nephew, Abbot John of Ravenna (1028–78), whose writings were among the leading devotional texts of the period.[13] Bec was particularly famed for its school after Lanfranc took it over; among its most distinguished alumni were Anselm, Ivo of Chartres, William Bona Anima of Rouen, and the future Bishop of Rochester, Gundulf, as well as the future prior of Christ Church, then abbot of Battle, Henry.[14] It was also a major centre for the devotion to the Virgin, which it began to promote early on, and equally active in compiling collections of papal decretals, which reached England from Bec after the Conquest.[15] Among its patrons in Normandy were Baldwin and Richard of Meulles, Hugh of Grantmesnil, and William of Vernon, all later closely involved in the patronage of English monastic houses and specially Canterbury.[16] A parallel example to that of the influence of Bec on St Stephen's at Caen is that of Jumièges on St Évroul, the other intellectual centre in Normandy.[17] The third such centre was Mont Saint Michel, refounded by Bishop Avitus of Avranches in 966 and dedicated on 16 October. It was a crossroads for influences from the south of Italy, Germany, and Flanders in the eleventh century, and from the north of Italy under the abbacy of Suppo of Fruttuaria (1033–48), who brought relics and probably some of the new monastic ideals from his former abbey.[18]

[11] *Jumièges: Congrès Scientifique du XIIIe Centenaire* (2 vols.; Rouen, 1955), *passim*.
[12] L. David, 'L'Histoire de l'abbaye St Wandrille de Fontenelle', in *L'abbaye St Wandrille, de Fontenelle* (St Wandrille, 1957), 3–18, and Grierson, 'Early Abbots of St Peter's', 133.
[13] Leclercq and Bonnes, *Un maître*, 31–106; Wilmart, *Auteurs spirituels*, 66–9.
[14] Gibson, *Lanfranc*, 34–7; C. Porée, *Histoire de l'abbaye du Bec* (2 vols.; Evreux, 1901), i. 30–233.
[15] Ibid. 29, 139.
[16] Ibid. 30.
[17] *Orderic*, i. 11–28.
[18] Laporte, 'L'Abbaye du Mont Saint Michel aux xe et xie siècles', in Laporte, *Millénaire*, 53–80, and Alexander, *Norman Illumination*, 86–126.

East of the royal domain lay the county of Champagne.[19] Some cities from that area were mentioned in English sources, though they were not under the authority of the count, but episcopally governed towns, where the bishop had comital power, and were gradually attracted within the orbit of royal protection. These were Laon, Langres, and Reims; while Châlons-sur-Marne was under the control of the count of Auxerre in the tenth century. At Châlons-sur-Marne, the fair is already mentioned as being in existence by 963; Italian merchants were beginning to be seen there, and it was on its way to becoming one of the great fairs of Champagne during the next three centuries.[20] The patron saints of Reims were St Rémi and St Nicasius, whose cults were centred on the two abbeys dedicated to them, which held their relics. Bishop Nicasius built the first cathedral in the fifth century and dedicated it to the Virgin. A hospice was attached to it, and it was rebuilt first under Bishop Ebbo, then again in 862 under Hincmar, when it acquired a western end (Westwork), a façade mosaic depicting Louis the Pious and Pope Stephen IV at the feet of Christ, and a roof covered in sheets of tin, probably imported from England. The church of Reims possessed lands in the dioceses of Metz, Mainz and Worms, and as far south as Provence, Limoges, and Poitiers. During the course of the tenth century, the cathedral school, run by the canons under Gerbert, who had been educated in Spain and Italy, was at its intellectual peak, and it was particularly renowned between the years 972 and 991. Gerbert's teaching, especially in the sciences of the quadrivium, was famous throughout Europe.[21] He had pupils from everywhere, such as Abbo and Constantius of Fleury, his works were available as far as Chartres and he had close links with the German Emperors and Empresses, the king of France, and bishops and abbots in Germany, France and Flanders, such as those of Tours, Fleury and St Peter's at Ghent. Before his career changed its course from the contested appointment as archbishop of Reims to the German and Italian worlds, he had already been abbot of Bobbio for a while.

Hincmar also rebuilt the basilica of St Rémi, originally built by the saint himself then dedicated to him in 627, and translated the saint's relics there in 852. The monastery attached to it was reformed from Gorze in the tenth century. The relics of the saint were solemnly translated anew in 1049 by Pope Leo IX during the council held in Reims.[22] Outside the walls of Reims itself were several other churches, the main one being dedicated to

[19] M. Bur, *La Formation du comté de Champagne* (Nancy, 1977).
[20] Lestocquoy, 'The Tenth Century', in *Études*, 48.
[21] On Gerbert's career, see Lattin, *Gerbert*, 1–20, 39–45, 59.
[22] R. W. Southern, *The Making of the Middle Ages* (London, 1953), 125–7.

St Thierry; within the walls were two nunneries dedicated to St Peter, chapels, and two hospices. By the tenth century, the monastic borough was increasingly prosperous once again, with two fairs; and in 990, Gislebert of Roucy abandoned his rights of public authority over the monastic borough to the monks of St Rémi. In the late tenth century, the town was, both intellectually and economically, exceptionally prosperous.[23]

At Laon, the churches of St Christopher (later St Vincent), St Hilary, St Peter, and the abbey of the Virgin and St John were all founded during the Merovingian era. The cathedral school was one of the most important centres of the Carolingian Renaissance and one of the last to survive; it was at its peak when Irish scholars were gathered there around John Scot Eriugena, as they were also in Auxerre.[24] Laon had an English connection since Eadgifu, wife of Charles the Simple and mother of Louis IV 'd'Outre-Mer', married there her second husband, Herbert of Vermandois, later Count of Troyes.[25]

The duchy of Burgundy was effectively founded by Count Richard (878–921). It gave two kings to France, the Dukes Raoul (923–36) and Robert II (996–1031), through alliances of its ducal family with the Capetians, but failed to remain a territorial and political unit.[26] It became further split into counties then castellanies during the course of the eleventh century, under the authority of counts such as that of Mâcon, then of local lords, both lay and ecclesiastical, of which the most powerful was the abbey of Cluny.[27] Other Burgundian cities mentioned in English sources are Auxerre, which had its own count, and had been a major Carolingian cultural centre, as well as an artistic one, exemplified by the wall-paintings depicting the life of St Stephen in the crypt of its main abbey, St Germain; Péronne, a monastery which had some links with England through the presence there of St Fursa, an Irish missionary who had worked in East Anglia and whose head was a major relic of Christ

---

[23] P. Desportes (ed.), *Histoire de Reims* (Toulouse, 1983), 63–135.

[24] J. J. Contreni, *The Cathedral School of Laon from 850 to 930: Its Manuscripts and Masters* (Munich, 1978).

[25] On Laon, see J. F. L. Devisme, *Histoire de la ville de Laon* (2 vols.; Laon, 1822, repr. 1980), i. 15–124.

[26] On the history of Burgundy, see J. Richard (ed.), *Histoire de la Bourgogne* (Toulouse, 1978), esp. J. Marilier and J. Richard, 'La Bourgogne du haut Moyen Age', 89–130, and P. Quarré and J. Richard, 'La Bourgogne à l'âge roman et gothique', 131–66.

[27] On the history of the duchy, see M. Chaume, *Les Origines du duché de Bourgogne* (Dijon, 1925–31), and J. Richard, *Les Ducs de Bourgogne et la formation du duché du XIᵉ au XIVᵉ siècle* (Dijon, 1954); a classic study of a county is that of G. Duby, *La Société aux XIᵉ et XIIᵉ siècles dans la région mâconnaise* (2 vols.; Paris, 1953), dealing also with the early development of Cluny. On Cluny, see G. de Valous, *Le Monachisme clunisien des origines au XVᵉ siècle* (2 vols.; Ligugé, 1935), and N. Hunt (ed.), *Cluniac Monasticism in the Central Middle Ages* (London, 1971).

Church at Canterbury; Autun; and Dijon, which came into the duchy of
Burgundy in the eleventh century. Autun venerated St Symphorian, its
first martyr, in the abbey built in the fifth century, where his relics had
been translated by the other saint of the city, Bishop Leodegarius (Léger),
c.680. Dijon's main ecclesiastical centre was the abbey of St Bénigne,
whose church was rebuilt from 1001 onwards by the reforming abbot
William of Volpiano on a Carolingian model with additions by Lombard
craftsmen in the north Italian architectural style, seen in particular in the
crypt.[28] William also brought there the customs of Cluny and the
spirituality of his own foundation of Fruttuaria from 989 onwards.

At Tours, the main saint of the city, Martin, was the patron-saint of
monasticism in Gaul, and was greatly venerated throughout Western
Europe. This veneration had already started during his lifetime, according
to his biographer Sulpicius Severus, and the cult developed rapidly after
St Martin's death when Severus' *Life*, which achieved an immense
popularity, began to circulate.[32] After the saint's death, a basilica was built
over his tomb at Tours, which became a major pilgrimage centre, almost
equal to Rome and Jerusalem. It was burnt down in 997, but again rebuilt
and dedicated on 4 July 1008. Already a patron saint of the Carolingians,
St Martin was maintained in that position by the Capetians, although St
Denis was an increasingly successful rival. Tours continued to flourish as
the centre of his cult, and its vast possessions stretched as far as Italy and
Germany. The devotion to St Martin was strong in both these areas, as the
numerous churches dedicated to him confirm.[33]

Chartres and Tours belonged to the count of Blois, and Angers to that
of Anjou. Chartres was particularly famed for its cathedral school under
its bishops Fulbert and Ivo. Another master at the time of Fulbert was
Berengar, under whom Lanfranc possibly studied for a while about 1035.[29]
The reputation of the school soared under Fulbert, possibly an Italian by
birth, who died in 1028 and who had been educated under Gerbert at
Reims,[30] while Ivo is known as one of the most important canonists of the
Middle Ages, whose works were found in English libraries by the end of
the century.[31]

[28] N. Stratford in *Glaber*, 300–2, and Fernie, *Architecture*, 157–9.

[29] Gibson, *Lanfranc*, 17–19.

[30] J. A. Clerval, *Les Écoles de Chartres au Moyen Âge* (Paris, 1895), 29–142; and see below, n.
112.

[31] The canonical collections are edited in P L 161, 47–1022, 1045–1344; and his letters in
J. Leclercq (ed.), *Yves de Chartres: Correspondance* (Paris, 1949). On Ivo, see R. Spandrel, *Ivo von
Chartres und seine Stellung in der Kirchengeschichte* (Stuttgart, 1962), 9–85 and App. ii, 180–98.

[32] On the cult of St Martin after his death, the relics, and the translations, see A. Lecoy de la
Marche, *St Martin* (Tours, 1881), 379–96, 423–7, 492–4. For the life of St Martin, see J. Fontaine
(ed.), *Sulpice Sévère: Vie de St Martin* (3 vols.; Paris, 1967–9).

[33] Apart from Monte Cassino, Rome had a church dedicated to him, S. Martino ai Monti, and

St Martin's influence had already made itself felt on the British Church. The first two known churches in the British Isles were dedicated to St Martin, St Martin's at Canterbury and Ninian's church at Whithorn in Galloway.[34] Veneration for St Martin, originally linked with Gaul, had increased when it found its way to Ireland in the fifth century, where most of the great Irish saints modelled themselves upon him, perhaps from St Patrick's time, and certainly in St Columba's case.[35] The regard for St Martin within the Irish Church cannot be better illustrated than by the inclusion of his name in the Canon of the Mass, for example, in the Bobbio Missal.[36] The Irish monks of Iona who converted England brought the cult with them and later Irish-style monks, such as St Cuthbert, continued to model themselves upon, and were moulded by their biographers into, the image of St Martin. Under this Irish influence, six churches at least were dedicated to the saint in early Anglo-Saxon England and Irish monks sometimes chose this patron saint for the abbeys and hospices which they founded on the Continent.[37] St Martin's cult in England was almost certainly further encouraged by the presence of Alcuin at Tours, and his writing of a Life of the saint.[38] Throughout the Anglo-Saxon period, St Martin provided a model for monastic bishops, an institution nowhere more important in the West than it was in England.

The liturgical cult of St Martin started at Tours with a feast on 11 November, the day of the saint's funeral.[39] Three other feasts were later added to this date: 4 July was the feast of the ordination or consecration of the saint, as well as the dedication of the basilica and the translation of

one of St Gregory's foundations in Sicily, S. Martino delle Scale in Palermo, was under his patronage. On S. Martino ai Monti, see Lecoy de la Marche, *St Martin*, 586–8. The cult was also important at Lucca, where the cathedral was dedicated to the saint in the early Middle Ages. ibid. 585–6. In Germany, Trier had a church of St Martin, and so had Liège. On the German cult and the churches at Trier and Cologne, ibid. 572–7. On the cult at Liège and the collegiate church, ibid. 570–1, and Kurth, *Notger*, i. 147–9.

[34] *BHE* 76–7, 222–3.

[35] On the Irish devotion to St Martin, see J. Ryan, *Irish Monasticism: Origins and Early Development* (London, 1931, repr. Shannon, 1972), 225, 345–58; L. Gougaud, *Christianity in Celtic Lands* (London, 1932), 63, 327; and especially P. Grosjean, 'Gloria postuma Scti Martini apud Scotos et Britannos', *AB* 55 (1937), 300–48. On St Patrick's veneration for the saint, see the *Vita Tertia*, edited in L. Bieler (ed.), *Four Latin Lives of St Patrick* (Dublin, 1971), 130, and Ryan, *Irish Monasticism*, 61–2, 95. On St Columba's veneration, see A. O. and M. O. Anderson (eds.), *Adomnán's Life of Columba* (London, 1961), some of which was copied almost literally by Adomnán from the *Vita Martini*, 186–7 and n. 11, and Introduction, 86.

[36] E.A. Lowe (ed.), *The Bobbio Missal*, ii (London, 1920), 10.

[37] Levison, *England and the Continent*, App. V, 259. St Martin comes fourth in Levison's list of patron saints, after St Peter, the Virgin, and St Andrew. An example of an Irish monastery dedicated to St Martin on the Continent was St Martin 'of the Scots' at Cologne, which Marianus Scotus entered in 1052, see *Florence*, i. 143.

[38] Edited in P L 101, 657–664.

[39] On the feasts of St Martin, see Lecoy de la Marche, *St Martin*, 595–602, 607–8.

the relics into it; 12 May was the feast of the *Subventio*, when the Vikings had failed to capture the city, owing to St Martin's protection; and 13 December celebrated the return of the relics after another, and this time successful, attack of the Vikings had compelled the monks to carry them away to safety.

In England, the 11 November feast was entered in all calendars, usually as a high-rank celebration. From the eleventh century onwards, it was given an Octave in all Winchester calendars, and in the Wells calendar, thereby indicating the existence of a special cult at Winchester. The second feast of 4 July is also found in all calendars, in capitals at Crowland and Worcester. The 11 November feast was celebrated with the Gregorian mass, tropes, hymns, benedictions, and the full office. The translation feast is also celebrated in all sacramentaries with the gradual, and there is a mass for the Octave of the *Natale* at Wells. In most cases the cult was simply due to St Martin's great reputation and established veneration in the West. It was a genuinely traditional cult in most English abbeys, inherited from the early Anglo-Saxon Church, but rather less prominent than it had been after the Conversion. Churches were still dedicated to him in the eleventh century: we hear of one at Oxford by 1043 and William I placed his first English foundation at Battle under his patronage.[40] The cult picked up again after the Conquest, under French influence; before this, it was less of a strong personal devotion than, for example, the cults of St Gregory and St Benedict, because, despite the strength of the institution of monastic bishops in late Anglo-Saxon England, it was less identified with English traditions. English tradition in the tenth and eleventh century was associated with the Roman rather than with the Irish mission or even with Gaulish influences.

St Brice was the second most popular saint after St Martin. A disciple of Martin, a monk at Marmoûtier and bishop of Tours between 397 and 444, he built the church of St Martin, where he was buried, and his cult began a few years after his death at Tours.

Around the middle of the eleventh century, under Count Geoffrey Martel of Anjou, most of the lands of the counts of Blois were taken over by their belligerent neighbours the counts of Anjou, although not Blois itself. Angers, capital of the counts, was under the patronage of the fifth-century bishops St Maurilius and St Albinus, to whom the main abbey was dedicated. The counts of Anjou exerted public authority from their castles and dominated the government of the Church. They reformed existing abbeys and founded new ones, such as St Nicholas' of Angers in 1020, on

[40] *Chronicon Abingdon*, i. 444; Searle, *Chronicle of Battle Abbey*, 36–7, 66–9.

the return of Fulk Nerra from one of his pilgrimages to the Holy Land.[41]

The other main monastic house on the Loire valley was Fleury. Founded in the seventh century, the abbey became a spiritual centre after its acquisition of the relics of St Benedict from Monte Cassino in 703, and a major cultural centre under the rule of Theodulf of Orléans (798–818). It was reformed by Odo of Cluny in 930 and was at the peak of its prestige at the turn of the tenth and eleventh centuries, under the abbacy of Abbo (988–1004). Abbo was known as a scholar, who had studied in Paris, Reims, and Orléans, and rivalled Gerbert of Reims. The school of Fleury commanded respect, which reached England: Oswald invited Abbo to Ramsey, where Abbo spent two years teaching, between 985 and 987. He became a friend of Dunstan and later kept in touch with English affairs. The Fleury school had expanded on a par with the library and *scriptorium* of the abbey and, after the fire of 974, the two monastic churches of St Peter and St Mary were rebuilt.[42] Bonneval and St Maurus of Glanfeuil are also mentioned in English sources.

Further south in Poitou, Poitiers and its numerous foundations and Limoges, which grew around the abbey of St Martial, provide the two furthermost examples of contacts with England. Both cities belonged to the duchy of Aquitaine. Poitiers' main churches were St Hilaire, Ste Radegonde, and the Holy Cross. At Limoges, the monks of St Martial were then attempting to have their patron saint recognized as the Apostle of Gaul.[43]

Neither important cities, such as Marseilles, or important abbeys, such as St Gilles, seem to have been directly visited, and we must assume that, once pilgrims to Rome had abandoned the sea route via Lyons and Marseilles used until the establishment of the Saracens in the western Mediterranean in the ninth century, these cities were no longer frequented by Englishmen. It is at the very end of the eleventh century, under Norman and French influence, that two saints venerated in the south of France appear in English sources once again: St Leonard of Noblac in Poitou and St Giles of Provence, both saints who were also particularly popular in Crusading circles; and St Faith of Conques. Conques, the centre of her cult, was one of the main stopping points on the route of the pilgrimage

---

[41] On the counts of Anjou, see O. Guillot, *Le Comte d'Anjou et son entourage au XIe siècle* (Paris, 1972); for St Nicholas', see Jones, *Nicholas of Myra*, 99–108, and *The Liturgy*, 65 n. 7.

[42] On the history of the abbey, school, and library, see P. Cousin, *Abbon de Fleury-sur-Loire* (Paris, 1954), 35–7; Guerreau-Jalabert, *Abbo Floriacensis*, 10–23, 147–75; and M. Mostert, *The Political Theology of Abbo of Fleury* (Hilversum, 1987), 25–36, and *The Library of Fleury* (Hilversum, 1989). On Abbo's career and writings, see Cousin, *Abbon*, 48–9, 60–4; Guerreau-Jalabert, *Abbo Floriacensis*, 24–9; and Mostert, *Theology*, 41–5.

[43] See below, ch. 7 and n. 153.

to Compostela; in 1034, the Norman abbey of Conches was founded by monks from Conques.

II. THE FACTUAL EVIDENCE FOR CONTACT

The axis extending from England and Germany to Rome and Byzantium was not the only source of Anglo-Saxon contacts with the Continent. Boniface, who had undertaken his mission to Germany at Pépin's request, after having reorganized the Frankish Church, was only one of the numerous Englishmen involved in the history of the Carolingian Empire. Before him, a few pilgrims on their way to Rome had travelled extensively through Gaul, for example, Benedict Biscop; and had even come close to Merovingian power, in the shape of Ebroin, the Mayor of the Palace in Neustria and Queen Balthild, in the case of Wilfrid.[44] An early Anglo-Saxon tradition led English princesses to become nuns at Chelles or Faremoutiers, and Queen Balthild had been an English slave-girl.[45] Benedict Biscop had brought books from Gaul and even masons to build the church at Monkwearmouth, and Wilfrid may have visited St Denis's; the stone masonry, columns, and side chapels in their churches were common in Gaulish architecture.[46] But the liturgical and artistic influences in the later eighth- and in the ninth-century exchanges between Gaul and England went essentially from England towards the Carolingian world.[47] These influences were faithful both to Rome and Ireland, and Boniface and Alcuin contributed to their diffusion by spreading English scholarship in the form of manuscripts sent to them from England,[48] which introduced stylistic features of eighth-century Insular art on the Continent, while also supporting the Roman liturgical elements within the reforms of the Carolingian Church. Alcuin's role in the development of Marian piety was considerable: he introduced the Irish-inspired English prayer anthologies of the type of the Book of Cerne on the Continent, which were at the origin of the *Libelli precum*, and thus promoted the devotion to the Virgin which they favoured; and he composed a votive mass for the Virgin which

---

[44] *Vita Abbatum Bedae*, 368–9; *Life of Wilfrid*, 14–15, 52–3.

[45] B. Krusch (ed.), *Vita Sanctae Balthildis*, MGH SSRM ii. 483.

[46] *Vita Abbatum Bedae*, 368–9; A. Lohaus, *Die Merowinger und England* (Munich, 1974), and Campbell, 'The First Century of Christianity in England', in *Essays*, 53–67.

[47] S. J. Crawford, *Anglo-Saxon Influence on Western Christendom 600–800* (Oxford, 1933), 32–71.

[48] On Boniface's constant requests to his English friends for manuscripts, see *Boniface*, 60–1, 63–4, 64–5, 116, 133–4, 168. It is interesting to see that nuns were also engaged in the copying of books.

established the precedent of the Saturday being dedicated to her, as well as writing *tituli* venerating her for various altars.[49]

Links with the area still known as the kingdom of France, and hence with the kings themselves, are scant throughout the two centuries of our period, and clearly attested only for King Aethelstan's reign.[50] Two of the king's half-sisters Eadhild and Eadgifu married respectively the son of King Odo, Hugh, and the Carolingian Charles known as 'the Simple'.[51] On the occasion of Eadhild's wedding, an embassy was sent by Hugh, led by Adolph, son of Count Baldwin of Flanders, who brought valuable gifts and relics to the English court. Among the latter was Charlemagne's spear, a lance reputed to have been Longinus' Lance which pierced Christ's side; the possession of this relic, equally claimed by the Ottonian Emperors under the name of St Maurice's Holy Lance, was to remain a point of contention between the kings of England and the German emperors until well into the Middle Ages. Other gifts brought by Hugh were perfumes, jewels, an alabaster vase decorated with human figures, a sword deemed to have belonged to Emperor Constantine, with an iron spike from the Crucifixion in its pommel, the banner of St Maurice, a diadem with jewels, and parts of the Crown of Thorns and of the Cross, enclosed in crystal.[52] There is no doubt that Aethelstan himself also sent numerous gifts of possibly metalwork and embroidery, two English skills renowned at the time, both to Hugh and to Charles. It is also more than probable that the embassy sent by Charles to obtain the hand of Eadgifu also brought presents, probably of relics, since Aethelstan had a reputation in Europe as a collector of relics, and possibly also of books. In William of Malmesbury's words, Aethelstan 'nemo legalius vel litterarius rempublicam administraverit'.[53] It is not impossible that the embassy could even have been led by Charles himself, since Richer dwelled on how charming this prince seems to have been thought by the English, 'anglos . . . mira benevolentia sibi adaegit'.[54] When Charles was imprisoned, his son Louis

[49] Barré, *Prières*, 8–76; id., 'L'Apport marial de l'Orient à l'Occident de St Ambroise à St Anselme', *Études mariales*, 19 (1962), 60–75; and T. H. Bestul, 'Continental Sources of Anglo-Saxon Devotional Writing', in Szarmach, *Sources*, 105–12.

[50] Prior to the 10th c., marital associations between English and Carolingian kings had already existed, when King Aethelwulf of Wessex married Judith, the daughter of Charles the Bald. He had spent some time at Charles' court on his way to Rome and the wedding had been celebrated by the archbishop of Reims. Judith came to England and, after Aethelwulf's death, married his son Aethelbald, a highly criticized action, which led to her leaving England after the latter's death, to return to France; on this, see *ASC*, 858, 43–4; *Asser*, chs. 13 and 17, pp. 10–12 and 16; and Grat, *Annales de St Bertin*, 854, 856, 858, 862, pp. 70, 73, 76, 87.

[51] *Aethelweard*, 2; *WMGR* i. 149–50; *Flodoard*, 926; *Richer*, i. 124–5.

[52] *WMGR* i. 149–51.

[53] Ibid. 144, 142. On Aethelstan as a collector of relics, see J. Armitage Robinson, *The Times of St Dunstan* (Oxford, 1923), 71–80.

[54] *Richer*, i. 36–7.

with his mother took refuge at King Edward the Elder's then at his uncle Aethelstan's courts until, in 936, he regained his throne with Aethelstan's help and reigned under the name of Louis 'd'Outre-Mer', that is to say, of England.[55] On this occasion too, English followers went to France with Louis, after having mixed for several years with the Frankish followers of Louis when he, as a child, came to England to be educated there. The return of Louis to France is described in French sources. Aethelstan sent Bishop Oda of Ramsbury (not yet archbishop of Canterbury) on a mission to Hugh, to be sure that the latter was willing to acknowledge Louis as king, after Hugh's embassy had come to England to ask for Louis' return.[56] Aethelstan continued to provide support for his nephew when Louis appeared to be in trouble with the 'inhabitants of the coast', possibly Bretons or Normans, who were said to have rebelled: an English fleet was sent to France in 939, to return to England when no rebellion was forthcoming.[57] Whether the said peoples returned to obedience before the fleet arrived, or the prospect of the English fleet was enough to prevent the rebellion, is not made clear. Later, when Louis was a prisoner, his wife Gerberga appealed to both her brother, the future Emperor Otto I, and to King Edmund, Louis' cousin, to help her husband; once again an English threat of war was made, the consequence of which was the deliverance of Louis.[58] We can guess at the opportunities of exchanges of goods and presents which some of these events allowed.[59]

After Aethelstan's and Edmund's time, the only intimation of contacts with the kings of France relates to an embassy of King Aethelred to the Emperor Henry III, at which King Robert of France was present, and an embassy of Henry I of France to Edward.[60] Glaber says that, at this meeting between Henry and Robert, presents were exchanged, with the offering of a Gospel-book covered with gold and precious stones and a relic of St Vincent, by Robert to Henry, and equally sumptuous presents from other kings, including Aethelred, to the Emperor; Aethelred also asked for help, though Glaber does not say for what purpose.[61] One surmises that it might have been against the Danes, but Glaber does not seem to have been all that well informed about the identity of English kings; he correctly indicates the nature of the war in England against the Danes, and

[55] *Richer*, 124–33; *Flodoard*, 936.
[56] Ibid. 936; *Richer*, i. 130–1.
[57] Ibid. 152–3.
[58] Ibid. 206–9; *Flodoard*, 946.
[59] On Louis, see P. Lauer, *Le Règne de Louis IV d'Outre-Mer* (Paris, 1900), 10–15, 131–43.
[60] *Vita Aedwardi*, 10; Edward may have spent some time at Henry's court before his recovery of the English throne, see Barlow, 'Edward', in *Norman Conquest*, 65.
[61] *Glaber*, 108.

Cnut's taking over of both the English Crown and Aethelred's widow, but makes Aethelred the Danish king and Cnut that of the West Saxons.[62] However, it is possible that the claim of Edward the Confessor's biographer of the king's ability to perform healing miracles may have been a parallel to the same claim made by Helgaud for King Robert.[63] Another parallel between the two kings could be said to be the heavy emphasis which both their hagiographers place on their charity and almsgiving: possibly a reflection of eleventh-century European spiritual trends, or even of the Continental background of Edward's hagiographer, it may nevertheless also be a conscious common feature.

We hear once again about Edward in French sources when Guibert of Nogent mentions the election at Laon of one Helinand, ex-chaplain of Edward.[64] Guibert again mentions England, this time to castigate it since he implies that the communal movement at Laon was at least partly inspired by English and Norman models;[65] this statement is particularly interesting in view of the argument sometimes put forward that English merchant guild organizations, of the kind we hear about at Exeter in the tenth century and at Canterbury in 1086, for example, exerted some influence on urban Continental developments, for example in the Rhineland and Norman cities.[66] Guibert was aware of the stories of at least two English saints, Edmund and Swithun, and he claimed to have been taught by Anselm before the latter came to England.

The surviving evidence of contacts between England and Brittany also comes from the time of Aethelstan. Among the refugees at Aethelstan's court, apart from Louis d'Outre-Mer, was also the count of Brittany Alan Crooked Beard, to whom Aethelstan stood sponsor and who was educated at the English court. Alan was in England between the years 931 and 936, when he recovered Brittany.[67] In c.926, a letter was sent from the prior Radbod and the monks of the abbey of St Samson at Dol, offering Aethelstan some relics of Samson's body and of SS Senator of Milan and Paternus and Scubilis of Avranches, and asking him for alms for their

[62] Ibid. 54–5.

[63] R. H. Bautier and G. Labory (eds.), *Helgaud de Fleury: Vie de Robert le Pieux* (Paris, 1965), 126–9; on this, see *Vita Aedwardi*, 122–3 n. 4 and Barlow, 'The King's Evil', in *Norman Conquest*, 23–47; further parallels between Edward and Robert are highlighted by Campbell, 'England', in *Essays*, 191–4.

[64] G. Bourgin (ed.), *Guibert de Nogent: Histoire de sa vie*, (Paris, 1907), 130–1.

[65] Ibid. 155–85, esp. 155–8.

[66] The best résumé on the guilds is that by G. Rosser, 'The Anglo-Saxon Gilds', in J. Blair (ed.), *Minsters and Parish Churches: The Local Church in Transition 950–1200* (Oxford, 1988), 31–4, esp. 32–3, which suggests a parallel between 11th-c. guilds and the 'Peace of God' associations on the Continent.

[67] R. Merlet (ed.), *La Chronique de Nantes (570 env.–1049)* (Paris, 1896), 82–3, also repr. in J. Delumeau (ed.), *Documents de l'histoire de la Bretagne* (Toulouse, 1971), 87.

abbey.[68] Aethelstan's answering letter is no longer extant, but the relics were duly received and sent by the king to the abbey he had founded at Milton.[69] Aethelstan's father, King Edward, had been himself a member of the confraternity of Dol.[70]

While the evidence for links with Brittany does not go beyond the end of the tenth century, that for exchanges of all kinds with Normandy only begins at the end of that same century, with an extant letter sent to King Edgar by the monks of St Ouen at Rouen, asking him for alms for their abbey.[71] Some time before, relics of St Ouen appear to have been sent to Archbishop Oda at Canterbury (942–58), and the abbey of St Ouen owned some land in England before the Conquest.[72] Under King Aethelred, these exchanges became more frequent. The king married a Norman princess, Emma, sister of the duke of Normandy Richard II, and in 1013 she took refuge at the Norman court with her son by Aethelred, the future Edward the Confessor.[73] One of the law codes ascribed to Aethelred mentions the presence of merchants from Rouen in London, trading in wine and fish.[74] Emma was in England in 1017, to marry again another king of England, the Danish Cnut, by whom she had another son, Harthacnut.[75] During the struggle for power between the latter and Harold, Cnut's son by an English concubine, Emma was sent away and took refuge in Flanders, but returned to England when her son Edward was called to the English throne in 1042.[76] Throughout the period, especially when she was Cnut's wife, her influence on cultural and religious affairs such as the commissioning of manuscripts, the collecting of relics, and the gifts of valuable objects to religious houses, was considerable. For example, together with Cnut, she sent manuscripts to Germany as presents to the Emperor, offered to Canterbury the relic of the arm of St Bartholomew, purchased from the visiting bishop of Benevento, and, on her own initiative, offered a valuable gift to Winchester.[77] The policies she favoured and encouraged both Cnut and Edward to pursue were heavily weighted in favour of Normandy. Edward himself seems to have had a preference for the people among whom he had been brought up,[78] and he was lavish with his gifts to

[68] *CSD* I. i. 39–40.
[69] Only those of Paternus may have been eventually given to Malmesbury, *WMGP* 398.
[70] *CSD* I. i. 39.
[71] Stubbs, *Memorials*, 363–4.
[72] Eadmer, 'De Reliquiis', 362–70, and on the Canterbury cult, see A. Wilmart, 'Les Reliques de St Ouen à Cantobéry', *AB* 51 (1933), 285–7; Sawyer, *Anglo-Saxon Charters*, no. 1015.
[73] *Encomium*, 32–3; *ASC*, CDE 1013, 93.
[74] Robertson, *Laws*, IV Aethelred 5 and 6, 73.
[75] *ASC*, CDE1017, 97 and CD1035, EF1036, 102–3.
[76] Ibid. CDEF1037, 104; CD1041, EF1040 and CD1042, EF1041, 106.
[77] See above, ch. 3, and ch. 4, p. 104 and *Annales monasterii de Wintonia*, 18.
[78] Barlow, 'Edward', in *Norman Conquest*, 63–83, 101–11, challenges this view by stating that

Norman friends, such as Earl Ralph 'the Timid' and his men in Hereford-shire, where they built at least one castle, at Hereford,[79] and with appointments of Norman ecclesiastics to English sees, Ulf at Dorchester in 1049, William at London in 1051, and Robert, abbot of Jumièges, first to London, then to Canterbury in 1051.[80] Other such appointments were those of Osbern 'Pentecost', Hugh, who later erected several castles in Mercia, a deacon Robert and his son-in-law Richard, the king's equerry Alfred, and one Anfrid *Ceocesfot*. He only renounced this policy under duress, when his opponents, led by the most powerful Earl Godwine and his family, forced him to do so in 1052. Unfortunate appointments, such as those of the archbishop of Canterbury Robert of Jumièges and the bishop of Dorchester Ulf, were revoked. Only those whom 'the king should wish to have with him, who were loyal to him and to all the people', i.e. Robert, Richard, Alfred, and Anfrid, were allowed to stay, the other 'Frenchmen who had promoted injustices and passed unjust judgments and given bad counsel in this country' were outlawed.[81]

Edward also inaugurated a regular policy of making donations of lands to Norman monastic houses, for example, to Fécamp and Jumièges, and he granted the abbey of St Michael's Mount in Cornwall to Mont Saint Michel.[82] This policy was pursued on a much larger scale after the Norman Conquest and grants were made by William I, William II, and various Norman barons such as the count of Mortain and Hugh of Grandmesnil, to Fécamp, the Holy Trinity at Caen, St Stephen's at Caen, St Wandrille, St Évroul, St Valéry, Mont Saint Michel, Séez, Bec, St Ouen at Rouen, Lire, Jumièges, Bernay, St Taurinus' at Évreux, La-Croix-St-Leufroy, and St Pierre-sur-Dive.[83] William I also gradually replaced English

Edward, who had been on sufferance at the Norman court, was rather embittered and did not look with great favour upon his Norman relations; this view seems to me rather at odds with the way the Anglo-Saxons perceived the situation, clearly seeing Edward's attitude as one of bias in favour of the Normans.

[79] *ASC*, E1051, 119; DE1052, 122; D1052, 124; *Florence*, i. 213; on the three castles built by Normans in England before the Conquest, Hereford, Ewias, and 'Richard's Castle' called Avreton in Domesday Book, see E. S. Armitage, *The Early Norman Castles of the British Isles* (London, 1912), 24, 161–2, 150–1, 192–3, and, more generally, R. Allen Brown, *English Castles* (3rd edn.; London, 1976), 40–9.

[80] Ibid. C1049, 114 and D1050, 115; D1052, 121; AC1050, D1051 and E1048, 115–16; *Florence*, i. 203, 207, 204. On Robert, see D. Douglas, 'Robert de Jumièges, Archevêque de Cantorbéry et la Conquête de l'Angleterre par les Normands', 283–6 and M. Chibnall, 'Les Relations entre Jumièges et l'Angleterre du xᵉ au xiiiᵉ siècles', 269–75, in *Jumièges*, i.

[81] *ASC*, CD1052, 124.

[82] P. L. Hull (ed.), *The Cartulary of St Michael's Mount: Hatfield House MS No. 315* (Exeter, 1962), pp. x-xiii; on the abbeys owning land in England before the Conquest, see Knowles, *Monastic Order*, App. VI, 703 and Matthew, *Norman Monasteries*, 19–26. See, for example, the charters of Cnut and Edward for Fécamp in Sawyer, *Anglo-Saxon Charters*, nos. 949, 982, and 1054.

[83] Knowles, *Monastic Order*, App. VI, 703, and Matthew, *Norman Monasteries*, 27–70.

bishops and abbots with Normans, but only in 1070–1 was there anything like a purge and some of the victims were declared or suspected rebels such as Aethelmaer of Elmham, Aethelric of Selsey, and Aethelsige of St Augustine's. Rather, he imposed Norman heads when approximately half a dozen Anglo-Saxon abbots fled the country after the Conquest, as did Seiwold of Bath and Aethelsige, or gradually, as Anglo-Saxon abbots died; 'in 1073 there were still a dozen English abbots ruling in the twenty-odd houses of which we have complete records', eight of whom were still alive in 1083, and several survived until the end of our period, such as Aelfsige of Bath († 1087), Aethelsige of Ramsey († 1087) and Aelfwold of Holme († 1089).[84] He did not attempt to replace systematically the monks and clergy, however, since this might have led to major conflicts between abbot and monks, as was the case in the notorious riot of the monks of Glastonbury in 1083 when their newly appointed Norman abbot Thurstan attempted to impose Norman liturgical customs in this most conservative and prestigious among English abbeys.[85] By the end of the eleventh century, when the last Anglo-Saxon ecclesiastic, Wulfstan of Worcester, had died in 1095, most of the abbots and bishops were of Continental origins, either Normans such as Gundulf of Rochester (1077–1108), a monk of Bec, William of St Calais at Durham (1081–96), four former monks from Mont Saint Michel who became abbots of St Augustine's, Hyde, Gloucester, and Cerne,[86] or Lotharingians, such as Robert of Hereford, Walcher of Durham, and Herbert Losinga bishop of Norwich, or Italians, as were Lanfranc and the recently appointed archbishop of Canterbury Anselm. By the beginning of the twelfth century, not only were most of the higher clergy of Norman descent, but a mixed type of ecclesiastic became more common, especially among monks. Representative examples of those were Eadmer, William of Malmesbury, and Orderic Vitalis, the latter two of mixed English and Norman parentage but educated by the Normans and even, in the case of Orderic, in Normandy at St Évroul.[87]

Apart from the links between the kings of England and France, others were growing with centres in Paris and in northern France. A letter written to King Edgar by the monks of Ste Geneviève in Paris, asking him for alms, has survived.[88] North of Paris, the two cities of Amiens and Beauvais were sometimes visited by pilgrims, and a castellan Hugh fled to England

---

[84] Knowles, *Monastic Order*, 111 and n. 4.
[85] *Florence*, ii. 16–17; *WMHG* 156–9; *Orderic*, ii. 270–1.
[86] C. R. Dodwell, *The Canterbury School of Illumination 1066–1200* (Cambridge, 1954), 8–14; Alexander, *Norman Illumination*, 58–82, 17.
[87] *Vita Anselmi*, 50; *WMGR* ii. 283; *Orderic*, vi. 552–5.
[88] Stubbs, *Memorials*, 366–8.

when he became entangled in a conflict with the bishop of Cambrai Gérard[89]. South-east of Paris, Péronne and its abbey were dedicated to St Fursa, whose relics rested there. The saint's head was at Canterbury, and English pilgrims such as Sigeric would have venerated this saint, both on account of the relic and also of the role he had played in the conversion of East Anglia, an episode described in detail by Bede in the *Historia Ecclesiastica*.[90] The city of Péronne itself was an Irish centre, since Fursa had been an Irishman, and hospices for Irish and English pilgrims were doubtless available there, as in another city of the same kind, Vercelli; one such may have been that of Doingt-sur-la-Cologne, a suburb of Péronne, mentioned by Sigeric in his diary.

The main abbey within northern France was probably the royal abbey of St Denis, north of Paris. In the late tenth century, Edith of Wilton developed a great devotion towards the saint and, when the abbey church of Wilton had to be rebuilt in 984, she asked Dunstan to consecrate it to St Denis.[91] About 1059, possibly as a result of both the presence of a monk of St Denis, Baldwin, at the English court as a doctor, and of the devotion of Edward's wife Edith, brought up at Wilton, for the saint, Edward granted the church and lands of Deerhurst to the French abbey.[92] A few years later, in 1065, Baldwin was appointed abbot of Bury, where he had a church or chapel built and dedicated to St Denis.[93] After the Conquest, William I contributed to the work of rebuilding St Denis's by donating some money for the building of a tower in 1075, which, however, collapsed in 1087.[94]

East of the royal domain were the lands of the count of Champagne. Langres was a city well known to the English, since the anonymous Jarrow author had narrated the pilgrimage of his abbot Ceolfrid, which ended when he died at Langres.[95] Some of his companions had remained there; Ceolfrid's tomb was there for later pilgrims to visit, although the body had been brought back to England a little later and, either through some of the monks of Jarrow who returned to England after having spent some time at Langres, or by some other means, Bede knew who the patron saints of this city were and included their names, Speusippus, Meleusippus, and Eleusippus, in his martyrology. Late Anglo-Saxon pilgrims went through Langres, which is perhaps entered in Sigeric's diary under the heading of

[89] *Gesta Pontificum Cameracensium: Continuatio*, ed. G. H. Pertz, MGH SS vii. 498–9.
[90] *BHE* 268–77; for the relic, see Eadmer, 'De Reliquiis', 365.
[91] Wilmart, 'Légende de Ste Édith', 86–7.
[92] *Religious Houses*, 64; Binns, *Monastic Dedications*, 96.
[93] Arnold, *Memorials of St Edmund's Abbey*, i. 56, ii. 3.
[94] Crosby, *The Abbey of St Denis*, 184.
[95] *Vita abbatum auctore anonimo*, 400.

'Oisma', the abbey of St Geosmes, very close to Langres itself. It possessed the relics of the three patron saints of the city and had been a prestigious and wealthy abbey in the ninth century, where Charles the Bald held a synod in 854.[96] A Langres missal of *c*.1060 contains some notes in Old English in the margins, implying either the passage of Anglo-Saxon pilgrims there or an exchange of books.

Reims was one of the cities with which England had some of its strongest ties. The archbishop of Reims Fulk had corresponded with King Alfred in his capacity of abbot of St Bertin, and had sent him Grimbald to help implement his programme to revive learning in England.[97] Almost a century later, one of Edith's teachers at Wilton had also been a monk from Reims, Radbod, and by the middle of the tenth century, a Reims manuscript of Bede's *De Temporum Ratione* was in England.[98] In 1049, three English ecclesiastics, Bishop Duduc of Wells, Abbot Wulfric of St Augustine's, and Abbot Aelfwine of Ramsey, were present at the papal council held at Reims by Pope Leo IX and, on that occasion, attended the second Translation of the body of St Rémi in the recently rebuilt basilica dedicated to him.[99] Reims had always been a major stop on the route of the Roman pilgrimage and Sigeric stopped there. So did a certain Burgheard in 1061–2, son of Earl Aelfgar, who died there on his return from Rome; the fact is known on account of the donation of land which his father made to St Rémi, where Burgheard was buried.[100]

The next set of lands which pilgrims to Rome crossed on their way belonged to the kingdom of Burgundy, and have been examined in a previous chapter. However, west of the kingdom of Burgundy was the duchy of Burgundy, with which the English Church also came into contact. At least two Anglo-Saxons knew the abbey of St Bénigne of Dijon: one because he 'retired' there to become a monk some time in the eleventh century, according to the chronicle of this monastery,[101] the other, Wulfric, abbot of St Augustine's at Canterbury, because Goscelin says of him that he wished to rebuild the rotunda of his abbey on the model of that of St Bénigne, which he may have visited when in Reims in 1049.[102] Further south, the customs of the abbey of Cluny, as they had been written down by the monk Bernard in 1067, served as a model for those of Lanfranc's *Monastic Constitutions*, alongside those of his own abbey of Bec,

[96] *Langres ancienne et moderne: Guide de Langres* (6th edn.; Langres, 1947), 19–20, 66.
[97] *CSD* i. i. 7–13.
[98] Wilmart, 'Légende de Ste Édith', 50; Rella, 'Continental', no. 21.
[99] See above, n. 22.
[100] Sawyer, *Anglo-Saxon Charters*, no. 1237.
[101] *Chronicon S. Benigni*, P L 141, 864.
[102] *HTA* 32–3.

either because he had learnt them from Cluny itself or, more probably, because he knew them from Fécamp, an abbey reformed by William of Volpiano, disciple of Cluny.[103] Before the eleventh century, some of these Cluniac customs had been already known in England through the intermediary of the monastery of Fleury, whose links with England were particularly close at the time of the monastic reform and which had itself been previously reformed from Cluny. They had been incorporated into the *Regularis Concordia*, together with customs from other Continental monasteries, in the same way as Lanfranc was to add some of them to the customs of Bec. The first properly speaking cluniac house, St Pancras', was not founded in England until 1070, by the Norman baron William of Warenne, at Lewes.[104] He had travelled to Cluny and been so impressed by monastic life there that he asked Abbot Hugh to sent him some monks from Cluny for his new foundation. The *Monastic Constitutions* of Lanfranc were soon to be known in other monastic cathedrals in England, Rochester, Durham, and Worcester, and in monasteries, beginning with St Albans under the abbacy of Paul, Anselm's nephew, Evesham, and Eynsham.[105]

Of all monastic houses and spiritual centres on the Loire valley, the most famous was without doubt Fleury. Reformed in the tenth century from Cluny itself, priding itself on the possession of the relics of St Benedict of Nursia, it was a centre of learning and spiritual fervour. For this reason, Bishop Aethelwold sent there his disciple Osgar;[106] and Oswald himself, together with Germanus, later to become abbot of Ramsey, spent some time at Fleury between 950 and 958, to learn the customs and liturgical observances which this abbey was reputed to enforce.[107] For that same reason, monks from Fleury were invited to England to take part in the reforming council of Winchester in 990–2, and to contribute to the compiling of the *Regularis Concordia*.[108] On another occasion, Abbo spent some time at Ramsey between 985 and 987 as a guest.[109] At least two manuscripts from that area, probably written at Fleury in the ninth

---

[103] M. D. Knowles (ed.), *Lanfranci Monachi Cantuariensis Constitutiones Monasticae* (London, 1951), pp. xi–xiii.

[104] Spurious foundation charter of Lewes in W. Dugdale, rev. J. Caley *et al.*, *Monasticon Anglicarum* (6 vols.; London, 1846), v.i. 12. The story about William's visit to Cluny is only found in this forged charter, see H. M. R. E. Mayr-Harting, *The Acta of the Bishops of Chichester 1075–1207* (Torquay, 1964), 78–9, but it was probably based on a genuine tradition.

[105] Knowles, *Monastic Order*, 123–4.

[106] Winterbottom, *Three Lives*, 21–2.

[107] *HCY* i. 413–19, 422–3, ii. 8–14.

[108] *RC* 71–2; see also Knowles, *Monastic Order*, 42, 46 n. 3; T. Symons in Parsons, *Tenth-Century*, however, does not debate this issue.

[109] *Chronicon Rameseiensis*, 42–3.

century, one of Boethius and one of Bede, reached England, the first one by the middle of the tenth century through Wales, the second in the eleventh century.[110]

Another well-known ecclesiastic and near contemporary of Abbo's was the bishop of Chartres Fulbert, to whom King Cnut sent some gifts, though we do not know on what occasion this took place.[111] Fulbert's main achievement was the establishment of a particularly flourishing cathedral school at Chartres. Bishop between 1007 and 1029, he had been a pupil of Gerbert at Reims, where he was trained in the seven liberal arts.[112] The cathedral school he helped build at Chartres, which became the first cathedral school to reach fame in the eleventh century, prepared students according to the same training, among the most renowned of whom was Berengar of Tours, who used dialectics in the controversy on the Eucharist which he carried on with Lanfranc until his death in 1088.[113] Fulbert himself was also interested in medicine, canon law, and contemporary politics, as his poems and particularly his letters show. One of these, sent to Duke William V of Aquitaine sometime before 1021, is important to historians since, in it, Fulbert describes for the first time, in an idealized version, the mechanisms, procedures, and *raison d'être* of what historiography has for a long time called the 'feudal social order'.[114]

Not far from Chartres was Tours, whose patron saint was also the most popular French saint throughout the early Middle Ages, St Martin. The annals of Evesham mention a vision of St Martin at Tours because a vision of St Ecgwin is identical to it.[115] Tours was a major European pilgrimage goal and shrine, and St Martin one of the great traditional saints in England. A ninth-century manuscript of Bede's commentary on Luke, from Tours, was in England, at Canterbury or Winchester, by the early eleventh century.[116] Another English traveller, Abbot Aelfsige of Peterborough, also toured this area when he accompanied Queen Emma on her exile c.1013, and bought at Bonneval the relics of the patron saint of the abbey, Florentinus, which he then offered to Peterborough.[117]

The main residence of the counts of Anjou was also a centre whose

---

[110] Rella, 'Continental', nos. 34 and 14.

[111] *WMGR* i. 226 and F. Behrends (ed.), *The Letters and Poems of Fulbert of Chartres* (Oxford, 1976), in a letter dated c.1018–20, 66–9.

[112] C. H. Haskins, *The Renaissance of the Twelfth Century* (Cambridge, Mass., 1927), 25–8.

[113] On the controversy with Lanfranc, see Gibson, *Lanfranc*, 63–97 and, especially, Montclos, *Lanfranc et Bérenger*; also now H. Chadwick, 'Ego Berengarius', *Journal of Theological Studies*, 40 (1989), 414–45.

[114] Behrends, *Letters*, 90–3.

[115] *Chronicon Evesham*, 51–4.

[116] Rella, 'Continental', no. 25.

[117] *Hugh Candidus*, 48–9.

attraction to Englishmen is known to us. Towards the end of the eleventh century, a young nun of Wilton, Eve, inflamed by the attractions of a more ascetic lifestyle, abandoned England to live as a hermit near the hermitage of her spiritual adviser Hervé, in the vicinity of Angers.[118] Also at the end of the eleventh century, two English houses, Spalding and Tyward-reath, were given to the monasteries of St Nicholas and SS Sergius and Bacchus of Angers in 1074 and *c*.1088, as dependencies.[119] The former, dedicated in 1020 by Count Fulk Nerra on his return from one of his pilgrimages to the Holy Land, reflects the count's interest in eastern devotions, which St Nicholas still was at the time.

In Poitiers, we hear of the presence of an English 'architect', Gauthier (Waldhere?) Coorland, working on the rebuilding of the church of the Holy Cross.[120] Further south, a group of texts from Limoges imply that a delegation of monks from St Martial went to England to try and secure the recognition of their patron saint as the 'Apostle of Gaul' *c*.1033, at a time when the issue was a hotly debated one in Aquitaine and France.[121] This visit was to have important consequences on the English liturgy. A claim has been made that, on his route to Rome, Cnut stopped at Limoges and initiated a friendship with the duke of Aquitaine William, which then prompted him to send to the duke a lavishly illuminated book of the Lives of the Saints.[122] Whether or not Cnut actually made this visit, which would have taken him by an unlikely route, such a manuscript was indeed sent during the course of an exchange of embassies. In fact, Adhémar of Chabannes seems to imply that such gifts passed between the duke and Cnut on several occasions, and the former was clearly aware of English internal affairs at this time.[123] Duke William's court was a brilliant one and ambassadors from the kings of France, Spain, Navarre, and the Emperor were present there, while William was also involved in Italian politics through the offer of Bishop Leo of Vercelli of the throne of Italy to the duke's son.[124] All these embassies implied mutual gifts of orna-ments, relics, possibly books, thus providing one of the most common forms and opportunities for reciprocal cultural influences at the time.

---

[118] A. Wilmart, 'Ève et Goscelin', *RB* 46 (1934), 414–38, 50 (1938), 42–83.

[119] Binns, *Monastic Dedications*, 105, 108.

[120] See above, ch. i n. 24.

[121] Above, ch. 1 n. 21.

[122] *Acta concilii Lemovicensis*, ii. 1369.

[123] *Adémar of Chabannes: Chronique*, ed. E. Pognon, in *L'An Mille* (Paris, 1947), 181, 193–4.

[124] *Adémar*, 182; Behrends, *Letters*, 186–7, 196–203. The geographical area called, in 12th c. style, 'Aquitaine' by G. Beech, 'England and Aquitaine in the Century before the Norman Conquest', *ASE* 19 (1990), 81–101, is none other than Poitou and the Limousin; his examples draw on the same material as I do.

III. CULTURAL EXCHANGES BETWEEN ENGLAND AND FRANCE

These exchanges took three forms: exchanges of books, of people, and of ideas. The first kind had been active during the late seventh and eighth centuries, and became so once again in the early tenth century. The first French manuscript that we know to have reached England is a Gospel-book from the abbey of Landévénnec in Brittany, and another Breton manuscript of the tenth century, a copy of Amalarius, was at Christ Church by the middle of the eleventh century.[125] Another Frankish manuscript, the psalter now British Library, Cotton Galba A. XVIII, belonged to Aethelstan. Contemporary with it was a manuscript of Philo Judaeus, 'On the Interpretation of Hebrew Names', which reached Malmesbury from St Médard of Soissons in the early tenth century.[126] A 'large number' of Frankish manuscripts were in England by the late tenth century, Gospel-books, standard Carolingian texts by Hrabanus, Chrodegang, Amalarius, and Smaragdus; Michael Wood has shown how Frankish scholars as well as texts and the heritage of the Carolingian renaissance were appropriated by Aethelstan and his clergy. They did this through imitation of the Carolingian models for biographies of the king, such as the now lost *Gesta Aethelstani*, just as Asser had modelled his Life of Alfred on Einhard; and through the deliberate emulation of Charlemagne, Louis the Pious, and Charles the Bald, evident from Aethelstan's acquisition of Charlemagne's relics and other artefacts associated with that Emperor, the portraying of Aethelstan in frontispiece pictures on the model of those found in Charles the Bald's books, and the patronage of art and learning.[127] From the time of Alfred English law-codes show Frankish inspiration; the entire peniten-tial tradition, which had been taken by the Carolingians from Anglo-Irish ecclesiastics in the first place, but lost in England, returned through the intermediary of the Frankish penitential of Halitgar, possibly via Brittany and Exeter.[128]

Towards the end of the tenth century, a sacramentary, written either at Winchcombe or at Ramsey—at any rate in one of Oswald's foundations—

---

[125] This MS, brought to Exeter, is now Oxford, Bodleian Library MS Auct. D.2.16; Rella, 'Continental', no.2.

[126] Wood, 'Making', 263.

[127] Ibid. 268 and more generally, 263–72.

[128] On the use of Carolingian law-codes in England, see C. P. Wormald, 'Aethelred the Lawmaker', in D. Hill (ed.), *Ethelred the Unready: Papers from the Millenary Conference* (Oxford, 1978), 71–7 and id., *The Making of English Law* (forthcoming), ch. 13. On the penitential movements and the manuscript transmission which makes it possible to follow the progress of the penitential tradition from Ireland to England and the Continent in the Carolingian period and back to England, until the age of the 'commonplace' books of the late 10th and 11th centuries, see Frantzen, Literature, 122–50.

was either sent to France or possibly taken back by Abbo, to Fleury. It was certainly there by the early eleventh century, when the first Fleury additions appear. About 1030, Cnut sent a lavishly illuminated book of Lives of the Saints to the duke of Aquitaine. Between 1062 and 1065, Earl Aelfgar donated a Gospel-book to St Rémi at Reims in memory of his son buried there.[129] These are only the best-known examples of manuscripts sent to and from England, but it is likely that many more travelled either way, in the baggage of ambassadors and clergy of various kinds, before the Conquest. Two early tenth-century Gospel-books from France were given by Aethelstan to Chester-le-Street and St Augustine's; a northeastern French manuscript of works by Jerome, Isidore, Cyprian, Cassiodorus, and Dionysius Exiguus was in England by the early tenth century, and another, written in the north-west of France in the second half of the tenth century, containing penitentials and works by Jerome, reached England at the turn of the tenth and eleventh centuries.[130] Another French compilation of the *Dionysio Hadriana* and the capitula of Ansegisus, of the tenth century, was at Worcester at the beginning of the eleventh.[131] The presence of prayers from a ninth-century northern French psalter brought to Canterbury in the tenth century in Arundel 155, from two other Continental manuscripts from Beauvais and Fleury in the Leofric Psalter, and from an Angers book in the Bury Psalter, further highlights these exchanges.[132] After 1066, or rather after 1071 and the rebellion of Hereward, a great many books from the library of Ely were sent to Normandy, as well as sacred vessels and other artefacts. Similar losses happened at Abingdon and probably other abbeys which resisted the Norman take-over.[133] William of Poitiers writes in almost lyrical fashion about the marvelling which took place when great quantities of Anglo-Saxon manuscripts reached Normandy.[134] Taken together with the only too rare descriptions of monastic libraries in England, such as that in the *Liber Eliensis*,[135] in Leofric's list, Candidus' *Peterborough Chronicle*, the two eleventh-century lists from Bury, the two lists from Worcester and Durham, and the guesses as to the probably considerable extent of those

---

[129] W. M. Hinkle, 'The Gift of an Anglo-Saxon Gospel Book to the Abbey of St Rémi, Rheims', *Journ. of the Brit. Archaeol. Assoc.*, 3rd ser. 33 (1970), 21–35.

[130] Rella, 'Continental', nos. 13, 18, 9, 26.

[131] Ibid. no. 29.

[132] Bestul, 'Continental', 115; Barré, *Prières*, 130.

[133] *Chronicon Abingdon*, i. 491.

[134] Foreville, *William of Poitiers*, 222–7.

[135] *LE* 224. 287 service-books are mentioned. The whole library was probably much larger since it contained also at least some theological, grammatical, and computistical works.

of Glastonbury, Winchester, Christ Church, and others,[136] it seems likely
that quite a few books left England at that time for Normandy, even though
allowance has to be made for losses in the later medieval period by fire,
theft, replacement and wanton destruction. Norman ecclesiastics, however, did not only remove English books, since until the end of the eleventh
century at least, the liturgical material, which was the core of Anglo-Saxon
book-production, remained in use for the purpose of celebration. They
also imported books from the Continent, in particular, copies of patristic
texts and of canon law. On account of their strong bias in favour of patristic
and theological writings, the production of such texts increased in
England. If we study the catalogues of two English libraries, Christ Church
and Durham, we can observe this change at work. In the eleventh century,
Christ Church possessed, apart from the service-books and the *Anglo-
Saxon Chronicle*, copies of Juvencus, Defensor, Arator, Isidore, Gregory's
Dialogues, Sedulius, Smaragdus, Amalarius and the Rule of St Benedict,
the *Regularis Concordia*, and Aldhelm. Durham had copies of Jerome,
Augustine, Prudentius, Cassiodorus, Julian of Toledo, Suetonius, Ennod-
ius, as well as service-books, Bede, and Aelfric. At the turn of the eleventh
and twelfth centuries, Christ Church acquired manuscripts of Eusebius,
Boethius, Orosius, Eutropius, Victor Vitensis, Ambrose, Augustine,
Haymo, the Rule of Chrodegang, collections of letters of the popes and of
Ivo of Chartres; and Durham is credited with manuscripts of the Pseudo-
Isidore, Berengaudus, Origen, Rabanus Maurus, Boethius, Gregory of
Nazianzus, John Chrysostom, another three of Ambrose, three of Jerome,
twelve of Augustine, four of Gregory the Great, two of Isidore, as well as
copies of excerpts from the Fathers, canon law collections, Ivo of Chartres,
and Anselm.[137] By the very end of the eleventh century, once the
generation of Anglo-Saxon monks and clergy steeped in the pre-Conquest,
more traditional and strongly Romanizing style of celebration, had gradually died away, Norman abbots and bishops began to reform the presentation and sometimes the content of the liturgical texts themselves. A
manuscript such as the Missal of St Augustine's, Canterbury, shows a very
clear, orderly, and standardized presentation of the liturgical text, with
different scripts and colours to differentiate the stages of the celebration.
This attempt at clarification and standardization of the liturgy, as well as
of theological and legal issues is one of the most obvious hallmarks of the

---

[136] Lapidge, 'Booklists', 57–8, 62–82; we hear, by chance, of the composition of the library of
a small church, that of Sherburn-in-Elmet, in the middle of the 11th c., ibid. 56–7, which has
nine service-books.

[137] On these libraries, see N. R. Ker, *Medieval Libraries of Great Britain: A List of Surviving
Books* (2nd edn.; London, 1964), and on Christ Church, Gibson, *Lanfranc*, 177–81.

programme of reforms of the papacy and the Church during the second half of the eleventh century. Whether the English Church, with its respect and allegiance to the papacy, would have implemented these reforms in any case is only a matter of academic interest; as it is, we can only observe that the reforming trend reached England through the intermediary of the Norman clergy.

Before the arrival of the Normans, whether as counsellors to King Edward from 1042 onwards or in the Conqueror's wake, other ecclesiastics from France had spent some time in England. Abbo of Fleury stayed at Ramsey, probably at the invitation of Oswald, who had spent several years at Fleury. Abbo was asked to write a Life of St Edmund and a treatise on grammar; and he wrote to Dunstan several times; about 1000–4, Abbot Wulfric of St Augustine's asked him to put into verse a Life of St Dunstan, now lost.[138] He carried out these tasks, and the rewriting of Dunstan's Life probably took place after his return to France. Eric John has shown how strong Abbo's influence was, not only on Byrhtferth of Ramsey, but also on Aelfric. The latter's choice of saints corresponded to the 'universalist' rather than the 'particularist' tradition and he appears to have been aware of the writings of Rather of Verona and of Flodoard, likely to have been made known to him by Abbo.[139]

Among the other monks who spent some time in England, Radbod of Reims and Baldwin of St Denis have already been mentioned. Before them another scholar, identified as Frédégaud of Brioude, was working in England at Canterbury.[140] Michael Lapidge has further shown the existence of a more subtle link between the two countries, when analysing the parallels between the cultural production of Aethelwold's school at Winchester and the circle of Robert of Rouen in a group of Winchester poems.[141]

After the Conquest, monks such as Orderic went to Normandy to be taught and monks trained in Norman abbeys became heads of some English houses. Such are the four monks of Mont Saint Michel Scolland, Ruald, Serlo, and William of Agorn at St Augustine's, Hyde, Gloucester, and Cerne, Paul at St Albans, and Henry of Bec, prior of Christ Church from 1070–5 to 1096, when he became abbot of Battle. By the time we

---

[138] Stubbs, *Memorials*, 378–80, 409; on the visit and works, see Cousin, *Abbon*, 60–4; Guerrau-Jalabert, *Abbo Floriacensis*, 24–9; Mostert, *Theology*, 21–2, 41–5, and 'Le Séjour d'Abbon de Fleury à Ramsey', *Bibliothèque de l'École des Chartes*, 144 (1987), 199–208; and Ridyard, *Royal Saints*, 63–9, 93–5.

[139] E. John, 'The World of Abbot Aelfric', in *Ideal and Reality*, 300–6.

[140] M. Lapidge, 'A Frankish Scholar in Tenth-Century England: Frithegod of Canterbury/Frédégaud of Brioude', *ASE* 17 (1988), 45–66.

[141] Lapidge, 'Three Latin Poems', 85–137.

reach the generation of William of Malmesbury, we find a mixed parentage of Saxon and Norman, combined with a by then standard Norman-reformed education.[142] The result, in William's writings and those of other scholars, such as Eadmer, is a certain pride in both their heritages, mixed with a somewhat amused indulgence in the Saxon peculiar culture. Altogether, it gives twelfth-century English scholars a European kinship which no English writer since Bede, Alcuin, and Aldhelm had enjoyed.

Two Anglo-Saxon writers, however, were shown by Georges Duby to have a much greater European influence than had been previously thought, in one area at least.[143] Aelfric and Wulfstan, and King Alfred before them in the annotations to his translation of Boethius' *Consolation of Philosophy*, developed in their homiletical writings a theological and social theory about the ordering of human society, based on the division of men into three orders: those who pray, those who fight and those who labour.[144] This theory of the three orders was adopted and further enriched by two French bishops, Adalbero of Laon and Gérard of Cambrai, in the years around 1025, as well as by Abbo of Fleury, who had been in England, and by a Norman writer, Dudo of St Quentin.[145] Significantly, recent research has shown that an important ideological synthesis had already been quite advanced in this respect in the works of Carolingian writers of the 'School of Auxerre', such as Haymo and Heiric, who had adapted ideas from Isidore of Seville;[146] Isidore was one of the most widely read, used, and regarded writers in seventh- and eighth-century Ireland,[147] and it may be no coincidence that Auxerre happened to be at the heart of an area of intense Irish missionary work and monastic foundations in the late Merovingian and early Carolingian periods.

IV. LITURGICAL AND DEVOTIONAL EXCHANGES BETWEEN ENGLAND AND FRANCE

Liturgical customs reached England from Cluny in the later tenth century and again in the later eleventh century, first through the intermediary of

---

[142] On this mixture in linguistic and cultural terms, see M. Chibnall, *Anglo-Norman England 1066–1166* (Oxford, 1986), 209–18.

[143] G. Duby, *The Three Orders: Feudal Society Imagined* (tr. Chicago, 1980), 99–109.

[144] W. J. Sedgefield (ed.), *King Alfred's Old English Version of Boethius' De Consolatione Philosophiae* (Oxford, 1899), 40–1; *Aelfric's Lives of the Saints*, ii. 120–5; Wulfstan's *Institutes of Polity* are edited by K. Jost (Berne, 1959).

[145] Duby, *Three Orders*, 13–80, 110–66, 83–92, 181–91.

[146] D. Iogna-Prat, 'Le 'Baptême' du schéma des trois ordres fonctionnels: l'apport de l'École d'Auxerre dans la seconde moitié du ixe siècle', *Annales ESC*, 41(1) (1986), 101–26, and E. Ortigues, 'L'Élaboration de la théorie des trois ordres chez Haymon d'Auxerre', *Francia*, 14 (1986), 27–43.

[147] Hillgarth, *Visigothic Spain*, 451–2, 447–8.

Fleury, which had adopted the Cluniac reform and passed it on to English monasteries in the *Regularis Concordia*, and secondly through Lanfranc, whose *Monastic Constitutions*, though influenced by Bec, also contained features from other Norman abbeys reformed by William of Volpiano, such as Fécamp and Jumièges.[148] Examples of customs of Cluny found in the *Monastic Constitutions* are: the celebration of the Trinity on the last Sunday before Advent, the celebration of Nones on Palm Sunday, parts of the office for Maundy Thursday copied directly from Bernard of Cluny, the celebration of masses for the Dead on the Vigil of All Saints, a devotion introduced by Odilo, and, on a more practical level, the existence of 'circumcitores' who went round the monastery checking on the good functioning of all duties and the preparation of the host by the sacrist.[149] One of the prayers for the Cross in the *Concordia* is of Carolingian origin, while another was subsequently adopted in France.[150] However, Patrick Wormald has emphasized the need to take into account the reformers' aquaintance with the Carolingian monastic reforms of Benedict of Aniane; six manuscripts of the Aachen *capitula* survive from England after 970, one of which is actually bound together with the *Regularis Concordia*.[151] Even more significant is the ideological impact of the Carolingian reforms, the idea of a custom to be enforced for all religious houses and endorsed by royal authority: Edgar and Aethelwold consciously adopted the Carolingian ideology of a 'Christian Empire, serving one God, one king and one Rule'.[152]

Other liturgical borrowings from France are the tropes and sequences of the mass, usually taken from the St Gall repertoire but, in some cases, from that of St Martial of Limoges, which may have been taught English monks by the envoys from St Martial about 1031, and from the north of France.[153] It is impossible to know whether other liturgical items were borrowed from particular French books which present a local version of the standard *Hadrianum*, since few are still extant, but there is no reason why this should not have happened. All we know is that liturgical forms, such as masses, benedictions, offices, or hymns for local patron saints were usually copied in Anglo-Saxon liturgical books from French books originating in the centres where specific saints were venerated. Unless there were relics of these saints in England, which prompted the writing of prayers in the churches which housed these relics—such as St Justus of Beauvais

---

[148] *MC, passim*; R. Graham, 'The Relations of Cluny to some Other Movements of Monastic Reform', in *English Ecclesiastical Studies* (London, 1929), 1–29.
[149] *MC* 9, 25, 32, 54, 65–7, 69–70.
[150] L. Gjerlow, *Adoratio Crucis* (Oslo, 1961), 13–29.
[151] Wormald, 'Aethelwold', 31.
[152] Ibid. 32.
[153] *Winchester Troper*, pp. xxxi–xxxii; Planchart, *Repertory*, i. 167–240.

at Winchester and St Ouen at Christ Church—liturgical forms are usually borrowed directly from the books of the relevant Continental abbeys. Thus, for example, the masses for St Denis or St Rémi were taken from St Denis or Reims sacramentaries, especially those for the secondary feasts of the Translation of St Rémi and the Invention of the Head of St Denis. St Denis' main feast of the *Natale* is found in all calendars, in bold letters in the calendar in Robert's missal. Three Winchester calendars enter the Octave of the feast. The very strong emphasis on the cult at Winchester is already perceptible. All sacramentaries have a mass for this feast, and Leofric added a second long mass in six parts to the already existing one in the missal, an addition itself made at Glastonbury before the book reached Exeter. There are collects at Durham and Worcester and benedictions at Exeter, Wells, Canterbury, and Winchester, where the feast is troped, and the missal of New Minster includes two masses for the Vigil and the Octave. The second feast of St Denis, the *Inventio capitis*, is entered in four New Minster calendars, and in two calendars from centres closely associated with New Minster at the time of their compilation: Sherborne and Worcester in the early eleventh century, and in the eleventh-century West Country calendar. The New Minster missal celebrated this feast with a mass, as did Giso's sacramentary. Whereas the texts for the masses of the *Natale*, Vigil, and Octave are those used at St Denis—with the exception of the Prefaces for the last two—the texts for the mass of the *Inventio* differ and seem to have been written in England. The Winchester connection is confirmed in the litanies, since the saint and his companions are entered in them all, and are placed particularly high in the list of martyrs in Winchester litanies. Although the New Minster possessed relics of the saint, the presence of relics did not necessarily make for a great popular cult. In this instance, the reasons for the Winchester veneration are of a different kind, and explain, indirectly, the Wells cult. The increasing prestige of St Denis in France and possibly also the existence of relics at Glastonbury and Abingdon may have been the original cause for the veneration that St Edith of Wilton, Edgar's daughter, acquired for the saint. She dedicated to him the church she built at Wilton in 984; this church was consecrated by St Dunstan, whose sojourn at St Peter's, Ghent may have also led him to support the cult of this saint, venerated at St Peter's because the reformer of this abbey Gérard of Brogne had spent some time as a visitor at St Denis's.[154] The late tenth-century southern English cult saw a renewal of its popularity in the mid-eleventh century,

[154] Wilmart, 'Légende de Ste Édith', 86–7; on the late 10th-c. English cult, see D. C. Hoare, 'The Cult of St Denys in England in the Middle Ages', M. Phil. thesis (Nottingham, 1978), 11–13, 117–19.

due in part to Queen Edith's devotion, since she had been educated at Wilton and rebuilt St Edith's church there in 1065, and in part to the presence at court of the monk Baldwin of St Denis, Edward's doctor and later abbot of Bury. Edward the Confessor partly rebuilt the church at Deerhurst in 1056 and granted it *c.*1059 to the abbey of St Denis,[155] whilst about 1080, Goscelin wrote Edith's Life emphasizing the saint's devotion to St Denis at Wilton. Meanwhile, Giso, one of Edward's chaplains, probably learnt about the cult at Winchester and took it with him when he became bishop of Wells in 1052. The underlying thread linking the promoters of the cult from Edith of Wilton to William I, who gave money to St Denis's itself for the building of a tower and offered a relic of the saint to Westminster, is their royal background. Edith was of royal blood and it is perhaps not surprising that she was devoted to this royal saint *par excellence*, which St Denis was becoming in France as patron saint of the Capetians. Edward and his Queen were probably aware of the royal overtones of the cult and this continuous connection may account for the success of the saint in the main royal city Winchester, even more than the existence of a relic at New Minster.[156]

In the same way, some of the secondary feasts of major saints of the Church celebrated in specific French centres were included in English liturgical texts. In some cases, such local feasts were only recorded in calendars, as was that of St Michael at Mont Saint Michel, which appears for the first time in the Wells calendar of 1061–88, being the feast of the dedication of that abbey. In other cases, the local feast, which would have been celebrated only in the centre whose patron saint was a major saint of the Church calendar—as for example, the local feast of the *Illatio* or *Tumulatio* of St Benedict at Fleury on 4 December or that of the *Subventio* of St Martin at Tours on 11 or 12 May—were entered in calendars especially at Oswald's foundations of Worcester and Evesham, possibly also at Ramsey and Pershore, from which no sources are extant. It comes as no surprise that Wulfstan's collectar should contain the only liturgical celebration for that feast. It is again the Worcester calendar which enters the Tours feast, in red, an entry which confirms the existence of direct links with the city of St Martin, links further demonstrated by the entries

---

[155] Hoare 'Cult of St Denys', 164–6, is somewhat confused in linking the grant of Deerhurst to St Denis and Edward's devotion to the saint: he ascribes the grant of Deerhurst first to Edward's devotion for St Denis as one of the Seven Sleepers of Ephesus, but he refuses to consider Queen Edith's devotion to the saint as an incentive, because her rebuilding of the church at Wilton took place in 1065. However, he notices that Edward's vision of the Seven Sleepers took place in 1060, after the re-foundation of Deerhurst, whilst ignoring that there had been a church dedicated to St Denis at Wilton since 984.

[156] Ridyard, *Royal Saints*, 140–75 insists on the royal nature of Edith's own cult but does not mention St Denis in this respect at all.

of several Touraine saints and special distinctions for St Brice in this calendar.[157]

The same applies to a variety of local saints, some only recorded in calendars and litanies, others with a proper cult in liturgical books. From Brittany, we have Wynwaloe of Landévénnec, Machutus of St Malo, and Samson of Dol; from Normandy, Wandrille and Ansbert of St Wandrille, Leufroy of La-Croix-St-Leufroy, Ouen, Gildard, Melanius, Nicasius and his companions Quirinus, Scubiculus, and Pientia of Rouen, Paternus of Avranches, Vigor of Bayeux, Taurinus of Évreux, Laudius of Coutances, and Valéry of Leuconay-St Valéry; from northern France, Aldegund of Maubeuge, Firmin of Amiens, Lucian and Justus of Beauvais, Denis, Quentin of St Quentin, Médard and Eligius of Noyon, Crispin, Crispinian, and Valerian of Soissons, and Geneviève, Germanus, and Maurus, all three associated with Paris. Further east are Rémi and Nicasius of Reims, and in Burgundy, Benignus of Dijon, Columba of Sens, Philibert of Tournus, Germanus of Auxerre, Léger and Symphorian of Autun, and Maiolus of Cluny; while from the Loire valley, we find the names of Brice of Tours, Maurilius, Lupus, and Albinus of Angers, Evurtius and Anianus of Orléans, Maurus of Glanfeuil, Launomarus of Corbion near Blois, Sulpicius and Ursinus of Bourges, Pavatus of Le Mans, Mamertus of Vienne whose cult was in fact stronger at Orléans than at Vienne, Florentinus of Bonneval, and Hilary and Radegund of Poitiers; and from further south, Foy of Conques, Léonard of Noblac, and Honoratus of Lérins and Marseilles.

The importance of these saints is clearly not equal. Some, such as Hilary, Quentin, and the two Germanus, began to be entered in English sources in the seventh century, for example in Bede's martyrology, and their presence is no sign of any particular veneration, especially since their celebrations are practically unchanged throughout the two centuries we are examining. Others were entered in some calendars and litanies in the late tenth century, at what must obviously have been a period of intense contacts with France, but never reached any further liturgical sources of a non-recording kind. Such are Samson, Evurtius, Benignus, Columba, Philibert and Maiolus. Hence, it seems that, at a time of frequent travel to France and to Rome, travellers encountered these names of the patron saints of monastic houses or churches where they stayed, and brought them back to England, to be recorded in a personal and somewhat whimsical

---

[157] This is the calendar of uncertain Worcester or Evesham provenance, whose origin I should ascribe to Evesham despite Atkins's, 'Investigation', 219–54 theory but in agreement with Wormald's, *Kalendars*, no. 18. Despite his own arguments, Atkins' theory itself confirms the Evesham provenance, since the vision of St Martin at Tours is described in the Evesham Chronicle, confirming the interest of this abbey in the Tours connection, 53–4.

manner in liturgical sources whose aim was comprehensiveness for the purpose of intercession. Only when such saints achieved incorporation in the liturgical books proper, can we say that their cult was established, thus demonstrating a closer relationship with the respective Continental centres, as in the case of Rémi, Maurus, Eligius, or Léger.

The study of these liturgical entries suggests several conclusions. It implies a difference in time and in the geography of the links with French centres, with one peak in the late tenth century, at the time of the monastic reform, and another around the 1030s and 1040s, under the reign of Cnut and the first years of Edward's reign. It also suggests that the privileged areas for such contacts shifted from the Wessex monasteries headed by Glastonbury and Winchester in the first period, to the Mercian abbeys in the west (Worcester and Evesham) and in the east (East Anglia and the Fens). Thirdly, it shows that these contacts were individual, that is proper to individual religious centres, whose members may have travelled, encountered a saint hitherto unknown to them, and introduced his or her cult into the records of their abbey on their way back. There these names often remained since, if it was an advantage to invoke as great a number of intercessors as possible, English monks were most careful and conservative in their liturgical celebrations. Only occasionally, when relics of such local foreign saints were available in England, did the writers of liturgical books introduce formulae for their celebration in their books, usually borrowed from the saint's native cult-centre, but sometimes written in England too. Such are the cases of St Justus at Winchester, St Austroberta and St Ouen at Christ Church, St Radegund at Exeter, and St Florentinus at Peterborough. In some cases, local Continental saints may not have been imported from their mother-church, because they had cults and relics in different monasteries with which we know, from other sources, English churches to have been in close contact. Ansbert and Wandrille had relics at St Peter's at Ghent; Benignus and Gengulf, two Burgundian saints recorded in a Winchester litany of the beginning of the eleventh century, were also venerated at Fécamp; and Sigismund of Agaune was highly regarded at Fleury, which may have led to the entry in the 'Winchcombe Sacramentary' litany, though he also appears in the Winchester litany.[158]

In view of the lack of direct contacts with Cluny attested in other sources before the late eleventh century, it is interesting to note the entries of

---

[158] On Sigismund, see D. Gremont and L. Donnat, 'Fleury, le Mont-Saint-Michel et l'Angleterre à la fin du Xᵉ et au début du XIᵉ siècle à propos du manuscrit d'Orléans n. 127(105)', in Laporte and Baudot, *Millénaire*, 764; the Winchester litany is that in a prayer-book from Nunnaminster, British Library Cotton MS Galba A. XIV.

Maiolus, one of the abbots of the abbey, and of Gérard of Roussillon, venerated there. We have to assume that some individuals may well have come into contact or even been to the abbey and that our only record of such a visit comes from Wells for Maiolus and Glastonbury in the eleventh century or Exeter for Gérard in this form. It is more than probable that Giso and Leofric, from whose churches these entries come, were closer to Cluny through their Lotharingian education, and more likely to be aware of its saints.

Even less evidence exists to confirm possible links between England and the other flourishing Burgundian abbey of Vézelay after 1050. The cult of St Mary Magdalene had been of some significance in England, through its Eastern and Irish connections, from the eighth century onwards. The *Natale* on 22 July, the main feast of the saint, is first found in Europe in the martyrology of Bede, and has clear oriental origins.[159] From then on, it is found in all calendars and martyrologies. The veneration for St Mary Magdalene in England, expressed by Bede when he chose to include this oriental date from Ephesus, where the saint was reputed to have died, and possibly reinforced by Willibald's visit to her shrine at Ephesus in the eighth century,[160] is further confirmed by three of the earliest appearances of this saint in art on two Northumbrian crosses, the Ruthwell Cross of the eighth century and the later Gosforth Cross in Cumberland, and in an eighth-century ivory.[161] She is shown at Christ's feet, kneeling, in the Ruthwell Cross; standing alongside with the other holy figures in the Gosforth Cross Crucifixion; and meeting Christ on Easter day on the ivory panel. Her cult was, at the time, associated with the veneration for the Cross and the Crucified Christ, a devotion which we know to have been very strong in England from the early Anglo-Saxon until the late Anglo-Saxon period. However, the eremitical legend was also known in the ninth century, since the Old English Martyrology mentions it;[162] but, although the eremitic connotations are present both in it and in the Ruthwell Cross, the association of the saint in England was primarily with the Cross and

[159] Saxer, *Culte*, 40–1.

[160] Talbot, *Missionaries*, 160; Thomas, 'Cult of the Saints' Relics', 430, suggested that the relic may have been brought back by Willibald from Ephesus.

[161] On St Mary Magdalene on the Ruthwell Cross, see Collingwood, *Northumbrian Crosses*, 84, pl. 101; Saxl, 'The Ruthwell Cross', 2, pl. 2b; and M. Schapiro, 'The Religious Meaning of the Ruthwell Cross' (1944) repr. in *Selected Papers*, 164. On St Mary on the Gosforth Cross, see Coatsworth, 'Iconography', 254, 316; C. A. Parker, *The Ancient Crosses at Gosforth, Cumberland* (London, 1896) and P. Wormald in J. Campbell (ed.), *The Anglo-Saxons* (Harmondsworth, 1991), 163; the agreement on the identification of the female figure with St Mary is far from being complete, see, for example, K. Berg, 'The Gosforth Cross', *JWCI* 21 (1958), 30–4, who takes the figure to represent Ecclesia. For the 8th-c. ivory diptych showing Christ meeting St Mary, now in the Musée de Cluny in Paris, see Beckwith, *Ivory Carvings*, pl. 18.

[1] Kotzor, *Das altenglische Martyrologium*, ii. 156–7, 330.

the Resurrection.[163] It is also in England that we find one of the first known references to a relic of St Mary Magdalene in the West in the possession of Exeter, to which it had been given by King Aethelstan.[164]

In England, after Bede's and the Old English martyrologies, the next entries for St Mary Magdalene's feast are found in several calendars, two of *c*.850, two of the late ninth or early tenth century, and in the late tenth-century Glastonbury calendar. This group covers the earliest evidence for the cult before it spread to the rest of Europe, and was entered, for example, in German calendars. It has already been suggested that Bede probably found the feast in Greek texts, since the date of 22 July is that of the celebration of the saint at Ephesus, the eastern town where her cult was at its strongest.

Victor Saxer described the cult as, at root, a 'création savante de cabinet' by Bede and, on account of the devotion of his fellow monks in England, a feast first limited to the monastic and clerical world, which was later to become a great popular one.[165] The cult developed in England from its eastern origins, via Italy, but possibly also via Ireland. It should be remembered that the Hieronymian Martyrology is one of the first sources in the West to enter a feast of the saint. The oldest recension of this martyrology comes from Auxerre, and it may be no coincidence that Auxerre had strong links with Ireland. A group of Irish monks in the eighth century gave a conference at Auxerre, praising St Mary Magdalene, an eulogy not altogether surprising to find being offered by those leading the most clearly eremitical style of life in Europe at that period.[166] The mention of the eremitical legend in the Old English martyrology may well be due to the Irish connection.

In the tenth century, the English cult developed around Aethelstan's gift of relics to Exeter. It is beyond doubt that the eleventh-century fame of the Vézelay cult further promoted the veneration for St Mary Magdalene, but the cult was already well established by then in England, the country which had preceded the rest of western Europe in this devotion, both because of the saint's role as the first witness of the Resurrection, and because of her importance as a model of a life of penance and contemplation. The popularity of her fellow saint, St Mary the Egyptian, also venerated as a hermit and penitent, became considerable in England after the arrival there of the Naples Life; and the similarities of the itineraries

---

[163] On the eremitical themes in the Ruthwell Cross, see Schapiro, 'Ruthwell Cross', 164.

[164] *Leofric Missal*, 3–5, and Saxer, *Culte*, 54.

[16] Saxer, *Culte*, 45.

[166] P. David, 'Un recueil de conférences monastiques irlandaises du VIIIe siècle', *RB* 49 (1937), 80.

of the Life of St Mary the Egyptian and the Life of St Mary Magdalene
are striking. The two saints remained closely associated in the eleventh
and twelfth centuries, for example, in litanies, and vernacular Lives of
both were written in Anglo-Norman.[167] However, we may infer from the
far greater popularity of St Mary Magdalene in England that, since St Mary
the Egyptian shared the eremitical and penitential attributes, the greater
importance of St Mary Magdalene was due to her Gospel association.

The English veneration for St Mary Magdalene before the Vézelay cult
began can be demonstrated not only from the texts and sculptures already
discussed, but especially from another image, which many historians
appear to have ignored. In the Benedictional of St Aethelwold, amongst
the surviving illustrated pages depicting the choirs of the saints in the order
in which they are cited in the litanies, we find a miniature showing the
Choir of the Virgins.[168] In a position of pre-eminence in the centre of the
whole choir stands one figure, the only figure not crowned, but haloed by
a pearled nimbus. She is painted in a size slightly larger than the other
Virgins, even than that of St Etheldreda, for whom the benedictional and
its author expressed a special devotion. She wears the same vestment as St
Etheldreda, patterned on gold, and identical to that of the Virgin Mary in
the Annunciation scene in the manuscript. Like St Etheldreda, she holds
a book bearing her name, of which only 'Scta Maria Ma' is now visible.
J. O. Westwood, Francis Wormald, and Robert Deshman clearly identify
this figure as 'Scta Maria Magdalena', which is all the more probable here
since the Virgin Mary, the other suggested identification, does not belong
to the choir of the Virgins.[169] Thus the two most important female saints
in the benedictional are St Etheldreda and St Mary Magdalene, both
virtually assimilated to the Virgin Mary herself, and, of the two, St Mary

---

[167] Baker, 'Vie', 152.

[168] *Benedictional of St Aethelwold*, fo. 1ᵛ.

[169] Westwood, *Facsimiles*, 133; F. Wormald, 'The Benedictional of St Ethelwold', in *Collected Writings*, 91; and Deshman, 'Iconography', 112–13. Against them, Warner in *Benedictional of St Aethelwold*, p. xvi, and J. B. L. Tolhurst, 'An Examination of Two Anglo-Saxon Manuscripts of the Winchester School: The Missal of Robert of Jumièges and the Benedictional of St Aethelwold', *Archaeologia*, 83 (1933), 42–3, say that she was not St Mary Magdalene. Warner suggested the reading 'Sca Maria Ma[ter Christi]', with which I do not agree because the Virgin Mary does not belong to the choir of the Virgins in the litanies, which the folios follow closely, and also because, when I examined the MS, there did not seem to be enough room for [ter Christi], whereas [gdalena] would fit perfectly:

SCA	MA[G
MA	DAL
RIA	ENA]

It is not impossible that, when Westwood examined the MS in the mid-19th c., some of the now faded gold letters were still visible, and even now, using ultra-violet light, I am not certain that a very faint trace of the G is not visible.

Magdalene, as the leader of the Choir of the Virgins, a position in which she is found in five litanies, appears to be more important. This miniature, which pre-dates the Vézelay cult and was possibly linked with the knowledge of Aethelstan's gift of relics, demonstrates that the cult of St Mary Magdalene in England was strong even before the eleventh century, at any rate at Winchester, and did not rely as much on the Vézelay relics as it did throughout western Europe.

The feast of 22 July is entered in most English calendars, except in two from Winchester, one from Wessex, and one from Worcester, dating from the first half of the eleventh century. It is distinguished in three calendars of Christ Church, Sherborne, and Crowland. The saint whose feast falls on the same day, St Wandrille, comes second in English calendars. Mary Magdalene is celebrated with masses at Exeter and St Augustine's, and with the gradual; in the 'Winchcombe Sacramentary' where a six-part mass was added in a later hand; and at Wells. Four collects for the office are found in Wulfstan's collectar, two full hours in Arundel 155, and the full office is included in Leofric's collectar and in Salisbury, Cathedral Library MS 157. The strong Exeter and south-western emphasis of the cult is immediately apparent. There may have been a mixture of two channels of influence promoting the cult: the prestige of the local relic at Exeter on the one hand, and the influence of Leofric's and Giso's devotion on the other. The latter would be a consequence of the development of the cult in eastern France and Germany, in such centres as Verdun, Besançon, Reims, Echternach, and throughout Flanders, in addition to the impact of Cluny, one of the promoters of the Vézelay cult, upon Lotharingian monasteries. The themes of the English cult are similar to those encompassed in one of the representative eleventh-century liturgical texts quoted by Saxer.[170] Wulfstan's collectar uses those of St Mary as the first witness of the Resurrection and of the remission of sins, the mass in Leofric's missal that of the best share being that of St Mary and not of St Martha, that is to say, the contemplative life; Giso's insists on love bringing forgiveness of sins. The most interesting grouping of these themes is contained in Leofric's collectar. Despite mentioning the 'love and forgiveness of sins' and the 'best share' themes, it provides essentially a narrative office, recalling three times the anointing of Christ, twice the remission of sins through tears and penance, and finally insisting on St Mary Magdalene as the first witness of the Resurrection, the 'Apostle of the Apostles'. Arundel 155 is no less concerned with the tears and penance and also recalls the Raising of Lazarus. Altogether, the compilers of English texts seem to have

---

[170] Saxer, *Culte*, App. I.

been more interested in the historical facts from the Gospel—the tears and love and remission of sins, the anointing of Christ, St Mary and St Martha, the witness to the Resurrection—than in the more apocryphal cult associated with the contemplative and eremitic life in the desert. This may have been due to the tendency of English liturgical texts to avoid the use of apocryphal themes, preferring the purely biblical. But it could also be interpreted as an indication of a desire to view and venerate St Mary Magdalene as a Gospel figure rather than as an essentially eremitic one, thus revealing a preference for one contemporary spiritual movement over the other, possibly on account of the older tradition in this country of St Mary Magdalene's cult.

Throughout the eleventh century in England the cult remained formal. There are no prayers addressed to the saint, although we find five long hymns in Rouen A.44, which is considerable even for this rather expansive hymnal. Her name ascends from the twenty-first and twentieth place respectively in the litanies in Harleian 863 and Galba A.XIV, to the fourth place in B. N. lat. 8824, the second in four litanies of the second half of the eleventh century, eventually reaching the first place in five litanies, most of them of the late eleventh century and from the south-west, for example, those in Additional 28188 and Vitellius E.XVIII. By the end of the century in Rouen A.44 and Vitellius A.VII, her name was entered on a separate line, in capitals, before the other Virgins, with its own prayer.

The Vézelay cult most certainly contributed to the development of the veneration for St Mary Magdalene during the second half of the eleventh century, and it is clear from the various manuscript sources that the fame of Vézelay reached English liturgical texts very quickly. However, the themes and preferences of the older English cult continued to be expressed in English books. This continuity is also visible in art, since the miniature depicting the saint at the foot of the Cross in the Crucifixion from Countess Judith's Gospel-book, now MS 709 in the Pierpont Morgan Library in New York, is clearly descended from the tradition of the Ruthwell Cross.[171] In the course of the twelfth century, Norman influence was to bring the more Continental themes of the cult to England, and was to enhance the devotion, developing it into one as popular as it had already become in the West during the late eleventh century.[172]

---

[171] New York, Pierpont Morgan Library MS 709, fo. 1ᵛ, reproduced in Temple, *ASM*, pl. 289. However, she describes this figure as being the donor, Countess Judith, 110, but such a representation would be an unusually early case of a donor being depicted in art. On this MS, see also Harssen, 'The Countess Judith'.

[172] There was also an altar dedicated to St Mary in Lanfranc's new church at Canterbury, see *Gervase*, i. 14. The first religious house dedicated to her was Beadlow-Beaulieu, in 1097 (moved to Millhook in 1119 and given to St Albans), followed by Barnstaple (1107) and King's Lynn,

St Mary Magdalene's cult answered the need for an eremitical, contemplative, and penitential saint, at a time when such spiritual movements were strong in western Europe. In England, she remained above all the Holy Woman of the Resurrection, as well as being the penitent at Christ's feet and the friend who could be associated with Christ's earthly life, even though, from the twelfth century onwards, the eremitical associations promoted by Vézelay and by the Norman tradition became predominant.[173] The Vézelay Translation undoubtedly played a part in the development of the cult in England, but it did not supersede the earlier Anglo-Saxon traditions and themes. There is no doubt that the rapid development and spread of the cult of this saint in relation to the alleged discovery of her relics at Vézelay in 1050 greatly contributed to making her into one of the major saints in England by the end of the eleventh century. Within fifty years, a devotion traditional in England on account of the saint's link with the Gospel, but still limited, became one of the main cults in both the official liturgy and private devotion.

The cult of Mary Magdalene was strongly supported by the Normans. They contributed to reinforcing the cults of Norman saints in England, such as that of St Ouen, and introduced cults popular in France from the mid-eleventh century onwards, such as those of St Faith of Conques, from both Conques and the Norman abbey at Conches, St Léonard of Noblac in Poitou, and St Giles of Provence. Léonard is entered only in the Worcester calendar in the second half of the eleventh century, but Faith was added to the Glastonbury calendar in the eleventh century and to the West Country one in the late eleventh century. She was entered in the twelfth century in one Winchester calendar; at Worcester with XII lessons; and at Crowland in green capitals. Her name is in the original hand in twelfth-century calendars, but also in the eleventh-century Wells calendar. The devotion to St Faith was essentially a twelfth-century feature. The saint appears twice in the liturgical texts themselves, in two masses at St Augustine's and Exeter. St Faith's name appears in three litanies from the

founded *c.*1100 by Herbert Losinga—who had been educated in Lotharingia, see Binns, *Monastic Dedications*, 110, 163, and *Religious Houses*, 98 on Barnstaple and 59 on Beadlow. From the 12th c. onwards, she became increasingly associated with the dedication of leper hospitals, the first of which was Colchester, dedicated in 1096–7, ibid. 353. Apart from the Lotharingians, bishop Gundulf of Rochester (1077–1108) was also reputed to have held St Mary Magdalene in great veneration, see R. Thomson (ed.), *The Life of Gundulf, Bishop of Rochester* (Toronto, 1977), 5–6, 12.

[173] A good illustration of the veneration for St Mary Magdalene within the new monastic eremitic orders of the 12th c. such as the Carthusians, is the episode relating St Hugh of Lincoln's devotion to the saint when he tried to acquire a relic of her at Fécamp by biting off a piece of bone from her arm, see D. L. Douie and [D.] H. Farmer (eds.), *Magna Vita Sancti Hugonis: The Life of St Hugh of Lincoln* (2 vols.; London, 1961–2, repr. 1986), ii. 169.

second half of the eleventh century. It was squeezed in after that of St Cecilia in the litany in Douce 296 and it was entered in ninth position, just after St Mary Magdalene, St Mary the Egyptian, and the Roman virgins in the litany in Vitellius E.XVIII.

The popularity of St Giles', mostly associated with the lepers and the lame in the later Middle Ages, was also due in part to the First Crusade and the devotion of the nobility to the saint, inspired by Raymond IV of Toulouse, one of the leaders of the Crusade, who greatly venerated St Giles. St Giles' cult is a case of a devotion relying on the popularity of the tenth-century Life of the saint, written to support the patronage of an increasingly wealthy abbey on account of its position on the pilgrimage routes to Rome, Jerusalem, and Compostela—that of St Gilles near Nîmes.[174] In England, St Giles was entered in six calendars, at Glastonbury, in the original hand, and at Christ Church, Sherborne, Worcester, Wells, and Crowland. The only liturgical celebration is a mass in four parts in the 'Leofric Missal'. An interest in the cult is evident in Leofric's and Giso's territory in the south-west, and Worcester and Crowland may have derived theirs from the two centres of Exeter and Wells. The presence of the saint in some Norman calendars may explain, in part, its success. By the end of the eleventh century and especially by the twelfth century, it was well on the way to becoming a major cult. St Giles' name was entered in four late eleventh-century litanies. The cult was promoted originally by St Gilles-de-Provence, a key centre of communications and ideally placed for pilgrims. The aristocratic devotion was due, to a certain extent, to the First Crusade and to Raymond of Toulouse, but in twelfth-century England it was essentially linked with the arrival of the Normans and, with them, of a popular French cult. This could explain the existence of urban churches such as St Giles', Cambridge, dedicated c.1092 by the Norman sheriff and his French wife, before the First Crusade.[175]

Equally popular after the First Crusade was another eastern saint, whose cult reached England from Normandy in the second half of the eleventh century, St Catherine. Her cult was still rather weak in the eleventh century, when she was entered only in one Winchester calendar and at Wells. In the twelfth century, her name was added at Christ Church, with XII lessons, at Worcester, and at Crowland in red capitals, whereas the twelfth-century calendars entered it with various distinctions everywhere. The only liturgical celebration for the saint in our period is found

---

[174] On the abbey of St Gilles and its role on the pilgrimage routes, see C. Brooke and W. Swaan, *The Monastic World 1000–1300* (London, 1974), 99, and V. and H. Hell, *The Great Pilgrimage of the Middle Ages: The Road to St. James of Compostella* (tr. London, 1966), 134. *The Vita Egidii* is edited in AASS, Sept I, 284–304.

[175] Brooke, 'The Churches', in Beales and Best, *History*, 55–6.

in the missal of St Augustine's, in which the mass mentions both the links of St Catherine with Mount Sinai, where Moses received the Law, and the famous myrrh or oil of St Catherine, which constituted one of the main relics together with the equivalent relic of St Nicholas. The office of St Catherine, written by Aimard at St Ouen in the early eleventh century, was clearly by then not adopted in England.[176]

The first signs of the new importance of the cult can be seen in the litanies. Her name is inserted, like that of St Faith in the same book, after St Lucy, in the litany from Douce 296, and it was also added between those of St Lucy and St Tecla in the Harleian 863 litany. We again find it in four other late eleventh-century litanies. By the early twelfth century it is placed before those of the Roman virgins themselves.

The cult was already active in Italy by the tenth century, since we encounter her name in various sources, for example, in litanies and frescos in Naples, Rome, and central Italy. However, it seems that this channel was not very successful in the case of St Catherine, since the English cult appears to have been linked to a greater extent with the Norman rather than with the Italian cult. The Norman veneration for St Catherine was due to the Translation of her relics to the abbey of La Trinité-au-Mont at Rouen. According to the *S. Catherinae virginis et martyris translatio et miracula Rothomagenses saeculi x*, this Translation was performed by St Simeon, a monk from Mount Sinai, who had come to Normandy to collect the alms offered by the dukes of Normandy to his monastery. This story was demonstrated by Robert Fawtier to have been impossible as it stands, but he admitted the presence of the relics at Rouen from the time of the first abbot of the monastery, Isembart (1033–53).[177] In any case, the devotion became a major cult in Normandy and the abbey of the Holy Trinity changed its name to St Catherine's in about 1120–40; and it was spread to the rest of western Europe by the Norman expansion from the mid-eleventh century onwards. Its relatively feeble presence in England before the twelfth century seems to indicate that in this case, it was indeed the Norman Conquest which acted as a major influence on the development of the cult. It may be that such a situation was more the result of chronology than of the Conquest itself, since the cult only began to be active in Normandy approximately ten years before the Conqueror crossed the Channel, and we may assume that it would have reached England in due course, as all Continental cults did, even without the arrival of the Normans. The Conquest may have speeded up the process, but it was

---

[176] Jones, *Nicholas of Myra*, 148.
[177] R. Fawtier, 'Les Reliques rouennaises de Ste Catherine', *AB* 41 (1923), 357–68.

accelerated even more by the Crusades. St Catherine's cult in England reflected the impact of the Conquest and the increasing fame of the saint of Mount Sinai after the First Crusade. This is the only case of an eastern saint whose cult took this route, since often such cults arrived in England via the south of Italy or Germany directly from the East, as did that of St Nicholas.

The devotional links with Normandy were not, however, one-sided. Late eleventh- and twelfth-century Norman calendars have entries for Anglo-Saxon saints: Edmund the Martyr at St Ouen and Fécamp, and a long list of English saints comprising Oswald, Edward, Kenelm, Cuthbert, Botulf, Dunstan, Aethelberht, Guthlac, Aelfheah, Mildburgh, and Werburgh at Évreux. When Lanfranc attempted to play down the cults of some Anglo-Saxon saints in his cathedral, the reason for his move was probably not a dislike for these saints themselves but, rather, the result of the by then prevailing ecclesiastical policy in the spirit of the Roman reform. These popularly proclaimed saints, venerated on a par with major figures of the Church, did not fit in with the more hierarchical views of the late eleventh-century policy, prevalent in the composition and emphases of the liturgical books of the period. By 1070, popular acclaim was no longer considered sufficient for sanctity. Lanfranc is made to appear devoted to Dunstan by Osbern: he is restored to health when ill by kissing Dunstan's stirrup, and it is Dunstan who encourages him in a vision, when he engages in the lawsuit at Penenden Heath.[178] His attempted rejection of the Canterbury saints was a result of these developments in ecclesiastical policy, which started around the middle of the eleventh century and were implemented forcefully by Norman rulers, rather than of contempt on their part for the saints of the conquered Church.[179]

Earlier than that, coronation *ordines* had been brought from England to France twice, first for the coronation of Judith when she married King Aethelwulf of Wessex in 856, and again in 936, for the coronation of Louis IV on his return from England; the first one was adapted by Hincmar from the earliest, possibly even seventh-century English *ordo*, the second was entered in the sacramentary of Ratold at Corbie, which included benedictions from Aethelwold's benedictional, and was subsequently used also by King Edgar.[180] The exchanges between the two countries in terms of royal rituals functioned both ways: it is the second coronation of Charles the

---

[178] Stubbs, *Memorials*, 151–2, 143–4.

[179] On the question of veneration of Anglo-Saxon saints after the Conquest, mentioned by Eadmer in the *Vita Anselmi*, 50–4, see S. J. Ridyard, '*Condigna Veneratio*: Post-Conquest Attitudes to the Saints of the Anglo-Saxons', *Anglo-Norman Studies*, 9 (1986), 179–206.

[180] Nelson, 'Ritual *Ordines*', 341–60, and 'Second English *Ordo*', 368, in *Politics*. These are the benedictions for the feasts of the Nativity of the Virgin, SS Cecilia, Clement, and Andrew.

Bald which inspired King Edgar's second coronation of 973, when he too acquired new territories; but the coronation of William I was performed under pressure from his English subjects, for whom authority could only proceed from kingship, whereas the Normans remained detached from it; William only used the ceremony of the *Laudes regiae* in England, not in Normandy.[181] The Carolingian ideas about the nature of royal and imperial power gained impetus in England, from the time of Alfred, whose biography Asser modelled on that of Charlemagne by Einhard, but the lesson was so well adopted that, by the end of the eleventh century, the idea of authority and royal coronation had become inseparable in the minds of the Anglo-Saxons.

V. ARTISTIC EXCHANGES BETWEEN ENGLAND AND FRANCE

The most considerable French source of influence on late Anglo-Saxon book illumination is to be found in the manuscripts illuminated at Reims in the ninth and early tenth centuries and, in particular, in one, of which two faithful copies were made in England within a hundred years of its arrival here, known as the Utrecht Psalter.[182] This manuscript reached England before 1000 and was copied for the first time at Christ Church, Canterbury, in the early eleventh century in the Harley Psalter.[183] The copy was faithful but not slavish: Hanns Swarzenski has shown how some among the scribes who contributed to it at different periods pushed further a few of the characteristic features of the Reims style by adding a greater 'dynamic vivacity' and colour drawings as opposed to the monochrome original model. Different devotional features are occasionally emphasized in England by choice of the scribe, as well as the initial choice of using the Roman rather than the Gallican version of the psalter, which was a characteristically English feature.[184] But in terms of book illumination, after the impulse of the Reims style in England in the late tenth century, the exchange of influences worked as much from England to France as in the other direction. English manuscripts reached various Norman abbeys both before and after the Conquest. The examples that we know are the books brought by Robert of Jumièges to Normandy when he fled from England, among which was the sacramentary from Winchester, and

---

[181] Nelson, 'Inauguration Rituals', 300, and 'Rites', 396–401, in *Politics and Ritual*.
[182] Van der Horst and Engelbreght, *Utrecht Psalter*.
[183] British Library MS Harley 603; on this MS, see *Golden Age*, no. 59, pp. 74–5.
[184] H. Swarzenski, *Monuments of Romanesque Art: The Art of Church Treasures in North-Western Europe* (2nd edn.; London, 1974), 22–3, 24–6; and J. Backhouse, 'The Making of the Harley Psalter', *British Library Journal*, 10 (1984), 97–113.

possibly also a late tenth-century benedictional;[185] and the books sent by
the Conqueror from Ely, Abingdon, and probably other abbeys to
Normandy. J. J. Alexander's study of the manuscripts produced at Mont
Saint Michel during the eleventh century has shown the extent of the
influence of the Anglo-Saxon style, as well as the role of intermediary
played by this abbey in conveying themes and stylistic features to England
from other parts of Europe from which books were acquired by the Mont,
such as Liège or northern Italy (Abbot Suppo had been a monk of
Fruttuaria).[186] The influence of Anglo-Saxon book illumination remained
considerable during the early twelfth century, especially in the areas of
France which were under the dominion of the Angevins after the accession
to the throne of Henry II, which explains the impact of the second
Winchester style on the Romanesque churches of Poitou, in particular on
the wall-paintings of St-Savin-sur-Gartempe, where the Creation scenes of
the Late Antique type had been transmitted through the intermediary of
Anglo-Saxon manuscripts of the kind of the illustrated Hexateuch and
Junius 11.[187]

   A variety of other artefacts left England after the Conquest, and Norman
chroniclers mention with particular relish the embroideries, probably of
the type of the tapestry of Bayeux, and the church vessels, book covers,
and other precious metal objects, of which English abbeys were full.
Glastonbury had vessels, images, and vestments, made of gold, silver, and
precious stones, in an eighth-century chapel; King Edgar gave it a
reliquary of gold, silver and ivory, King Harthacnut another reliquary,
and Abbot Brihtwald numerous gifts.[188] At Abingdon, Cnut gave the
abbey gifts and Abbot Aethelwine made a reliquary and cross; but the
ornaments and a Gospel-book were removed to Normandy, as were those
of Malmesbury.[189] At Ramsey, Oswald offered two crosses and at Evesham
Abbot Manni made two reliquaries and illuminated two missals and two
psalters.[190] Gifts were made to Winchester by kings, noblemen—Gytha,
Earl Godwine's wife, presented ornaments—and bishops, especially
Stigand, who gave a cross and two gold and silver images.[191] At Peterborough, we have a long list of ornaments: a great gold and silver cross

---

[185] The benedictional of Aethelgar, known as the 'Benedictional of Archbishop Robert', may
have been removed by Robert or by Queen Emma when she left England for Normandy *c.*1013,
and given by her to her brother Robert, archbishop of Rouen, *BAR*, pp. xiv–xvi.
   [186] Alexander, *Norman Illumination*, 11, 86–126.
   [187] G. Henderson, 'The Sources of the Genesis Cycle at St-Savin-sur-Gartempe', *Journ. of the
Brit. Archaeol. Assoc.*, 3rd ser. 26 (1963), 18–25.
   [188] *WMHG* 102–3, 130–1, 134–5, 138–9.
   [189] *Chronicon Abingdon* i. 443, 447; *WMGP*, 432.
   [190] *Chronicon Rameseiensis*, 48–9, and *Chronicon Evesham*, 87.
   [191] *Annales monasterii de Wintonia*, 26, 29–30.

over the altar, two gold and silver candlesticks, an altar table of gold, silver, and precious stones, over a dozen gold and silver book-bindings and reliquaries, purple vestments embroidered with gold, other gold, silver, and gem-studded crosses and vessels; many were taken by the first Norman abbot Turold to Normandy and given to the abbey of Préaux, then to the cathedral of Beauvais when he was appointed bishop there; though, in 1102–3, when thieves came to Peterborough, they still found enough crosses, candlesticks, and chalices of gold to steal.[192] The list of similar possessions in the *Liber Eliensis* is too long to be cited,[193] and most churches had at least a few such ornaments. Renowned as embroiderers and goldsmiths, English craftsmen probably exerted a stronger influence on the development of the applied arts in France than they have been credited with previously, even before the massive arrival there of artefacts from England after the Conquest. Long before, we hear that Abbo had obtained an English silver reliquary, which he brought back to Fleury.[194]

In architecture, influences also went both ways to a certain extent, but French, particularly Norman, architecture was of greater importance for the evolution of English art. It is possible that Coorland, the English architect working on the Holy Cross at Poitiers, brought some Anglo-Saxon inspiration to France;[195] and, in one respect, we know that it was an English innovation, the cushion capital, which remained the standard carved capital in Anglo-Norman England, rather than the Norman volute capital.[196] Outside the main areas, the Normans had little influence on sculpture, which retained the flat relief tympana and the abstract patterns of the pre-Conquest period.[197]

English architects had found inspiration in France previously, since the late Anglo-Saxon churches were modelled essentially on their Carolingian counterparts, with a double apse and a raised Westwork, and two axial towers above the church, the style found in France, Lotharingia, and Flanders.[198] Abbot Wulfric of St Augustine's found inspiration at St Bénigne of Dijon for the rotunda he intended to build in his own abbey,

[192] *Hugh Candidus*, 87.
[193] *LE* 194–7, 223–4.
[194] Cousin, *Abbon*, 64.
[195] Gauthier's involvement in the rebuilding of St Hilaire may have been due to the interest of Cnut and Emma in this church, itself probably a result of Fulbert of Chartres' patronage of it; Cnut and Fulbert had corresponded and, if Cnut went through Chartres on his way to Rome, he would have met Fulbert and seen the cathedral being rebuilt, see R. Gem, 'A Recension in English Architecture during the Early Eleventh Century and its Effect on the Development of the Romanesque Style', *Journ. of the Brit. Archaeol. Assoc.*, 38 (1975), 39–40.
[196] G. Zarnecki, *English Romanesque Sculpture 1066–1140* (London, 1951), 12–13.
[197] Ibid. 13–14.
[198] Clapham, *English Romanesque Architecture*, i. 77–97, and Fernie, *Architecture*, 74–153.

and Norman architecture inspired Westminster; after the Conquest, Battle was modelled on Marmoutier near Tours, and Tournus.[199] In both religious and military architecture, the Normans contributed considerably during the last years of the eleventh century. The main buildings of cathedrals and abbeys were pulled down, to make room for new, much larger and more solid buildings on the model of Norman abbeys such as Bernay and Jumièges, a model already adopted by Edward for his rebuilding of the abbey-church of Westminster, and St Étienne of Caen, which inspired Lanfranc's new cathedral at Christ Church.[200] Before the end of the century, new cathedrals were being built at Canterbury, York, Lincoln, Old Sarum, Rochester, Durham, Winchester, St Paul's in London, Chichester, Chester, and Norwich; and new abbey-churches at St Albans, Gloucester, Ely, York, Battle, St Augustine's at Canterbury, Bury, and Tewkesbury; even Wulfstan began the rebuilding of his church at Worcester. The traditional view that we do not know what the Anglo-Saxon cathedrals of, for example, Winchester or Christ Church looked like, since the only pre-Conquest buildings still left are precisely those of small churches from villages where the Norman lords were not able to summon the money or the willingness to rebuild in Norman style, has been supplemented by recent research. This emphasized the relative lack of interest of the Anglo-Saxons for the size of the buildings, in favour of their lavish decoration, and their preferences for building new churches next to the old ones within the same compound, Roman-style, when the need to fit in more people arose, rather than pulling down the old churches to build a larger one.[201] It remains true, however, that even the largest of these Anglo-Saxon churches are not visible any longer, whereas the written sources occasionally imply a fairly considerable-sized building, when describing its decoration of rood-screens, statues or crucifixes. The Norman clergy was more interested in size and length than in decoration. They extended the nave and choir, added chapels around the ambulatory and a central tower rather than an axial one.[202] The main contribution of

---

[199] Clapham, *English Romanesque Architecture*, ii. 2–15.

[200] Sulcard of Westminster, 'Prologus de construccione Westmonasterii', 90–1; *Vita Aedwardi*, 44–6, and Gibson, *Lanfranc*, 163; on Westminster, see Fernie, *Architecture*, 155–7. Apart from the classic study by Clapham, *English Romanesque Architecture*, the best recent discussions of Romanesque architecture in England are those by R. Gem, 'English Romanesque Architecture', in G. Zarnecki, J. Holt, and T. Holland (eds.), *English Romanesque Art 1066–1200* (London, 1984), 27–37; 'The English Parish Church in the Eleventh and Early Twelfth Centuries: A Great Rebuilding?', in Blair, *Minsters*, 21–30; 'England and the Resistance to Romanesque Architecture', in C. Harper-Bill *et al.* (eds.), *Studies in Medieval History Presented to R. Allen Brown* (Woodbridge, 1989), 129–39; and 'A Recension in English Architecture', 28–49. See also Barlow, 'The Effects of the Norman Conquest', in *Norman Conquest*, 183–4.

[201] See, for example, Dodwell, *Anglo-Saxon Art*, 42–3, 231–4.

[202] Clapham, *Architecture After the Conquest*, 36–9.

English Romanesque was to be the development of the ribbed stone vaulting, seen at Durham. With the introduction of the Romanesque style of building, which reached this country late but developed quickly, the twelfth-century Norman settlers contributed to bringing English architecture within the mainstream of contemporary European building. However, in those places where buildings were not directly under the patronage and influence of the new masters, the local architects and masons often resisted anything but the most commonplace of innovations; by the twelfth century, church building re-integrated some of the Anglo-Saxon characteristics, thus giving birth to a mixed style combining native features and innovations.[203]

[203] Gem, 'English Parish Church', 25–8, and 'England and the Resistance', 132–8.

CONCLUSION

No event in English history has imposed itself more thoroughly on the historical perceptions of scholars as well as laymen than the Norman Conquest. One of the effects has been to leave the impression of an English Church that was somehow more distinct, even isolated, before the Battle of Hastings than afterwards. There seems little doubt that the whole pace of cultural communication was increasing in eleventh-century Europe, so that it is surely true that the English Church, like other European Churches, was more fully integrated into the spiritual lifestyle of western Christendom in the twelfth century than it had been in the tenth. None the less, the very speed and scale of change in Europe as a whole raises insistent questions about how much of what happened (in the sphere of papal reform, monastic observance, liturgical homogeneity, intellectual development, and architectural ambition) would have happened anyway, whoever had won the Battle of Hastings. And what remains beyond doubt, elements of Norman and reforming propaganda notwithstanding, is that the English Church of the century and a half before 1066 was never isolated, whether by circumstance or design. The changes that came after 1066 were real enough in the political arena but not in the cultural one before 1100. And most of these cultural changes were more or less experienced by parts of Europe that suffered no humiliating defeats in the process.

The Anglo-Saxon and early Anglo-Norman Church could be defined as a mixture of indigenous characteristics inherited from the past with an influx of contemporary foreign elements. This work is a study of the European connections of the English Church. But the considerable role of the national heritage from the early Anglo-Saxon period in the cultural, liturgical, devotional and artistic fields must never be forgotten or overlooked. The English attitude in this respect was one of pride in both past and contemporary achievements, even when the English regarded some foreign cultural features as superior to their own, in the field of hagiography for instance. Hence, the borrowing of Continental elements, when it took place, was never indiscriminate, but prompted by a deliberate choice: some areas of influence appeared to be more appropriate than others at particular times. The choice to take or leave, as well as how much to take and how to incorporate it within the English tradition, was an ever-present one.

Unsurprisingly, then, the pattern of these exchanges was not simple, nor was their development continuous. Two peak periods during the tenth century, the first under Aethelstan and the second during the age of the monastic revival, saw an increase in the number of foreign elements in England. These periods were each followed by about three decades of less intense exchanges, during which the imported features were either rejected or more deeply incorporated into the life of the English Church. There was a fresh influx of European elements under Cnut and during the first years of Edward the Confessor's reign. Thereafter, communications with the Continent remained steady but not particularly intense in cultural terms until the very last years of the eleventh century, when the effects of the Conquest were to make themselves more obviously felt over Anglo-Saxon culture. Only in the early twelfth century do we find a genuine attempt at merging rather than superimposing the two cultures, Saxon and Norman, with a return to some of the Anglo-Saxon traditions, mixed with Norman influences.

Just as the chronological development did not follow a steady line, so the geographical connections also changed according to the period. After Aethelstan's multiple and extensive European contacts, one area came to the fore of English interest at the end of the tenth century: the Ottonian Empire, particularly Lotharingia (that is to say the Rhineland and eastern French centres), and the north of Italy. German influence remained present throughout the first half of the eleventh century, but gave way increasingly to links with northern and central France and, from the 1040s onwards, with Normandy. The only area of influence whose success remained unchallenged throughout the period, culturally speaking, was Rome. Meanwhile, partly thanks to Rome and the Empire, an unbroken interest in Byzantium and its production was taken during the tenth and the first half of the eleventh centuries in England.

In addition to the *when* and *where* of its sources of influence, the English Church made yet another choice: the *what*. It did not borrow the same kind of features from these varied geographical areas. Ottonian Germany became a model on account of its concept of Christological kingship (possibly inspired at first by English ideological views) and in the example it could provide for bishops such as Aethelwold, Ealdred, Stigand and Wulfstan to act as great patrons of art and learning. Both Germany and Italy were potential spiritual models for a strong individual New Testament-oriented piety, which manifested itself in the devotional life and in the iconography. Meanwhile, France, and even Flanders, though much nearer and more frequented by Englishmen than Germany, Rome and even Byzantium, seem to have had less impact on English culture. This could be the result of sometimes hostile relations on the political scene, especially with Flanders. But it could also be seen as a sign of general decline in stature of these areas in the context of Europe as a whole during our period. English ecclesiastics were clearly not interested in importing foreign features just because these were foreign, but were only tempted by what they thought was of particular interest. Models, if any, were therefore often to be found in those areas which could be described as the 'high spots' of European culture in the tenth and eleventh centuries, Germany, Italy, and Byzantium. It could be claimed that only a civilization which had itself become especially refined and discerning would be able to make such specific choices. One cannot insist too strongly on the fact that England herself sustained one of these times of cultural apogee in contemporary Europe, and chose what she found most worth while in European culture because she herself was in a position to give a great deal to the Continent. Without any doubt, she did so throughout these two centuries, both as an example and as a source of inspiration.

BIBLIOGRAPHY

I. PRIMARY SOURCES

This is a bibliography of works used, rather than a comprehensive survey of the field; only the main items of relevant material have been included. The list of MSS contains mostly the unpublished codices which I have used though, in some cases, a few published ones are included when having seen the MS has proved to be essential to my conclusions. Primary works are entered under the name of the editor but cross-references are provided for major authors. The place-names in the list of manuscripts normally refer to the *scriptorium* in which the book was written.

1. *Manuscripts*

Besançon, Bibliothèque Municipale
14: Gospel-book, end 10th c., Old Minster, Winchester.

Boulogne-sur-mer, Bibliotèque Municipale
9: Gospel-book, 11th c., St Vaast, Arras.
11: Gospel-book, c.989–1008, St Bertin, AS illumination.
16: Bede: sermons; 12th c. fragments of the Life of St Dunstan, 10th c., St Bertin – Arras.
20: Psalter, c.989–1008, St Bertin, AS illumination.
106: Saints' Lives, 10–11th cc., St Bertin.
107: Saints' Lives, 11th c., St Bertin.

Cambridge, Corpus Christi College Library
9: Legendary, (and calendar), mid-11th c., Worcester.
23: Prudentius, late 10th c., Christ Church, Canterbury.
41: Sacramentary, 1st half of 11th c., Exeter.
44: Pontifical, (litanies), 11th c., ? St Augustine's, Canterbury, ? Ely.
57: Rule of St Benedict and Martyrology, 10th–11th cc., Abingdon.
146: Pontifical and Benedictional, (litanies), beg. 11th c., Worcester.
163: Pontifical (litanies), mid-11th c., copied at Winchester from a Cologne Pontifical.
190: Penitential and Miscellanea Liturgica, 1st half of 11th c., Exeter.
196: Fragment of Martyrology pp. 1–110, 3rd quarter of 11th c., Exeter.
198: Homilies (Anglo-Saxon), 10th–11th cc., ? Worcester.
253: Augustine's Confessions and Miscellanea Liturgica, 11th c., Canterbury.
270: Missal, late 11th c., St Augustine's, Canterbury.
361: Gregory's Pastoral Care and Miscellanea Liturgica, 11th c., Malmesbury.
389: Jerome's Life of St Paul and Felix's Life of St Guthlac, 10th c., addns. c.1070, St Augustine's, Canterbury.
391: Collectar (with calendar, hymns and canticles, and litany), 'Portiforium of St Wulfstan', 2nd half of 11th c., Worcester.
411: Psalter (litany), end of 10th c., St Augustine's, Canterbury.
421: Homilies (Anglo-Saxon), 2nd quarter of 11th c., English.
422: Sacramentary and Ritual (calendar and litany), 'The Red Book of Darley', mid-11th c., Winchester and Sherborne (calendar).

473: Troper, 'Winchester Troper', 1st half of 11th c., Old Minster, Winchester.

Cambridge, Fitzwilliam Museum Library
88—1972: Gospel lectionary, 11–12th cc., St Augustine's, Canterbury.

Cambridge, Pembroke College Library
23, 24, 25: Homiliary, 11th c., Bury St Edmunds.
301: Gospel-book, 'Pembroke Gospels', *c*.1020, addns. 2nd half of 11th c., ? Canterbury.
302: Gospel lectionary, 'Hereford Gospels', *c*.1050, ? Canterbury, ? Hereford.
312 C, nos. 1, 2: Psalter fragments, mid-11th c., English.

Cambridge, Sidney Sussex College Library
100 (Part II): Pontifical and Miscellanea Liturgica, 1st half of 11th c., Winchester, then Durham.

Cambridge, St John's College Library
35: Gregory's Homilies on Ezekiel and note on the Three Maries, 11th c., English.
59: Psalter (litany), 10–11th cc., Ireland.
73: Gospel-book and Gospel lists, 11–12th cc., ? Bury, ? St Augustine's, Canterbury.
164: Translation of St Benedict at Fleury and sermon, 10–11th cc., St Augustine's, Canterbury.

Cambridge, Trinity College Library
B.1.40: Augustine *De LXXXIII Quaestionibus*, 11–12th cc., St Augustine's, Canterbury.
B.10.4: Gospel-book and Gospel lectionary, 'Trinity Gospels', 1st quarter of 11th c., ? Christ Church, Canterbury.
B.14.3: Arator *Historia apostolica*. Flyleaves 1–4: 9th c. mass for St Ambrose written at Nonantola, 10–11th cc., Christ Church, Canterbury.
B.16.3: Hrabanus Maurus *De laudibus sanctae crucis*, 2nd quarter of 10th c., south of England.
O.3.55: Life of St Cuthbert and list of relics, beg. 12th c., Durham.
R.15.14: Pseudo-Boethius, Antiphonary and Tonal, end of 10th c., St Vaast, Arras.
R.15.32: Computistica, (calendar), 11th c., Winchester, then moved to St Augustine's, Canterbury.

Cambridge, University Library
Ff.1.23: Psalter, mid-11th c., ? Winchcombe.
Gg.5.35: Miscellanea Theologica and Hrabanus Maurus, *De laude sanctae crucis*, mid-11th c., St Augustine's, Canterbury.
Ii.2.11: Gospel-book, 3rd quarter 11th c., Exeter.
Ii.2.19 and Kk.4.13: Homiliary, end of 11th c., Norwich.
Kk.5.32: Computistica and calendar, late 11th c., West Country.

Copenhagen, Royal Library
G.K.S.10.2°: Gospel book, late 10thc., New Minster, Winchester, then ? Peterborough.

Damme, Musée van Maerlant, now P. Getty Museum, California
9: Gospel lectionary fragment, *c*.1000, Canterbury.

Durham, Cathedral Library
A.III.29, B.II.2 and B.II.31: Homiliary, end of 11th c., Durham.

A.IV.19: Collectar, 'Durham Collectar', beg. 10th c., south of England, then Chester-le-Street and Durham.

B.III.32: Hymnal, 1st half of 11th c., Christ Church, Canterbury.

B.IV.24: Rule of St Benedict, Martyrology, Lanfranc's *Decretum*, and confraternity book, 2nd half of 11th c., Durham.

Durham, University Library

Cosin V.v.6: Gradual, end of 11th c., Christ Church, Canterbury.

Florence, Biblioteca Medicea Laurenziana

Amiatino 1: Bible Pandect, beg. 8th c., Jarrow.

Pluteo XVII.20: Gospel lectionary, 1st half 11th c., Christ Church, Canterbury.

Hanover, Kestner Museum

WM xxia 36: Gospel-book, *c.*1020, Christ Church, Canterbury.

Ivrea, Biblioteca Capitolare

31(LXXXVI): Sacramentary, end 10th c., Ivrea.

London, British Library

Additional 28188: Pontifical and Benedictional (litanies), 2nd half of 11th c., Exeter.

Additional 30337: Exultet Roll, 12th c., south of Italy.

Additional 34890: Gospel-book and Gospel lectionary, 'Grimbald Gospels', *c.*1020, Christ Church, Canterbury.

Additional 37517: Psalter and Hymnal (calendar and litany), 'Bosworth Psalter', end of 10th c., Canterbury.

Additional 40000: Gospel-book and lists, confraternity book, beg. of 10th c., Brittany, addns. 10th to 15th cc., Thorney.

Additional 47967: Orosius (King Alfred's transln.), 1st half of 10th c., Winchester.

Additional 49598: Benedictional, 'St Aethelwold's', 2nd half of 10th c., Old Minster, Winchester.

Additional 57337: Pontifical and Benedictional (litany), 10–11th cc., ? south of England, then ? Durham.

Arundel 60: Psalter (calendar and litany), 2nd half of 11th c., New Minster, Winchester.

Arundel 91: Legendary, 11–12th cc., St Augustine's, Canterbury.

Arundel 155: Psalter (calendar and litany), 1st quarter of 11th c., Christ Church, Canterbury.

Cotton Caligula A.XIV: Troper, 'Canterbury Troper' or 'Hereford Troper', mid-11th c., Christ Church, Canterbury.

Cotton Caligula A.XV: Computistica, 2nd half of 11th c., Christ Church, Canterbury.

Cotton Claudius A.III, fos. 31–86 and 106–50: Pontifical and Benedictional (litany), 'Claudius Pontifical', 10–11th cc., Worcester or York.

Cotton Claudius A.III, fos. 9–18 and 87–105: Pontifical (litany), 'Claudius Pontifical', 2nd half of 11th c., ? Christ Church, Canterbury, ? Worcester.

Cotton Domitian VII: Confraternity book, 'Liber Vitae of Durham', 9th c. onwards, Lindisfarne, Chester-le-Street, Durham.

Cotton Galba A.XIV and Cotton Nero A.II: Prayer-book (litanies), beg. 11th c., Nunnaminster, Winchester.

Cotton Galba A.XVIII: Psalter (litany and martyrology), 'Aethelstan's Psalter', 9th c., northern France; then beg. 10th c., Winchester.

Cotton Julius A.VI: Computistica and Hymnal, early and mid-11th c., Christ Church, Canterbury.

Cotton Nero A.III: Miscellanea Theologica and Liturgica (and calendar), 11th c., Wessex.

Cotton Nero E.I: Passional, *c*.1060, Worchester.

Cotton Tiberius A.II: Gospel-book and Gospel lists, 9th c., ? north east France, ? Germany, then Christ Church, Canterbury.

Cotton Tiberius A.III: Consuetudinary and Prayer-book (litany), mid-11th c., Christ Church, Canterbury.

Cotton Tiberius B.I: Poetical Menology, 10th c., English.

Cotton Tiberius B.V: 'Marvels of the East', calendar, Sigeric's Itinerary, 1st half of 11th c., ? Winchester.

Cotton Tiberius C.I, fos. 43–203: Pontifical (litany), Germany, 1st half of 11th c., then south of England.

Cotton Tiberius C.III: Rule of St Benedict, Regularis Concordia, offices, 1st half-mid 11th c., Christ Church, Canterbury.

Cotton Tiberius C.VI: Psalter, mid-11th c., Old Minster, Winchester.

Cotton Titus D.XXVI and D.XXVII: Collectar and offices (calendar and litany), 1st half of 11th c., New Minster, Winchester.

Cotton Vespasian A.VIII: Charter of King Edgar to New Minster, 966, New Minster, Winchester.

Cotton Vespasian D.XII: Hymnal, mid-11th c., Christ Church, Canterbury.

Cotton Vitellius A.VII: Pontifical (litanies), 1st half of or mid-11th c., Canterbury.

Cotton Vitellius A.XII: Miscellanea Theologica and Liturgica (and calendar), late 11th c., Exeter.

Cotton Vitellius A.XVIII: Sacramentary and Benedictional (calendar and litany), 2nd half of 11th c., Wells.

Cotton Vitellius C.XII: Martyrology, 11–12th cc., fos. 114–57, St Augustine's, Canterbury.

Cotton Vitellius E.XII fos. 116–60: Pontifical (litany), Germany, 1st half of 11th c., addns. York and Exeter, 2nd half of 11th c.

Cotton Vitellius E.XVIII: Psalter (and calendar), mid-11th c., New Minster, Winchester.

Harley 76: Gospel-book and Gospel lists, 'Bury Gospels', 1st half of 11th c., Bury, ? Christ Church, Canterbury.

Harley 603: Psalter, early 11th c., and addns., Christ Church, Canterbury.

Harley 652: Homiliary, 11–12th cc., St Augustine's, Canterbury.

Harley 863: Psalter (litany and addn. of a 12th c. martyrology), 2nd half of 11th c., Exeter.

Harley 1117: Lives of St Cuthbert; fos. 43–4, 63–6 services, 2nd half of 10th or early 11th c., Christ Church, Canterbury.

Harley 2892: Benedictional, 1st half of 11th c., Christ Church, Canterbury.

Harley 2904: Psalter (litany), end of 10th c., 'Harley Psalter', ? Ramsey, ? Winchester.

Harley 2961: Collectar, mid-11th c., 'Leofric Collectar', Exeter.

Harley 3271: Grammatical treatises; fols. 114^{r-v} Office for the Invention of St Stephen, 1st half of 11th c., English.

Landsdowne 383: Psalter (litany), 1st half of 12th c., Shaftesbury.

Royal 1.D.IX: Gospel-book and Gospel lists, *c*.1020, Christ Church, Canterbury.

Royal 1.E.VI: Gospel-book, *c*.1000, St Augustine's, Canterbury.

Royal 1.E.VII: Bible (2 vols.) *c*.1050–70, Christ Church, Canterbury.
Royal 2.B.V.: Psalter, 10th c., addn. of services 2nd half of 11th c., Winchester.
Royal 2.C.III: Hymnal, end of 11th c., Rochester.
Royal 6.A.VII: Life of St Gregory, early 11th c., Worcester.
Stowe 2: Psalter, mid-11th c., New Minster, Winchester.
Stowe 944: Gospel lectionary and confraternity book, 'Liber Vitae of New Minster', 1st half of 11th c., New Minster, Winchester.

London, College of Arms
Arundel 52: Gospel lectionary fragment, c.980, Winchester.

London, Lambeth Palace Library
427: Psalter, 1st half of 11th c., English.

London, Society of Antiquaries
154: Sacramentary fragment, end 10th c., Winchester.

Monte Cassino, Archivio della Badia
BB 437,439: Gospel-book, *c*.1050, English.
HH.9.9: Life of St Benedict, 1071–2, Monte Cassino.

New York, Pierpont Morgan Library
708: Gospel-book, 2nd half of 11th c., English.
709: Gospel-book, 2nd half of 11th c., English.
827: Continental Gospel-book, addns. by English artist at Fleury and St Bertin, 11th c.
869: Gospel-book, *c*.990–1000, Christ Church, Canterbury.

Orléans, Bibliothèque Municipale
123: Psalter and Breviary, 12th c., Fleury.
127: Sacramentary (litany), 'Winchcombe Sacramentary', 2nd half of 10th c., addns early 11th c., Winchcombe, possibly for Fleury.
175: Gregory's Homilies on Ezekiel, late 10th c., Fleury, AS illumination.

Oxford, Bodleian Library
Auct. D.2.16: Gospel-book, 10th c., Landévénnec, moved to Exeter.
Bodley 155: Gospel-book and Gospel lists, 10–11th cc.
Bodley 572: Miscellanea Theologica and Liturgica, 10–11th cc., Cornish or Welsh, then ? Winchester, then ? Canterbury.
Bodley 579: Sacramentary, Pontifical and Benedictional, Ritual (litany and calendar), 'Leofric Missal', northern France, 2nd half of 9th c.; Glastonbury, 2nd half of 10th c.; Exeter, mid-11th c.
Bodley 718: Penitentials (litany), 10–11th cc., Exeter.
Bodley 775: Troper and Gradual (litany), 'Winchester Troper', mid-11th c., Old Minster, Winchester.
Digby 39: Legendary, late 11th c., Abingdon.
Douce 296: Psalter (litany and calendar), mid-11th c., Crowland.
Fell 1, 3, 4: Legendary, end of 11th to early 12th c., Salisbury.
Hatton 48: Rule of St Benedict, 8th c., English.
Hatton 113: Homiliary (and calendar), 2nd half of 11th c., Worcester (? Evesham calendar).
Junius 11: Old English poetry, end 10th–beg. 11th c., ? Canterbury.
Junius 27: Psalter, beg. 10th c., ? Winchester.

Lat. lit. B.2: Lectionary, 2nd half of 11th c., Stavelot.

Laud. lat. 81: Psalter (litany), 2nd half of 11th c., English.

Laud. lit. F.5: Gospel lectionary, 'St Margaret's Gospel', 1st half or mid-11th c., Scotland, then Durham.

Laud. Misc. 482: Manual and Penitential (litany), 'Penitential of Egbert', mid-11th c., Worcester.

Tanner 3: Gregory's Dialogues, 2nd quarter of 11th c., ? Worcester.

Oxford, Wadham College Library
2: Gospel-book, *c.*1020–31, English.

Paris, Bibliothèque Nationale
grec 510: Sermons of Gregory of Naziansus, late 9th c., Constantinople.

lat. 272: Gospel-book and Gospel lists, 2nd half of 10th c., English.

lat. 943: Pontifical and Benedictional (litanies), 'Sherborne Pontifical', 2nd half of 10th c., ? Christ Church, Canterbury.

lat. 987: Benedictional, last quarter of 10th c., Winchester, possibly for Christ Church, Canterbury where it was at the beg. of 11th c.

lat. 6401: Boethius, end 10th c., Fleury, miniature by English artist.

lat. 7299: Calendar, 10–11th cc., English, fos. 3–12.

lat. 8824: Psalter (litany), mid-11th c., English.

lat. 10575: Pontifical and Benedictional (litanies), 'Pontifical of Egbert', mid-10th c., English.

Reims, Bibliothèque Municipale
9: Gospel-book, *c.*1060, English.

Rome, Vatican City, Biblioteca Apostolica Vaticana
Archiv. San Pietro F.12: Sacramentary (Gregorian, monastic), 11th c., Rome.

Borgia lat. 359: Epistolary and Gradual, 11th c., St Étienne of Besançon.

Chigi. C.VI.173: Breviary (calendar and litany), 10–11th cc., central Italian monastery.

Chigi. D.V.77: Breviary (Hymnal and offices), end of 11th c., San Vincenzo al Vulturno.

Ottobon. lat. 67: Bede, *De Temporibus*, and calendar, 11th c., St Denis.

Ottobon. lat. 313: Sacramentary (Gregorian), and Pontifical, 9th c., Paris.

Palat. lat. 485: Sacramentary (and calendar), 9–10th cc., Lorsch.

Palat. lat. 493: Missale Gallicanum Vetus, 8th c., Luxeuil.

Palat. lat. 1341: Varia and calendar, 10–11th cc., Trier–Lorsch.

Palat. lat. 1448: Computistica and calendar, 9th c., Mainz.

Regin. lat. 12: Psalter (litany and calendar), mid-11th c., Bury, ? Christ Church, Canterbury.

Regin. lat. 15: Gospel lectionary, beg. 11th c., Lorraine, Trier or Echternach.

Regin. lat. 257: Missale Francorum, beg. 8th c., Paris, Corbie, Soissons.

Regin. lat. 316: Sacramentary (Gelasian), Pontifical, and Ritual, 8th c., France.

Regin. lat. 317: Missale Gothicum, 7th–8th cc., Autun.

Regin. lat. 318; Saints' Lives and sermons, 9th–10th cc., Fleury.

Regin. lat. 338: Hymnal, Pontifical, and Ritual, 10th–11th cc., ? English.

Regin. lat. 465: Saints' Lives, 11th c., St Aubin of Angers.

Regin. lat. 466: Passions and offices, 11th c., St Thierry, Reims.

Regin. lat. 537: Saints' Lives and sermons, 12th c., Liège.

Regin. lat. 573: Saints' Lives, 11th c., ? Fontenelle-St Wandrille.

Regin. lat. 1263: Calendar, 11th c., St Mesmin de Micy, near Orléans.

Regin. lat. 1573: Calendar, 11th c., St Pierre of Ferrières-en-Gâtinais (diocese of Sens).

Regin. lat. 1864: Saints' Lives, 11th–12th cc., St Médard of Soissons.

Rossi. 204: Sacramentary (and calendar), 11th c., Austria, for St Maurice of Augsburg.

Urbin. lat. 585: Psalter and Collectar (Hymnal, calendar) 11–12th cc., Monte Cassino.

Urbin. lat. 602: Troper, 11–12th cc., Monte Cassino.

Vatic. lat. 84: Psalter, 10th c., Nonantola.

Vatic. lat. 645: Varia and calendar, 11th c., St Quentin en Vermandois.

Vatic. lat. 1189: Legendary and Homiliary, 10th–11th cc., Rome, monastery of San Gregorio *in Clivo Scauri*.

Vatic. lat. 1202: Life of St Benedict, 1071–2, Monte Cassino.

Vatic. lat. 1272: Missal, 11th c., Subiaco.

Vatic. lat. 3784: Exultet Roll, 11th c., Monte Cassino.

Vatic. lat. 3806: Sacramentary (and calendar), offices, Pontifical, 11th c., Fulda.

Vatic. lat. 5771: Legendary, 10th–11th cc., Bobbio.

Vatic. lat. 6080: Missal, 11th c., Chiusi.

Vatic. lat. 8565: Saints' Lives, 11th–12th cc., Malmédy.

Vatic. lat. 9820: Exultet Roll, 981–7, St Mary and St Peter's, Benevento.

Rouen, Bibliothèque Municipale

A.21: Gospel-book, 2nd half of 11th c., Abingdon.

A.27: Pontifical and Benedictional (litanies), 'Lanalet Pontifical', 1st half of 11th c., St Germans–Crediton.

A.44: Psalter and Hymnal (litany), end of 11th c., St Augustine's, Canterbury.

A.287: Sacramentary, 11th c., St Évroul.

A.290: Calendar, 10–11th cc., Jumièges.

A.328: Calendar, 12th c., Fécamp.

Y.6: Sacramentary (calendar, litany), 'Missal of Robert of Jumièges', 1st half of 11th c., ? Winchester, ? Christ Church, Canterbury.

Y.7: Pontifical and Benedictional (litanies), 'Benedictional of Archbishop Robert', end of 10th c., New Minster, Winchester.

Y.21: Calendar, 12th c., St Ouen, Rouen.

Y.41: Saints' Lives, end of 11th c., St Ouen, Rouen.

Y.196: Sacramentary, 11th c., Fontenelle-St Wandrille.

Salisbury, Cathedral Library

89: Gregory of Nazianzus; addn. of a litany, 11th c., English.

150: Psalter (calendar, litany) 'Salisbury Psalter', *c*.969–1006, prov. Salisbury.

157: Augustine, Isidore, etc.; fos. 90–1 Office of St Mary Magdalene, mid- or 2nd half of 11th c., ? south of England.

179: Homiliary, end of 11th c., Salisbury.

180: Psalter (litany), 10th c., Brittany, then Salisbury.

Worcester, Cathedral Library

F.91: Gospel lectionary, 11th c., English.

F.92: Homiliary, 2nd half of 11th c., English.

F.173: Sacramentary (litany), 1st half of 11th c., Old Minster, Winchester, then Worcester.

Q.5: Varia (Bede, Priscian) and Miscellanea Liturgica, 11th c., Worcester.

York Minster, Chapter Library
Add. 1: Gospel-book, 'York Gospels', 10–11th cc., Christ Church, Canterbury.

2. *Printed Sources*

ABBO of Fleury, see under Guerreau-Jalabert.

ABBO of Paris, 'Siège de Paris par les Normands', in Guizot, *Collection*, 7–66.

ADALBERO of Laon, see under Carozzi.

ADAM OF BREMEN, see under Schmeidler.

ADÉMAR of Chabannes, *Chronique*, in Pognon, *An Mille*, 145–209.

ADO's *Martyrology*, see under Quentin.

ADOMNÁN, see under Anderson, Meehan.

AELFRIC, see under Pope, Skeat, Thorpe.

AETHELWOLD, see under Winterbottom.

ALCUIM, see under Godman.

ALDHELM, see under Lapidge.

ALEXANDER, J. J. G. (ed.), *Insular Manuscript: Sixth to the Ninth Century*, vol. i of *A Survey of Manuscripts Illuminated in the British Isles* (London, 1978).

AMIET, J. R. (ed.), *The Benedictionals of Freising* (HBS 88; London, 1974).

ANDERSON, A. O., and ANDERSON, M. O. (eds. and trs.), *Adomnán's Life of Columba* (London, 1961).

ANDRIEU, M. (ed.), *Les Ordines Romani du haut Moyen Âge* (5 vols.; Spicilegium sacrum Lovaniense, 11, 23–4, 28–9; Louvain, 1931, 1948–51, 1956–61, repr. 1960–5).

ANSELM, see under Southern.

ARDO SMARAGDUS, *Diadema Monachorum*, P L 102, 593–690.

ARNOLD, T. (ed.), *Symeonis Monachi Opera Omnia* (2 vols.; RS; London, 1882–5). [Includes *Historia Dunelmensis Ecclesiae*, i. 3–135; *Historia Regum*, ii. 3–283; *Historia de Sancto Cuthberto*, i. 196–214].

—— (ed.), *Memorials of St Edmund's Abbey* (3 vols.; RS; London, 1890–6).

ARNOLD-FORSTER, F. M., *Studies in Church Dedications, or England's Patron Saints* (3 vols.; London, 1899).

ASSER, see under Keynes, Stevenson.

AVERY, M., *The Exultet Rolls of Southern Italy* (Princeton, 1936).

BANNISTER, H. M. (ed.), *'Missale Gothicum'* (2 vols.; HBS 52, 54; London, 1917, 1919).

BANTING, H. M. J. (ed.), *Two Anglo-Saxon Pontificals* (HBS 104; London, 1989).

BARKER, N., *et al* (eds.), *The York Gospels* (The Roxburghe Club; London, 1986).

BARLOW, F. (ed. and tr.), *Vita Aedwardi Regis qui apud Westmonasterium requiescit S. Bertini monacho ascripta: The Life of King Edward who Rests at Westminster Attributed to a Monk of St Bertin* (Nelson's Medieval Texts; London, 1962).

BATELY, J. (ed.), *The Old English Orosius* (EETS 6th ser.; Oxford, 1980).

BAUTIER, R. H., and LABORY, G. (eds.), *Helgaud de Fleury: Vie de Robert le Pieux: Epitoma vitae regis Rotberti pii* (Paris, 1965).

—— —— (eds.), *André de Fleury: Vie de Gauzlin, abbé de Fleury* (Paris, 1969).

BECKER, J. (ed.), *Liudprandus: Opera*, MHG SRG (Hanover and Leipzig, 1915).

BECKWITH, J., *Ivory Carvings in Early Medieval England* (London, 1972).

—— *Ivory Carvings in Medieval England 700–1200* (Catalogue of the Victoria and Albert Museum Exhibition, 1974).

BEDE, see under Colgrave, Dubois, Hurst, Plummer, Quentin.

BEHRENDS, F. (ed. and tr.), *The Letters and Poems of Fulbert of Chartres* (Oxford, 1976).

BEISSEL, S. (ed.), *Der heilige Bernward Evangelienbuch im Dome zu Hildesheim*, (Hildesheim, 1891).

Benedictional of St Thierry (Reims), P L 78. 605–28.

BERNWARD OF HILDESHEIM, *Vita Bernwardi episcopi Hildesheimensis auctore Thangmaro presbytero*, P L 140, 385–442.

BETHURUM, D. (ed.), *The Homilies of Wulfstan* (Oxford, 1957).

BIELER, L. (ed.), *Four Latin Lives of St Patrick* (Scriptores Latini Hiberniae, 8; Dublin. 1971).

BIRCH, W. DE G. (ed.), *Cartularium Saxonicum: A Collection of Charters relating to Anglo-Saxon History* (4 vols.; London, 1885–99, repr. New York, 1964).

—— (ed.), *Liber Vitae: Register and Martyrology of New Minster and Hyde Abbey, Winchester* (Hampshire Record Society, 5; London, 1892).

BLAKE, E. O. (ed.), *Liber Eliensis* (RHS Camden, 3rd series, 92; London, 1962).

BLOCH, M. (ed.), 'Vita beati ac gloriosi regis Anglorum Eadwardi: la Vie de S. Édouard le Confesseur par Osbert de Clare', *AB* 41 (1923), 5–63.

BÖCKLER, A. (ed.), *Das goldene Evangelienbuch Heinrichs III* (Berlin, 1933).

BOINET, A., *La Miniature carolingienne: ses origines, son développement* (Paris, 1913).

BONIFACE, see under Emerton.

BOURGIN, G. (ed.), *Guibert de Nogent: Histoire de sa vie* (Paris, 1907).

BOURQUE, E., *Étude sur les sacramentaires romains* (Studi d'antichità cristiana, 20, 25 pt. i: Les Textes primitifs; Vatican City, 1948; pt. ii: Les Textes remaniés, 2 vols.; Quebec, 1952; Vatican City, 1958).

BRENNER, E., 'Der altenglische Junius Psalter', *Anglistische Forschungen*, 23 (Heidelberg, 1908).

BRESSLAU, H. (ed.), *Die Werke Wipos: Gesta Chuonradi II Imperatoris*, MGH SRG (Hanover and Leipzig, 1915).

BRETT, M., BROOKE, C. N. L., and WINTERBOTTOM, M. (eds.), rev. from JOHNSON, C., *Hugh the Chanter: The History of the Church of York 1066–1127* (Oxford Medieval Texts; Oxford, 1990).

BROOKS, K. R. (ed.), *Andreas and the Fates of the Apostles* (Oxford, 1961).

BROU, L. (ed.), *The Psalter Collects from V–VIth Century Sources, edited from the Papers of the late A. Wilmart* (HBS 83; London, 1949).

BROWN, T. J., WORMALD, F., ROSS, A. S. C., and STANLEY, E. G. (eds.), *The Durham Ritual: Durham Cathedral Library A.IV.19* (EEMF 16; Copenhagen, 1969).

BRÜCKMANN, J., 'Latin Manuscript Pontificals and Benedictionals in England and Wales', *Traditio*, 29 (1973), 391–458.

BRUYLANTS, P., *Les Oraisons du missel romain* (2 vols.; Louvain, 1952, repr. 1965).

BULST, N. (ed.), with FRANCE, J., and REYNOLDS, P. (trs.), *Rodulfi Glabri Historiarum Libri Quinque: Rodulfus Glaber, 'The Five Books of the Histories'* (Oxford, 1989).

CAGIN, P. (ed.), *Sacramentaire gélasien d'Angoulême* (Angoulême, 1919).

CAMPBELL, A. (ed.), *Encomium Emmae Reginae* (RHS Camden, 3rd series, 72; London, 1949).

—— (ed.), *Frithegodi Monachi Breviloquium Vitae Beati Wilfredi et Wulfstani Cantoris Narratio Metrica de Sancto Swithuno* (Thesaurus Mundi; Zurich, 1950).

—— (ed.), *Chronicon Æthelwardi: The Chronicle of Æthelweard* (Nelson's Medieval Texts; London, 1962).

CAROZZI, C. (ed.), *Adalbéron de Laon: Poème au roi Robert* (Paris, 1979).

CECCHELLI, C., FURLANI, G., and SALMI, M., (eds.), *The Rabbula Gospels: Facsimile Edition of the Miniatures of the Syriac MS Plut. I.56 in the Medicean Laurentian Library* (Olten, 1959).

CHAMBERS, R. W., *et al.* (eds.), *The Exeter Book of Old English Poetry* (London, 1933).

CHAVASSE, A. (ed.), *Le Sacramentaire gélasien, Vaticanus Reginensis 316, sacramentaire présbytéral en usage dans les titres romains au VIIe siècle* (Tournai, 1958).

CHEVALLIER, U. (ed.), *Repertorium Hymnologicum* (6 vols; Louvain, 1892–1920).

—— *Sacramentaire et martyrologe de l'abbaye de Saint Rémy: Martyrologe, calendrier ordinaire et prosaire de la métropole de Reims (VIIIe–XIIIe siècles)* (Paris, 1900).

CHIBNALL, M. (ed. and tr.), *The Ecclesiastical History of Orderic Vitalis* (6 vols.; Oxford Medieval Texts; Oxford, 1968–80).

CLAYTON, M. (ed.), '*Assumptio Mariae*: An Eleventh-Century Anglo-Latin Poem from Abingdon', *AB* 104 (1987), 419–26.

CLOVER, V. H., and GIBSON, M. (eds. and trs.), *The Letters of Lanfranc, Archbishop of Canterbury* (London, 1979).

COENS, M. (ed.), 'Anciennes litanies des saints', *AB* 54 (1936), 5–37; 55 (1937), 49–69; 59 (1941), 272–98; 62 (1944), 126–68.

COLGRAVE, B. (ed. and tr.), *The Life of Bishop Wilfrid by Eddius Stephanus* (Cambridge, 1927).

—— (ed. and tr.), *'Two Lives' of St Cuthbert: A Life by an Anonymous Monk of Lindisfarne and Bede's Prose Life* (Cambridge, 1940, repr. 1985).

—— (ed. and tr.), *Felix's Life of St Guthlac* (Cambridge, 1956, repr. 1985).

—— (ed. and tr.), *The Earliest Life of Gregory the Great, by an Anonymous Monk of Whitby* (Lawrence, 1968, repr. Cambridge, 1985).

COLGRAVE, B., and MYNORS, R. A. B. (eds. and trs.), *Bede's Ecclesiastical History of the English People* (Oxford Medieval Texts; Oxford, 1969).

—— *et al.* (eds.), *The Paris Psalter: MS Bibliothèque Nationale fonds latin 8824* (EEMF 8; Copenhagen, 1958).

CONSTANTINE PORPHYROGENITUS, *Constantin VII Porphyrogénète: Le Livre des Cérémonies* (2 vols.; Paris, 1967).

DALTON, O. M. (ed. and tr.), *Gregory of Tours: History of the Franks* (2 vols.; Oxford, 1927).

DARLINGTON R. R. (ed.), *The Vita Wulfstani of William of Malmesbury: To which are Added the Extant Abridgements of this Work and the Miracles and Translations of St Wulfstan* (RHS Camden, 3rd series, 40; London, 1928).

—— (ed.), 'Winchcombe Annals 1049–1181', *A Medieval Miscellany for Doris Mary Stenton*, ed. P. M. Barnes and C. F. Slade (Pipe Roll Society, n.s. 36; London, 1962), 111–38.

DAWES, E. A. S. (ed. and tr.), *The Alexiad of the Princess Anna Comnena* (London, 1967).

DELEHAYE, H. (ed.), *Synaxarium Ecclesiae Constantinopolitanae*, AASS, Novembris, Propylaeum (Brussels, 1902).

DELISLE L., *Rouleaux des Morts du IXe au XVe siècle* (Société de l'Histoire de France; Paris, 1866).

—— *Mémoire sur d'anciens sacramentaires* (Mémoires de l'Académie des Inscriptions et Belles-Lettres, 32(1); Paris, 1886).

DESHUSSES, J. (ed.), 'Le Bénédictionnaire Gallican du VIIIe siècle', *Ephemerides Liturgicae*, 77 (1963), 169–82.

—— (ed.), *Le Sacramentaire grégorien: ses principales formes d'après les plus anciens manuscrits* (3 vols.; Spicilegium Friburgense, 16, 24, 28; Fribourg, 1971, 1979, 1982).

DEWALD, E. T. (ed.), *The Stuttgart Psalter* (Princeton, 1930).

DEWICK, E. S., and FRERE, W. H. (eds.), *The Leofric Collectar* (2 vols.; HBS 45, 56; London, 1914, 1921).

DOBLE, G. H. (ed.), *Pontificale Lanaletense* (HBS 74; London, 1937).

DODWELL, C. R., and CLEMOES, P. (eds.), *The Old English Illustrated Hexateuch: British Library Cotton Claudius B.IV* (EEMF 18; Copenhagen, 1974).

DOUGLAS, D. C., and GREENAWAY, G. W. (eds.), *English Historical Documents*, ii: 1042–1189 (London, 1953, 2nd edn. 1981).

DOUIE, D. L., and FARMER, [D.] H. (eds.), *Magna Vita Sancti Hugonis: The Life of St Hugh of Lincoln* (2 vols.; Nelson's Medieval Texts; London, 1961–2, repr. Oxford Medieval Texts; Oxford, 1986).

DREVES, G. M., and BLUME, C. (eds.), *Analecta Hymnica Medii Aevi* (55 vols.; Leipzig, 1886–1912; Indices, 3 vols.; Berne, 1978).

DUBOIS, J. (ed.), *Le Martyrologe d'Usard: texte et commentaire* (Subsidia Hagiographica, 40; Brussels, 1965).

—— and RENAUD, G. (eds.), *Édition pratique des martyrologes de Bède, de l'Anonyme lyonnais, et de Florus* (Paris, 1976).

DUCHESNE, L. (ed.), *Le Liber Pontificalis* (2 vols.; Paris, 1886–92, and vol. iii, rev. C. Vogel (Paris, 1957).

—— (ed.), *Commentarius in Martyrologium Hieronymianum*, AASS, Novembris II, ii, 1931.

DUGDALE, W., *Monasticon Anglicanum*, rev. ed. with adds. by J. Caley, H. Ellis, and B. Bandinel (6 vols.; London, 1817–30, repr. 1846).

DUMAS, A., and DESHUSSES, J. (eds.), *Liber Sacramentorum Gellonensis* (Corpus Christianorum Series Latina, 159, 159A; Turnhout, 1981).

DUMVILLE, D. and KEYNES, S. (gen. eds.), *The Anglo-Saxon Chronicle: A Collaborative Edition*, vol. iii, ed. J. Bately (Cambridge, 1986) and vol. iv, ed. S. Taylor (Cambridge, 1983).

DUNSTAN, see under Stubbs.

EADMER, see under Rule, Southern, Wilmart.

EARLE, J., and PLUMMER, C. (eds.), *Two of the Saxon Chronicles Parellel* (2 vols.; Oxford, 1892, 1899, repr. 1952).

EBNER, A. (ed.), *Quellen und Forschungen zur Geschichte und Kunstgeschichte des Missale Romanum im Mittelalter* (Iter Italicum; Freiburg, 1896, repr. Graz, 1957).

EDMUND, see under Arnold, Winterbottom.

EDWARD, see under Barlow, Bloch.

EHWALD, R. (ed.), *Aldhelm: De virginitate*, MGH, AA xv, 226–323 (verse), 350–471 (prose).

EMERTON, E. (ed. and tr.), *The Letters of St Boniface* (New York, 1940).

ESPOSITO, M. (ed.), 'La Vie de Sainte Vulfhilde par Goscelin de Cantorbéry', *AB* 32 (1913), 10–26.

FARMER, D. H. (ed.), *The Rule of St Benedict: Oxford, Bodleian Library MS Hatton 48* (EEMF 15; Copenhagen, 1968).

FLODOARD, see under Lauer, Lejeune.

FLORENCE OF WORCESTER, see under Thorpe.

Florus' Martyrology, see under Dubois, Quentin.

FONTAINE, J. (ed.), *Sulpice Sévère: Vie de St Martin* (3 vols.; Sources Chrétiennes, 133–5; Paris, 1967–9).

FOREVILLE, R. (ed. and tr.), *Guillaume de Poitiers: Histoire de Guillaume le Conquérant* (Paris, 1952).

FÖRSTER, M. (ed.), *Die Vercelli Homilien*, in C. W. M. Grein (ed.), *Bibliothek der angelsächsischen Prosa* (1st edn. R. P. Wülker, 13 vols.; Cassel and Göttingen, 1872–1933, xii; repr. Darmstadt, 1964).

—— *Der Vercelli Codex CXVII nebst Abdruck einiger altenglischen Homilien der Handschrift* (Halle, 1913).

FRANZ, G., and RONIG, F. J. (eds.), *Codex Egberti der Stadtbibliothek Trier: Entstehung und Geschichte der Handschrift* (Wiesbaden, 1984).

FRERE, W. H. (ed.), *The Winchester Troper* (HBS 8; London, 1894).

—— *Studies in Early Roman Liturgy*, i. The Kalendar; ii. The Roman Gospel-Lectionary; iii. The Roman Epistle-Lectionary (Alcuin Club Collections, 28, 30, 32; Oxford and London, 1930–5).

FULBERT of Chartres, see under Behrends.

GAGE, J., 'A Dissertation on St Aethelwold's Benedictional', *Archaeologia*, 24 (1832), 1–117.

GAMBER, K., *Codices liturgici latini antiquiores* (2 vols.; Spicilegii Friburgensis subsidia 1; 2nd edn.; Friboug, 1968).

—— DOLD, A., and BISCHOFF, B., *Sakramentartypen: Versuch einer Gruppierung der Handschriften und Fragmente bis zur Jahrtausendwende* (Texte und Arbeiten, 49–50; Beuron, 1958).

GASQUET, F. A., and BISHOP, E. (eds.), *The Bosworth Psalter* (London, 1908).

GERBERT, see under Lattin.

GERCHOW, J. (ed.), *Die Gedenküberlieferung der Angelsachsen* (Berlin and New York, 1988).

GERVASE OF CANTERBURY, see under Stubbs.

GILES, J. A. (ed.), *Lanfranci Archiepiscopi Cantuariensis Opera Omnia* (2 vols.; Oxford, 1844).

GISO OF WELLS, for the *History*, see under Hunter.

GLABER, see under Bulst.

GNEUSS, H. (ed.), *Hymnar und Hymnen im englischen Mittelalter: Studien zur Überlieferung, Glossierung und Übersetzung lateinischer Hymnen in England* (Tübingen, 1968).

GODMAN, P. (ed. and tr.), *Alcuin: The Bishops, Kings and Saints of York* (Oxford Medieval Texts; Oxford, 1982).

GOLDSCHMIDT, A. (ed.), *Die Elfenbeinskulpturen aus der Zeit der karolingischen und sächsischen Kaiser VIII–XI Jahrhundert* (4 vols.; Berlin, 1914–26).

GOODWIN, C. W. (ed.), *The Anglo-Saxon Legends of St Andrew and St Veronica* (Cambridge Antiquarian Society Octavo Pubs., 1; Cambridge, 1851).

GOSCELIN, *Historia Translationis S. Augustini Episcopi Anglorum Apostoli: Aliorumque sanctorum qui in ipsius monasterio Cantuariensi quiescebant, auctore Gocelino ejusdem loci monachi aequali*, P L 155, 13–46.

—— *Miracula Sancti Augustini episcopi Cantuariensis*, AASS Maii VI, 375–411.

—— *Miracula Sancti Ivonis*, in *Chronicon Rameseiensis*, pp. lix-lxxxiv.

—— *Wulfhild*: see under Esposito.

—— *Swithun*: see under Sauvage.

—— *Wulfsige* and the '*Liber Confortatorius*': see under Talbot.

—— *Edith*: see under Wilmart.

GOULBOURN, E. M., and SYMONDS, H. (eds. and trs.), *The Life, Letters and Sermons of Bishop Herbert de Losinga* (2 vols.; London, 1878).

GRANSDEN, A. (ed. and tr.), *Chronicle of Bury St Edmunds 1212–1301* (Nelson's Medieval Texts; London, 1964).

—— *The Customary of the Benedictine Abbey of Bury St Edmunds in Suffolk* (HBS 99; London, 1973).

GRANT, R. J. S. (ed.), 'Cambridge, Corpus Christi College 41: The Loricas and the Missal', *Costerus*, n.s. 17 (Amsterdam, 1973).

—— (ed.), *Three Homilies from Corpus Christi College Cambridge MS 41: The Assumption, St Michael and the Passion* (Tecumseh, 1982).

GRAT, F., VIELLIARD, J., and CLEMENCET, S. (eds.), *Les Annales de St Bertin* (Paris, 1964).

GREENWELL, W. (ed.), *The Pontifical of Egbert, Archbishop of York AD 732–766* (Surtees Society, 27; London, 1853).

GRÉGOIRE, R., *Les Homéliaires du moyen âge: inventaire et analyse des manuscrits* (RED series maior, 6; Rome, 1966).

—— 'Repertorium liturgicum Italicum', *Studi medievali*, 3rd series, 9 (1968), 465–592; with addenda in 11 (1970), 537–56, 14 (1973), 1123–32.

GREGORY THE GREAT, *Vita S. Gregorii papae, auctore Paulo Diacono*, P L 75, 41–60.

—— *Vita S. Gregorii papae, auctore Joanne Diacono*, ibid. 59–242.

—— *Dialogues*: see under de Vogüé, Moricca.

—— *Letters*: see under Norberg.

For the *Life* by a monk of Whitby, see under Colgrave.

GRIMALDI, G., *Descrizione della basilica antica di San Pietro in Vaticano, Cod. Barberini lat. 2733*, ed. R. Niggl (Vatican City, 1972).

GRIMME, E. G. (ed.), *Das Evangeliar Kaiser Otto III im Domschatz zu Aachen* (Freiburg, Basel, Vienna, 1984).

GUERREAU-JALABERT, A. (ed.), *Abbo Floriacensis Quaestiones Grammaticales* (Paris, 1982).

GUIBERT DE NOGENT, see under Bourgin.

GUIZOT, M. (ed. and tr.), *Collection de mémoires relatifs à l'histoire de France* (Paris, 1824).

HADDAN, A. W., and STUBBS, W. (eds.), *Councils and Ecclesiastical Documents Relating to Great Britain and Ireland* (3 vols.; Oxford, 1869–71).

HALLINGER, K. (ed.), 'Regularis Concordia Anglicae Nationis', in 'Consuetudinum saeculi X/XI/XII', *Monumenta Non-Cluniacensia, Corpus Consuetudinum Monasticarum, VII/3* (Siegburg, 1984), 61–147.

HALPHEN, L., and POUPARDIN, R. (eds.), *Chronique des comtes d'Anjou et des seigneurs d'Amboise* (Paris, 1969).

HAMILTON, N. E. S. A. (ed.), *William of Malmesbury: De Gestis Pontificum Anglorum libri quinque* (RS; London, 1870).

HAMPSON, R. T., *Medii Aevi Kalendarium: Or Dates, Charters and Customs of the Middle Ages* (2 vols.; London, 1841).

HANDSCHIN, J., 'The Two Winchester Tropers', *Journal of Theological Studies*, 37 (1936), 34–49, 156–72.

HARIULF, see under Lot.

HARMER, F. E. (ed.), *Anglo-Saxon Writs* (Manchester, 1952).

HARTZELL, K. D., 'An Unknown English Benedictine Gradual of the Eleventh Century', *ASE* 4 (1975), 131–44.

—— 'A St Albans Miscellany in New York', *Mittellateinsches Jahrbuch*, 10 (1975), 20–61.

HASKINS, C. H. (ed.), 'A Canterbury Monk at Constantinople, *c.*1090', *EHR* 25 (1910), 293–5.

HEARNE, T. (ed.), *Hemingi Chartularium ecclesiae Wigornensis* (2 vols.; Oxford, 1723).

HEIMING, O. (ed.), 'Die ältesten ungedruckten Kalender der mailändischen Kirche', in *Colligere fragmenta: Festschrift Alban Dold zum 70. Geburtstag am 7.7.1952*, ed. B. Fischer and V. Fiala Texte und Arbeiten; 1. Abteilung, 2. Beiheft; Beuron, 1952), 214–35.

HELGAUD DE FLEURY, see under Bautier.

HERZFELD, G. (ed.), *An Old English Maryrology* (EETS 116; London, 1900).

HESBERT, R. J., *Corpus Antiphonalium Officii* (6 vols.; RED series maior, 7–12; Rome, 1963–79).

HICKES, G., *Menologium seu Calendarium Poeticum ex Hickensiano Thesaurus: Or the Poetical Calendar of the Anglo-Saxons*, ed. and tr. S. Fox (London, 1830).

HOFFMANN, H. (ed.), *Chronica Monasterii Casinensis: Die Chronik von Montecassino*, MGH SS xxxiv (Hanover, 1980).

HOFMEISTER, A. (ed.), *Instituta Regalia . . . Camerae Regum Longobardorum*, MGH SS xxx (2). 1444–60.

HOLDER-EGGER, O. (ed.), *Vita Bernwardi Hildesheimensis Episcopi auctore Thangmari*, MGH SS iv. 754–82.

—— (ed.), *Folcuini Diaconi Gesta Abbatum Sithiensium*, MGH SS xiii. 607–63.

—— (ed.), *Miracula Sancti Ursmari*, MGH SS xv(2). 837–42.

—— (ed.), *Lamperti Monachi Hersfeldensis Opera*, MGH SRG (Hanover and Leipzig, 1894).

HOLTZMANN, W. (ed.), *Papsturkunden in England* (3 vols.; Abhandlung der Gesellschaft der Wissenschaften zu Göttingen, Philologisch-Historische Klasse, Neue Folge, Band 25, 1–2; Dritte Folge, 14–15, 33; Berlin and Göttingen, 1930–52).

HROSWITH of Gandersheim, see under de Winterfeld.

HUGH CANDIDUS, see under Mellows.

HUGH THE CHANTER, see under Brett.

HUGHES, A. (ed.), *The Portiforium of St Wulfstan* (2 vols.; HBS 89–90; London, 1958–60).

—— (ed.), *The Bec Missal* (HBS 94; London, 1963).

HULL, P. L. (ed.), *The Cartulary of St Michael's Mount: Hatfield House MS No. 315* (Devon and Cornwall Record Society, n.s., 5; Exeter, 1962).

HUNTER, J. (ed.), Giso of Wells, 'Historiola de primordiis episcopatus Somersetensis', in *Ecclesiastical Documents* (Camden Society; London, 1840), 9–20.

HURST, D. (ed.), 'In Marci Evangelium Expositio', in *Bedae Venerabilis Opera*, ii (3) (Corpus Christianorum Series Latina, 120; Turnhout, 1960), 431–648.

—— (ed.), 'De Temporum Ratione Liber LXVI: Chronica Maiora seu de Sex Aetatibus Mundi', in *Bedae Venerabilis Opera*, vi (2) (Corpus Christianorum Series Latina, 123B; Turnhout, 1977), 263–544.

IVO OF CHARTRES, *Canonical Collections*, PL 161, 47–1022, 1045–1344.

—— Letters: see under Leclercq.

JAMES, M. R. (ed. and tr.), *The Apocryphal New Testament* (2nd edn.; Oxford, 1953).
JOHN OF GORZE, see under Pertz.
JOST, K. (ed.), *Wulfstan's Institutes of Polity* (Berne, 1959).

KAHSNITZ, R., MENDE, U., and RÜCKER, E. (eds.), *Das goldene Evangelienbuch von Echternach* (Frankfurt, 1989).
KENDRICK, T. D., *et al.* (eds.), *Evangeliorum Quattuor Codex Lindisfarnensis* (2 vols.; Olten, 1960).
KER, N. R., *Catalogue of Manuscripts Containing Anglo-Saxon* (Oxford, 1957).
KEYNES, S. D., and LAPIDGE, M. (trs.), 'Asser's Life of King Alfred', in *Alfred the Great* (Harmondsworth, 1983), 67–110.
KEYSER, C. E., *A List of Norman Tympana and Lintels . . . in the Churches of Great Britain* (4 vols.; 2nd edn.; London, 1927).
KNOWLES, M. D. (ed.), *Lanfranci monachi Cantuariensis Constitutiones Monasticae* (Nelson's Medieval Texts; London, 1951).
—— (ed.), *Decreta Lanfranci monachis Cantuariensibus transmissa* (Siegburg, 1967), vol. iii of *Corpus Consuetudinum Monasticarum*, gen. ed. K. Hallinger.
KÖHLER, W. R. W. (ed.), *Drogo-Sakramentar: manuscrit latin 9428, Bibliothèque Nationale, Paris: Vollständige Faksimile-Ausgabe im Originalformat* (2 vols.; Graz, 1974).
KORHAMMER, P. M. (ed.), *Die monastischen Cantica im Mittelalter and ihre altenglischen Interlinearversionen* (Münchener Universitäts—Schriften, 6; Munich, 1976).
KOTZOR, G. (ed.), *Das altentglische Martyrologium* (2 vols.; Bayerische Akademie der Wissenschaften, Philologisch-Historische Klasse Abhandlungen, n.s. 88; Munich, 1981).
KRAUS, F. X. (ed.), *Die Miniaturen des Codex Egberti in der Stadtbibliothek zu Trier* (Freiburg, 1884).
KRUSCH, B. (ed.), *Vita Sanctae Balthildis*, MGH SSRM ii. 482–588.
LAMBOT, C. (ed.), *Northern Italian Services of the XIth Century* (HBS 67; London, 1931).
LAMPERT of Hersfeld, see under Holder-Egger.
LANFRANC, see under Giles, Knowles, Clover.
—— 'Acta Lanfraci', in Earle and Plummer, *Two Saxon Chronicles*, i. 287–92; tr. EHD ii, 631–5.
LAPIDGE, M., and HERREN, M. (eds. and trs.), *Aldhelm: The Prose Works* (Cambridge, 1979).
LAPIDGE, M., and WINTERBOTTOM, M. (eds. and trs.), *Wulfstan of Winchester: Life of St Aethelwold*, (Oxford Medieval Texts; Oxford, 1991).
LAPPENBERG, I. M., rev. KURZE, F. (ed.), *Thietmari Merseburgensis Episcopi Chronicon*, MGH SRG (Hanover, 1889).
LATOUCHE, R. (ed. and tr.), *Richer: Histoire de France (888–995)* (2 vols.; Paris, 1967, 1964).
LATTIN, H. P. (ed. and tr.), *The Letters of Gerbert* (New York, 1961).
LAUER, P. (ed.), *Les Annales de Flodoard* (Paris, 1906).
LECLERCQ, H., and HEFELE, C. J., *Histoire des conciles d'après les documents originaux* (11 vols.; Paris, 1911).
LECLERCQ, J. (ed.), *Yves de Chartres: Correspondance* (Paris, 1949).
LEGG, J. W. (ed.), *Three Coronation Orders* (HBS 19; London, 1900).
LEHMANN-BROCKHAUS, O. (ed.), *Schriftquellen zur Kunstgeschichte des 11. und 12.*

Jahrhunderts für Deutschland, Lothringen und Italien (2 vols.; Berlin, 1938).

—— (ed.), *Lateinische Schriftquellen zur Kunst in England, Wales und Schottland vom Jahre 901 bis zum Jahre 1307* (Veröffentlichungen des Zentralinstituts für Kunstgeschichte in München, 1; 5 vols.; Munich, 1955–60).

LEJEUNE, M., *et al.* (eds.), *Histoire de l'Église de Reims* (2 vols.; Reims, 1854).

LEMARIÉ, J., 'Textes relatifs au culte de l'Archange et des Anges dans les bréviaires manuscrits du Mont-Saint-Michel', *Sacris Erudiri*, 13 (1962), 113–52.

—— 'Textes liturgiques concernant le culte de St Michel', *Sacris Erudiri*, 14 (1963), 277–85.

LEROQUAIS , V. (ed.), *Les Sacramentaires et les missels manuscrits des bibliothèques publiques de France* (3 vols. and Pls.; Paris, 1924).

—— (ed.), *Les Bréviaires manuscrits des bibliothèques publiques de France* (5 vols. and Pls.; Paris, 1934).

—— (ed.), *Les Pontificaux manuscrits des bibliothèques publiques de France* (4 vols. and Pls.; Paris, 1937).

—— (ed.), *Les Psautiers manuscrits latins des bibliothèques publiques de France* (2 vols. and Pls.; Mâcon, 1940–1).

LEVILLAIN, L. (ed.), *Correspondance de Loup de Ferrières* (2 vols.; Paris, 1907).

LIEBERMANN, F. (ed.), *Ungedruckte anglo-normannische Geschichtsquellen* (Strasburg, 1879).

—— (ed.), *Die Heiligen Englands: Angelsächsisch und Lateinisch* (Hanover, 1889).

—— (ed.), *Die Gesetze der Angelsachsen* (3 vols.; Halle, 1903–1916).

LIETZMANN, H. (ed.), *Das Sacramentarium Gregorianum nach dem Aachener Urexemplar* (Münster, 1921, repr. 1967).

LINDELÖF, U. L., (ed.), *Der Lambeth-Psalter* (2 vols.; Acta Societatis Scienticarum Fennicae, 35 (1), 43 (3); Helsinki, 1909–14).

—— (ed.), *Rituale Ecclesiae Dunelmensis: The Durham Collectar* (Surtees Society, 140: London, 1927).

LITTLEHALES, H. (ed.), *English Fragments from Latin Medieval Service Books* (EETS extra series, 90; London, 1903).

LIUTPRAND of Cremona, see under Becker.

LOEW, E. A. (ed.), *Die ältesten Kalendarien aus Monte Cassino* (Quellen und Untersuchungen zur lateinische Philologie des Mittelalters, 3(3); Munich, 1908).

LOHMANN, H. E. (ed.), rev. HIRSCH, P., *Widukindi monachi Corbeiensis rerum gestarum saxonicarum libri tres*, MGH SRG (Hanover, 1935).

LOSINGA, see under Goulbourn.

LOT, F. (ed.), *Hariulf: chronique de l'abbaye de St Riquier* (Paris, 1894).

LOTTER, F. (ed.), *Die Vita Brunonis des Ruotger* (Bonn, 1958).

LOWE, E. A. (ed.), *The Bobbio Missal* (3 vols.; HBS 53, 58, 61; London, 1917, 1920, 1924).

—— (ed.), *Codices Latini Antiquiores* (Oxford, 1934–66).

LUARD, H. R. (ed.), *Annales Monasterii de Wintonia (AD 519–1277)*, in *Annales Monastici*, ii. 3–125 (RS; London, 1865).

McCANN, J. (ed.), *The Rule of St Benedict, in Latin and English* (London, 1952).

McGURKE, P. (ed.), 'The Metrical Calendar of Hampson: A New Edition', *AB* 104 (1986), 79–125.

—— *et al.* (eds.), *An Eleventh Century Anglo-Saxon Illustrated Miscellany: British Library Cotton Tiberius B.V.* (EEMF 21; Copenhagen, 1983).

MACRAY, W. D. (ed.), *Chronicon Abbatiae de Evesham ad annum 1418* (RS; London, 1863).
—— (ed.), *Chronicon Abbatiae Rameseiensis* (RS; London, 1886).
MAGNANI, L., *Le miniature dell'Sacramentario d'Ivrea e di altri codici warmondiani* (Rome, 1934).
MALLARDO, D. (ed.), 'Il Calendario Marmoreo di Napoli', *Ephemerides Liturgicae*, 58–60 (1944–6), 115–77, 233–94, 217–92.
MANSI, J. M. (ed.), *Sacrorum Conciliorum Nova et Amplissima Collectio* (31 vols.; Florence and Venice, 1759–98).
MARX J. (ed.), *Guillaume de Jumièges: Gesta Normannorum Ducum* (Paris, 1914).
MAYR-HARTING, H. M. R. E. (ed.), *The Acta of the Bishops of Chichester 1075–1207* (Torquay, 1964).
MEARNS, J. (ed.), *Early Latin Liturgical Hymnaries: An Index of Hymns in Hymnaries Before 1100* (Cambridge, 1913).
MEEHAN, D. (ed.), *Adomnán: De Locis sanctis* (Scriptores Latini Hiberniae, 3; Dublin, 1958).
MELLOWS, W. T. (ed.), *The Chronicle of Hugh Candidus, a Monk of Peterborough: With La Geste de Burch*, ed. A. Bell (Oxford, 1949).
Menologio: Il Menologio di Basilio II: Codex Vaticano Greco 1613 (2 vols.; Turin, 1907). Also pubished in J. P. Migne, Patrologia Graeca 117 (Paris, 1864), 19–614.
MERLET, R. (ed.), *La Chronique de Nantes (570 env.–1049)* (Paris, 1896).
METZ, P. (ed.), *The Golden Gospels of Echternach* (London, 1957).
MIESGES, P. (ed.), *Der Trierer Festkalender: Seine Entwicklung und seine Verwendung zu Urkundendatierungen: Ein Beitrag zur Heortologie und Chronologie des Mittelalters* (Trierisches Archiv Erg., 15; Trier, 1915).
Missale S. Eligii, P L 78, 25–582.
MÖLLER, E. (ed.), *Corpus Benedictionum Pontificalium* (2 vols. in 4; Corpus Christianorum Series Latina, 162, 162A–C; Turnhout, 1971–9).
—— (ed.), *Corpus Praefationum* (2 vols. in 5; Corpus Christianorum Series Latina, 161 and 161A–D; Turnhout, 1980–1).
MOHLBERG, K. (ed.), *Das Fränkische Sacramentarium Gelasianum in alamannischer Überlieferung (Codex Sangall. No. 348)* (St Galler Sakramentar-Forschungen I, 3, verbesserte Auflage; Liturgiewissenschaftliche Quellen und Forschungen, 1/2; Münster, 1971).
MOHLBERG, L. C. (ed.), *Missale Gothicum (Vat. Reg. Lat. 317)* (RED series maior, Fontes, 5; Rome, 1961).
—— et al. (eds.), *Sacramentarium Veronense (Cod. Bibl. Capit. Veron. LXXXV [80])* (RED series maior, Fontes, 1; Rome, 1956).
—— (eds.), *Missale Francorum* (RED series maior, Fontes, 2; Rome, 1957).
—— (eds.), *Missale Gallicanum Vetus* (RED series maior, Fontes, 3; Rome, 1958).
—— (eds.), *Liber Sacramentorum Romanae Aecclesiae Ordinis Anni Circuli (Sacramentarium Gelasianum)* (RED series maior, Fontes, 4; Rome, 1960).
MOLINIER, A. (ed.), *Les Sources de l'histoire de France: des origines aux guerres d'Italie, 1494* (6 vols.; Paris, 1901–6).
MORICCA, U. (ed.), *Gregorii Magni Dialogorum Libri IV* (Fonti per la Storia d'Italia; Rome, 1924).
MORRIS, R. (ed. and tr.), *The Blickling Homilies of the Tenth Century* (EETS 58, 63, 73; London, 1874–80).

MORTET, V., and DESCHAMPS, P. (eds.), *Recueil de textes relatifs à l'histoire de l'architecture . . . en France, au moyen–âge* (Paris, 1911–29).

MUIR, B. J. (ed.), *A Pre-Conquest English Prayer-Book* (HBS 103; London, 1988).

MURATORI, L. A. (ed.), *Litugia Romana Vetus . . . Gregorianum* (2 vols.; Venice, 1748).

NAPIER, A. S. (ed.), *The Old English Versions of the Enlarged Rule of Chrodegang, the Capitula of Theodulf and the Epitome of Benedict of Aniane* (EETS o.s. 150; London, 1916).

NEEDHAM, G. I. (ed.), *Lives of Three English Saints* (London, 1966).

NORBERG, D. (ed.), *Sancti Gregorii Magni Registrum Epistularum* (2 vols.; Corpus Christianorum Series Latina, 140, 140A; Turnhout, 1982).

NORMAN, H. W. (ed.), *The Anglo-Saxon Version of the Hexameron of St Basil and the Saxon Remains of St Basil's 'Admonitio ad Filium Spiritualem'* (London, 1848).

OBERTYNSKI, Z. (ed.), *The Cracow Pontifical* (HBS 100; London, 1977).

OESS, G., 'Der altenglische Arundel Psalter', *Anglistische Forschungen*, 30 (Heidelberg, 1910).

OHLGREN, T. H. (ed.), *Insular and Anglo-Saxon Illuminated Manuscripts: An Iconographic Catalogue c. AD 625–1100* (New York, 1986).

OMONT, H., *Miniatures des plus anciens manuscrits grecs de la Bibliothèque Nationale du VIᵉ au XIVᵉ siècle* (Paris, 1929).

ORDERIC VITALIS, see under Chibnall

OROSIUS (King Alfred's Translation), see under Bately.

OSWALD, see under Raine.

OURY, G., 'Les Messes de St Martin dans les sacramentaires gallicans, romano-francs, et milanais', *Études grégoriennes*, 5 (1962), 73–97.

PERTZ, G. H. (ed.), MGH SS iv [contains *Annales S. Maximini Trevirensis*, 6–7; *Annales Virdunenses*, 7–8; *Annales Leodienses*, 9–20; *Vita Brunonis altera*, 275–9; *Vita Johannis abbatis Gorziensis auctore Johanne abbate S. Arnulphi*, 335–7; *Gerhardi Vita S. Oudalrici episcopi*, 384–419; *Vita Deoderici episcopi Mettensis auctore Sigeberto Gemblacensi*, 462–83; *Widrici Vita S. Gerardi episcopi Tullensis*, 490–505; *Vita S. Adalberti episcopi auctore Johanne Canapario*, 581–95; *Purchardi Carmen de gestis Witigowonis abbatis*, 622–32; *Vita Adalberonis II Mettensis episcopi auctore Constantino abbate*, 659–72; *Vita Balderici episcopi Leodiensis auctore monacho S. Jacobi Leodiensis*, 725–38; *Vita Heriberti archiepiscopi Coloniensis auctore Lantberto*, 740–53].

—— (ed.), MGH SS vii [contains *Gesta pontificum Cameracensium*, 402–525; *Anselmi Gesta episcoporum Leodiensis*, 189–234].

PICARD, B. (ed.), *Das altenglische Aegidiusleben in ms Corpus Christi College Cambridge 303* (Freiburg, 1981).

PIPER, P. (ed.), *Libri confraternitatum Sancti Galli, Augiensis, Fabariensis*, MGH (Berlin, 1984).

PLANCHART, A. E., *The Reportory of Tropes at Winchester* (2 vols.; Princeton, 1977).

PLUMMER, C. (ed.), *Venerabilis Baedae Opera Historica* (2 vols.; Oxford, 1896). [Includes the Lives of the Abbots by Bede and by an anonymous author].

—— (ed.), *Irish Litanies* (HBS 62; London, 1925).

POGNON, E. (ed.), *L'An Mille* (Paris, 1947).

POPE, J. C. (ed.), *Homilies of Aelfric: A Supplementary Collection* (2 vols.; EETS 259, 260; London, 1967–8).

POTTER, K. R. (ed. and tr.), *William of Malmesbury: Historia Novella* (Nelson's Medieval Texts; London, 1955).

PUNIET, P. DE, 'Le Sacramentaire romain de Gellone', *Ephemerides Liturgicae*, 51 (1937), 13–63.

QUENTIN, H., *Les Martyrologes historiques du moyen-âge: étude sur la formation du martyrologe romain* (2nd edn.; Paris, 1908).

RAINE, J. (ed.), *The Historians of the Church of York and its Archbishops* (3 vols.; RS; London, 1879–94). [Includes the Lives of Oswald by an anonymous author and by Eadmer, and the Chronicle of the Archbishops of York.]

RICHER, see under Latouche.

RICHTER, G., and SCHONFELDER, A. (eds.), *Sacramentarium Fuldense saeculi X* (HBS 101; London, 1912 repr.).

RILEY, H. T. (ed.), *Gesta Abbatum Monasterii Sancti Albani a Thoma Walsingham* (3 vols.; RS; London, 1867–9).

ROBERTSON, A. J. (ed.), *The Laws of the Kings of England from Edmund to Henry I* (Cambridge, 1925).

—— (ed.), *Anglo-Saxon Charters* (Cambridge, 1939, repr. 1956).

ROBINSON, J. Armitage (ed.), *Flete's History of Westminster Abbey* (Cambridge, 1906).

ROLLASON, D. W. (ed.), 'Lists of Saints' Resting-Places in Anglo-Saxon England', *ASE* 7 (1978), 61–93.

—— (ed.), 'Goscelin of Canterbury's Account of the Translation and Miracles of St Mildrith (BHL 5961/4): An Edition with Notes', *Mediaeval Studies*, 48 (1986), 139–210.

RULE, M. (ed.), *Eadmeri Historia Novorum in Anglia* (RS; London, 1884). Books i–iv tr. G. Bosanquet (London, 1964).

—— (ed.), *The Missal of St Augustine's Abbey, Canterbury* (Cambridge, 1896).

SAUERLAND, H. V., and HASELOFF, A. (eds.), *Der Psalter Erzbischof Egberts von Trier* (2 vols.; Trier, 1901).

SAUVAGE, E. P. (ed.), 'Sancti Swithuni Wintoniensis episcopi translatio et miracula auctore Lantfredo monacho Wintoniensi', *AB* 4 (1885), 367–410.

—— (ed.), 'Vita Sancti Swithuni Wintoniensis episcopi auctore Goscelino, monacho Sithiensi', *AB* 7 (1888), 373–80.

SAWYER, P. H. (ed.), *Anglo-Saxon Charters: An Annotated List and Bibliography* (Royal Historical Society Guides and Handbooks, 8; London, 1968).

SCHIEL, H. (ed.), *Codex Egberti der Stadtbibliothek Trier* (Basel, 1960).

SCHMEIDLER, B. (ed.), *Adam von Bremen: Hamburgische Kirchengeschichte*, MGH SRG (Hanover and Leipzig, 1917).

SCHMITT, F. S. (ed.), *S. Anselmi Opera Omnia* (6 vols.; Edinburgh, 1946–61).

SCHOLZ, B. W. (ed.), 'Sulcard of Westminster, "Prologus de construccione Westmonasterii"', *Traditio*, 20 (1964), 59–91.

SCHRAMM, P. E., and MÜTHERICH, R., *Denkmale der deutschen Könige und Kaiser. Ein Beitrag zur Herrschergeschichte von Karl dem Großen bis Friedrich II 798–1250* (Munich, 1962).

SCOTT, J. (ed. and tr.), *The Early History of Glastonbury: An Edition, Translation and Study of William of Malmesbury's 'De Antiquitate Glastonie Ecclesie'* (Woodbridge, 1981).

SEARLE, E., (ed. and tr.), *The Chronicle of Battle Abbey* (Oxford Medieval Texts; Oxford, 1980).

SEDGEFIELD, W. J. (ed.), *King Alfred's Old English Version of Boethius' De Consolatione Philosophiae* (Oxford, 1899).

SIMEON THE HERMIT, *Vita Sancti Simeoni monachi et eremitae*, AASS Jul. VI, 319–37.

SISAM, C. (ed.), *The Vercelli Book* (EEMF 19; Copenhagen, 1976).

—— and SISAM, K. (eds.), *The Salisbury Psalter* (EETS o.s. 242; London, 1959).

SKEAT, W. W. (ed.), *Aelfric's Lives of the Saints: Being a Set of Sermons on Saints' Days* (2 vols. in 4 parts; EETS o.s. 76, 82, 94, 114; London, 1881–1900).

SOLESMES, BÉNÉDICTINS DE (eds.), *Le Graduel romain: édition critique, ii. Les Sources* (Solesmes, 1957).

SOPHRONIUS, *De Scta Maria Aegyptiaca et S. Zosima presb. monacho (Life of St Mary the Egyptian)*, AASS, Aprilis I, 67–83.

SOUTHERN, R. W. (ed. and tr.), *Eadmeri monachi Cantuariensis Vita Sancti Anselmi archiepiscopi Cantuariensis: The Life of St Anselm Archbishop of Canterbury by Eadmer* (Oxford Medieval Texts; Oxford, 1972).

STANTON, R. (ed.), *A Menology of England and Wales* (London, 1887).

STEVENSON, J. (ed.), *Liber Vitae Ecclesiae Dunelmensis* (Surtees Society 13; London, 1841).

—— (ed.), *The Latin Hymns of the Anglo-Saxon Church* (Surtees Society, 23; London, 1851).

—— (ed.), *Chronicon Monasterii de Abingdon* (RS; 2 vols.; London, 1858).

STEVENSON, W. H., *Asser: Life of King Alfred . . .* (Oxford, 1904, rev. edn. 1959).

STOKES, W. (ed.), *The Martyrology of Oengus the Culdee* (HBS 29; London, 1905).

STUBBS, W. (ed.), *Memorials of St Dunstan Archbishop of Canterbury* (RS; London, 1874). [Includes the Lives of St Dunstan by the 'B' author, Adelard, Osbern, Eadmer, and William of Malmesbury, and Sigeric's Itinerary].

—— (ed.), *The Historical Works of Gervase of Canterbury* (2 vols.; RS; London, 1879–80). [Includes *Chronica*, i. 3–594; *Gesta Regum*, ii. 3–106; *Actus Pontificum Cantuariensis Ecclesiae*, ii. 325–414.]

—— (ed.), *William of Malmesbury: De Gestis Regum Anglorum libri quinque* (2 vols.; RS; London, 1887–9.).

SWANTON, M. (ed. and tr.), *The Dream of the Rood* (New York and Manchester, 1970).

SWITHUN, see under Campbell, Needham, Sauvage.

SYMEON OF DURHAM, see under Arnold.

SYMONS, T. (ed. and tr.), *Regularis Concordia Anglicae Nationis Monachorum Sanctimonialiumque: The Monastic Agreement of the Monks and Nuns of the English Nation* (Nelson's Medieval Classics; London, 1953).

SZARMACH, P. E. (ed.), *Vercelli Homilies IX–XXIII* (Toronto, 1981).

TALBOT, C. H. (tr.), *The Anglo Saxon Missionaries in Germany: Being the Lives of St Willibrord, Boniface, Sturm, Leoba and Lebuin together with the Hodoeporicon of St Willibald and a Selection of Correspondence of St Boniface* (London, 1954).

—— (ed.), 'The *Liber Confortatorius* of Goscelin of Saint Bertin', *Studia Anselmiana*, 37 (1955), 1–117.

—— (ed.), 'The Life of Saint Wulfsin of Sherborne by Goscelin', *RB* 69 (1959), 68–85.

TEMPLE, E. (ed.), *Anglo-Saxon Manuscripts 900–1066*, vol. ii of *A Survey of Manuscripts Illuminated in the British Isles* (London, 1976).

THIETMAR of Meerseburg, see under Lappenberg.

THOMSON, R. (ed.), *The Life of Gundulf, Bishop of Rochester* (Toronto Medieval Latin Texts, 7; Toronto, 1977).

THORPE, B. (ed.), *The Homilies of the Anglo-Saxon Church: The First Part Containing the Sermones Catholici, or Homilies of Aelfric, in the Original Anglo-Saxon with an English Version* (Aelfric Society; 2 vols.; London, 1844–6).

—— *Florence of Worcester: Chronicon ex Chronicis* (2 vols.; London, 1848–9).

TOLHURST, J. B. L. (ed.), *The Monastic Breviary of Hyde Abbey, Winchester*, vi (HBS 80; London, 1942).

TURNER, D. H. (ed.), *The Missal of the New Minster, Winchester* (HBS 93; London, 1962).

—— (ed.), *The Claudius Pontificals* (HBS 97; London, 1971).

VACANDARD, E., 'Principaux écrits sur St Ouen du VIIe au XVIIe siècle', *AB* 20 (1901), 165–76.

VALENTINI, R., and ZUCCHETTI, G. (eds.), *Codice topografico della città di Roma* (4 vols.; Fonti per la storia d'Italia; Rome, 1940–53).

VAN DER HORST, K., and ENGELBREGHT, J. H. A. (eds.), *The Utrecht Psalter* (2 vols.; Graz, 1984).

VOGEL, C., and ELZE, R. (eds.), avec utilisation des collations laissées par M. Andrieu, *Le Pontifical romano-germanique du dixième siècle* (3 vols. in 2; Studi e Testi, 226, 227, 269; Rome, 1969–72).

VOGUÉ, A. DE, and ANTIN, P. (eds.), *Grégoire le Grand: Dialogues* (2 vols.; Sources Chrétiennes, 251–60; Paris, 1978–9).

—— and NEUFVILLE, J. (eds.), *La Règle de St Benoît* (6 vols.; Sources Chrétiennes, 181–6; Paris, 1971–2).

WARNER, G. F., *The Stowe Missal* (2 vols.; HBS 31–2; London, 1906–15).

—— and WILSON, H. A. (eds.), *The Benedictional of St Æthelwold* (Facsimile edited for the Roxburghe Club; Oxford, 1910).

WARREN, F. E. (ed.), *The Leofric Missal as Used in the Cathedral of Exeter AD 1050–1072* (Oxford, 1883, repr. Farnborough, 1968).

—— (ed.), *The Antiphonary of Bangor* (2 vols., HBS 4, 10; London, 1893, 1895).

WEST, R. C. (ed.), *Western Liturgies* (London, 1938).

WHITELOCK, D. (ed.), *Anglo-Saxon Wills* (Cambridge, 1930).

—— (ed.), *English Historical Documents*, i: *c*.500–1042 (London, 1955, 2nd edn. 1979).

—— BRETT, M., and BROOKE, C. N. L., (eds.), *Councils and Synods: With Other Documents Relating to the English Church*, vol. 1, pt. i: AD 871–1066; pt. ii: 1066–1204 (Oxford, 1981).

—— DOUGLAS, D. C., and TUCKER, S. I., *The Anglo-Saxon Chronicle: A Revised Translation* (London, 1961).

WIDUKIND of Corvey, see under Lohmann.

WIELAND, G. (ed.), *The Canterbury Hymnal* (Toronto Medieval Latin Texts, 12; Toronto, 1982).

WILDHAGEN, K. (ed.), *Der Cambridger Psalter* (Bibliothek der Angelsächsische Prosa, 7; Hamburg, 1910).

WILLIAM OF JUMIÈGES, see under Marx.

WILLIAM OF MALMESBURY, see under Darlington, Hamilton, Scott, Stubbs.

WILLIAM OF POITIERS, see under Foreville.

WILKINSON, J. (ed.), *Jerusalem Pilgrims before the Crusades* (Jerusalem, 1977).

WILMART, A. (ed.), 'Le "Comes" de Murbach', *RB* 30 (1913), 25–69.

—— (ed.), 'Les Reliques de St Ouen à Cantorbéry', *AB* 51 (1933), 285–92.

—— (ed.), 'Eadmeri Cantuariensis Cantoris Nova Opuscula de Sanctorum Veneratione et Obsecratione', *Revue des Sciences Religieuses*, 15 (1935), 184–219, 354–79. [Comprising *Ascriptum de Ordinatione Beati Gregorii Anglorum Apostoli*, 207–19; *De Reliquiis Sancti Audoeni et Quorundam Aliorum Sanctorum quae Cantuariae in Aecclesia Domini Salvatoris Habentur*, 362–70; *Insipida quaedam Divinae Dispensationis Consideratio Edita ab Eadmero Magno Peccatore de Beatissimo Gabriele Archangelo*, 371–9.]

—— 'La Légende de Ste Édith en prose et en vers par le moine Goscelin', *AB* 56 (1938), 5–101, 265–307.

—— *Precum Libelli Quattuor Aevi Carolini* (Rome, 1940).

WILSON, H. A. (ed.), *The Gelasian Sacramentary: Liber Sacramentorum Romanae Ecclesiae* (Oxford, 1894).

—— (ed.), *The Missal of Robert of Jumièges* (HBS 11; London, 1896).

—— (ed.), *The Benedictional of Archbishop Robert* (HBS 24; London, 1903).

—— (ed.), *The Gregorian Sacramentary under Charles the Great* (HBS 49; London, 1915).

—— (ed.), *The Calendar of St Willibrord* (HBS 55; London, 1918).

WINTERBOTTOM, M. (ed.), *Three Lives of English Saints* (Toronto Medieval Latin Texts; Toronto, 1972).

WINTERFELD, P. DE (ed.), *Hrosvithae Opera*, MGH SRG (Berlin, 1902).

WIPO, see under Bresslau.

WOOLLEY, R. M. (ed.), *The Canterbury Benedictional* (HBS 51; London, 1917).

WORMALD, F. (ed.), *English Kalendars Before AD 1100* (HBS 72; London, 1934).

—— (ed.), *English Benedictine Kalendars After AD 1100* (2 vols.; HBS 77, 81; London, 1939, 1946).

—— (ed.), 'The English Saints in the Litany in Arundel MS 60', *AB* 64 (1946), 72–86.

—— (ed.), 'An English Eleventh-Century Psalter with Figures, British Museum Cotton MS Tiberius C.VI', *The Thirty-Eighth Volume of the Walpole Society*, 1960–2 (Glasgow, 1962), repr. in Wormald, *Collected Writings*, 123–37.

—— (ed.), *The Winchester Psalter* (London, 1973).

WULFSTAN, see under Bethurum, Darlington, Jost.

YERKES, D. (ed.), *The Old English Life of Machutus* (Toronto, 1984).

ZILLIKEN, G. (ed.), *Der Kölner Festkalender: Seine Entwicklung und seine Verwendung zu Urkundendatierungen: Ein Beitrag zur Heortologie und Chronologie des Mittelalters*, *Bonner Jahrbücher des Vereins von Alterthumsfreunden*, 119 (Bonn, 1910).

II. SECONDARY LITERATURE

Abbaye St Wandrille de Fontenelle, L' (Fontenelle, 1957)

ABRAMS, L., and CARLEY, J. P. (eds.), *The History and Archaeology of Glastonbury Abbey: Essays in Honour of the Ninetieth Birthday of C. A. Ralegh Radford* (Woodbridge, 1991).

ACHELIS, H., *Die Katakomben von Neapel* (Leipzig, 1936).

ADAMSKI, H. J., *Die Christussaüle im Dom zu Hildesheim* (Hildesheim, 1979).

ADDEO, A., *Pavia e Sant'Agostino* (Pavia, 1950).

ALEXANDER, J. J. G., *Norman Illumination at Mont Saint Michel 966–1100* (Oxford, 1970).

ALEXANDER, J. W., 'Herbert of Norwich 1091–1119', *Studies in the History of Norman England*, 6 (1969), 115–232.

ALLEN BROWN, R., *English Castles* (3rd edn.; London, 1976).

ANCONA, P. d', *La Miniature italienne du Xe au XIVe siècle* (Paris and Brussels, 1925).

Angli e Sassoni al di qua e al di là del mare (Settimane, 1984; 2 vols.; Spoleto, 1986).

ANGOLD, M., *The Byzantine Empire 1025–1206: A Political History* (London and New York, 1984).

ARMELLINI, M., rev. CECCHELLI, C., *Le chiese di Roma dal secolo IV al secolo XIX* (2 vols.; Rome, 1942).

ARMITAGE, E. S., *The Early Norman Castles of the British Isles* (London, 1912).

ARNALDI, G., *Le origini dello stato della Chiesa* (Turin, 1987).

—— *Natale 875; Politica, Ecclesiologia, Cultura del papato altomedievale* (Rome, 1990).

ARONSTAM, R. A., 'Pope Leo IX and England', *Speculum*, 49 (1974), 535–41.

—— 'Penitential Pilgrimages to Rome', *Archivio Storico Pontificio*, 13 (1975), 65–83.

Art mosan, L', (Paris, 1953).

Art mosan et arts anciens du pays de Liège (Liège, 1951).

ATKINS, Sir I., 'An Investigation of two Anglo-Saxon Kalendars (Missal of Robert of Jumièges and St Wulfstan's Homiliary)', *Archaeologia*, 78 (1928), 219–54.

—— 'The Church of Worcester from the Eighth to the Twelfth Century', *The Antiquaries Journal*, 17(4) (1937), 371–91, 20 (1940), 1–38.

ATROSHENKO, V. I., and COLLINS, J., *The Origins of the Romanesque: Near Eastern Influences on European Art 4th–12th Centuries* (London, 1990).

AUBERT, E., *Trésor de l'Abbaye de St Maurice d'Agaune* (Paris, 1872).

AUDA, A., *L'École musicale liégeoise au Xe siècle; Étienne de Liège* (Brussels, 1923).

AURENHAMMER, H., *Lexikon der christlichen Ikonographie A-Chr* (Vienna, 1959–67).

AVAGLIANO, F. (ed.), *Una grande abbazia altomedioevale nel Molise: S. Vincenzo al Vulturno* (Miscellanea Cassinese, 51; Montecassino, 1985).

AVERY, M., and INGUANEZ, M., *Miniature cassinensi del secolo XI illustranti la 'Vita di San Benedetto'* (Monte Cassino, 1934).

AYTON, A., and DAVIES, V., 'Ecclesiastical Wealth in England in 1086', in W. J. Shiels and D. Wood (ed.), *Studies in Church History*, 24 (Oxford, 1988), 47–60.

BACKHOUSE, J., 'The Making of the Harley Psalter', *British Library Journal*, 10 (1984), 97–113.

—— , TURNER, D. H., and WEBSTER, L. (eds.), *The Golden Age of Anglo-Saxon Art 966–1066* (London, 1984).

BADAWI, A., *Coptic Art and Archaeology* (Cambridge, Mass., 1978).

BAIX, F., *L'Abbaye et la principauté de Stavelot–Malmédy* (Brussels, 1981).

BAKER, A. T., 'Vie de Ste Marie l'Égyptienne', *Revue des Langues Romanes*, 59 (1916–17), 145–401.

BAKER, D. (ed.), *Byzantium and the West in the Middle Ages* (Edinburgh, 1973).

BAKER, E. P., 'The Cult of St Alban of Cologne', *The Archaeological Journal*, 94 (1937), 207–56.

BALDWIN-BROWN, G., *The Arts in Early England* (6 vols.; London, 1937).

—— , and CHRISTIE, A. H., 'St Cuthbert's Stole and Maniple at Durham', *Burlington Magazine*, 23 (1913), 3–17, 67–72.

BARKER, E. R., *Rome of the Pilgrims and Martyrs* (London, 1913).

BARLOW, F., *The Feudal Kindom of England 1042–1216* (London, 1955).

—— 'Two Notes: Cnut's Second Pilgrimage and Queen Emma's Disgrace in 1043', *EHR* 73 (1958), 649–51, repr. *Norman Conquest*, 49–56.

—— 'Edward the Confessor's Early Life, Character and Attitudes', *EHR* 80 (1965), 225–51, repr. *Norman Conquest*, 57–83.

—— 'The Vita Aedwardi (Book II): The Seven Sleepers', *Speculum*, 40 (1965), 385–97, repr. *Norman Conquest*, 99–111.

—— *Edward the Confessor* (London, 1970).

—— *The English Church 1000–1066* (2nd edn.; London, 1979).

—— *The English Church 1066–1154: A History of the Anglo–Norman Church* (London, 1979).

—— *The Norman Conquest and Beyond* (London, 1983).

——, DEXTER, K., ERSKINE, A. M., and LLOYD, L. J. (eds.), *Leofric of Exeter: Essays in Commemoration of the Foundation of Exeter Cathedral Library in AD 1072* (Exeter, 1972).

BARRÉ, H., 'L'Apport marial de l'Orient à L'Occident de St Ambroise à St Anselme', *Études mariales*, 19 (1962), 27–89.

—— *Prières anciennes de Occident à la Mère du Sauveur des origines à St Anselme* (Paris, 1963).

BATELY, J. M., 'Grimbald of St Bertin's', *Medium Aevum*, 35 (1966), 1–10.

BATES, D., *Normandy Before 1066* (London, 1982).

—— *William the Conqueror* (London, 1989).

BATTISCOMBE, C. F. (ed.), *The Relics of St Cuthbert* (Oxford, 1956).

BAUMSTARK, A., *Comparative Liturgy* (tr. London, 1958).

BECKWITH, J., *Coptic Sculpture* (London, 1963).

—— *Early Medieval Art: Carolingian, Ottonian, Romanesque* (London, 1964).

—— *The Art of Constantinople: An Introduction to Byzantine Art 330–1453* (2nd edn.; London, 1968).

—— *Early Christian and Byzantine Art* (London, 1970).

BEECH, G., 'The Participation of Aquitanians in the Conquest of England, 1066–1100', *Anglo-Norman Studies*, 9 (1986), 1–24.

—— 'England and Aquitaine in the Century Before the Norman Conquest', *ASE* 19 (1990), 81–101.

BEISSEL, S., *Geschichte der Trieren Kirchen, ihrer Reliquien und Kunstschätze* (Trier, 1887–9).

—— *Der heilige Bernward von Hildesheim als Künstler und Förderer der deutschen Kunst* (Hildesheim, 1895).

BELLI BARSALI, I., 'La topografia di Lucca nei secoli VIII–X', *Atti del 5. Congresso Internazionale di Studi sull'Alto Medioevo (Lucca)* (Spoleto, 1973), 461–554.

BENATI, P., *Sta Cecilia nella leggenda e nell'arte* (Milan, 1928).

BENSON, G. R., and TSELOS, D. T., 'New Lights on the Origins of the Utrecht Psalter', *The Art Bulletin*, 13 (1931), 13–53.

BERG, K., 'The Gosforth Cross', *JWCI* 21 (1958), 27–43.

BERLIÈRE, U., 'L'Étude des réformes monastiques des Xᵉ et XIᵉ siècles', *Bulletin de l'Académie Royale de Belgique, Lettres* (1932).

BERTAUX, E., *L'Art dans l'Italie méridionale de la fin de l'Empire romain à la conquête de Charles d'Anjou* (2 vols.; Paris and Rome, 1903, repr. 1968).

BERTELLI, C., *La Madonna del Pantheon* (Rome, 1961).

—— *La Madonna di Santa Maria in Trastevere* (Rome, 1961).

BERTOLINI, O., *Roma di fronte a Bisanzio e ai Longobardi* (Bologna, 1941).

BESTUL, T. H., 'St Anselm and the Continuity of Anglo-Saxon Devotional Traditions', *Annuale Medievale*, 18 (1977), 20–41.

—— 'Continental Sources of Anglo-Saxon Devotional Writing', in Szarmach, *Sources*, 103–26.

BEUMANN, H., 'Das Kaisertum Otto des Große: Ein Rückblick nach Tausend Jahren', *Historische Zeitschrift*, 195 (1962), 529–73.

BEUMANN, H., *Die Ottonen* (Stuttgart, 1987).

BEURATH, H., *Die Kaiserin Theophano* (Stuttgart and Berlin, 1940).

BEYERLE, K., *Die Kultur der Abtei Reichenau* (2 vols.; Munich, 1925).

BIDDLE, M. (ed.), *Winchester in the Early Middle Ages: An Edition and Discussion of the Winton Domesday* (Oxford, 1976).

BINDING, G., *Bischof Bernward als Architekt der Michaeliskirche in Hildesheim* (Cologne, 1987).

BINNS, A. M., *Monastic Dedications of England and Wales 1066–1216* (Woodbridge, 1989).

BISCHOFF, B., 'Das griechische Element in der abendländischen Bildung des Mittelalters', *Byzantinische Zeitschrift*, 44 (1951), 27–55.

BISCHOFF, B., *Paläographie des römischen Altertums und des abendländischen Mittelalters* (Berlin, 1979).

BISHOP, E., *Liturgica Historica: Papers on the Liturgy and Religious Life of the Western Church*, ed. R. H. Connolly and K. Sisam (Oxford, 1918).

BISHOP, T. A. M., 'The Copenhagen Gospel Book', *Nordisk Tidskrift for Bok- och Bibliotheksvasen*, 54 (1967), 33–41.

BLAIR, J. (ed.), *Ministers and Parish Churches: The Local Church in Transition 950–1200* (Oxford, 1988).

BLAKE, D., 'The Chapter of Exeter', *Journal of Medieval History*, 8 (1982), 1–11.

BLOCH, H., *Monte Cassino in the Middle Ages* (3 vols.; Rome, 1987).

BLOCH, M., *Les Rois thaumaturges* (3rd edn.; Paris, 1983).

BLOCH, P., and SCHNITZLER, H., *Die ottonische Kölner Malerschule* (2 vols.; Düsseldorf, 1970).

BLUMENTHAL, U.-R., *The Investiture Contest: Church and Monarchy from the Ninth to the Twelfth Century* (Philadelphia, 1988).

BOASE, T. S. R., *English Art 1066–1216* (Oxford, 1853).

BOCCOLINI, I., 'L'iconographia di S. Benedetto', in *S. Gregorio Magno, Vita e miracoli di S. Benedetto* (Rome, 1954).

BODDEN, M. C., 'Evidence for Knowledge of Greek in Anglo-Saxon England', *ASE* 17 (1988), 217–46.

BÖCK, H., *Einsiedeln: Das Kloster und seine Geschichte* (Zurich and Munich, 1989).

BÖHMER, H., *Kirche und Staat in England und in der Normandie im XI. und XII. Jahrhundert* (Leipzig, 1899).

BOLGAR, R. R. (ed.), *Classical Influences on European Culture* AD 500–1500 (Cambridge, 1971).

BONNER, G. (ed.), *Famulus Christi* (London, 1976).

——, ROLLASON, D., and STANCLIFFE, C. (eds.), *St Cuthbert: His Cult and Community to AD 1200* (Woodbridge, 1989).

BORNSCHEUER, L., *Miseriae Regum: Untersuchungen zum Krisen- und Todesgedanken in der Herrschaftstheologischen Vorstellung der ottonisch–salischen Zeit* (Berlin, 1968).

BOSHOF, E., *Das Erzstift Trier und seine Stellung zu Königtum und Papstum in ausgehenden 10. Jahrhundert: Der Pontifikat des Theuderichs* (Cologne and Vienna, 1972).

BOSL, K., GIEYSZTOR, A., GRAUS, F., POSTAN, M. M., SEIBT, F., and BARRACLOUGH, G. (eds.), *Eastern and Western Europe in the Middle Ages* (London, 1970).

BOUARD, M. DE (ed.) *Histoire de la Normandie* (Toulouse, 1970).

BOUSSARD, J., *The Civilization of Charlemagne* (London, 1968).

—— *Nouvelle histoire de Paris: De la fin du siège de 885–886 à la mort de Philippe Auguste* (Paris, 1976).

BOUTÉMY, A., 'Un grand enlumineur du Xᵉ siècle: l'abbé Odbert de St Bertin', *Annales de la Fédération Archéologique et Historique de la Belgique*, 32 (1947), 247–54.

—— 'Odbert de St Bertin et la Seconde Bible de Charles le Chauve', *Scriptorium*, 4 (1950), 101–2.

—— 'L'Enluminure anglaise de l'époque saxonne (Xᵉ et XIᵉ siècles) et la Flandre française', *Bulletin de la Société Nationale des Antiquaires de France*, (1956), 42–50.

—— 'Un monument capital de l'enluminure anglo-saxonne: le manuscrit 11 de Boulogne-sur-Mer', *Cahiers de Civilisation Médiévale*, 1(2) (1958), 179–82.

BOYLE, L., *St Clement's, Rome* (Rome, 1989).

BRAUNFELS, W., *Die Welt der Karolinger und ihre Kunst* (Munich, 1964).

—— (ed.), *Lexikon der christlichen Ikonographie* (8 vols.; Freiburg, 1968–76)

——, and SCHNITZLER, H. (eds.), *Karl der Grosse: Lebenswerk und Nachleben* (3 vols.; iii, *Karolingische Kunst*, Düsseldorf, 1965).

BRENK, B., *Die frühchristlichen Mosaiken in S. Maria Maggiore zu Rom* (Wiesbaden, 1975).

BROOKE, C. N. L., 'Gregorian Reform in Action: Clerical Marriage in England 1050–1200', *Cambridge History Journal*, 12 (1956), 1–21.

—— 'Archbishop Lanfranc, the English Bishops and the Council of London of 1075', *Collectanea S. Kuttner*, ed. G. Forchielle and A. M. Stickler (Bologna, 1967).

—— *Europe in the Central Middle Ages 962–1154* (2nd edn.; London, 1987).

—— and KEIR, G., *London 800–1216: The Shaping of a City* (London, 1975).

——, and SWAAN, W., *The Monastic World 1000–1300* (London, 1974).

BROOKE, R., and BROOKE C., 'I vescovi di Inghilterra e Normandia nel secolo XI: contrasti', *Le istituzioni ecclesiastiche della 'societas christiana' dei secoli XI–XII; diocesi, pievi e parrochie* (Atti della sesta settimana internazionale di studio, Milan, 1974).

—— —— *Popular Religion in the Middle Ages: Western Europe 1000–1400* (London, 1984).

BROOKE, Z. N., *The English Church and the Papacy from the Conquest to the Reign of John* (Cambridge, 1931).

BROOKS, N., *The Early History of the Church of Canterbury: Christ Church from 597 to 1066* (Leicester, 1984).

BROWN, J. A., *The Normans and the Norman Conquest* (2nd edn.; Woodbridge, 1985).

BROWN, P., *The Cult of the Saints: Its Rise and Function in Latin Christianity* (London, 1981).

BROWNRIGG, L. L., 'Manuscripts Containing English Decoration 871–1066, Catalogued and Illustrated: A Review', *ASE* 7 (1978), 239–65.

BRUCE-MITFORD, R. L. S., 'The Reception by the Anglo-Saxons of Mediterranean Art Following their Conversion from Ireland and Rome', *Settimane*, 14 (1967), 797–825.

—— *The Art of the Codex Amiatinus* (Jarrow Lecture, 1967).

—— (ed.), *The Sutton Hoo Ship Burial* (4 vols.; London, 1983).

BRÜCK, A. P. (ed.), *Willigis und sein Dom: Festschrift zur Jahrtausendfeier des Mainzer Domes 975–1975* (Mainz, 1975).

BRÜHL, K., 'Die Kaiserpfalz bei St Peter und die Pfalz Ottos III auf dem Palatin', *Quellen und Forschungen aus Italienischen Archiven und Bibliotheken*, 34 (1954), 1–30.

—— *Fodrum, Gistum, Servitium Regis* (2 vols.; Cologne and Vienna, 1968).

BUCHTAL, H., 'Some Representations from the Life of St Paul in Byzantine and Carolingian Art', *Tortulae: Studien zu altchristlichen und byzantinischen Monumenten*, ed. W. N. Schuhmacher (Rome, Freiburg, and Vienna, 1966), 43–8.

BULLOUGH, D., 'Urban Change in Early Medieval Italy: The Example of Pavia', *Papers of the British School at Rome*, 34 (1966), 82–130.

—— *The Age of Charlemagne* (2nd edn.; London, 1973).

—— 'Alcuin and the Kingdom of Heaven: Liturgy, Theology and the Caroligian Age', in V. R. Blumenthal (ed.), *Caroligian Essays* (Washington, 1980).

BULST, N., *Untersuchungen zu den Klosterreformen Wilhelms von Dijon (962–1031)* (Bonn, 1973).

BUNJES, H., *et al.* (eds.), *Die kirchlichen Denkmäler der Stadt Trier* (Düsseldorf, 1938).

BUR, M., *La Formation du comté de Champagne* (Nancy, 1977).

BURRIDGE, A. W., 'L'Immaculée Conception dans la théologie de l'Angleterre médiévale', *Revue d'Histoire Ecclésiastique*, 32 (1936), 570–97.

BUTLER, C., 'St Dunstan's Kyrie', *Downside Review*, 5 (1885), 49–51.

BUTLER, L. A. S., and MORRIS, R. K. (eds.), *The Anglo-Saxon Church* (CBA Research Report 60; Cambridge, 1986).

BÜTTNER, H., 'Erzbischof Willigis von Mainz', in *Zur Frühmittelalterlichen Reichsgeschichte am Rhein, Main und Neckar*, ed. A. Gerlich (Darmstadt, 1975), 301–13.

CABROL, F., *The Books of the Latin Liturgy* (London, 1932).

——, and LECLERCQ, J., *Dictionnaire d'archéologie chrétienne et de liturgie* (15 vols.; Paris, 1907–53).

CAHEN, C., *Orient et Occident au temps des Croisades* (Paris, 1983).

CAMES, G., *Byzance et la peinture romane de Germanie: apports de l'art grec posticonoclaste à l'enluminure et à la fresque ottoniennes et romanes de Germanie dans les thèmes de majesté et les Évangiles* (Paris, 1966).

CAMBELL, J. (ed.), *The Anglo-Saxons* (Oxford, 1982).

—— *Essays in Anglo-Saxon History* (London, 1986).

CANCELLIERI, F., 'La visita de' sacri limini ed il denaro di S. Pietro', *Giornale Arcadico*, 10 (1821), 264–82.

CANTOR, N. F., *Church, Kingship and Lay Investiture in England 1089–1135* (Princeton, 1958).

CAPELETTI, G., *Le chiese d'Italie dalla loro origine sino ai nostri giorni* (21 vols.; Venice, 1844–70).

CAPITANI, O., 'Chiese e monaseri pavesi nel secolo X', *Pavia capitale di regno: Atti del 4° congresso internazionale di studi sull'alto medioevo 1967* (Spoleto, 1969).

CARLEY, J. P., 'John Leland and the Contents of English Pre-Dissolution Monasteries: Glastonbury Abbey', *Scriptorium*, 40 (1987), 107–20.

—— *Glastonbury Abbey: The Holy House at the Head of the Moors Adventurous* (Woodbridge, 1988).

CASAGRANDE, M., *I codici warmondiani e la cultura a Ivrea fra X e XI secolo* (Pavia, 1971–4).

CASPAR, E., *Geschichte des Papsttums von des Anfängen bis zum Höhe der Weltherrschaft* (Tübingen, 1930–3).

CASSON, S., 'Byzantine and Anglo-Saxon Sculpture', *Burlington Magazine*, 61 (1932), 265–74, 62 (1933), 26–36.

CATHER, S., PARK, D., and WILLIAMSON, P., *Early Medieval Wall Painting and Painted Sculpture in England* (B. A. R. 216; Oxford, 1990).

CAVALLO, G., *Rotoli di Exultet dell'Italia meridionale* (Bari, 1973).

CECCHELLI, C., *Iconografia di San Pietro* (Rome, 1937).

—— *I mosaici della basilica di Sta Maria Maggiore* (Turin, 1956).

CHADWICK, H., 'Ego Berengarius', *Journal of Theological Studies*, 40 (1989), 414–45.

CHADWICK, N. K. (ed.), *Studies in Early British History* (Cambridge, 1954).

CHAPLAIS, P., *England and her Neighbours 1066–1453: Essays in Honour of P. Chaplais*, ed. M. Jones and M. Vale (London, 1989).

CHAPMAN, J., 'À propos des martyrologes: B. Les Fêtes de St Benoît aux VII–IXᵉ siècles', *RB* 20 (1903), 295–313.

CHARLAND, P. V., *Madame Ste Anne et son culte au Moyen Âge* (2 vols.; Paris, 1911–13).

CHASSINAT, E., (ed.), *Le Monastère et la nécropole de Baouît* (Mémoires de l'Institut Français d'Archéologie Orientale du Caire, 12; Cairo, 1904).

CHAUME, M., *Les Origines du duché de Bourgogne* (Dijon, 1925–31).

CHAUSSIER, F., *Histoire de l'abbaye de Gorze* (Metz, 1894).

CHELINI, J., *L'Aube du Moyen Âge: naissance de la chrétieneté occidentale: la vie religieuse des laïcs dans l'Europe carolingienne (750–900)* (Paris, 1991).

CHIBNALL, M., *The World of Orderic Vitalis* (Oxford, 1984).

—— *Anglo-Norman England 1066–1166* (Oxford, 1986).

Chiesa e Riforma nella spiritualità del secolo XI (Todi, 1968).

CHOUX, J., *La Lorraine chrétienne au Moyen Âge* (Metz, 1981).

CHRISTIE, A. G. I., *English Medieval Embroidery* (Oxford, 1938).

CIGGAAR, K., 'England and Byzantium on the Eve of the Norman Conquest (The Reign of Edward the Confessor)', *Anglo-Norman Studies*, 5 (1982), 78–96.

CILENTO, N., *Civilà napoletana del medioevo nei secoli VI–XIII* (Naples, 1969).

CLANCHY, M. T., *England and its Rulers 1066–1272* (Harmondsworth, 1983).

CLAPHAM, A. W., *English Romanesque Architecture* (2 vols.; Oxford, 1930–4, repr. 1965).

CLARK, J. M., *The Abbey of St Gall as a Centre of Literature and Art* (Cambridge, 1926).

CLAUDE, D., *Geschichte des Erzbistums Magdeburg bis in der 12. Jahrhundert* (2 vols.; Cologne and Vienna, 1972).

CLAYTON, M., 'Feasts of the Virgin in the Liturgy of the Anglo-Saxon Church', *ASE* 13 (1984), 209–33.

—— *The Cult of the Virgin Mary in Anglo-Saxon England* (Cambridge, 1990).

CLEMOES, P., *The Cult of St Oswald on the Continent* (Jarrow Lecture, 1983).

—— *Learning and Literature in Anglo-Saxon England: Studies Presented to P. Clemoes on the Occasion of his Sixty-Fifth Birthday*, ed. M. Lapidge and H. Gneuss (Cambridge, 1985).

CLERVAL, J. A., *Les Écoles de Chartres au Moyen Âge* (Paris, 1895).

COATSWORTH, E., 'Late Pre-Conquest Sculptures with the Crucifixion South of the Humber', in Yorke, *Æthelwold*, 161–93.

COLGRAVE, B., 'The Earliest Life of St Gregory the Great written by a Whitby Monk', *Celt and Saxon: Studies in the Early British Border*, ed. N. K. Chadwick (Cambridge, 1963), 119–37.

COLLINGWOOD, W. G., *Northumbrian Crosses of the Pre-Norman Age* (London, 1927).

COLLINS, R., and GODMAN, P., *Charlemagne's Heir: New Perspectives on the Reign of Louis the Pious* (Oxford, 1989).

COMPTON, P., *Harold the King* (Hale, 1961).

CONANT, K. J., *Carolingian and Romanesque Architecture 800–1200* (3rd edn.; Harmondsworth, 1973).

CONSOLI, G., *Sant'Agata vergine e martire catanese* (Catania, 1951).

CONTI, P. M., *Luni nell'alto medioevo* (La Spezia, 1967).

CONTRENI, J. J., *The Cathedral School of Laon from 850 to 930: Its Manuscripts and Masters* (Münchener Beiträge für Mediävistik und Renaissanceforschungen, 29; Munich, 1978).

COOPER, J., 'The Last Four Anglo-Saxon Archbishops of York', *Borthwick Papers*, 38 (1970), 23–9.

CORBET, P., 'La Diffusion du culte de St Gilles au Moyen Age (Champagne, Lorraine, Nord de la Bourgogne)', *Annales de l'Est*, 32 (1980), 3–42.

—— *Les Saints ottoniens* (Sigmaringen, 1986).

Corbie, Abbaye Royale: volume du XIIIe Centenaire (Lille, 1963).

CORBLET, J., *Hagiographie du diocèse d'Amiens* (5 vols.; Amiens, 1869–75).

COUSIN, P., *Abbon de Fleury-sur-Loire: Un savant, un pasteur, un martyr à la fin du Xe siècle* (Paris, 1954).

COWDREY, H. E. J., *The Age of Abbot Desiderius: Montecassino, the Papacy and the Normans in the Eleventh and Early Twelfth Centuries* (Oxford, 1983).

—— *Popes, Monks and Crusaders* (London, 1984).

—— 'The Gregorian Reform in the Anglo-Norman Lands and in Scandinavia', *Studi Gregoriani*, 13 (1985), 321–52.

—— 'Count Simon of Crépy's Monastic Conversion' (forthcoming).

CRAMP, R., 'The Anglo-Saxons and Rome', *Transactions of the Architectural and Archaeol. Societies of Durham and Northumberland*, n.s. 3 (1974), 27–37.

CRAWFORD, S. J., *Anglo-Saxon Influence on Western Christendom 600–800* (Oxford, 1933).

CROCQ, C. DE, *Le Premier Saint de la Flandre française: St Winnoc, patron de Bergues* (Lille, 1944).

CROQUINSON, J., 'Les Origines de l'iconographie grégorienne', *Cahiers Archéologiques*, 12 (1962), 249–62.

CROSBY, S. McK., *The Abbey of St Denis 475–1122* (New Haven, 1942), i.

Culte et les reliques de St Benoît et de Ste Scholastique, Le (Paris, 1980).

Cultura antica nell'occidente latino dal VII all'XI secolo, La (*Settimane*, 1974; 2 vols.; Spoleto, 1975).

CUTLER, A., *The Aristocratic Psalters in Byzantium* (Paris, 1984).

DALES, D., *Dunstan Saint and Statesman* (Cambridge, 1988).

DARLINGTON, R. R., *Anglo-Norman Historians* (London, 1947).

—— 'The Anglo-Saxon Period', in C. R. Dodwell (ed.), *The English Church and the Continent* (London, 1959).

DAUPHIN, H., 'Le Renouveau monastique en Angleterre au Xe siècle et ses rapports avec la réforme de St Gérard de Brogne', *RB* 70 (1960), 177–203.

—— 'L'Érémitisme en Angleterre aux XIe et XIIe siècles', *L'eremitismo in Occidente nei secoli XI e xii* (Milan, 1965), 271–310.

DAVID, P., 'Un recueil de conférences monastiques irlandaises du VIIIe siècle', *RB* 49 (1937), 62–89.

DAVID, H. F., 'The Origins of the Devotion to Our Lady's Immaculate Conception', *Dublin Review*, 118 (1954), 375–92.

DAVIS, R. H. C., 'The Monks of St Edmund 1021–1148', *History*, 40 (1955), 227–39.

—— *Studies in Medieval History Presented to R. H. C. Davis*, ed. H. Mayr-Harting and R. I. Moore (London, 1985).

DEANESLY, M., *The Pre-Conquest Church in England* (London, 1961).

—— *Augustine of Canterbury* (London, 1964).

DEBRAY, C., *et al.* (eds.), *Histoire des territoires ayant formé le département du Pas-de-Calais* (Arras, 1946).

DEICHMANN, F. W., *Frühchristliche Bauten und Mosaiken von Ravenna* (Baden-Baden, 1958).

DELBONO, F., *Gli Anglosassoni e il continente* (Elia, 1975).

DELEHAYE, H., *Les Légendes grecques des saints militaires* (Paris, 1909).

—— 'Hagiographie napolitaine', *AB* 59 (1941), 1–33.

DELPIERRE, M., *L'Iconographie de Marie Madeleine* (Paris, 1948).

DELUMEAU, J., *Histoire de la Bretagne* (Toulouse, 1969).

DEMUS, O. F., *Byzantine Mosaic Decoration: Aspects of Monumental Art in Byzantium* (London, 1948).

—— *The Church of St Mark's in Venice* (Dumbarton Oaks Studies, 4; Cambridge, Mass., 1960).

—— *Byzantine Art and the West* (New York, 1970).

DESHMAN, R., 'Anglo-Saxon Art After Alfred', *Art Bulletin*, 56(2) (1974), 176–200.

—— '"Christus rex and magi reges": Kingship and Christology in Ottonian and Anglo-Saxon Art', *Frümittelalterliche Studien*, 10 (1986), 367–405.

—— 'The Leofric Missal and Tenth-Century English Art', *ASE* 6 (1977), 145–73.

—— *Anglo-Saxon and Anglo-Scandinavian Art: An Annotated Bibliography* (Boston, 1984).

—— 'Servants of the Mother of God in Byzantine and Medieval Art', *Word and Image*, 5 (1989), 33–70.

DESPORTES, P. (ed.), *Histoire de Reims* (Toulouse, 1983).

DEVISME, J. F. L., *Histoire de la ville de Laon* (2 vols.; Laon, 1822, repr. 1980).

DICKINS, B., 'The Cult of St Olave', *Saga-Book of the Viking Society*, 12 (1937), 33–80.

DODWELL, C. R., *The Canterbury School of Illumination 1066–1200* (Cambridge, 1954).

—— *Painting in Europe 800–1200* (Harmondsworth, 1971).

—— 'Losses of Anglo-Saxon Art in the Middle Ages', *Bulletin of the John Rylands Library*, 56 (1973), 74–92.

—— *Anglo-Saxon Art: A New Perspective* (Manchester, 1982).

—— , and TURNER, D. H., *Reichenau Reconsidered: A Re-Assessment of the Place of Reichenau in Ottonian Art* (London, 1965).

DOLAN, D., *Le Drame liturgique de Pâques en Normandie et en Angleterre au Moyen Âge* (Publications de l'Université de Poitiers, Letters et Sciences Humaines, 16; Paris, 1975).

DONALDSON, C., *Martin of Tours: Paris Priest, Mystic and Exorcist* (London, 1980).

DOREZ, L., *Les Manuscrits à peintures de la bibliothèque de Lord Leicester* (Paris, 1908).

DOUGLAS, D. C., *William the Conqueror: The Norman Impact upon England* (London, 1964).

DUBY, G., *La Société aux XIᵉ et XIIᵉ siècles dans la région mâconnaise* (2 vols.; Paris, 1953).

—— *The Three Orders: Feudal Society Imagined* (tr., Chicago, 1980).

DUCKETT, E. S., *St Dunstan of Canterbury: A Study of Monastic Reform in the Tenth Century* (New York, 1955).

DUDDEN, F. H., *Gregory the Great: His Place in History and in Thought* (2 vols.; London, 1905).

DUFRENNE, S., 'Les Copies anglaises du Psautier d'Utrecht', *Scriptorium*, 18 (1964), 185–97.

—— *Les Illustrations du Psautier d'Utrecht: sources et apport carolingien* (Paris, 1978).

DUNBABIN, J., *France in the Making 843–1180* (Oxford, 1985).

DUNNING, G. C., 'Trade Relations between England and the Continent in the Late-Anglo-Saxon Period', *Dark Age Britain: Studies Presented to E. T. Leeds*, ed. D. B. Harden (London, 1956), 218–33.

DUPRÉ-THESEIDER, E., 'La "grande rapina dei corpi santi" dall'Italia al tempo di Ottone I', *Festscrift für P. E. Schramm*, ed. P. Classen (Wiesbaden, 1964) i. 420–32.

DUSERRE, J., *Les Origines de la dévotion à St Joseph* (Montreal, 1954).

DVORNIK, F., *The Idea of Apostolicity in Byzantium and the Legend of the Apostle Andrew* (Cambridge, Mass., 1958).

EARLE, J., Legends of St Swithun and Sancta Maria Aegyptiaca (London, 1861).

EBERSOLT, J., *La Miniature byzantine* (Paris and Brussels, 1926).

—— *Orient et Occident: Recherches sur les influences byzantines et orientales en France avant les Croisades* (2nd edn.; Paris, 1954).

EHRLE, F., 'Ricerche su alcune antiche chiese del Borgo di S. Pietro', *Dissertazione della Pontificia Accademia Romana di Archeologia*, ser. ii, 10 (1910), 1–43.

English Illuminated Manuscripts 700–1500 (Brussels, 1973).

ESPINAS, G., *Les Origines du capitalisme, iii. Deux fondations de villes dans l'Artois et la Flandre française (X^e–XVe siècles): Saint-Omer, Lannoy du Nord* (Lille and Paris, 1946).

ETTINGHAUSEN, R., 'Foundation-Moulded Leatherwork: A Rare Egyptian Technique also used in Britain', in *Studies in Islamic Art and Architecture in Honour of Prof. K. A. C. Creswell* (Cairo, 1965), 63–71.

EVANS, G. R., 'Mens Devota: The Literary Community of the Devotional Works of John of Fécamp and St Anselm', *Medium Aevum*, 43 (1974), 105–15.

—— *Anselm and a New Generation* (Oxford, 1980).

EWIG, E., 'Der Martinuskult im Frühmittelalter', *Archiv für mittelrheinische Kirchengeschichte*, 14 (1962), 11–30.

FABRE, P., 'Recherches sur le denier de St Pierre au Moyen Âge', in *Mélanges G.-B. de Rossi* (Paris and Rome, 1892).

FARMER, D., 'Two Biographies by William of Malmesbury', in *Latin Biography*, ed. T. A. Dorey (London, 1967), 157–76.

FAWTIER, F., 'Les Reliques rouennaises de Ste Catherine', *AB* 41 (1923), 357–68.

FERNIE, E., *The Architecture of the Anglo-Saxons* (London, 1983).

—— 'The Effect of the Conquest on Norman Architectural Patronage', *Anglo-Norman Studies*, 9 (1986), 71–85.

FERRARI, G., *Early Roman Monasteries* (Studi d'antichità cristiana, 23; Rome, 1957).

FICHTENAU, H., *Lebensordnungen des 10. Jahrhunderts: Studien über Denkart und Existenz im einstigen Karolingerreich* (2 vols.; Monographien zur Geschichte des Mittelalters, 30; Stuttgart, 1984).

FINUCANE, R., *Miracles and Pilgrims: Popular Beliefs in Medieval England* (London, 1977).

FISHER, E. A., *The Greater Anglo-Saxon Churches: An Architectural Historical Study* (London, 1962).

FLAMION, J., *Les Actes apocryphes de l'Apôtre André* (Louvain, 1911).

FLECKENSTEIN, J., *Die Hofkapelle der deutschen Könige* (2 vols.; Stuttgart, 1966).

FLICHE, A., *La Réforme grégorienne* (3 vols.; Louvain, 1924–37).

—— , and MARTIN, V. (eds.), *Histoire de l'église depuis les origines jusqu'à nos jours* (vols. 4–13; Paris, 1948–64).

FLICOTEAUX, E., *La Noël d'Été et le culte de Jean Baptiste* (Bruges, 1932).

FOCILLON, H., *The Year 1000* (New York, 1961).

FÖRSTER, M., 'The Donations of Leofric to Exeter', in *The Exeter Book of Old English Poetry*, ed. R. W. Chambers *et al.* (London, 1933), 10–32.

—— *Zur Geschichte des Reliquienkultus in Altengland* (Munich, 1943), 63–80.

FOHLEN, C., (ed.), *Histoire de Besançon* (2 vols.; Besançon, 1964).

FOURNIER, P., and LE BRAS, G., *Histoire des collections canoniques en Occident* (Paris, 1931), i.

FRANCASTEL, P. (ed.), *L'Art mosan: journées d'études, Paris 1952* (Paris, 1953).

FRANCHI DE CAVALIERI, P., 'Sant'Agnese nella tradizione e nella leggenda', *Studi e Testi*, 221 (1962), 293–354.

FRANTZEN, A. J., *The Literature of Penance in Anglo-Saxon England* (New Brunswick, 1983).

FREEMAN, E. A., *History of the Norman Conquest* (6 vols.; Oxford, 1867–79).

FRIEND, A. M., 'Portraits of the Evangelists in Greek and Latin Manuscripts', *Art Studies*, 5 (1927), 115–47, 7 (1929), 3–29.

FUHRMANN, H., *Germany in the High Middle Ages c.*1050–1200 (Cambridge, 1986).

FUIANO, M., *La cultura a Napoli nell'alto medioevo* (Naples, 1961).

—— *Napoli nel medioevo XI–XIII* (Naples, 1972).

GABORIT-CHOPIN, D., *La Décoration des manuscrits à St Martial de Limoges et en Limousin du IXᵉ au XIIᵉ siècle* (Paris, 1969).

GAEDHE, J., and MÜTHERICH, F., *Carolingian Painting* (New York, 1977).

GALASSI, G., *Roma o Bisanzio* (Rome, 1953).

GALASSI PALUZZI, C., *La basilica di San Pietro* (Bologna, 1975).

GALASSO, G. (ed.), *Storia d'Italia* (Turin, 1980), i, ii.

GARANA, O., *Sta Lucia nella tradizione, nella storia, nell'arte* (Syracuse, 1958).

GARBER, J., *Wirkungen der frühchristlichen Gemäldezyklen der alten Peters und Pauls-Basiliken in Rome* (Berlin and Vienna, 1918).

GARMONSWAY, G. N., *Canute and his Empire* (London, 1964).

GARNETT, G. S., '*Franci et Angli*': the Legal Distinction Between Peoples After the Conquest', *Anglo-Norman Studies*, 8 (1985), 109–37.

GASQUET, F. A., *A History of the Venerable English College, Rome* (London, 1920).

GATCH, M. McC., *Preaching and Theology in Anglo-Saxon England: Aelfric and Wulfstan* (Toronto, 1977).

GAY, J., *L'Italie méridionale et l'Empire Byzantin depuis l'avènement de Basile I jusqu'à la prise de Bari par les Normands (867–1071)* (Paris and Rome, 1904).

GEARY, P. J., '*Furta Sacra': Thefts of Relics in the Central Middle Ages* (Princeton, 1978).

GEM, R., 'A Recension in English Architecture during the Early Eleventh Century and its Effect on the Development of the Romanesque Style', *Journ. of the Brit. Archaeol. Assoc.*, 38 (1975), 28–49.

—— 'L'Architecture pré-romane et romane en Angleterre', *Bulletin Monumental*, 143 (1984), 233–72.

—— 'The English Parish Church in the Eleventh and Early-Twelfth Century: A Great Rebuilding?', in Blair, *Minsters*, 21–30.

—— 'England and the Resistance to Romanesque Architecture', in C. Harper-Bill *et al.* (eds.), *Studies in Medieval History Presented to R. Allen Brown* (Woodbridge, 1989), 129–39.

—— 'Documentary References to Anglo-Saxon Painted Architecture', in Cather, Park, and Williamson (eds.), *Early Medieval Wall Painting*, 1–16.

GÉNICOT, L. F., *Les Églises mosanes du XIᵉ siècle* (Louvain, 1972).

GIBBS, M., 'The Decrees of Agatho and the Gregorian Plan for York', *Speculum*, 48(2) (1973), 213–46.

GIBSON, M., *Lanfranc of Bec* (Oxford, 1978).

GJERLØW, L., *Adoratio Crucis* (Oslo, 1961).

GNEUSS, H., 'A Preliminary List of Manuscripts Written and Illuminated in England up to 1100', *ASE* 9 (1982), 1–60.

GODFREY, J., 'The Defeated Anglo-Saxons Take Service with the Eastern Emperor', *Anglo-Norman Studies*, 1 (1978), 63–74.

GOLDSCHMIDT, A., *German Illumination* (2 vols.; Florence and Paris, 1928).

—— 'English Influence on Medieval Art of the Continent', in *Medieval Studies in Memory of A. Kingsley Porter*, ed. W. R. W. Köhler (2 vols.; Cambridge, Mass., 1939), ii. 709–22.

——, and WEITZMANN, K., *Die byzantinischen Elfenbeinskulpturen des X–XIII Jahrhunderts* (2 vols.; Berlin, 1930–34).

GORDON, E., *Eynsham Abbey 1005–1228: A Small Window into a Large Room* (Chichester, 1990).

GOUGAUD, L., *Christianity in Celtic Lands* (London, 1932).

—— 'Sur les routes de Rome et du Rhin avec les "peregrini" insulaires', *Revue d'Histoire Ecclésiastique*, 29(1) (1933), 253–71.

—— *Les Saints irlandais hors d'Irlande* (Louvain, 1936).

—— 'Inventaire des manuscrits provenant d'anciennes bibliothèques monastiques de Grande Bretagne', *Revue d'Histoire Ecclésiastique*, 33 (1937), 789–91.

GRABAR, A., *Martyrium: Recherches sur le culte des reliques et l'art chrétien antique* (3 vols.; Paris, 1946).

—— *Byzantium* (London, 1966).

—— *L'art de la fin de l'Antiquité* (3 vols.; Paris, 1968).

—— *Christian Iconography: A Study of its Origins* (London, 1969).

—— *L'Art du moyen âge en Occident: influences byzantines et orientales* (London, 1980).

——, and NORDENFALK, C., *Early Medieval Painting from the Fourth to the Eleventh Century* (Geneva, 1957).

GRABOIS, A., 'Anglo-Norman England and the Holy Land', *Anglo-Norman Studies*, 7 (1984), 132–41.

GRAF, A., *Roma nella memoria e nelle immaginazioni del Medio Evo* (2 vols.; Turin, 1882).

GRAHAM, R., *English Ecclesiastical Studies* (London, 1929).

GRANSDEN, A., *Historical Writing in England c.500 to c.1307* (London, 1974).

—— 'Baldwin, Abbot of Bury St Edmunds, 1065–1097', *Anglo-Norman Studies*, 4 (1981), 65–76.

GRAVES, E. B., *A Bibliography of English History to 1485* (Oxford, 1975).

GREENHALGH, M., *The Survival of Roman Antiquities in the Middle Ages* (London, 1989).

GRÉGOIRE, R., *Homéliaires liturgiques médiévaux: analyse des manuscrits* (Bibliotheca degli studi medievali, 12; Spoleto, 1980).

GREGOROVIUS, F., *A History of the City of Rome in the Middle Ages* (8 vols.; tr., London, 1894–1902).

GRIERSON, P., 'A Visit of Earl Harold to Flanders in 1056', *EHR* 51 (1936), 90–7.

—— 'The Early Abbots of St Peter's, Ghent', *RB* 48 (1936), 129–46.

—— The Early Abbots of St Bravo's, Ghent', *RB* 49 (1937), 29–61.

—— 'Grimbald of St Bertin's', *EHR* 55 (1940), 529–61.

—— 'Les Livres de l'abbé Seiwold de Bath', *RB* 52 (1940), 96–116.

—— 'Relations between England and Flanders before the Norman Conquest', *TRHS* 4th ser. 23 (1941), 71–112, repr. in Southern, *Essays*, 61–92.

GRISAR, H., *Die römische Kapelle Sancta Sanctorum und ihr Schatz* (Freiburg, 1908).

—— *History of Rome and the Popes in the Middle Ages* (3 vols.; London, 1911–12.).

GRODECKI, L., *L'Architecture ottonienne* (Paris, 1980).

—— MÜTHERICH, F., TARALON, J., and WORMALD, F. (eds.), *Le Siècle de l'An Mil* (Paris, 1973).

GROSJEAN, P., 'Gloria postuma Scti Martini apud Scotos et Britannos', *AB* 55 (1937), 300–48.

——, 'La Prétendue origine irlandaise du culte de St Joseph en Occident', *AB* 72 (1954), 357–62.

GROSSO, O., *S. Giorgio nell'arte* (Milan, 1962).

GRUENEISEN, W. DE, *Sainte Marie Antique* (Rome, 1911).

GUILLOT, O., *Le Comte d'Anjou et son entourage au XIe siècle* (Paris, 1972).

GUILLOU, A., 'Art et religion dans l'Italie grecque médiévale', in *La Chiesa greca in Italia dall VIII al XVI secolo* (Padua, 1972), 725–58.

—— *Culture et Société en Italie Byzantine* (London, 1978).

GUTBERLET, S. H., *Die Himmelfahrt Christi in der bildenden Kunst von den Anfängen bis ins hohe Mittelalter* (Leipzig and Strasburg, 1935).

HAIGH, G. T., *The History of Winchcombe Abbey* (London, 1950).

HALL, J. R., 'Some Liturgical Notes on Aelfric's *Letter to the Monks of Eynsham*', *Downside Review*, 93 (1975), 297–303.

HALLAM, E., *Capetian France 987–1328* (London, 1980).

HALLINGER, K., *Gorze–Kluny: Studien zu den monastischen Lebensformen und Gegensätzen im Hochmittelalter* (Studia Anselmiana, 22–5, 2 vols.; Rome, 1950–1).

—— 'Papst Gregor der Grosse und der heilige Benedikt', *Studia Anselmiana*, 42 (1957), 231–319.

HALPHEN, L., *Charlemagne and the Carolingian Empire* (Amsterdam, 1977).

HALSALL, M., 'Vercelli and the *Vercelli Book*', *Proceedings of the Medieval Languages Association*, 84 (1969), 1545–7.

HAMILTON, B., *Monastic Reform, Catharism and the Crusades (900–1300)* (London, 1979).

HANDSCHIN, J., 'The Two Winchester Tropers', *Journal of Theological Studies*, 37 (1936), 34–49, 156–72.

HARRISON, M., *A Temple for Byzantium: The Discovery and Excavation of Anicia Juliana's Palace Church in Istanbul* (London, 1989).

HARSSEN, M., 'The Countess Judith of Flanders and the Library of Weingarten Abbey', *Papers of the Bibliographical Society of America*, 24 (1930), 1–13.

HARVEY, J., *English Medieval Architecture* (2nd rev. edn.; London, 1984).

HASKINS, C. H., *The Renaissance of the Twelfth Century* (Cambridge, Mass., 1927).

HAUCK, A., *Kirchengeschichte Deutschlands* (8th edn.; Leipzig and Berlin, 1958), i, ii.

HAVERKAMP, A., *Medieval Germany 1056–1273* (Oxford, 1988).

HEIMBÜCHER, M., *Die Orden und Kongregationen der Katholischen Kirche* (3 vols.; 2nd edn.; Paderborn, 1907–8).

HEITZ, C., *Recherches sur les rapports entre architecture et liturgie à l'époque carolingienne* (Paris, 1963).

—— *L'Architecture religieuse carolingienne* (Paris, 1980).

HENDERSON, G., 'The Sources of the Genesis Cycle at St-Savin-sur-Gartempe', *Journ. of the Brit. Archaeol. Assoc.*, 3rd ser. 26 (1963), 11–26.

—— *Early Medieval Style and Civilisation* (London, 1972).

—— *Losses and Lacunae in Early Insular Art* (York, 1982).

HENRY, F., *Irish High Crosses* (Dublin, 1964).

HERMANIN, F., *L'arte in Roma dal secolo VIII al XIV* (Bologna, 1945).

HERRIN, J., *The Formation of Christendom* (Oxford, 1987).

HERZBERG, A. J., *Der heilige Mauritius: Ein Beitrag zur Geschichte der deutschen Mauritius-Verehrung* (Düsseldorf, 1936).

HERZOG, E., *Die ottonische Stadt: Die Anfänge der mittelalterlichen Stadtbaukunst in Deutschland* (Berlin, 1964).

HIGGIT, J., 'The Iconography of St Peter in Anglo-Saxon England and the St Cuthbert's Coffin', in Bonner, *St Cuthbert*, 267–85.

HILL, D. (ed.), *Æthelred the Unready: Papers from the Millenary Conference* (B. A. R. 59; Oxford, 1978).

—— *An Atlas of Anglo-Saxon England* (Oxford, 1981).

HILL, J., 'St George before the Conquest', *Report of the Society of the Friends of St George's and the Descendants of the Knights of the Garter*, 6 (1985–6), 284–95.

—— 'Pilgrim Routes in Medieval Italy', *Bolletino del CIRVI*, 5 (1) (1986), 3–22.

HILLER, H., *Otto der Grosse und seine Zeit* (Munich, 1980).

HILLGARTH, J., *Visigothic Spain, Byzantium and the Irish* (London, 1985).

HINKLE, W. M., 'The Gift of an Anglo-Saxon Gospel-Book to the Abbey of St Rémi, Rheims', *Journ. of the Brit. Archaeol. Assoc.*, 3rd ser. 33 (1970), 21–35.

HLAWITSCHKA, E., *Lotharingien und das Reich an der Schwelle der deutschen Geschichte* (Stuttgart, 1968).

—— *Die Anfänge des Hauses Habsburg–Lothringen* (Saarbrücken, 1969).

HOFFMANN, H., *Buchkunst und Königtum im ottonischen und frühsalischen Reich* (Stuttgart, 1986).

HOHLER, C., 'Les Saints insulaires dans le missel de l'archevêque Robert', in *Jumièges*, i. 293–308.

HOLTZMANN, R., 'Otto der Grosse und Magdeburg', *Aufsätze zur deutschen Geschichte im Mittelmeerraum*, ed. A. Timm (Darmstadt, 1962), 1–33.

HOLTZMANN, W., *König Heinrich I und die heilige Lanze* (Berlin, 1947).

HOMBURGER, O., *Die Anfänge der Malschule von Winchester im X. Jahrhundert* (Leipzig, 1912).

—— 'L'Art carolingien de Metz et l'école de Winchester', *Gazette des Beaux-Arts*, 62 (1963), 35–46.

HOMO, L., *Rome médiévale* (Paris, 1934).

HOOPER, N., 'Edgar the Ætheling: Anglo-Saxon Prince, Rebel and Crusader', *ASE* 14 (1985), 197–214.

HOWARD-JOHNSTON, J. (ed.), *Byzantium and the West c.850–c.1200* (Amsterdam, 1988).

HUBERT, J., *L'Art préroman* (Paris, 1938).

—— *L'Architecture religieuse du haut Moyen Âge en France* (Paris, 1952).
——, PORCHER, J., and VOLBACH, W., *Carolingian Art* (tr. London, 1970).
HUDSON, P., *Archeologia urbana e programmazione della ricerca: L'esempio di Pavia* (Florence, 1981).
HUELSEN, C., *Le chiese di Roma nel Medio Evo* (Florence, 1927).
HUGHES, A., *Medieval Manuscript for Mass and Office: A Guide to their Organization and Terminology* (Toronto, 1982).
HUHN, E. H., *Geschichte Lothringens* (2 vols.; 2nd edn.; Berlin, 1877).
HUNT, N. (ed.), *Cluniac Monasticism in the Central Middle Ages* (London, 1971).
HUNTER, M., 'Germanic and Roman Antiquity and the Sense of the Past in Anglo-Saxon England', *ASE* 3 (1974), 29–50.
HUYGHEBAERT, N., 'Moines grecs et italiens en Lotharingie, VIIIᵉ–XIIᵉ siècles', *Miscellanea Tornacensia: mélanges d'Archéologie et d'Histoire; Annales du Congrès archéologique et historique de Tournai 1949*, ed. J. Cassart, (Brussels, 1951), 95–111.
HYDE, J. K., *Society and Politics in Medieval Italy: The Evolution of the Civil Life 1000–1350* (London, 1973).

IOGNA-PRAT, D., 'Le "Baptême" du schéma des trois ordres fonctionnels: l'apport de l'École d'Auxerre dans la seconde moitié du IXᵉ siècle', *Annales ESC*, 41(1)(1986), 101–26.
——, and PICARD, J-C. (eds.), *Religion et culture autour de l'An Mil: royaume capétien et Lotharingie* (Paris, 1990).
—— JEUDY, C., and LOBRICHON, G. (eds.), *L'École caroligienne d'Auxerre de Muretach à St Rémi 830–908; Entretiens d'Auxerre 1989* (Paris, 1991).

JACOBI, J., 'Erzbischof Poppo von Trier', *Archiv für mittelrheinische Kirchengeschichte*, 13 (1961), 9–26.
JAMES, E., *The Origins of France* (London, 1982).
JANTZEN, H., *Ottonische Kunst* (Hamburg, 1959).
JENKINS, R., *Byzantium: The Imperial Centuries AD 610–1071* (Toronto, Buffalo, and London, 1987).
JENSEN, O., 'The "Denarius Sancti Petri" in England', *TRHS* n.s. 15 (1901), 171–98.
JOHN, E., *Orbis Britanniae and Other Studies* (Leicester, 1966).
—— 'The World of Abbot Aelfric', in *Ideal and Reality*, 300–16.
JONES, A. E. E., *Anglo-Saxon Worcester* (Worcester, 1958).
JONES, C. W., 'A Legend of St Pachomius', *Speculum*, 18 (1943), 197–210.
—— *Saints' Lives and Chronicles in Early England* (New York, 1947).
—— 'The *Scriptorium* of Corbie', *Speculum*, 22 (1947), 191–204 and 375–94.
—— *The Saint Nicholas Liturgy and its Literary Relationships (Ninth to Twelfth Centuries)* (Berkeley, 1963).
—— *St Nicholas of Myra, Bari and Manhattan: Biography of a Legend* (London and New York, 1978).
Jumièges: Congrès scientifique du XIIIᵉ Centenaire (2 vols.; Rouen, 1955).
JUNG, J., 'Das Itinerar des Erzbischofs Sigeric und die Strasse von Rom über Siena nach Lucca', *Mitteilungen des Instituts für Österreichische Geschichtsforschung*, 25 (1904), 1–90.
JUNG-INGLESSIS, E.-M., *Römische Madonnen: Über die Entwicklung der Marienbilder in Rom, von den Anfängen bis in die Gegenwart* (Sankt Ottilien, 1989).

KAFTAL, H., *Iconography of the Saints in Italian Art* (4 vols.; Florence, 1965–85).

KANTOROWICZ, E., 'Ivories and Litanies', *JWCI* 5 (1942), 56–81.

KARTSONIS, A. D., *Anastasis: The Making of an Image* (Princeton, 1986).

KEHRER, H., *Die 'Heiligen Drei Könige' in der Legende und in her deutschen bildenden Kunst bis Albrecht Dürer* (Strasburg, 1904).

KEMPF, T., 'Benna Treverensis Canonicus de Sancti Paulini Patrocinio', *Mainz und der Mittelrhein in der europäischen Kunstgeschichte: Studien für W. F. Volbach zu seinem 70. Geburtstag* (Mainz, 1966), 179–84.

KENDRICK, T. D., *Anglo-Saxon Art to 900* (London, 1938).

—— *Late-Saxon and Viking Art* (London, 1949).

KENNEDY, V. L., *The Saints of the Canon of the Mass* (Studi d'antichità cristiana, 14; Rome, 1954).

KENTENICH, G., *Geschichte der Stadt Trier von ihrer Gründung bis zur Gegenwart* (Trier, 1915).

KER, N. R., *Medieval Libraries of Great Britain: A List of Surviving Books* (2nd edn.; London, 1964).

—— *Books, Collectors and Libraries: Studies in the Medieval Heritage* (London, 1985).

KEYNES, S. D., *The Diplomas of King Æthelred 'the Unready' 978–1016* (Cambridge, 1980).

—— 'King Athelstan's Books', in *Learning and Literature*, 143–201.

KEYSER, C. E., 'Note on a Sculptured Tympanum at Kingswinford Church, Staffordshire, and Other Early Representations in England of St Michael the Archangel', *The Archaeological Journal*, 62 (1905), 137–46.

KEYSERLINGK, A. Graf von, *Vergessene Kulturen in Monte Gargano* (Nüremberg, 1968).

KIRBY, D. P. (ed.), *St Wilfred at Hexham* (Newcastle, 1974).

KIRK, J., *The Alfred and Minster Lovell Jewels* (Oxford, 1948).

KIRSCH, J. P., *Die heilige Cecilia in der römischen Kirche des Altertums* (Paderborn, 1910).

—— , *Die stadtrömische christlichen Festkalender im Altertum: Textkritische Untersuchungen zu den römischen 'Depositiones' und dem Martyrologium Hieronymianum* (Münster, 1924).

KITZINGER, E., *Die Buchmalerei des frühen Mittelalters* (Munich, 1972).

—— *The Art of Byzantium and the Medieval West* (Indiana U. P., 1976).

—— *Early Medieval Art in the British Museum* (3rd edn.; London, 1983).

—— , and GALASSI, G., *Roma e Bisanzio* (2nd edn.; Rome, 1953).

—— , and MCINTYRE, D., *The Coffin of St Cuthbert, Durham* (Oxford, 1950).

KLEINSCHMIDT, H., *Untersuchungen über das englische Königtum im 10. Jahrhundert* (Göttingen, 1979).

KLUKAS, A. W., 'The Architectural Implications of the "Decreta Lanfranci"', *Anglo-Norman Studies*, 6 (1983), 136–71.

—— 'Liturgy and Architecture: Deerhurst Priory as an Expression of the *Regularis Concordia*', *Viator*, 15 (1984), 81–106.

KNOWLES, D., 'The Norman Plantation', *Downside Review*, 49 (1931), 441–56.

—— 'The Cultural Influence of English Medieval Monasticism', *Cambridge History Journal*, 7 (1943), 146–59.

—— *The Monastic Order in England* (2nd edn.; Cambridge, 1963).

—— , and HADCOCK, R. NEVILLE (eds.), *Medieval Religious Houses: England and Wales* (London and New York, 1971).

—— , and OBOLENSKI, D. (eds.), *The Christian Centuries; A New History of the Catholic Church* (London, 1968), ii: *The Middle Ages*.

—— LONDON, V. C. M., and BROOKE, C. N. L., (eds.), *Heads of Religious Houses: England and Wales 940–1216* (Cambridge, 1972).

KÖHLER, W. R. W., cont. MÜTHERICH, F., *Die karolingische Miniaturen im Auftrage des deutschen Vereins für Kunstwissenschaft* (6 vols.; Berlin, 1930–77).

KÖRNER, S., *The Battle of Hastings, England and Europe 1035–1066* (Bibliotheca Historica Lundensis, 14; Gleerup, 1964).

KORHAMMER, M., *Die monastischen Cantica im Mittelalter* (Texte und Untersuchungen zur englischen Philologie, 6; Munich, 1976).

KOTTJE, R., and MAURER, H. (eds.), *Monastische Reformen im 9. und 10. Jahrhundert* (Sigmaringen, 1989).

KRAUTHEIMER, R., *Early Christian and Byzantine Architecture* (3rd edn.; Harmondsworth, 1979).

—— *Rome: Profile of a City 312–1308* (Princeton, 1980).

—— *Three Christian Capitals: Topography and Politics* (London, 1983).

—— , et al., *Corpus Basilicarum Christianarum Romae: The Early Christian Basilicas of Rome IV–IXth Centuries* (5 vols.; Vatican City, 1937–70).

KÜNSTLE, K., *Ikonographie der christlichen Kunst* (2 vols.; Freiburg, 1926–8).

KUNZE, K., 'Studien zur Legende Mariae Aegyptiacae', *Philologische Studien und Quellen*, 49 (1969).

KURTH, G., *Notger de Liège et la civilisation au Xe siècle* (2 vols.; Paris, Brussels, and Liège, 1905).

—— *La Cité de Liège au Moyen Âge* (3 vols.; Paris, 1909).

LABANDE, E. R., 'Recherches sur les pélerins dans l'Europe des XI–XIIe siècles', *Cahiers de Civilisation Médiévale*, 1 (1958), 158–69 and 339–47.

LAISTNER, M. L. W., *Thought and Letters in Western Europe AD 500 to 900* (2nd edn.; London, 1957).

LAMB, J. W., *St Wulfstan Prelate and Patriot: A Study of His Life and Times* (London, 1933).

LANCIANI, R., *The Destruction of Ancient Rome* (New York and London, 1899).

Langres ancienne et moderne: Guide de Langres (6th edn.; Langres, 1947).

LAPIDGE, M., 'Three Latin Poems from Æthelword's School at Winchester', *ASE* 1 (1972), 85–137.

—— 'Some Latin Poems as Evidence for the Reign of Æthelstan', *ASE* 9 (1981), 93–7.

—— 'The Origin of CCC 163', *Transactions of the Cambridge Bibliographical Society*, 8 (1981), 18–28.

—— 'Ealdred of York and the MS Cotton Vitellius E.XII', *Yorkshire Archaeological Journal*, 55 (1983), 11–25.

—— 'Surviving Booklists from Anglo-Saxon England', in *Learning and Literature*, 33–89.

—— 'Litanies of the Saints in Anglo-Saxon Manuscripts; A Preliminary List', *Scriptorium*, 40 (1986), 264–77.

—— 'The School of Theodore and Hadrian', *ASE* 15 (1986), 45–72.

—— 'A Frankish Scholar in Tenth-Century England: Frithegod of Canterbury/ Frédégaud of Brioude', *ASE* 17 (1988), 45–66.

LAPORTE, J., and BAUDOT, M. (eds.), *Millénaire monastique du Mont-Saint-Michel* (3 vols.; Paris, 1966–71).

LARSON, L. M., *Canute the Great 995c–1035 and the Rise of Danish Imperialism during the Viking Age* (New York, 1912).

LASKO, P., *Ars Sacra 800–1200* (Harmondsworth, 1972).

LAUER, P., *Le Règne de Louis IV d'Outre-Mer* (Paris, 1900).

—— 'Le Trésor du Sancta Sanctorum', *Monuments et Mémoires publiés par l'Académie des Inscriptions et Belles-Lettres*, 15 (1906), 7–140.

—— *Le Palais du Latran: étude archéologique et historique* (Paris, 1911).

LAWRENCE, A., 'The Influence of Canterbury on the Collection and Production of Manuscripts at Durham in the Anglo-Norman Period', in A. Borg and A. Martindale (eds.), *The Vanishing Past: Studies of Medieval Art, Liturgy and Metrology Presented to Christopher Hohler* (B.A.R. Inter. ser. 111; Oxford, 1981), 95–103.

LAWRENCE, C. H. (ed.), *The English Church and the Papacy in the Middle Ages* (London, 1965).

LAWRENCE, M. 'Maria Regina', *The Art Bulletin*, 7 (1924–5), 150–61.

LAZAREV, V., *Storia della pittura bizantina* (Turin, 1967).

LECHNER, J. and EISENHOFER, L., *The Liturgy of the Roman Rite* (tr. London, 1961).

LECLERCQ, H., *St Benoît sur Loire, les reliques, le monastère, l'église* (Paris, 1925).

LECLERCQ, J., *St Pierre Damien ermite et homme d'Église* (Rome, 1960).

—— 'Les Relations entre le monachisme oriental et le monachisme occidental dans le Haut Moyen Âge', *Millénaire du Mont Athos*, ii (Chevetogne, 1964), 49–80.

——, and BONNES, J. P., *Un maître de la vie spirituelle au xie siècle: Jean de Fécamp* (Paris, 1946).

——, VANDENBROUCKE, F., COGNET, L., and BOUYER, L., *A History of Christian Spirituality, ii: The Spirituality of the Middle Ages* (London, 1968).

LECOY DE LA MARCHE, A., *St Martin* (Tours, 1881).

LEMARIGNIER, J.-F., *Le Gouvernement royal aux premiers temps capétiens (987–1108)* (Paris, 1965).

LE MOYNE DE LA BORDERIE, A., *Histoire de la Bretagne* (6 vols.; Paris, 1898–1914, repr. 1972).

LE PATOUREL, J., *The Norman Empire* (Oxford, 1976).

LESTOCQUOY, J., *Le Diocèse d'Arras* (Arras, 1949).

—— *Études d'histoire urbaine: villes et abbayes: Arras au Moyen Âge* (Arras, 1966).

LETHBRIDGE, T. C., 'Byzantine Influence in Late-Saxon England', *Proceedings of the Cambridge Antiquaries Society*, 43 (1950), 2–6.

LEVISON, W., *Das Werden der Ursula-Legende* (Cologne, 1928).

—— *England and the Continent in the Eighth Century* (Oxford, 1946).

—— *Aus rheinischer und fränkischer Frühzeit: Ausgewählte Aufsätze* (Düsseldorf, 1948).

LEVRON, J., *Les Saints du pays angevin* (Angers, 1943).

LEYSER, H. *Hermits and the New Monasticism: A Study of Religious Communities in Western Europe 1000–1150* (London, 1984).

LEYSER, K. J., *Rule and Conflict in an Early Medieval Society: Ottonian Germany* (London, 1979).

—— *Medieval Germany and its Neighbours 900–1250* (London, 1982).

—— 'Die Ottonen und Wessex', *Frühmittelalterliche Studien*, 17 (1983), 73–97.

LIESS, R., *Die Frühromanischen Kirchenbau des 11. Jahrhunderts in der Normandie* (Munich, 1967).

LLEWELLYN, P., *Rome in the Dark Ages* (London, 1971).

—— 'The Roman Church in the Seventh Century: The Legacy of Gregory the Great', *JEH* 25 (1974), 363–80.

—— 'The Popes and the Constitution in the Eighth Century', *EHR* 101 (1986), 42–67.

LOHAUS, A., *Die Merowinger und England* (Müncher Beiträge zur Mediävistik und Renaissanceforschung, 19; Munich, 1974).

LOISEL, A., *Un missel et un bénédictionnaire anglo-saxons de la bibliothèque de Rouen* (Paris, 1912).

LOMAX, D. W., 'The First English Pilgrims to Santiago de Compostela', *Studies Presented to R. H. C. Davis*, ed. R. I. More and H. R. M. E. Mayr-Harting (London, 1985), 165–75.

LOMBARD-JOURDAN, A., *'Montjoie et St Denis!'; le Centre de la Gaule aux origines de Paris et de St Denis* (Paris, 1989).

LONGHURST, M., *English Ivories* (Harmondsworth, 1926).

LOOMIS, L. HIBBARD, 'The Holy Relics of Charlemagne and King Æthelstan: The Lances of Longinus and Mauricius', *Speculum*, 25 (1950), 440–56.

—— 'The Æthelstan Gift-Story: Its Influence on English Chronicles and Carolingian Romances', *Modern Languages Association Publications*, 67(1) (1952), 521–37.

LOPEZ, R., 'Le Problème des relations anglo-byzantines du VIIe au Xe siècle', *Byzantion*, 18 (1948), 139–62.

LOYN, H. R., *Anglo-Saxon England and the Norman Conquest* (London, 1962).

—— 'Peter's Pence', *Friends of Lambeth Palace Library Annual Report* 1984, 10–29.

Lucca, Il Volto Santo e la civiltà altomedioevale (Atti del convegno internazionale di studi, Lucca, 1982; Lucca, 1984).

LUCOT, P., *St Joseph, étude historique sur son culte* (Paris, 1875).

MACCARINI, P. A., 'William the Conqueror and the Church of Rome (from the *Epistolae)*', *Anglo-Norman Studies*, 6 (1983), 172–87.

MCCLENDON, C. B., *The Imperial Abbey of Farfa* (New Haven, 1987).

MACFARLANE, L. J., *The Vatican Archives, with Special Reference to Sources for British Medieval History* (London, 1959).

MCKITTERICK,. R., *The Frankish Church and the Carolingian Reforms 789–895* (London, 1977).

—— *The Frankish Kingdoms under the Carolingians 751–987* (London, 1983).

—— *The Carolingians and the Written Word* (Cambridge, 1989).

MACK SMITH, D., *A History of Sicily: Medieval Sicily 800–1713* (London, 1968).

MAGOUN, F. P., Jr., 'An English Pilgrim Diary of the Year 990', *Mediaeval Studies*, 2 (1940), 231–52.

—— 'The Rome of Two Northern Pilgrims: Archbishop Sigeric of Canterbury and Abbot Nikolas of Munkathverà', *Harvard Theological Review*, 33 (1940), 267–89.

MAÎTRE, L. A., *Les Écoles épiscopales et monastiques en Occident avant les universités 768–1180* (Paris, 1866).

MÂLE, E., *The Early Churches of Rome* (tr. London, 1960).

MANCINI, A., *Storia di Lucca* (Lucca, 1849, repr. 1975).

MANGO, C., 'La culture grecque et l'Occident au VIIIe siècle', *Settimane*, 20 (1973), 683–721.

—— *Byzantium: The Empire of New Rome* (London, 1980).

—— *Byzantine Architecture* (London, 1986).

MANITIUS, M., *Geschichte des lateinischen Literatur des Mittelalter* (3 vols.; Munich, 1911–31).

MARENBON, J., *From the Circle of Alcuin to the School of Auxerre* (Cambridge, 1981).

MARKUS, R. A., *Bede and the Tradition of Ecclesiastical Historiography* (Jarrow Lecture, 1975).

MARTIN, K., *Die ottonische Wandbilder der St Georgskirche Reichenau–Oberzell* (2nd edn., Sigmaringen, 1975).

MARUCCHI, O., *Eléments d'archéologie chrétienne, iii: Églises et basiliques de Rome* (Paris and Rome, 1902).

MASON, E., *St Wulfstan of Worcester c. 1008–1095* (Oxford, 1990).

MATTHES, D., *Die Heiratsurkunde der Kaiserin Theophanu* (Stuttgart, 1980).

MATTHEW, D. J. A., *The Norman Monasteries and their English Possessions* (London, 1962).

MATTHIAE, G., *Le chiese di Roma dal IV al X secolo* (Rome, 1962).

—— *Musaici medievali di Roma* (2 vols.; Rome, 1962).

—— *La pittura romana del medioevo* (2 vols.; Rome, 1965–6).

MAURER, H. (ed.), *Die Abtei Reichenau; Neue Beiträge zur Geschichte und Kultur des Inselklosters* (Sigmaringen, 1974).

MAYR-HARTING, H., *The Coming of Christianity to Anglo-Saxon England* (London, 1972).

MEISEN, K., *Nikolauskult und Nikolausbrauch im Abendlande; Eine kulturgeographisch-volkskundliche Untersuchung* (Düsseldorf, 1981).

MENDE, U., *Die Bronzetüren des Mittelalters* (Munich, 1983).

MEYVAERT, P., *Bede and Gregory the Great* (Jarrow Lecture, 1964).

—— 'Bede and the Church Paintings at Wearmouth–Jarrow', *ASE* 8 (1979), 63–77.

—— , and VIRCILLO-FRANKLIN, C., 'Has Bede's Version of the "Passio S. Anastasii" Come Down to us in "BHL" 408?', *AB* 100 (1982), 373–400.

MICHELI, G. L., *L'Enluminure du Haut Moyen Âge et les influences irlandaises; histoire d'une influence* (Brussels, 1939).

MILLAR, E. G., *English Illuminated Manuscripts from the Tenth to the Twelfth Century* (Paris and Brussels, 1926).

Millénaire de Cluny (2 vols.; Mâcon, 1910).

MITCHELL, H. P., 'Flotsam of Later Anglo-Saxon Art' i, ii, iii, *Burlington Magazine*, 42 (1923), 63–72, 162–9, 303–5.

—— 'English or German?—A Pre-Conquest Gold Cross', *Burlington Magazine*, 47 (1925), 324–30.

Monachesimo e la Riforma Ecclesiastica (1049–1122), Il, (Milan, 1971).

Moneta dall'antichità ad oggi, La, pub. by Regione Val d'Aosta and the Circolo Numismatico Valdostano (Aosta, 1984).

MONTCLOS, J. DE, *Lanfranc et Bérenger: la controverse eucharistique du XIe siècle* (Spicilegium Sacrum Lovaniense, 37; Louvain, 1971).

MOORE, W. J., *The Saxon Pilgrims to Rome and the Schola Saxonum* (Fribourg, 1937).

MOREAU, E. DE, *Saint Amand, apôtre de la Belgique et du Nord de la France* (Brussels, 1927).

—— *Histoire de l'Église en Belgique* (6 vols.; 2nd edn.; Brussels, 1945–52), i and ii.

MORETON, B., *The Eighth Century Gelasian Sacramentary: A Study in Tradition* (Oxford, 1976).

MORETUS, H., 'Les Deux anciennes Vies de St Gregoire', *AB* 26 (1907), 66–72.

MOREY, C. R., *Lost Mosaics and Frescoes of Rome in the Medieval Period* (Princeton, 1915).

MORGAN, M. M., *The English Lands of the Abbey of Bec* (Oxford, 1946).

MORIN, G., 'La Liturgie à Naples au temps de Grégoire le Grand d'après deux évangéliaires du VIIe siècle', *RB* 8 (1891), 481–93, 529–37.

MORRIS, C., *The Papal Monarchy: The Western Church from 1050 to 1250* (Oxford, 1989).

MORRIS, R., *The Church in British Archaeology* (Oxford, 1983).

MOSTERT, M., *The Political Theology of Abbo of Fleury* (Hilversum, 1987).

—— 'Le Séjour d'Abbon de Fleury à Ramsey', *Bibliothèque de l'École des Chartes*, 144 (1987), 199–208.

—— *The Library of Fleury* (Hilversum, 1989).

MUNDY, J. H., *Europe in the High Middles Ages 1150–1309* (London, 1973).

MUÑOZ, A., *Il codice purpureo di Rossano ed il Frammento Sinopense* (Rome, 1907).

—— *La basilica di San Lorenzo fuori le Mura* (Rome, 1944).

MUSSET, L., Relations et échanges d'influences dans l'Europe du Nord-Ouest (X–XIe siècles)', *Cahiers de Civilisation Médiévale*, 1 (1958), 63–82.

—— 'Rouen et l'Angleterre vers l'An Mil', *Annales de Normandie*, 24 (1974), 287–90.

NELSON, J. L., *Politics and Ritual in Early Medieval Europe* (London, 1986).

——, and GIBSON, M. (eds.), *Charles the Bald, Court and Kingdom* (B. A. R.; Oxford, 1981).

NERSESSIAN, S. DER, *Armenian Art* (London, 1978).

NEUSS, W., and ÖDIGER, F. W., *Geschichte des Erzbistums Köln* (3 vols.; Cologne, 1964).

NILGEN, U., 'Maria Regina: Ein politischer Kultbildtypus?', *Römisches Jahrbuch für Kunstgeschichte*, 19 (1981), 1–33.

NITTI DE VITO, F., *La Leggenda della Translazione di San Nicola da Mira a Bari: I Marinai* (Trani, 1902).

NORDENFALK, C., 'Abbas Leofsinus', *Acta Archaeologica*, 4 (1933), 49–83.

—— 'The Draped Lectern', in *Intuition und Kunstwissenschaft: Festschrift für Hanns Swarzenski zum 70. Geburtstag am 30. August 1973*, ed. P. Bloch *et al.* (Berlin, 1973), 81–97.

NORDHAGEN, P. J., *The Codex Amiatinus and the Byzantine Element in the Northumbrian Renaissance* (Jarrow Lecture, 1977).

—— *Studies in Byzantine and Early Medieval Painting* (London, 1990).

NORTIER, G., *Les Bibliothèques médiévales des abbayes bénédictines de Normandie* (Paris, 1971).

OAKESHOTT, W., *Classical Inspiration in Medieval Art* (London, 1959).

—— *The Mosaics of Rome from the Third to the Fourteenth Century* (London, 1967).

Occident et Orient au Xe siècle (Paris, 1979).

Ó'CARRÁGAIN, É. , 'Liturgical Innovations Associated with Pope Sergius and the Iconography of the Ruthwell and Bewcastle Crosses', in R. T. Farrell (ed.), *Bede and Anglo-Saxon England* (B. A. R. 46; Oxford, 1978), 131–47.

OGILVY, J. D. A., *Books Known to Anglo-Latin Writers from Aldhelm to Alcuin 670–804* (The Medieval Academy of America; Cambridge, Mass., 1936).

—— *Books Known to the English 597–1066* (Cambridge, Mass., 1967).

—— *The Place of Wearmouth and Jarrow in Western Cultural History* (Jarrow Lecture, 1968).

OHNESORGE, W., *Konstantinopel und der Okzident: Gesammelte Aufsätze zur Geschichte der byzantinisch-abendländischen Beziehungen und des Kaisertums* (Darmstadt, 1966).

OKASHA, E., and O'REILLY, J., 'An Anglo-Saxon Portable Altar: Inscription and Iconography', *JWCI* 47 (1984), 32–51.

OMAN, C., 'An Eleventh-Century English Cross', *Burlington Magazine*, 96 (1954), 382–4.

—— *English Church Plate 597–1830* (London, 1957).

OMONT, H. (ed.), *Évangiles avec peintures byzantines du xiᵉ siècle* (2 vols.; Paris, 1908).

ONOFRIO, C. D', *Visitiamo Roma mille anni fà: La città dei Mirabilia* (Rome, 1988).

ORLANDI, M., *Antiche monete in Val d'Aosta* (Aosta, 1983).

ORTENBERG, V., 'Archbishop Sigeric's Pilgrimage to Rome in 990', *ASE* 19 (1990), 197–246.

—— 'An Unknown Late Anglo-Saxon Text About Old St Peter's in Rome', *The Antiquaries Journal*, 70 (1990) 115–20.

ORTIGUES, E., 'L'Élaboration des trois ordres chez Haymon d'Auxerre', *Francia*, 14 (1986), 27–43.

OSBORNE, J., 'Early Medieval Wall-Paintings in the Catacombs of San Valentino, Rome', *Papers of the British School at Rome*, 49 (1981), 82–90.

—— 'Early Medieval Painting in S. Clemente, Rome: The Madonna and Child in the Niche', *Gesta*, 20 (1981), 299–310.

OSHEIM, D. J., *An Italian Lordship: The Bishopric of Lucca in the Late Middle Ages* (Berkeley, 1977).

OSTROGORSKI, G., *A History of the Byzantine State* (tr. Oxford, 1968).

OTRANTO, G., and CARLETTI, C., *Il Santuario di S. Michele arcangelo sul Gargano dalle origini al X secolo* (Bari, 1990).

OTTONE, T. DA, *La leggenda di Sta Caterina vergine e martire d'Alessandria* (Genoa, 1940).

PARISOT, R., *Les Origines de la Haute Lorraine et sa première maison ducale 953–1033* (Paris, 1909).

PARISSE, M., *La Lorraine monastique au Moyen Âge* (Nancy, 1981).

PARKER, C. A., *The Ancient Crosses at Gosforth, Cumberland* (London, 1896).

PARSONS, D. (ed.), *Tenth-Century Studies: Essays in Commemoration of the Millenium of the Council of Winchester and 'Regularis Concordia'* (London and Chichester, 1975).

PARTNER, P., *The Lands of St Peter: The Papal State in the Middle Ages and the Early Renaissance* (London, 1972).

PASCHINI, P., 'Ricerche agiografice: S. Cristina di Bolsena', *Rivista d'Archeologia Cristiana*, 2 (1925), 167–94.

Pellegrinaggi e culto dei santi in Europa fino alla prima Crociata (Convegni del Centro di Studi sulla Spiritualità Medievale, 4; Todi, 1963).

PENCO, G., *Storia del monachesimo in Italia* (Rome, 1961), i.

—— *Storia della Chiesa in Italia* (2 vols.; 2nd edn.) Milan, 1978), i.

PESCI, B., 'L'Itinerario Romano di Sigerico Archivescovo di Canterbury e la lista dei Papi da lui portata in Inghilterra (anno 990)', *Rivista di Archeologia Cristiana*, 13 (1936), 43–61.

PFAFF, R. W., *Medieval Latin Liturgy: A Select Bibliography* (Toronto, 1982).

PIETRANGELI, C. (ed.), *S. Paolo fuori le Mura a Roma* (Florence, 1989).

PIETRI, C., *Roma Christiana* (2 vols.; Paris and Rome, 1976).

PIVA, P., *La cattedrale doppia: Una tipologia architettonica e liturgica del Medioevo* (Bologna, 1990).

PLANITZ, H., *Die deutsche Stadt im Mittelalter* (Graz and Cologne, 1954).

PONTIFEX, D., 'St Dunstan and his First Biography', *Downside Review*, 51 (1933), 20–40 and 309–25.

POOLE, R. L., 'Burgundian Notes: the Alpine Son-in-Law of Edward the Elder', *EHR* 26 (1911), 313–17.

PORÉE, C., *Histoire de l'abbaye du Bec* (2 vols.; Évreux, 1901).

PORTER, A. KINGSLEY, *Medieval Studies in Memory of A. Kingsley Porter*, ed. W. R. W. Köhler (2 vols.; Cambridge, Mass., 1939).

Povertà e ricchezza nella spiritualità dei secoli XI e XII (Todi, 1969).

PRANDI, A., *Il complesso monumentale della basilica celimontana dei SS Giovanni e Paolo* (Vatican City, 1953).

PRICOCO, S. (ed.), *Storia della Sicilia e Tradizione Agiografica nella Tarda Antichità: Atti del Convegno di Studi Catania, 20–22 maggio 1986* (Catania, 1986).

PRIOR, E. S., and GARDNER, A., *An Account of Mediaeval Figure Sculpture in England* (Cambridge, 1912).

QUASTEN, J., 'Oriental Influences in the Gallican Liturgy', *Traditio*, 1 (1943), 55–78.

RAMSAY, R. L., 'Theodore of Mopsuestia in England and Ireland', *Zeitschrift für keltische Philologie*, 8 (1912), 452–97.

RAW, B., 'The Probable Derivation of Most Illustrations in Junius 11 from an Illustrated Old Saxon Genesis', *ASE* 5 (1976), 133–48.

—— *Anglo-Saxon Crucifixion Iconography and the Art of the Monastic Revival* (Cambridge, 1990).

RÉAU, L., *Iconographie de l'art chrétien* (6 vols.; Paris, 1955–8).

REIL, J., *Die frühchristlichen Darstellungen der Kreuzigung Christi* (Leipzig, 1904).

—— *Christus am Kreuz in der Bildkunst der Karolingerzeit* (Leipzig, 1930).

RELLA, F. A., 'Continental Manuscripts Acquired for English Centres in the Tenth and Early Eleventh Centuries: A Preliminary Checklist', *Anglia*, 98 (1980), 107–16.

RENET, A., *St Lucien et les autres saints du Beavaisis* (2 vols.; Beauvais, 1892–3).

REPETTI, E., *Dizionario geografico fisico storico della Toscana* (5 vols.; Florence, 1833–46).

REYNOLDS, L. D., and WILSON, N. G., *Scribes and Scholars* (Oxford, 1967).

REUTER, T., 'The "Imperial Church System" of the Ottonian and Salian Rulers: A Reconsideration', *JEH* 33 (1982), 347–74.

Rhein und Maas: Kunst und Kultur 800–1400 (Cologne, 1972).

RICE, D. TALBOT, *Byzantine Art* (Oxford, 1935).

—— *Byzantine Painting and Development in the West before AD 1200* (London, 1948).

—— *English Art 871–1100* (Oxford, 1952).

RICHARD, J., *Les Ducs de Bourgogne et la formation du duché du XIe au XIVe siècle* (Dijon, 1954).

—— (ed.), *Histoire de la Bourgogne* (Toulouse, 1978).

RICHARDS, J., *The Popes and the Papacy in the Early Middle Ages 476–752* (London, 1979).

—— *Consul of God: The Life and Times of Gregory the Great* (London, 1980).

RICHÉ, P., *Éducation et culture dans l'Occident barbare VIe–VIIIe siècle* (Paris, 1962).

—— *Les Écoles et l'enseignement aux VIIIe–XIIe siècles* (Paris, 1979).

RICKERT, M., *Painting in Britain: The Middle Ages* (Harmondsworth, 1954).

RIDYARD, S. J., '*Condigna Veneratio*: Post-Conquest Attitudes to the Saints of the Anglo-Saxons', *Anglo-Norman Studies*, 9 (1986), 179–206.

—— *The Royal Saints of Anglo-Saxon England* (Cambridge, 1988).

ROBINSON, I., *The Papacy 1073–1198* (Cambridge, 1990).

ROBINSON, J. ARMITAGE, 'Lanfranc's Monastic Constitutions', *Journal of Theological Studies* 10 (1909), 375–88.

—— *The Saxon Bishops of Wells: A Historical Study in the Tenth Century* (British Academy Suppl. Papers, 4; London, 1918).

—— 'The Saxon Abbots of Glastonbury', *Somerset Historical Essays* (London, 1921), 26–53.

—— *The Times of St Dunstan* (Oxford, 1923).

ROJDESTVENSKI, O., *Le Culte de St Michel et le Moyen Âge latin* (Paris, 1922).

ROLLASON, D., *Saints and Relics in Anglo-Saxon England* (Oxford, 1989).

Roma e l'età carolingia (Atti delle giornate di studio 3–8 maggio 1976, cura dell'Instituto di storia dell'arte dell'università di Roma; Rome, 1976).

ROMEO, S., *Sant'Agata e il suo culto* (Catania, 1922).

ROSENFELD, H. F., *Der heilige Christoforus, seine Verehrung und seine Legende* (Leipzig, 1937).

ROSE-TROUP, F., 'The Ancient Monastery of St Mary and St Peter at Exeter', *Trans. Devonshire Assoc. for the Advancement of Science, Literature and Art*, 63 (1931), 179–220.

ROSS, M. C., 'An Eleventh-Century English Bookcover', *The Art Bulletin*, 22 (1940), 83–5.

ROSSER, G., 'The Anglo-Saxon Gilds', in Blair, *Minsters*, 31–4.

ROSSI, G. B. DE, *Roma sotterranea cristiana descritta ed illustrata* (2 vols.; Rome 1864–97).

—— *La Bibbia offerta da Ceolfrido Abbate al sepolcro di San Pietro* (Rome, 1887).

ROUND, J. H., *The Commune of London and other Studies* (London, 1899).

RUPRICH-ROBERT, V., *L'Architecture normande aux XI*[e] *et XII*[e] *siècles en Normandie et en Angleterre* (Paris, 1884–9, repr. 1971).

RYAN J., *Irish Monasticism: Origins and Early Development* (London, 1931, repr. Shannon, 1972).

—— 'The Early Irish Church and the See of St Peter', *Settimane*, 7(2) (1960), 549–74.

SABBE, E., 'Les Relations économiques entre l'Angleterre et le Continent au haut Moyen Âge', *Le Moyen Âge*, 56 (1950), 169–93.

Saint Chrodegang: communications présentées au colloque tenu à Metz à l'occasion du douzième centenaire de sa mort (Metz, 1967).

Saint Germain d'Auxerre: intellectuels et artistes dans l'Europe carolingienne IXe*–XI*[e] *siècles* (Auxerre, 1990).

SANSTERRE, J. M., *Les Moines grecs et orientaux à Rome aux époques byzantine et carolingienne (milieu du VI*[e]*-fin du IX*[e] *siècle)* (Académie Royale de Belgique, Mémoire de la classe des lettres 2e série, 66(1); Brussels, 1983).

SANTIFALLER, L., 'Zur Geschichte des ottonisch–salischen Reichskirchensystem', *Abhandlungen der phil.-hist. Klasse der österreichischen Akademie der Wissenschaften, Sitzungsberichte* 229 (1954).

SAUNDERS, O. E., *English Illumination* (2 vols.; Florence and London, 1928).

SAUVEL, T., 'Le Crucifiement de St Pierre', *Bulletin Monumental*, 97 (1938), 337–52.

SAWYER, P. H., 'The Wealth of England in the Eleventh Century', *TRHS* 5th ser. 15 (1965), 145–64.

SAXER, V., *Le Culte de Marie Madeleine en Occident des origines à la fin du Moyen Âge* (2nd edn.; Auxerre, 1959).

SAXL, F., 'The Ruthwell Cross', *JWCI* 6 (1942), 1–19.

—— , and WITTKOWER, R., *British Art and the Mediterranean* (London, 1942).

SCHAPIRO, M., 'The Image of the Disappearing Christ: The Ascension in English Art around the Year 1000' (1943), repr. in *Late Antique, Early Christian and Medieval Art: Selected Papers* (3 vols.; London, 1980), iii. 267–87.

—— , 'The Religious Meaning of the Ruthwell Cross' (1944), repr. *Selected Papers*, iii. 150–95.

SCHEFFEL, P. H., *Verkehrungsgeschichte der Alpen* (2 vols.; Berlin, 1914).

SCHETTINI, F., *La basilica di San Nicola di Bari* (Bari, 1967).

SCHIEFFER, T., *Winifred-Bonifatius und die christliche Grundlegung Europas* (Freiburg, 1954).

SCHILLER, G., *Iconography of Christian Art* (2 vols.; tr. London, 1971–2).

SCHMITZ, P., *Histoire de l'ordre de St Benoît* (7 vols.; Maredsous, 1942), i and ii.

—— 'L'Influence de St Benoît d'Aniane dans l'histoire de l'ordre de St Benoît', *Settimane*, 4 (1957), 401–16.

SCHNEIDER, F., *Rom und Romgedanke im Mittelalter* (Munich, 1926).

SCHNITZLER, H., 'Hieronymus und Gregor in der ottonische Kölner Buchmalerei', *Kunstgeschichtliche Studien für H. Kaufmann*, ed. W. Braunfels (Berlin, 1956), 11–18.

—— *Karolingische und ottonische Kunst: Werden, Wesen, Wirkung* (Wiesbaden, 1957).

SCHRAMM, P. E., *Kaiser, Rom und Renovatio* (Leipzig and Berlin, 1929).

SCHUSTER, I., *La basilica e il monastero di S. Paolo fuori le Mura* (Turin, 1934).

SCHWARZMAIER, H., *Lucca und das Reich bis zum Ende des 11. Jahrhunderts* (Tübingen, 1972).

SEDLMAYR, H., *Saint-Martin de Tours im 11. Jahrhundert* (Munich, 1970).

SEITZ, J., *Das Josephfest in der lateinischen Kirche in seiner Entwicklung bis zum Konzil von Trient dargestellt* (Freiburg, 1908).

SELMER, C., 'Israel, ein unbekannter Schotte des 10. Jahrhunderts', *Studien und Mitteilungen zur Geschichte des Benediktinerordens*, 62 (1950), 69–86.

SEVCENKO, N. P., *The Life of St Nicholas in Byzantine Art* (Turin, 1983).

SHEPARD, J., 'The English and Byzantium: A Study of their Role in the Byzantine Army in the Later Eleventh Century', *Traditio*, 29 (1973), 53–92.

SHORR, D. C., 'The Mourning Virgin and St John', *The Art Bulletin*, 22 (1940), 61–9.

SISAM, K., *Studies in the History of Old English Literature* (Oxford, 1953).

SMALLEY, B., *The Study of the Bible in the Middle Ages* (3rd edn.; Oxford, 1983).

SMITH, R. A. L., 'The Early Community of St Andrews at Rochester 604–c.1080', *EHR* 60 (1945), 289–99.

SOUTHERN, R. W., 'The First Life of Edward the Confessor', *EHR* 58 (1943), 385–400.

—— *The Making of the Middle Ages* (London, 1953).

—— *St Anselm and his Biographer* (Cambridge, 1963).

—— *Essays in Medieval History* (London, 1968).

—— *Western Society and the Church in the Middle Ages* (Harmondsworth, 1970).

—— *Medieval Humanism and Other Studies* (Oxford and New York, 1970).

SPEER, E., *Quedlinburg und seine Kirchen* (Berlin, 1971).

SPANDREL, R., *Ivo von Chartres und seine Stellung in der Kirchengeschichte* (Stuttgart, 1962).

SPIEGEL, G. M., 'The Cult of St Denis and Capetian Kingship', in *Saints and their Cults*, ed. S. Wilson (Cambridge, 1983), 141–68.

STACPOOLE, A. J., 'Regularis Concordia', *Ampleforth Journal*, 76 (1971), 30–49.

STENTON, F. M., *The Early History of the Abbey of Abingdon* (Reading, 1913).

—— *Anglo-Saxon England* (3rd edn.; Oxford, 1971).

STEVENS, W. O., *The Cross in the Life and Literature of the Anglo-Saxons* (Yale Studies in English, 22; New Haven, 1904).

STONE, L., *Sculpture in Britain: The Middle Ages* (Harmondsworth, 1972).

STOPANI, R., *Le grande vie di pellegrinaggio del mediovo: Le strade per Roma* (Florence, 1986).

Storia di Pavia, a cura della Banca del Monte di Lombardia (Società pavese di storia patria; Milan, 1987).

Storia d'Italia, ii: Della caduta dell'Impero romano al secolo XVIII (Turin, 1974).

STROUD, D. I., 'The Provenance of the Salisbury Psalter', *The Library*, 6th ser., 1(3) (1979), 225–35.

SWARZENSKI, H., 'The Anhalt–Morgan Gospels', *The Art Bulletin*, 31(2) (1949), 77–83.

—— *Monuments of Romanesque Art: The Art of Church Treasures in North-Western Europe* (2nd edn.; London, 1974).

SYMONS, T., 'The Regularis Concordia', *Downside Review*, 40 (1922), 15–30.

—— 'The Monastic Observance of the Regularis Concordia', *Downside Review*, 44 (1926), 157–71.

—— 'The Sources of the Regularis Concordia', *Downside Review*, 59 (1941), 14–36, 143–70, 264–89.

—— 'The English Monastic Reform of the Tenth Century', *Downside Review*, 60 (1942), 1–22, 196–222, 268–79.

—— 'The Regularis Concordia and the Council of Winchester', *Downside Review*, 80 (1962), 140–56.

—— 'Notes on the Life and Work of St Dunstan', *Downside Review*, 80 (1962), 250–61, 355–66.

SZARMACH, P. Z., and DARROW OGGINS, V. (eds.), *Sources of Anglo-Saxon Culture* (Studies in Medieval Culture, 20; Kalamazoo, Mich., 1986).

—— , and HUPPÉ, B. F. (eds.), *The Old English Homily and its Background* (Albany, 1978).

Tardo Antico e Alto Medioevo: la forma artistica nel passagio dall'Antichità al medioevo (Rome, 1968).

TAYLOR, H. M., 'The Anglo-Saxon Cathedral Church at Canterbury', *Archaeologia*, 126 (1969), 101–30.

—— , and TAYLOR, J., *Anglo-Saxon Architecture* (3 vols.; London, 1965–78).

TEA, E., *La basilica di Sta Maria Antiqua* (Milan, 1937).

TELLENBACH, G., *Church, State and Christian Society at the Time of the Investiture Contest* (Oxford, 1940).

Temps chrétien de la fin de l'Antiquité au Moyen Âge, III–XIIIe siècles, Le, Colloque CNRS 1981 (Paris, 1984).

TESTINI, P., *Le catacombe e gli antichi cimiteri cristiani in Roma* (Bologna, 1966).

THOMPSON, A. HAMILTON, *Bede: His Life, Time and Writings* (Oxford, 1935).

THOMPSON, R., *William of Malmesbury* (Woodbridge, 1987).

THURSTON, H., 'The Oldest Life of Gregory', *The Month*, 104 (1904), 337–53.

TOLHURST, J. B. L., 'An Examination of Two Anglo-Saxon Manuscripts of the Winchester School: The Missal of Robert of Jumièges and the Benedictional of St Æthelwold', *Archaeologia*, 83 (1933), 27–44.

TOMMASINI, A. M., *Irish Saints in Italy* (tr. London, 1937).

TOUBERT, P., *Histoire du Haut Moyen Âge et de l'Italie médiévale* (London, 1987).

TOUT, M. I., 'The Legend of St Ursula and the Eleven Thousand Virgins', in *Historical Essays*, ed. T. F. Tout and J. Tait (Manchester, 1907), 17–56.

TOYNBEE, J. M. C., and WARD-PERKINS, J., *The Shrine of St Peter and the Vatican Excavations* (London, 1956).

TRONZO, W., 'Two Roman Wall Decorations', *Dumbarton Oaks Papers* 41 (1987), 489–92.

TSCHAN, F. J., *St Bernward of Hildesheim* (3 vols.; Notre Dame, 1943, 1951–2).

TSELOS, D., 'English MS Illustration and the Utrecht Psalter', *The Art Bulletin*, 41 (1959), 137–49.

TURNER, C. H., 'The Earliest List of Durham Manuscripts', *Journal of Theological Studies*, 19 (1917–18), 121–32.

TYLER, J. E., *The Alpine Passes: The Middle Ages 962–1250* (Oxford, 1930).

ULLMANN, W., *The Growth of Papal Government in the Middle Ages* (3rd edn., London, 1970).

VACANDARD, E., 'Les Principaux écrits sur St Ouen du VIIe au XVIIe siècle', *AB* 20 (1901), 165–76.

VALOUS, G. DE, *Le Monachisme clunisien des origines au XVe siècle: vie intérieure des monastères et organisation de l'ordre* (2 vols.; Ligugé, 1935).

VAN BERCHEM, M., and CLOUZOT, E., *Mosaïques chrétiennes du IVe au IXe siècle* (Geneva, 1924).

VAN DEN BOSCH, J., *Capa, basilica, monasterium et le culte de St Martin à Tours* (Nimejgen, 1959).

VAN DER ESSEN, L., *Étude critique sur les Vitae des saints mérovingiens de l'ancienne Belgique* (Louvain and Paris, 1907).

—— *Le siècle des saints (625–739)* (Brussels, 1948).

VAN DIJK, S. J. P., 'The Origin of the Latin Feast of the Conception of the Blessed Virgin Mary', *Dublin Review*, 118 (1954), 251–67, 428–42.

—— 'The Urban and Papal Rites in Seventh and Eighth-Century Rome', *Sacris Erudiri*, 12 (1961), 411–87.

VASILIEV, A. A., 'The Opening Stages of the Anglo-Saxon Immigration to Byzantium in the Eleventh Century', *Annales de l'Institut Kondakov (Seminarium Kondakovianum)*, 9 (1937), 39–70.

VAUCHEZ, A., *La Spiritualité du Moyen Âge occidental VIIe–XIIe siècle* (Paris, 1975).

VERGNOLLE, E., *St Benoît sur Loire et la sculpture du XIe siècle* (Paris, 1985).

VERHEYEN, E., *Das Goldene Evangelienbuch der Echternach* (Munich, 1963).

VÉZIN, G., *L'Adoration et le cycle des Mages dans l'art chrétien primitif* (Paris, 1950).

VIAUD, G., *La Liturgie des Coptes d'Égypte* (Paris, 1978).

VIELLIARD, J., 'Notes sur l'iconographie de St Pierre', *Le Moyen Âge*, 2nd ser. 39 (1929), 1–16.

VIELLIARD, R., *Recherche sur les origines de la Rome chrétienne* (Rome, 1959).

VOLBACH, W. F., *Elfenbeinarbeiten der Spätantike und des frühen Mittelalters* (Mainz, 1952).

—— 'Les Ivoires sculptés de l'époque carolingienne au XIIe siècle', *Cahiers de Civilisation Médiévale*, 1(2) (1958), 17–26.

VOLLRATH, H., *Die Synoden Englands bis 1066* (Paderborn, 1985).

WAETZOLDT, S., *Die Kopien des 17. Jahrhunderts nach Mosaiken und Wandmalereien in Rom* (Vienna and Munich, 1964).

WALLACE-HADRILL, J. M., 'Rome and the Early English Church: Some Questions of Transmission', *Settimane*, 7 (2) (1960), 519–48.

—— *A Carolingian Renaissance Prince: The Emperor Charles the Bald* (London, 1980).

—— *The Frankish Church* (Oxford, 1983).

—— *Ideal and Reality in Anglo-Saxon Society: Studies Presented to J. M. Wallace-Hadrill*, ed. P. Wormald, D. Bullough, and R. Collins (Oxford, 1983).

—— *Bede's Ecclesiastical History of the English People: A Historical Commentary* (Oxford, 1989).

WALLACH, L., *Alcuin and Charlemagne: Studies in Carolingian History and Literature* (New York, 1959).

WARD-PERKINS, B., *From Classical Antiquity to the Middle Ages: Urban Public Buildings in Northern and Central Italy* (Oxford, 1984).

WARD-PERKINS, J., 'The Shrine of St Peter and its Twelve Spiral Columns', *Journal of Roman Studies*, 12 (1952), 21–33.

WARREN, F. E., 'An Anglo-Saxon Missal at Worcester', *The Academy*, 28 (1885), 394–5.

WEBB, D. M., 'The Holy Face of Lucca', *Anglo-Norman Studies*, 9 (1986), 227–37.

WEBB, G., *Architecture in Britain: The Middle Ages* (Harmondsworth, 1956).

WEBER, R., *Le Psautier Romain et les autres psautiers latins* (Rome, 1953).

WEISBACH, W., 'Les Images des Évangélistes dans l'Évangéliaire d'Otton III et leur rapport avec l'Antiquité', *Gazette des Beaux Arts*, 81 (1939), 131–52.

WEITZMANN, K., *Die byzantinische Buchmalerei des 9. und 10. Jahrhunderts* (Berlin, 1935).

—— 'The Narrative and Liturgical Gospel Illuminations', *Studies in Classical and Byzantine Manuscript Illumination*, ed. H. L. Kessler (Chicago and London, 1971), 247–70.

—— 'Various Aspects of Byzantine Influence on the Latin Countries from the Sixth to the Twelfth Century', in *Art in the Medieval West*.

—— *Late Antique and Early Christian Book Illumination* (London, 1977).

—— *The Age of Spirituality: Late Antique and Early Christian Art: Third to Seventh Century* (New York, 1979).

—— *Art in the Medieval West and its Contacts with Byzantium* (London, 1982).

WELLESZ, E., 'Eastern Elements in English Ecclesiastical Music', *JWCI* 5 (1942), 44–55.

WENGER, A., *L'Assomption de la T. S. Vierge dans la tradition byzantine du vi⁰ au ix⁰ siècle: études et documents* (Paris, 1955).

WESSEL, K., *Koptische Kunst* (Recklinghausen, 1963).

WEST, R. C., *Western Liturgies* (London, 1938).

WESTERMANN-ANGERHAUSEN, H., 'Spolie und Umfeld in Egberts Trier', *Zeitschrift für Kunstgeschichte*, 50 (1987), 305–36.

WESTWOOD, J. O., *Facsimiles of the Miniatures and Ornaments of Anglo-Saxon and Irish Manuscripts* (London, 1868).

WICKHAM, C., *Early Medieval Italy: Central Power and Local Society 400–1000* (London, 1981).

WILDHAGEN, K., 'Studien zum Psalterium Romanum in England und zu seinen Glossierungen', *Festschrift für L. Morsbach*, ed. F. Holthausen and H. Spies (Studien zur englischen Philologie, 50; Halle, 1913), 418–72.

—— 'Das Psalterium Gallicanum in England und seine altenglischen Glossierungen', *Englische Studien*, 54 (1920), 35–45.

WILMART, A., 'Le Couvent et la bibliothèque de Cluny vers le milieu du XIe siècle', *Revue Mabillon*, 11 (1921), 89–124.

—— 'Les Livres de l'abbé Otbert', *Bulletin Historique de la Société des Antiquaires de la Morinie*, 14 (1922–4), 169–88.

—— *Auteurs spirituels et textes dévots du Moyen Âge latin* (Paris, 1932).

—— 'Les Reliques de St Ouen à Cantorbéry', *AB* 51 (1933), 285–92.

—— 'Ève et Goscelin', *RB* 46 (1934), 414–38, 50 (1938), 42–83.

WILPERT, G., *Fractio Panis: la plus ancienne représentation du sacrifice eucharistique à la 'Cappella Greca'* (Paris, 1896).

———— *Roma sotterranea: Le pitture delle catacombe romane illustrate* (2 vols.; Rome, 1903).

WILPERT, J., rev. SCHUHMACHER, W. N., *Die römischen Mosaiken der christlichen Bauten vom IV zum XIII Jahrhundert* (Freiburg, Basle, and Vienna, 1976).

WILSON, D. M., 'Anglo-Saxon Ornamental Metalwork', *Catalogue of Antiquities of the Later Saxon Period*, i (British Museum; London, 1964).

—— *The Anglo-Saxons* (2nd edn.; Harmondsworth, 1971).

WILSON, N. G., *Scholars of Byzantium* (London, 1983).

WOLPERS, T., *Die englische Heiligenlegende des Mittelalters* (Tübingen, 1964).

WOOD, M., 'The Making of Æthelstan's Empire: An English Charlemagne?', in *Ideal and Reality*, 250–64.

WORMALD, C. P., 'Æthelred the Lawmaker', in Hill, *Æthelred*, 47–80.

—— *Bede and the Conversion of England: The Charter Evidence* (Jarrow Lecture, 1984).

—— 'Æthelwold and his Continental Counterparts: Contacts, Comparison, Contrast', in Yorke, *Æthelwold*, 13–42.

—— 'In Search of King Offa's "Law-Code"', in I. Wood and N. Lund (eds.), *People and Places in Northern Europe 500–1600* (Woodbridge, 1991), 25–45.

WORMALD, F., 'The English Saints in the Litany in Arundel 60', *AB* 64 (1946), 72–86.

—— *English Drawings of the Tenth and Eleventh Centuries* (London, 1952).

—— 'The Liturgical Calendar of Glastonbury Abbey', *Festschrift B. Bischoff*, ed. J. Autenrieth and F. Brünhölzl (Stuttgart, 1971), 325–45.

—— 'Fragments of a Tenth-Century Sacramentary from the Binding of the Winton Domesday', in M. Biddle (ed.), *Winchester in the Early Middle Ages: An Edition and Discussion of the Winton Domesday* (Oxford, 1976), 541–9.

—— *Collected Writings, i: Studies in Medieval Art from the Sixth to the Twelfth Centuries*, ed. J. J. G. Alexander, T. J. Brown, and J. Gibbs (Oxford, 1984).

WORRINGER, P., 'Über den Einfluss der Angelsächsischen Buchmalerei auf die frühmittelalterliche Monumentalplastik des Kontinents', *Schriften der Königsburger gelehrten Gesellschaft* (1931).

YORKE, B., (ed.), *Bishop Æthelwold: His Career and Influence* (Woodbridge, 1988).

ZARNECKI, G., *English Romanesque Sculpture 1066–1140* (London, 1951).

—— *The Monastic Achievement* (London, 1972).

—— *Art of the Medieval World* (New York, 1975).

—— HOLT, J., and HOLLAND, T. (eds.), *English Romanesque Art* (Catalogue of the Hayward Gallery Exhibition; London, 1984).

ZENDER, M., *Räume und Schichten Mittelalterlichen Heiligenverehrung in ihrer Bedeutung für die Volkskunde* (Düsseldorf, 1959).

ZIMMERMAN, G., 'Bamberg als königlicher Pfalzort', *Jahrbuch für Fränkische Landesforschung*, 19 (1959), 203–22.

ZIMMERMANN, H. (ed.), *Otto der Grosse* (Darmstadt, 1976).

ZWÖLFER, T., *Sankt Peter, Apostelfürst und Himmelspförter: Seine Verehrung bei den Angelsächsen und Franken* (Stuttgart, 1929).

III. UNPUBLISHED DISSERTATIONS

COATSWORTH, E., 'The Iconography of the Crucifixion in Pre-Conquest Sculpture in England', Ph. D. thesis (Durham, 1979).

DESHMAN, R., 'The Iconography of the Full-Page Miniatures of the Benedictional of St Æthelwold', Ph.D. thesis (Princeton, 1969).

DRAGE, E. M., 'Bishop Leofric and Exeter Cathedral Chapter (1050–1072): A Reassessment of the Manuscript Evidence', D.Phil. thesis (Oxford, 1978).

GARNETT, G. S., 'Royal Succession in England: 1066–1154', Ph.D. thesis (Cambridge, 1987).

HARRIS, R. M., 'The Marginal Drawings of the Bury St Edmunds Psalter', Ph.D. thesis (Princeton, 1960).

HOARE, D. C., 'The Cult of St Denys in England in the Middle Ages,' M.Phil. thesis (Nottingham, 1978).

MOSFORD, S., 'A Critical Edition of the *Vita Gregorii Magni* by an Anonymous Member of the Community of Whitby', D.Phil. thesis (Oxford, 1988).

THOMAS, I. G., 'The Cult of the Saints' Relics in Medieval England', Ph.D. thesis (London, 1975).

The following relevant works have been published too late for me to be able to consult them:

EUW, A., and SCHREINER, P. (eds.), *Kaiserin Theophanu († 991): Begegnung des Ostens und Westens um die Wende des ersten Jahrtausends: Gedenkschrift dem Kölner Schnütgen-Museum zum 1000. Todesjahr der Kaiserin* (Cologne, 1991).

GALLISTL, B., *Die Bronzetüren Bischof Bernwards im Dom zu Hildesheim* (Freiburg, 1990).

LEONARDI, C., and MENESTO, E. (eds.), *La tradizione dei tropi iturgici* (Atti dei convegni sui tropi liturgici Paris 1985 and Perugia 1987; Spoleto, 1991).

MAYR-HARTING, H., *Ottonian Book Illumination: An Historical Study, i: Themes* (London, 1991).

MICK, E., *Köln im Mittelalter* (Cologne, 1990).

Salier und ihr Reich 1024–1125, Die (Katalog zur Austellung, Speyer; Sigmaringen, 1991).

WEINFURTER, S. (ed.), *Die Salier und das Reich* (3 vols.; Sigmaringen, 1991).

INDEX